Contents

Plan Your Trip   4

Explore Berlin   72

Understand Berlin   227

Survival Guide   265

Berlin Maps   291

(left) **Reichstag p78**
Home of the German
parliament

(above) **Spree River-
bank** Popular for picnics

(right) **Remnant of the
Berlin Wall p34** Symbol
of a divided Germany.

Welcome to Berlin

Berlin's combo of glamour and grit is bound to mesmerise anyone keen to explore its vibrant culture, fabulous food and tangible history.

High on History

Bismarck and Marx, Einstein and Hitler, JFK and Bowie, they've all shaped – and been shaped by – Berlin, whose richly textured history stares you in the face at every turn. This is a city that staged a revolution, was headquartered by Nazis, bombed to bits, divided in two and finally reunited – and that was just in the 20th century! Walk along remnants of the Berlin Wall, marvel at the splendour of a Prussian palace, visit Checkpoint Charlie or stand in the very room where the Holocaust was planned. Berlin is like an endlessly fascinating 3D textbook where the past is very much present wherever you go.

Party Paradise

Forget about New York – Berlin is the city that truly never sleeps. Sometimes it seems as though Berliners are the lotus eaters of Germany, people who love nothing more than a good time. The city's vast party spectrum caters for every taste, budget and age group. From tiny basement clubs to industrial techno temples, chestnut-canopied beer gardens to fancy cocktail caverns, saucy cabarets to ear-pleasing symphonies – Berlin delivers hot-stepping odysseys, and not just after dark and on weekends but pretty much 24/7. Pack your stamina!

Cultural Trendsetter

When it comes to creativity, the sky's the limit in Berlin, Europe's newest start-up capital. In the last 20 years, the city has become a giant lab of cultural experimentation thanks to an abundance of space, cheap rent and a free-wheeling spirit that nurtures and encourages new ideas. Top international performers grace its theatre, concert and opera stages; international art-world stars like Olafur Eliasson and Jonathan Meese make their home here; and Clooney and Hanks shoot blockbusters in the German capital. High-brow, low-brow and everything in between – there's plenty of room for the full arc of cultural expression.

Laidback Lifestyle

Berlin is a big multicultural metropolis but deep down it maintains the unpretentious charm of an international village. Locals follow the credo 'live and let live' and put greater emphasis on personal freedom and a creative lifestyle than on material wealth and status symbols. Cafes are jammed at all hours, drinking is a religious rite and clubs keep going until the wee hours or beyond. Size-wise, Berlin is pretty big but its key areas are wonderfully compact and easily navigated on foot, by bike or by using public transport.

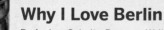

Why I Love Berlin

By Andrea Schulte-Peevers, Writer

Berlin is a bon vivant, passionately feasting on the smorgasbord of life, never taking things – or itself – too seriously. To me, this city is nothing short of addictive. It embraces me, inspires me, accepts me and makes me feel good about myself, the world and other people. I enjoy its iconic sights, its vast swathes of green, its sky bars and chic restaurants, but I love its gritty sides more. There's nothing static about Berlin: it's unpredictable, unpretentious and irresistible. And it loves you back – if you let it in.

For more about our writer, see p320

Top: Open-air bar in Monbijou Park on the Spree River

Berlin's
Top 10

Brandenburger Tor (p80)

1 Prussian kings, Napoleon and Hitler have marched through this neoclassical royal city gate that was once trapped east of the Berlin Wall. Since 1989 it has gone from a symbol of division and oppression to the symbol of a united Germany. The landmark, which overlooks the stately Pariser Platz with its embassies and banks, is at its most atmospheric – and photogenic – at night when light bathes its stately columns and proud Goddess of Victory sculpture in a mesmerising golden glow.

⊙ *Historic Mitte*

Reichstag (p78)

2 This famous Berlin landmark has been set on fire, bombed, left to crumble, and wrapped in fabric before emerging as the home of the German parliament (the Bundestag) and focal point of the reunited country's government quarter. The plenary hall can only be seen on guided tours but, with advance booking, you're free to catch the lift to the dazzling glass dome designed by Lord Norman Foster. Enjoy not only the fabulous views, but learn about the building and surrounding landmarks on a free audio tour.

⊙ *Historic Mitte*

CANADASTOCK/SHUTTERSTOCK ©

MBBIRDY/GETTY IMAGES ©

Berlin Wall (p34)

3 Few events in history have the power to move the entire world. The Kennedy assassination. The moon landing. The events of 9/11. And, of course, the fall of the Berlin Wall in 1989. If you were old enough back then, you may remember the crowds of euphoric revellers cheering and dancing at the Brandenburg Gate. Although little is left of the physical barrier, its legacy lives on in the imagination, and in such places as Checkpoint Charlie (p88), the Gedenkstätte Berliner Mauer (p177) and the East Side Gallery (p166). TOP LEFT: GRAFFITI AT THE EAST SIDE GALLERY

⊙ *Scheunenviertel*

Nightlife (p53)

4 The techno temple Berghain may be Berlin's most famous club, but when it comes to nightlife, the entire city is your oyster. Gothic raves to hip-hop hoedowns, craft-beer pubs to riverside bars, beer gardens to underground dives – finding a party to match your mood is a snap. Not into hobnobbing with hipsters at hot-stepping bars or clubs? Why not relive the roaring twenties in a high-kicking cabaret, indulge your ears with symphonic strains in iconic concert halls or point your highbrow compass towards one of three opera houses? LEFT: A BEACH BAR PARTY IN MONBIJOU PARK

🍷 *Drinking & Nightlife*

Museumsinsel (p96)

5 Berlin's 'Louvre on the Spree', this imposing ensemble of five treasure houses is the undisputed highlight of the city's museum landscape. Declared a Unesco World Heritage site, Museum Island represents 6000 years of art and cultural history, from the Stone Age to the 19th century. Feast your eyes on majestic antiquities at the Pergamonmuseum and Altes Museum, report for an audience with Egyptian queen Nefertiti at the Neues Museum, take in 19th-century art at the Alte Nationalgalerie and marvel at medieval sculptures at the Bode-Museum. ABOVE: A WALL RELIEF AT PERGAMONMUSEUM

⊙ *Museumsinsel & Alexanderplatz*

Holocaust Memorial *(p81)*

6 Listen to the sound of your footsteps and feel the presence of uncounted souls as you make your way through the massive warped labyrinth that is Germany's central memorial to the Jewish victims of the Nazi-orchestrated genocide. New York architect Peter Eisenman poignantly captures this unspeakable horror with a maze of 2711 tomblike concrete plinths of varying heights that rise from an unsettlingly wavy ground. The memorial's abstract narrative contrasts with the graphic and emotional exhibits in the subterranean information centre.

◉ *Historic Mitte*

Street Art & Alternative Living *(p44)*

7 Berlin has world-class art, cultural events galore and increasingly sophisticated dining – but so do most other capital cities. What makes this metropolis different is the unbridled climate of openness and tolerance that fosters experimentation, a DIY ethos and a thriving subculture. Hip and funky Kreuzberg, Friedrichshain and northern Neukölln are all trend-setting laboratories of diversity and creativity. No surprise, then, that some of the city's finest street art is brightening up the streetscapes around here. RIGHT: STREET ART DEPICTING REFUGEE CHILDREN

☆ *The Berlin Art Scene*

7

8

Potsdamer Platz
(p115)

8 No other area around town better reflects the 'New Berlin' than this quarter forged from the death-strip that separated East and West Berlin for 28 years. The world's biggest construction site through much of the 1990s, Potsdamer Platz 2.0 is a postmodern take on the historic area that until WWII was Berlin's equivalent of Times Square. A cluster of plazas, offices, museums, cinemas, theatres, hotels and flats, it shows off the talents of seminal architects of our times, including Helmut Jahn and Renzo Piano.

⊙ *Potsdamer Platz & Tiergarten*

Schloss Charlottenburg *(p191)*

9 We can pretty much guarantee that your camera will have a love affair with Berlin's largest and loveliest remaining royal palace. A late-baroque jewel inspired by Versailles, it backs up against an idyllic park, complete with carp pond, rhododendron-lined paths, two smaller palaces and a mausoleum. The palace itself is clad in a subtle yellow favoured by the royal Hohenzollern family and adorned with slender columns and geometrically arranged windows. A copper-domed tower overlooks the forecourt and the equestrian statue of the Great Elector Friedrich Wilhelm.

⊙ *City West & Charlottenburg*

Kulturforum *(p118)*

10 Conceived in the 1950s, the Kulturforum was West Berlin's answer to Museumsinsel and is a similarly enthralling cluster of cultural venues, albeit in modern buildings. One of the city's most important art museums, the Gemäldegalerie, wows fans with Old Masters from Rembrandt to Vermeer. Other museums zero in on prints and drawings, arts and crafts, and musical instruments. Next door, the Berliner Philharmoniker, one of the world's finest orchestras, has its home base in a honey-coloured free-form concert hall designed by Hans Scharoun. ABOVE: NEUE NATIONALGALERIE (P122), KULTURFORUM

⊙ *Potsdamer Platz & Tiergarten*

What's New

Food & Drink

The global street-food phenomenon has fully engulfed Berlin, with some early purveyors already trading their mobile kitchens for brick-and-mortar restaurants. Craft-beer culture also continues to gain traction in Berlin, fuelled by pioneering local breweries such as Heidenpeters, Vagabund and Brlo, many of which operate their own taprooms. There's also a growing number of craft-beer bars, often with dozens of varieties on tap and dozens more in bottles.

Museum Closures

The north wing and the Pergamon Altar at the Pergamonmuseum are closed for an extensive facelift until 2019. The Neue Nationalgalerie will also remain closed for renovation until at least 2018. (p97 & p122)

Schloss Charlottenburg

Frederick the Great's sumptuous state apartments in the Neuer Flügel have reopened; now it's the **Alter Flügel** that's closed for a facelift, probably until mid-2017. (p192)

Kunsthaus Dahlem

In the suburb of Dahlem, the Kunsthaus Dahlem presents postwar German sculpture in the monumental studio of Nazi-era artist Arno Breker, including works by Gerhard Marcks, Bernhard Heiliger and Jeanne Mammen. (p212)

Spy Museum

As the Cold War 'capital of spies', it's only appropriate that Berlin now has a dedicated Spy Museum, complete with lipstick pistols, an Enigma deciphering machine and a Bond exhibit. (p121)

The Gate

Opposite the Brandenburger Tor, The Gate lets visitors dip into Berlin's often turbulent history during a digital-age whirlwind tour enhanced by sound effects and emotional music. (p85)

Erlebnis Europa

The members, mysteries and vagaries of the EU are in the spotlight at the interactive Erlebnis Europa exhibit, with a 360° cinema where visitors can attend a session of the European Parliament. (p86)

Humboldt Forum

The reconstruction of the Prussian royal city palace opposite Museumsinsel is now well under way. Learn more about its future use as a museum and cultural venue at the Humboldt-Box. (p109)

Unter den Linden

The grand boulevard is a giant construction zone as Berlin builds a new U-Bahn line and the Berlin City Palace; completion of the refurb of the Staatsoper Unter den Linden opera house has also been delayed. (p88)

Neues Palais in Potsdam

After extensive restoration, highlights of the Neues Palais in Park Sanssouci – such as the Grotto Hall, the Marble Hall and the Lower Royal Suite – are once again open to visitors. (p207)

For more recommendations and reviews, see **lonelyplanet. com/germany/berlin**

Need to Know

For more information, see Survival Guide (p265)

Currency
Euro (€)

Language
German

Visas
Generally not required for tourist stays of up to 90 days (or at all for EU nationals); some nationalities need a Schengen visa.

Money
ATMs widespread. Cash is king; credit cards are not widely used.

Mobile Phones
➡ Mobile phones operate on GSM900/1800.

➡ Local SIM cards can be used in unlocked European and Australian phones.

➡ US multiband phones also work in Germany.

Time
Central European Time (GMT/UTC plus one hour).

Tourist Information
Visit Berlin (www.visitberlin.de) has branches at the airports, the main train station, the Brandenburg Gate, the TV Tower and on Kurfürstendamm, plus a call centre (☑030-2500 2333; ☺9am-7pm Mon-Fri, 10am-6pm Sat, 10am-2pm Sun) for information and bookings.

Daily Costs

Budget: Less than €100
➡ Dorm bed or peer-to-peer rental: €10–30

➡ Doner kebab: €3–4

➡ Club cover: €5–15

➡ Public-transport day pass: €7

Midrange: €100–200
➡ Private apartment or double room: €80–120

➡ Two-course dinner with wine: €25–40

➡ Guided tour: €10–20

➡ Museum admission: €20

Top end: More than €200
➡ Upmarket apartment or double in top-end hotel: from €160

➡ Gourmet two-course dinner with wine: €70

➡ Cab ride: €25

➡ Cabaret ticket: €50–80

Advance Planning

Two to three months before Book tickets for the Berliner Philharmonie, the Staatsoper, Sammlung Boros and other top-flight events.

One month before Book online tickets for the Reichstag dome, the Neues Museum and the Pergamonmuseum.

Two weeks before Reserve a table at trendy or Michelin-starred restaurants, especially for Friday and Saturday dinners.

Useful Websites

➡ **Lonely Planet** (www.lonelyplanet.com/germany/berlin) Destination information, hotel bookings, traveller forum and more.

➡ **Visit Berlin** (www.visitberlin.de) Official tourist authority info.

➡ **Museumsportal** (www.museumsportal-berlin.de) Gateway to the city's museums.

➡ **Resident Advisor** (www.residentadvisor.net) Guide to parties and clubbing.

➡ **Exberliner** (www.exberliner.com) Expat-geared monthly English-language Berlin culture magazine.

➡ **Stil in Berlin** (www.stilinberlin.de) City blogs with up-to-the-minute tips on food, fashion, style and art.

WHEN TO GO

July and August are busy and warm but often rainy. May, June, September and October offer plenty of festivals and cooler weather. Winters are quiet.

°C/°F Temp

Rainfall Inches/mm

PLAN YOUR TRIP NEED TO KNOW

Arriving in Berlin

Tegel Airport TXL express bus to Alexanderplatz (40 minutes) and bus X9 for City West (eg Kurfürstendamm, 20 minutes), €2.70; taxi €25.

Schönefeld Airport Airport-Express trains (RB14 or RE7) to central Berlin twice hourly (30 minutes), and S9 trains every 20 minutes for Friedrichshain and Prenzlauer Berg, €3.30; taxi €40 to Alexanderplatz.

Hauptbahnhof Main train station in the city centre; served by S-Bahn, U-Bahn, tram, bus and taxi.

Zentraler Omnibus Bahnhof (ZOB) The central bus station is on the western city edge. U-Bahn U2 to city centre (eg Bahnhof Zoo eight minutes, Alexanderplatz 28 minutes), €2.70; taxi €18.

For much more on **arrival** see p266

Getting Around

➡ **U-Bahn** Most efficient way to travel; operates 4am to 12.30am and all night Friday, Saturday and public holidays. From Sunday to Thursday, half-hourly night buses take over in the interim.

➡ **S-Bahn** Less frequent than U-Bahn trains but with fewer stops, and thus useful for longer distances. Same operating hours as the U-Bahn.

➡ **Bus** Slow but useful for sightseeing on the cheap. Run frequently 4.30am to 12.30am; half-hourly night buses in the interim. MetroBuses (designated eg M1, M19) operate 24/7.

➡ **Tram** Only in the eastern districts; MetroTrams (designated eg M1, M2) run 24/7.

➡ **Cycling** Bike lanes and rental stations abound; bikes allowed in specially marked U-Bahn and S-Bahn carriages.

➡ **Taxi** Can be hailed; fairly inexpensive; avoid during daytime rush hour.

➡ **Uber** The only Uber option is uberTaxi. Prices are identical to regular taxis, including a surcharge of €1.50 for cash-free payments.

For much more on **getting around** see p268

Sleeping

Berlin has over 137,000 hotel rooms but the most desirable properties book up quickly, especially in summer and around major holidays, festivals and trade shows; prices soar and reservations are essential during these periods. Otherwise, rates are mercifully low by Western capital standards. Options range from luxurious ports of call to ho-hum international chains, trendy designer boutique hotels to Old Berlin–style B&Bs, happening hostels to handy self-catering apartments.

Useful Websites

➡ **Lonely Planet** (lonelyplanet. com/germany/hotels) Lonely Planet's online booking service with insider lowdown on the best places to stay.

➡ **Visit Berlin** (www.visitberlin. de) Official Berlin tourist office books rooms at partner hotels with a best-price guarantee.

➡ **Boutique Hotels Berlin** (www.boutiquehotels-berlin. com) Booking service for about 20 handpicked boutique hotels.

➡ **Berlin30** (www.berlin30. com) Online low-cost booking agency for hotels, hostels, apartments and B&Bs.

For much more on **sleeping** see p217

First Time Berlin

For more information, see Survival Guide (p265)

Checklist

➡ Ensure your passport is valid for at least four months past your arrival date

➡ Check airline baggage restrictions

➡ Inform your debit-/credit-card company of your upcoming trip

➡ Organise travel insurance

➡ Check if your mobile/cell phone will work in Germany and the cost of roaming

➡ If taking prescription medicine, bring enough for your entire trip and put it in your carry-on

What to Pack

➡ Good walking shoes – Berlin is best appreciated on foot

➡ Umbrella or rain jacket – rain is possible any time of year

➡ Small daypack

➡ Travel adapter plug

➡ Sun hat and sunglasses

➡ Curiosity and a sense of humour

Top Tips for Your Trip

➡ Plan on doing most of your sightseeing by foot. Only by walking will you truly experience Berlin. To cover larger areas quickly, rent a bicycle. Otherwise, public transport is the best way of getting around.

➡ Go local – Berlin's spirit reveals itself to those walking around a neighbourhood, people-watching in a park or simply being curious about local food and drink.

➡ There is no curfew, so pace your alcohol intake on bar-hops and in clubs to keep your stamina up.

➡ When picking a place to stay, consider which type of experience you're most keen on – shopping, clubbing, museums, the outdoors, urban cool, partying, history – then choose a neighbourhood to match.

What to Wear

The short answer is: whatever you want. Berlin is an extremely casual city when it comes to fashion. Basically anything goes, including jeans at the opera or a little black dress in a beer garden. Individuality trumps conformity and expensive labels at any time. In fact, flaunting your own style – any style – is often the ticket for making it past a picky club bouncer. Venues or restaurants with official dress codes are extremely rare.

Berlin weather is immensely changeable, even in summer, so make sure you bring layers of clothing. A waterproof coat and sturdy shoes are a good idea for all-weather sightseeing. Winters can get fiercely cold, so be sure you bring your favourite gloves, hat, boots and heavy coat.

Be Forewarned

Berlin is one of the safest capital cities in the world, but that doesn't mean you should let your guard down.

➡ Pickpocketing has dramatically increased, so watch your belongings, especially in tourist-heavy areas, in crowds and at events.

➡ Crime levels have risen notably around Kottbusser Tor in Kreuzberg and the RAW Gelände in Friedrichshain.This includes drug dealing, pickpocketing, assault and sexual assault. Exercise caution.

➡ Carry enough cash for a cab ride back to wherever you're staying.

Money

Germany is still largely a cash-based society. International chain hotels, department stores, supermarkets and taxis usually accept credit cards, but make it a habit to enquire first.

ATMs are ubiquitous in all neighbourhoods. Machines do not recognise pins with more than four digits. Debit cards featuring the MasterCard or Visa logos are fairly widely used. Chip-and-pin is most common, but contactless payment systems have also started popping up.

Taxes & Refunds

Value-added tax (VAT, *Mehrwertsteuer*) is a 19% sales tax levied on most goods. The rate for food, books and services is usually 7%. VAT is always included in the price. If your permanent residence is outside the EU, you may be able to partially claim back the VAT you paid on purchased goods.

Tipping

➡ **Hotels** Room cleaners €1 to €2 per day, porters the same per bag.

➡ **Restaurants** For good service 5% to 10%.

➡ **Bars/Pubs** 5% to 10% for table service, rounded to the nearest euro, no tip for self-service.

➡ **Taxis** 10%, always rounding to a full euro.

➡ **Toilet attendants** €0.50.

It's considered rude to leave the tip on the table. Instead, tell the server the total amount you want to pay. If you don't want change back, say '*Stimmt so*' (that's fine).

Language

You can easily have a great time in Berlin without speaking a word of German. In fact, some bars and restaurants in expat-heavy Kreuzberg and Neukölln have entirely English- (and sometimes Spanish-) speaking staff. Many restaurant and cafe menus are now available in English and German (and sometimes only in English).

 Do you accept credit cards?
Nehmen Sie Kreditkarten?
nay·men zee kre·deet·kar·ten

Cash is still king in Germany, so don't assume you'll be able to pay by credit card – it's best to enquire first.

 Which beer would you recommend?
Welches Bier empfehlen Sie?
vel·khes beer emp·fay·len zee

Who better to ask for advice on beer than the Germans, whether at a beer garden, hall, cellar or on a brewery tour?

 Can I get this without meat?
Kann ich das ohne Fleisch bekommen?
kan ikh das aw·ne flaish be·ko·men

In the land of *Wurst* and *Schnitzel* it may be difficult to find a variety of vegetarian meals, especially in smaller towns.

 Do you speak English?
Sprechen Sie Englisch?
shpre·khen zee eng·lish

Given Berlin's cosmopolitan tapestry, the answer will most likely be 'yes' but it's still polite not to assume and to ask first.

 Do you run original versions?
Spielen auch Originalversionen?
shpee·len owkh o·ri·gi·nahl·fer·zi·aw·nen

German cinemas usually run movies dubbed into German – look for a cinema that runs subtitled original versions.

Etiquette

Although Berlin is fairly informal, there are a few general rules worth keeping in mind when meeting strangers.

➡ **Greetings** Shake hands and say '*Guten Morgen*' (before noon), '*Guten Tag*' (between noon and 6pm) or '*Guten Abend*' (after 6pm). Use the formal '*Sie*' (you) with strangers and only switch to the informal '*du*' and first names if invited to do so. With friends and children, use first names and '*du*'.

➡ **Asking for help** Germans use the same word – *Entschuldigung* – to say 'excuse me' (to attract attention) and 'sorry' (to apologise).

➡ **Eating and drinking** At the table, say '*Guten Appetit*' before digging in. Germans hold the fork in the left hand and the knife in the right hand. To signal that you have finished eating, lay your knife and fork parallel across your plate. If drinking wine, the proper toast is '*Zum Wohl*'; with beer it's '*Prost*'.

Top Itineraries

Day One

Historic Mitte (p76)

 One day in Berlin? Follow this whirl-wind itinerary to take in all the key sights. Book ahead for an early lift ride up to the dome of the **Reichstag**, then snap a picture of the **Brandenburg Gate** before exploring the maze of the **Holocaust Memorial** and admiring the contemporary architecture of **Potsdamer Platz**. View the **Berlin Wall remnants**, then head to **Checkpoint Charlie** to ponder the full extent of the Cold War madness.

 Lunch Renew your energies at Augustiner am Gendarmenmarkt (p90).

Historic Mitte (p76)

After lunch, soak up the glory of **Gendarmenmarkt**, drop by **Rausch Schokoladenhaus** for a chocolate treat and get a dose of retail therapy at the **Friedrichstadtpassagen**. Follow Unter den Linden east to **Museumsinsel** and spend at least an hour marvelling at the antiquities in the **Pergamonmuseum**. Beer-o'clock! Head over to **Strandbar Mitte** on the river.

Dinner Book ahead for dinner at Katz Orange (p138).

Scheunenviertel (p129)

After dinner, stroll over to the all-ages **Clärchens Ballhaus** for a spin on the dance floor or process the day's impressions over a nightcap at **Buck and Breck**.

Day Two

Prenzlauer Berg (p175)

 Spend a couple of hours coming to grips with what life in Berlin was like when the Wall still stood by exploring the **Gedenkstätte Berliner Mauer**. Take a quick spin around **Mauerpark**, then grab a coffee at **Bonanza Coffee Heroes** and poke around the boutiques on Kastanienallee.

Lunch W-der Imbiss (p183) and District Môt (p137) are buzzy pit stops.

Museumsinsel & Alexanderplatz (p94)

Start the afternoon by budgeting at least an hour for your audience with Queen Nefertiti and other treasures at the stunning **Neues Museum**, then relax while letting the sights drift by on a one-hour **river cruise** around Museumsinsel. Pop into the nearby **Humboldt-Box** to find out what to expect from the Prussian royal city palace that's being rebuilt opposite the museums. Enjoy the views over a coffee or cocktail on the top-floor panorama terrace of the **Humboldt-Terrassen**.

 Dinner Head to Kreuzberg and have a Turkish dinner at Defne (p154).

Kreuzberg & Neukölln (p145)

After dinner, go bar-hopping around Kottbusser Tor, try cocktails at **Würgeengel**, beer at **Möbel Olfe** or a little dancing at **Monarch Bar**.

Day Three

City West & Charlottenburg (p189)

 Day three starts at **Schloss Charlottenburg**, where the Neuer Flügel (New Wing) and the palace garden are essential stops. Take the bus to Zoologischer Garten and meditate upon the futility of war at the **Kaiser-Wilhelm-Gedächtniskirche**, then – assuming it's not Sunday – satisfy your shopping cravings along **Kurfürstendamm** and its side streets. Keep your wallet handy and drop by shopping malls **Bikini Berlin** and **KaDeWe**.

> **Lunch** Enjoy a casual lunch in the KaDeWe (p69) food hall.

Kreuzberg & Neukölln (p145)

Spend an hour or two at the amazing Daniel Libeskind–designed **Jüdisches Museum**, then head down to the wide open fields of **Tempelhofer Feld** to see how an old airport can be recycled into a sustainable park and playground. Have a break at the **Luftgarten** beer garden or find a favourite cafe among the many in northern Neukölln.

> **Dinner** Make a reservation at eins44 (p155) a Neukölln culinary hotspot.

Kreuzberg & Neukölln (p145)

You're already in party central, so hit the bars on Weserstrasse (**Thelonius** or **TiER** are recommended) and its side streets, then hit the dance floor at **Griessmühle** if you want to extend your evening.

Day Four

Potsdam (p113)

 There's plenty more to do in Berlin proper, but we recommend you spend the better part of the day exploring the parks and royal palaces in Potsdam, a mere 40-minute S-Bahn ride away. Buy online tickets for your favourite time slot to see **Schloss Sanssouci**, a rococo jewel of a palace. Afterwards, explore the surrounding park and its many smaller palaces at leisure. The **Chinesisches Haus** is a must-see.

> **Lunch** Have lunch at the exotic Drachenhaus (p208) in the park.

Potsdam (p113)

Continue your park explorations or head to Potsdam's old town for a spin around the **Holländisches Viertel** (Dutch Quarter). If you've still got room, have a *Flammkuchen* (Alsatian pizza) at **Maison Charlotte**, otherwise head back to Berlin and enjoy a well-deserved drink at **Prater** beer garden.

> **Dinner** Pull up a stool at Prenzlauer Berg's lovely Umami (p183).

Prenzlauer Berg (p175)

 After dinner, enjoy a stroll around beautiful Kollwitzplatz. Still got stamina? Turn your evening into a bar-hop, perhaps stopping at **Bryk Bar** or **Becketts Kopf** for fine cocktails.

If You Like...

Museums

Pergamonmuseum A treasure trove of monumental architecture from ancient civilisations. (p97)

Neues Museum Pay your respects to Queen Nefertiti, star of the Egyptian collection, then explore other priceless artefacts from ancient Troy and elsewhere. (p101)

Jüdisches Museum Comprehensive exhibits going beyond the Holocaust in tracing the rich history of Jews in Germany. (p147)

Museum für Naturkunde Meet giant dinos in Berlin's own 'Jurassic Park', then learn about the universe, evolution and even the anatomy of a housefly. (p134)

Deutsches Technikmuseum Plenty of planes, trains, boats and automobiles, plus the world's first computer and other techno gems. (p149)

Clubbing

Berghain/Panorama Bar Big, bad Berghain is still Berlin's dancing den of iniquity. (p172)

://about blank Wild, trashy, unpredictable and with a great garden for daytime partying. (p172)

Ritter Butzke Labyrinthine party house for extended electro-house dance-a-thons. (p157)

Clärchens Ballhaus Salsa, tango, ballroom, disco and swing's the thing in this campy retro ballroom. (p138)

KitKatClub Hedonistic pleasure pit for sexually adventurous latex and leather lovers. (p159)

House of Weekend Views and barbecue on rooftop terrace and top DJs. (p112)

TURTIX/GETTY IMAGES ©

Berliner Dom (p108)

Views

Fernsehturm Check off the landmarks from the needle-like TV Tower, Germany's tallest building. (p106)

Reichstag Dome Book ahead for the lift to the landmark glass dome atop German's historic parliament building. (p78)

Panoramapunkt Catch Europe's fastest lift at Potsdamer Platz for top views of the city centre. (p116)

Berliner Dom Climb into Berlin's largest church dome for gobsmacking views of Museum Island and the Humboldt Forum construction site. (p108)

Park Inn Panorama Terrasse Put yourself at eye level with the TV Tower on this open-air rooftop lounge atop the Park Inn Hotel. (p110)

Weltballon Berlin Soar above Berlin in this tethered hot-air balloon near Checkpoint Charlie. (p93)

Cold War History

Gedenkstätte Berliner Mauer Find out all about the Berlin Wall in a 1.4km long indoor-outdoor exhibit. (p177)

Stasimuseum Learn about the machinations of East Germany's secret police in its historic headquarters. (p171)

Stasi Prison Take a tour for a behind-the-scenes look at East Berlin's most notorious prison. (p171)

East Side Gallery Wander along the longest remaining stretch of Berlin Wall, now a street art canvas. (p166)

Tränenpalast Feel the emotional impact of the Berlin Wall at this 'Palace of Tears' border-crossing pavilion. (p88)

WWII Sites

Topographie des Terrors Peels away the layers of brutality of the Nazi regime on the site of the SS and Gestapo command centres. (p85)

Holocaust Memorial Germany's central memorial to the Nazi-orchestrated genocide of European Jews is a haunting site indeed. (p81)

Sachsenhausen A visit to one of Nazi Germany's first concentration camps, in Oranienburg just north of Berlin, will leave no one untouched. (p209)

Gedenkstätte Deutscher Widerstand Tells the stories of the brave German Nazi resistance, including Stauffenberg's failed 'Operation Valkyrie'. (p123)

Haus der Wannsee-Konferenz Get shivers while standing in the very room where Nazi leaders discussed the 'final solution'. (p214)

Modern Architecture

Jüdisches Museum Daniel Libeskind's astonishing zigzag-shaped architectural metaphor for Jewish history in Germany. (p147)

Neues Museum David Chipperfield's reconstructed New Museum ingeniously blends old and new into something bold and beautiful. (p101)

Sony Center Helmut Jahn's svelte glass-and-steel complex is the most striking piece of architecture on Potsdamer Platz. (p115)

IM Pei Bau Relentlessly geometrical, glass-spiral-fronted museum annexe by the 'Mandarin of Modernism'. (p82)

For more top Berlin spots, see the following:
→ Eating (p47)
→ Drinking & Nightlife (p53)
→ Gay & Lesbian Berlin (p60)
→ Entertainment (p64)
→ Shopping (p69)

Quirky Experiences

Badeschiff Cool off in summer in this river barge turned swimming pool with attached beach club. (p163)

Museum der Unerhörten Dinge Examine the way you look at museums in this mind-bending exhibit of curiosities. (p33)

Roses The wildest, wackiest and campiest bar in Kreuzberg (hint: pink fur on the walls). (p161)

Monster Ronson's Ichiban Karaoke Loosen your throat and your inhibitions to hang with the crowd. (p173)

Monsterkabinett Descend into a dark and bizarre underworld inhabited by a small army of endearingly spooky mechanical monsters. (p135)

Art Collections

Gemäldegalerie An Aladdin's cave of Old Masters has heads turning in its expansive Kulturforum space. (p118)

Sammlung Boros World-class private collection of contemporaries in a rambling WWII bunker. (p133)

Hamburger Bahnhof Sweeping survey of post-1950 global art in a spectacularly converted train station. (p131)

Museum Berggruen Priceless Picassos plus works by Klee and

Giacometti in a newly expanded building. (p193)

Brücke-Museum Groundbreaking canvases by 'The Bridge', Germany's first modern-artist group (1905–13). (p212)

Bauhaus Archiv Showcase of works by key teachers of the school that was the midwife of modern architecture and design. (p123)

Royal Encounters

Schloss Charlottenburg This pretty Prussian power display delivers a glimpse into the sumptuous lifestyles of the rich and royal. (p191)

Schloss Sanssouci The most famous palace in Park Sanssouci drips in opulence and overlooks vine-draped terraces and a big fountain. (p203)

Berliner Dom The royal court church has impressive dimensions, a palatial design and elaborately carved sarcophagi for the remains of kings and queens. (p108)

Pfaueninsel Romantic island with a fanciful palace and strutting peacocks, built by a king for tête-à-têtes with his mistress. (p213)

Music

Berliner Philharmonie Berlin's most iconic classical concert venue and home of the world-famous Berliner Philharmoniker. (p128)

Bearpit Karaoke Feel-good Sunday karaoke event in the Mauerpark. (p185)

Konzerthaus This Schinkel-built jewel graces Gendarmenmarkt and is a fabulous classical music venue. (p92)

Sonntagskonzerte Intimate concerts amid the faded glamour of a century-old mirror-clad ballroom. (p142)

Astra Kulturhaus This midsize concert hall with commie-era decor draws big rock, pop and electro names. (p173)

Markets

Flohmarkt am Mauerpark Gets deluged with visitors in summer but still offers a primo urban archaeology experience. (p187)

Street Food Thursday Global bites, local craft beer and people-watching in a 19th-century market hall. (p155)

Türkischer Markt Berlin meets the Bosphorus at this bustling canal-side farmers' market with budget-priced produce. (p162)

Nowkoelln Flowmarkt Hipster market with lots of handmade treasures and impromptu concerts. (p163)

Kollwitzplatzmarkt Discerning gourmets can source the finest morsels for that ultimate picnic. (p188)

Parks & Gardens

Tiergarten Take pleasure in getting lost amid the lawns, trees and paths of one of the world's largest city parks. (p122)

Schlossgarten Charlottenburg Stake out a picnic spot near the carp and ponder royal splendours. (p191)

Park Sanssouci Find your favourite corner away from the crowds for a little time 'without cares'. (p204)

Volkspark Friedrichshain Rambling 'people's park' offering plenty of diversions and covering two 'mountains' made from WWII debris. (p169)

Viktoriapark Pint-sized park atop Berlin's highest 'peak', the 66m-high Kreuzberg; with beer garden and playground. (p150)

Naughty Berlin

KitKatClub Dive in and be as nice or nasty as you desire – but do follow the dress code. (p159)

Insomnia Worship at the altar of hedonism at this sassy, sexy dance club with performances and playrooms. (p159)

Schwarzer Reiter Classy purveyor of anything boys and girls with imagination might need for a fun encounter. (p143)

Lab.oratory The place for gays to live out their most frisky, completely uncensored, fantasies. (p173)

Other Nature Discover alternative pleasures at this sex shop with a feminist and queer focus. (p163)

1920s & Cabaret

Chamäleon Varieté Intimate former ballroom delivering an alchemy of acrobatics, artistry and sex appeal. (p142)

Bar Jeder Vernunft Gorgeous mirrored tent that makes you feel as if you're on the set of *Cabaret*. (p200)

Friedrichstadt-Palast Europe's largest revue theatre has long-legged beauties putting on sparkly Old Vegas–style shows. (p142)

1. Absinth Depot Berlin Make a date with the 'green fairy' at this eccentric libation station. (p144)

Prinzipal Burlesque-themed bar with occasional shows, and cocktails named after famous performers. (p161)

Month By Month

January

New Year's Eve may be wrapped up, but nighttime hotspots show no signs of slowing down, especially not during Fashion Week. Cold weather invites extended museum visits and foraging at the Internationale Grüne Woche (Green Week) food fair.

🔒 Berlin Fashion Week

Twice a year (again in July), international fashion folk book up all the trendy hotels (and restaurants) while here to present or assess next season's threads. See www.fashion-week-berlin.com for public events.

🍴 Internationale Grüne Woche

Find out about the latest food trends and gorge on global morsels at this nine-day fair (www.gruene woche.de) of food, agriculture and gardening.

February

Days are still dark but Berlin perks up when glamour comes to town during the famous film festival. A full theatre, opera, concert and party schedule also tempts people out of the house.

✦ Transmediale

Digital-media art gets full bandwidth at this edgy festival (www.transmediale.de), which investigates the links between art, culture and technology through exhibitions, conferences, screenings and performances.

✦ Berlinale

Berlin's international film festival (www.berlinale.de) draws stars, starlets, directors, critics and the world's A-to-Z-list celebrities for two weeks of screenings and glamorous parties around town. The best ones go home with a Golden or Silver Bear.

March

Could there be spring in the air? This is still a good time to see the sights without the crowds, but hotel rooms fill to capacity during the big tourism fair.

✦ Internationale Tourismus Börse

Take a virtual trip around the globe at the world's largest international travel expo (www.itb-berlin.de); it's trade-only during the week but open to the public at the weekend.

☆ Maerzmusik

'Music' or 'soundscapes'? You decide after a day at this contemporary music festival (www.berlinerfestspiele.de), which explores and celebrates a boundary-pushing palette of sounds – from orchestral symphonies to experimental recitals.

April

Life starts moving outdoors as cafe tables appear on pavements and you begin to see budding trees on walks in the park. Hotels get busy over the Easter holidays.

✥ Achtung Berlin

Flicks about Berlin, and at least partially produced in the city, compete for the New Berlin Film Award at this festival (achtungberlin. de). Screenings are often attended by writers, directors, producers and actors.

☆ Festtage

Daniel Barenboim, music director of Berlin's internationally renowned Staatsoper opera house, brings the world's finest conductors, soloists and orchestras together for this 10-day highbrow hoedown of gala concerts and operas (www. staatsoper-berlin.de).

✥ Gallery Weekend

Join collectors, critics and other art aficionados in keeping tabs on the Berlin art scene on a free hop around 40 of the city's best galleries (www.gallery-weekend-berlin.de) over the last weekend in April.

May

Spring is in, making this a fabulous month to visit Berlin. Time for beer gardens, picnics and walks among blossoming trees. White asparagus appears in markets and on menus. Don't forget your sunglasses!

✥ Karneval der Kulturen

Every Whitsuntide (Pentecost) weekend, the Carnival of Cultures (www.karneval-berlin.de) celebrates Berlin's multicultural tapestry

with four days of music, dance, art and culture, culminating in a raucous parade of flamboyantly dressed performers shimmying through the streets of Kreuzberg.

☆ Theatertreffen

The Berlin Theatre Meeting is a three-week showcase of new productions by emerging and established German-language ensembles from Germany, Austria and Switzerland (www. theatertreffen-berlin.de).

June

Festival season kicks into high gear around the summer solstice with plenty of al fresco events, thanks to a rising temperature gauge.

✥ Berlin Biennale

This biennial curated forum for contemporary art explores international trends and invites newcomers to showcase their work around town for about eight weeks (www.berlin biennale.de). The next is in 2018.

☆ Fête de la Musique

Summer starts with good vibrations thanks to hundreds of free concerts during this global music festival (www.fetedela musique.de) that first came online in Paris in 1982. Held each year on 21 June.

✥ Christopher Street Day

No matter what your sexual persuasion, come out and paint the town pink at this huge pride parade (www. csd-berlin.de/en) featuring

floats often decorated with queer political statements and filled with naked torsos writhing to techno beats. Sometimes held in July.

July

Hot summer days send Berliners scurrying to the lakes in town or the surrounding countryside. Gourmets rejoice in the bounty of fresh local produce in the markets. Expect long lines at main sights and attractions.

☆ Classic Open Air Festival

Five nights, five al fresco concerts – from opera to pop – delight an adoring crowd hunkered on bleachers before the palatial backdrop of the Konzerthaus (www.classicopenair.de) on Gendarmenmarkt.

☆ Wassermusik

The Haus der Kulturen der Welt makes waves with this popular series of water-themed concerts (www. hkw.de/wassermusik) held on its roof terrace and combined with related events like markets and movies.

🔒 Berlin Fashion Week

Local and international designers present next year's spring fashions during the summer edition of Berlin's fashion fair (www.fashion-week-berlin.com).

August

More outdoor fun than anyone can handle with concerts in parks, daytime clubbing, languid boat

(Top) Karneval der Kulturen (p24), in Kreuzberg, celebrates multiculturalism

(Bottom) A Christmas market at Gendarmenmarkt (p83)

rides, beach-bar partying, lake swimming and a huge beer festival.

🍷 Berliner Bierfestival

Who needs Oktoberfest when you can have the 'world's longest beer garden' (www.bierfestival-berlin.de)? As the bands play on, pick your poison from some 340 breweries representing 90 countries with over 2000 beers along 2.2km of Karl-Marx-Allee.

☆ Tanz im August

Step out gracefully to this three-week dance festival (www.tanzimaugust.de), which attracts loose-limbed talent and highly experimental choreography from around the globe.

🎆 Lange Nacht der Museen

Culture meets entertainment during the Long Night of the Museums (www.lange-nacht-der-museen.de) when around 80 museums welcome visitors between 6pm and 2am.

September

Kids are back in school but there's still plenty of partying to be done and often fine weather to enjoy. As days get shorter, the new theatre, concert and opera season begins.

🎆 Berlin Art Week

This contemporary art fair (www.berlinartweek.de) combines art exhibits, fairs and awards with talks, film and tours. It also provides a chance to see private collections, project spaces and artist studios.

🏃 Berlin Marathon

Sweat it out with the other 40,000 runners or just cheer 'em on during Germany's biggest street race (www.berlin-marathon.com), which has seen nine world records set since 1977.

☆ Musikfest Berlin

World-renowned orchestras, choirs, conductors and soloists come together for 21 days of concerts (www.berlinerfestspiele.de) at the Philharmonie and other venues.

🍺 Braufest Berlin

This free festival (www.braufest-berlin.de) celebrates Berlin's growing craft-beer scene with two days of tastings of new-wave suds, music and partying.

October

It's getting nippy again and trees start shedding their summer coats, but Berlin keeps a bright disposition, and not only during the Festival of Lights.

✨ Festival of Lights

For two weeks Berlin is all about 'lightseeing' during this shimmering festival (www.festival-of-lights.de) when historic landmarks such as the TV Tower, the Berliner Dom and the Brandenburg Gate sparkle with illuminations, projections and fireworks.

✨ Porn Film Festival

Vintage porn, Japanese porn, indie porn, sci-fi porn – the 'Berlinale' of sex (www.pornfilmfestivalberlin.de) brings alternative skin flicks out of the smut corner and on to the big screen.

✨ Tag der deutschen Einheit

Raise a toast to reunification on 3 October, the German national holiday celebrated with street parties across town – from the Brandenburg Gate to the Rotes Rathaus (town hall).

November

A great time to visit if you don't like crowds and are keen on snapping up hotel bargains. Weather-wise it's not the prettiest of months, but don't let that darken your mood.

☆ JazzFest Berlin

This top-rated jazz festival (www.berlinerfestspiele.de) has doo-wopped in Berlin since 1964 and presents fresh and big-time talent in dozens of performances all over town.

December

Days are short and cold but the mood is festive, thanks to dressed-up shop windows, illuminated streets and facades, and Christmas markets redolent with the aroma of roast almonds and mulled wine.

🎁 Christmas Markets

Pick up shimmering ornaments or indulge in mulled wine at dozens of Yuletide markets held throughout the city.

✨ Nikolaus

On St Nicholas' Day (6 December) children leave their shoes outside their door to receive sweets if they've been nice, or a stone if they've been naughty; eventually this developed into Santa's international rounds. Germans are pretty attached to the original – all kinds of clubs hold Nikolaus parties, complete with costumed St Nicks.

✨ Silvester

New Year's Eve is the time to hug strangers, coo at fireworks, guzzle bubbly straight from the bottle and generally misbehave. The biggest public bash is at the Brandenburg Gate.

MAY DAY/MYFEST

May Day demonstrations used to be riotous affairs with heavily armed police and leftist groups facing off in Kreuzberg, complete with flying stones and burning cars. Although an official 'Revolutionary May Day' demonstration still draws as many as 15,000 anticapitalist, antifascist protesters, it's now considerably more peaceful. This is due partly to an enormous police presence, and partly to the alternative, largely apolitical Myfest, held in Kreuzberg since 2003. It runs from noon to midnight. The actual Revolutionary May Day demonstration starts at 6pm at Lausitzer Platz. RevolutionaryBerlin Tours (www.revolutionaeres berlin.wordpress.com) runs English-language walking tours about the May Day Riots on request.

With Kids

Travelling to Berlin can be child's play, especially if you keep a light schedule and involve them in day-to-day planning. There's plenty to do to keep youngsters occupied, from zoos to kid-oriented museums. Parks and imaginative playgrounds abound in all neighbourhoods, as do public pools.

A Lego giraffe outside Legoland Discovery Centre (p116)

Museums

Museum für Naturkunde (Museum of Natural History)

Meet giant dinosaurs, travel through space back to the beginning of time and find out why zebras are striped in this wonderful museum (p134).

Science Center Spectrum

Toddlers to teens get to play with, experience and learn about such concepts as balance, weight, water, air and electricity by pushing buttons, pulling levers and otherwise engaging in dozens of hands-on science **experiments** (Map p314, A3; ☑030-9025 4284; www.sdtb.de; Möckernstrasse 26; adult/concession/under 18 €8/4/free after 3pm; ☺9am-5.30pm Tue-Fri, 10am-6pm Sat & Sun; ℙ; Ⓤ Möckernbrücke, Gleisdreieck) (p149).

Deutsches Technikmuseum (German Museum of Technology)

Next to the Science Center Spectrum, the collection here is so vast, it is best to concentrate time and energy on two or three sections that interest your tech-loving kids the most. The one-hour kid-geared audioguide tour provides a good introduction (p149).

Madame Tussauds

Kids of any age are all smiles when posing with the waxen likeness of their favourite pop star or celluloid celebrity (p86).

Legoland Discovery Centre

The milk-tooth set delights in this Lego wonderland (p116) with rides, entertainment and interactive stations.

Computerspielemuseum (Computer Games Museum)

Teens can get their kicks in this universe of computer games (p167) – from Pac-Man to World of Warcraft.

Mauermuseum (Wall Museum)

Teenagers with an interest in history and a decent attention span may enjoy the ingenious homemade contraptions used to escape from East Germany (p89).

Loxx am Alex Miniatur Welten

Berlin in miniature built around a huge model railway (p107).

Parks, Pools & Playgrounds

Park am Gleisdreieck

This family-friendly park (p150) is packed with fun zones including adventure playgrounds, basketball courts, a huge skate park and a nature garden.

Kollwitzplatz

This square (p179) sports three playgrounds for different age groups, including one with giant wooden toys. All get busy in the afternoon and on weekends. Cafes and ice-cream parlours are just a hop, skip and jump away.

Kinderbad Monbijou

Keep cool on hot days splashing about this family-friendly public **pool** (Map p302, B5; ☎030-2219 0011; www.berliner-baeder.de; Oranienburger Strasse 78; adult/child €5.50/3.50; 🕒11am-7pm mid-Jun–early Sep; 🚋M1, [S]Hackescher Markt, Oranienburger Strasse) in the Scheunenviertel.

Animals

Berlin Zoo & Aquarium

If the 20,000 furry, feathered and finned friends fail to enchant the little ones, there's also always the enormous adventure playground (p195).

NEED TO KNOW

➡ **Child minding services** Get an English-speaking babysitter at Babysitter Express (www.babysitter-express.de) or Welcome Kids (www.welcome-kids.de).

➡ **Public transport** Children under six travel free and those between six and 14 pay the concession fare.

➡ **Entrance fees** Many museums, monuments and attractions are free to anyone under age 18, but the cut-off might also be age 12 or 14.

Tierpark Berlin

Expect plenty of ooh and aah moments when kids watch baby elephants at play or see lions and tigers being fed at this vast animal **park** (☎030-515 310; www.tierpark-berlin.de; adult/concession/child 4-15yr €13/9/6; 🕒zoo 9am-6.30pm Apr-Sep, to 6pm Mar & Oct, to 4.30pm Nov-Feb, palace 11am-5pm Tue & Thu-Sun; [U]Tierpark).

Sealife Berlin

At Sealife (p107), little ones get to press their noses against dozens of fish-filled tanks, solve puzzles and even touch starfish and sea anemones – ever so gently, of course.

Domäne Dahlem

Kids can interact with their favourite barnyard animals, help collect eggs, harvest potatoes or just generally watch daily farm life unfold at this fun working **farm** (☎030-666 3000; www.domaene-dahlem.de; Königin-Luise-Strasse 49; adult/concession/under 18 grounds €2/1/free, museum €4/2/free; 🕒grounds 8am-8pm May-Sep, to 7pm Oct-Apr, museum 10am-5pm Tue-Sun; [P] 👪; [U]Dahlem-Dorf).

Eating Out with Kids

It's fine to eat out as a family any time of the day, especially in cafes, bistros and pizzerias. Many offer a limited *Kindermenü* (children's menu) or *Kinderteller* (children's dishes) to meet small appetite requirements. If they don't, most will be happy to serve half-size portions or prepare a simple meal. Popular dishes include schnitzel, *Pommes mit Ketchup or Mayonnaise* (fries with ketchup or mayo), *Nudeln mit Tomatensosse* (noodles with tomato sauce) and *Fischstäbchen* (fish sticks).

Large malls have food courts while larger department stores feature self-service cafeterias. Farmers markets also have food stalls. Bakeries selling scrumptious cakes and sandwiches are plentiful. The most popular snacks-on-the-run are bratwurst in a bun or doner kebab (sliced meat tucked into a pita pocket with salad and sauce).

Baby food, infant formula, soya and cow's milk, disposable nappies (diapers) and the like are widely available in supermarkets and chemists (drugstores).

Like a Local

Local life in Berlin is not as settled upon as in other cities but is defined to some extent by the enormous influx of neo-Berliners from abroad and other parts of Germany. As such, it's comparatively easy to mingle with locals and to partake in their customs.

MARK READ/LONELY PLANET ©

Weinbar Rutz (p138)

Dining Like A Local

Berliners love to dine out and, taking advantage of the city's many reasonably priced cafes and restaurants, do so quite frequently. This can mean scarfing down a quick doner at the local kebab joint or indulging in a four-course meal in a foodie hotspot. Eating out is rarely just about getting fed but is also a social experience. Meeting friends or family over a meal is considered a great way to catch up, engage in heated discussions or exchange the latest gossip.

Going out for breakfast has been a beloved pastime for years, although the trend seems to have peaked. Enjoying a meal out at lunchtime is no longer the domain of just desk jockeys and business people on expense accounts as many restaurants (including Michelin-starred ones) now offer daily specials or set menus at reduced prices. The traditional German afternoon-coffee-and-cake ritual is not practised widely in Berlin, and is pretty much the realm of more mature generations. The main going-out meal is dinner, with restaurant tables usually filled at 7.30pm or 8pm. Since it's customary to stretch meals to two hours and then linger over a last glass of wine, restaurants – for now – only count on one seating per table per night. Servers will not present you with the bill until you ask for it.

Partying Like a Local

Most Berliners start the night around 9pm or 10pm in a pub or bar, although it's also common to meet at someone's home for a few cheap drinks in a ritual called *'Vorglühen'* (literally 'preglowing'). Once out on the town, people either stay for a few drinks at the same place or pop into several spots, before moving on to a club around 1am or 2am at the earliest.

In most pubs and bars, it's common practice to place orders with a server rather than pick up your own drinks at the bar. Only do the latter if that's what everyone does or if you see a sign saying *'Selbstbedienung'* (self-service). It is not expected (nor customary) to buy entire rounds for everyone at the table.

Once in the club, how long one stays depends on individual stamina and alcohol and drug consumption. Hardy types stagger

MARK READ/LONELY PLANET ©

Picnickers on the Spree River

out into the morning sunshine, although the most hardcore may last even longer. Since some clubs don't close at all on weekends, it's becoming increasingly popular to start the party in the daytime and go home at, say 11pm, for a normal night's sleep. But don't feel bad if that's not your thing. Partying in Berlin does indeed take some practice...

Shopping Like a Local

Berliners pretty much fulfil all their shopping needs in their local *Kiez* (neighbourhood). There will usually be three or four supermarkets within walking distance. Most people don't get all their grocery shopping done in one fell swoop but rather make several smaller trips spread over the course of the week. Since some supermar-

NEED TO KNOW

For many Berliners, the preferred way of getting around town is by bicycle, so why not join them and rent your own two-wheeler? Alternatively, and especially in bad weather, take advantage of Berlin's excellent public transport system. For sightseeing on the cheap, hop aboard bus 100 or 200.

kets have started home delivery, ordering online is becoming more popular.

The local farmers' market is the preferred source of fresh produce and speciality products like handmade noodles, artisanal cheese and Turkish cheese spreads. Days start with fresh *Brötchen* (rolls) bought from the bakery around the corner. Non-food needs are also met locally where possible, be it stationery, gifts, flowers, books, hardware, wine or what have you.

Clothing will come from a mix of places that may include high-street chains, indie boutiques, vintage stores, flea markets and, of course, online shops. When Berliners venture out of their neighbourhoods to shop, it's usually to buy big-ticket items like furniture or vehicles, or speciality items not available locally. There are a few big malls in the city centre, such as LP12 Mall of Berlin (p128) and Alexa (p112), but generally these are more commonly located in the suburbs.

Living Like a Local

The typical Berlin dwelling is a spacious rented two-bedroom flat on at least the 1st floor of a large early-20th-century apartment building (no one wants to live at street level), probably facing on to a

Hinterhof (back courtyard) full of bicycles and coloured recycling bins. The apartment itself has very high ceilings, large windows and, as often as not, stripped wooden plank floors. The kitchen will almost invariably be the smallest room in the house and right next to the bathroom. Some kitchens have small pantries and/or storage rooms.

Berlin flats are usually nicely turned out, whatever the style favoured by the occupant. Much attention is paid to design, though comfort is also considered. At least one item of furniture will come from a certain Swedish furniture chain. Depending on income, the rest may come from the Stilwerk design centre, Polish crafters, a flea market or eBay – or any combination thereof.

Relaxing Like a Local

Although they are passionate about their city, Berliners also love to get out of town, especially in summer. If they're not jetting off to Mallorca or Mauritius, they will at least try to make it out to a local lake on a sunny day. There are dozens right in town, including the **Plötzensee** (☑0176 3441 8634, 030-8964 4787; www.strandbad-ploetzensee. de; Nordufer 26; adult/concession €5/3; ⊙9am-7pm May-Sep; 🚌M13, 50) in Wedding, the Weissensee near Prenzlauer Berg, the vast Müggelsee (p215) in Köpenick and the Wannsee (p214) in Zehlendorf – all easily reached by public transport. Hundreds more are just a quick car or train ride away in the surrounding countryside of Brandenburg. Everyone's got their favourite body of water and, having staked out the perfect spot, tends to return there time and again.

With equally easy access to some fabulous parks, Berliners love heading for the greenery to work on their tan, relax in the shade, play Frisbee or catch up on their reading. Some parks have sections where barbecuing is permitted.

Sightseeing Like a Local

Most locals – especially more recent arrivals – are very appreciative of Berlin's cultural offerings and keep tabs on the latest museum and gallery openings, theatre productions and construction projects. It's quite common to discuss the merits of the latest play or exhibit at dinner tables.

Although they love being a tourist in their own city, Berliners stay away from the big-ticket sights in summer when the world comes to town. More likely they will bide their time until the cold and dark winter months or visit on late-opening nights for smaller crowds. The annual Lange Nacht der Museen (Long Night of the Museums, usually in August), when dozens of museums stay open past midnight, brings out culture vultures by the tens of thousands.

Local Obsessions

Soccer

Many Berliners live and die by the fortunes of the local soccer team, Hertha BSC, which has seen its shares of ups and downs in recent years. After a brief stint in *2. Fussball-Bundesliga* (Second Soccer League), the team returned to the top-level Bundesliga in the 2013–14 season – much to the relief of locals. Still, true fans don't quit the team when it's down and, during the season, many will inevitably don their blue-and-white fan gear to make the trek out to the Olympic Stadium (p200) for home games.

Berlin's other major team, 1. FC Union, plays in the second league and has an especially passionate following in the eastern parts of the city.

The Weather

Many locals are hobby meteorologists who will never pass up a chance to express their opinion on tomorrow's weather or on whether it's been a good summer so far, whether the last winter was mild or brutal, what to expect from the next one, and so on... So if you run out of things to say to a local, get the conversation going again by mentioning the weather. Other popular topics are rising rents, the perceived ineptitude of the local government or the much delayed opening of the Berlin Brandenburg Airport.

For Free

It's no secret that you can get more bang for your euro in Berlin than in any other Western European capital. Better still, there are plenty of ways to stretch your budget further by cashing in on some tip-top freebies, including such sights as the Reichstag dome and Holocaust Memorial.

A remnant of the Berlin Wall, East Side Gallery (p166)

Free History Exhibits

Given that Germany has played a disproportionate role in 20th-century history, it's only natural that there are plenty of memorial sites and exhibits shedding light on various (mostly grim) milestones. Best of all, they're all free.

World War II

Study up on the SS, Gestapo and other organisations of the Nazi power apparatus at the Topographie des Terrors (p85) exhibit, then see the desk where WWII ended with the signing of Germany's unconditional surrender at the Deutsch-Russisches Museum Berlin-Karlshorst (p216). You can stand in the very room where the 'final solution' was planned at the Haus der Wannsee-Konferenz (p214), get shivers while walking around the Sachsenhausen (p209) concentration camp, then pay your respects to Jewish Nazi victims at the Holocaust Memorial (p81). German resistance against the Nazis is the focus of the Gedenkstätte Deutscher Widerstand (p123), the Gedenkstätte Stille Helden (p141) and the Museum Blinden-werkstatt Otto Weidt (p141).

Cold War

The East Side Gallery (p166) may be the longest surviving section of the Berlin Wall, but to get the full picture of the Wall's physical appearance and human impact swing by the Gedenkstätte Berliner Mauer (p177) and the Tränenpalast (p88). For an eyeful of what daily life was like behind the Iron Curtain, drop by the new Museum in der Kulturbrauerei (p179). At Checkpoint Charlie (p88), an outdoor exhibit chronicles milestones in Cold War history. For the Cold War years from the point of view of the western Allies, swing by the Alliierten-Museum (p212).

Free Museums & Galleries
State Museums

Admission to the permanent exhibits at Berlin's state museums – including the Pergamonmuseum (p97), Neues Museum (p101), Gemäldegalerie (p118) and Hamburger Bahnhof (p131) – is free for anyone under 18.

Niche Museums

Although the blockbuster state museums do charge admission to adults, a few niche museums don't. Learn about the history of German democracy at the Deutscher Dom (p83), life during the Biedermeier at the Knoblauchhaus (p109), and Berlin's equivalent of Oskar Schindler at the Museum Blindenwerkstatt Otto Weidt (p141). Free art can be enjoyed at the Daimler Contemporary (p117) and unusual objects at the **Museum der Unerhörten Dinge** (Museum of 'Unheard of' Things; ☏030-781 4932, 0175 410 9120; www. museumderunerhoertendinge.de; Crellestrasse 5-6; admission free; ☺3-7pm Wed-Fri; Ⓤ Kleistpark, Ⓢ Julius-Leber-Brücke) FREE. Military and aeroplane buffs can travel to the city outskirts for the Militärhistorisches Museum – Flugplatz Berlin-Gatow (p211).

Sometimes Free

Museums offering free admission at certain times include the Akademie der Künste (p125) from 3pm to 7pm Tuesday; Deutsche Bank KunstHalle (p86) on Mondays; Museum für Film und Fernsehen (p116) from 4pm to 8pm Thursday; and the Märkisches Museum (p109), Ephraim-Palais (p109) and Nikolaikirche (p108) on the first Wednesday of the month.

Free Guided Tours

Many museums and galleries include free multilingual audioguides in the admission price; some also offer free guided tours, although these are usually in German.

Alternative Berlin Tours (p270), New Berlin Tours (p270) and Brewer's Berlin Tours (p270) are English-language walking tour companies that advertise 'free' guided tours, although guides depend on tips.

Free Music

Free gigs and music events take place all the time, in pubs, bars, parks and churches. See the listings magazines for what's on during your stay.

Summer Concerts

In summer, many of Berlin's parks and gardens ring out with the free sound of jazz, pop, samba and classical music. Case in point: the lovely Teehaus im Englischen

---

Garten (p124) presents two Sunday concerts (at 4pm and 7pm) in July and August.

Karaoke

The Mauerpark is a zoo-and-a-half on hot summer Sundays, thanks largely to the massively entertaining outdoor Bearpit Karaoke (p185), which sees thousands of spectators cramming on to the stone bleachers to cheer and applaud crooners of various talent levels.

Classical

At 1pm on Tuesdays from September to mid-June, the foyer of the Berliner Philharmonie (p128) fills with music lovers for free lunchtime chamber-music concerts. Students of the prestigious Hochschule für Musik Hanns Eisler (p92) also show off their skills at several free recitals weekly. At 12.30pm from Tuesday to Sunday, you can enjoy free organ recitals at the Matthäuskirche (p122) in the Kulturforum. The Französischer Dom (p83) on Gendarmenmarkt has free organ concerts at the same time from Tuesday to Friday.

Rock & Jazz

For one-off free concerts, check the listings magazines. Jazz fans can bop gratis at A-Trane (p201) on Mondays and at the late-night jam session after 12.30am on Saturday. On Wednesdays, b-Flat (p143) has its own free jam sessions. **Kunstfabrik Schlot** (Map p304, C1; ☏030-448 2160; www.kunstfabrik-schlot.de; Invalidenstrasse 117, Schlegelstrasse 26; tickets €3-20; ☺daily; Ⓢ Nordbahnhof, Ⓤ Naturkundemuseum) is the go-to freebie on most Mondays and Thursdays.

MPAYNE13/BUDGET TRAVEL ©

A remnant of the Berlin Wall

◉ The Berlin Wall

It's more than a tad ironic that Berlin's most popular tourist attraction is one that no longer exists. For 28 years the Berlin Wall, the most potent symbol of the Cold War, divided not only a city but the world.

The Beginning

Shortly after midnight on 13 August 1961, East German soldiers and police began rolling out miles of barbed wire that would soon be replaced with prefab concrete slabs. All of a sudden, streets were cut in two, transportation between the city halves was halted and East Germans, including commuters, were no longer allowed to travel to West Berlin.

The Berlin Wall was a desperate measure launched by the German Democratic Republic (GDR, East Germany) to stop the sustained brain-and-brawn drain the country had experienced since its 1949 founding. Some 3.6 million people had already headed to western Germany, putting the GDR on the brink of economic and political collapse. The actual construction of the Wall, came as a shock to many: only a couple of months before that fateful August day, GDR head of state Walter Ulbricht had declared at a press conference that there were no plans to build a wall.

The Physical Border

Euphemistically called the 'Anti-Fascist Protection Barrier', the Berlin Wall was an instrument of oppression that turned West Berlin into an island of democracy within a sea of socialism. It consisted of a 43km-long inner-city barrier separating West from East Berlin and a 112km border between West Berlin and East Germany. Each reinforced concrete segment was 3.6m high, 1.2m wide and weighed 2.6 tonnes. In some areas, the border strip included the Spree River or canals.

Continually reinforced and refined over time, the Berlin Wall eventually grew into a complex border-security system consisting of not one, but two, walls: the main wall abutting the border with West Berlin and the so-called hinterland security wall, with the 'death strip' in between. A would-be escapee who managed to scale the hinterland wall was first confronted with an electrified fence that triggered an alarm. After this, he or she would have to contend with guard dogs, spiked fences, trenches and other obstacles. Other elements included a patrol path with lamp posts that would flood the death strip with glaring light at night. Set up at regular intervals along the entire border were 300 watchtowers staffed by guards with shoot-to-kill orders. Only nine towers remain, including the one at Erna-Berger-Strasse (p117) near Potsdamer Platz.

In West Berlin, the Wall came right up to residential areas. Artists tried to humanise the grey concrete scar by covering it in colourful graffiti. The West Berlin government erected viewing platforms, which people could climb to peek across into East Berlin.

Escapes

There are no exact numbers, but it is believed that of the nearly 100,000 GDR citizens who tried to escape, hundreds died in the process, many by drowning, suffering fatal accidents or committing suicide when caught. More than 100 were shot and killed by border guards – the first only a few days after 13 August 1961. Guards who prevented an escape were rewarded with commendations, promotions and bonuses.

The first person to be shot at the Wall was 24-year-old trained tailor Günter Litfin. The Wall had been in existence for only 11 days when a hailstorm of bullets ripped through his body as he tried to swim to freedom across a 40m-wide canal on 24 August 1961, a Sunday. Since 2003, his brother Jürgen Litfin has kept Günter's legacy alive with a **memorial exhibit** (☎030-2362 6183; www.gedenkstaetteguenterlitfin.de; Kieler Strasse 2; 🕒tours half-hourly 11.30am-1.30pm Sun-Thu Mar-Oct; [S]Naturkundemuseum, Hauptbahnhof, 🚆Hauptbahnhof,) [FREE] in a GDR watchtower near where he was killed. It's a bit off the beaten path but well worth visiting, not only to see the inside of this rare border relic but mainly for a chance to meet this outspoken eyewitness to history.

Another famous incident illustrating the barbarity of the shoot-to-kill order occurred on 17 August 1962 when 18-year-old would-be escapee Peter Fechter was shot and wounded and then left to bleed to death as East German guards looked on. There's a memorial (p86) in his honour on Zimmerstrasse, near Checkpoint Charlie. Behind the Reichstag, on the southern bank of the Spree River, the seven white crosses of the Gedenkort Weisse Kreuze (p86) commemorate the Wall victims, as does the emotional 'Window of Remembrance' at the Gedenkstätte Berliner Mauer (p177). This memorial features the names and photographs of all the people who were shot or died in an accident while attempting to escape.

The Gedenkstätte Berliner Mauer runs along 1.4km of Bernauer Strasse, which was literally split in two by the Berlin Wall, with one side of apartment buildings on the western side and the other in the east. As the barrier was erected, many residents on the eastern side decided to flee spontaneously by jumping into rescue nets or sliding down ropes, risking severe injury and death. Bernauer Strasse was also where several escape tunnels were dug, most famously Tunnel 29 in 1962, so named because 29 people managed to flee to the West before border guards detected the route.

The fact that there was no limit to the ingenuity of would-be escapees is documented at the Mauermuseum (p89) near Checkpoint Charlie. On display are several original contraptions used to flee East Germany, including a hot air balloon, a hollow surfboard, a specially rigged car and even a homemade mini-submarine.

The End

The Wall's demise came as unexpectedly as its creation. Once again the GDR was losing its people in droves, this time via Hungary, which had opened its borders with Austria. Thus emboldened, East Germans took to the streets by the hundreds of thousands, demanding improved human rights and an

The Berlin Wall

The construction of the Berlin Wall was a unique event in human history, not only for physically bisecting a city but by becoming a dividing line between competing ideologies and political systems. It's this global impact and universal legacy that continue to fascinate people more than a quarter century after its triumphant tear-down. Fortunately, plenty of original Wall segments and other vestiges remain, along with museums and memorials, to help fathom the realities and challenges of daily life in Berlin during the Cold War.

Our illustration points out the top highlights you can visit to learn about different aspects of these often tense decades. The best place to start is at the **Gedenkstätte Berliner Mauer ❶** for an excellent introduction to what the inner-city border actually looked liked and what it meant to live in its shadow. Reflect upon what you've learned while relaxing on the former death strip that is now the **Mauerpark ❷** before heading to the emotionally charged exhibit at the **Tränenpalast ❸**, an actual border crossing

OLIVER HOFFMANN/GETTY IMAGES ©

Brandenburg Gate
People around the world cheered as East and West Berliners partied together atop the Berlin Wall in front of the iconic city gate which today is a photogenic symbol of united Germany.

Tränenpalast
This modernist 1962 glass-and-steel border pavilion was dubbed 'Palace of Tears' because of the many tearful farewells that took place outside the building as East Germans and their western visitors had to say goodbye.

Bernauer Strasse

Chausseestr

JOHN FREEMAN/GETTY IMAGES ©

Potsdamer Platz
Nowhere was the death strip as wide as on the former no-man's-land around Potsdamer Platz from which sprouted a new postmodern city quarter in the 1990s. A tiny section of the Berlin Wall serves as a reminder.

Unter den Linden

LONELY PLANET/GETTY IMAGES ©

Checkpoint Charlie
Only diplomats and foreigners were allowed to use this border crossing. Weeks after the Wall was built, US and Soviet tanks faced off here in one of the hottest moments of the Cold War.

Leipziger Str

pavilion. Relive the euphoria of the Wall's demise at the **Brandenburg Tor** ❹, then marvel at the revival of **Potsdamer Platz** ❺ that was nothing but death strip wasteland until the 1990s. The Wall's geopolitical significance is the focus at **Checkpoint Charlie** ❻, which saw some of the tensest moments of the Cold War. Wrap up with finding your favourite mural motif at the **East Side Gallery** ❼.

It's possible to explore these sights by using a combination of walking and public transport, although a bike ride is actually the best method for getting a sense of the former Wall's erratic flow through the central city.

FAST FACTS

- » **Beginning of construction:** 13 August 1961
- » **Total length:** 155km
- » **Height:** 3.6m
- » **Weight of each segment:** 2.6 tonnes
- » **Number of watchtowers:** 300

❷ ....

Remnants of the Wall →

DAVID PEEVERS/GETTY IMAGES ©

Gedenkstätte Berliner Mauer
Germany's central memorial to the Berlin Wall and its victims exposes the complexity and barbaric nature of the border installation along a 1.4km stretch of the barrier's course.

Alexanderplatz

Alexanderstr

Mauerpark
Famous for its flea market and karaoke, this popular park actually occupies a converted section of death strip. A 30m segment of surviving Wall is now an official practice ground for budding graffiti artists.

JOHN FREEMAN/GETTY IMAGES ©

East Side Gallery
Paralleling the Spree for 1.3km, this is the longest Wall vestige. After its collapse, more than a hundred international artists expressed their feelings about this historic moment in a series of colourful murals.

EWAIS/SHUTTERSTOCK ©

❼

end to the dictatorship of the SED (Sozial-istische Einheitspartei Deutschland), the single party in East Germany. A series of demonstrations culminated in a gathering of half a million people on Alexanderplatz on 4 November 1989, vociferously demand-ing political reform. Something had to give.

It did, on 9 November, when government spokesperson Günter Schabowski an-nounced during a press conference on live TV that all travel restrictions to the West would be lifted. When asked by a reporter when this regulation would come into ef-fect, he nervously shuffled his papers look-ing for the answer, then responded with the historic words: 'As far as I know, immedi-ately.' In fact, the ruling was not supposed to take effect until the following day, but no one had informed Schabowski.

The news spread through East Berlin like wildfire, with hundreds of thousands head-ing towards the Wall. Border guards had no choice but to stand back. Amid scenes of wild partying and mile-long parades of GDR-made Trabant cars, the two Berlins came together again.

Today

The dismantling of the hated border forti-fications began almost immediately and by now the city halves have visually merged so perfectly that it takes a keen eye to tell East from West. Fortunately, there's help in the form of a **double row of cobblestones** with bronze plaques inscribed 'Berliner Mauer 1961-1989' that guides you along 5.7km of the Wall's course. Also keep an eye out for the **Berlin Wall History Mile**, which consists of 32 information panels set up along the course of the Wall. They draw attention, in four languages, to specific events that took place at each location. Berlin's division, the construction of the Wall, how the Wall fell, and the people who died at the Wall are all addressed. For de-tails, see www.berlin.de/mauer/en/history/history-mile.

Only about 2km of the actual concrete barrier still stands today; most famous is the 1.3km stretch that is now the East Side Gallery (p166). But there are plenty of other traces scattered throughout the city, including lamps, patrol paths, fences, perimeter defences, switch boxes and so on. Most are so perfectly integrated they're only discernible to the practised eye. A brilliant source for tracking down these fragments is the **Memorial Landscape Berlin Wall** (www.berlin-wall-map.com), an interactive Geographic Information System (GIS) that documents all remaining bits and pieces, no matter how small.

Tours

Fat Tire Bike Tours (p270) and Berlin on Bike (p270) offer guided trips along the course of the Wall. If you're feeling ambi-tious, rent a bike for a DIY tour of all or part of the 160km-long **Berliner Mauer-weg** (Berlin Wall Trail), a signposted walk-ing and cycling path that runs along the former border fortifications, with 40 multi-lingual information stations posted along the way. For a description and route maps in English, go to www.berlin.de/mauer/en/wall-trail.

The Berlin Wall by Neighbourhood

These original Wall remnants, museums and memorials keep the legacy of the Berlin Wall alive.

➡ **Historic Mitte** asisi Panorama Berlin, Ben Wagin installation at Marie-Elisabeth-Lüders-Haus, BlackBox Kalter Krieg, Brandenburger Tor, Checkpoint Charlie, Gedenkort Weisse Kreuze (White Crosses Memorial Site), Mauermuseum, Parlament der Bäume (Parliament of Trees), Peter Fechter Memorial, Tränenpalast.

➡ **Potsdamer Platz & Tiergarten** Wall remnants at Potsdamer Platz, Wall section at Niederkirchner Strasse (next to Topographie des Terrors), Watchtower Erna-Berger-Strasse.

➡ **Friedrichshain** East Side Gallery.

➡ **Prenzlauer Berg** Gedenkstätte Berliner Mauer, Mauerpark.

Topographie des Terrors (p85)

Historical Museums & Memorials

From its humble medieval beginnings, Berlin's history – especially its key role in major events of the 20th century – has created a rich and endlessly fascinating tapestry. It's also extremely well documented in numerous museums, memorial sites and monuments, many of them in original historic locations that are open to the public.

The Evolution of Berlin & Germany

Trace Berlin's evolution from its medieval birth to today's modern metropolis at the traditional Märkisches Museum (p109), or head to the Story of Berlin (p195) for a more experiential and multimedia approach, providing insight into Berlin's various epochs. If you like your history in a nutshell (or in 20 minutes), take in the multimedia show, The Gate (p85).

For a comprehensive survey of German history from the early Middle Ages to the present, visit the Deutsches Historisches Museum (p82). Berlin's Jewish history gets the spotlight at the Jüdisches Museum (p147).

The Third Reich

Few periods shaped the fate of Berlin as much as its 12-year stint as capital of Nazi Germany. Numerous museums and memorial sites, almost all of them free, keep the memory alive. For insight into the sinister machinations of the Nazi state, visit the Topographie des Terrors (p85). Nazi leaders decided on the implementation of the so-called 'final solution' in a lakeside villa that is now the Haus der Wannsee-Konferenz (p214).

The unfathomable impact of Nazi terror is emotionally documented at the Ort der Information (p81) and at the Sachsenhausen (p209)

ANDERSPHOTO/SHUTTERSTOCK ©

NEED TO KNOW

Tickets

Admission to many museums and memorial sites, including Gedenkstätte Berliner Mauer, Topographie des Terrors, and Gedenkstätte Deutscher Widerstand, is free (p32). Major museums that charge admission include the Jüdisches Museum, The Gate, Spy Museum, Deutsches Historisches Museum, Mauermuseum, Story of Berlin and Schloss Cecilienhof.

Opening Hours

➜ Core museum hours are 10am to 6pm, with some major venues open until 8pm.

➜ Closed Monday: Märkisches Museum, Ort der Information, Schloss Cecilienhof, Deutsch-Russisches Museum Berlin-Karlshorst, Tränenpalast, AlliiertenMuseum and Museum in der Kulturbrauerei.

concentration camp. The brave locals who tried to stand up against the Nazis are commemorated at the Gedenkstätte Deutscher Widerstand (p123), the Gedenkstätte Stille Helden (p141) and the Museum Blindenwerkstatt Otto Weidt (p141).

When WWII finally came to an end, the German surrender was signed at what is now the Deutsch-Russisches Museum Berlin-Karlshorst (p216), whose exhibits present WWII from the point of view of the Soviet Union. Two giant monuments honour the vast number of Russian soldiers who died in the Battle of Berlin: the Sowjetisches Ehrenmal Treptow (p151) and the Sowjetisches Ehrenmal Tiergarten (p84). To see where the victorious Allies hammered out Germany's postwar fate, visit **Schloss Cecilienhof** (☏0331-969 4200; www.spsg.de; Im Neuen Garten 11; tours adult/concession €6/5; ☉10am-6pm Tue-Sun Apr-Oct, to 5pm Nov-Mar; ☒603) in nearby Potsdam.

The Cold War

After World War II, Berlin was caught in the cross hairs of the Cold War superpowers – the US and the USSR – as epitomised in the city's division and the construction of the Berlin Wall. The longest surviving vestige of this barrier is the street-art festooned East Side Gallery (p166). To deepen your understanding of the physical appearance of the border fortifications and their human toll, the Gedenkstätte Berliner

Mauer (p177) and the Tränenpalast (p88) are essential stops.

Daily life behind the Iron Curtain is documented in interactive fashion at the DDR Museum (p108), while the free new Museum in der Kulturbrauerei (p179) follows a comparatively traditional approach to the same subject. Both exhibits also address the role of East Germany's Ministry of State Security (the Stasi) in shoring up the power base of the country's regime. Learn more at the Stasimuseum (p171) and on a guided tour of the Stasi Prison (p171) where regime critics were incarcerated.

Near Checkpoint Charlie (p88), the famous border crossing, you can learn about the daring attempts by East Germans to escape to the West at the privately run Mauermuseum (p89). For a take on the Cold War in Berlin from the perspective of the occupying Western allies, visit the AlliiertenMuseum (p212). Berlin's legacy as the capital of spies is the subject of the Spy Museum (p121) on Leipziger Platz.

Historical Museums & Memorials by Neighbourhood

➜ **Historic Mitte** BlackBox Kalter Krieg, Deutsches Historisches Museum, Mauermuseum, Ort der Information, Sowjetisches Ehrenmal Tiergarten, The Gate, Topographie des Terrors, Tränenpalast.

➜ **Museumsinsel & Alexanderplatz** DDR Museum, Märkisches Museum.

➜ **Potsdamer Platz & Tiergarten** Berlin Story Museum, Berlin Wall Watchtower Erna-Berger-Strasse, Gedenkstätte Deutscher Widerstand, Spy Museum.

➜ **Scheunenviertel** Gedenkstätte Stille Helden, Museum Blindenwerkstatt Otto Weidt.

➜ **City West & Charlottenburg** Kaiser-Wilhelm-Gedächtniskirche, Story of Berlin.

➜ **Kreuzberg & Neukölln** Jüdisches Museum.

➜ **Prenzlauer Berg** Gedenkstätte Berliner Mauer, Jüdischer Friedhof Schönhauser Allee, Museum in der Kulturbrauerei.

➜ **Outer Berlin** AlliiertenMuseum, Deutsch-Russisches Museum Berlin-Karlshorst, Gedenkstätte Plötzensee, Haus der Wannsee-Konferenz, Sachsenhausen, Stasi Prison, Stasimuseum, Sowjetisches Ehrenmal Treptow.

➜ **Potsdam** Memorial Leistikowstrasse (KGB Prison), Schloss Cecilienhof.

Lonely Planet's Top Choices

Gedenkstätte Berliner Mauer (p177) Indoor-outdoor multimedia exhibit which vividly illustrates the history, physical appearance and impact of the Berlin Wall.

Topographie des Terrors (p85) Gripping examination of the origins of Nazism, its perpetrators and its victims, on the site of the SS and Gestapo headquarters.

Jüdisches Museum (p147) Daniel Libeskind's contorted building is a striking backdrop for this thorough survey of the history and cultural heritage of Jews in Germany.

Gedenkstätte und Museum Sachsenhausen (p209) No book or movie comes close to the emotional impact of actually standing in a concentration camp.

Deutsches Historisches Museum (p82) Charts German history in the European context from the Middle Ages to the present, in a former Prussian armoury.

Best in Historic Locations

Stasi Prison (p171) Former inmates lead tours of this infamous jail, which had a starring role in the Academy Award–winning *The Lives of Others*.

Stasimuseum (p171) The headquarters of East Germany's feared and loathed Ministry of State Security are now a museum.

Tränenpalast (p88) Explains why tears of goodbye once flowed in this Friedrichstrasse border pavilion.

Gedenkstätte und Museum Sachsenhausen (p209) North of Berlin, this early concentration camp served as a model for many others.

Best for Jewish Remembrance

Jüdisches Museum (p147) Engagingly laid out chronicle and celebration of nearly 2000 years of Jewish life in Germany.

Ort der Information (p81) Chilling exhibit below the Holocaust Memorial examining personal aspects of this unfathomable chapter in human history.

Museum Blindenwerkstatt Otto Weidt (p141) Learn how one heroic man saved untold Jewish lives.

Gleis 17 Memorial (p213) Haunting train tracks memorialise the departure point for trains heading to the concentration camps.

Mendelssohn Exhibit (p89) A homage to one of Berlin's most prominent Jewish families.

Best for Kids

DDR Museum (p108) Highly experiential and hands-on journey into daily life behind the Iron Curtain.

Story of Berlin (p195) Plenty of engaging visuals and a tour of an atomic bunker make this one a winner with teens.

Mauermuseum (p89) Outdated exhibit with a fascinating collection of ingenious, original contraptions used by East Germans to escape their country.

Best for Momentous Moments

Haus der Wannsee-Konferenz (p214) Get the shivers in the very room where Nazi leaders planned the systematic annihilation of European Jews on 20 January 1942.

Deutsch-Russisches Museum Berlin-Karlshorst (p216) With the stroke of a pen WWII ended on 8 May 1945 with the signing of the German surrender at this former seat of the Soviet Military Administration.

Schloss Cecilienhof (p40) The Potsdam Conference brought Stalin, Truman and Attlee to this pretty palace between 17 July and 2 August 1945 to divvy Germany up into four occupation zones.

Gedenkstätte Deutscher Widerstand (p123) Stand in the rooms where army officer Claus von Stauffenberg and his cohorts planned the ill-fated assassination of Hitler.

Best for Architecture

Jüdisches Museum (p147) Daniel Libeskind's structures are never just buildings, they're also moving metaphors, as beautifully illustrated by Berlin's Jewish Museum.

Märkisches Museum (p109) This imposing red-brick pile is a clever mash-up of actual historic buildings from the surrounding state of Brandenburg.

Deutsches Historisches Museum (p82) Highlights of this ex-armoury are the baroque dying-warrior sculptures in the courtyard and the modern annex by IM Pei.

Bauhaus Archiv (p123)

The Berlin Art Scene

Art aficionados will find their compass on perpetual spin in Berlin. Home to 440 galleries, scores of world-class collections and some 33,000 international artists, it has assumed a pole position on the global artistic circuit. Adolescent energy, restlessness and experimental spirit combined and infused with an undercurrent of grit are what give this 'eternally unfinished' city its street cred.

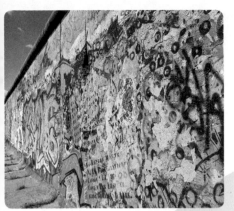
Berlin Wall (p34)

Major Art Museums

Berlin's most famous art museums are administered by the Staatliche Museen Berlin (Berlin State Museums; www.smb. museum). The main locations:

Gemäldegalerie (p118) Encyclopedic collection of European painting from the 13th to the 18th century – Rembrandt, Caravaggio and Vermeer included; at the Kulturforum.

Alte Nationalgalerie (p104) Neoclassical, Romantic, impressionist and early modernist art, including Caspar David Friedrich, Adolf Menzel and Monet; on Museumsinsel.

Hamburger Bahnhof (p131) International contemporary art – Warhol to Rauschenberg to Beuys; east of the Hauptbahnhof.

Museum Berggruen (p193) Classical modernist art, mostly Picasso and Klee; near Schloss Charlottenburg.

Sammlung Scharf-Gerstenberg (p193) Surrealist art by Goya, Magritte, Jean Dubuffet, Max Ernst and more; near Schloss Charlottenburg.

Neue Nationalgalerie (p122) Early 20th-century art, especially German expressionists. It's part of the Kulturforum but is closed for renovation until at least 2018; selections are on view at Hamburger Bahnhof's Neue Galerie until then.

Aside from these heavy hitters, Berlin teems with smaller museums specialising in a particular artist or genre. You can admire the colourful canvases of artist group Die Brücke in a lovely museum (p212) on the eastern edge of the Grunewald forest; see the paintings of Max Liebermann while standing in

NEED TO KNOW

Tickets

➡ Generally, buy tickets at the gallery or museum; prebook for the hottest tickets (p43).

➡ Commercial galleries do not charge admission. Most hold *vernissage* (opening) and *finissage* (closing) parties.

➡ The Berlin Museum Pass (€24, concession €12) buys admission to about 50 museums and galleries for a three-day period. Available at participating museums and the tourist offices.

Advance Planning

➡ Blockbuster visiting shows often sell out so it's best to prepurchase tickets online. Same goes for Pergamonmuseum and Neues Museum.

➡ Most private collections require advance registration; reserve months ahead for the Sammlung Boros.

Opening Hours

➡ The big museums and galleries are typically open from 10am to 6pm, with extended viewing one day a week, usually Thursday. Many are closed on Mondays.

➡ Commercial galleries tend to be open from noon to 6pm Tuesday to Saturday and by appointment.

Tours

GoArt! Berlin (www.goart-berlin.de) runs customised tours that demystify Berlin's art scene by opening doors to private collections, artist studios and galleries or by taking you to exciting street-art locations. Also does art consulting.

Websites

➡ **Museumsportal** (www.museums portal.de) is a gateway to the city's museums and galleries.

➡ Search online for 'Berliner Kunstfaltplan' for a comprehensive overview of the latest commercial gallery shows.

the very studio where he painted them in the Liebermann-Villa am Wannsee (p214); or take a survey of a century of Berlin-made art in the Berlinische Galerie (p149).

The main exhibition spaces without their own collections are the Martin-Gropius-Bau (p121) and the Haus der Kulturen der Welt (p84). Both mount superb temporary and travelling art shows, the latter with a special focus on contemporary arts from non-European cultures and societies.

Two museums train the spotlight on women: the Käthe-Kollwitz-Museum (p195), which is dedicated to one of the finest and most outspoken early-20th-century German artists, and the **Das Verborgene Museum** (Hidden Museum; Map p316; ☎030-313 3656; www.dasverborgenemuseum.de; Schlüterstrasse 70; adult/concession €2/1; 🕐3-7pm Thu & Fri, noon-4pm Sat & Sun; [S]Savignyplatz, [U]Ernst-Reuter-Platz), which champions lesser-known German female artists from the same period.

There are also corporate collections like the Deutsche Bank KunstHalle (p86) or the Daimler Contemporary (p117) and private ones like Me Collectors Room (p134) and the must-see Sammlung Boros (p133).

Commercial Art Galleries

The **Galleries Association of Berlin** (www.berliner-galerien.de) counts some 400 galleries within the city. In addition, there are at least 200 noncommercial showrooms and off-spaces that regularly show new exhibitions. Although the orientation is global, it's well worth keeping an eye out for the latest works by major contemporary artists living and working in Berlin, including Thomas Demand, Jonathan Meese, Via Lewandowsky, Isa Genzken, Tino Sehgal, Esra Ersen, John Bock and the artist duo Ingar Dragset and Michael Elmgreen.

PUBLIC ART

Free installations, sculptures and paintings? Absolutely. Public art is big in Berlin, which happens to be home to the world's longest outdoor mural, the 1.3km-long **East Side Gallery** (p166). No matter which neighbourhood you walk in, you're going to encounter public art on a grand scale. Daimler City (p121), in the Potsdamer Platz area, offers especially rich pickings, including works by Keith Haring, Mark Di Suvero and Frank Stella.

Galleries cluster in four main areas:

Scheunenviertel (Mitte) Auguststrasse and Linienstrasse were the birthplaces of Berlin's post-Wall contemporary art scene. Some pioneers have since moved on to bigger digs but key players like Eigen+Art, neugerriemschneider, Kicken and Galerie Neu remain. Another seminal contender on nearby Museumsinsel is Contemporary Fine Arts. Other galleries to keep an eye on include KOW and Mehdi Chouakri.

Checkpoint Charlie area (northern Kreuzberg) A number of key galleries hold forth on Zimmerstrasse, Charlottenstrasse, Rudi-Dutschke-Strasse and Markgrafenstrasse, including Galerie Krone, Galerie Thomas Schulte and Galerie Barbara Thumm. A bit further east, on Lindenstrasse, the Galerienhaus (www.galerienhaus.com) houses 11 contemporary art galleries.

Potsdamer Strasse (Schöneberg) In recent years, the gritty area around Potsdamer Strasse and Kurfürstenstrasse has emerged as one of Berlin's most dynamic art quarters with a great mix of established galleries and newcomers. Heavy hitters include Galerie Isabella Bortolozzi, Loock Galerie and Galerie Thomas Fischer.

Around Savignyplatz (Charlottenburg) In the traditional gallery district in the western city centre, standouts include Camera Work, Galerie Michael Schulz, Galerie Max Hetzler and Galerie Brockstedt.

Street Art & Where to Find It

Stencils, paste-ups, throw-ups, burners and bombings. These are some of the magic words in street art and graffiti, the edgy art forms that have helped shape the aesthetic of contemporary Berlin. A capital of street art, the city is the playground of such international heavyweights as Blu, JR, Os Gemeos, Romero, Shepard Fairey and ROA, along with local talent like Alias, El Bocho and XOOOOX. Every night, hundreds of hopeful next-gen artists haunt the streets, staying one step ahead of the police as they aerosol their screaming visions, often within seconds.

There's street art pretty much everywhere, and the area around U-Bahn station Schlesisches Tor in Kreuzberg has some house-wall-size classics, including Pink Man (p149) by Blu and Yellow Man (p149) by the Brazilian twins Os Gemeos. Skalitzer Strasse is also a fertile hunting ground with Victor Ash's Astronaut (p149) and ROA's Nature Morte (p149) being highlights (you

TOP FIVE BERLIN ART BLOGS

Berlin Art Link (www.berlinartlink. com) Online magazine delving into the contemporary art scene via studio visits and artist interviews, reviews and event listings.

Street Art Berlin (www.streetartbln. com) Keeps tabs on new works, profiles Berlin artists and posts about events.

Art News (www.artnews.org) Lists new exhibitions by opening date, closing date and venue.

Art Berlin (www.artberlin.de) Opens the door to the city's art scene by portraying artists, galleries, collections, exhibits and fairs; in German only.

Berlin Art Parasites (www.artparasites. com) Navigates through the Berlin art jungle with reviews, artist profiles and offbeat opinion pieces.

The Berlin Art Scene by Neighbourhood

➡ **Historic Mitte** Akademie der Künste – Pariser Platz, Contemporary Fine Arts, Deutsche Bank KunstHalle, galleries around Checkpoint Charlie, Haus der Kulturen der Welt. (p78)

➡ **Museumsinsel & Alexanderplatz** Alte Nationalgalerie. (p104)

➡ **Potsdamer Platz & Tiergarten** Bauhaus Archiv, Daimler Contemporary, Gemäldegalerie, Martin-Gropius-Bau, Neue Nationalgalerie, public art in DaimlerCity. (p115)

➡ **Scheunenviertel** Hamburger Bahnhof, Me Collectors Room, Sammlung Boros, Sammlung Hoffmann, street art, top-notch galleries around Auguststrasse. (p131)

➡ **City West & Charlottenburg** C/O Berlin, high-end galleries around Savignyplatz, Käthe-Kollwitz-Museum, Museum Berggruen, Museum für Fotografie, Sammlung Scharf-Gerstenberg. (p191)

➡ **Kreuzberg & Neukölln** Best for street art; also Berlinische Galerie, Galerienhaus. (p147)

➡ **Friedrichshain** East Side Gallery, RAW Gelände.

can even spot them on the north side of the tracks when riding the above-ground U1). There's also a new work by street-art super-star Shepard Fairey called **Make Art Not War** on Mehringplatz.

Across the Spree River in Friedrichshain, the RAW Gelände has plenty of great stuff, especially at the Urban Spree (p167) bar and gallery. Around Boxhagener Platz you'll find works by Boxi, Alias and El Bocho. In Mitte, there's plenty of art underneath the S-Bahn arches, although the undisputed hub is the courtyard of Haus Schwarzenberg (p141). Prenzlauer Berg has the Mauerpark, where budding artists may legally polish their skills along a section of the Berlin Wall. In the entryway of the Tuntenhaus at Kastanienallee 86 are nice works by Alias and El Bocho. You'll also pass by plenty of graffiti when riding the circle S41/S42.

Alternative Berlin Tours (p270) runs an artist-led, four-hour street-art workshop and walking tour (€18). A good book on the subject is *Street Art in Berlin* by Kai Jakob (2015).

Galleries with an urban art focus include **Open Walls** (www.openwallsgallery.com) on Schröderstrasse near the Scheunenviertel and **Circle Culture Gallery** (www. circleculture-gallery.com) at Potsdamer Strasse 68.

BPK - BILDAGENTUR FÜR KUNST, KULTUR UND GESCHICHTE MARCEL JOLIBOIS/GETTY IMAGES ©

Contemporary art museum Hamburger Bahnhof (p131)

Lonely Planet's Top Choices

Gemäldegalerie (p118) Sweeping survey of Old Masters from Germany, Italy, France, Spain and the Netherlands from the 13th to the 18th centuries.

Hamburger Bahnhof (p131) Warhol, Beuys and Twombly are among the many legends aboard the contemporary-art express at this former train station.

Sammlung Boros (p133) Book months' ahead for tickets to see this stunning cutting-edge private collection housed in a WWII bunker.

Martin-Gropius-Bau (p121) First-rate travelling exhibits take up residence in this gorgeous Renaissance-style building.

Best Single-Artist Galleries

Käthe-Kollwitz-Museum (p195) Representative collection of works by Germany's greatest female artist, famous for her haunting depictions of war and human loss and suffering.

Liebermann-Villa am Wannsee (p214) Charming exhibit set up in the lakeside summer home of the great German impressionist and leading Berlin Secession founder Max Liebermann.

Dalí – Die Ausstellung (p121) Private collection showcasing lesser-known drawings, illustrated books and sculptures by the famous Catalan surrealist.

Best Artistic Genre Galleries

Museum Berggruen (p193) Picasso, Klee and Giacometti

form the heart of this stunning classical-modernist collection donated to the city by Heinz Berggruen.

Sammlung Scharf-Gerstenberg (p193) Across from Museum Berggruen, this space delves into the fantastical worlds conjured up by Goya, Max Ernst, Magritte and other giants of the surrealist genre.

Alte Nationalgalerie (p104) The 3rd floor of this venerable art temple is packed with Romantic masterpieces by such genre practitioners as Caspar David Friedrich, Karl Friedrich Schinkel and Carl Blechen.

Brücke-Museum (p212) Forest-framed gem focusing on German expressionism, with works by Karl Schmidt-Rottluff, Ernst Ludwig Kirchner and other members of the Bridge, Germany's first modern-artist group.

Bauhaus Archiv (p123) Offers comprehensive insight into the pioneering modernist school and its main teachers and practitioners.

Best Private Collections

Sammlung Boros (p133) The latest works by established and emerging artists displayed in a labyrinthine WWII bunker.

Sammlung Hoffmann (p134) Every Saturday, artficionados can join a tour of long-time collector Erika Hoffmann's private loft.

Me Collectors Room (p134) Thomas Olbricht's 'cabinet of curiosities', plus exhibits drawn from his own collection and from other international collectors.

Best Art Museum Architecture

Bauhaus Archiv (p123) Walter Gropius himself drew up the blueprints for this complex distinguished by its curved shed-roof silhouette. It's currently getting an annex.

Hamburger Bahnhof (p131) Flanked by two towers and centred on a cathedral-like hall, this 19th-century train station is home to one of Germany's finest contemporary art collections.

Neue Nationalgalerie (p122) Ludwig Mies van der Rohe's templelike final masterpiece is as edgy today as it was at its 1967 opening (note: exhibits closed for renovation).

Best Art Exhibition Halls

Martin-Gropius-Bau (p121) Top of the heap with headline-making travelling art exhibits from all fields of creative endeavour.

Haus der Kulturen der Welt (p84) Mounts shows with a special focus on non-European cultures and societies.

Akademie der Künste (p86) Berlin's oldest arts institution (founded in 1696) presents genre-hopping exhibits drawn from its archives in two locations.

Deutsche Bank KunstHalle (p86) Shines the spotlight on the art scene in emerging countries and examines the effects of globalisation on the art world.

SEAN GALLUP/STAFF/GETTY IMAGES ©

Street Food at the Markthalle Neun (p162)

Eating

If you crave traditional German comfort food, you'll certainly find plenty of places to indulge in pork knuckles, smoked pork chops and calf's liver in Berlin. These days, though, 'typical' local fare is lighter, healthier, more creative, and more likely to come from an organic eatery, an ethnic restaurant or a gourmet kitchen (including 20 flaunting 26 Michelin stars between them).

Food Trends

Just like with art and fashion, Berliners are always onto the next hot thing when it comes to food. You'll find plenty culinary obsessions in the capital.

MODERN REGIONAL CUISINE

The organic, slow-food and locavore movements are stronger than ever in Berlin with such ingredients as apple-fed pork from the Havelland, fish from the Müritz Lake District or wild boar from the Schorfheide increasingly showing up on menus around Berlin. Some restaurants even go so far as to use *only* regional ingredients – so no pepper, lemons or chocolate. Whatever is in season not only reaches the plates but is also preserved for future use through pickling, brining and fermentation, thereby picking up on another global food trend.

STREET FOOD

Street food and food trucks have been part of Berlin's culinary scene for years now, not just in random locations at markets, parties and events around town but also at regular gatherings.

NEED TO KNOW

Price Ranges

The following price ranges refer to the average cost of a main course.

€ less than €10

€€ €10 to €20

€€€ more than €20

Opening Hours

Cafes 8am to 8pm

Restaurants 11am to 11pm

Fast-food joints 11am to midnight or later

Bills & Tipping

➡ It's customary to add between 5% and 10% for good service.

➡ Tip as you hand over the money, rather than leaving it on the table (as this is considered rude). For example, if your bill comes to €28 and you want to give a €2 tip, say '€30'. If you have the exact amount and don't need change, just say 'Stimmt so' (that's fine).

Reservations

Reservations are essential at the top eateries and are recommended for midrange restaurants – especially for dinner and at weekends. Book the trendiest places four or more weeks in advance. Many restaurant websites now offer an online booking function. Berliners tend to linger at the table, so if a place is full at 8pm it's likely that it will stay that way for a couple of hours.

Late-Night & Sunday Shopping

➡ One handy feature of Berlin culture is the Spätkauf (Späti in local vernacular), which are small neighbourhood stores stocked with the basics and open from early evening until 2am or later.

➡ Some supermarkets stay open until midnight; a few are even open 24 hours.

➡ Shops and supermarkets in major train stations (Hauptbahnhof, Ostbahnhof, Friedrichstrasse) are open late and on Sunday.

Still going strong is Street Food Thursday (p155) at Markthalle Neun in Kreuzberg, the year-round event that started the craze back in 2013. From spring to autumn, it is joined by a number of alfresco schemes like Bite Club (p155), which sets up on Fridays on the Spree next to the Badeschiff and makes for a tasty place to get your stomach in shape for a long weekend of partying. Roughly once a month, it is grill and grind at Burgers & Hip Hop (p155), which has a residency at Prince Charles club on Moritzplatz. Up in Prenzlauer Berg, Street Food auf Achse (p183) draws scores of street food fans to the Kulturbrauerei on Sunday.

The street food experience has proven so successful for some chefs that they've taken their concept to a bricks-and-mortar level. Graduates from Markthalle Neun include Fräulein Kimchi (p183), **Bun Bao** (Map p306; ☑030-2349 6218; www.bao-burger.de; Kollwitzstrasse 84; burgers €6.70-8.40; ☺noon-10pm Sun-Thu, to 11pm Fri & Sat; ☏; 🚃M2, M10, ⓊEberswalder Strasse), Koshary Lux (p198) and Chicha (p153).

NEXT-LEVEL BURGERS & PIZZAS

Carnivores rejoice: once a humble fast-food staple, burgers have of late been elevated into the pantheon of culinary greats. Hardly a day seems to pass without the opening of yet another pattie temple, further fuelling locals' obsession with the hunt for the perfect burger. Any twist on the familiar is cheered, be it yak or wild-boar burgers, unusual homemade sauces like chipotle beetroot mayo or red wine barbecue sauce, or out-there toppings like caramelised kimchi, ramen noodles, foie gras or rice crackers.

Artesanal pizza, too, has foodies in a headlock these days. A new breed of pizzerias is familiarising the uninitiated with the Neapolitan original: a perfect crust topped with ingredients that have never seen the inside of a can and tickled to perfection in a ferociously hot cupola furnace.

VEGAN, RAW & JUICES

Vegan restaurants are spreading faster than rabbits on Viagra in Berlin. It helps that the world's first all-vegan supermarket chain, Veganz, opened here in 2011, and that the growing number of expats import foodie concepts from home (if the sudden ubiquitousness of avocado sandwiches is any indication). Only slowly making inroads are detox trends like raw food and cold-press juice cleanses; **Rawtastic** (Map p306; ☑0172 439 1287; www.rawtastic.de; Danziger Strasse 16; mains €11-14; ☺10am-10pm Sun-Thu, 10am-11pm

Fri, noon-11pm Sat; ☎; ⓜM1, ⓤEberswalder Strasse) ranks among the pioneers. For a comprehensive list of vegetarian and vegan restaurants in Berlin, search on www.happy cow.net.

NOSE TO TAIL

An antithesis to the vegan avalanche is the nose-to-tail trend where recipes star not just filet cuts but such low-brow animal parts as tongue, heart or bone marrow. The holistic approach is a logical segue to the farm-to-table and orchard-to-bottle movements that have been spinning the culinary compass lately.

ISRAELI FOOD

Until a couple of years ago, hummus was practically unknown by German palates but thanks to a growing crop of restaurants like Hummus & Friends (p136) and Kanaan (p179) serving the velvety chickpea puree and other Israeli staples like shakshuka, sabich and tabbouli, they're getting an education. The hunt is also on for the city's best pastrami with Mogg (p137) and Louis Pretty (p153) both being serious contenders.

Eating Like a Local

Restaurants are often formal places with full menus, crisp white linen and high prices. Some restaurants are open for lunch and dinner only, but more casual places tend to be open all day. Same goes for cafes, which usually serve both coffee and alcohol, as well as light meals, although ordering food is not obligatory. Many cafes and restaurants offer inexpensive weekday 'business lunches' that usually include a starter, main course and drink for under €10.

English menus are now quite common, and some places (especially those owned by neo-Berliners from the US, UK or around Europe) don't even bother with German menus at all. When it comes to paying, sometimes the person who invites pays, but very often Germans go Dutch and split the bill. This might mean everyone chipping in at the end of a meal or asking the server to pay separately (*getrennte Rechnung*).

Handy speed-feed shops, called *Imbiss,* serve all sorts of savoury fodder, from sausage-in-a-bun to *Döner Kebab* and pizza. Many bakeries serve sandwiches alongside pastries.

Locals love to shop at farmers markets and nearly every *Kiez* (neighbourhood) runs at least one or two during the week.

LOCAL SPECIALITIES YOU SHOULD TRY – AT LEAST ONCE

Pfannkuchen Known as 'Berliner' in other parts of Germany, these donut-like pastries are made from a yeasty dough, stuffed with a dollop of jam, deep fried and tossed in granulated sugar.

Currywurst This classic cult snack, allegedly invented in Berlin in 1949, is a smallish fried or grilled *Wiener* sliced into bite-sized ringlets, swimming in a spicy tomato sauce and dusted with curry powder. It's available '*mit*' or '*ohne*' (ie with or without) its crunchy epidermis and traditionally served on a flimsy plate with a plastic toothpick for stabbing.

Döner Spit-roasted meat may have been around forever, but the idea of serving it in a lightly

---

TOP FIVE BERLIN BLOGS ABOUT FOOD & MORE

It's no secret that Berlin is a fast-changing city and so it's only natural that the food scene also develops at lightning speed. Fortunately there are a number of passionate foodies keeping an eye on new openings and developments and generously sharing them on their (English-language) blogs. If you read German, also check out Mit Vergnügen (www. mitvergnuegen.com) and Berlin Ick Liebe Dir (www.berlin-ick-liebe-dir.de).

Berlin Food Stories (www.berlinfoodstories.com) Excellent up-to-the-minute site by a dedicated food lover who keeps tabs on new restaurants and visits each one several times before writing honest, mouthwatering reviews.

Stil in Berlin (www.stilinberlin.de) One of the longest-running city blogs (since 2006), Mary Sherpe's 'baby' keeps track of developments in food, fashion, style and art.

CeeCee (www.ceecee.cc) Stylish blog keeps tabs on what's hot and what's not across Berlin's culinary and cultural spectrum.

I Heart Berlin (www.iheartberlin.com) Long-running blog spreads the love about cool places and upcoming events.

Eating by Neighbourhood

Prenzlauer Berg
Lively cafe scene, comfy neighbourhood eateries (p179)

Scheunenviertel
Trendy, progressive eating for all budgets (p136)

Potsdamer Platz & Tiergarten
Fine dining in five-star hotels (p124)

Fernsehturm

Friedrichshain
Mostly cheap eats with pockets of sophistication (p168)

City West & Charlottenburg
Excellent Asian, Italian and other international fare (p197)

Historic Mitte
Swanky, cosmopolitan, Michelin-starred dining (p89)

Museumsinsel & Alexanderplatz
Tourist-geared fast food and traditional German (p110)

Spree River

Kreuzberg & Neukölln
Eclectic ethnic and creative contemporary options (p152)

toasted bread pocket with copious amounts of fresh salad and a healthy drizzle of yoghurt-based *Kräuter* (herb), *scharf* (spicy) or *Knoblauch* (garlic) sauce was allegedly invented by a Turkish immigrant in 1970s West Berlin.

Boulette Called *Frikadelle* in other parts of Germany, this cross between a meatball and a hamburger is eaten with a little mustard and an optional dry roll. The name is French for 'little ball' and might have originated during Napoleon's occupation of Berlin in the early 19th century.

Eisbein or Grillhaxe Boiled or grilled pork hock typically paired with sauerkraut and boiled potatoes.

Königsberger Klopse This classic dish may have its origin in Königsberg in eastern Prussia (today's Kaliningrad in Russia), but it has of late made a huge comeback on Berlin menus. It's a simple but elegant plate of golf-ball-sized veal meatballs in a caper-laced white sauce served with a side of boiled potatoes and beetroot.

I SCREAM ICE CREAM

Berlin is nirvana for ice-cream lovers with countless home-grown parlours popping up as soon as the last winter winds have died down. With locals being increasingly healthy and carb-conscious, frozen-yoghurt shops have finally made some major inroads as well. Everyone's got their favourite stop for frozen delights; some of ours include **Caffe e Gelato** (p128) and **Fräulein Frost** (Map p312; ☎030-9559 5521; Friedelstrasse 39; ☻1pm-eve Mon-Fri, noon-eve Sat & Sun, closing time depends on weather; ☞; ⓤSchönleinstrasse).

Lonely Planet's Top Choices

Restaurant Tim Raue (p90) Berlin's top toque is famous for his mash-up of Asian and Western flavours.

Einsunternull (p138) Gourmet food deconstructed to the essentials using regional ingredients.

Restaurant Faubourg (p197) Elevated French cuisine, sensitively interpreted and served in an eye-candy setting.

Katz Orange (p138) Cosy country-style farm-to-table lair in gorgeously recycled brewery.

Restaurant am Steinplatz (p198) German classics reinterpreted for the 21st century amid 1920s glamour.

Best by Budget

€

Street Food Thursday (p155) Global treats at a weekly street-food fair in a 19th-century market hall.

Hummus & Friends (p136) Hip Tel Aviv import makes kosher hummus and more next to the New Synagogue.

W-der Imbiss (p183) Perfect yin and yang of Italian-Indian cooking amid tiki decor.

Burgermeister (p155) Succulent two-fisted burgers and fries doused in homemade sauces in a former public latrine.

€€

Umami (p183) Sharp Indochine nosh for fans of the classics and the innovative amid sensuous lounge decor.

Der Hahn ist tot! (p185) Succulent *coq au vin* and more French faves at wallet-friendly prices.

Ishin (p90) Sushi may be the star of the show, but this unas-

suming cafeteria also rocks the rice bowls.

Cafe Jacques (p154) Empty tables are as rare as hen's teeth in this cande-lit cocoon with top Mediterranean food and wine.

€€€

Restaurant Tim Raue (p90) Eponymous gourmet kitchen of bad boy turned double Michelin-star chef.

Katz Orange (p138) This stylish 'cat' fancies anything that's regional, seasonal and creative amid chic country decor.

Restaurant Faubourg (p197) Creative, modern French cuisine beautifully presented amid Bauhaus-inspired decor.

Pauly Saal (p137) Time-honoured regional dishes reinterpreted in modern Michelin-decorated fashion.

Best by Cuisine

Berlin Classics

Weinbar Rutz (p138) Fabulous wine complements the soulful goodness of Michelin-chef-interpreted local fare.

Zur Letzten Instanz (p110) Has done a roaring trade with local rib-stickers since 1621.

Max und Moritz (p153) Industrial-weight platters and local brews in charmingly decorated centenarian pub.

Modern German

3 Schwestern (p153) Inspired regional dishes with international influences in historic hospital reborn as artist quarter.

Restaurant am Steinplatz (p198) Diverse and sometimes surprising array of ingredients find their destination in superb creations.

eins44 (p155) Neukölln fine-dining pioneer with clever but

unfussy French-leaning food in a pimped-up old distillery.

Traditional German

Augustiner am Gendarmenmarkt (p90) Go the whole hog at this famous Munich beer hall transplant.

Henne (p153) No misty-eyed nostalgia, just the ultimate roast chicken, and that since 1907.

Schwarzwaldstuben (p136) Oldies but goodies from Germany's south amid delightfully irreverent decor.

Oderquelle (p185) Consistent and inspired port of call for flawlessly executed favourites.

Asian

Zenkichi (p138) Japanese morsels for the soul in a sophisticated izakaya with sake sommelier.

Chutnify (p182) South Indian street food so perky it may get you off your Prozac.

Umami (p183) Modern Vietnamese food that sings with freshness and creativity.

Good Friends (p198) Berlin's best Chinese restaurant delivers a taste-bud tingling culinary journey.

Italian

Masaniello (p153) Classic neighbourhood pizza joint churns out giant pies and Chianti by the gallon.

Lavanderia Vecchia (p155) Palate-pleasing and waist-expanding 13-course indulgence in a converted industrial laundry.

Muret La Barba (p136) Wine-shop-cum-restaurant where meals have all the flavours of Italy locked inside them.

Standard – Serious Pizza (p183) Handmade Neapolitan-style pizza cooked in fiercely hot oven.

Vegetarian

Lucky Leek (p183) Richly satisfying meatfree dishes in stylish-minimalist Prenzlauer Berg haunt.

Cookies Cream (p91) Clandestine meatfree kitchen tiptoes between hip and haute.

Kanaan (p179) Funky Israeli-Palestinian co-production serves divine hummus, shakshuka and sabich.

Vöner (p168) Has been serving vegan doner long before the animal-free trend went mainstream.

Best for Breakfast

Anna Blume (p181) The three-tiered 'Anna Blume Special' at this floral charmer is the perfect greet-the-day choice.

Tomasa (p152) Classics and homemade specialities served until a hangover-friendly 4pm in a rambling old villa with garden.

Cabslam – California Breakfast Slam (p154) Bloodshot party eyes disappear quickly with *huevos rancheros,* eggs benedict and other West Coast faves.

Cafe am Neuen See (p128) Sleepyheads love the quiet Tiergarten park setting for leisurely alfresco breakfast served until 4pm.

Best for Burgers

Burgermeister (p155) This patty-and-bun joint in a former historic toilet is a hugely popular pit stop on a budget.

The Butcher (p198) New kid on the block pimps up ground Angus with cocktails and DJs.

The Bird (p185) Expat favourite makes cooked-to-order burgers, now in two locations.

Berlin Burger International (p154) Giant, sloppy, delicious.

Best Farmers Markets

Türkischer Markt (p162) Bazaar-like canal-side market with bargain-priced produce and a bonanza of Mediterranean deli fare (olives, feta etc).

Kollwitzplatzmarkt (p188) Posh player with velvety gorgonzola, juniper-berry smoked ham, homemade pesto and other exquisite morsels. The Thursday market is smaller and all organic. Kids' playground nearby.

Markt am Winterfeldtplatz (p126) Local institution with quality produce alongside artsy-crafty stuff and global snack stands.

Best Middle Eastern

Wolff & Eber (p197) A convincing, if unlikely, mash-up of Syrian and local cuisine in a literary salon setting.

Defne (p154) Turkish delights beyond the doner kebab, on the terrace in summer.

Habba Habba (p182) This hole-in-the-wall stuffs Middle Eastern wraps with unexpected meatless ingredients.

Koshary Lux (p198) Snack place specialising in perky street food from Morocco to Yemen.

Maroush (p153) Fingerlickin' felafel; makes an excellent stop on a bar hop.

Best for Romance

Spindler & Klatt (p156) If your date doesn't make you swoon, the riverside setting should still make for an unforgettable evening.

Café am Neuen See (p128) Tiergarten beer garden where you can take your sweetie on a spin on the adjoining lake.

Zenkichi (p138) Booths shielded by bamboo blinds for extra privacy to savour sublime Japanese fare.

Cafe Jacques (p154) Fine wine, candlelight and, above all, mouthwatering Mediterranean fare are the hallmarks of a romantic night out.

Cookies Cream (p91) Herbivore haven where you'll get kudos and kisses merely for finding the entrance.

Best Michelin-Starred Restaurants

Restaurant Tim Raue (p90) The outpost by Berlin's rebel-turned-top-toque ranks among the best 50 in the world.

Restaurant Richard (p156) Arty decor combines with supreme classic French cooking in this relaxed gourmet lair.

Reinstoff (p138) Experimental culinary perfection in the sophisticated-industrial setting of a former light-bulb factory.

Horváth (p154) Unfussy Kreuzberg restaurant dishes up creatively fine-tuned dishes inspired by Austrian cuisine.

Clärchens Ballhaus (p138)

Drinking & Nightlife

As one of Europe's primo party capitals, Berlin offers a thousand and one scenarios for getting your cocktails and kicks (or wine or beer, for that matter). From cocktail lairs and concept to craft beer pubs and rooftop lounges – the next thirst parlour is usually within stumbling distance.

NEED TO KNOW

Opening Hours

➡ Pubs are open from around noon to midnight (later on weekends).

➡ Trendy places and cocktail bars open around 7pm or 8pm until the last tippler leaves.

➡ Clubs open at 11pm or midnight and fill up around 1am or 2am

Costs

Big clubs like Berghain/Panorama Bar or Watergate will set you back €12 to €15 admission, but there are plenty of others that charge between €5 and €10. Places that open a bit earlier don't charge admission until a certain hour, usually 11pm or midnight. Student discounts are virtually unheard of, but some of the more mainstream clubs run 'Ladies Nights' when women get in free.

Dress Code

Berlin's clubs are very relaxed. In general, individual style almost always beats high heels and Armani. Cocktail bars and some disco-style clubs may prefer a more glam look, but in pubs anything goes.

What's On?

For the latest scoop, scan the listings in *Zitty* (www.zitty.de), *Tip* (www.tip-berlin. de), *030* (www.berlin030.de) or Ex-Berliner (www.exberliner.com); sift through flyers in shops, cafes, clubs and bars; and check internet platforms such as Resident Advisor (www.residentadvisor.net) and blogs like I Heart Berlin (www.iheartberlin.de).

Bars & Pubs

Berlin is a notoriously late city: bars stay packed from dusk to dawn and beyond, and some clubs don't hit their stride until 4am. The lack of a curfew never created a tradition of binge drinking, which is why many party folk prefer to pace their alcohol consumption and thus manage to keep going until the wee hours. Of course there's no denying that illegal drugs can also play their part...

Edgier, more underground venues cluster in Kreuzberg, Friedrichshain, Neukölln and up-and-coming outer boroughs like Wedding (north of Mitte) and Lichtenberg (east of Friedrichshain). Places in Charlottenburg, Mitte and Prenzlauer Berg tend to be quieter, close earlier and are thus more suited for date nights than dedicated drinking. Generally, the emphasis here is on style and atmosphere and some proprietors have gone to extraordinary lengths to come up with special design concepts.

The line between cafe and bar is often blurred, with many changing stripes as the hands move around the clock. Alcohol, however, is served (and consumed) pretty much all day. Some bars have happy hours that usually run from 6pm to 9pm.

Although still lower than in other major capital cities, drinks prices have crept up over the last couple of years. To cater to the truly cash-strapped, some of Berli's latenight convenience stores (called *Spätkauf* or *Späti* for short) have started to put out tables on the sidewalks for patrons to gather and consume their store-bought beverages.

BEER GARDENS, BEACH & ROOFTOP BARS

Berliners are sun cravers and as soon as the first rays spray their way into spring, outdoor tables show up faster than you can pour a pint of beer. The most traditional places for outdoor chilling are of course the beer gardens with long wooden benches set up beneath leafy old chestnuts and with cold beer and bratwurst on the menu. In 2002, Berlin also jumped on the 'sandwagon' with the opening of its first beach bar, Strandbar Mitte (p140), in a prime location on the Spree River. Many that followed have since been displaced by development, which has partly fuelled another trend: rooftop bars. Outdoor boozing grounds tend to open from May to October, weather permitting.

COCKTAIL BARS

Dedicated cocktail bars are booming in Berlin and new arrivals have measurably elevated the 'liquid art' scene. Dedicated drinking dens tend to be elegant cocoons with mellow lighting and low sound levels, helmed by mix-meisters capable of applying their classic training to boundary-pushing experimental riffs. A good cocktail will set you back between €10 and €15. Most bars and pubs serve cocktails too, but of the Sex on the Beach and Cosmopolitan variety. Prices are lower (between €7 and €9) and

Above: Sunseekers on the Spree River

Right: Watermelon mojitos at one of Berlin's prolific cocktail bars

quality can be hit or miss due to mediocre mixing talents and/or inferior spirits.

ETIQUETTE
Table service is common, and you shouldn't order at the bar unless you intend to hang out there or there's a sign saying *Selbstbedienung* (self-service). In traditional German pubs, it's customary to keep a tab instead of paying for each round separately. In bars with DJs €1 or €2 is usually added to the cost of your first drink. Tip bartenders about 5%, servers 10%. Drinking in public is legal and widely practised, especially around party zones. Try to be civilised about it, though. No puking on the U-Bahn, please!

Clubbing
Since the 1990s, Berlin's club culture has taken on near-mythical status and, to no small degree, contributed to the magnetism of the German capital. It has incubated trends and sounds, launched the careers of such internationally renowned DJs as Paul van Dyk, Ricardo Villalobos, Ellen Allien and Paul Kalkbrenner, and put Berlin firmly on the map of global music fans who turn night into day in the over 200 clubs in this curfew-free city.

What distinguishes the Berlin scene from other party capitals is a focus on independent, non-mainstream niche venues, run by owners or collectives with a creative rather than a corporate background. The shared goal is to promote a diverse, inclusive and progressive club culture rather than to maximize profit. This is also reflected in a door policy that strives to create a harmonious balance in terms of age, gender and attitude.

Electronic music in its infinite varieties continues to define Berlin's after-dark action but other sounds like hip-hop, dancehall, rock, swing and funk have also made inroads. The edgiest clubs have taken up residence in power plants, transformer stations, abandoned apartment buildings and other repurposed locations.

The scene is in constant flux as experienced club owners look for new challenges and a younger generation of promoters enters the scene with new ideas and impetus. Overall, though, rising costs, development and noise complaints have shifted the focus away from heavily gentrified Prenzlauer Berg and Mitte down to Kreuzberg, Neukölln and Friedrichshain. However, as these districts too become more and more hyped, the wildest parties are staged even further afield in such boroughs as Lichtenberg, Treptow and Wedding.

WHEN TO GO
Whatever club or party you're heading for, don't bother showing up before 1am un-

---

A TASTE OF BERLIN

In recent years a flurry of indie boutique beverage purveyors has cropped up in Berlin. Look for them at kiosks, cool bars, pubs and even supermarkets. Here are our favourites:

Berliner Brandstifter Berliner Vincent Honrodt is the man behind the Brandstifter Korn, a premium schnapps that gets extraordinary smoothness from a seven-stage filtering process. It also makes a mean gin.

Original Berlin Cidre OBC is made from 100% German apples by two Berliners, Urs Breitenstein and Thomas Godel. There are three varieties: the dry OBC Strong, the sweet OBC Classic and the fruity OBC Rose.

Adler Berlin Dry Gin Crafted by the **Preussische Spirituosen Manufaktur** (☎030-4502 8537; www.psmberlin.de; Seestrasse 13; 1-/2hr tour €10/15; ⊙shop 11am-7pm Mon-Fri, tours by arrangement; 🚌50, M13) that already served Kaiser Wilhelm II, this creamy and balanced gin is aromatised with juniper, lavender, coriander, ginger and lemon peel.

Our/Berlin Made with Berlin water and German wheat, this smooth vodka is distilled in small batches at Flutgraben 2 on the Kreuzberg–Treptow border and sold in stylish bottles right there and in select shops.

Berliner Luft The mamba-green peppermint schnapps has gained cult status despite tasting like mouthwash. Consumed as a shot, it's a popular method to get blasted fast.

Wostok This Kreuzberg-made certified organic lemonade comes in six flavours, including the pine-scented Tannenwald based on an original 1973 Soviet soft drink recipe.

less you want to have a deep conversation with a bored bartender. And don't worry about closing times – Berlin's famously long nights have gotten even later of late and, thanks to a growing number of after parties and daytime clubs, not going home at all is definitely an option at weekends. In fact, savvy clubbers put in a good night's sleep, then hit the dance floor when other people head for Sunday church or afternoon tea.

AT THE DOOR

Doors are notoriously tough at Berlin's best clubs (eg Watergate, Berghain/Panorama Bar, Magdalena and Salon zur Wilden Renate) as door staff strive to sift out people that would feel uncomfortable with the music, the vibe or the libertine ways past the door. Except at some disco-type establishments, flaunting fancy labels and glam cocktail dresses can actually get in the way of your getting in. Wear something black and casual. If your attitude is right, age rarely matters. Be respectful in the queue, don't drink and don't talk too loudly (seriously!). Don't arrive wasted. As elsewhere, large groups (even mixed ones) have a lower chance of getting in, so split up if you can. Stag and hen parties are rarely welcome. If you do get turned away, don't argue. And don't worry, there's always another party somewhere...

Drinks
BEER

Predictably, beer is big in Berlin and served – and consumed – almost everywhere all day long. Most places pour a variety of local, national and imported brews, including at least one draught beer (*vom Fass*) served in 300mL or 500mL glasses. In summer, drinking your lager as an Alster, Radler or Diesel (mixed with Sprite, Fanta or Coke, respectively) is a popular thirst quencher.

Beer has been brewed in Berlin since the Middle Ages, reaching its peak in the 19th century when there used to be hundreds of breweries, especially in Prenzlauer Berg. Today, the only commercial one left is the **Berliner Kindl-Schultheiss Brauerei** (030-960 9579; www.berliner-kindl.de; Indira-Gandhi-Strasse 66-69; tours €5, with beer tasting €9, with beer tasting & food from €12; 10am, 2pm & 5.30pm Mon-Thu; M13 to Betriebshof Indira-Gandhi-Strasse), which produces the Berliner Pilsner, Schultheiss, Berliner Kindl and Berliner Bürgerbräu brands. For a behind-the-scenes look, book a guided tour

(in German) – preferably followed by a beer tasting – via its website.

Other German and imported beers are widely available. There's plenty of Beck's and Heineken around but for more flavour look for Jever Pilsener from northern Germany, Rothaus Tannenzäpfle from the Black Forest, Zywiec from Poland, and Krušovice and Budweiser from the Czech Republic. American Budweiser is practically nonexistent here.

WINE

Oenophiles can rejoice as there is finally a respectable crop of wine bars in Berlin. Many are bar-shop hybrids and some also serve food. Run by wine enthusiasts, they have an egalitarian rather than elitist mood, with wines for all budgets. Some specialise in *vin naturel* ('natural wine', ie organically grown and handled with minimal chemical interference), which often looks cloudy and tastes a bit tart at first. But then...

In regular pubs and bars the quality of wine ranges from drinkable to abysmal, which is probably why so many Germans drink it with fizzy water, called a *Weinschorle*. Wine is usually served in 200mL glasses. However, in more sophisticated bars, as well as in a growing number of restaurants, better-quality wine is now served in mere 100mL glasses.

Sparkling wine comes in 100mL flutes. Depending on where a place sees itself on the trendiness scale, it will offer German *Sekt,* Italian Prosecco or French *cremant.* In clubs it's often served on the rocks (*Sekt auf Eis*). Champagne is trendy among the monied set.

In winter, and especially on the Christmas markets, *Glühwein* (mulled wine) is a popular beverage to stave off the chills.

Party Miles
FRIEDRICHSHAIN

RAW Gelände & Revaler Strasse The skinny-jeanster set invades the gritty clubs and bars along the 'techno strip' set up in a former train repair station. Live concerts at Astra Kulturhaus, techno-electro at Suicide Circus, eclectic sounds at Cassiopeia and various off-kilter bars in between.

Ostkreuz Draw a bead on this cool party zone by staggering through the dark trying to find the entrance to Salon zur Wilden Renate or ://about blank.

Drinking & Nightlife by Neighbourhood

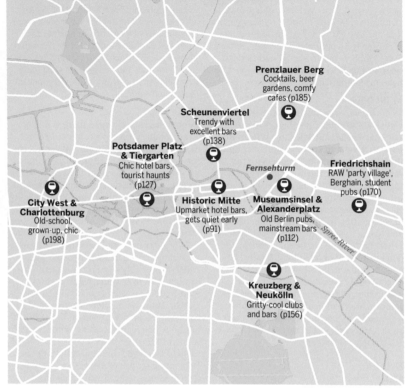

Prenzlauer Berg
Cocktails, beer gardens, comfy cafes (p185)

Scheunenviertel
Trendy with excellent bars (p138)

Potsdamer Platz & Tiergarten
Chic hotel bars, tourist haunts (p127)

Fernsehturm

Friedrichshain
RAW 'party village', Berghain, student pubs (p170)

City West & Charlottenburg
Old-school, grown-up, chic (p198)

Historic Mitte
Upmarket hotel bars, gets quiet early (p91)

Museumsinsel & Alexanderplatz
Old Berlin pubs, mainstream bars (p112)

Spree River

Kreuzberg & Neukölln
Gritty-cool clubs and bars (p156)

Ostbahnhof Hardcore partying at Berghain/ Panorama Bar and mellow chilling at Yaam.

Simon-Dach-Strasse If you need a cheap buzz, head to this well-trodden booze strip popular with field-tripping school groups and stag parties.

KREUZBERG & NEUKÖLLN

Weserstrasse The main party drag in hyped Neukölln hood is packed with an eclectic mix of pubs and bars, from trashy to stylish.

Kottbusser Tor & Oranienstrasse Grunge-tastic area perfect for dedicated drink-a-thons with a punky-funky flair.

Schlesische Strasse Freestyle strip where you could kick off with beers at Birgit&Bier, catch a band at Lido, heat up the dance floor at Watergate, then chill in the morning sun at Club der Visionäre.

Skalitzer Strasse Eclectic drag with small clubs and some quality cocktail bars just off it.

SCHEUNENVIERTEL

Torstrasse This noisy strip is where Berlin demonstrates that it too can grow up. A globe-spanning roster of monied creatives populates the chic drinking dens with their well-thought-out bar concepts, shabby to sleek decor and drinks made with top-shelf spirits.

Oranienburger Strasse Tourist zone where you have to hopscotch around sex workers and pub crawlers to find the few remaining thirst parlours worth your money.

Lonely Planet's Top Choices

Berghain/Panorama Bar (p172) Hyped but still happening Holy Grail of techno clubs with DJ royalty every weekend.

Clärchens Ballhaus (p138) Hipsters mix it up with grannies for tango and jitterbug in a kitsch-glam 1913 ballroom.

Club der Visionäre (p158) Summers wouldn't be the same without chilling and dancing in this historic canal-side boat shed.

Prater Biergarten (p185) Berlin's oldest beer garden still rocks beneath the chestnuts after 175 years in business.

Würgeengel (p160) Fun crowd keeps the cocktails and conversation flowing in a genuine '50s setting.

Best Clubs

Berghain/Panorama Bar (p172) Big bad Berghain is still the best in town.

://about blank (p172) Gritty techno hot spot with enchanting summer garden.

Sisyphos (p172) Summer-only party village in retired dog food factory.

Salon zur wilden Renate (p172) Psychedelic home of flashy-trashy electro parties in an abandoned apartment building.

Ritter Butzke (p157) Low-key but high-calibre electro club in ex-factory keeps it real with mostly local DJs and a crowd that appreciates them.

Best Cocktail Bars

Schwarze Traube (p158) Pint-sized drinking parlour with bespoke cocktails.

Becketts Kopf (p187) Wait for Godot while sipping supreme classics and seasonal inspirations.

Thelonius (p157) Neukölln drinking reaches new heights at this perfect trifecta of soft sounds, lovely light and expert cocktails.

Bar am Steinplatz (p198) Newbies and seasoned imbibers will be impressed by the supreme libations in this classy den.

Buck and Breck (p140) Cocktail classics for grown-ups in a speakeasy-style setting.

Best Craft Beer Pubs

Hopfenreich (p159) Berlin's first craft beer bar also has tastings, tap takeovers and guest brewers.

Castle Pub (p186) Irish pub turned craft beer hub with international kegged and bottled beers and a tiny resident microbrewery.

Herman (p186) Laid-lair specialises in Belgian suds from tap and bottle with over 100 on offer.

Pier (p141) This upscale craft beer bar inspired by Coney Island also serves American snacks.

Best Last Drinks

Mein Haus am See (p142) Any time is a good time to stumble into this 24/7 bar at Rosenthaler Platz.

Roses (p161) This 'Queen of Camp' is the ultimate on Kreuzberg's roster of eccentric trash dive bars.

August Fengler (p187) When the party shuts down in Prenzlauer Berg, Fengler keeps going...and going...

Kumpelnest 3000 (p128) Kitschy dive bar in a former brothel; not for the faint-of-heart.

Best Rooftop Bars

Klunkerkranich (p157) Hipster spot with urban garden and great sunset views atop Neukölln shopping centre.

Deck 5 (p187) Beach vibe with a view from the top parking deck of a Prenzlauer Berg shopping mall.

House of Weekend (p112) Club-affiliate delivers cocktails and barbecue at eye level with the TV Tower.

Monkey Bar (p199) Trendy West Berlin lair with exotic tiki drinks and a view of the baboons of the Berlin Zoo.

Best Wine Bars

Briefmarken Weine (p170) Oenophile den in former stamp shop for grown-up Italian wine fanciers.

Vin Aqua Vin (p158) Eliminates wine bar trepidation with casual vibe and wallet-friendly vintages.

Cordobar (p140) German and Austrian vintages get the spotlight at this chic Mitte hangout with upscale bar bites.

Otto Rink (p160) For relaxed but demanding wine fans with a penchant for German wines.

Christopher Street Day (p62)

Gay & Lesbian Berlin

Berlin's legendary liberalism has spawned one of the world's biggest, most divine and diverse LGBTIQ playgrounds. Anything goes in 'Homopolis' (and we do mean anything!), from the highbrow to the hands-on, the bourgeois to the bizarre, the mainstream to the flamboyant. Except for the most hard-core places, gay spots get their share of opposite-sex and straight patrons.

Gay in Berlin

Generally speaking, Berlin's gayscape runs the entire spectrum from mellow cafes, campy bars and cinemas to saunas, cruising areas, clubs with darkrooms and all-out sex venues. In fact, sex and sexuality are entirely everyday matters to the unshockable city folks and there are very few, if any, itches that can't be quite openly and legally scratched. As elsewhere, gay men have more options for having fun, but grrrrls of all stripes won't feel left out either.

History

Berlin's emergence as a gay capital has roots in 1897 when sexual scientist Magnus Hirschfeld founded the Scientific Humanitarian Committee, the world's first homosexual advocacy group. Gay life thrived in the wild and wacky 1920s, driven by a demi-monde that drew and inspired writers like Christopher Isherwood, until the Nazis put an end to the fun in 1933. Postwar recovery came slowly, but by the 1970s the scene was firmly re-established, at least in the western city. From 2001 to 2014, Berlin was governed by an openly gay mayor, Klaus Wowereit. To learn more about Berlin's LGBTIQ history, visit the Schwules Museum (p123).

Parties & Clubbing

Berlin's scene is especially fickle and venues and dates may change at the drop of a hat, so make sure you always check the websites or the listings magazines for the latest scoop. One important alternative queer party space is **Südblock** (www.suedblock. org) at Kottbusser Tor in Kreuzberg, which is famous for its inclusive programming and diverse clientele.

Long-running gay party places include Connection (p199), SchwuZ (p158), Berghain (p172) and Lab.oratory (p173), but there are also lots of regular parties held in various other locations. A selection follows. Unless noted, all are geared towards men.

Cafe Fatal All comers descend on SO36 (p157) for the ultimate rainbow tea dance, which goes from 'strictly ballroom' to 'dirty dancing' in a flash. If you can't tell a waltz from a foxtrot, come at 7pm for free lessons. Sundays.

Chantals House of Shame (www.facebook.com/ChantalsHouseofShame) Trash diva Chantal's louche lair at Bassy (p186) is a beloved institution, not so much for the glam factor as for the over-the-top drag shows and the hotties who love 'em. Thursdays.

Gayhane Geared towards gay and lesbian Muslims, but everyone's welcome to rock the kasbah when this 'homoriental' party takes over SO36 (p157) with Middle Eastern beats and belly dancing. Last Saturday of the month.

Gegen (www.gegenberlin.com) Counter-cultural party at KitKatClub (p159) brings in anti-trendy types for crazy electro and wacky art performances. First Friday of every other month.

Girls Town (www.girlstown-berlin.de) Suse and Zoe's buzzy girl-fest takes over Gretchen (p156) in Kreuzberg with down-and-dirty pop, electro, indie and rock. Second Saturday of every other month, September to May.

GMF (www.gmf-berlin.de) Berlin's premier techno-house Sunday club, currently at 2BE Club (Klosterstrasse 44) is known for excessive SM (standing and modelling) with lots of smooth surfaces. Predominantly boyz, but girls OK.

Irrenhaus (www.ninaqueer.com) The name means 'insane asylum' and that's no joke. Party hostess with the mostest, trash queen Nina Queer, puts on nutty, naughty shows at Kreuzberg's **Musik & Frieden** (Map p312; 📞030-2391 9994; www.

NEED TO KNOW

Magazines

➡ **Blu** (www.blu.fm) Online and freebie print magazine with searchable, up-to-the-minute location and event listings.

➡ **L-Mag** (www.l-mag.de) Bimonthly magazine for lesbians.

➡ **Out in Berlin** (www.out-in-berlin. com) Up-to-date free English/German booklet and website, often found at tourist offices.

➡ **Siegessäule** (www.siegessaeule.de) Free weekly lesbigay 'bible'.

Websites

➡ **Gay Berlin4u** (www.gayberlin4u. com)

➡ **GayCities Berlin** (www.berlin.gay cities.com)

➡ **Patroc Gay Guide** (www.patroc.de/ berlin)

Tours

➡ **Queer Berlin** (p270) Long-running tour company Original Berlin Walks taps into the city's LGBTIQ legacy on tours through Kreuzberg and Schöneberg.

➡ **Berlinagenten** (p271) Customised gay-lifestyle tours (nightlife, shopping, luxury, culinary).

➡ **Lügentour** (www.luegentour.de) An interactive and humorous walking tour takes you back to the lesbigay scene in 1920s Schöneberg; alas in German only.

➡ **Schröder Reisen Comedy Bus** (www.comedy-im-bus.de) Outrageous comedy bus tours led by trash drag royalty Edith Schröder (aka Ades Zabel) and friends.

Help

➡ **Mann-O-Meter** (www.mann-o-meter. de) Gay men's information centre.

➡ **Maneo** (www.maneo.de) Gay victim support centre and gay-attack hotline.

➡ **Lesbenberatung** (www.lesbenbera tung-berlin.de) Lesbian resource centre.

musikundfrieden.de; Falckensteinstrasse 48; ⊗hours vary; Ⓤ Schlesisches Tor), which are not for the faint-of-heart. Expect the best. Fear the worst. Third Saturday of the month.

L-Tunes (www.l-tunes.com) Lesbians get their groove on in the dancing pit of SchwuZ (p158). With speed-dating lounge and darkroom. Last Saturday of the month.

Mermaids (www.mermaids-party.de) This steamy summer-only party draws lesbians and their queer and straight friends. Check the website for dates and location. Usually third Saturday of the month, May to September.

Propaganda (www.propaganda-party.de) Currently at the **Puro Sky Lounge** (Map p316; ☑030-2636 7875; www.puroberlin.de; Tauentzienstrasse 9-12; ⊗10pm-6am Thu, 11pm-6am Sat; ⓤKurfürstendamm) in Charlottenburg, this New York–style house and electro party-and-a-half draws fashionable see-and-be-scenesters with its big sound and buff and bronzed go-go dancers. First Saturday of the month.

Revolver (www.facebook.com/RevolverParty Global) This London export hosted by Oliver and Gary is a sizzling and sexy party at the KitKatClub (p159) with no special dress code required. On the second Friday of the month.

Rose Kennedy (www.ninaqueer.de) Another Nina Queer production, this one lures revellers for a night of pop and house in changing locations, such as Birgit&Bier (p159) or **Brunnen 70** (Map p306; www.brunnen70.de; Brunnenstrasse 70; ⊗from 11pm Fri & Sat; ⓤVoltastrasse). Every fourth Saturday of the month.

Festivals & Events

Leather & Fetish Week (www.blf.de) Europe's biggest fetish fest whips the leather, rubber, skin and military sets out of the dungeons and into the clubs over the long Easter weekend. It culminates with the crowning of the 'German Mr Leather'.

Lesbisch-Schwules Stadtfest (www.stadtfest.berlin) The Lesbigay City Festival takes over the Schöneberg rainbow village in June, with bands, food, info booths and partying.

Christopher Street Day (www.csd-berlin.de) Later in June, hundreds of thousands of people of various sexual persuasions paint the town pink with a huge semipolitical parade and more queens than a royal wedding.

Kreuzberg Pride (www.transgenialercsd.wordpress.com) Also known as Transgenialer CSD, Kreuzberg celebrates this alternative version of Christopher Street Day, although not every year. Check the website.

Lesbischwules Parkfest (www.parkfest-friedrichshain.de) The gay community takes over the Volkspark Friedrichshain for this delightfully noncommercial festival in August.

Folsom Europe (www.folsomeurope.info) The leather crowd returns in early September for another weekend of kinky partying.

Hustlaball (www.hustlaball.de) The party year wraps up in October with a weekend of debauched fun in the company of porn stars, go-gos, trash queens, stripping hunks and about 3000 other men who love 'em.

Gay & Lesbian Berlin by Neighbourhood

➡ **Museumsinsel & Alexanderplatz** GMF, the best gay Sunday party, currently has a residency at the 2BE Club at Klosterstrasse 44.

➡ **Scheunenviertel** Gets a mixed crowd, but its trendy bars and cafes (especially near Hackescher Markt and on Torstrasse) also draw a sizeable contingent of gay customers.

➡ **Kreuzberg & Neukölln** Hipster central. Things are comparatively subdued in the bars and cafes along main-strip Mehringdamm. Around Kottbusser Tor and along Oranienstrasse the crowd skews younger, wilder and more alternative, and key venues stay open till sunrise and beyond. For a DIY subcultural vibe, head across the canal to northern Neukölln.

➡ **Friedrichshain** This area is thin on gay bars but is still a de rigueur stop on the gay nightlife circuit thanks to clubs like Berghain, the hands-on Lab.oratory and ://about blank.

➡ **Prenzlauer Berg** East Berlin's pink hub before the fall of the Wall has a few surviving relics as well as a couple of popular cruising dens and fun stations for the fetish set, mostly around the Schönhauser Allee S-/U-Bahn station.

➡ **Schöneberg** The area around Nollendorfplatz (Motzstrasse and Fuggerstrasse especially) has been a gay mecca since the 1920s. Institutions like **Tom's Bar** (www.tomsbar.de; Motzstrasse 19; ⊗10pm-6am; ⓤNollendorfplatz), Connection (p199) and **Hafen** (http://hafen-berlin.de; Motzstrasse 19; ⊗from 8pm) pull in the punters night after night, and there's also plenty of nocturnal action for the leather and fetish set.

Lonely Planet's Top Choices

GMF (p61) Glamtastic Sunday club with pretty people in stylish and central location.

Roses (p161) Plush, pink, campy madhouse – an essential late-night stop on a lesbigay bar hop.

Möbel Olfe (p160) Old furniture shop recast as busy drinking den; standing room only on (unofficial) gay Thursdays.

Chantals House of Shame (p186) Eponymous trash-drag diva's weekly parties run wild and wicked.

SchwuZ (p158) LGBTIQ club with different parties – great for scene newbies.

Best Venues by Day of the Week

Monday
Monster Ronson's Ichiban Karaoke (p173) Loosen those lungs and get louche.

Tom's Bar (p62) Two-for-one drinks.

Kino International (p173) Queer movies during 'Mongay'.

Tuesday
Rauschgold (p161) 'Time Tunnel' retro party.

Himmelreich (p171) Smart cocktails and 'ladies' only.

Möbel Olfe (p160) Comfortably cheerful femme fave.

Wednesday
Himmelreich (p171) Two-for-one drinks for a lesbigay crowd.

Thursday
Möbel Olfe (p160) Manly men get-together.

Chantals House of Shame (p186) Over-the-top drag-queen party.

Friday
SchwuZ (p158) Weekend warm-up.

Lab.oratory (p173) Two-for-one drinks, no dress code.

Saturday
SchwuZ (p158) Good for newbies.

Berghain (p172) Advanced partying.

Sunday
GMF (p61) Hot-stepping weekend wrap-up.

Cafe Fatal @ SO36 (p157) All-ages tea dance.

Best Gay Bars

Möbel Olfe (p160) Relaxed Kreuzberg joint goes into gay turbodrive on Thursdays; femmes dominate at Tuesday's Mädchendisko.

Himmelreich (p171) This '50s retro lounge is a lesbigay-scene stalwart in Friedrichshain.

Roses (p161) Over-the-top late-night dive with camp factor and strong drinks.

Coven (p140) Stylish Mitte bar with industrial decor and strong drinks.

Best Lesbian Bars

Himmelreich (p171) Women's Lounge on Tuesdays brings cool chicks to this comfy Friedrichshain bar.

Möbel Olfe (p160) Pop, disco and rock music get lesbians and their friends into party mood on Tuesdays.

L-Tunes (www.l-tunes.com) Flirting, dancing and making out at legendary **SchwuZ** (p158) on the last Saturday of the month.

Best for Camp

Rauschgold (p161) Small glitter-glam bar for all-night fun with pop, karaoke and drag shows.

Roses (p161) This pink-fur-walled kitsch institution is an unmissable late-night fuelling stop.

Best Sex Clubs/ Darkrooms

Lab.oratory (p173) Fetish-oriented experimental play zone in industrial setting below Berghain.

Greifbar (p186) Friendly cruising bar in Prenzlauer Berg with video, darkroom and private areas.

Connection Club (p199) Legendary dance club in Schöneberg with Berlin's largest cruising labyrinth.

Dancers perform at Friedrichstadt-Palast Berlin (p142)

☆ Entertainment

Berlin's cultural scene is lively, edgy and the richest and most varied in the German-speaking world. With three state-supported opera houses, five major orchestras – including the world-class Berliner Philharmoniker – scores of theatres, cinemas, cabarets and concert venues, you've got enough entertainment options to last you a lifetime.

Classical Music

Classical-music fans are truly spoilt in Berlin. Not only is there a phenomenal range of concerts throughout the year, but most of the major concert halls are architectural and acoustic gems of the highest order. Trips to the Philharmonie or the Konzerthaus are a particular treat, and regular concerts are also organised in churches like the Berliner Dom and such palaces as Schloss Charlottenburg.

Top of the pops is, of course, the world-famous Berliner Philharmoniker (p128), which was founded in 1882 and counts Hans Bülow, Wilhelm Furtwängler and Herbert von Karajan among its music directors. Since 2002, Sir Simon Rattle has continued the tradition. He will be succeeded by Russia-born Kirill Petrenko in 2019.

Though not in quite the same lofty league, the other orchestras are certainly no musical slouches either. Treat your eyes to concerts by the Berliner Symphoniker, the Deutsches Symphonie-Orchester, the Konzerthausorchester and the Rundfunk-Sinfonieorchester Berlin. Note that most venues take a summer hiatus (usually July and August).

A special treat are the Sunday concerts (p142) in a historic mirror hall above Clärchens Ballhaus in the Scheunenviertel.

Opera

Not many cities afford themselves the luxury of three state-funded opera houses, but then opera has been popular in Berlin ever since the first fat lady loosened her lungs. Today fans can catch some of Germany's biggest and best performances here. Leading the pack in the prestige department is the **Staatsoper Unter den Linden** (Map p296; ✆030-2035 4554; www.staatsoper-berlin.de; Bismarckstrasse 110; 🚌100, 200, TXL, ⓤFranzösische Strasse), the oldest among the three, founded by Frederick the Great in 1743. The hallowed hall hosted many world premieres, including Carl Maria von Weber's *Der Freischütz* and Alban Berg's *Wozzeck*. Giacomo Meyerbeer, Richard Strauss and Herbert von Karajan were among its music directors. Since reunification, Daniel Barenboim has swung the baton. (Note that until completion of the current long-term renovation, performances take place in the Schiller Theater in Charlottenburg.)

The Komische Oper (p92) opened in 1947 with *Die Fledermaus* by Johann Strauss and still champions light opera, operettas and dance theatre. Across town in Charlottenburg, the Deutsche Oper Berlin (p199) entered the scene in 1912 with Beethoven's *Fidelio*. It was founded by local citizens keen on creating a counterpoint to the royal Staatsoper.

Film

Berliners keep a wide array of cinemas in business, from indie art houses and tiny neighbourhood screens to stadium-style megaplexes with the latest technology. Mainstream Hollywood movies are dubbed into German, but numerous theatres also show flicks in their original language, denoted in listings by the acronym 'OF' (*Originalfassung*) or 'OV' (*Originalversion*); those with German subtitles are marked 'OmU' (*Original mit Untertiteln*). The Cinestar Original (p128) at the Sony Center in Potsdamer Platz only screens films in the original English.

Food and drink may be taken inside the auditoriums, although you are of course expected to purchase your beer and popcorn (usually at inflated prices) at the theatre. Almost all cinemas also add a sneaky

NEED TO KNOW

Ticket Bookings

➡ Early bookings are always advisable but essential in the case of the Berliner Philharmoniker, the Staatsoper and big-name concerts.

➡ Some venues let you book tickets online for free or only a small surcharge using a credit card. Pick them up before the show at the box office.

Ticket Agencies

➡ **Theaterkasse** Ticket outlets commonly found in shopping malls charge hefty fees.

➡ **Eventim** (www.eventim.de) The main online agency.

➡ **Hekticket** Half-price tickets for same-day performances online, by phone and in person at its outlets near Zoo Station (✆030-230 9930; www.hekticket.de; Hardenbergstrasse 29d) and Alexanderplatz (Alexanderstrasse 1).

➡ **Koka 36** (✆030-6110 1313; www.koka36.de) For indie concerts and events.

Discount Tickets

➡ Some theatres sell unsold tickets at a discount 30 minutes or an hour before curtain. Some restrict this to students.

➡ It's fine to buy spare tickets from other theatregoers but show them to the box-office clerk before forking over any cash.

➡ The ClassicCard (www.classiccard.de) offers savings for classical-music aficionados under 30.

Resources

➡ **Tip** (www.tip-berlin.de) Biweekly listings magazine (in German).

➡ **Zitty** (www.zitty.de) Biweekly listings magazine (in German).

➡ **Ex-Berliner** (www.ex-berliner.de) Expat-oriented English-language monthly.

➡ **Gratis in Berlin** (www.gratis-in-berlin.de) Free events (in German).

➡ **Berlin Bühnen** (www.berlin-buehnen.de) Browse by genre (theatre, opera, dance etc).

Überlängezuschlag (overrun supplement) of €0.50 to €1.50 for films longer than 90 minutes. There's also a surcharge for 3D movies plus a €1 rental fee if you don't have your own glasses. Seeing a flick on a *Kino-tag* (film day, usually Monday or Tuesday) can save you a couple of euros.

From May to September, alfresco screenings are a popular tradition, with classic and contemporary flicks spooling off in *Freiluftkinos* (open-air cinemas). Come early to stake out a good spot and bring pillows, blankets and snacks. Films are usually screened in their original language with German subtitles, or in German with English subtitles. Here are some of our favourites:

Freiluftkino Insel im Cassiopeia (Map p308; ☑030-3512 2449; www.freiluftkino-insel.de; Revaler Strasse 99; tickets €7; ◉around 9.30pm Mon, Tue, Thu & Sun; ⓰M10, M13, Ⓢ Warschauer Strasse, Ⓤ Warschauer Strasse) Free blankets; Friedrichshain.

Freiluftkino Friedrichshain (p173) In the open-air amphitheatre at Volkspark Friedrichshain.

Freiluftkino Kreuzberg (Map p312; ☑030-2936 1628; www.freiluftkino-kreuzberg.de; Mariannenplatz; tickets €7; ◉daily May-early Sep; Ⓤ Kottbusser Tor) In the courtyard of Kunstquartier Bethanien.

Open-Air Kino Mitte (p142) In the courtyard of Haus Schwarzenberg.

Berlin also plays host to most German and international movie premieres and, in February, stages the single most important event on Germany's film calendar, the **Berlinale** (www.berlinale.de; ◉Feb). Founded in 1951 on the initiative of the Western Allies, around 400 films are screened in theatres around town, with some of them competing for the Golden and Silver Bear trophies.

Dozens of other film festivals take place throughout the year, including Achtung Berlin, featuring movies made in Berlin and, yes, the Porn Film Festival. For the entire schedule, see http://berliner-film festivals.de.

Live Rock, Pop, Jazz & Blues

Berlin's live-music scene is as diverse as the city itself. There's no Berlin sound as such, but many simultaneous trends, from punk rock to hardcore rap and hip-hop, reggae to sugary pop and downtempo jazz. With four clubs – Musik & Frieden, Bii Nuu, Lido and Privatclub – the area around Schlesisches Tor U-Bahn station in Kreuzberg is sound central. Another prime venue, the Astra Kulturhaus, is just across the river in Friedrichshain. Some venues segue smoothly from concert to party on some nights. With scores of pubs and bars also hosting concerts, you're never far from a musical good time.

International top artists perform at various venues around town:

Columbiahalle (Map p314; ☑030-6981 2814; http://columbiahalle.berlin; Columbiadamm 13-21; Ⓤ Platz der Luftbrücke) Originally a gym for members of the US air-force, this hall now packs in up to 3500 people for rock and pop concerts.

Kindl-Bühne Wuhlheide (www.kindl-buehne-wuhlheide.de; An der Wuhlheide 187; ◉May-Sep; Ⓢ Wuhlheide) This 17,000-seat outdoor stage in the shape of an amphitheatre was built in the early 1950s and is a popular venue for German pop and rock concerts.

Mercedez-Benz Arena (Map p308; ☑tickets 030-206 070 8899; www.mercedes-benz-arena-berlin.de; Mühlenstrasse 12-30; Ⓢ Ostbahnhof, Warschauer Strasse, Ⓤ Warschauer Strasse) Berlin's professional ice hockey and basketball teams play their home games at this state-of-the-art Friedrichshain arena that's also the preferred venue of international entertainment stars.

Olympiastadion (p200) With a seating capacity of nearly 75,000, the storied Olympic Stadium has hosted top music acts, the premier league soccer team Hertha BSC and even the Pope.

Tempodrom (Map p314; ☑tickets 01806 554 111; www.tempodrom.de; Möckernstrasse 10; Ⓢ Anhalter Bahnhof) This mid-sized hall in an eye-catching tent-shaped building has great acoustics and eclectic programming from concerts to snooker championships.

Waldbühne Berlin (☑01806 570 070; www.waldbuehne-berlin.de; Glockenturmstrasse 1; ◉May-Sep; Ⓢ Pichelsberg) Built for the 1936 Olympics, this 22,000-seat open-air amphitheatre in the woods is a magical place for summer concerts.

Cabaret

The light, lively and lavish variety shows of the Golden Twenties have been undergoing a sweeping revival in Berlin. Get ready for an evening of dancing and singing, jugglers, acrobats and other entertainers. A popular venue is the Bar Jeder Vernunft (p200) and its larger sister Tipi am Kanzleramt (p92) whose occasional reprise of the musical *Cabaret* plays to sell-out audiences. In the heart of the 'East End' theatre district, Friedrichstadtpalast (p142) is Europe's largest revue theatre and the realm of leggy dancers and Vegas-worthy technology. The nearby Chamäleon Varieté (p142) is considerably more intimate. Travelling shows camp out at the lovely **Wintergarten Varieté** (☎030-588 433; www.wintergarten-variete.de; Potsdamer Strasse 96; ticket prices vary; ⓤKurfürstenstrasse).

These 'cabarets' should not be confused with *Kabarett,* which are political and satirical shows with monologues and skits.

Theatre

Get ready to smell the greasepaint and hear the roar of the crowd; with more than 100 stages around town, theatre is a mainstay of Berlin's cultural scene. Add in a particularly active collection of roaming companies and experimental outfits and you'll find there are more than enough offerings to satisfy all possible tastes. Kurfürstendamm in Charlottenburg and the area around Friedrichstrasse in Mitte (the 'East End') are Berlin's main drama drags.

Most plays are performed in German, naturally, but of late several of the major stages – including Schaubühne (p201), Volksbühne (p142) and Gorki (p92) – have started using English subtitles in some of their productions. There's also the English Theatre Berlin (p162), which has some pretty innovative productions often dealing with socio-political themes, including racism, identity and expat-related issues.

Many theatres are closed on Monday and from mid-July to late August.

The **Berliner Theatertreffen** (Berlin Theatre Meeting; www.theatertreffen-berlin.de), in May, is a three-week-long celebration of new plays and productions that brings together top ensembles from Germany, Austria and Switzerland.

Live Comedy

Berlin's vast expat community fuels a lively English-language comedy scene with everything from stand-up to sketch and musical comedy being performed around town. Upcoming events are posted on www.comedyinenglish.de. The Kookaburra (p187) comedy club does English-language shows some nights.

Dance

With independent choreographers and youthful companies consistently promoting experimental choreography, Berlin's independent dance scene is thriving as never before. The biggest name in choreography is Sasha Waltz, whose company Sasha Waltz & Guests has a residency at the cutting-edge Radialsystem V (p173). Other indie venues include the **Sophiensaele** (Map p302; ☎030-283 5266; www.sophiensaele.com; Sophienstrasse 18; tickets €10-15; ⓜM1, ⓢHackescher Markt, ⓤWeinmeisterstrasse), **Dock 11** (Map p306; ☎030-448 1222; www.dock11-berlin.de; Kastanienallee 79; tickets vary; ⓜM1, ⓤEberswalder Strasse) and Hebbel am Ufer (p161). The latter, in cooperation with Tanzwerkstatt Berlin, organises **Tanz im August** (www.tanzimaugust.de), Germany's largest contemporary dance festival, which attracts loose-limbed talent and highly experimental choreography from around the globe.

In the mainstream, the Staatsballett Berlin (Berlin State Ballet) performs both at the Staatsoper and at the Deutsche Oper Berlin.

Entertainment by Neighbourhood

→ **Historic Mitte** Tops for classical music and opera. (p92)

→ **Potsdamer Platz & Tiergarten** State-of-the-art multiplexes, art-house cinema, casino. (p128)

→ **Scheunenviertel** Cabaret, comedy, cinema and the 'East End' theatre district. (p142)

→ **Kreuzberg & Neukölln** Live music, off-theatre, art-house cinemas. (p161)

→ **Friedrichshain** Live music, outdoor cinema. (p173)

→ **Prenzlauer Berg** Live music. (p187)

→ **City West & Charlottenburg** Theatre, opera, jazz and indie screens. (p199)

Lonely Planet's Top Choices

Berliner Philharmonie (p128) One of the world's top orchestras within its own 'cathedral of sound'.

Staatsoper im Schiller Theater (p199) Top-ranked opera house.

Babylon (p142) Diverse and intelligent film programming in a 1920s building.

Lido (p161) Head-bobbing platform for indie bands, big names included.

Best Classical Music

Berliner Philharmonie (p128) The one and only. Enough said.

Konzerthaus Berlin (p92) Schinkel-designed concert hall festooned with fine sculpture; a festive backdrop for fine symphonies.

Sonntagskonzerte (p142) Intimate concerts amid charmingly faded 1920s grandeur.

Berliner Dom (p108) Former court church host concerts, sometimes played on the famous Sauer organ.

Best for Rock & Punk

SO36 (p157) Venerable club fixture has been rocking the crowd since the 1970s.

Wild at Heart (p161) Friendly biker-style dive with loud music and cheap beers.

Bassy (p186) Dedicated to pre-1969 sounds from swing to surf to psychedelic.

Best for Jazz & Blues

A-Trane (p201) Occasionally hosts jazz A-listers and has a rollicking Saturday night jam session.

Yorckschlösschen (p162) Easy-going and long-running, this knick-knack-filled club draws a no-nonsense, all-comers crowd.

b-Flat (p143) Intimate jazz joint mixing it up with Balkan beats and a through-the-roof jam session on Wednesday.

Best Cinemas

Babylon (p142) Art-house cinema in protected 1920s Bauhaus building with restored theatre organ.

Cinestar Original (p128) The best place to see English-language blockbusters in the original language.

Arsenal (p128) Arty fare from around the world in the original language, often with English subtitles.

Freiluftkino Friedrichshain (p173) Classics, indies, documentaries and blockbusters under the stars in the vast Volkspark Friedrichshain.

Kino Central (p142) At the funky Haus Schwarzenberg, this small indie house plays new and classic art-house fare; also outdoors in summer.

Best Live-Music Venues

Lido (p161) Great for catching tomorrow's headliners of the rock-indie-electro-pop persuasions.

Privatclub (p159) Small retro joint with an anything-goes booking policy.

Astra Kulturhaus (p173) Clued-in bookers fill this rambling space with everything from big-name artists to electro swing parties.

Waldbühne (p66) Berliner Philharmoniker to the Rolling Stones: they've all rocked this enchanting outdoor amphitheatre near the Olympic Stadium.

Best Cabaret

Chamäleon Varieté (p142) Historic variety theatre in the Hackesche Höfe presents mesmerising contemporary spins on acrobatics, dance, theatre, magic and music.

Bar Jeder Vernunft (p200) An art nouveau mirrored tent provides a suitably glam backdrop for high-quality entertainment.

Tipi am Kanzleramt (p92) There's not a bad seat in the house at this festive dinner theatre in a tent on the edge of the Tiergarten park.

Best for Free Entertainment

Bearpit Karaoke (p185) A huge crowd turns out to sing and cheer on Sunday at the Mauerpark.

Berliner Philharmonie (p128) Free Tuesday lunchtime concerts in the foyer of this famous concert hall.

Hochschule für Musik Hanns Eisler (p92) The gifted students of this conservatory show off their talent.

A-Trane Jazz Jam (p201) Mondays bring down the house in the well-established jazz club.

Französischer Dom Organ Recitals (p83) Lovely lunch break in historic church at 12.30pm Tuesday to Friday.

Teehaus im Englischen Garten (p124) Jazz to hip-hop concerts on summer Sundays at this charming Tiergarten beer garden.

PETER PTSCHELINZEW/GETTY IMAGES ©

Bikini Berlin (p201)

Shopping

Berlin is a great place to shop, and we're definitely not talking malls and chains. The city's appetite for the individual manifests in small neighbourhood boutiques and buzzing markets that are a pleasure to explore. Shopping here is as much about visual stimulus as it is about actually spending your cash, no matter whether you're ultrafrugal or a power-shopper.

Where to Shop

Berlin's main shopping boulevard is Kurfürstendamm (Ku'damm) in the City West and Charlottenburg, which is largely the purview of mainstream retailers (from H&M to Prada). Its extension, Tauentzienstrasse, is anchored by **KaDeWe** (www.kadewe.de; Tauentzienstrasse 21-24; ☑030-212 10; 10am-8pm Mon-Thu, ◷10am-9pm Fri, 9.30am-8pm Sat), continental Europe's largest department store. Standouts among the city's dozens of other shopping centres are the concept mall Bikini Berlin and the vast new LP12 Mall of Berlin at Leipziger Platz.

Getting the most out of shopping in Berlin, though, means venturing off the high street and into the *Kieze* (neighbourhoods). This is where you'll discover a cosmopolitan cocktail of indie boutiques stirred by the city's zest for life, envelope-pushing energy and entrepreneurial spirit.

Home-Grown Designers

Michael Michalsky may be Berlin's best-known fashion export, but hot on his heels are plenty of other fashion-forward local designers such as C.Neeon, Anna von Griesheim, Firma Berlin, Esther Perbandt,

NEED TO KNOW

Opening Hours

➜ Malls, department stores, supermarkets are open 9.30am to 8pm or 9pm; some supermarkets are 24 hours.

➜ Boutiques and other smaller shops have flexible hours, usually from 11am to 7pm weekdays, and to 4pm or 5pm Saturday.

Taxes & Refunds

If your permanent residence is outside the EU, you may be able to partially claim back the 19% value-added tax (VAT, *Mehrwertsteuer*) you have paid on goods purchased in stores displaying the 'Tax-Free for Tourists' sign.

Clothing Sizes

For women's clothing sizes, a German size 36 equals a size 6 in the US and a size 10 in the UK, then increases in increments of two, making size 38 a US 8 and UK 12, and so on.

Sunday Shopping

Stores are closed on Sunday, except for some bakeries, flower shops, souvenir shops and supermarkets in major train stations, including Hauptbahnhof, Friedrichstrasse and Ostbahnhof. Shops may also open from 1pm to 8pm on two December Sundays before Christmas and on a further six Sundays throughout the year, the latter being determined by local government.

C'est Tout, Claudia Skoda, Kostas Murkudis, Kaviar Gauche, Potipoti and Leyla Piedayesh. In typical Berlin style, they walk the line between originality and contemporary trends in a way that more mainstream labels do not.

New names on the watch list include Hien Li, Sadak, Julian Zigerli, Marina Hoermanseder and Jen Gilpin. Trend-pushers also include Umasan's vegan fashion, schmidttakahashi's take on upcycling, and high-end sustainable fashion by Christine Mayer. When it comes to accessories, look for eyewear by ic! Berlin and Mykita, bags by Liebeskind and Ta(u)sche, shoes by Trippen, and hats by Fiona Bennett and Rike Feurstein.

Flea Markets

Flea markets are like urban archaeology: you'll need plenty of patience and luck when sifting through other people's cast-offs, but oh, the thrill, when finally unearthing a piece of treasure! Berlin's numerous hunting grounds set up on weekends (usually Sunday) year-round – rain or shine – and are also the purview of fledgling local fashion designers and jewelry makers. The most famous market is the weekly Flohmarkt am Mauerpark (p187) in Prenzlauer Berg, which is easily combined with a visit to nearby Trödelmarkt Arkonaplatz (p188).

Shopping by Neighbourhood

➜ **Historic Mitte** Souvenir shops on Unter den Linden; top-flight retailers, concept stores and galleries on and around Friedrichstrasse. (p92)

➜ **Museumsinsel & Alexanderplatz** Eastern Berlin's mainstream shopping hub, plus a weekend collectables market. (p112)

➜ **Potsdamer Platz & Tiergarten** Two big malls and little else. (p128)

➜ **Scheunenviertel** Edgy international labels alongside local designers and accessories in chic boutiques and concept stores. (p143)

➜ **Kreuzberg & Neukölln** Vintage fashion and streetwear along with music and accessories, all in indie boutiques. (p162)

➜ **Friedrichshain** Up-and-coming area centred around Boxhagener Platz, site of a Sunday flea market; antiques market at Ostbahnhof. (p174)

➜ **Prenzlauer Berg** Fashionable boutiques and accessories on Kastanienallee, children's stores around Helmholtzplatz and a fabulous flea market. (p187)

➜ **City West & Charlottenburg** Mainstream on Kurfürstendamm, indie boutiques in the side streets, concept stores at Bikini Berlin, and homewares on Kantstrasse. (p201)

Lonely Planet's Top Choices

KaDeWe (p69) The ultimate consumer temple seemingly has everything every heart desires.

Bikini Berlin (p201) Edgy shopping in a revitalised 1950s landmark building near Zoo Station.

Galeries Lafayette (p93) French *je ne sais quoi* in an uberstylish building by Jean Nouvel.

Dussmann – Das Kulturkaufhaus (p92) The mother lode of books and music with high-profile author readings and signings.

Rausch Schokoladenhaus (p93) Palace of pralines and chocolate, plus ingenious model-sized replicas of famous Berlin landmarks – made of chocolate, of course.

Hard Wax (p162) Key music stop for electro heads.

Best Berlin Fashion & Accessories

Claudia Skoda Women (p144) Berlin style icon has kept women looking fab in knitwear since partying with Bowie & Co in the '70s.

lala Berlin (p144) Big city fashion label that reflects the idiosyncractic Berlin spirit.

IC! Berlin (p144) Unbreakable and stylish eyewear for the fashion-forward.

Trippen (p143) Handmade designer footwear that's sustainable, ergonomic and stylish.

Ta(u)sche (p187) Sturdy, chic and customisable messenger bags by dynamic local designer duo.

Best Bookshops

Another Country (p162) Quirkily run English-language bookstore/library/community living room.

Pro Qm (p144) Floor-to-ceiling shelves crammed with tomes on art, architecture and design.

Hundt Hammer Stein (p143) Expertly curated literary bookshop run by well-read staff.

Dussmann – Das Kulturkaufhaus (p92) Vast literature and music emporium with extended shopping hours.

Best Flea Markets

Flohmarkt am Mauerpark (p187) The mother of all markets is overrun but still a good show.

Nowkoelln Flowmarkt (p163) This internationally flavoured hipster market is also a showcase of local creativity.

Flohmarkt am Boxhagener Platz (p174) Fun finds are bound to abound at this charmer on a leafy square.

RAW Flohmarkt (p174) True bargains still about at this little market on the grounds of a railway repair station turned party zone.

Best Gastro Delights

KaDeWe Food Hall (p69) Mindboggling bonanza of gourmet treats from around the world.

Markthalle Neun (p162) Revitalised historic market hall with thrice-weekly farmers market and global bites during Street Food Thursday.

Bonbonmacherei (p143) Willy Wonka would feel right at home in this old-fashioned candy kitchen.

Best Malls & Department Stores

Bikini Berlin (p201) The city's first concept mall with hip stores and views of the monkeys at Berlin Zoo.

LP12 Mall of Berlin (p128) Huge new high-end shopping quarter with 270 stores alongside apartments, a hotel and offices.

Alexa (p112) Vast all-purpose mall with all the usual highstreet chains and an exhibit of Berlin in miniature.

KaDeWe (p69) The largest department store in continental Europe.

Best Quirky Shops

1. Absinth Depot Berlin (p144) Make your acquaintance with the Green Fairy at this quaint Old Berlin–style shop.

Käthe Wohlfahrt (p201) Where it's Christmas 365 days of the year so you can stock up on things that shine and glitter in July.

Ampelmann Galerie (p144) The little traffic-light guy that helps you across the street now has his own franchise.

Explore Berlin

BERLIN'S
TOP SIGHTS

Neighbourhoods at a Glance

❶ Historic Mitte p76

A cocktail of culture, commerce and history, Mitte packs it in when it comes to blockbuster sights: the Reichstag, the Brandenburg Gate, the Holocaust Memorial and Checkpoint Charlie are all within its confines. Cutting through it all is the grand boulevard Unter den Linden, large sections of which are currently torn up for construction of a new U-Bahn line.

❷ Museumsinsel & Alexanderplatz p94

This historic area is sightseeing central, home to world-class museums, including the unmissable Pergamonmuseum. The Berliner Dom watches serenely over it all, including the reconstruction of the Berlin City Palace across the street. Nearby, learn about life under socialism in the DDR Museum, then gain a dif-

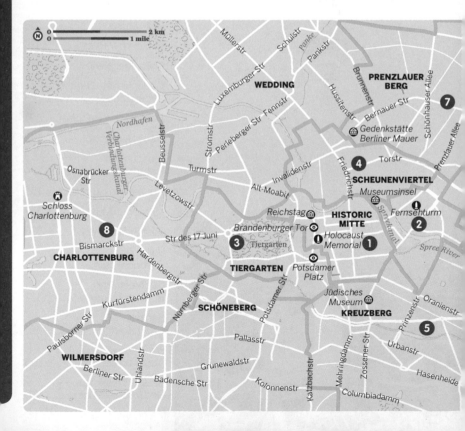

ferent perspective from the top of the Fernsehturm on socialist-era Alexanderplatz.

[3] Potsdamer Platz & Tiergarten p113

This new quarter, forged from ground once bisected by the Berlin Wall, is a showcase of contemporary architecture and home to cinemas and shopping. Culture lovers should not skip the Kulturforum museums, especially the Gemäldegalerie and the world-class Berliner Philharmonie. The leafy Tiergarten makes for a perfect sightseeing break.

[4] Scheunenviertel p129

With its boutique-lined lanes and charming courtyards like the Hackesche Höfe, the Scheunenviertel is fashionista central. It teems with progressive bars and restaurants, making it a pleasure to explore after dark as well. This is Berlin's traditional Jewish quarter, whose revival is symbolised by the gleaming dome of the rebuilt Neue Synagoge on Oranienburger Strasse. For contemporary art check out the galleries along Auguststrasse, the Hamburger Bahnhof and Sammlung Boros art museums.

[5] Kreuzberg & Neukölln p145

Kreuzberg and northern Neukölln across the canal are Berlin's most dynamic and hip neighbourhoods. With the Jewish Museum and the German Museum of Technology, the area has a couple of big sights, but its main draw is in its eclectic shopping, and a glut of excellent eateries and nightlife reflect its multicultural demographic.

[6] Friedrichshain p164

The former East Berlin district of Friedrichshain is famous for such high-profile GDR-era relics as the longest surviving stretch of Berlin Wall (the East Side Gallery), the socialist boulevard Karl-Marx-Allee and the former Stasi headquarters. It also has Berlin's most rambunctious nightlife scene with a glut of clubs and bars holding forth along Revaler Strasse and around the Ostkreuz train station.

[7] Prenzlauer Berg p175

Splendidly well-groomed Prenzlauer Berg is one of Berlin's most charismatic residential neighbourhoods, filled with cafes, historic buildings and indie boutiques. On Sundays, the world descends on its Mauerpark for flea marketeering, summertime karaoke and chilling in the sun. It's easily combined with a visit to the Gedenkstätte Berliner Mauer.

[8] City West & Charlottenburg p189

The glittering heart of West Berlin during the Cold War, Charlottenburg is a big draw for shopaholics, royal groupies and art lovers. Its main sightseeing attraction is Schloss Charlottenburg with its park and adjacent art museums. About 3.5km southeast of here City West, around Zoologischer Garten (Zoo Station), is characterised by Berlin's biggest shopping boulevard, the Kurfürstendamm.

Historic Mitte

GOVERNMENT QUARTER | PARISER PLATZ & UNTER DEN LINDEN | FRIEDRICHSTRASSE & CHECKPOINT CHARLIE | GENDARMENMARKT

Neighbourhood Top Five

❶ **Brandenburger Tor** (p80) Snapping a selfie with this famous landmark and symbol of German reunification.

❷ **Gendarmenmarkt** (p83) Taking in the architectural symmetry of this gorgeous square before indulging in a gourmet meal at one of the stellar restaurants in its vicinity.

❸ **Holocaust Memorial** (p81) Absorbing the stillness and presence of uncounted souls at this haunting site before putting it all in perspective at the underground exhibit.

❹ **Reichstag** (p78) Standing in awe of history at Germany's government building, then pinpointing the sights while meandering up its landmark glass dome.

❺ **Topographie des Terrors** (p8) Understanding the machinations of Nazi Germany at this haunting exhibit standing on the one-time site of the Gestapo and SS headquarters.

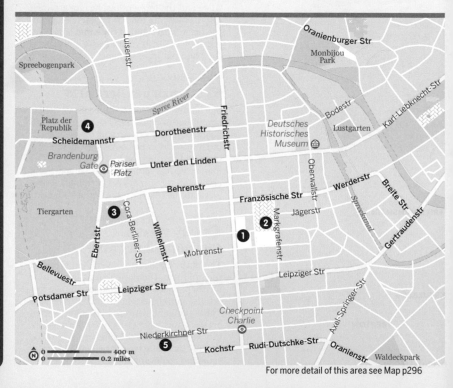

For more detail of this area see Map p296

Explore: Historic Mitte

With the mother lode of sights clustered within a walkable area, the most historic part of Berlin is naturally a prime port of call for most first-time visitors. Book ahead for access to the Reichstag dome, then snap a picture of the Brandenburger Tor and commune with lost souls at the Holocaust Memorial before dipping into Berlin's Prussian past on a stroll along the normally grand boulevard Unter den Linden. These days, though, expect to hopscotch around several major construction sites on account of a new U-bahn line, the renovation of the State Opera House and the rebuilding of the Berlin City Palace as a cultural centre called Humboldt Forum.

Unaffected by the temporary turmoil is Friedrichstrasse, which bisects Unter den Linden and runs north into the 'East End' theatre district and south to Checkpoint Charlie. Gendarmenmarkt, Berlin's most beautiful square, is just one block east and is surrounded by ritzy restaurants and fancy shops. Its Konzerthaus provides high-brow after-dark diversion, but aside from a few posh bars, this area is pretty devoid of nightlife action.

Local Life

➜**Glamour shopping** Brand-name bunnies flock to Friedrichstrasse. Aside from boutiques, the Friedrichstadtpassagen (p88), led by the stunningly designed Galeries Lafayette, beckon with top-flight Berlin and international designers.

➜**High-brow culture** Music and theatre fans are drawn to this part of town to take in concerts at the Konzerthaus Berlin (p92), theatre at the Gorki (p92), and opera at the Komische Oper (p92).

➜**Power of words** What's better than a night off sitting in front of the TV? Browsing a bookstore, of course. Open until 11pm, Dussmann (p92), the self-titled 'cultural department store', is an eldorado for bookworms and also has a huge music selection.

Getting There & Away

➜**Bus** Buses 100 and 200 run along most of Unter den Linden from Alexanderplatz.

➜**S-Bahn** S1 and S2/25 stop at Brandenburger Tor and Friedrichstrasse.

➜**U-Bahn** Stadtmitte (U2, U6), Französische Strasse (U6) and Hausvogteiplatz (U2) are all convenient for Gendarmenmarkt. For Unter den Linden, get off at Brandenburger Tor (U5), Friedrichstrasse (U6) or Französische Strasse (U6).

➜**Tram** The M1 travels from Museumsinsel to Prenzlauer Berg via Friedrichstrasse.

Lonely Planet's Top Tip

There is definitely a mystique of Checkpoint Charlie, so by all means drop by to take a look. However, in order to truly understand what it was like to cross between West and East Berlin, swing by the excellent – and free – exhibit in the **Tränenpalast** (p88), an actual border pavilion, a bit north on Friedrichstrasse.

⊙ Best Landmarks

➜ Brandenburger Tor (p80)

➜ Reichstag (p78)

➜ Holocaust Memorial (p81)

➜ Gendarmenmarkt (p83)

For reviews, see p84.➜

✕ Best Places to Eat

➜ Augustiner am Gendarmenmarkt (p90)

➜ Crackers (p91)

➜ Restaurant Tim Raue (p90)

➜ Ishin (p90)

For reviews, see p89.➜

☐ Best Places for Drinking

➜ Bar Tausend (p91)

➜ Berliner Republik (p91)

➜ Lost in Grub Street (p91)

For reviews, see p91.➜

TOP SIGHT
REICHSTAG

It's been burned, bombed, rebuilt, buttressed by the Berlin Wall, wrapped in fabric and finally turned into the modern home of the German parliament by Norman Foster: the Reichstag is one of Berlin's most iconic buildings. Its most eye-catching feature is the glistening glass dome, which draws more than three million visitors each year.

Dome

Resembling a giant glass beehive, the sparkling cupola is open at the top and bottom and sits right above the plenary chamber as a visual metaphor for transparency and open-ness in politics. A lift whisks you to the rooftop terrace from where you can easily pinpoint such sights as the curvaceous House of World Cultures and the majestic Berliner Dom (Berlin Cathedral) or marvel at the enormous dimensions of Tiergarten park. To learn more about these and other landmarks, the Reichstag building and the workings of parliament, pick up a free multilingual audioguide as you exit the lift. The commentary starts automatically as you mosey up the dome's 230m-long ramp, which spirals around a mirror-clad cone that deflects daylight down into the plenary chamber.

Home of the Bundestag

Today, the Reichstag is the historic anchor of the new federal government quarter built after reunification. The Bundestag, Germany's parliament, has hammered out its policies here since moving from the former German capital of Bonn to Berlin in 1999. The parliament's arrival followed a complete architectural revamp master-

DON'T MISS
- ➡ The dome
- ➡ The facade
- ➡ The free audioguide

PRACTICALITIES
- ➡ Map p296, C3
- ➡ www.bundestag.de
- ➡ Platz der Republik 1, Visitors' Service, Scheidemannstrasse
- ➡ admission free
- ➡ ⊘lift ride 8am–midnight, last entry 10pm, Visitors' Service 8am-8pm Apr-Oct, to 6pm Nov-Mar
- ➡ ⊒100, Ⓢ Brandenburger Tor, Hauptbahnhof, Ⓤ Brandenburger Tor, Bundestag

minded by Lord Norman Foster, who preserved only the building's 19th-century shell and added the landmark glass dome.

Main Facade

Stylistically, the monumental west-facing main facade borrows heavily from the Italian Renaissance, with a few neo-baroque elements thrown into the mix. A massive staircase leads up to a portico curtained by six Corinthian columns and topped by the dedication 'Dem Deutschen Volke' (To the German People), which wasn't added until 1916. The bronze letters were designed by Peter Behrens, one of the fathers of modern architecture, and cast from two French cannons captured during the Napoleonic Wars of 1813–15. The original dome, made of steel and glass and considered a high-tech marvel at the time, was destroyed during the Reichstag fire in 1933.

Historic Milestones

The grand old structure was designed by Paul Wallot and completed in 1894 when Germany was still a constitutional monarchy known as the Deutsches Reich (German Empire), hence the building's name. Home of the German parliament from 1894 to 1933 and again from 1999, the hulking building will likely give you more flashbacks to high-school history than any other Berlin landmark. On 9 November 1919, parliament member Philipp Scheidemann proclaimed the German republic from one of its windows. In 1933, the Nazis used a mysterious fire as a pretext to seize dictatorial powers. A dozen years later, victorious Red Army troops raised the Soviet flag on the bombed-out building, which stood damaged and empty on the western side of the Berlin Wall throughout the Cold War. In the late 1980s, megastars including David Bowie, Pink Floyd and Michael Jackson performed concerts on the lawn in front of the building.

The Wall collapsed soon thereafter, paving the way to German reunification, which was enacted here in 1990. Five years later the Reichstag made headlines once again when the artist couple Christo and Jeanne-Claude wrapped the massive structure in silvery fabric. It had taken an act of the German parliament to approve the project, which was intended to mark the end of the Cold War and the beginning of a new era. For two weeks starting in late June 1995, visitors from around the world flocked to Berlin to admire this unique sight. Shortly after the fabric came down, Lord Norman Foster set to work.

An extensive photographic exhibit at the bottom of the dome captures many of these historic moments.

VISITING THE DOME

Free reservations for visiting the Reichstag dome must be made at www.bundestag.de. Book early, and prepare to show picture ID, pass through a metal detector and have your belongings X-rayed. Guided tours and lectures can also be booked via the website. If you haven't prebooked, swing by the Service Centre near the Reichstag to enquire about remaining tickets for that day or the next two. You can also reach the rooftop by making reservations at the Dachgartenrestaurant Käfer.

It was the night of 27 February 1933: the Reichstag was ablaze. In the aftermath, a Dutch anarchist named Marinus van der Lubbe was arrested for arson without conclusive proof. Historians regard the incident as a pivotal moment in Hitler's power grab. Claiming that the fire was part of a large-scale Communist conspiracy, the Nazis pushed through the 'Reichstag Fire Decree', quashing civil rights and triggering the persecution of political opponents. The true events of that night remain a mystery. Its impact on history does not.

RICOWDE/GETTY IMAGES/MOMENT RF©

TOP SIGHT
BRANDENBURGER TOR

The Brandenburger Tor is Berlin's most famous – and most photographed – landmark. Trapped right behind the Berlin Wall during the Cold War, it went from symbol of division to epitomising German reunification when the hated barrier fell in 1989. It now serves as a photogenic backdrop for raucous New Years' Eve parties, concerts, festivals and mega-events like FIFA World Cup finals.

Commissioned by Prussian king Friedrich Wilhelm II, the gate was completed in 1791 as a symbol of peace and a suitably impressive entrance to the grand boulevard Unter den Linden. Architect Carl Gotthard Langhans looked to the Acropolis in Athens for inspiration for this elegant triumphal arch, which is the only surviving one of 18 city gates that once ringed historic Berlin.

The neoclassical sandstone structure stands 26m high, 65.5m wide and 11m deep and punctuates Pariser Platz, a harmoniously proportioned square framed by banks, a luxury hotel and the US, British and French embassies. The gate is fronted by 12 Doric columns and divided into five passageways. The wider central passage was reserved for the king and his entourage; common folk had to use the four narrower ones.

Crowning the Brandenburg Gate is the *Quadriga,* Johann Gottfried Schadow's famous sculpture of a winged goddess piloting a chariot drawn by four horses. After trouncing Prussia in 1806, Napoleon kidnapped the lady and held her hostage in Paris until she was freed by a gallant Prussian general in 1815. Afterwards, the goddess, who originally represented Eirene (the goddess of peace), was promoted to Victoria (the goddess of victory) and equipped with a new trophy designed by Karl Friedrich Schinkel: an iron cross wrapped into an oak wreath and topped with a Prussian eagle.

DON'T MISS

- Quadriga
- View from Pariser Platz at sunset

PRACTICALITIES

- Brandenburger Gate
- Map p296, C3
- Pariser Platz
- [S]Brandenburger Tor, [U]Brandenburger Tor

FRANK WALDECKER/LOOK-FOTO/GETTY IMAGES ©

TOP SIGHT
HOLOCAUST MEMORIAL

The Denkmal für die ermordeten Juden Europas (Memorial to the Murdered Jews of Europe) was officially dedicated in 2005. Colloquially known as Holocaust Memorial, it's Germany's central memorial to the Nazi-planned genocide during the Third Reich. For the football-field-sized space, New York architect Peter Eisenman created 2711 sarcophagi-like concrete stelae (slabs) of equal size but various heights, rising in sombre silence from undulating ground.

You're free to access this massive concrete maze at any point and make your individual journey through it. At first it may seem austere, even unemotional. But take time to feel the coolness of the stone and contemplate the interplay of light and shadow, then stumble aimlessly among the narrow passageways, and you'll soon connect with a metaphorical sense of disorientation, confusion and claustrophobia.

For context, visit the subterranean **Ort der Information** (Information Centre; Map p296; ☎030-7407 2929; www.holocaust-mahnmal.de; Cora-Berliner-Strasse 1; audioguide adult/concession €4/2; 🕒10am-8pm Tue-Sun Apr-Sep, to 7pm Oct-Mar, last admission 45min before closing; [S]Brandenburger Tor, [U]Brandenburger Tor) [FREE], which movingly lifts the veil of anonymity from the six million Holocaust victims. A graphic timeline of Jewish persecution during the Third Reich is followed by a series of rooms documenting the fates of individuals and families. The most visceral is the darkened Room of Names, where the names and years of birth and death of Jewish victims are projected onto all four walls while a solemn voice reads their short biographies. Poignant and heart-wrenching, these exhibits will leave no one untouched.

DON'T MISS

- Field of Stelae
- Ort der Information
- Room of Names

PRACTICALITIES

- Memorial to the Murdered European Jews
- Map p296, C4
- ☎030-2639 4336
- www.stiftung-denkmal.de
- Cora-Berliner-Strasse 1
- audioguide adult/concession €4/2
- 🕒field 24hr, information centre 10am-8pm Tue-Sun Apr-Sep, to 7pm Oct-Mar, last entry 45min before closing
- [S]Brandenburger Tor, [U]Brandenburger Tor

TOP SIGHT
DEUTSCHES HISTORISCHES MUSEUM

If you're wondering what the Germans have been up to for the past 1500 years, take a spin around this engaging museum in the baroque Zeughaus, formerly the Prussian arsenal. Upstairs, displays concentrate on the period from the 1st century AD to the end of WWI in 1918, while the ground floor tracks the 20th century all the way through to German reunification.

DON'T MISS

- Nazi globe
- Schlüter's sculptures in the courtyard
- IM Pei Exhibition Hall

PRACTICALITIES

- German Historical Museum
- Map p296, G3
- ☎030-203 040
- www.dhm.de
- Unter den Linden 2
- adult/concession/under 18 €8/4/free
- 🕐10am-6pm
- 📶
- 🚌100, 200, [S]Hackescher Markt, [U]Hausvogteiplatz

Permanent Exhibit

All the major milestones in German history are dealt with in a European context and examine political history as it was shaped by rulers. The timeline begins with the coronation of Charlemagne, the founding of the Holy Roman Empire and everyday life in the Middle Ages. It then jumps ahead to Martin Luther and the Reformation and the bloody Thirty Years' War and its aftermath, addresses Napoleon and the collapse of the Holy Roman Empire in 1806, and the founding of the German Empire in 1871. WWI, which brought the end of the monarchy and led to the Weimar Republic, is a major theme, as are of course the Nazi era and the Cold War. The exhibit ends in 1994 with the withdrawal of Allied troops from German territory.

Displays are a potpourri of documents, paintings, books, dishes, textiles, weapons, furniture, machines and other objects ranging from the sublime to the trivial. One of the oldest objects is a 3rd-century Roman milestone. There's also splendid medieval body armour for horse and rider and a felt hat once worn by Napoleon I. Among the more unusual objects is a pulpit hourglass, which was introduced after the Reformation to limit the length of sermons to one hour. A startling highlight is a big globe that originally stood in the Nazi Foreign Office, with a bullet hole where Germany should be. Among the newer objects is a 1985 Robotron, the first PC made in East Germany.

The Building

The rose-coloured Zeughaus, which was used as a weapons depot until 1876, was a collaboration of four architects: Johann Arnold Nering, Martin Grünberg, Andreas Schlüter and Jean de Bodt. Completed in 1730, it is the oldest building along Unter den Linden and a beautiful example of secular baroque architecture. This is in no small part thanks to Schlüter's magnificent sculptures, especially those in the glass-covered courtyard whose facades are festooned with heads of dying soldiers, their faces contorted in agony. Although intended to represent vanquished Prussian enemies, they actually make more of a pacifist statement for modern viewers.

IM Pei Exhibition Hall

High-calibre temporary exhibits take up a spectacular contemporary **annexe** (Map p296; ☎030-203 040; www.dhm.de; Hinter dem Giesshaus 3; exhibits adult/concession/under 18 €8/4/free; 🕐10am-6pm; [U]Hausvogteiplatz) designed by Chinese-American architect IM Pei. Fronted by a glass spiral, it's an uncompromisingly geometrical space, made entirely from triangles, rectangles and circles, yet imbued with a sense of lightness achieved through an airy atrium and generous use of glass.

RUDYBALASKO/GETTY IMAGES ©

TOP SIGHT
GENDARMENMARKT

The graceful Gendarmenmarkt is widely considered Berlin's prettiest square and – surrounded by luxury hotels, fancy restaurants and bars – shows off the city at its ritziest. It was laid out around 1690 and named after the *Gens d'Armes*, an 18th-century Prussian regiment of French Huguenots who settled here after being expelled from France in 1685.

The 1705 **Französischer Dom** (French Cathedral; Map p296; www.franzoesischer-dom.de; Gendarmenmarkt; church free, museum adult/concession €3.50/2, tower adult/child €3/1; ⊙church & museum noon-5pm Tue-Sun, tower 10am-7pm Apr-Oct, noon-5pm Jan-Mar, last entry 1hr before closing; Ⓤ Französische Strasse) was built by Huguenot refugees and consists of two buildings: the soaring domed tower, which was added by Carl von Gontard in 1785, and the attached Französische Kirche (French Church), a copy of the Huguenots' mother church in Charenton. There's a small Huguenot museum on the ground floor of the tower whose viewing platform is reached via 284 steps.

The **Deutscher Dom** (German Dome; Map p296; ☎030-2273 0431; www.bundestag.de/deutscherdom; Gendarmenmarkt 1; ⊙10am-7pm Tue-Sun May-Sep, to 6pm Oct-Apr; Ⓤ Französische Strasse, Stadtmitte) **FREE** wasn't much of a looker being topped by Gontard's dazzling galleried dome in 1785. Built as the Neue Kirche (New Church) between 1702 and 1708 for German-speaking congregants, it is now home to an exhibit charting Germany's path to parliamentary democracy. English audioguides and tours are available.

One of Karl Friedrich Schinkel's finest buildings, the 1821 Konzerthaus (p92) rose from the ashes of Carl Gotthard Langhans' Schauspielhaus (National Theatre). Schinkel kept the surviving walls and columns and added a grand staircase leading to a raised columned portico. The building is fronted by an elaborate sculpture of 18th-century poet and playwright Friedrich Schiller. For an inside look at this beacon of Berlin high-brow culture, catch a concert or take a guided tour (€3, in German) at 1pm on Saturday.

DON'T MISS

➜ Free organ recital in the Französische Kirche

➜ Climbing the tower of the Französischer Dom

➜ Concert at the Konzerthaus

PRACTICALITIES

➜ Map p296, F4

➜ Ⓤ Französische Strasse, Stadtmitte

◉ SIGHTS

Berlin's historic centre flanks the boulevard Unter den Linden and handily packs a lot of blockbuster sights into a compact frame. A visit here is easily combined with a stroll around the Tiergarten to the west, a look at the new Potsdamer Platz city quarter to the south or a spin around the stunners of Museum Island just east of here.

◉ Government Quarter

REICHSTAG
HISTORIC BUILDING
See p78.

PAUL-LÖBE-HAUS
NOTABLE BUILDING
Map p296 (www.bundestag.de; Konrad-Adenauer-Strasse; ☒100, ⓢHauptbahnhof, ⓤBundestag, Hauptbahnhof) The glass-and-concrete Paul-Löbe-Haus houses offices for the Bundestag's parliamentary committees. It's filled with modern art that can be viewed only during free guided tours (in German) at 2pm and 4pm on Saturday and Sunday. Advance online registration is required.

BUNDESKANZLERAMT
NOTABLE BUILDING
Map p296 (Federal Chancellery; Willy-Brandt-Strasse 1; ⊘closed to public; ☒100, ⓤBundestag) The Federal Chancellery, Germany's 'White House', is a sparkling, modern compound designed by Axel Schultes and Charlotte Frank and consisting of two parallel office blocks flanking a central white cube. Eduardo Chillida's rusted-steel *Berlin* sculpture graces the eastern forecourt. The best views of the entire building are from the Moltkebrücke (bridge) or the northern Spree River promenade.

MARIE-ELISABETH-LÜDERS-HAUS
NOTABLE BUILDING
Map p296 (www.bundestag.de; Schiffbauerdamm; ⊘galleries 11am-5pm Tue-Sun; ⓢHauptbahnhof, ⓤBundestag, Hauptbahnhof) Home to the parliamentary library, this recently expanded, extravagant structure has a massive tapered stairway, a flat roofline jutting out like a springboard and giant circular windows. In the basement is an art installation (p86) by Ben Wagin featuring original segments of the Berlin Wall.

Accessible from the Luisenstrasse entrance is the Kunst-Raum, which presents politically infused contemporary art.

STRASSE DES 17 JUNI
STREET
Map p296 (ⓢBrandenburger Tor, ⓤBrandenburger Tor) The boulevard bisecting Tiergarten was named Street of 17 June in honour of the victims of the bloodily quashed 1953 workers' uprising in East Berlin. It originally linked two royal palaces and was turned into a triumphal road under Hitler.

SOWJETISCHES EHRENMAL TIERGARTEN
MEMORIAL
Map p296 (Soviet War Memorial; Strasse des 17 Juni; ⊘24hr; ⓢBrandenburger Tor, ⓤBrandenburger Tor) FREE The imposing Soviet War Memorial is flanked by two Russian T-34 tanks said to have been the first to enter the city in 1945. It was built by German workers on order of the Soviets and completed just months after the end of the war. More than 2000 Red Army soldiers are buried behind the colonnade.

HAUS DER KULTUREN DER WELT
NOTABLE BUILDING
Map p296 (House of World Cultures; ☒030-3978 7175; www.hkw.de; John-Foster-Dulles-Allee 10; ⊘exhibits 11am-7pm Wed-Mon; 🅿🛜; ☒100, ⓢHauptbahnhof, ⓤBundestag, Hauptbahnhof) This highly respected cultural centre showcases contemporary non-European art, music, dance, literature, films and theatre, and also serves as a discussion forum on zeitgeist-reflecting issues. The gravity-defying parabolic roof of Hugh Stubbins' extravagant building, designed as the American contribution to a 1957 architectural exhibition, is echoed by Henry Moore's sculpture *Butterfly* in the reflecting pool.

Computerised chime concerts ring out at noon and 6pm daily from the nearby 68-bell carillon, and live concerts take place Sunday at 3pm from May to September (also at 2pm in December). The cost of admission varies.

DENKMAL FÜR DIE IM NATIONALSOZIALISMUS ERMORDETEN SINTI UND ROMA EUROPAS
MEMORIAL
Map p296 (Memorial to the Sinti & Roma of Europe Murdered under the Nazi Regime; www.stiftung-denkmal.de; Scheidemannstrasse; ⊘24hr; ☒100, ⓢBrandenburger Tor, ⓤBrandenburger Tor) FREE Inaugurated in 2012, this memorial commemorates the Sinti and Roma victims of the Holocaust and consists of a fountain with a submersed stone decorated daily with a fresh flower. It was designed by Israeli sculptor Dani Karavan.

TOP SIGHT
TOPOGRAPHIE DES TERRORS

In the same spot where once stood the most feared institutions of Nazi Germany (including the Gestapo headquarters, the SS leadership and, during the war, the Reich Security Main Office) this compelling exhibit dissects the anatomy of the Nazi state. It discusses the stages of terror and persecution, puts a face on the perpetrators and details the impact these brutal institutions had on all of Europe. From their desks, top Nazi commanders like Himmler and Heydrich hatched Holocaust plans and organised the systematic persecution of political opponents, many of whom suffered torture and death in the Gestapo prison.

From spring to autumn, another exhibit called 'Berlin 1933–1945: Between Propaganda & Terror' opens in a trench against glassed-in foundations of the Gestapo prison cells. It looks at how the Nazis were able to turn liberal Berlin into a nexus of their leadership's political power and how life changed for local residents as a result. In addition, a self-guided tour of the historic grounds takes you past 15 information stations with photos, documents and 3D graphics as well as a 200m stretch of the Berlin Wall along Niederkirchner Strasse. Admission is free.

DON'T MISS

- Model of the grounds in the foyer
- Diagram of the concentration camp system

PRACTICALITIES

- Topography of Terror
- Map p296, D7
- ☎030-2548 0950
- www.topographie.de
- Niederkirchner Strasse 8
- 🕘10am-8pm, grounds close at dusk or 8pm at the latest
- [S]Potsdamer Platz, [U]Potsdamer Platz

DENKMAL FÜR DIE IM NATIONALSOZIALISMUS VERFOLGTEN HOMOSEXUELLEN MEMORIAL

Map p296 (Memorial to the Homosexuals Persecuted under the Nazi Regime; www.stiftung-denkmal.de; Ebertstrasse; 🕘24hr; [S]Brandenburger Tor, Potsdamer Platz, [U]Brandenburger Tor, Potsdamer Platz) [FREE] Since 2008 this memorial has trained the spotlight on the tremendous suffering of Europe's gay community under the Nazis. The freestanding, 4m-high, off-kilter concrete cube was designed by Danish-Norwegian artists Michael Elmgreen and Ingar Dragset. A looped video plays through a warped, narrow window.

Pariser Platz & Unter den Linden

BRANDENBURGER TOR LANDMARK

See p80.

HOLOCAUST MEMORIAL MEMORIAL

See p81.

DEUTSCHES HISTORISCHES MUSEUM MUSEUM

See p82.

PARISER PLATZ SQUARE

Map p296 (Pariser Platz; [S]Brandenburger Tor, [U]Brandenburger Tor) Lorded over by the landmark Brandenburg Gate, this elegant square was completely flattened in WWII, then spent the Cold War just trapped east of the Berlin Wall. Look around: the US, French and British embassies, banks and a luxury hotel have returned to their original sites and once again frame the bustling plaza, just as they did during its 19th century heyday.

THE GATE MULTIMEDIA SHOW

Map p296 (☎030-236 078 436; www.thegate-berlin.de; Pariser Platz 4a; adult/concession/child €12/9/6; 🕘10am-8pm; [S]Brandenburger Tor, [U]Brandenburger Tor) Get the gist of Berlin's often turbulent history in 20 minutes without opening a book in this new whirlwind multimedia show. Using sound effects along with historical footage and documents projected onto 87 screens arranged in a U-shape, this digital-age time capsule ticks off all the major milestones –

revolutions, war, Hitler, Kennedy, the Berlin Wall, reunification – in an often emotional but historically accurate format. You're free to watch it more than once or deepen your knowledge in the attached traditional exhibit.

AKADEMIE DER KÜNSTE – PARISER PLATZ
ARTS CENTRE

Map p296 (Academy of Arts; ☎030-200 571 000; www.adk.de; Pariser Platz 4; admission varies; 🕐building 10am-10pm, exhibits vary; [S]Brandenburger Tor, [U]Brandenburger Tor) The only building on Pariser Platz with a glass facade is the Academy of Arts, which was designed by Günter Behnisch. The Academy is one of Berlin's oldest cultural institutions, founded in 1696 by the later King Friedrich I as the Prussian Academy of Arts. It presents a varied program of high-brow readings, lectures, workshops and exhibits, many of them free.

HITLER'S BUNKER
HISTORIC SITE

Map p296 (cnr In den Ministergärten & Gertrud-Kolmar-Strasse; 🕐24hr; [S]Brandenburger Tor, [U]Brandenburger Tor) Berlin was burning and Soviet tanks advancing relentlessly when Adolf Hitler committed suicide on 30 April 1945, alongside Eva Braun, his long-time female companion, hours after their marriage. Today, a parking lot covers the site, revealing its dark history only via an information panel with a diagram of the vast bunker network, construction data and the site's post-WWII history. The interior was blown up and sealed off by the Soviets in 1947. The 2004 movie *The Downfall* chronicles Hitler's last days at the Führerbunker.

ERLEBNIS EUROPA
MUSEUM

Map p296 (Europa Experience; www.erlebnis-europa.de; Unter den Linden 78; 🕐10am-6pm; [S]Brandenburger Tor, [U]Brandenburger Tor) [FREE] In times when many question the future of the EU, a new permanent exhibit works hard to make a case for a united Europe. Funded by the European Commission, you can learn more about each member country, find out how the EU works and what it's like to be a European citizen – in 24 languages. Attend a session of the European Parliament in the 360° cinema or take a selfie and send an electronic postcard from 'Europe'.

WALL VICTIMS MEMORIALS

The Berlin Wall ran right through this area, which is why there are several memorials honouring those unfortunate souls who died trying to scale it in escaping to the West.

Mahnmal im Marie-Elisabeth-Lüders-Haus (Berlin Wall Memorial at the German Bundestag; Map p296; ☎030-2273 2027; www.bundestag.de/mauermahnmal; Schiffbauerdamm; 🕐11am-5pm Tue-Sun; 🚌TXL, [U]Bundestag) In the basement of the Marie-Elisabeth-Lüders Haus, this installation by Ben Wagin runs along the original course of the Berlin Wall. It consists of original segments, each painted with a year and the number of people killed at the Wall in that year. Enter from the Spree Promenade. If it's closed, you can easily sneak a peak through the window.

Gedenkort Weisse Kreuze (White Crosses Memorial; Map p296; Reichstagufer; 🚌100, [U]Bundestag) The Berlin Wall ran right behind the Reichstag. In 1971 a group of West Germans erected seven white crosses on the southern bank of the Spree River, which still belonged to West Berlin. It commemorates East Germans who died in their attempt to escape to the West.

Wall Memorial 'Parlament der Bäume' (Parliament of Trees; Map p296; cnr Schiffbauerdamm & Adele-Schreiber-Krieger-Strasse; 🕐24hr; [U]Bundestag) Conceived by Berlin-based artist Ben Wagin in 1990, this environmental art installation is a quiet garden of remembrance for those who died at the Berlin Wall and stands on the spot of the original border strip. It consists not only of trees but also memorial stones, pictures, text and 58 original pieces of the border fortification which list the names of 258 victims.

Peter Fechter Memorial (Map p296; Zimmerstrasse; 🕐24hr; [U]Kochstrasse) A famous incident illustrating the barbarity of the shoot-to-kill order occurred on 17 August 1962 when 18-year-old would-be escapee Peter Fechter was shot and wounded and then left to bleed to death as East German guards looked on. A simple memorial pillar marks the site where he died on Zimmerstrasse, just east of Checkpoint Charlie.

MADAME TUSSAUDS MUSEUM

Map p296 (☎01806-545 800; www.madametussauds.com/berlin; Unter den Linden 74; adult/child 3-14yr €23.50/18.50; ⏲10am-7pm year round, 9.30am-7.30pm Aug, last entry 1hr before closing; 🚌100, [S]Brandenburger Tor, [U]Brandenburger Tor) At this legendary wax museum the world's biggest pop stars, Hollywood legends, sports heroes and historical icons stand still – very still – for you to snap their picture. Sure, it's an expensive haven of kitsch and camp, but where else can you have a candlelit dinner with George Clooney, play piano with Beethoven or visit the land of Azeroth from the movie *Warcraft*? Avoid wait times and save money by buying tickets online.

DEUTSCHE BANK KUNSTHALLE GALLERY

Map p296 (☎030-202 0930; www.deutsche-bank-kunsthalle.de; Unter den Linden 13-15; adult/concession/under 18 €4/3/free, Mon free; ⏲10am-8pm; 🚌100, 200, TXL, [U]Französische Strasse) This small exhibition hall by American architect Richard Gluckman is a platform for contemporary art, especially from emerging art centres in Africa, China, India and South America. The three to four exhibits per year (also in cooperation with international guest curators) often push artistic boundaries and examine the effects of a globalised society. One exhibit presents Deutsche Bank's 'Artist of the Year'.

HUMBOLDT UNIVERSITÄT ZU BERLIN NOTABLE BUILDING

Map p296 (☎030-2093 2951; www.hu-berlin.de/en; Unter den Linden 6; 🚌100, 200, TXL, [U]Französische Strasse) Marx and Engels studied here and the Brothers Grimm and Albert Einstein taught here, at Berlin's oldest university, founded in 1810 and housed in a palace built by Frederick the Great for his brother Heinrich. Statues of the uni's founder, philosopher Wilhelm von Humboldt, and his explorer brother Alexander flank the main entrance.

REITERDENKMAL FRIEDRICH DER GROSSE MONUMENT

Map p296 (Unter den Linden 6; 🚌100, 200, TXL) Seemingly surveying his domain, Frederick the Great cuts a commanding figure on horseback in this famous 1850 monument that kept sculptor Christian Daniel Rauch busy for a dozen years. The plinth is decorated with a parade of German military men, scientists, artists and thinkers.

BEBELPLATZ SQUARE

Map p296 (Bebelplatz; 🚌100, 200, TXL, [U]Hausvogteiplatz) In 1933 the Nazi German Student League organised the first full-blown public book burning in Germany. Works by Brecht, Mann, Marx and others deemed 'subversive' went up in flames on this treeless square. Named for August Bebel, the co-founder of Germany's Social Democratic Party (SPD), it was originally laid out in the 18th century under King Frederick the Great.

Originally called Opernplatz (Opera Square), it was intended to be the hub of the Forum Fridericianium, a cultural centre envisioned by the king. Money woes meant that only some of the buildings could be realised: the Staatsoper Unter den Linden (State Opera House), the Alte Königliche Bibliothek (Old Royal Library), a palace for the king's brother Heinrich (now the Humboldt Universität zu Berlin) and the copper-domed St-Hedwigs-Kathedrale.

ST-HEDWIGS-KATHEDRALE BERLIN CHURCH

Map p296 (☎030-203 4810; www.hedwigs-kathedrale.de; Hinter der Katholischen Kirche 3; ⏲10am-5pm Mon-Sat, 1-5pm Sun; 🚌100, 200, [U]Hausvogteiplatz) This copper-domed church (1773) was commissioned by Frederick the Great, designed by Knobelsdorff, modelled after the Pantheon in Rome and named for the patron saint of Silesia. Restored after WWII, its circular, modern interior is lidded by a ribbed dome and accented with Gothic sculpture and an altar cross made of gilded and enamel-decorated ivory. It was Berlin's only Catholic post-Reformation house of worship until 1854. During WWII, St Hedwig was a centre of Catholic resistance led by Bernard Lichtenberg, who died en route to the Dachau concentration camp in 1943; he is buried in the crypt.

ALTE BIBLIOTHEK HISTORIC BUILDING

Map p296 (Bebelplatz; ⏲9am-9.30pm Mon-Fri, to 6pm Sat, 1-6pm Sun; 🚌100, 200, TXL, [U]Hausvogteiplatz) Thanks to its curvaceous facade, this handsome baroque building is nicknamed *Kommode* (chest of drawers). Built under Frederick the Great to shelter the royal book collection, it has been part of the Humboldt University since 1914. It now houses the university's law school. Lenin used to hit the books in the Reading Room behind the central columns.

Note that on Saturday and Sunday the entrance is at Unter den Linden 9.

STAATSOPER UNTER DEN LINDEN
HISTORIC BUILDING

Map p296 (☏030-2035 4555; www.staatsoper
-berlin.de; Bebelplatz; 📮100, 200, TXL, ⓊHaus-
vogteiplatz) Berlin's opulent state opera was
commissioned as the royal opera house by
Frederick the Great and designed by his
friend and master architect Georg Wenzel-
slaus von Knobelsdorff. It has graced Bebelplatz since 1742 and risen from the ashes
three times. Since 2010, the building has
again undergone large-scale modernisation.
Until reopening, performances take
place at the Schiller Theater in the western
district of Charlottenburg.

NEUE WACHE
MEMORIAL

Map p296 (New Guardhouse; Unter den Linden 4;
◷10am-6pm; 📮100, 200, TXL) FREE This columned, temple-like neoclassical structure
(1818) was Karl Friedrich Schinkel's first
important Berlin commission. Originally a
memorial to the victims of anti-Napoleonic
wars, it is now Germany's Central Memorial for the Victims of War and Dictatorship.
Its austere interior is dominated by Käthe
Kollwitz' heart-wrenching sculpture of a
mother cradling her dead soldier son.

Buried beneath are the remains of an
unknown soldier, a Nazi resistance fighter
and soil from nine European battlefields
and concentration camps.

SCHLOSSBRÜCKE
BRIDGE

Map p296 (Palace Bridge; Unter den Linden; 📮100,
200, TXL) Marking the transition from Unter
den Linden to Museum Island, the Palace
Bridge is considered among Berlin's prettiest. Designed by Karl Friedrich Schinkel in
the 1820s, it is decorated with eight marble
sculptures depicting the life and death of a
warrior. Alas, empty royal coffers kept them
from being chiselled until the late 1840s, a
few years after the master's death.

⊙ Friedrichstrasse & Checkpoint Charlie

TRÄNENPALAST
MUSEUM

Map p296 (☏030-4677 7790; www.hdg.de; Reichstagufer 17; ◷9am-7pm Tue-Fri, 10am-6pm Sat &
Sun; Ⓢ Friedrichstrasse, ⓊFriedrichstrasse) FREE
During the Cold War, tears flowed copi-
ously in this glass-and-steel border-crossing
pavilion where East Berliners had to bid
adieu to family visiting from West Germany
– hence its moniker 'Palace of Tears'. The
exhibit uses original objects (including the
claustrophobic passport control booths and
a border auto-firing system), photographs
and historical footage to document the division's social impact on the daily lives of Germans on both sides of the border.

FRIEDRICHSTADTPASSAGEN
ARCHITECTURE

Map p296 (Friedrichstrasse, btwn Französische
Strasse & Mohrenstrasse; ◷10am-8pm Mon-Sat;
🅿🛜; ⓊFranzösische Strasse, Stadtmitte) Even
if you're not part of the Gucci and Prada bri-
gade, the architectural wow factor of this
trio of shopping complexes (called *Quar-
tiere*) is undeniable. Highlights are Jean
Nouvel's shimmering glass funnel inside
the Galeries Lafayette (p93), the dazzling-
ly patterned art deco–style Quartier 206
and John Chamberlain's tower made from
crushed cars in Quartier 205.

CHECKPOINT CHARLIE
HISTORIC SITE

Map p296 (cnr Zimmerstrasse & Friedrichstrasse;
◷24hr; ⓊKochstrasse) FREE Checkpoint
Charlie was the principal gateway for foreigners and diplomats between the two Berlins from 1961 to 1990. Unfortunately, this
potent symbol of the Cold War has degener-
ated into a tacky tourist trap, though a free
open-air exhibit that illustrates milestones
in Cold War history is one redeeming aspect.

ASISI PANORAMA BERLIN
GALLERY

Map p296 (☏030-355 5340; www.asisi.de;
Friedrichstrasse 205; adult/concession/child
€10/8/4; ◷10am-6pm, last entry 30min before
closing; ⓊKochstrasse) Artist Yadegar Asisi is
famous for creating bafflingly detailed monumental photographic panoramas. At 15m
high and 60m wide, his latest creation depicts the bleakness of everyday life along the
Berlin Wall on a random day in the 1980s.
Standing on a scaffold in the West, visitors get to look across the death strip and
contemplate what it was like to live in the
shadow of barbed wire and guard towers.

BLACKBOX KALTER KRIEG
MUSEUM

Map p296 (☏030-216 3571; www.bfgg.de; Friedrichstrasse 47; adult/concession €5/3.50;
◷10am-6pm; ⓊKochstrasse) This small pop-
up museum chronicles the history of the Cold
War. Using photographs, maps, original footage and recordings and various memorabilia,
it seeks to explain how the Berlin Wall fit into
the conflict and how surrogate conflicts in
Korea and Vietnam fuelled the tension between the US and the Soviet Union.

MAUERMUSEUM MUSEUM

Map p296 (Haus am Checkpoint Charlie; ☎030-253 7250; www.mauermuseum.de; Friedrichstrasse 43-45; adult/concession €12.50/9.50, audioguide €3.50; ⏲9am-10pm; [U]Kochstrasse) The Cold War years, especially the history and horror of the Berlin Wall, are engagingly, if haphazardly, documented in this privately run tourist magnet. Open since 1961, the ageing exhibit is still strong when it comes to telling the stories of escape attempts to the West. Original devices used in the process, including a hot-air balloon, a one-person submarine and a BMW Isetta, are crowd favourites.

TRABI MUSEUM MUSEUM

Map p296 (☎030-3020 1030; www.trabi-museum.com; Zimmerstrasse 14-15; adult/child under 12 €5/free; ⏲10am-6pm; [U]Kochstrasse) If you were lucky enough to own a car in East Germany, it would most likely have been a Trabant (Trabi in short), a tinny two-stroker whose name ('satellite' in English) was inspired by the launch of the Soviet Sputnik in 1956. The small exhibit displays the entire production line of Trabis, including rare wooden and racing versions.

MUSEUM FÜR KOMMUNIKATION BERLIN MUSEUM

Map p296 (☎030-202 940; www.mfk-berlin.de; Leipziger Strasse 16; adult/concession/under 17 €4/2/free; ⏲9am-8pm Tue, 9am-5pm Wed-Fri, 10am-6pm Sat & Sun; [U]Mohrenstrasse, Stadtmitte) Three cheeky robots welcome you to this elegant, neo-baroque museum, which takes you on an entertaining romp through the evolution of communication, from smoke signals to computers. Admire such rare items as a Blue Mauritius stamp or one of the world's first telephones, test milestones in communication techniques, or ponder the impact of information technology on our daily lives.

DEUTSCHES CURRYWURST MUSEUM MUSEUM

Map p296 (☎030-8871 8647; www.currywurstmuseum.com; Schützenstrasse 70; adult/concession/child 6-13yr incl sausage snack €11/8.50/7; ⏲10am-6pm; [U]Stadtmitte, Kochstrasse) Bright, fun and interactive, this museum is entirely dedicated to the *Currywurst*, Berlin's beloved cult snack. Sniff out curry secrets in the Spice Chamber, listen to *Currywurst* songs and learn about the wurst's history. Tickets include a wurst tasting in the snack bar.

MENDELSSOHN EXHIBIT MUSEUM

Map p296 (☎030-8170 4726; www.jaegerstrasse.de; Jägerstrasse 51; donations welcome; ⏲noon-6pm; [U]Französische Strasse, Hausvogteiplatz) [FREE] The Mendelssohns are one of the great German family dynasties, starting with the *pater familias,* Jewish Enlightenment philosopher Moses Mendelssohn (1729–86). The bank founded by his son Joseph in 1795 grew into Berlin's largest private banking house and moved into the city's 'Wall Street' on Jägerstrasse in 1890. An exhibit in its former counter hall traces the fate and history of this influential family, who was forced into bankruptcy by the Nazis, prompting many members to flee Germany.

🍴 EATING

Historic Mitte is awash with swanky restaurants where the decor is fabulous, the crowds cosmopolitan and menus stylish. Sure, some places may be more sizzle than substance, but the see-and-be-seen punters don't seem to mind. The area also has several Michelin-starred restaurants.

🍴 Government Quarter

BERLIN PAVILLON INTERNATIONAL €

Map p296 (☎030-2065 4737; www.berlin-pavillon.de; Scheidemannstrasse 1; mains €3.50-9; ⏲8am-9pm; 🚌100, [S]Brandenburger Tor, [U]Brandenburger Tor, Bundestag) For quick feeds, this tourist-geared, self-service cafeteria on the edge of Tiergarten comes in rather handy for breakfast, cakes and simple hot dishes. In summer, the beer garden offers shaded respite.

DACHGARTENRESTAURANT KÄFER IM BUNDESTAG INTERNATIONAL €€€

Map p296 (☎030-2262 9933; www.feinkost-kaefer.de/berlin; Platz der Republik 1; mains €19.50-36; ⏲9am-4.30pm & 6.30pm-midnight; 🚌100, [U]Bundestag) While politicians debate treaties and taxes in the plenary hall below, you can enjoy breakfast and hot meals with a regional bent at the rooftop restaurant of the Reichstag building. Reservations here also give you direct access to the landmark glass dome crowning the building; book at least two weeks ahead.

✗ Pariser Platz & Unter den Linden

CAFE EINSTEIN   CAFE €€
Map p296 (📞030-204 3632; www.einsteinudl.de; Unter den Linden 42; mains €12.50-16.50; ⊙7am-10pm; 🚌100, 200, TXL, Ⓢ Brandenburger Tor, Friedrichstrasse, Ⓤ Brandenburger Tor, Friedrichstrasse) One of Berlin's few coffeehouses with big-city flair, this cosmo spot is great for scanning the power-crowd for famous politicians, artists or actors – discreetly, please – while enjoying some of the city's best coffee or noshing on homemade apple strudel or international favourites like vitello tonato or roast beef. The changing photography exhibits also provide great conversation fodder.

ZWÖLF APOSTEL   ITALIAN €€
Map p296 (www.12-apostel.de; Georgenstrasse 2; pizza €10-15, mains €16.50-22.50; 🚋M1, Ⓢ Friedrichstrasse, Ⓤ Friedrichstrasse) A pleasant pit stop between museums, this place beneath the railway arches has over-the-top religious decor and tasty thin-crust pizzas named after the 12 apostles, plus good-value lunch specials.

ISHIN   JAPANESE €€
Map p296 (📞030-2067 4829; www.ishin.de; Mittelstrasse 24; sushi platter €8.50-21, bowl €5.80-7.60; ⊙11.30am-10pm Mon-Fri, noon-10pm Sat; Ⓢ Friedrichstrasse, Ⓤ Friedrichstrasse) The ambience is a bit ho-hum but who cares if the sushi is super-fresh, the rice bowls generously topped with fish or meat, and the green tea free and bottomless. Prices drop a bit during happy hour (all day Wednesday and Saturday, and until 4pm on other days).

There's another **branch** (Map p296; 📞030-6050 0172; Charlottenstrasse 16; Ⓤ Kochstrasse) near Checkpoint Charlie.

CAFE IM DEUTSCHEN HISTORISCHEN MUSEUM   GERMAN €€
Map p296 (📞030-2064 2744; www.kofler kompanie.com/restaurants/cafe-im-deutschen -historischen-museum; Unter den Linden 2; mains €8.50-17; ⊙10am-6pm; 🚌100, 200, TXL, Ⓢ Hackescher Markt, Ⓤ Hausvogteiplatz) Even if history leaves you cold, this cafe inside the German Historical Museum is a lovely spot for breakfast, cakes, a snack or a full meal, especially in summer when the Spree-facing terrace opens.

✗ Gendarmenmarkt

★AUGUSTINER AM GENDARMENMARKT   GERMAN €€
Map p296 (📞030-2045 4020; www.augustiner -braeu-berlin.de; Charlottenstrasse 55; mains €6.50-26.50; ⊙10am-2am; Ⓤ Französische Strasse) Tourists, concert-goers and hearty-food lovers rub shoulders at rustic tables in this authentic Bavarian beer hall. Soak up the down-to-earth vibe right along with a mug of full-bodied Augustiner brew. Sausages, roast pork and pretzels provide rib-sticking sustenance, but there's also plenty of lighter (even meat-free) fare as well as good-value lunch specials.

GOODTIME   THAI €€
Map p296 (📞030-2007 4870; www.goodtime -berlin.de; Hausvogteiplatz 11; mains €11-23.50; ⊙noon-midnight; 🍴; Ⓤ Hausvogteiplatz) Sweep on down to this busy dining room with a garden courtyard for fragrant Thai and Indonesian dishes. Creamy curries, succulent shrimp, roast duck or an entire *rijstafel* spread (an elaborate buffet-style meal) all taste flavourful and fresh, if a bit easy on the heat to accommodate German stomachs.

BORCHARDT   FRENCH €€€
Map p296 (📞030-8188 6262; www.borchardt -restaurant.de; Französische Strasse 47; 2-course lunch Mon-Fri €14, dinner mains €20-40; ⊙11.30am-1am; Ⓤ Französische Strasse) Jagger, Clooney and Redford are among the celebs who have tucked into dry-aged steaks and plump oysters in the marble-pillared dining hall of this Berlin institution, first established in 1853 by a caterer to the Kaiser. No dish, however, moves as fast as the Wiener Schnitzel, a wafer-thin slice of breaded veal fried to crisp perfection. Since the kitchen stays open until midnight, it's a popular late-dining spot in these parts.

✗ Friedrichstrasse & Checkpoint Charlie

★RESTAURANT TIM RAUE   ASIAN €€€
Map p296 (📞030-2593 7930; www.tim-raue. com; Rudi-Dutschke-Strasse 26; 3-/4-course lunch €48/58, 8-course dinner €198, mains €55-66; ⊙noon-3pm & 7pm-midnight Wed-Sat; Ⓤ Kochstrasse) Now here's a twin Michelin starred restaurant we can get our mind around. Un-

stuffy ambience and a reduced design with walnut and Vitra chairs perfectly juxtapose with Raue's brilliant Asian-inspired plates that each shine the spotlight on a few choice ingredients. His interpretation of Peking duck is a perennial bestseller. Popular at lunchtime too. The kitchen closes at 1pm for lunch service and 9pm for dinner. Book at least a couple of weeks in advance for dinner.

CRACKERS
INTERNATIONAL €€€

Map p296 (www.crackersberlin.com; mains €16-36; ☺7pm-1am; 🚌100, 200, TXL, ⓤFranzösische Strasse) With Crackers, Berlin nightlife impresario Heinz 'Cookie' Gindullis transformed his former club Cookies into a cosmopolitan gastro-cathedral with an appropriately lofty ceiling. The kitchen is helmed by Stephan Hentschel who treats patrons to a menu featuring such tasties as slow-cooked rack of veal or sea bass ceviche. On weekends, DJs heat up the vibe.

NOBELHART & SCHMUTZIG
INTERNATIONAL €€€

Map p296 (☎030-2594 0610; www.nobelhartundschmutzig.com; Friedrichstrasse 218; 10-course menu €80; ☺6.30pm-midnight; ⓤKochstrasse) 'Brutally local' is the motto at the Michelin-starred restaurant of star sommelier Billy Wagner. All ingredients hail – without exception – from producers in and around Berlin and the nearby Baltic Sea. Hence, no pepper or lemons. The intellectually ambitious food is fresh and seasonal or naturally preserved by using such traditional methods as pickling, brining and fermenting.

COOKIES CREAM
VEGETARIAN €€€

Map p296 (☎030-2749 2940; www.cookiescream.com; Behrenstrasse 55; mains €25, 3-course menu €44; ☺6.30pm-1am Tue-Sat; ☎; ⓤFranzösische Strasse) Kudos if you can locate this chic herbivore haven right away. Hint: it's upstairs past a giant chandelier in the service alley of the Westin Grand Hotel. Ring the bell to enter an elegantly industrial loft for flesh-free, flavour-packed dishes from current-harvest ingredients.

🍷 DRINKING & NIGHTLIFE

Since Historic Mitte isn't a residential area, bars and nightlife cater mostly to visitors and are often confined to the hotels. Notable exceptions are a few riverside haunts along Schiffbauerdamm, off Friedrichstrasse, which are also popular with the local post-theatre crowd.

LOST IN GRUB STREET
BAR

Map p296 (☎030-2060 3780; www.lostingrubstreet.de; Jägerstrasse 34; ☺7pm-late Tue-Sat; ⓤHausvogteiplatz) This cocktail bar packs a punch, so to speak. The focus here is on 'Big Bowls': huge stainless steel vessels filled with potent punch for classy and convivial sharing for two to 12 people. If that's not your thing, opt for a 'short drink', creative cocktails made from such unusual cocktail ingredients as chocolate, carrot or jalapeños. Reservation recommended.

BAR TAUSEND
BAR

Map p296 (☎030-2758 2070; www.tausendberlin.com; Schiffbauerdamm 11; ☺7.30pm-late Tue-Sat; ⓢFriedrichstrasse, ⓤFriedrichstrasse) No sign, no light, no bell, just an anonymous steel door tucked under a railway bridge leads to one of Berlin's chicest bars. Behind it, flirty frocks sip raspberry mojitos alongside London Mule–cradling three-day stubbles. The eye-catching decor in the tunnel-shaped space channels '80s glam while DJs and bands fuel the vibe. The restaurant in back serves Asian-German cuisine.

BERLINER REPUBLIK
PUB

Map p296 (☎030-3087 2293; www.die-berliner-republik.de; Schiffbauerdamm 8; ☺10am-6am; 🛜; ⓢFriedrichstrasse, ⓤFriedrichstrasse) Just as in a mini–stock exchange, the price of beer (18 varieties on tap!) fluctuates with demand after 5pm at this tourist-friendly riverside pub. Everyone goes Pavlovian when a heavy brass bell rings, signalling rock-bottom prices. In summer, seats on the terrace are the most coveted. A full menu of home-style Berlin and German provides sustenance.

FELIX CLUBRESTAURANT
CLUB

Map p296 (☎030-301 117 152; www.felix-clubrestaurant.de; Behrenstrasse 72; ☺from 11pm Mon, Thu, Fri & Sat; ⓢBrandenburger Tor, ⓤBrandenburger Tor) Once past the velvet rope of this tricked-out 'premium club', you too can shake your booty to high-octane hip-hop, dance and disco beats, sip Champagne cocktails, watch the crowd from the gallery and flirt up a storm. On Monday, women get free entry, a glass of Prosecco until midnight and a men's strip show.

⭐ ENTERTAINMENT

KOMISCHE OPER
OPERA

Map p296 (Comic Opera; ☑tickets 030-4799 7400; www.komische-oper-berlin.de; Behrenstrasse 55-57; tickets €10-159; ⊘box office 11am-7pm Mon-Sat, 1-4pm Sun; 🚇100, 200, TXL, UFranzösische Strasse) Opera, operetta, musical, ballet and concerts from many periods are the bread and butter of the high-profile theatre with its tiered neo-baroque auditorium. Seats feature an ingenious subtitling system that gives you the option of reading along in German or English. Tickets can be purchased online or at the **box office** (Map p296; Unter den Linden 41; ⊘11am-7pm Mon-Sat, 1-4pm Sun; 🚇100, 200, TXL, UFranzösische Strasse, Friedrichstrasse) on Unter den Linden.

KONZERTHAUS BERLIN
CLASSICAL MUSIC

Map p296 (☑tickets 030-203 092 101; www. konzerthaus.de; Gendarmenmarkt 2; tickets €15-79; UStadtmitte, Französische Strasse) This top-ranked concert hall – a Schinkel design from 1821 – counts the Konzerthausorchester Berlin as its 'house band', but also hosts international soloists, thematic concert cycles, children's events and concerts by the Rundfunk-Sinfonieorchester Berlin.

TIPI AM KANZLERAMT
CABARET

Map p296 (☑tickets 030-3906 6550; www. tipi-am-kanzleramt.de; Grosse Querallee; tickets €30-50; 🚇100, SHauptbahnhof, UBundestag) Tipi stages a year-round program of high-calibre cabaret, dance, acrobatics, musical comedy and magic shows starring German and international artists. It's all staged in a huge and festively decorated permanent tent stationed between the Federal Chancellory and the House of World Cultures on the edge of Tiergarten park. Pre-show dinner is available.

GORKI
THEATRE

Map p296 (☑030-2022 1115; www.gorki.de; Am Festungsgraben 2; tickets €10-34; 🚇100, 200, TXL, 🚇M1, 12, SFriedrichstrasse, UFriedrichstrasse) Artistic director Shermin Langhoff has made the smallest of Berlin's four state-funded theatres the dedicated home of the so-called 'post-migrant theatre'. The ensemble cast, which looks like a Benetton ad, puts on classic and original productions that examine such issues as integration, identity, transition and discrimination. All performances have English subtitles.

ADMIRALSPALAST
PERFORMING ARTS

Map p296 (☑tickets 030-2250 7000; www. admiralspalast.de; Friedrichstrasse 101; 🚇M1, SFriedrichstrasse, UFriedrichstrasse) This beautifully restored 1920s 'palace' stages crowd-pleasing international plays, concerts and comedy shows in its glamorous historic main hall. More intimate programs like readings or comedy shows are presented on the smaller studio stage on the 4th floor. Many performances are suitable for non-German speakers, but do check ahead. Ticket prices vary.

HOCHSCHULE FÜR MUSIK HANNS EISLER
CLASSICAL MUSIC

Map p296 (☑tickets 030-203 092 101; www.hfm-berlin.de; Charlottenstrasse 55; UStadtmitte, Französische Strasse) The gifted students at Berlin's top-rated music academy populate several orchestras, a choir and a big band, which collectively stage as many as 400 performances annually, most of them in the **Neuer Marstall** (New Royal Stables; Map p300; Schlossplatz 7; 🚇100, 200, TXL, UHausvogteiplatz), where the Prussian royals once kept their coaches and horses. Many concerts are free or low-cost.

🛍 SHOPPING

There are some souvenir shops along Unter den Linden and around Checkpoint Charlie, but for fancy fashion and accessories, make a beeline to Friedrichstrasse with its dazzling Friedrichstadtpassagen and Galeries Lafayette.

DUSSMANN – DAS KULTURKAUFHAUS
BOOKS, MUSIC

Map p296 (☑030-2025 1111; www.kulturkaufhaus.de; Friedrichstrasse 90; ⊘9am-midnight Mon-Fri, to 11.30pm Sat; 🚇; SFriedrichstrasse, UFriedrichstrasse) It's easy to lose track of time in this cultural playground with wall-to-wall books (with an extensive English section), DVDs and CDs, leaving no genre unaccounted for. Bonus points for the free reading-glass rentals, downstairs cafe and performance space used for concerts, political discussions and high-profile book readings and signings.

RAUSCH SCHOKOLADENHAUS FOOD
Map p296 (☎0800 030 1918; www.rausch.de;
Charlottenstrasse 60; ◷10am-8pm Mon-Sat,
11am-8pm Sun; ⓤStadtmitte) If the Aztecs
thought of chocolate as the elixir of the
gods, then this emporium of truffles and
pralines must be heaven. Bonus: the chocolate volcano and giant replicas of Berlin
landmarks like the Brandenburg Gate or
the TV Tower. The upstairs cafe-restaurant
has views of Gendarmenmarkt and serves
sinful drinking chocolates and cakes as
well as dishes prepared and seasoned with
cocoa.

GALERIES LAFAYETTE DEPARTMENT STORE
Map p296 (☎030-209 480; www.galerieslafay
ette.de; Friedrichstrasse 76-78; ◷10am-8pm
Mon-Sat; ⓤFranzösische Strasse) Stop by the
Berlin branch of the exquisite French fashion emporium if only to check out the show-
stealing interior (designed by Jean Nouvel,
no less), centred on a huge glass cone
shimmering with kaleidoscopic intensity.
Around it wrap three circular floors filled
with fancy fashions, fragrances and accessories, while glorious gourmet treats await
in the basement food hall.

**RITTER SPORT BUNTE
SCHOKOWELT** FOOD
Map p296 (☎030-2009 5080; www.ritter
-sport.de; Französische Strasse 24; ◷10am-7pm
Mon-Wed, to 8pm Thu-Sat, to 6pm Sun; ⚑;
ⓤFranzösische Strasse) Fans of Ritter Sport's
colourful square chocolate bars can pick up
limited edition, organic and diet varieties
in addition to all the classics at this flagship store. Upstairs, a free exhibit explains
the journey from cocoa bean to finished
product, but a bigger hit is the chocolate
station where you can create your person-
alised bars.

**VIELFACH – DAS
KREATIVKAUFHAUS** DEPARTMENT STORE
Map p296 (☎030-9148 4678; www.fachmiete.
de; Zimmerstrasse 11; ◷11am-7pm Mon-Fri,
to 4pm Sat; ⓤKochstrasse) Pick up unique
gifts or souvenirs handmade in Germany
at this store where artists and craftspeo-
ple can rent shelf space to display beauty
products, stuffed animals, bags, ceramics,
photographs and lots of other pretty things.
The store occupies a beautifully renovated
listed building near Checkpoint Charlie.

FRAU TONIS PARFUM BEAUTY
Map p296 (☎030-2021 5310; www.frau-tonis-
parfum.com; Zimmerstrasse 13; ◷10am-6pm
Mon-Sat; ⓤKochstrasse) Follow your nose to
this scent-sational made-in-Berlin perfume
boutique and pick up a custom blend to
match your type – classic, extravagant or
modern. Bestsellers include the sprightly
'Berlin Summer' with hints of mint and
lemon balm.

BERLIN STORY BOOKS
Map p296 (☎030-2045 3842; www.berlinstory.
de; Unter den Linden 40; ◷10am-7pm Mon-Sat,
to 6pm Sun; ☒100, 200, TXL, ⓈFriedrichstrasse,
ⓤFriedrichstrasse, Französische Strasse) Never
mind the souvenirs, this store's ammo is
its broad selection of Berlin-related books,
maps, DVDs, CDs and magazines, in English and a dozen other languages, some
published in-house. A free exhibition 'The
Making of Berlin' tracks 800 years of city
history and includes a 30-minute movie.

**ANTIK- UND BUCHMARKT
AM BODEMUSEUM** ANTIQUES, MARKET
Map p296 (www.antik-buchmarkt.de; Am Kupfergraben; ◷11am-5pm Sat & Sun; ☒M1, 12,
Ⓢfatty Hackescher Markt, ⓤHackescher Markt) This
book and collectible market has about 60
vendors in a gorgeous setting with Museum
Island as a backdrop. Book worms have
plenty of boxes to sift through alongside a
smattering of furniture, toys, coins, bric-a-
brac and old photographs.

🏃 SPORTS &
ACTIVITIES

WELTBALLON BERLIN VIEWPOINT
Map p296 (☎030-5321 5321, wind conditions
030-226 678 811; www.air-service-berlin.de;
cnr Wilhelmstrasse & Zimmerstrasse; adult/
concession/child 3-10yr €20/17/7; ◷10am-10pm
Apr-Oct, 11am-6pm Nov-Mar; ⓤKochstrasse)
Drift up but not away for about 15 minutes
aboard this helium-filled balloon that remains tethered to the ground as it lifts you
noiselessly 150m into the air for panoramas
of the historic city centre. Your pilot will
help you pinpoint all the key sights. Con-
firm ahead as flights are cancelled in windy
conditions.

HISTORIC MITTE SPORTS & ACTIVITIES

Museumsinsel & Alexanderplatz

ALEXANDERPLATZ | SCHLOSSPLATZ | NIKOLAIVIERTEL

Neighbourhood Top Five

1 **Pergamonmuseum** (p97) Time-travelling through ancient Greece and Babylon to the Middle East at this glorious museum.

2 **Neues Museum** (p101) Making a date with Nefertiti and her royal entourage at the stunningly rebuilt repository.

3 **Berlin by Boat** (p112) Letting the sights drift by while enjoying cold drinks on the deck of a Spree River tour boat.

4 **DDR Museum** (p108) Dipping behind the Iron Curtain at this interactive exhibit.

5 **Fernsehturm** (p106) Getting high on the knock-out views from the top of Germany's tallest structure.

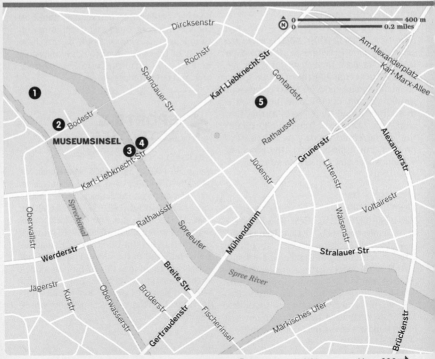

For more detail of this area see Map p300 ➡

Explore: Museumsinsel & Alexanderplatz

This historic area packs most of eastern Berlin's trophy sights into a compact frame and is best explored on foot in the daytime when museums and shops are open. A good place to start is on vast and amorphous Alexanderplatz, a mainstream shopping hub and home to Germany's most prominent landmark, the 368m-high Fernsehturm (TV Tower). In clear weather it's well worth taking the speedy lift to the viewing platform to get your bearings.

The open area west of the TV Tower links up with the Nikolaiviertel, Berlin's medieval birthplace, which was first torn down, then rebuilt by the East German government. The surrealism of this pseudo-quaint quarter can be a hoot, but don't expect to find too many Berliners patronising the pricey cafes and souvenir shops.

Better save your energy for the stunning treasures of the five museums on Museumsinsel (Museum Island). If you only have time for one or two, focus on the Pergamonmuseum with its monumental antiquities or the Egyptian collection at the Neues Museum. For more recent – and local – history, take a spin around the DDR Museum, which playfully captures the contradictions of daily life in East Germany.

Local Life

Late-night openings Clued-up locals know that the best time to see the Museumsinsel collections without the crowds is on Thursday evening, when all five museums stay open until 8pm.

Shopping Big shopping centres are scarce in central Berlin, which probably explains the enormous local popularity of the Alexa (p112) megamall. It harbours practically every chain under the sun and stays open until 9pm.

Drinks with a view There are few better places for summertime sunset cocktails than the rooftop terrace of the House of Weekend (p112) club, with the entire glittering city at your feet.

Getting There & Away

Bus M48 and 200 link Alexanderplatz with Potsdamer Platz; bus 247 goes to the Nikolaiviertel.

S-Bahn S5, S7/75 and S9 all converge at Alexanderplatz.

U-Bahn U2, U5 and U8 stop at Alexanderplatz. Other main stops are Klosterstrasse and Märkisches Museum (U2) and Jannowitzbrücke (U8).

Tram M4, M5 and M6 connect Alexanderplatz with Marienkirche and Hackescher Markt.

Lonely Planet's Top Tip

It would take superhuman stamina to visit all five museums on Museumsinsel in one day, so don't even try; concentrate your energy on those that interest you most. Skip the worst crowds by arriving first thing in the morning, late in the afternoon or on Thursdays, when all museums stay open until 8pm.

Best Places to Eat

➡ Udon Kobo Ishin (p110)
➡ Dolores (p110)
➡ Brauhaus Georgbräu (p112)
➡ Zur Letzten Instanz (p110)

For reviews, see p110.

Best Places to Drink

➡ House of Weekend (p112)
➡ Club Avenue (p112)

For reviews, see p112.

Best Non-Museum Sights

➡ Berliner Dom (p108)
➡ Humboldt-Box (p109)
➡ Fernsehturm (p106)
➡ Marienkirche (p107)
➡ Nikolaiviertel (p108)

For reviews, see p107.

MUSEUMSINSEL & ALEXANDERPLATZ

CANADASTOCK/SHUTTERSTOCK ©

TOP SIGHT
MUSEUMSINSEL

Walk through ancient Babylon, meet an Egyptian queen or be mesmerised by Monet's landscapes. Welcome to Museumsinsel, Berlin's famous treasure trove of 6000 years' worth of art, artefacts, sculpture and architecture from Europe and beyond. Spread across five grand museums built between 1830 and 1930, the complex covers the northern half of the Spree island where Berlin's settlement began in the 13th century.

Berlin's Louvre

The first repository to open was the **Altes Museum** (Old Museum), completed in 1830 next to the Berlin Cathedral and the Lustgarten park. Today it presents Greek, Etruscan and Roman antiquities. Behind it, the **Neues Museum** (New Museum) showcases the Egyptian collection, most famously the bust of Queen Nefertiti, and also houses the Museum of Pre- and Early History. The temple-like **Alte Nationalgalerie** (Old National Gallery) trains the focus on 19th-century European art. The island's top draw is the **Pergamonmuseum**, with its monumental architecture from ancient worlds, including the namesake Pergamon Altar. The **Bode-Museum**, at the island's northern tip, is famous for its medieval sculptures.

Museumsinsel Masterplan

In 1999 the Museumsinsel repositories collectively became a Unesco World Heritage Site. The distinction was at least partly achieved because of a master plan for the renovation and modernisation of the complex, which is expected to be completed in 2025 under the aegis of British architect David Chipperfield. Except for the Pergamon, whose exhibits are currently being reorganised, the restoration of the museums themselves has been completed. Construction is also well under way on the **James-Simon-Galerie**, a colonnad-

➡ Ishtar Gate
➡ Bust of Nefertiti
➡ Berliner Goldhut
➡ *Praying Boy*
➡ Sculpture by Tilman Riemenschneider

PRACTICALITIES

➡ Map p300, A3
➡ ☎030-266 424 242
➡ www.smb.museum
➡ day tickets for all 5 museums adult/ concession/under 18 €18/9/free
➡ ⊙varies by museum
➡ 🚌100, 200, TXL, Ⓤ Hackescher Markt, Friedrichstrasse

ed modern foyer named for an early-20th-century German-Jewish philanthropist. It will serve as the visitor centre with ticket desks, a cafe, a shop and direct access to the Pergamonmuseum and the Neues Museum. It will also lead to the 'Archaeological Promenade', a subterranean walkway set to link the Altes Museum with the Bode-Museum in the north. For more details see www.museumsinsel-berlin.de.

Pergamonmuseum

Berlin's top museum attraction, the **Pergamonmuseum** (Map p300; ☎030-266 424 242; www.smb.museum; Bodestrasse 1-3; adult/concession €12/6; 🕙10am-6pm Fri-Wed, to 8pm Thu; 🚌100, 200, TXL, [S]Hackescher Markt, Friedrichstrasse) opens a fascinating window on to the ancient world. Completed in 1930, the palatial three-wing complex presents a rich feast of classical sculpture and monumental architecture from Greece, Rome, Babylon and the Middle East in three collections: the Collection of Antiquities, the Museum of the Ancient Near East and the Museum of Islamic Art. Most of the pieces were excavated and spirited to Berlin by German archaeologists around the turn of the 20th century.

The Pergamonmuseum is the fourth treasure chest on Museumsinsel to undergo extensive, gradual restoration work that will leave some sections closed for years. The north wing and the hall containing the namesake Pergamon Altar will be off limits until 2019. This will be followed by the closure of the south wing, presumably until 2025. A fourth wing facing the Spree River will be added so that in future all parts of the museum can be experienced on a continuous walk.

During the restoration, the museum entrance is off Bodestrasse, behind the Neues Museum.

Antikensammlung

The Antikensammlung (Collection of Classical Antiquities) presents artworks from ancient Greece and Rome here and at the Altes Museum. Since the Pergamon Altar is currently closed to the public, the main sight is now the 2nd-century AD **Market Gate of Miletus**. Merchants and customers once flooded through the splendid 17m-high gate into the bustling market square of this wealthy Roman trading town in modern-day Turkey. A strong earthquake levelled much of the town in the early Middle Ages, but German archaeologists dug up the site between 1903 and 1905 and managed to put the puzzle back together. The richly decorated marble gate blends Greek and Roman design features and is the world's single largest monument ever to be reassembled in a museum.

TOP TIPS

- ➡Avoid culture fatigue by focusing on just two of the five museums in a single day.
- ➡If you plan on visiting more than one museum, save money by buying the Museumsinsel ticket (€18, concession €9), good for one-day admission to all five museums.
- ➡Admission is free for those under 18.
- ➡Arrive early or late on weekdays, or skip the queues by purchasing your ticket online.
- ➡Make use of the excellent multi-language audioguides included in the admission price.
- ➡In good weather, the lawns of the Lustgarten, outside the Altes Museum, are an inviting spot to chill.

Pergamon was the capital of the Kingdom of Pergamon, which reigned over vast stretches of the eastern Mediterranean in the 3rd and 2nd centuries BC. Inspired by Athens, its rulers, the Attalids, turned their royal residence into a major cultural and intellectual centre. Draped over a 330m-high ridge were grand palaces, a library, a theatre and glorious temples dedicated to Trajan, Dionysus and Athena.

Museumsinsel

Navigating around this five-museum treasure repository can be daunting, so we've created this itinerary to help you find the must-see highlights while maximising your time and energy. You'll need at least four hours and a Museumsinsel ticket for entry to all museums.

Start in the Altes Museum by admiring the roll call of antique gods guarded by a perky bronze statue called the **Praying Boy** ❶, the poster child of a prized collection of antiquities. Next up, head to the Neues Museum for your audience with **Queen Nefertiti** ❷, the star of the Egyptian collection atop the grand central staircase.

One more floor up, don't miss the dazzling Bronze Age **Berliner Goldhut** ❸ (room 305). Leaving the Neues Museum, turn left for the Pergamonmuseum. With the namesake altar off limits until 2019, the first major sight you'll see is the **Ishtar Gate** ❹. Upstairs, pick your way through the Islamic collection, past carpets, prayer niches and a caliph's palace to the intricately painted **Aleppo Room** ❺.

Jump ahead to the 19th century at the Alte Nationalgalerie to zero in on paintings by **Caspar David Friedrich** ❻ on the 3rd floor and precious sculptures such as Schadow's **Statue of Two Princesses** ❼ on the ground floor. Wrap up your explorations at the Bodemuseum, reached in a five-minute walk. Admire the foyer with its equestrian statue of Friedrich Wilhelm, then feast your eyes on European sculpture without missing masterpieces by **Tilman Riemenschneider** ❽ and his contemporaries in room 109.

FAST FACTS

» **Oldest object:** 700,000-year-old Paleolithic hand axe at Neues Museum

» **Newest object:** piece of barbed wire from Berlin Wall at Neues Museum

» **Oldest museum:** Altes Museum, 1830

» **Most popular museum in Germany:** Pergamonmuseum (750,000 visitors)

» **Total Museumsinsel visitors (2013):** 2.42 million

Sculptures by Tilman Riemenschneider (Room 109, Bodemuseum)
Dazzling detail and great emotional expressiveness characterise the wooden sculptures by late-Gothic master carver Tilman Riemenschneider as in this portrayal of *St Anne and Her Three Husbands* from around 1510.

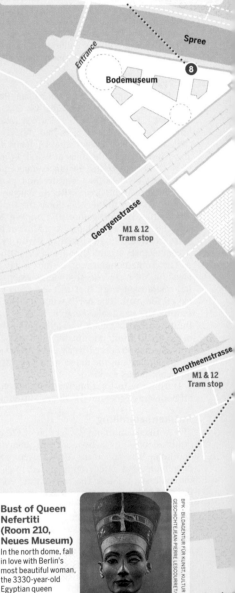

Bust of Queen Nefertiti (Room 210, Neues Museum)
In the north dome, fall in love with Berlin's most beautiful woman, the 3330-year-old Egyptian queen Nefertiti, she of the long graceful neck and timeless good looks – despite the odd wrinkle and missing eye.

Aleppo Room (Room 16, Pergamonmuseum)

A highlight of the Museum of Islamic Art, this richly painted, wood-panelled reception room from a Christian merchant's home in 17th-century Aleppo, Syria, combines Islamic floral and geometric motifs with courtly scenes and Christian themes.

Ishtar Gate (Room 9, Pergamonmuseum)

Draw breath as you enter the 2600-year-old city gate to Babylon with soaring walls sheathed in radiant blue glazed bricks and adorned with ochre reliefs of strutting lions, bulls and dragons representing Babylonian gods.

Pergamonmuseum

Spree

Alte Nationalgalerie

5 **4** **6** **7** **2**

Entrance

Entrance

Entrance

Neues Museum

3

Bodestrasse

1

Altes Museum

Entrance

Berliner Dom

Lustgarten

Paintings by Caspar David Friedrich (Top Floor, Alte Nationalgalerie)

A key artist of the romantic period, Caspar David Friedrich put his own stamp on landscape painting with his dark, moody and subtly dramatic meditations on the boundaries of human life vs the infinity of nature.

Statue of Two Princesses (Ground Floor, Alte Nationalgalerie)

Johann Gottfried Schadow captures Prussian princesses (and sisters) Luise and Friederike in a moment of intimacy and thoughtfulness in this double marble statue created in 1795 at the height of the neoclassical period.

Berliner Goldhut (Room 305, Neues Museum)

Marvel at the Bronze Age artistry of the Berlin Gold Hat, a ceremonial gold cone embossed with ornamental bands believed to have been used in predicting the best times for planting and harvesting.

Praying Boy (Room 5, Altes Museum)

The top draw at the Old Museum is the *Praying Boy*, ancient Greece's 'Next Top Model'. The life-size bronze statue of a young male nude is the epitome of physical perfection and was cast around 300 BC in Rhodes.

Also from Miletus is a beautifully restored **floor mosaic** starring Orpheus, a gifted musician from ancient Greek mythology whose lyre-playing charmed even the beasts surrounding him. It originally graced the dining room of a 2nd-century Roman villa.

Vorderasiatisches Museum

Step through the Gate of Miletus and travel back 800 years to yet another culture and civilisation: Babylon during the reign of King Nebuchadnezzar II (604–562 BC). You're now in the Museum of the Ancient Near East, where it's impossible not to be awed by the magnificence of the **Ishtar Gate**, the **Processional Way** leading to it and the facade of the **king's throne hall**. All are sheathed in radiant blue glazed bricks and adorned with ochre reliefs of strutting lions, bulls and dragons representing Babylonian gods. They're so striking, you can almost hear the roaring and fanfare as the procession rolls into town.

Other treasures from the collection include the colossal statue of the weather god Hadad (775 BC, room 2) from Syria and the nearly 5000-year-old cone mosaic temple facade from Uruk (room 5).

Museum für Islamische Kunst

Top billing in the Museum of Islamic Art upstairs belongs to the facade from the **Caliph's Palace of Mshatta** (8th century, room 9) in today's Jordan, which was a gift to Kaiser Wilhelm II from Ottoman Sultan Abdul Hamid II. A masterpiece of early Islamic art, it depicts animals and mythical creatures frolicking peacefully amid a riot of floral motifs in an allusion to the Garden of Eden.

Other rooms feature fabulous ceramics, carvings, glasses and other artistic objects as well as the brightly turquoise 11th-century **prayer niche** from a mosque in Konya,

....

PERGAMONMUSEUM

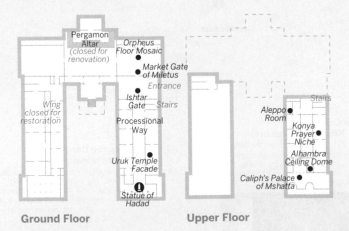

Ground Floor

Upper Floor

Neues Museum

Turkey, and an intricately patterned cedar-and-poplar **ceiling dome** from the Alhambra in Spain's Granada.

Capping a tour of the museum is the **Aleppo Room** (room 16). Guests arriving in this richly painted, wood-panelled reception room would have had no doubt as to the wealth and power of its owner, a Christian merchant in 17th-century Aleppo, Syria. The paintings depict both Christian themes and courtly scenes like those portrayed in Persian book illustrations, suggesting a high level of religious tolerance.

Neues Museum

David Chipperfield's reconstruction of the bombed-out **Neues Museum** (New Museum; Map p300; ☎030-266 424 242; www.smb.museum; Bodestrasse 1-3; adult/concession €12/6; ⏰10am-6pm, to 8pm Thu; 🚌100, 200, TXL, [S]Hackescher Markt) is the residence of Queen Nefertiti, the showstopper of the **Ägyptisches Museum** (Egyptian Museum) alongside the equally enthralling **Museum für Vor- und Frühgeschichte** (Museum of Pre- and Early History). As if piecing together a giant jigsaw puzzle, the British architect incorporated every original shard, scrap and brick he could find into the new building. This brilliant blend of the historic and modern creates a dynamic space that beautifully juxtaposes massive stairwells, domed rooms, muralled halls and high ceilings. Museum tickets are only valid for admission during a designated half-hour time slot. Skip the queue by buying advance tickets online.

TAKE A BREAK

Allegretto (Map p300; ☎030-2804 2307; www.allegretto-neuesmuseum.de; Bodestrasse 1; dishes €3-10; ⏰10am-6pm Fri-Wed, to 8pm Thu; 🚌100, 200, TXL, [S]Hackescher Markt) at the Neues Museum serves salads, Arabic dishes and soups, plus coffee and homemade cakes.

The Pergamonmuseum was purpose-built between 1910 and 1930 to house the massive amounts of ancient art and archaeological treasure excavated by German scientists at such sites as Babylon, Assur, Uruk and Miletus. Designed by Alfred Messel, the building was constructed by his close friend Ludwig Hoffmann following Messel's death, and was later badly pummelled in WWII. Lots of objects were whisked to the Soviet Union as war booty but most were returned in 1958.

A short walk away, **Zwölf Apostel** (p90) does breakfast and also has lunchtime pizza specials at heavenly prices.

Ägyptisches Museum

Most visitors come to the Neues Museum for an audience with the eternally gorgeous Egyptian queen **Nefertiti**. Her bust was created around 1340 BC by the court sculptor Thutmose. Extremely well preserved, the sculpture was part of the treasure trove unearthed around 1912 by a Berlin expedition of archaeologists who were sifting through the sands of Armana, the royal city built by Nefertiti's husband, King Akhenaten (r 1353–1336 BC).

Another famous work is the so-called **Berlin Green Head** – the bald head of a priest carved from smooth green stone. Created around 400 BC in the Late Egyptian Period, it shows Greek influence and is unusual in that it is not an actual portrait of a specific person but an idealised figure meant to exude universal wisdom and experience.

Museum für Vor- und Frühgeschichte

Within this collection, pride of place goes to the **Trojan antiquities** discovered by archaeologist Heinrich Schliemann in 1870 near Hisarlik in modern-day Turkey. However, most of the elaborate jewellery, ornate weapons and gold mugs on display are replicas because the originals became Soviet war booty after WWII and remain in Moscow. Exceptions are the three humble-looking 4500-year-old silver jars proudly displayed in their own glass case.

One floor up the grand staircase, just past Nefertiti and the precious **papyrus collection** (room 211), is another head turner: the bronze **Xanten Youth** (room 202), which served as a dumb waiter in a Roman villa. The massive sculpture of the **sun god Helios** in the south dome (room 203) also has its admirers.

The exhibit on the top floor travels back even further to the stone, bronze and iron ages. Highlights include the 45,000-year-old **fossilised skull** of an 11-year-old Neanderthal boy found in 1909 in Le Moustier, as well as a newly added reconstruction of his face. The biggest crowds of all gather around the 3000-year-old **Berliner Goldhut** (Berlin Gold Hat, room 305). Resembling a wizard's hat, it is covered in elaborate bands of astronomical symbols and must indeed have struck the Bronze Age people as something magical. It's one of only four of its kind unearthed worldwide.

Altes Museum

Architect Karl Friedrich Schinkel pulled out all the stops for the grand neoclassical **Altes Museum** (Old Museum; Map p300; ☎030-266 424 242; www.smb.museum; Am Lustgarten; adult/concession €10/5; 🕒10am-6pm Tue, Wed & Fri-Sun, to 8pm Thu; 🚌100, 200, TXL, [S]Friedrichstrasse, Hackescher Markt), which was the first exhibition space

THE MYSTERY OF PRIAM'S TREASURE

Heinrich Schliemann (1822–90) was not a particularly careful or skilled archaeologist but he was certainly one of the luckiest. Obsessed with the idea of uncovering Homer's Troy, he hit the mother lode in 1873 near Hisarlik in today's Turkey, putting paid to the belief that the town mentioned in the *Iliad* was mere myth. He also famously unearthed a hoard of gold and silver vessels, vases and jewellery, which he believed had once belonged to King Priam. The fact that it later turned out to be a good thousand years older than Homer's Troy doesn't make the find any less spectacular.

Schliemann illegally smuggled the cache to Berlin, had to pay a fine to the Ottoman Empire and eventually donated it to Berlin's ethnological museum. In a strange twist of fate, the treasure was carted off as WWII war booty by the Soviets, who remained mum about its whereabouts until 1993. It remains at the Pushkin Museum in Moscow to this day, leaving only replicas in Berlin.

to open on Museumsinsel in 1830. A curtain of fluted columns gives way to a Pantheon-inspired rotunda that's the focal point of a prized antiquities collection. In the downstairs galleries, sculptures, vases, tomb reliefs and jewellery shed light on various facets of life in ancient Greece, while upstairs the focus is on the Etruscans and Romans. Top draws include the *Praying Boy* bronze sculpture, Roman silver vessels and portraits of Caesar and Cleopatra.

Greeks

This chronologically arranged exhibit spans all periods in ancient Greek art from the 10th to the 1st centuries BC. Among the oldest items is a collection of bronze helmets, but it's the monumental statues and elaborate vases that show the greatest artistry.

Among the first eye-catchers is the strapping **Kouros** (room 2), a nude male with a Mona Lisa smile and a great mop of hair. In the next gallery, all eyes are on the **Berlin Goddess**, a beautifully preserved funerary statue of a wealthy young woman in a fancy red dress. The finely carved **Seated Goddess of Tarent** (room 9) is another highlight.

The biggest crowd-pleaser is the **Praying Boy** (room 5), an idealised young male nude sculpted in Rhodes around 300 BC and brought to Berlin by Frederick the Great in 1747. Both Napoleon and Stalin took a fancy to the pretty boy and temporarily abducted him as war booty to Paris and Moscow, respectively. Today, his serene smile once again radiates through the museum's soaring **rotunda**, which is lidded by a grand coffered and frescoed ceiling. Light filters through a central skylight illuminating 20 large-scale statues representing a who's who among antique gods, including Nike, Zeus and Fortuna.

Etruscans & Romans

The museum's Etruscan collection is one of the largest outside Italy and contains some stunning pieces. Admire a circular shield from the grave of a warrior alongside amphorae, jewellery, coins and other items from daily life dating back as far as the 8th century BC. Learn about the Etruscan language by studying the **tablet from Capua** and about funerary rites by examining the highly decorated **cinerary urns** and **sarcophagi**.

Ensuing rooms are dedicated to the Romans. There's fantastic sculpture, a superb 70-piece silver table service called the **Hildesheim Treasure** and busts of Roman leaders, including Caesar and Cleopatra. An adults-only **erotic cabinet** (behind a closed door, no less) brims with not-so-subtle depictions of satyrs, hermaphrodites and giant phalli.

OPEN-AIR CONCERTS

In July and August, classical open-air concerts take place at 8.30pm on Sundays outside the Bode-Museum, between Monbijoustrasse and Am Kupfergraben. Admission is free but show up early to admire the scenic surrounds and stake out a good spot. Check www.sonntagskonzerte.de for the schedule. There's also nightly outdoor tango, salsa and swing dancing at riverside **Strandbar Mitte** (p140), across from the museum.

Looking like a baptismal font for giants, the massive granite basin outside the Altes Museum was designed by Karl Friedrich Schinkel and carved from a single slab by Christian Gottlieb Cantian. It was considered an artistic and technical feat back in the 1820s. The original plan to install it in the museum's rotunda had to be ditched when the bowl ended up being too massive to fit its dimensions. Almost 7m in diameter, it was carved in situ from a massive boulder in Brandenburg and transported via a custom-built wooden railway to the Spree and from there by barge to Berlin.

Bode-Museum

Mighty and majestic, the **Bode-Museum** (Map p300; ☎030-266 424 242; www.smb.museum; cnr Am Kupfergraben & Monbijoubrücke; adult/concession €12/6; ⏰10am-6pm Tue, Wed & Fri-Sun, to 8pm Thu; [S]Hackescher Markt, Friedrichstrasse) has pushed against the northern tip of Museumsinsel like a proud ship's bow since 1904. The gloriously restored neobaroque beauty presents several collections in mostly naturally lit galleries.

The building, designed by Ernst von Ihne, was originally named Kaiser-Friedrich-Museum before being renamed for its first director, Wilhelm von Bode, in 1956. It's a beautifully proportioned architectural composition built around a central axis. Sweeping staircases, interior courtyards, frescoed ceilings and marble floors give the museum the grandeur of a palace.

The tone is set in the grand domed entrance hall where visitors are greeted by Andreas Schlüter's monumental sculpture of Great Elector Friedrich Wilhelm on horseback. From here head straight to the central Italian Renaissance-style basilica, where all eyes are on a colourfully glazed terracotta sculpture by Luca della Robbia. This leads to a smaller domed, rococo-style hall with marble statues of Frederick the Great and his generals. The galleries radiate from both sides of this axis and continue upstairs.

Skulpturensammlung

The majority of rooms showcase the Bode's Sculpture Collection, which former British Museum director Neil MacGregor hailed as 'the most comprehensive display of European sculpture anywhere'. The works span the arc of artistic creativity from the early Middle Ages to the late 18th century, with a special focus on the Italian Renaissance. There are priceless masterpieces like Donatello's **Pazzi Madonna**, Giovanni Pisano's **Man of Sorrows** relief, and the portrait busts of Desiderio da Settignano. Staying on the ground floor, you can cruise from the Italians to the Germans by admiring the 12th-century **Gröninger Empore**, a church gallery from a former monastery that is considered a major work of the Romanesque period.

Most of the German sculptures are upstairs, including a clutch of works by the late-Gothic master carver Tilman Riemenschneider. Highlights include the exquisite **St Anne and Her Three Husbands** as well as the **Four Evangelists**. Compare Riemenschneider's emotiveness to that of his contemporaries Hans Multscher and Nicolaus Gerhaert van Leyden also displayed here. The monumental **knight-saints** from the period of the Thirty Years' War (17th century) are another standout on this floor.

Museum für Byzantinische Kunst

Before breaking for coffee at the elegant cafe, pop back down to the ground floor where the Museum of Byzantine Art takes up just a few rooms off the grand domed foyer. It presents mainly western Roman and Byzantine art from the 3rd to the 15th centuries. The elaborate Roman sarcophagi, the ivory carvings and the mosaic icons point to the high level of artistry in these early days of Christianity.

Münzsammlung

Coin collectors will get a kick out of the Numismatic Collection on the 2nd floor. With half a million coins – and counting – it's one of the largest of its kind in the world, even if only a small fraction can be displayed at one time. The oldest farthing is from the 7th century BC and displayed in a special case alongside the smallest, largest, fattest and thinnest coins.

Alte Nationalgalerie

The Greek temple–style **Alte Nationalgalerie** (Old National Gallery; Map p300; ☎030-266 424 242; www.smb.museum; Bodestrasse 1-3; adult/concession €12/6; ⏰10am-6pm

Bode-Museum

Tue, Wed & Fri-Sun, to 8pm Thu; 🚌100, 200, TXL, [S]Hackescher Markt), open since 1876, is a three-storey showcase of first-rate 19th-century European art. It was a tumultuous century, characterised by revolutions and industrialisation that brought about profound changes in society. Artists reacted to the new realities in different ways. While German Romantics like Caspar David Friedrich sought solace in nature and Nazarenes like Anselm Feuerbach turned to religious subjects, the epic canvases of Adolf Menzel and Franz Krüger glorified moments in Prussian history, and the impressionists focused on light and aesthetics.

Johann Gottfried Schadow's **Statue of Two Princesses** and a bust of Johann Wolfgang von Goethe are standout sculptures on the ground floor. In the next galleries, Adolf Menzel gets the star treatment – look for his famous **A Flute Concert of Frederick the Great at Sanssouci**, showing the king playing the flute at his Potsdam palace.

The 2nd floor shows impressionist paintings by such famous French artists as Monet, Degas, Cézanne, Renoir and Manet, whose **In the Conservatory** is considered a masterpiece. Among the Germans, there's Arnold Böcklin's **Isle of Death** and several canvases by Max Liebermann.

Romantics rule the top floor where all eyes are on Caspar David Friedrich's mystical landscapes and the Gothic fantasies of Karl Friedrich Schinkel. Also look for key works by Carl Blechen and portraits by Philipp Otto Runge and Carl Spitzweg.

LUSTGARTEN

The Lustgarten (Pleasure Garden), as the patch of green fronting the Altes Museum is called, has seen as many makeovers as Madonna. It started as a royal kitchen garden and became a military exercise ground before being turned into a pleasure garden by Schinkel. The Nazis held mass rallies here, the East Germans ignored it. Restored to its Schinkel-era appearance, it's now a favourite resting spot for footweary tourists.

The banker JHW Wagener was an avid collector of art and a generous man who, in 1861, bequeathed his entire collection of 262 paintings to the Prussian state to form the basis of a national gallery. Just one year later, William I commissioned Friedrich August Stüler to design a suitable museum. He came up with the Alte Nationalgalerie, an imposing temple-like structure perched on a pedestal and fronted by a curtain of Corinthian columns. The entrance is reached via a sweeping double staircase crowned by a statue of King Friedrich Wilhelm IV on horseback.

TOP SIGHT
FERNSEHTURM

No matter where you are in Berlin, look up and chances are you'll see the Fernsehturm. Germany's tallest structure, the TV Tower is as iconic to the city as the Eiffel Tower is to Paris, has been soaring 368m high (including the antenna) since 1969. Pinpoint city landmarks from the panorama platform at 203m – views are stunning on clear days.

Ordered by East German government leader Walter Ulbricht in the 1950s, the tower was built not only as a transmitter for radio and TV programs but also as a demonstration of the GDR's strength and technological prowess. However, it ended up becoming a bit of a laughing stock when it turned out that, when struck by the sun, the steel sphere below the antenna produces the reflection of a giant cross. This inspired a popular joke (not appreciated by the GDR leadership) that the phenomenon was the 'Pope's revenge' on the secular socialist state for having removed crucifixes from churches.

The tower's rocketlike shape was inspired by the space race of the 1960s and in particular the launch of the first satellite, the Soviet Sputnik. The tower is made up of the base, a 250m-high shaft, the 4800-ton sphere and the 118m-high antenna. Its original location was supposed to be the Müggelberg hills on the city's southeastern edge. Construction had already begun when the authorities realised that the tower would be in the flight path of the planned airport at nearby Schönefeld. Ulbricht then decided on its current location.

DON'T MISS

➡ Sunset cocktails at Sphere (p110)

PRACTICALITIES

➡ TV Tower
➡ Map p300, C3
➡ ☎030-247 575 875
➡ www.tv-turm.de
➡ Panoramastrasse 1a
➡ adult/child €13/8.50, premium ticket adult/child €19.50/12
➡ ⊙9am-midnight Mar-Oct, 10am-midnight Nov-Feb, last ascent 11.30pm
➡ 🛜
➡ 🚌100, 200, TXL, Ⓢ Alexanderplatz, Ⓤ Alexanderplatz

⊙ SIGHTS

It's practically impossible to visit Berlin without spending time in this area, which packs some of Berlin's must-see sights into a very compact frame. Explore the city's beginnings in the Nikolaiviertel, then jump to the future at the construction site of the Berlin City Palace, skip around superb museums, take a river cruise and keep an eye on it all from atop the TV Tower.

MUSEUMSINSEL   MUSEUM
See p96.

⊙ Alexanderplatz

FERNSEHTURM   LANDMARK
See p106.

MARIENKIRCHE   CHURCH
Map p300 (www.marienkirche-berlin.de; Karl-Liebknecht-Strasse 8; ⊙10am-6pm; 🚌100, 200, TXL, 🆂Hackescher Markt, Alexanderplatz, 🆄Alexanderplatz) This Gothic brick gem has welcomed worshippers since the 13th century, making it one of Berlin's oldest surviving churches. A faded *Dance of Death* fresco in the vestibule inspired by a 15th-century plague leads to a relatively plain interior enlivened by elaborate epitaphs and a baroque alabaster pulpit by Andreas Schlüter (1703).

NEPTUNBRUNNEN   FOUNTAIN
Map p300 (Rathausplatz; 🚌100, 200, TXL, 🆄Klosterstrasse) This elaborate fountain was designed by Reinhold Begas in 1891 and depicts Neptune holding court over a quartet of buxom beauties symbolising the rivers Rhine, Elbe, Oder and Vistula. Kids get a kick out of the water-squirting turtle, seal, crocodile and snake.

ROTES RATHAUS   HISTORIC BUILDING
Map p300 (Red Town Hall; Rathausstrasse 15; ⊙closed to the public; 🆂Alexanderplatz, 🆄Alexanderplatz, Klosterstrasse) The hulking Rotes Rathaus is the office of Berlin's senate and governing mayor. The structure blends Italian Renaissance elements with northern German brick architecture and is framed by a terracotta frieze that illustrates Berlin milestones until 1871.

SEALIFE BERLIN   AQUARIUM
Map p300 (📞0180-666 690 101; www.visitsealife.com; Spandauer Strasse 3; adult/child €18/14.50; ⊙10am-7pm, last admission 6pm; 🚌100, 200, TXL, 🆂Hackescher Markt, Alexanderplatz) Sharks dart, moray eels lurk and spider crabs scuttle in this rambling aquarium; other crowd favourites include smile-inducing seahorses, ethereal jellyfish and Ophira the Octopus. Visits conclude with a slow lift ride through the Aquadom, a 25m-high cylindrical tropical fish tank. Check the website for online savings.

LOXX AM ALEX MINIATUR WELTEN BERLIN   MUSEUM
Map p300 (📞030-4472 3022; www.loxx-berlin.de; Grunerstrasse 20, 3rd fl, Alexa shopping mall; adult/concession/child €13/12/8; ⊙10am-8pm; 🚌100, 200, TXL, 🆂Alexanderplatz, 🆄Alexanderplatz) If you want to see Mum and Dad turn into little kids, take them to this huge model

---

THE BRAVE WOMEN OF ROSENSTRASSE

Rosenstrasse is a small, quiet, nondescript street where one of the most courageous acts of civilian defiance against the Nazis took place. It was at Nos 2–4, outside a Jewish welfare office, where hundreds of local women gathered in freezing rain in the middle of the winter of 1943. They all had one thing in common: they were Christians whose Jewish husbands had been locked inside for deportation to Auschwitz. Until that time, Jews married to non-Jewish Germans had enjoyed a certain degree of protection – but no more. 'Give us our husbands back', the women shouted – unarmed, unorganised and leaderless but with one voice. When the police threatened to shoot them, they shouted even louder. It took several weeks, but eventually they were heard. Propaganda minister Joseph Goebbels personally ordered the release of every single prisoner.

Today a pale-pink sandstone memorial called **Block der Frauen** (Map p300; Rosenstrasse; 🆂Hackescher Markt, Alexanderplatz, 🆄Alexanderplatz), by the late Jewish-German artist Inge Hunzinger, marks the site of the building while information pillars provide further background. The incident was movingly recounted in Margarethe von Trotta's 2003 feature film *Rosenstrasse*.

TOP SIGHT
DDR MUSEUM

How did regular East German Joes and Janes spend their day-to-day lives? The 'touchy-feely' DDR Museum does an entertaining job of pulling back the iron curtain on an extinct society. In hands-on fashion you'll learn how, under socialism, kids were put through collective potty training, engineers earned little more than farmers, and everyone, it seems, went on nudist holidays. You get to rummage through school bags, open drawers and cupboards or watch TV in a 1970s living room. And it's not only kids who love squeezing behind the wheel of a Trabant (Trabi) car for a virtual drive through a concrete-slab housing estate.

The more sinister sides of life in the GDR are also addressed, including chronic supply shortages, surveillance by the Stasi (secret police) and the SED party's monopoly on power. You can stand in a re-created prison cell, or imagine what it was like to be in the cross hairs of a Stasi officer by sitting on the victim's chair in a tiny, windowless interrogation room.

For a taste of the GDR, drop by the museum restaurant to try a *Grilletta, Ketwurst* or *Broiler*, as burgers, hot dogs and grilled chicken were called in East Germany.

DON'T MISS

- Trabi ride
- Stasi interrogation room

PRACTICALITIES

- GDR Museum
- Map p300, B4
- ☎030-847 123 731
- www.ddr-museum.de
- Karl-Liebknecht-Strasse 1
- adult/concession €7/5
- 🕙10am-8pm Sun-Fri, to 10pm Sat
- 🚌100, 200, TXL, [S]Hackescher Markt

railway where digitally controlled trains zip around central Berlin in miniature. Tour the Brandenburg Gate, visit Angela Merkel in the Chancellory or see planes take off and land at the already completed Loxx Airport. All has been recreated on a scale of 1:87 and more scenes are added all the time.

Schlossplatz & Nikolaiviertel

BERLINER DOM CHURCH

Map p300 (Berlin Cathedral; ☎030-2026 9136; www.berlinerdom.de; Am Lustgarten; adult/concession/under 18 €7/5/free; 🕙9am-8pm Apr-Oct, to 7pm Nov-Mar; 🚌100, 200, TXL, [S]Hackescher Markt) Pompous yet majestic, the Italian Renaissance–style former royal court church (1905) does triple duty as house of worship, museum and concert hall. Inside it's gilt to the hilt and outfitted with a lavish marble-and-onyx altar, a 7269-pipe Sauer organ and elaborate royal sarcophagi. Climb up the 267 steps to the gallery for glorious city views.

For more dead royals, albeit in less extravagant coffins, drop below to the crypt. Skip the cathedral museum unless you're interested in the building's construction. Multilanguage audioguides rent for €3.

NIKOLAIVIERTEL AREA

Map p300 (btwn Rathausstrasse, Breite Strasse, Spandauer Strasse & Mühlendamm; [U]Klosterstrasse) [FREE] Commissioned by the East German government in celebration of Berlin's 750th birthday, the twee Nicholas Quarter is a half-hearted attempt at re-creating the city's medieval birthplace around its oldest surviving building, the 1230 Nikolaikirche. The maze of cobbled lanes is worth a quick stroll, while several olde-worlde-style restaurants provide sustenance.

NIKOLAIKIRCHE MUSEUM

Map p300 (☎030-2400 2162; www.stadtmuseum.de; Nikolaikirchplatz; adult/concession/under 18 €5/3/free; 🕙10am-6pm; 🚌M48, [U]Klosterstrasse) The late-Gothic Church of St Nicholas (1230) is Berlin's oldest surviving building and is now a museum documenting the architecture and history of the church. Grab the free audioguide for the scoop on the octagonal baptismal font or to find out why the building is nicknamed the 'pantheon of prominent Berliners'.

EPHRAIM-PALAIS MUSEUM

Map p300 (☑030-2400 2162; www.stadtmuseum. de; Poststrasse 16; adult/concession/under 18 €6/4/free; ☺10am-6pm Tue & Thu-Sun, noon-8pm Wed; ☐248, M48, ☑Klosterstrasse) Once the home of Veitel Heine Ephraim – court jeweller and coin minter to Frederick the Great – this pretty, pint-size 1766 town palace hosts changing exhibits focusing on aspects of Berlin's artistic and cultural legacy.

KNOBLAUCHHAUS MUSEUM

Map p300 (☑030-2400 2162; www.stadtmuseum. de; Poststrasse 23; donation requested; ☺10am-6pm Tue-Sun; ☑Klosterstrasse) FREE This private rococo home features a series of painstakingly restored period rooms that impart a sense of how the well-to-do lived, dressed and spent their days during the Bieder-meier period.

MÄRKISCHES MUSEUM MUSEUM

Map p300 (☑030-2400 2162; www.stadtmuseum. de; Am Köllnischen Park 5; adult/concession/under 18 €5/3/free; ☺10am-6pm Tue-Sun; ☑Märkisches Museum) This old-school history museum is a rewarding stop for anyone keen on learning how the medieval trading village of Berlin-Cölln evolved into today's metropolis. The exhibits take you on a virtual walk through the city's streets and quarters, from the medieval Klosterviertel to the socialist Stalinallee boulevard. Paintings and sculpture, artefacts, furniture and objects from daily life illustrate the urban evolution.

BERLIN CITY PALACE: BACK TO THE FUTURE

In the heart of Berlin, across from the Berlin Cathedral and the famous museums of Museumsinsel, looms Berlin's biggest construction site: the **Humboldt Forum** (Berlin City Palace; Map p300; Schlossplatz; ☐100, 200, TXL, ☑Klosterstrasse), an art and cultural centre built to look like an exact replica of the baroque Berliner Stadtschloss (Berlin City Palace), but with a modern interior. Mired in controversy, construction finally kicked off in July 2013 after two decades of debate. The concrete shell, including the dome, was completed in 2015, while the project should be completed in 2019.

Although barely damaged in WWII, the grand palace where Prussian rulers had made their home since 1443 was blown up by East Germany's government in 1950 to drop the final curtain on Prussian and Nazi rule. To emphasise the point, the new communist rulers built their own modernist parliament – called Palast der Republik (Palace of the Republic) – on top of the ruins 26 years later. Riddled with asbestos, it too had a date with the wrecking ball in 2006.

The Stadtschloss 2.0 comes with a projected price tag of €590 million, with most of the bill to be footed by the federal government. The design by Italian architect Franco Stella has three sides of the facade looking like a baroque blast from the past, thus visually completing the historic ensemble of Museumsinsel, Berliner Dom and the Neuer Marstall (New Royal Stables). Only the facade facing the Spree River will be without baroque adornments.

How exactly the space will be used is still under discussion, especially since the 2015 appointment of Neil MacGregor, the outgoing director of the British Museum in London, as its foundational artistic director. What seems to be decided is that it will be a centre of global culture and the new home of the Museum of Ethnology and the Museum of Asian Art – both currently in the outer suburb of Dahlem. The focus on world cultures is also reflected in the name – Humboldt Forum – which channels the 19th-century geographers, naturalists, travellers and brothers Wilhelm and Alexander von Humboldt.

Pending the Forum's completion, the futuristic, advertising-clad **Humboldt-Box** (Map p300; ☑0180 503 0707; www.humboldt-box.com; Schlossplatz 5; ☺10am-7pm Apr-Nov, to 6pm Dec-Mar; ☐100, 200, TXL, ☑Hausvogteiplatz) FREE quite literally opens a panoramic window on to the ambitious project from its top level, which is also home to a nice cafe-restaurant called **Humboldt-Terrassen** (Map p300; ☑030-2062 5076; www.humboldt-terrassen.de; Schlossplatz 5; mains €6-10; ☎; ☐100, 200, TXL, ☑Hausvogteiplatz). On the other floors, interactive displays introduce various exhibition concepts, chronicle the palace's history and explain the state-of-the-art construction technology used in its reconstruction. A highlight is a fantastically detailed model that shows how the historic palace fit into the old city centre around 1900.

MUSEUMSINSEL & ALEXANDERPLATZ SIGHTS

🍴 EATING

With its abundant fast-food outlets, Alexanderplatz itself is not exactly a foodie haven, although there is a respectable self-service cafeteria in the Galeria Kaufhof (p112). Otherwise, try the food court in the Alexa (p112) mall, the traditional German restaurants in the Nikolaiviertel or head straight to the Scheunenviertel for better options.

🍴 Alexanderplatz

DOLORES CALIFORNIAN €

Map p300 (☎030-2809 9597; www.dolores-online.de; Rosa-Luxemburg-Strasse 7; burritos from €4.50; 🕒11.30am-10pm Mon-Sat, 1-10pm Sun; 📶🌶; 🚌100, 200, [S]Alexanderplatz, [U]Alexanderplatz) Dolores is a bastion of California-style burritos – fresh, authentic and priced to help you stay on budget. The menu is organised module-style: select your favourite combo of marinated meats (the lime coriander chicken is yummy) or tofu, rice, beans, veggies, cheese and salsa, and the cheerful staff will build it on the spot. Great homemade lemonade, too.

UDON KOBO ISHIN JAPANESE €€

Map p300 (☎030-6800 4007; www.ishin.de; Litfass-Platz 1; soups €7-12; 🕒noon-2.30pm & 6-9.30pm Mon-Fri, 2-9.30pm Sat; 🚋M1, [S]Hackescher Markt) The simple goodness of a big, steaming bowl of udon noodles (made in the open kitchen), swimming in a fragrant broth and topped with shiitakes, tofu, chicken, radishes, fish – what have you – is celebrated at this airy modern cantina-style eatery, which also serves good, value-priced sushi.

ZUR LETZTEN INSTANZ GERMAN €€

Map p300 (☎030-242 5528; www.zurletzteninstanz.de; Waisenstrasse 14-16; mains €9-19; 🕒5pm-1am Mon, noon-1am Tue-Sat, noon-10pm Sun; [U]Klosterstrasse) Oozing folksy Old Berlin charm, this rustic eatery has been an enduring hit since 1621 and has fed everyone from Napoleon to Beethoven to Angela Merkel. Although the restaurant is now tourist-geared, the food quality is reassuringly high when it comes to such local rib-stickers as *Grillhaxe* (grilled pork knuckle) and *Bouletten* (meat patties).

HOFBRÄUHAUS BERLIN GERMAN €€

Map p300 (☎030-679 665 520; www.hofbraeu-wirtshaus.de/berlin; Karl-Liebknecht-Strasse 30; mains €6-20; 🕒10am-1am Sun-Thu, to 2am Fri & Sat; 👪; 🚌100, 200, TXL, [S]Alexanderplatz, [U]Alexanderplatz) Popular with coach tourists and field-tripping teens, this giant beer hall with 2km of wooden benches serves the same litre-size mugs of beer and big plates of German fare as the Munich original. A brass band and Dirndl- and Lederhosen-clad servers add further faux authenticity.

SPHERE GERMAN €€€

Map p300 (☎030-247 5750; www.tv-turm.de/en/bar-restaurant; Panoramastrasse 1; mains lunch €9.50-18.50, dinner €14.50-28.50; 🕒10am-midnight; 🚌100, 200, TXL, [S]Alexanderplatz, [U]Alexanderplatz) Berlin's highest restaurant may not take demanding taste buds for a spin but it will take you around in a full circle within one hour. The revolving eatery, 207m up the iconic TV Tower (p106), delivers classic Berlin cuisine along with sweeping city views.

LOCAL KNOWLEDGE

EYE-POPPING VIEWS ON A BUDGET

If you don't want to drop the steep fee for a ride up the TV Tower, your next best option is heading up to the rooftop **Park Inn Panorama Terrasse** (Map p300; ☎030-238 90; Alexanderplatz 7; €4; 🕒noon-10pm Apr-Oct, to 6pm Nov-Mar, weather permitting; [S]Alexanderplatz, [U]Alexanderplatz), the open-air lounge of the Park Inn Hotel, for sweeping city views some 150m above Alexanderplatz. Grab a sunlounger and relax with a cold beer or look on as gutsy base-flyers leap off the edge of the building (Friday to Sunday only).

🍴 Nikolaiviertel

ZUM NUSSBAUM GERMAN €€

Map p300 (☎030-242 3095; Am Nussbaum 3; mains €8-16; 🕒noon-midnight; [U]Klosterstrasse) This is one of the last remaining Old Berlin-style inns in central Berlin. The original Nussbaum was built in 1507 on a nearby site and was a favourite watering hole of writers and artists, including the caricaturist Heinrich Zille, until it was destroyed in WWII. What you see today is a faithful replica, down to the namesake walnut tree and the heaping platters of classic local fare.

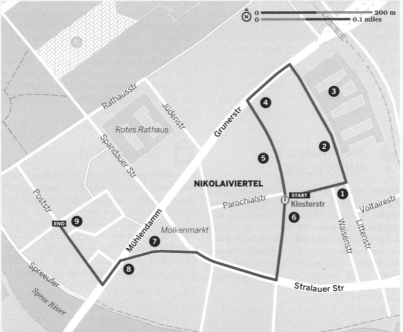

Neighbourhood Walk
Back to the Roots

START KLOSTERSTRASSE U-BAHN
END NIKOLAIVIERTEL
LENGTH 1.3KM; ONE HOUR

This walk charts Berlin history from its medieval beginnings to the early 20th century. From U-Bahn station Klosterstrasse, walk east on Parochialstrasse. Note Berlin's oldest restaurant, **❶ Zur Letzten Instanz** (p110), which has been serving pork knuckle for nearly 400 years, then turn left on Littenstrasse and stop at a crude 8m-long pile of boulders and bricks. It's what's left of **❷ Stadtmauer**, the city wall built around 1250 to protect the first settlers from marauders. Looming above is the monumental **❸ Justizgebäude Littenstrasse**, a 1912 courthouse with a grand art nouveau foyer.

On your left, the Gothic **❹ Franziskaner Klosterkirche** (Franciscan Monastery Church), once a prestigious school for such luminaries as Schinkel and Bismarck, is now used for outdoor art exhibits and concerts. Follow Littenstrasse north, turn

left on Grunerstrasse and left again on Klosterstrasse. The big building on your right is **❺ Altes Stadthaus** (Old City Hall), whose distinctive 87m-high domed tower is crowned by the goddess Fortuna. Keep going on Klosterstrasse to the 17th-century **❻ Parochialkirche**, which manages to be at once graceful and monumental. Designed by the same architect as Schloss Charlottenburg, it burnt out in WWII and, though restored, deliberately still reveals the scars of war.

Turn right on Stralauer Strasse, which leads to **❼ Molkenmarkt**, Berlin's oldest square and one-time thriving marketplace. The ornate building at No 2 is the historic **❽ Alte Münze**, the old mint turned event location. Note the decorative frieze depicting the evolution of metallurgy and coin minting.

Across the street, the **❾ Nikolaiviertel** (p108) may look medieval, but don't be fooled: it was built in the 1980s by the East German government to celebrate Berlin's 750th birthday. The 1230 Nikolaikirche and a handful of small museums are worth a look.

BRAUHAUS GEORGBRÄU　　GERMAN €€

Map p300 (☏030-242 4244; http://brauhaus-georgbraeu.de; Spreeufer 4; mains €6-14; ☺12pm-midnight; ⓊKlosterstrasse) Long before the craft beer craze reached Berlin, this cosy brewpub already churned out its own light and dark Georg-Bräu. In winter, the woodsy beer hall is perfect for tucking into hearty Berlin-style fare, while in summer tables in the riverside beer garden are golden.

🍷 DRINKING & NIGHTLIFE

Aside from a few tourist-oriented bars outdoors on Alexanderplatz and inside a clutch of hotels, there are few imbibing stations to be found in this area. For beer and Old Berlin flair, head to the restaurants in the Nikolaiviertel. For better options altogether, take the short stroll over to the Scheunenviertel.

CLUB AVENUE　　CLUB

(☏0174 600 3000; www.avenue-berlin.com; Karl-Marx-Allee 34; ☺from 10pm Thu, from 11pm Fri & Sat; ⓊSchillingstrasse) This high-octane club has taken up residency at Café Moskau, a protected East Berlin landmark. Dress to impress the door staff in order to gyrate on the dance floor to hip-hop, house or disco, depending on the night. The classy retro interior is the work of the decorating team behind Berghain/Panoramabar.

HOUSE OF WEEKEND　　CLUB

Map p300 (☏0152 2429 3140; www.houseof weekend.berlin; Am Alexanderplatz 5; ☺roof garden from 7pm, weather permitting; ⓈAlexanderplatz, ⓊAlexanderplatz) In summer the House of Weekend wows with sundowners, private cabanas and 360° views from its sophisticated rooftop terrace. At 11pm, the 15th floor opens for hot-stepping electro with the occasional excursion into hip-hop and dubstep courtesy of top local and visiting DJs. New: six private lounges with table service behind the DJ booth.

🛍 SHOPPING

Alexanderplatz is the hub of mainstream shopping in the eastern centre with department stores on and around the square itself and the massive Alexa shopping mall making sure that you can pick up a rainbow of goods in one compact area. Souvenir and trinket collectors should check out the little shops in the Nikolaiviertel.

GALERIA KAUFHOF　　DEPARTMENT STORE

Map p300 (☏030-247 430; www.galeria-kaufhof. de; Alexanderplatz 9; ☺9.30am-8pm Mon-Wed, to 10pm Thu-Sat; ⓈAlexanderplatz, ⓊAlexanderplatz) A full makeover by the late John P Kleihues turned this former GDR-era department store into a glitzy retail cube, complete with a glass-domed light court and a sleek travertine skin that glows green at night. There's little you won't find on the five football-field-size floors, including a gourmet supermarket on the ground floor.

ALEXA　　MALL

Map p300 (☏030-269 3400; www.alexacentre. com; Grunerstrasse 20; ☺10am-9pm Mon-Sat; ⓈAlexanderplatz, ⓊAlexanderplatz) Power shoppers love this XXL mall, which cuts a rose-hued presence near Alexanderplatz. The predictable range of high-street retailers is here, plus a few more-upmarket stores like Swarovski, Crumpler, Adidas Neo and North Face. Good food court for a bite on the run.

AUSBERLIN　　GIFTS & SOUVENIRS

Map p300 (☏030-4199 7896; www.ausberlin.de; Karl-Liebknecht-Strasse 9; ☺10am-8pm Mon-Sat; ☏; 🚌100, 200, TXL, ⓈAlexanderplatz, ⓊAlexanderplatz) 'Made in Berlin' is the motto of this hip shop where you can source the latest BPitch or Ostgut CD, eccentric ubo jewellery, wittily printed linen bags and all sorts of other knick-knacks (antimonster spray anyone?) designed right here in this fair city.

BERLIN BY BOAT

A lovely way to experience Berlin from April to October is on the open-air deck of a river cruiser. Several companies run relaxing Spree spins through the city centre from landing docks on the eastern side of Museumsinsel, for example outside the DDR Museum and from the Nikolaiviertel. Sip refreshments while a guide showers you with titbits (in English and German) as you glide past grand old buildings, beer gardens and the government quarter. Prices vary slightly by company, but expect the one-hour tour to cost between €12 and €14.

Potsdamer Platz & Tiergarten

POTSDAMER PLATZ | KULTURFORUM | TIERGARTEN & DIPLOMATENVIERTEL

Neighbourhood Top Five

1 **Gemäldegalerie** (p118) Feeling your spirit soar while perusing an Aladdin's cave of Old Masters – from Rembrandt to Vermeer.

2 **Sony Center** (p115) Stopping for a beer and people-watching beneath the magnificent canopy of this glass-and-steel landmark designed by Helmut Jahn.

3 **Panoramapunkt** (p116) Catching Europe's fastest lift to take in Berlin's impressive cityscape and enjoy refreshments in the sky.

4 **Tiergarten** (p122) Getting lost amid the lawns, trees and leafy paths of this sprawling city park with its ponds, monuments and beer gardens.

5 **Gedenkstätte Deutscher Widerstand** (p123) Admiring the brave people who stood up to the Nazis at this memorial exhibit in the offices where the 20 July 1944 assassination attempt on Hitler was plotted.

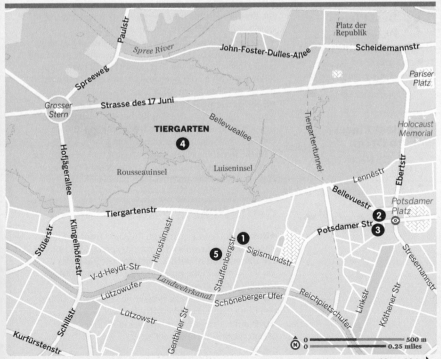

For more detail of this area see Map p294➡

Lonely Planet's Top Tip

For an unusual perspective of the Sony Center, enter the Museum für Film und Fernsehen and take the lift to the 9th floor, then rub shoulders with students and faculty of the German Film and Television Academy (DFFB) in their modern sky-lounge **cafeteria** (p116) with lovely terrace seating. Hot meals from noon to 2.30pm, coffee and snacks at other times.

◉ Best for Architecture

➡ Sony Center (p115)
➡ Berliner Philharmonie (p122)
➡ Bauhaus Archiv (p123)

For reviews, see p121.➡

✕ Best Places to Eat

➡ Joseph-Roth-Diele (p124)
➡ Qiu (p124)
➡ Weilands Wellfood (p124)

For reviews, see p124.➡

⊟ Best Places to Drink

➡ Café am Neuen See (p128)
➡ Fragrances (p127)
➡ Solar (p127)

For reviews, see p127.➡

Explore: Potsdamer Platz & Tiergarten

Despite the name, Potsdamer Platz is not really a square but Berlin's newest quarter, forged in the '90s from terrain once bifurcated by the Berlin Wall. A collaborative effort by the world's finest architects, it is a vibrant showcase of urban renewal. The area itself is rather compact and quickly explored – unless you choose to linger in the shopping mall, see Berlin from above from the Panoramapunkt or dive into German film history at the Museum für Film und Fernsehen.

A visit to Potsdamer Platz is easily combined with the nearby Kulturforum complex, where you can mingle with masters old and modern in several museums, then head south to the up-and-coming gallery strip on Potsdamer Strasse. Further west, the Diplomatenviertel (Diplomatic Quarter) doubles as a showcase of contemporary architecture, while a bit east Leipziger Platz has sprouted the huge and fancy LP12 Mall of Berlin. If your head is spinning after all that stimuli, the leafy paths of the vast Tiergarten, Berlin's equivalent of New York's Central Park, should provide a restorative antidote.

Local Life

➡**Concerts** The free Tuesday lunchtime concerts at the Berliner Philharmonie (p128) lure a wider range of music fans. From September until June.

➡**Tiergarten** When the sun is out, Berliners just want to get outdoors to the sweeping lawns, shady paths and romantic corners of the Tiergarten (p122) park, then follow up with a cold beer and pizza at the beer garden of Café am Neuen See (p128).

➡**Beer-garden concerts** On Sundays in July and August, the Teehaus im Englischen Garten (p124) turns into a big garden party with free rock, pop and jazz concerts (www.konzertsommer-berlin.de).

➡**Traffic light** The clock-tower-shaped replica of Europe's first traffic light, from 1924, at the corner of Potsdamer Platz and Stresemannstrasse is a popular meeting point.

Getting There & Away

➡**Bus** No 200 comes through en route from Bahnhof Zoologischer Garten and Alexanderplatz; M41 links the Hauptbahnhof with Kreuzberg and Neukölln via Potsdamer Platz; and the M29 connects with Checkpoint Charlie.

➡**S-Bahn** S1 and S2 link Potsdamer Platz with Unter den Linden and the Scheunenviertel.

➡**U-Bahn** U2 stops at Potsdamer Platz and Mendelssohn-Bartholdy-Park.

TOP SIGHT
POTSDAMER PLATZ

The rebirth of the historic Potsdamer Platz was Europe's biggest building project of the 1990s, a showcase of urban renewal masterminded by such top international architects as Renzo Piano and Helmut Jahn. An entire city quarter sprouted on terrain once bifurcated by the Berlin Wall and today houses offices, theatres and cinemas, hotels, apartments and museums.

Until WWII sucked all life out of the area, Potsdamer Platz was Berlin's central traffic, entertainment and commercial hub. Its modern reinterpretation is again divided into three sections, of which the **Sony Center** is the flashiest and most visitor-friendly, with a central plaza canopied by a glass roof that erupts in changing colours after dark. Segments from the Berlin Wall stand in the corner of Potsdamer Strasse and Ebertstrasse. Across Potsdamer Strasse, **DaimlerCity** has big hotels, a shopping mall, sprinkles of public art and entertainment venues that host movie premieres and galas during the Berlinale film festival in February. The **Beisheim Center**, with the Ritz-Carlton Hotel, is modelled after classic American skyscrapers.

DON'T MISS

➡ Panoramapunkt

➡ View of Sony Center from Helene-Schwarz-Cafe

➡ Museum für Film und Fernsehen

➡ Berlin Wall remnants

PRACTICALITIES

➡ Map p294, G5

➡ Alte Potsdamer Strasse

➡ 🚌200, Ⓢ Potsdamer Platz, Ⓤ Potsdamer Platz

Sony Center

Designed by Helmut Jahn, the visually dramatic **Sony Center** (Map p294; Potsdamer Strasse; 🛜; 🚌200, Ⓢ Potsdamer Platz, Ⓤ Potsdamer Platz) is fronted by a 26-floor, glass-and-steel tower that's the highest building on Potsdamer Platz. It integrates rare relics from Potsdamer Platz' prewar era, such as a section of the facade of the **Hotel Esplanade** (visible from Bellevuestrasse) and the opulent **Kaisersaal**, whose 75m move to its current location required some wizardly technology. The heart of the Sony Center is a central plaza canopied by a tentlike glass roof with supporting beams radiating like bicycle spokes. The plaza and its many cafes lend themselves to hanging out and people-watching.

VIEW FROM THE TOP

Europe's fastest lift, **Panoramapunkt** (Map p294; ☑030-2593 7080; www.panoramapunkt.de; Potsdamer Platz 1; adult/concession €6.50/5, without wait €10.50/8; ⊙10am-8pm Apr-Oct, to 6pm Nov-Mar; ⬚M41, 200, ⓈPotsdamer Platz, ⓊPotsdamer Platz), yo-yoes up and down the red-brick postmodern Kollhof Tower. From the bilevel viewing platform at a lofty 100m, you can pinpoint the sights, make a java stop in the 1930s-style cafe, enjoy sunset from the terrace and check out the exhibit that explores the quarter's history.

In WWII Potsdamer Platz suffered 80% destruction and plunged into a coma, only to be bisected by the Berlin Wall in 1961. Today, a double row of cobblestones indicates the course of the Wall, and a few Berlin Wall segments outside the Potsdamer Platz train station entrance feature explanatory texts about other Wall-related memorial sites. An original Berlin Wall Watchtower (p117) is just a short walk away on Erna-Berger-Strasse (off Stresemannstrasse).

Museum für Film & Fernsehen

From silent movies to sci-fi, Germany's long and illustrious film history gets the star treatment at the engaging **Museum für Film und Fernsehen** (Map p294; ☑030-300 9030; www.deutsche-kinemathek.de; Potsdamer Strasse 2; adult/concession €7/4.50, free 4-8pm Thu; ⊙10am-6pm Tue, Wed & Thu-Sun, to 8pm Thu; ⬚200, ⓈPotsdamer Platz, ⓊPotsdamer Platz). The tour kicks off with an appropriate sense of drama as it sends you through a dizzying mirrored walkway that conjures visions of *The Cabinet of Dr Caligari*. Major themes include pioneers and early divas, silent-era classics such as Fritz Lang's *Metropolis*, Leni Riefenstahl's groundbreaking Nazi-era documentary *Olympia*, German exiles in Hollywood and post-WWII movies. Stealing the show, as she did in real life, is femme fatale Marlene Dietrich, whose glamour lives on through her original costumes, personal finery, photographs and documents. The **TV exhibit** upstairs has more niche appeal but is still fun if you always wanted to know what *Star Trek* sounds like in German.

Make use of the excellent audioguide (€2) as you work your way through various themed galleries. Admission is free from 4pm to 8pm Thursdays.

The museum is part of the Filmhaus, which also harbours a film school, the Arsenal cinema (p128), a library, a museum shop and the **Helene-Schwarz-Cafe** (Map p294; ☑030-7202 4799; www.dffb.de; Potsdamer Strasse 2; dishes €3.50-8; ⊙9am-3.30pm Mon-Fri; ⬚200, ⓊPotsdamer Platz, ⓈPotsdamer Platz) on the top floor with a superb view of the Sony Center from above.

Legoland Discovery Centre

The **Legoland Discovery Centre** (Map p294; ☑01806-6669 0110; www.legolanddiscoverycentre.de/berlin; Potsdamer Strasse 4; €18.50; ⊙10am-7pm, last admission 5pm; ⬚200, ⓈPotsdamer Platz, ⓊPotsdamer Platz) is an indoor amusement park made entirely of those little coloured plastic building blocks that many of us grew up with. Cute but low-tech, it's best suited for kids aged three to eight. Skip the promotional introductory film and head straight to such adventure stations as Ninjago to battle snakes and brave a laser labyrinth, or Merlin's Magic Library to become a wizard apprentice and 'fly' through a magical potion room. Other 'thrills' include the 4D cinema (with tactile special effects), a slow-mo ride through the Dragon's Castle, and a 'torture-tickle chamber'. New: Space Mission, where kids can build their own shuttle, explore galaxies and meet aliens. Grown-ups will have fun marvelling at a Berlin in miniature at Miniland, which uses more than two million Lego bricks to recreate major landmarks.

The website has tickets deals and combination tickets with other attractions.

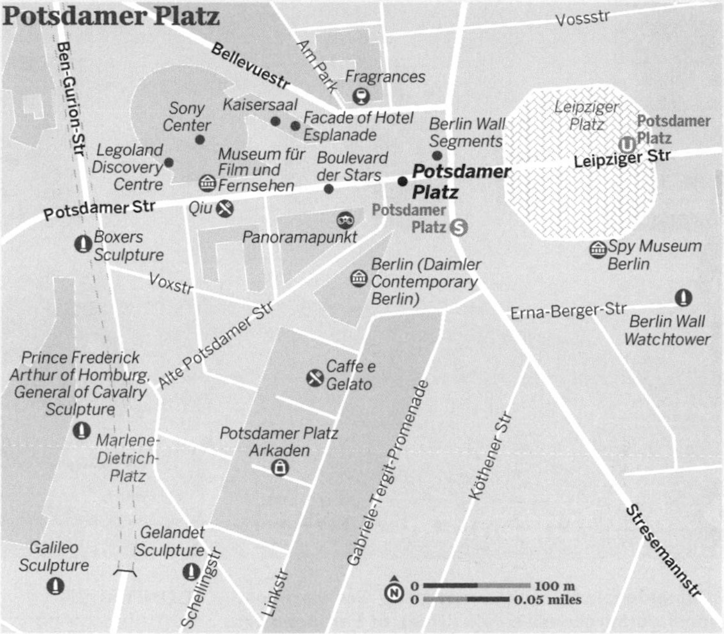
Potsdamer Platz
Vossstr
Bellevuestr
Am Park
Ben-Gurion-Str
Fragrances
Sony Center
Kaisersaal
Facade of Hotel Esplanade
Berlin Wall Segments
Leipziger Platz
Potsdamer Platz
Leipziger Str
Legoland Discovery Centre
Museum für Film und Fernsehen
Boulevard der Stars
Potsdamer Platz
Potsdamer Str
Qiu
Potsdamer Platz
Boxers Sculpture
Panoramapunkt
Spy Museum Berlin
Berlin (Daimler Contemporary Berlin)
Voxstr
Erna-Berger-Str
Berlin Wall Watchtower
Alte Potsdamer Str
Prince Frederick Arthur of Homburg, General of Cavalry Sculpture
Caffe e Gelato
Marlene-Dietrich-Platz
Potsdamer Platz Arkaden
Gabriele-Tergit-Promenade
Köthener Str
Stresemannstr
Gelandet Sculpture
Galileo Sculpture
Schellingstr
Linkstr
0 100 m
0 0.05 miles

Daimler Contemporary Berlin

Ring the bell to be buzzed into the free **Daimler Contemporary Berlin** (Map p294; ☎030-2594 1420; www.art.daimler.com; Alte Potsdamer Strasse 5, Weinhaus Huth, 4th fl; 🕒11am-6pm; 🚌200, [S]Potsdamer Platz, [U]Potsdamer Platz) [FREE], a loft-style gallery showcasing first-rate international abstract, conceptual and minimalist art. It's on the top floor of the 1912 **Weinhaus Huth**, which was one of the first steel-frame buildings in town and the only Potsdamer Platz structure that survived WWII intact.

Boulevard der Stars

Berlin's own version of Hollywood's Walk of Fame, the **Boulevard der Stars** (Boulevard of the Stars; Map p294; www.boulevard-der-stars-berlin.de; Potsdamer Strasse; 🕒24hr; 🚌200, [U]Potsdamer Platz, [S]Potsdamer Platz) [FREE] honours dozens of German TV and film actors (including Marlene Dietrich, Werner Herzog and Romy Schneider) with brass stars embedded in a red-asphalt 'carpet' along Potsdamer Strasse. A cute gimmick is the Pepper's Ghost cameras, which create a holographic image of the celebrity hovering above their brass star. Feel free to step next to it and snap a picture.

Berlin Wall Watchtower

The mushroom-shaped Berlin Wall Watchtower Erna-Berger-Strasse (Map p294 (🕒24hr; 🚌M41, 200, [U]Potsdamer Platz, [S]Potsdamer Platz) [FREE] is one of the few remaining border watchtowers set up along the Berlin Wall. Guards had to climb up a slim round shaft via an iron ladder to reach the octagonal observation perch on top. Introduced in 1969, this cramped model was later replaced by larger, square towers.

TOP SIGHT
GEMÄLDEGALERIE

The Gemäldegalerie ranks among the world's finest and most comprehensive collections of European art from the 13th to the 18th centuries. Expect to feast your eyes on masterpieces by Titian, Goya, Botticelli, Holbein, Gainsborough, Canaletto, Hals, Rubens, Vermeer and many other Old Masters. You're sure to find your favourites as you explore the galleries, most of them beautifully lit by muted daylight.

The gallery's opening in a purpose-built Kulturforum space in 1998 marked the happy reunion of a collection separated by the Cold War for half a century. Some works had remained at the Bode-Museum in East Berlin, the rest went on display in the West Berlin suburb of Dahlem. Today, about 1500 paintings span the arc of artistic vision over five centuries. Dutch and Flemish painters, including Rembrandt, are especially well represented, as are exponents of the Italian Renaissance. Another focus is on German artists from the late Middle Ages, and there's also a sprinkling of British, French and Spanish masters.

East Wing: German, Dutch & Flemish Masters

The exhibit kicks off with religious paintings from the Middle Ages and moves quickly to the Renaissance and works by two of the era's most famous artists: Albrecht Dürer and Lucas Cranach the Elder. A standout in Room 2 is Dürer's **Portrait of Hieronymus Holzschuher** (1526), a Nuremberg patrician, career politician and strong supporter of the Reformation. Note how the artist brilliantly lasers in on his

DON'T MISS

➡ Rembrandt Room (Room X)
➡ *Amor Victorius* (Room XIV)
➡ *Dutch Proverbs* (Room 7)
➡ *Fountain of Youth* (Room III)

PRACTICALITIES

➡ Gallery of Old Masters
➡ Map p294, E5
➡ ☎030-266 424 242
➡ www.smb.museum/gg
➡ Matthäikirchplatz
➡ adult/concession €10/5
➡ ⏱10am-6pm Tue, Wed & Fri, 10am-8pm Thu, 11am-6pm Sat & Sun
➡ ♿
➡ 🚌M29, M48, M85, 200, ⓢPotsdamer Platz, ⓤPotsdamer Platz

friend's features with utmost precision, down to the furrows, wrinkles and thinning hair.

One of Cranach's finest works is **Fountain of Youth** (1546) in Room III, which illustrates humankind's yearning for eternal youth. Old crones plunge into a pool of water and emerge as dashing hotties – no need for plastic surgeons! The transition is also reflected in the landscape, which is stark and craggy on the left and lush and fertile on the right.

A main exponent of the Dutch Renaissance was Pieter Bruegel the Elder who here is represented with the dazzling **Dutch Proverbs** (1559) in Room 7. The moralistic yet humorous painting crams more than 100 proverbs and idioms into a single seaside village scene. While some point up the absurdity of human behaviour, others unmask its imprudence and sinfulness. Some sayings are still in use today, among them 'swimming against the tide' and 'armed to the teeth'.

North Wing: Dutch 17th-Century Paintings

The first galleries in the north wing feature some exceptional portraits, most notably Frans Hals' **Malle Babbe** (1633) in Room 13. Note how Hals ingeniously captures the character and vitality of his subject 'Crazy Barbara' with free-wielding brushstrokes. Hals met the woman with the near-demonic laugh in the workhouse for the mentally ill where his son Pieter was also a resident. The tin mug and owl are symbols of Babbe's fondness for tipple.

Another eye-catcher is **Woman with a Pearl Necklace** (1662) in Room 18, one of the most famous paintings by Dutch realist Jan Vermeer. It depicts a young woman studying herself in the mirror while fastening a pearl necklace around her neck, an intimate moment beautifully captured with characteristic soft brushstrokes.

The real highlight of the north wing awaits in the octagonal Room X, which is dedicated to Rembrandt and dominated by the large-scale **Mennonite Minister Cornelius Claesz Anslo** (1641), which shows the preacher in conversation with his wife. The huge open Bible and his gesturing hand sticking out in almost 3D-style from the centre of the painting are meant to emphasise the strength of his religious convictions. Also note Rembrandt's small self-portrait next to it.

West Wing: Italian Masterpieces

The first galleries in the west wing stay in the 17th and 18th centuries. Crowds often form before Canaletto's **Il Campo di Rialto** (1758–63) in Room XII, which depicts the arcaded main market square of

The building housing this encyclopedic art collection was designed by the Munich firm Hilmer & Sattler and is essentially a postmodern interpretation of the clear lines and stark symmetry of the Schinkel era. The entrance sits atop a sloping piazza, while rooms radiate from the football-field-size central foyer anchored by a fountain designed by Walter De Maria.

POTSDAMER PLATZ & TIERGARTEN GEMÄLDEGALERIE

GEMÄLDEGALERIE

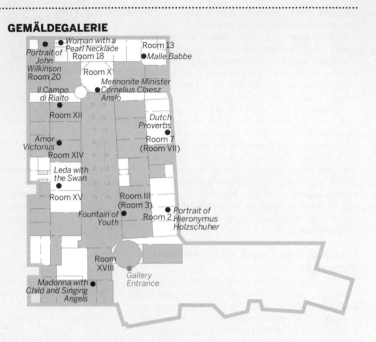

the artist's home town, Venice, with stunning precision and perspective. Note the goldsmith shops on the left, the wig-wearing merchants in the centre and the stores selling paintings and furniture on the right.

Older by 150 years is Caravaggio's delightful **Amor Victorius** (1602/3) in Room XIV. Wearing nothing but a mischievous grin, a pair of black angel wings and a fistful of arrows, this cheeky Amor means business. Note the near-photographic realism achieved by the dramatic use of light and shadow.

The next galleries travel back to the Renaissance when Raphael, Titian and Correggio dominated Italian art. The latter's **Leda with the Swan** (1532) in Room XV is worth a closer look. Judging by her blissed-out expression, Leda is having a fine time with that swan who, according to Greek mythology, is none other than Zeus himself. The erotically charged nature of this painting apparently so incensed its one-time owner Louis of Orleans that he cut off Leda's head with a knife. It was later restored.

Lest you think that all West Wing paintings have a naughty subtext, let us draw your attention to Sandro Botticelli's **Madonna with Child and Singing Angels** (1477) in Room XVIII. This circular painting (a format called a *tondo*) shows Mary flanked by two sets of four wingless angels. It's an intimate moment that shows the Virgin tenderly embracing – perhaps even about to breastfeed – her child. The white lilies are symbols of her purity.

⊙ SIGHTS

Sights in this compact area are handily clustered around Potsdamer Platz itself and in the adjacent Kulturforum museum complex. The Diplomatic Quarter is just west of here, the Tiergarten park to the north. It's all easily explored on foot.

⊙ Potsdamer Platz

POTSDAMER PLATZ AREA
See p115.

MARTIN-GROPIUS-BAU GALLERY
Map p294 (✆030-254 860; www.gropiusbau.de; Niederkirchner Strasse 7; cost varies, under 16 free; ☺10am-7pm Wed-Mon; 🚌M41, ⓈPotsdamer Platz, ⓊPotsdamer Platz) With its mosaics, terracotta reliefs and airy atrium, this Italian Renaissance–style exhibit space named for its architect (Bauhaus founder Walter Gropius' great-uncle) is a celebrated venue for high-calibre travelling shows. Whether it's a David Bowie retrospective, the latest works of Ai Weiwei or an ethnological exhibit on the mysteries of Angkor Wat, it's bound to be well curated and utterly fascinating.

DALÍ – DIE AUSSTELLUNG MUSEUM
Map p294 (✆0700-3254 237 546; www.dali berlin.de; Leipziger Platz 7; adult/concession €12.50/9.50; ☺noon-8pm Mon-Sat, 10am-8pm Sun; 🚌200, ⓈPotsdamer Platz, ⓊPotsdamer Platz) If you only know Salvador Dalí as the painter of melting watches, burning giraffes and other surrealist imagery, this private collection will likely open new perspectives on the man. Here, the focus is on his graphics, illustrations, sculptures, drawings and films, with highlights including etchings on the theme of Tristan and Isolde and epic sculptures like *Surrealist Angel*, as well as the *Don Quixote* lithographs.

SPY MUSEUM BERLIN MUSEUM
Map p294 (✆030-2062 0354; www.spymuseum berlin.com; Leipziger Platz 9; adult/concession €18/14; ☺10am-8pm, last entry 7pm; 🚌200, ⓈPotsdamer Platz, ⓊPotsdamer Platz) This interactive private museum not only documents the history of spying from ancient Egypt to the 20th century, it also displays hundreds of ingenious tools of the trade, including a lipstick pistol, an umbrella camera and an ultra-rare Enigma cipher machine. Learn about famous spies, get to encrypt a message and explore an entire section about James Bond, his women and his adversaries.

⊙ Kulturforum

GEMÄLDEGALERIE GALLERY
See p118.

DAIMLERCITY PUBLIC SCULPTURE TOUR

DaimlerCity is not only a postmodern urban landscape also packed with large-scale public sculptures. Several blue-chip artists explore the relationship between art and urban spaces and inject visual appeal into this otherwise rather austere city quarter.

Prince Frederick Arthur of Homburg, General of Cavalry Sculpture (Map p294; Marlene-Dietrich-Platz; ☺24hr; 🚌200, ⓈPotsdamer Platz, ⓊPotsdamer Platz) Frank Stella's otherworldly *Prince Frederick Arthur of Homburg, General of the Cavalry* (1999) is made of white-silver aluminium, steel carbon and fibreglass and explores the relationships of space, colour and form in a three-dimensional setting.

Galileo Sculpture (Map p294; Eichhornstrasse; ☺24hr; ⓈPotsdamer Platz, ⓊMendelssohn-Bartholdy-Platz, Potsdamer Platz) In the middle of a pond is Mark Di Suvero's *Galileo*, an abstract jumble of rusted steel T-beams assembled into a gravity-defying sculpture.

Gelandet Sculpture (Map p294; Schellingstrasse; ☺24hr; ⓈPotsdamer Platz, ⓊMendelssohn-Bartholdy-Platz, Potsdamer Platz) Crane your neck to spot Auke de Vries's *Gelandet* (Landed, 2002), a dronelike iron sculpture teetering on the edge of the roof of the DaimlerServices building (the one with the square tower with the green top).

Boxers Sculpture (Map p294; cnr Eichhornstrasse & Potsdamer Strasse; ☺24hr; 🚌200, M41, ⓈPotsdamer Platz, ⓊPotsdamer Platz) This 1987 sculpture by the American artist Keith Haring shows two cut-steel stick figures – one blue, one red – seemingly punching each other out. Or are they embracing each other? You decide.

KUNSTGEWERBEMUSEUM MUSEUM

Map p294 (Museum of Decorative Arts; ☎030-266 424 242; www.smb.museum; Matthäikirchplatz; adult/concession/under 18 €8/4/free; ⏰10am-6pm Tue-Fri, 11am-6pm Sat & Sun; 🚌M29, M48, M85, 200, [S]Potsdamer Platz, [U]Potsdamer Platz) This prized collection of European design, fashion and decorative arts from the Middle Ages to today is part of the Kulturforum museum cluster. Feast your eyes on exquisitely ornate reliquaries, portable altars, chests and leather wallpaper, as well as *Jugendstil* and Bauhaus classics by Henry van de Velde and Wilhelm Wagenfeld. Pride of place goes to the Fashion Gallery with classic designer outfits and accessories from the past 150 years.

KUPFERSTICHKABINETT GALLERY

Map p294 (Museum of Prints and Drawings; ☎030-266 424 242; www.smb.museum/kk; Matthäikirchplatz; adult/concession €6/3; ⏰10am-6pm Tue-Fri, 11am-6pm Sat & Sun; 🚌M29, M48, M85, 200, [S]Potsdamer Platz, [U]Potsdamer Platz) One of the world's largest and finest collections of art on paper, this gallery shelters a bonanza of hand-illustrated books, illuminated manuscripts, drawings and prints produced mostly in Europe from the 14th century onward – Dürer to Rembrandt to Schinkel, Picasso to Giacometti and Gerhard Richter.

BERLINER PHILHARMONIE ARCHITECTURE

Map p294 (☎030-2548 8156; www.berliner-philharmoniker.de; Herbert-von-Karajan-Strasse 1; tours adult/concession €5/3; ⏰tours 1.30pm Sep-Jun; 🚌M29, M48, M85, 200, [S]Potsdamer Platz, [U]Potsdamer Platz) A masterpiece of organic architecture, Hans Scharoun's 1963 iconic, honey-coloured concert venue is the home base of the prestigious Berliner Philharmoniker. The auditorium feels like the inside of a finely crafted instrument and boasts supreme acoustics and excellent sight lines from every seat.

MATTHÄUSKIRCHE CHURCH

Map p294 (Church of St Matthews; ☎030-262 1202; www.stiftung-stmatthaeus.de; Matthäikirchplatz; ⏰11am-6pm Tue-Sun; 🚌M29, M48, M85, [S]Potsdamer Platz, [U]Potsdamer Platz) [FREE] Standing a bit lost and forlorn within the Kulturforum, the Stüler-designed Matthäuskirche (1846) is a beautiful neo-Romanesque confection with alternating bands of red and ochre brick and a light-flooded, modern sanctuary filled with artworks, including the subterranean sculpture *Steps* by Micha Ullman. Views from the tower of the Kulturforum and Potsdamer Platz are free but only so-so. A nice time to visit is for the free 20-minute organ recitals at 12.30pm Tuesday to Sunday.

MUSIKINSTRUMENTEN-MUSEUM MUSEUM

Map p294 (Musical Instruments Museum; ☎030-2548 1178; www.mim-berlin.de; Tiergartenstrasse 1, enter via Ben-Gurion-Strasse; adult/concession/under 18 €6/3/free; ⏰9am-5pm Tue, Wed & Fri, 9am-8pm Thu, 10am-5pm Sat & Sun; 🚌200, [S]Potsdamer Platz, [U]Potsdamer Platz) This darling museum is packed with fun, precious and rare sound machines, including the glass harmonica invented by Ben Franklin, a flute played by Frederick the Great, and Johann Sebastian Bach's harpsichord. Stop at the listening stations to hear what some of the more obscure instruments sound like.

NEUE NATIONALGALERIE GALLERY

Map p294 (www.neue-nationalgalerie.de; Potsdamer Strasse 50; ⏰closed for renovation; 🚌200, [U]Potsdamer Platz, [S]Potsdamer Platz) This fabulous collection of early-20th-century art will not be on view during renovations being undertaken by David Chipperfield that are expected to last until 2018 or 2019. The building itself is a late masterpiece by Ludwig Mies van der Rohe. All glass and steel and squatting on a raised platform, it echoes a postmodern Buddhist temple.

[i] KULTURFORUM COMBINATION TICKET

A Kulturforum area ticket (Bereichskarte) costs €12 (concession €6) and includes same-day admission to the Gemäldegalerie, the Kunstgewerbemuseum, the Kupferstichkabinett and the Musikinstrumenten-Museum. Admission to all museums is free to anyone under 18.

Tiergarten & Diplomatenviertel

★TIERGARTEN PARK

(Strasse des 17 Juni; 🚌100, 200, [S]Potsdamer Platz, Brandenburger Tor, [U]Brandenburger Tor) [FREE] Berlin's rulers used to hunt boar and pheasants in the rambling Tiergarten until garden architect Peter Lenné landscaped the grounds in the 18th century. Today it's

TOP SIGHT
GEDENKSTÄTTE DEUTSCHER WIDERSTAND

If you've seen the movie *Valkyrie* you know the story of Claus von Stauffenberg, the poster boy of the German resistance against Hitler and the Third Reich. The very rooms where senior army officers led by Stauffenberg plotted their bold but ill-fated assassination attempt on the Führer on 20 July 1944 are now home to the German Resistance Memorial Centre. The building itself, the historic Bendlerblock, harboured the Wehrmacht high command from 1935 to 1945 and today is the secondary seat of the German defence ministry (the primary is still in Bonn).

Aside from detailing the Stauffenberg-led coup, the centre also comprehensively documents the efforts of many other Germans who risked their lives opposing the Third Reich for ideological, ethical, religious or military reasons. Most were just regular folks, such as students Hans and Sophie Scholl of the White Rose, or the craftmaker Georg Elser; others were prominent citizens like the artist Käthe Kollwitz and the theologian Dietrich Bonhoeffer.

In the yard, a sculpture marks the spot where Stauffenberg and three of his co-conspirators were executed right after the failed coup. Admission is free.

DON'T MISS

➡ Stauffenberg exhibit
➡ White Rose exhibit
➡ Stauffenberg memorial statue

PRACTICALITIES

➡ Map p294, D5
➡ ☎030-2699 5000
➡ www.gdw-berlin.de
➡ Stauffenbergstrasse 13-14
➡ ⊙9am-6pm Mon-Wed & Fri, 9am-8pm Thu, 10am-6pm Sat & Sun
➡ ☐M29, M48,
Ⓢ Potsdamer Platz,
Ⓤ Potsdamer Platz, Kurfürstenstrasse

---

one of the world's largest urban parks, popular for strolling, jogging, picnicking, Frisbee tossing and, yes, nude sunbathing and gay cruising (especially around the Löwenbrücke). It is bisected by a major artery, the Strasse des 17 Juni. Walking across the entire park takes about an hour, but even a shorter stroll has its rewards.

SIEGESSÄULE MONUMENT
Map p294 (Victory Column; Grosser Stern; adult/concession €3/2.50; ⊙9.30am-6.30pm Mon-Fri, to 7pm Sat & Sun Apr-Oct, 10am-5pm Mon-Fri, to 5.30pm Sat & Sun Nov-Mar; ☐100, 200, ⓤHansaplatz, ⓈBellevue) Like arms of a starfish, five roads merge into the Grosser Stern roundabout at the heart of the huge Tiergarten (p122) park. The Victory Column at its centre is crowned by a gilded statue of the goddess Victoria in celebration of 19th-century Prussian military triumphs. Today it is also a symbol of Berlin's gay community. Climb 285 steps for sweeping views of the park.

BAUHAUS ARCHIV MUSEUM
Map p294 (☎030-254 0020; www.bauhaus.de; Klingelhöferstrasse 14; adult/concession/under 18 incl audioguide Wed-Fri €7/4/free, Sat-Mon €8/5/free; ⊙10am-5pm Wed-Mon; ☐100, ⓤNollendorfplatz) Founded in 1919, the Bauhaus was a seminal school of avant-garde architecture, design and art. This avant-garde building, designed by Bauhaus' founder Walter Gropius, presents paintings, drawings, sculptures, models and other objects and documents by such famous artist-teachers as Klee, Feininger and Kandinsky. There's a decent cafe and good gift shop. A building expansion by Berlin architect Volker Staab is planned to open in 2021.

SCHWULES MUSEUM MUSEUM
(Gay Museum; ☎030-6959 9050; www.schwulesmuseum.de; Lützowstrasse 73; adult/concession €7.50/4; ⊙2-6pm Mon, Wed, Fri & Sun, to 8pm Thu, to 7pm Sat; ☐M29, ⓤNollendorfplatz, Kurfürstenstrasse) In a former print shop, this nonprofit museum is one of the largest and most important cultural institutions documenting LGBTIQ culture around the world, albeit with a special focus on Berlin and Germany. Changing exhibits on gay icons, artists, gender issues and historical themes keep the space dynamic.

HANSA STUDIOS: BOWIE'S BIG HALL BY THE WALL

Complete this analogy: London is to Abbey Road as Berlin is to...well? **Hansa Studios** (Map p294; www.meistersaal-berlin.de; Köthener Strasse 38; ⊠M41, ⓤPotsdamer Platz, ⓈPotsdamer Platz) , of course, that seminal recording studio that has exerted a gravitational pull on international artists since the Cold War. The only way to get access (and find out why Depeche Mode's Martin Gore stripped down naked for the recording of a love song) is with the highly recommended Berlin Music Tours (p271).

The 'Big Hall by the Wall' was how David Bowie fittingly dubbed its glorious Studio 2, better known as the Meistersaal (Masters' Hall). As you look through arched windows, imagine Bowie looking over the concrete barrier and perhaps waving at the gun-toting guards in their watchtowers. In the late '70s, the White Duke recorded his tortured visions for the seminal album *Heroes* here, after completing *Low*, both part of his Berlin Trilogy. Bowie also produced *The Idiot* and *Lust for Life* with his buddy Iggy Pop, who he bunked with at Hauptstrasse 155 in Schöneberg.

There's a long list of other music legends who have taken advantage of the special sound quality at Hansa Studios, including Nina Hagen, Nick Cave, David Byrne, Einstürzende Neubauten, Die Ärzte, Snow Patrol, Green Day, REM and The Hives. Depeche Mode produced three albums here – *Construction Time Again*, *Some Great Reward* and *Black Celebration* – between 1983 and 1986.

DIPLOMATENVIERTEL — AREA
Map p294 (Diplomatic Quarter; ⊠M29, 200, ⓈPotsdamer Platz, ⓤPotsdamer Platz) In the 1920s, a quiet villa-studded colony south of the Tiergarten evolved into Berlin's embassy quarter. After WWII the obliterated area remained in a state of quiet decay while the embassies all set up in the West German capital of Bonn. After reunification, many countries rebuilt on their historic lots, accounting for some of Berlin's boldest new architecture, which can be nicely explored on a leisurely wander.

 **EATING**

The best restaurants on Potsdamer Platz are in the hotels. For a quick nibble, head to the food courts on the lower floor of the Potsdamer Platz Arkaden (p128) mall and the 2nd floor of the LP12 Mall of Berlin (p128). The beer gardens tucked within Tiergarten park also serve food and are destinations in their own right.

JOSEPH-ROTH-DIELE — GERMAN €
Map p294 (☎030-2636 9884; www.joseph-roth-diele.de; Potsdamer Strasse 75; dishes €4-12; ⊗10am-midnight Mon-Fri; ⓤKurfürstenstrasse) Named for an Austrian Jewish writer, this wood-panelled salon time-warps you back to the 1920s, when Roth used to live next door. Walls decorated with bookshelves and quotations from his works draw a literary,

chatty crowd, especially at lunchtime when two daily changing €5 specials supplement the hearty menu of German classics.

WEILANDS WELLFOOD — INTERNATIONAL €
Map p294 (☎030-2589 9717; www.weilands-wellfood.de; Marlene-Dietrich-Platz 1; mains €5-10; ⊗10am-8pm Mon-Fri, noon-8pm Sat & Sun; ⓢ⏸; ⊠200, ⓈPotsdamer Platz, ⓤPotsdamer Platz) The wholewheat pastas, vitamin-packed salads and fragrant wok dishes at this jazzy self-service bistro are perfect for health- and waist-watchers but don't sacrifice a thing to the taste gods. Sit outside by the little pond, ideally outside of the office lunch rush.

QIU — INTERNATIONAL €€
Map p294 (☎030-590 051 230; www.qiu.de; Potsdamer Strasse 3, Mandala Hotel; 2-course lunches €16; ⊗noon-1am Sun-Wed, to 3am Thu-Sat; ⓟ; ⊠200, ⓈPotsdamer Platz, ⓤPotsdamer Platz) The two-course business lunch (noon to 3pm Monday to Friday) at this stylish bar-lounge at the Mandala Hotel (p222) also includes soup or salad, a nonalcoholic beverage, and coffee or tea. We call that a steal. Typical dishes are organic pork ribs, plaice fillet and wild garlic risotto. It's also a nice spot for coffee or cocktails.

TEEHAUS IM ENGLISCHEN GARTEN — INTERNATIONAL €€
Map p294 (☎030-3948 0400; www.teehaus-tiergarten.com; Altonaer Strasse 2; mains €8-17; ⊗10am-11pm; ⊠100, ⓈBellevue, ⓤHansaplatz)

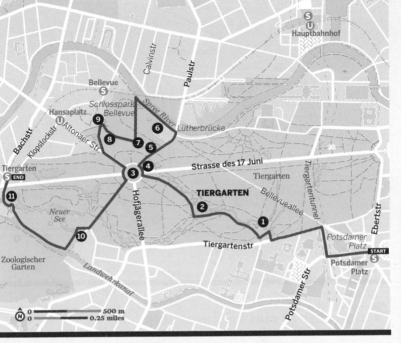

Neighbourhood Walk
A Leisurely Tiergarten Meander

START POTSDAMER PLATZ
END TIERGARTEN S-BAHN STATION
LENGTH 5KM; TWO HOURS

A ramble around Tiergarten delivers a relaxing respite from the sightseeing track. From Potsdamer Platz, make your way to **1 Luiseninsel**, an enchanting gated garden dotted with statues and seasonal flower beds. Not far away is **2 Rousseauinsel**, a memorial to 18th-century French philosopher Jean-Jacques ('Back to Nature') Rousseau. It was modelled after his actual burial site near Paris and placed on a teensy island in a sweet little pond.

At the heart of the park, engulfed by traffic, the imposing **3 Siegessäule** (p123) is crowned by a gilded statue of the goddess Victoria and commemorates Prussian military triumphs enforced by Iron Chancellor Otto von Bismarck. Nearby is the colossal monument **4 Bismarck Denkmal**.

Following Spreeweg north takes you past the oval **5 Bundespräsidialamt**, the offices of the German president, to their residence in **6 Schloss Bellevue** (Spreeweg 1; closed to public), a snowy-white neoclassical royal palace built for the younger brother of Frederick the Great in 1785.

Follow the path along the Spree, then turn left into the **7 Englischer Garten** (English Garden) created in the '50s in commemoration of the 1948 Berlin Airlift. At its heart, overlooking a pretty pond, the thatched-roof **8 Teehaus im Englischen Garten** (p124) hosts free summer concerts in its beer garden. Afterwards, check out the latest art exhibit at the nearby **9 Akademie der Künste** (☎030-200 572 000; Hanseatenweg 10; www.adk.de; building ☺10am-10pm, exhibits vary).

Walk south back through the park, crossing Altonaer Strasse and Strasse des 17 Juni, to arrive at the Neuer See with **10 Café am Neuen See** (p128) at its south end. Stroll north along the Landwehrkanal via the **11 Gaslaternenmuseum**, an open-air collection of 90 historic gas lanterns, and wrap up your tour at Tiergarten S-Bahn station.

Local Life
Saunter Around Schöneberg

Schöneberg flaunts a mellow middle-class identity but has a radical pedigree rooted in the squatter days of the '80s. Stroll from Viktoria-Luise-Platz through Berlin's original gay quarter and along streets lined with boho cafes and indie boutiques to ethnically flavoured Hauptstrasse. The best days to walk this route are Wednesdays or Saturdays when farmers' market sets up below the Church of St Matthew on Winterfeldtplatz square.

❶ Viktoria-Luise-Platz

Soak up the laid-back vibe of Schöneberg's prettiest square, Viktoria-Luise-Platz, a classic baroque-style symphony of flower beds, big old trees, a lusty fountain and benches where locals swap gossip or watch kids at play. The hexagonal square is framed by several inviting cafes and historic town houses whose facades, with their sculpture and ornamentation, invite closer inspection. Those at numbers 7, 12 and 12a are especially noteworthy.

❷ Nollendorfplatz & the 'Gay Village'

In the early 20th century, Nollendorfplatz was a bustling urban square filled with cafes, theatres and people on parade. Then as now, it was also the gateway to Berlin's historic gay quarter, where British writer

Christopher Isherwood penned *Berlin Stories* (the inspiration for *Cabaret*) while living at Nollendorfstrasse 17. Rainbow flags still fly proudly, especially along Motzstrasse and Fuggerstrasse. A memorial plaque at Nollendorfplatz U-Bahn station commemorates Nazi-era LGBT victims.

❸ Chocophile Alert

Winterfeldt Schokoladen (☎030-2362 3256; www.winterfeldt-schokoladen.de; Goltzstrasse 23; ⊙9am-8pm Mon-Fri, 9am-6pm Sat, noon-7pm Sun; ⓊNollendorfplatz) stocks a vast range of international handmade gourmet chocolates, all displayed in the original oak fixtures of a 19th-century pharmacy, which doubles as a cafe. Kosher, raw and gluten-free chocolates are among the more unusual choices.

❹ Boutique Hopping
Goltzstrasse and its extension Akazienstrasse teem with indie boutiques selling everything from vintage clothing to slinky underwear, antique books to handmade jewellery, exotic teas to cooking supplies. No high-street chain in sight! Wedged in between are charismatic cafes, many with pavement terraces.

❺ Double Eye
Local coffee lovers are addicted to the award-winning espresso of **Double Eye** (Akazienstrasse 22; 🕐8.30am-6.30pm Mon-Fri, 9am-6pm Sat; [U]Eisenacher Strasse), which is why no one seems to mind the inevitable out-the-door queue. Prices are fair, and all coffee can be ordered as 'mild' or 'strong'. Since there are few seats, this is more of a grab-and-go cafe, though.

❻ Möve im Felsenkeller
An artist hang-out since the 1920s, woodsy **Möve im Felsenkeller** (☎030-781 3447; Akazienstrasse 2; 🕐4pm-1am Mon-Fri, noon-2am Sat; [U]Eisenacher Strasse) is where Jeffrey Eugenides penned his 2002 bestseller *Middlesex* (upstairs, at the round table in the corner). A stuffed seagull dangling from the ceiling keeps an eye on patrons seeking inspiration from the six beers on tap. Gentrification has threatened the survival of this Old Berlin gem, but so far the owners have been able to stave off closure.

❼ Hauptstrasse
Chic boutiques give way to grocers and doner kebab shops along main artery Hauptstrasse. The Turkish supermarket **Öz-Gida** (☎030-7871 5291; www.ozgida.de; Hauptstrasse 16; 🕐8am-8pm Mon-Sat; [U]Kleistpark) is known citywide for its olive selection, cheese spreads and quality meats. In the '70s, David Bowie and Iggy Pop shared a pad at Hauptstrasse 155.

Not even many Berliners know about this enchanting reed-thatched teahouse tucked into the northwestern corner of Tiergarten park. It's best in summer, when the beer garden overlooking an idyllic pond seats up to 500 people for cold beers and a global roster of simple, tasty dishes.

🍷 DRINKING & NIGHTLIFE

The nicest bars are in the hotels and quite pricey. For a bit more action, head to the places ringing the Sony Center's central plaza. In summer, Tiergarten beckons with its beer gardens. If you need a final nightcap, try the dive bars on Potsdamer Strasse.

STUE BAR BAR

Map p294 (☎030-311 7220; www.das-stue-com; Drakestrasse 1; 🕐noon-1am Sun-Thu, to 2am Fri & Sat; 🚌100, 106, 200) In the Stue hotel (p222), light installations and animal sculptures pave the way to the glam bar where serious mixologists give classic cocktails from the 1920s and '30s a contemporary makeover. Also available: rare whiskys and cognacs and a wine gallery stocked with 400 German, Austrian and Spanish vintages. Live music on Fridays.

FRAGRANCES COCKTAIL BAR

Map p294 (☎030-337 777; www.ritzcarlton.com; Potsdamer Platz 3; 🕐from 7pm Wed-Sat; 📶; 🚌200, [S]Potsdamer Platz, [U]Potsdamer Platz) Berlin cocktail maven Arnd Heissen's newest baby is the world's first 'perfume bar', a libation station where he mixes potable potions mimicking famous scents. The black-mirrored space in the **Ritz-Carlton** (d from €190-435; [P]🚭❄@📶🏊👪) is a like a 3-D menu where adventurous drinkers sniff out their favourite from among a row of perfume bottles, then settle back into flocked couches to enjoy exotic blends served in unusual vessels, including a birdhouse.

SOLAR BAR

Map p294 (☎0163 765 2700; www.solar-berlin.de; Stresemannstrasse 76; 🕐6pm-2am Sun-Thu, to 3am Fri & Sat; [S]Anhalter Bahnhof) Watch the city light up from this 17th-floor glass-walled sky lounge above a posh restaurant (mains €18 to €37). With its dim lighting, soft black leather couches and breathtaking views, it's a great spot for a date or sunset drinks. Getting there aboard an exterior glass lift is half the fun. The entrance is behind the Pit Stop auto shop.

CAFÉ AM NEUEN SEE
BEER GARDEN

(☑030-254 4930; www.cafeamneuensee.de; Lichtensteinallee 2; ⊙restaurant 9am-11pm, beer garden 11am-late Mon-Fri, 10am-late Sat & Sun; ⌨200, ⓤZoologischer Garten, ⓢZoologischer Garten, Tiergarten) Next to an idyllic pond in Tiergarten, this restaurant gets jammed year-round for its sumptuous breakfast and seasonal fare, but it really comes into its own during beer garden season. Enjoy a microvacation over a cold one and a pretzel or pizza, then take your sweetie for a spin in a rowing boat.

KUMPELNEST 3000
BAR

Map p294 (☑030-261 6918; www.kumpelnest3000.com; Lützowstrasse 23; ⊙7pm-5am or later; ⓤKurfürstenstrasse) A former brothel, this trashy bat cave started out as an art project and would be kooky and kitsch enough to feature in a 1940s Shanghai noir thriller. Famous for its wild, debauched all-nighters, it attracts a hugely varied crowd, including the occasional celebrity (Kate Moss, U2, Karl Lagerfeld).

☆ ENTERTAINMENT

BERLINER
PHILHARMONIE
CLASSICAL MUSIC

Map p294 (☑tickets 030-254 888 999; www.berliner-philharmoniker.de; Herbert-von-Karajan-Strasse 1; tickets €30-100; ⌨M29, M48, M85, 200, ⓢPotsdamer Platz, ⓤPotsdamer Platz) This world-famous concert hall has supreme acoustics and, thanks to Hans Scharoun's terraced vineyard configuration, not a bad seat in the house. It's the home turf of the Berliner Philharmoniker, who will be led by Sir Simon Rattle until 2018. One year later, Russia-born Kirill Petrenko will pick up the baton as music director.

Chamber-music concerts take place at the adjacent Kammermusiksaal. From September to June, free lunchtime concerts take place in the foyer of the Philharmonie at 1pm on Tuesdays.

CINESTAR ORIGINAL IM
SONY CENTER
CINEMA

Map p294 (☑030-2606 6400; www.cinestar.de; Potsdamer Strasse 4, Sony Center; tickets €6.50-13.50, 3D glasses €1; ⌨200, ⓢPotsdamer Platz, ⓤPotsdamer Platz) A favourite among English-speaking expats and Germans, this state-of-the-art cinema with nine screens, comfy seats and the top technology shows the latest Hollywood blockbusters in 2D and 3D, all in English, all the time. Buy tickets online to skip the queue.

ARSENAL
CINEMA

Map p294 (☑030-2695 5100; www.arsenal-berlin.de; Potsdamer Strasse 2, Sony Center; tickets €7.50; ⌨200, ⓢPotsdamer Platz, ⓤPotsdamer Platz) The antithesis of popcorn culture, this arty twin-screen cinema features a bold global flick schedule that hopscotches from Japanese satire to Brazilian comedy and German road movies. Many films have English subtitles.

🛍 SHOPPING

Shopping in this district is limited to its two malls.

LP12 MALL OF BERLIN
MALL

Map p294 (www.mallofberlin.de; Leipziger Platz 12; ⊙10am-9pm Mon-Sat; ☎; ⌨200, ⓤPotsdamer Platz, ⓢPotsdamer Platz) This spanking new retail quarter is tailor-made for black-belt mall rats. More than 270 shops vie for your shopping euros, including flagship stores by Karl Lagerfeld, Hugo Boss, Liebeskind, Marc Cain, Muji and other international high-end brands alongside the usual high-street chains like Mango and H&M. Free mobile phone recharge station on the 2nd floor.

POTSDAMER PLATZ ARKADEN
MALL

Map p294 (☑030-255 9270; www.potsdamerplatz.de/potsdamer-platz-arkaden; Alte Potsdamer Strasse 7; ⊙10am-9pm Mon-Sat; ☎🍴; ⓢPotsdamer Platz, ⓤPotsdamer Platz) All your basic shopping cravings will be met at this attractive indoor mall with 130 shops spread over three floors. The basement has supermarkets, a chemist and numerous fast-food outlets. Ice cream fans flock to **Caffe e Gelato** (Map p294; ☑030-2529 7832; www.caffe-e-gelato.de; scoops €1.70; ⊙10am-10.30pm Mon-Thu, to 11pm Fri, to midnight Sat, 10.30am-10pm Sun) on the 1st floor.

Scheunenviertel

HACKESCHER MARKT AREA | HAUPTBAHNHOF & ORANIENBURGER TOR | TORSTRASSE

Neighbourhood Top Five

❶ Sammlung Boros (p133) Glimpsing high drama, abstract mind-benders and glowing colour among the contemporary artworks at this bunker-turned-art museum.

❷ Hackesche Höfe (p135) Exploring fashion boutiques, shops, galleries and cafes in this charismatic courtyard maze.

❸ Clärchens Ballhaus (p138) Strutting your stuff to salsa, tango, ballroom, waltz and swing at this funky retro ballroom.

❹ Neue Synagoge (p132) Admiring the exotic architecture and studying up on the quarter's Jewish history at this local landmark.

❺ Museum für Naturkunde (p134) Sizing yourself up next to giant dinos at Berlin's mini Jurassic Park in the city's Museum of Natural History.

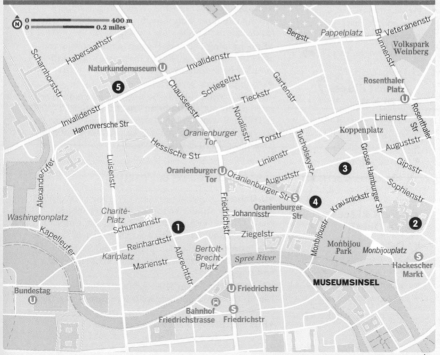

For more detail of this area see Map p302 ➡

Lonely Planet's Top Tip

If you can't make it on to *Dancing with the Stars*, at least you can dance *under* the stars in Berlin. From May to September, riverside Strandbar Mitte (p140) invites you to tango, swing or waltz on a wooden dance floor while the Spree courses past and lights bathe the ornamented facade of the Bode-Museum in a romantic glow. There's no charge, but a €4 donation for the DJ is requested. Check the website for dance lessons and foul-weather cancellations.

Best Jewish History Sites

- Neue Synagoge (p132)
- Museum Blindenwerkstatt Otto Weidt (p141)
- Gedenkstätte Stille Helden (p141)
- Friedhof Grosse Hamburger Strasse (p139)

For reviews, see p132.

Best Places to Eat

- Einsunternull (p138)
- Katz Orange (p138)
- Pauly Saal (p137)
- Chèn Chè (p136)

For reviews, see p136.

Best Places to Drink

- Clärchens Ballhaus (p138)
- Strandbar Mitte (p140)
- Buck and Breck (p140)
- Cordobar (p140)

For reviews, see p138.

Explore: Scheunenviertel

Scheunenviertel packs bunches of charisma into its relatively compact size and is a joy to explore by day and night. Don't expect any blockbuster sights staring you in the face, though: its greatest charms reveal themselves in the labyrinth of quiet lanes fanning out from its main drags, Oranienburger Strasse and Rosenthaler Strasse.

Embark on an aimless wander and you'll constantly stumble upon the unexpected here: an idyllic courtyard or boundary-pushing gallery, a fashion-forward boutique, a fancy wine bar or a glam belle époque ballroom. A distinctive feature of the quarter is its *Höfe* – interlinked courtyards filled with cafes, shops and drinking temples.

Since the 1990s, the Scheunenviertel has also reprised its historic role as Berlin's main Jewish quarter, with the Neue Synagoge as its shining beacon. Gritty Torstrasse, meanwhile, delivers a roll call of trendy restaurants, bars and boutiques that lure a cashed-up creative crowd of locals, expats and visitors.

The area between the Hauptbahnhof and Friedrichstrasse harbours two of Berlin's contemporary arts highlights: the Hamburger Bahnhof and the Sammlung Boros. North of the Hauptbahnhof itself, a new city quarter called Europa-City is slowly getting off the drawing board.

Local Life

- **Shopping** Find out what keeps Berlin designers' sewing machines humming by prowling the backstreets for the shops of fashion-forward local-labels.
- **Bar-hopping** Play it cool when joining hotties and hopefuls for a classy buzz in Torstrasse's doorstaff-guarded booze burrows.
- **Monbijoupark** Set out a picnic, sip a beer in Strandbar Mitte (p140) – Berlin's first beach bar – or catch a play at the **Monbijou Theater** (Map p302; ☎030-288 866 999; www.monbijou-theater.de; Monbijoustrasse 3b; tickets €14-22; ⏰May-Sep; 🚋M1, [S]Oranienburger Strasse, Hackescher Markt) in this riverfront park.

Getting There & Away

- **U-Bahn** Weinmeisterstrasse (U8) is the most central station. Rosenthaler Platz (U8), Rosa-Luxemburg-Platz (U2) and Oranienburger Tor (U6) are closer to Torstrasse and the northern Scheunenviertel.
- **S-Bahn** Hackescher Markt (S5, S7 and S9) and Oranienburger Strasse (S2) stations are both good jumping-off points.
- **Tram** M1 runs from Museumsinsel (Museum Island) to Prenzlauer Berg and stops throughout the Scheunenviertel.
- **Bus** No 142 runs along Torstrasse.

TOP SIGHT
HAMBURGER BAHNHOF

Berlin's contemporary art museum opened in 1996 in the former Hamburger Bahnhof railway station, whose loft and grandeur are the perfect foil for this Aladdin's cave of paintings, sculptures and installations. The museum's inventory spans the entire arc of post-1950 artistic movements from conceptual art and pop art to minimal art, Arte Povera and Fluxus.

Permanent loans from three collectors – Erich Marx, Friedrich Christian Flick and Egidio Marzona – form the core of the collection. Seminal works by such major players as Andy Warhol, Cy Twombly, Anselm Kiefer, Robert Rauschenberg and Bruce Nauman are presented in changing configurations in both the main museum and the adjacent 300m-long **Rieckhallen** (Rieck Halls). The entire ground floor of the main building's west wing is dedicated to the ultimate artistic boundary-pusher, Joseph Beuys. New since November 2015 is the **Neue Galerie**, which presents changing modern art exhibits drawn from the collection of the New National Gallery, which is closed for renovation until at least 2019. High-calibre temporary exhibits also help keep things fluid.

Trains first rolled through the Hamburger Bahnhof in 1874, but after only 32 years the station had become too small and was turned into a traffic museum. After WWII the building stood empty until the late Josef Paul Kleihues was hired in 1989 to create an exhibition space. He kept the elegant exterior, which at night is bathed in the light of a Dan Flavin installation. The interior, though, was gutted and turned into modern minimalist galleries that orbit the central hall with its exposed iron girders.

DON'T MISS

➡ Andy Warhol's *Chairman Mao* (1975)
➡ Anselm Kiefer's *Volkszählung* (Census, 1991)
➡ Joseph Beuys' *The End of the Twentieth Century* (1983)
➡ Robert Rauschenberg's *Pink Door* (1954)

PRACTICALITIES

➡ Map p304, A2
➡ ☏030-266 424 242
➡ www.smb.museum
➡ Invalidenstrasse 50-51
➡ adult/concession €14/7
➡ ⊙10am-6pm Tue, Wed & Fri, 10am-8pm Thu, 11am-6pm Sat & Sun
➡ 🚋M5, M8, M10, Ⓢ Hauptbahnhof, Ⓤ Hauptbahnhof

TOP SIGHT
NEUE SYNAGOGE

The gleaming gold dome of the Neue Synagoge is the most visible symbol of Berlin's revitalised Jewish community. Architect Eduard Knoblauch looked to the Alhambra in Granada for inspiration, which explains the exotic Moorish design elements, including the elaborate facade and the shiny dome. Consecrated on Rosh Hashanah in 1866, the building seated 3200 people, making it Germany's largest synagogue.

During the 1938 Kristallnacht (Night of the Broken Glass) pogroms, local police chief Wilhelm Krützfeld prevented a gang of SA (Sturmabteilung, a militia of the Nazi party) troopers from setting it on fire, an act of civil courage commemorated by a plaque affixed to the main facade. The German Wehrmacht eventually desecrated the synagogue anyway by using it as a warehouse, although it was not destroyed until hit by bombs in 1943. After the war, the ruin lingered until reconstruction began in 1988 on the 50th anniversary of Kristallnacht.

Rededicated in 1995, today's Neue Synagoge is not so much a house of worship (although prayer services do take place), but a museum and place of remembrance called **Centrum Judaicum**. In addition to temporary presentations, a permanent exhibit features architectural fragments and objects recovered from the ruins of the building before its reconstruction. They include a Torah scroll and an eternal lamp, and help tell the history of the building and the people associated with it.

DON'T MISS

➜ The facade
➜ The dome
➜ Torah scroll

PRACTICALITIES

➜ Map p302, B4
➜ ☑030-8802 8300
➜ www.centrum judaicum.de
➜ Oranienburger Strasse 28-30
➜ adult/concession €5/4
➜ ⏰10am-6pm Mon-Fri, to 7pm Sun, closes 3pm Fri & 6pm Sun Oct-Mar
➜ ⓜM1, ⓤOranienburger Tor, ⓢOranienburger Strasse

SIGHTS

Art, architecture and Jewish history characterise this charming quarter. Start your explorations at the Hackesche Höfe courtyard ensemble, then meander the narrow lanes, perhaps with a focus on Grosse Hamburger Strasse, Auguststrasse and Alte Schönhauser Strasse. For contemporary art, head west of Friedrichstrasse to the Hamburger Bahnhof and Sammlung Boros.

Hackescher Markt Area

NEUE SYNAGOGE — SYNAGOGUE

See p132.

HECKMANN HÖFE — HISTORIC SITE

Map p302 (Oranienburger Strasse 32; ⏲24hr; 🚋M1, [S]Oranienburger Strasse) [FREE] For a retreat from the urban frenzy, skip on over to this idyllic courtyard complex linking Oranienburger Strasse with Auguststrasse. A sweet treat is Bonbonmacherei (p143), an old-fashioned candy kitchen and shop.

JÜDISCHE MÄDCHENSCHULE — HISTORIC BUILDING

Map p302 (www.maedchenschule.org; Auguststrasse 11-13; ⏲hours vary; 🚋M1, [S]Oranienburger Strasse, [U]Oranienburger Tor) [FREE] This 1920s former Jewish girls' school reopened in 2012 as a cultural and culinary centre in a sensitively restored New Objectivity structure by Alexander Beer, who died at Theresienstadt concentration camp. Two galleries – **Michael Fuchs** and **Grüntuch Ernst Lab** – and the Museum the Kennedys have set up shop in the former classrooms, while the ground floor has the Jewish deli Mogg (p137) and the Michelin-starred Pauly Saal (p137).

MUSEUM THE KENNEDYS — MUSEUM

Map p302 (☎030-2065 3570; www.thekennedys.de; Auguststrasse 11-13; adult/concession €5/2.50; ⏲10am-6pm Tue-Fri, 11am-6pm Sat & Sun; 🚋M1, [S]Oranienburger Strasse, [U]Oranienburger Tor) US president John F Kennedy has held a special place in German hearts since his defiant *'Ich bin ein Berliner!'* solidarity speech in 1963. This private exhibit addresses the president's continued mystique as well as such topics as the Berlin visit and his assassination in Dallas through photographs, documents, video footage and memorabilia.

BUNKER ART

The Nazi-era bunker **Sammlung Boros** (Boros Collection; Map p304; ☎030-2759 4065; www.sammlung-boros.de; Reinhardtstrasse 20; adult/concession €12/6; ⏲tours 3-6.30pm Thu, 10am-6.30pm Fri-Sun; 🚋M1, [S]Friedrichstrasse, [U]Oranienburger Tor, Friedrichstrasse) shelters one of Berlin's finest private contemporary art collections. Advertising guru Christian Boros acquired the behemoth in 2003 and converted it into a shining beacon of art. Book online (weeks, if not months, ahead!) to join a guided tour (also in English) of works by such hotshots as Wolfgang Tillmans, Olafur Eliasson and Ai Weiwei, and to pick up fascinating nuggets about the building's past incarnations.

Exhibits are drawn from all media – sculpture to painting, video to photography, installations to drawing – with many of them site-specific. The exhibition kicks off with Boros' favourite (and Berlin resident) Olafur Eliasson, whose brass-and-mirror *Orientation Star* is cleverly juxtaposed with *Colour Experiment No 10*. A major eye-catcher is Ai Weiwei's 6m-tall *Tree*, whose installation required cutting out ceilings and walls. Boros is also big on championing new artists, which is why not-yet-household names like Alicja Kwade, Klara Lidén, Thea Djordjadze, Michael Sailstorfer and Danh Vo are also featured quite prominently.

During the tour you'll be peppered with historical details of the war-scarred shelter with its preserved original fittings, pipes, steel doors and vents. Built for 2000 people, its dank rooms crammed in twice as many during the heaviest air raids towards the end of WWII. After the shooting stopped, the Soviets briefly used it as a POW prison before it assumed a more benign role as a fruit and vegetable storeroom in East Berlin, a phase that spawned the nickname 'Banana Bunker'. In the 1990s, the claustrophobic warren saw some of Berlin's naughtiest techno raves and fetish parties.

TOP SIGHT
MUSEUM FÜR NATURKUNDE

Fossils and minerals don't quicken your pulse? Well, how about Tristan, one of the best-preserved *Tyrannosaurus rex* skeletons in the world? Or Oskar, the 12m-high *Brachiosaurus branchai*, the Guinness Book–certified world's largest mounted dino? At Berlin's Museum of Natural History, the two Jurassic superstars are joined by a dozen other extinct buddies, including the ferocious allosaurus and a spiny-backed kentrosaurus, all of them about 150 million-year-old migrants from Tanzania. Clever 'Juraskopes' bring some of them back to virtual flesh-and-bone life.

Beyond the dinosaurs you can journey deep into space or clear up such age-old mysteries as why zebras are striped and why peacocks have such beautiful feathers. Surprises include massively magnified insect models – wait until you see the mind-boggling anatomy of an ordinary house fly! A spooky highlight is the wet collection: one million ethanol-preserved animals floating in 276,000 glass jars displayed in a huge glowing glass cube in its own darkened hall.

A crowd favourite among the taxidermic animals is Knut, the polar bear whose birth at the Berlin Zoo in 2006 caused global 'Knutmania'. The cuddly giant died unexpectedly in 2011.

DON'T MISS
→ Tristan the *T rex*
→ Oskar the *Brachiosaurus*
→ Archaeopteryx

PRACTICALITIES
→ Museum of Natural History
→ Map p304, B1
→ ☑030-2093 8591
→ www.naturkunde museum.berlin
→ Invalidenstrasse 43
→ adult/concession incl audioguide €8/5
→ ☺9.30am-6pm Tue-Fri, 10am-6pm Sat & Sun
→ ☒M5, M8, M10, 12, ⓊNaturkundemuseum

KW INSTITUTE FOR CONTEMPORARY ART   GALLERY
Map p302 (☑030-243 4590; www.kw-berlin.de; Auguststrasse 69; adult/concession €6/4; ☺noon-7pm Wed-Mon, to 9pm Thu; ☒M1, ⓈOranienburger Strasse, ⓊOranienburger Tor) In an old margarine factory, nonprofit KW helped ensure the fate of the Scheunenviertel as Berlin's original post-Wall art district. It continues to stage groundbreaking exhibits reflecting the latest – and often radical – trends in contemporary art. Reduced admission (€4) Thursday after 6pm with free tour at 6pm.

ME COLLECTORS ROOM   GALLERY
Map p302 (☑030-8600 8510; www.me-berlin. com; Auguststrasse 68; adult/concession/under 18 €7/4/free; ☺noon-6pm Tue-Sun; ☎; ☒M1, ⓈOranienburger Strasse) Created by private collector Thomas Olbricht, this modern space showcases not only his own art collection from the 16th century to today, but also serves as a platform for other collectors to present their works in themed group shows. The only permanent feature is the *Wunderkammer,* a global 'cabinet of curiosities' that includes rare postage stamps, art-nouveau objects and toys.

SAMMLUNG HOFFMANN   GALLERY
Map p302 (☑030-2849 9120; www.sammlung -hoffmann.de; Sophienstrasse 21; tours €10; ☺11am-4pm Sat Sep-Jul; ⓊWeinmeisterstrasse) Blink and you'll miss the doorway leading to the Sophie-Gips-Höfe, a trio of courtyards linking Sophienstrasse and Gipsstrasse. The former sewing-machine factory now harbours shops, offices and flats as well as this stellar contemporary art collection in a private home, which is open for guided 90-minute tours every Saturday. Book several days ahead.

RAMONES MUSEUM   MUSEUM
Map p302 (☑030-7552 8889; www.ramones museum.com; Krausnickstrasse 23; €4.50; ☺10am-10pm; ☎; ☒M1, ⓈOranienburger Strasse) They sang 'Born to Die in Berlin', but the legacy of punk pioneers the Ramones is kept very much alive in the German capital, thanks to this eclectic collection of memorabilia. Look for Marky Ramone's drumsticks and Johnny Ramone's jeans amid signed album covers, posters, flyers, photographs and other flotsam and jetsam. The on-site cafe also hosts the occasional concert.

TOP SIGHT
HACKESCHE HÖFE

The Hackesche Höfe is the largest and most famous of the courtyard ensembles peppered throughout the Scheunenviertel. Built in 1907 it lingered through the city's division before being put through a total makeover in the mid-1990s. In 1996 the eight interlinked courtyards reopened to great fanfare with a congenial mix of cafes, galleries, indie boutiques and entertainment venues.

The main entrance off Rosenthaler Strasse leads to **Court I**, prettily festooned with ceramic tiles by art-nouveau architect August Endell. One of Berlin's best cabarets, the **Chamäleon Varieté** (p142), is located here in a historic art-nouveau ballroom. It presents a fun and innovative mix of acrobatics, music, dance and comedy – no German skills required! Cinephiles flock upstairs to the **Hackesche Höfe Kino** (Map p302; ☑030-283 4603; www.hoefekino.de; tickets €7.50-9), an art-house cinema in the same building.

Shoppers can look forward to galleries and the flagship shops of Berlin designers. If you're a fan of the little characters on Berlin traffic lights, stock up on souvenirs at **Ampelmann Berlin** (p144) in Court V. Court VII leads off to the **Rosenhöfe**, a frilly art nouveau–inspired courtyard with a sunken rose garden.

DON'T MISS

➡ Endell's art-nouveau facade in Court I
➡ Berlin designer boutiques

PRACTICALITIES

➡ Map p302, C4
➡ ☑030-2809 8010
➡ www.hackesche-hoefe.com
➡ enter from Rosenthaler Strasse 40/41 or Sophienstrasse 6
➡ admission free
➡ ⓂM1, ⓈHackescher Markt, ⓊWeinmeisterstrasse

MONSTERKABINETT GALLERY
Map p302 (☑0152 1259 8687; www.monster kabinett.de; Rosenthaler Strasse 39, 2nd courtyard; tours adult/concession €8/5; ⊙tours 6-10pm Thu, 4-10pm Fri & Sat; ⓂM1, ⓈHackescher Markt) If you want to meet 'Püppi' the techno-loving go-go dancer or 'Orangina' the twirling six-legged doll, you need to descend a steep spiral staircase into Hannes Heiner's surrealist underground world. Inspired by his dreams, the artist has fashioned a menagerie of mechanical robot-monsters and assembled them in a computer-controlled art and sound installation that will entertain, astound and perhaps even frighten you just a little bit.

⊙ Hauptbahnhof & Oranienburger Tor

HAMBURGER BAHNHOF – MUSEUM FÜR GEGENWART MUSEUM
See p131.

BERLINER MEDIZINHISTORISCHES MUSEUM MUSEUM
Map p304 (Berlin Museum of Medical History; ☑030-450 536 156; www.bmm-charite.

de; Charitéplatz 1; adult/concession €7/3.50; ⊙10am-5pm Tue, Thu, Fri & Sun, to 7pm Wed & Sat; ⓈHauptbahnhof, ⓊHauptbahnhof) This Charité Hospital–run museum chronicles 300 years of medical history in an anatomical theatre, a pathologist's dissection room, a laboratory and a historical patients' ward. The heart of the exhibit, though, is a grisly specimen hall whose 750 pathological-anatomical wet and dry preparations are essentially a 3D medical textbook on human disease and deformity.

DOROTHEENSTÄDTISCHER FRIEDHOF CEMETERY
Map p304 (Chausseestrasse 126; ⊙8am-dusk, closes 8pm May-Aug; ⓊOranienburger Tor, Naturkundemuseum) FREE This compact 18th-century cemetery is the place of perpetual slumber for a veritable roll call of famous Germans, many of them buried beneath artistic tombstones. Karl Friedrich Schinkel, in fact, designed his own. Brecht, who lived next door, chose to be buried here, allegedly to be close to his idols, the philosophers Hegel and Fichte. A map by the entrance shows grave locations.

🍴 EATING

The Scheunenviertel packs in so much culinary variety you could eat your way around the world in a day. Practically all tastes, budgets and food neuroses are catered for in eateries ranging from comfy neighbourhood joints to big-city dining shrines, health-nut havens to ho-hum tourist joints, and a growing number of Michelin-starred establishments.

🍴 Hackescher Markt Area

HUMMUS & FRIENDS ISRAELI €

Map p302 (☎030-5547 1454; www.hummus-and-friends.com; Oranienburger Strasse 27; mains €7.50-8.50; 🕒9.30am-midnight; 🚊M1, [S]Oranienburger Strasse) 'Make Hummus, Not Walls' is the motto at this vegan and kosher kitchen next to the Neue Synagoge (p132). The eponymous chickpea dip, whipped up with special beans from Galilee, is naturally the menu star. Also try the paper-wrapped oven-roasted cauliflower with creamy tahini.

HOUSE OF SMALL WONDER INTERNATIONAL €

Map p304 (☎030-2758 2877; www.houseofsmallwonder.de; Johannisstrasse 20; dishes €4-11; 🕒9am-5pm; 📶; [U]Oranienburger Tor, [S]Oranienburger Strasse, Friedrichstrasse) A wrought-iron staircase spirals up to this whimsical brunch and lunch cafe where plants are potted in birdcages and the ceiling is made of opaque glass panels. The menu features comfort food inspired by American, Japanese and European tastes and includes sandwiches (top choice: avocado and goat's cheese), home-baked goods and such eccentric mains as Okinawan Taco Rice.

BARCOMI'S DELI CAFE €

Map p302 (☎030-2859 8363; www.barcomis.de; Sophienstrasse 21, Sophie-Gips-Höfe, 2nd courtyard; dishes €2.60-12; 🕒9am-9pm Mon-Sat, 10am-9pm Sun; 📶; [U]Weinmeisterstrasse) Join latte-rati, families and expats at this New York–meets-Berlin deli for custom-roasted coffee, wraps, bagels with smoked salmon, creative sandwiches and possibly the best brownies and cheesecake this side of the Hudson River.

★CHÈN CHÈ VIETNAMESE €€

Map p302 (☎030-2888 4282; www.chenche-berlin.de; Rosenthaler Strasse 13; dishes €6.50-11; 🕒noon-midnight; 🌱; 🚊M1, [U]Rosenthaler Platz) In this exotic Vietnamese tea room you can settle down in the charming Zen garden or beneath the hexagonal chandelier made from the torn pages of a herbal medicine book. The compact menu features healthy and meticulously presented *pho* (soups), curries and noodle dishes served in traditional clay pots. Exquisite tea selection and small shop.

MURET LA BARBA ITALIAN €€

Map p302 (☎030-2809 7212; www.muretlabarba.de; Rosenthaler Strasse 61; mains €12.50-25; 🕒10am-midnight Mon-Fri, noon-midnight Sat & Sun; 🚊M1, [U]Rosenthaler Platz) This wine shop–bar-restaurant combo oozes the kind of rustic authenticity that instantly transports cognoscenti to Italy. The food is hearty, inventive and made with top ingredients imported from the motherland. All wine is available by the glass or by the bottle (corkage fee €10).

CECCONI'S ITALIAN €€

Map p302 (☎030-405 044 680; www.cecconisberlin.com; Torstrasse 1; mains €12-30; 🕒11.30am-midnight Sun-Thu, to 1am Fri & Sat; 📶; 🚊M2, M4, M5, M6, M8, [U]Rosa-Luxemburg-Platz) Open to all despite being set within the members-only Soho House, Cecconi's oozes metropolitan flair with red leather, marble floors, an open kitchen and a suitably sophisticated clientele. Aside from pasta, pizza and risotto dishes – some pimped up with lobster and truffle – the menu also checks the superfoods box with its quinoa and chia salads, while also featuring carnivore-pleasing grilled meats.

STORE KITCHEN INTERNATIONAL €€

Map p302 (☎030-405 044 550; www.thestores.com; Torstrasse 1; dishes €5-12; 🕒10am-7pm Mon-Wed, to late Thu-Sat; 📶; [U]Rosa-Luxemburg-Platz) This is the kind of impossibly trendy yet welcoming place that had food fanciers in a headlock the moment it opened inside hipper-than-thou lifestyle and fashion temple the Store, on the ground floor of the members club Soho House (but it's open to all). Head here if you crave salads, sandwiches and light meals that capture the latest global food trends while using local suppliers.

SCHWARZWALDSTUBEN GERMAN €€

Map p302 (☎030-2809 8084; www.schwarzwaldstuben-berlin.com; Tucholskystrasse 48; mains €7-16; 🕒9am-midnight; 🚊M1, [S]Oranienburger Strasse) In the mood for a Hansel and Gretel moment? Then join the other 'lost kids' for satisfying slow food from the southwest German regions of Baden and Swabia. Tuck

ROSENTHALER PLATZ: SNACK CENTRAL

For feeding hunger pangs on the quick and cheap, choices could not be greater than in the area around Rosenthaler Platz. Here's our personal hit list:

Côcô (Map p302; ☑030-5547 5188; www.co-co.net; Rosenthaler Strasse 2; sandwiches €5.50-6.50; ⊙11am-10pm Mon-Thu, to 11pm Fri & Sat, noon-10pm Sun; ☎; 🚇M1, ⓊRosenthaler Platz) This hip little joint sells banh mi - Vietnamese sandwiches with marinated meats, pâtes, spicy sauces and fresh herbs in a toasted baguette.

Rosenburger (Map p302; ☑030-2408 3037; Brunnenstrasse 196; burgers €3.50-7; ⊙11am-3am Sun-Thu, to 5am Fri & Sat; 🚇M1, 12, ⓊRosenthaler Platz) This burger joint is especially busy from the early evening onwards. Organic meat costs a bit more.

Rosenthaler Grill und Schlemmerbuffet (Map p302; ☑030-283 2153; Torstrasse 125; dishes €2.80-7; ⊙24hr; 🚇M1, 12, ⓊRosenthaler Platz) Excellent doner joint with outdoor seating and nonstop service.

into gut-filling platters of *spaetzle* (mac 'n' cheese), *Maultaschen* (ravioli-like pasta), giant schnitzel or a daily special. Dine amid rustic and tongue-in-cheek forest decor or grab a table on the pavement.

DISTRICT MÔT
VIETNAMESE €€

Map p302 (☑030-2008 9284; www.district mot.com; Rosenthaler Strasse 62; dishes €8-19; ⊙noon-1am Sun-Thu, to 2am Fri & Sat; ☎; 🚇M1, ⓊRosenthaler Platz) At this colourful mock-Saigon street-food parlour, patrons squat on tiny plastic stools around wooden tables where rolls of toilet paper irreverently stand in for paper napkins. The small-plate menu mixes the familiar (steamy *pho* noodle soup, papaya salad) with the adventurous (stewed eel, deep-fried silk worms). The tabletop seafood or meat barbecue is a special treat.

MOGG
DELI €€

Map p302 (☑0176 6496 1344; www.moggmogg. com; Auguststrasse 11-13; mains €7-14.50; ⊙11am-10pm Mon-Fri, 10am-10pm Sat & Sun; ☎; 🚇M1, ⓈOranienburger Strasse) At Berlin's first New York–style Jewish deli, home-cured and smoked pastrami on rye feeds tummy and soul in an arty 1930s-inspired setting with purple-topped benches and Finnish designer chairs. The menu also features other staples such as matzo ball soup, *shakshuka* and a killer cheesecake, alongside nontraditional deli picks like bruléed chicken liver and salmon with shaved fennel.

TADSHIKISCHE TEESTUBE
RUSSIAN €€

Map p302 (☑030-204 1112; www.tadshikische -teestube.de; Oranienburger Strasse 27, KunstHof; mains €7-12; ⊙4-11pm Mon-Fri, noon-midnight Sat & Sun; 🚇M1, ⓈOranienburger Strasse) Treat yourself to a Russian tea ceremony complete with silvery samovar, biscuits and vodka, or tuck into hearty Russian blini (pancakes) or *vareniki* (dumplings) while reclining amid plump pillows, hand-carved sandalwood pillars and heroic murals in this original Tajik tea room. The authentic space was gifted by the Soviets to the East German government in 1974.

KOPPS
VEGAN €€

Map p302 (☑030-4320 9775; www.kopps-berlin. de; Linienstrasse 94; dinner mains €16-19, brunch €13.50; ⊙6pm-midnight daily, 9.30am-4pm Sat & Sun; ☎; 🚇M1, ⓊRosenthaler Platz) 'German vegan' has not been an oxymoron since Kopps opened as Berlin's first high-end, animal-product-free restaurant. Locals love the early bird dinner (€19 for three courses, no reservations) from 6pm to 7.30pm and the weekend brunch buffet. The space is sparse but stylish, with bluish-grey walls, recycled doors and mirrors in unexpected places.

★PAULY SAAL
GERMAN €€€

Map p302 (☑030-3300 6070; www.paulysaal. com; Auguststrasse 11-13; 2-/3-/4-course lunches €36/46/56, 4-/7-course dinners €76/97; ⊙noon-2pm & 6-9.30pm Tue-Sat, bar to 2.30am; 🚇M1, ⓈOranienburger Strasse, ⓊOranienburger Tor) Since taking the helm at this Michelin-starred outpost, Arne Anker has given the cuisine a youthful and lighter edge while still following the seasonal-regional credo. Only multicourse menus are served, even at lunch. Nothing has changed about the stunning venue: the edgy-art-decorated gym of a former Jewish girls' school (p133) in a Bauhaus building. On balmy days, sit beneath the old schoolyard's leafy trees.

ZENKICHI　　　　JAPANESE €€€

Map p304 (☑030-2463 0810; www.zenkichi.de; Johannisstrasse 20; tasting menus €45-65, small plates €6-29; ⊗6pm-midnight; ☑; ⓤOranienburger Tor, Friedrichstrasse, ⓢFriedrichstrasse) Tokyo meets Berlin via Brooklyn at this lantern-lit basement izakaya, which serves faithful gourmet Japanese fare and supreme sake in cosy booths shielded by wooden bamboo blinds for extra privacy. Opt for the seasonally changing eight-course *omakase* (chef's) menu or compose your own culinary symphony from the small-plate à la carte menu. Superb sake selection, too.

✖ Hauptbahnhof & Oranienburger Tor

REINSTOFF　　　INTERNATIONAL €€€

Map p304 (☑030-3088 1214; www.reinstoff. eu; Schlegelstrasse 26c; 5-course menus €110, additional courses €22; ⊗7pm-late Tue-Sat; ⓤNaturkundemuseum, ⓢNordbahnhof) With two Michelin stars to his name, Daniel Achilles creates poetry on a plate and pairs it punctiliously with wines from Germany and Spain. Clear lines and a glass bubble canopy give the space, in a former lamp factory, an elegant, unhurried ambience.

GRILL ROYAL　　　STEAK €€€

Map p304 (☑030-2887 9288; www.grillroyal.com; Friedrichstrasse 105b; steaks €27-120; ⊗6pm-late; ☎; ⓢFriedrichstrasse, ⓤFriedrichstrasse) With its airy dining room, original look-at-me art, polyglot staff and open kitchen, Grill Royal ticks all the boxes of a chic metropolitan restaurant. A platinum card is a handy accessory if you want to slurp your oysters and tuck into aged prime steaks in the company of A-listers, power politicians, pouty models and 'trust-afarians'.

✖ Torsstrasse

★EINSUNTERNULL　　INTERNATIONAL €€€

Map p304 (☑030-2757 7810; www.einsunternull. com; Hannoversche Strasse 1; 3-/4-/5-course lunch menus €29/37/45, 6-course dinner menus €77, additional courses €10; ⊗noon-2pm Tue-Sat, 7-11pm Mon-Sat; ⓜM1, ⓤOranienburger Tor) The name means 'one below zero' but the food at Einsunternull is actually happening hot. Adventurous palates get to embark on a regional-seasonal journey that combines time-tested techniques like fermentation with next-gen flavour blends like carrot, anise and walnut.

★KATZ ORANGE　　INTERNATIONAL €€€

Map p302 (☑030-983 208 430; www.katz orange.com; Bergstrasse 22; mains €18-29; ⊗6-11pm; ⓜM8, ⓤRosenthaler Platz) ✔ With its gourmet, organic farm-to-table menu, stylish country flair and top-notch cocktails, the 'Orange Cat' hits a gastro grand slam. It will have you purring for such perennial faves as Duroc pork that's been slow-roasted for 12 hours (nicknamed 'candy on bone'). The setting in a castle-like former brewery is stunning, especially in summer when the patio opens.

★WEINBAR RUTZ　　GERMAN €€€

Map p304 (☑030-2462 8760; www.rutz -restaurant.de; Chausseestrasse 8; mains €16-25; ⊗4-11pm Tue-Sat, food from 6.30pm; ⓤOranienburger Tor) Below his high-concept gourmet temple, Michelin-starred Marco Müller operates this fairly casual wine bar where the menu has a distinctly earthy and carnivorous bent. Many of the meats and sausages are sourced from Berlin and surrounds and come in two sizes. Great selection of wines by the glass.

🍷 DRINKING & NIGHTLIFE

This area has plenty of bars to match the demands of its creative, international and well-heeled residents and visitors. Torsstrasse is an especially fertile hunting ground, but there are also some cute wine bars, gay haunts and offbeat watering holes tucked into the quiet side lanes.

🍷 Hackescher Markt Area

★CLÄRCHENS BALLHAUS　　CLUB

Map p302 (☑030-282 9295; www.ballhaus.de; Auguststrasse 24; ⊗11am-late; ⓜM1, ⓢOranienburger Strasse) Yesteryear is right now at this late, great 19th-century dance hall where groovers and grannies hoof it across the parquet without even a touch of irony. There are different sounds nightly – salsa to swing, tango to disco – and a live band on Saturday. Dancing kicks off from 9pm

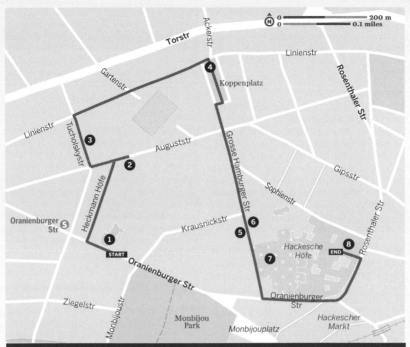

🏃 Neighbourhood Walk
Traces of Jewish Life in the Scheunenviertel

START NEUE SYNAGOGE
END HAUS SCHWARZENBERG
LENGTH 1.5KM; ONE TO THREE HOURS

This easy walk takes you past vestiges, memorials and revitalised sites of Jewish life throughout the Scheunenviertel. It starts at the rebuilt ❶**Neue Synagoge** (p132), inaugurated in 1866 as Germany's largest Jewish house of worship and now a museum and community centre. Take the Heckmann Höfe to Auguststrasse and turn right to find yourself at the ❷**Jüdische Mädchenschule** (p133), a Bauhaus-style Jewish girls' school turned gallery and restaurant space.

Double back on Auguststrasse, then turn right on Tucholskystrasse, perhaps stopping for a bite at the kosher ❸**Beth Cafe** at No 40. Turn right on Linienstrasse and continue to Koppenplatz with Karl Biedermann's art installation ❹**Der Verlassene Raum** (The Deserted Room). Follow Grosse Hamburger Strasse and note the facades still scarred by bullet and shrapnel holes along the walkway leading to the Sophienkirche. A bit further on, look on your right for the ❺**Missing House**, Christian Boltanski's 1990 memorial installation on the site of a bombed-out apartment building. The structure opposite, at No 27, was a ❻**Jewish Boys' School** founded in 1788. The Nazis turned it and the adjacent Jewish seniors' home into a deportation centre in 1942. The home was destroyed in a bombing raid shortly before the war ended, but the school building survived.

A few steps south, the ❼**Friedhof Grosse Hamburger Strasse** was Berlin's first Jewish cemetery. Some 2700 people were buried here between 1672 and 1827, including Enlightenment philosopher Moses Mendelssohn. Outside the cemetery is a memorial stone to the deported Jews as well as a haunting sculpture group by Will Lammert showing 13 fatigued women.

The tour concludes at street-art decorated ❽**Haus Schwarzenberg** (p141), which harbours three small museums dealing with the fate of Jews under the Nazis.

or 9.30pm. Easy door but often packed, so book a table.

Pizza and German staples provide sustenance all day long (in summer in the pretty garden; pizza €5.50 to €12, mains €6.50 to €18).

★ STRANDBAR MITTE   BAR
Map p302 (📞030-2838 5588; www.strandbar-mitte.de; Monbijoustrasse 3; dancing €4; ⊙10am-late May-Sep; 🚇M1, ⓢOranienburger Strasse) With a full-on view of the Bode-Museum, palm trees and a relaxed ambience, Germany's first beach bar (since 2002) is great for balancing a surfeit of sightseeing stimulus with a reviving drink and thin-crust pizza. At night, there's dancing under the stars with tango, cha-cha, swing and salsa, often preceded by dance lessons.

★ BUCK AND BRECK   COCKTAIL BAR
Map p302 (www.buckandbreck.com; Brunnenstrasse 177; ⊙7pm-late; 🚇M1, ⓤRosenthaler Platz) Liquid maestro Gonçalo de Sousa Monteiro and his team treat grown-up patrons to libational flights of fancy in their clandestine cocktail salon with classic yet friendly flair. Historical concoctions are a strength, including the eponymous bubbly-based cocktail Buck and Breck, named for mid-19th-century US president James Buchanan and his VP John Breckinridge.

★ CORDOBAR   WINE BAR
Map p302 (📞030-2758 1215; www.cordobar.net; Grosse Hamburger Strasse 32; ⊙6pm-2am Tue-Sat; 🚇M1, ⓢHackescher Markt, Oranienburger

STUMBLING UPON HISTORY

If you lower your gaze, you'll see them all over town but nowhere are they more concentrated than in the Scheunenviertel: small brass paving stones in front of house entrances. Called *Stolpersteine* (stumbling blocks), they are part of a nationwide project by Berlin-born artist Gunter Demnig and are essentially mini-memorials honouring the people (usually Jews) who lived in the respective house before being killed by the Nazis. The engravings indicate the person's name, birth year, year of deportation, the name of the concentration camp where they were taken and the date they perished.

Strasse) At this joint effort of a music producer, a movie director and two sommeliers, characterful German and Austrian vintages dominate the well-curated wines-by-the-glass list, which is kept in a frequent state of flux. The selection of satisfyingly experimental small plates (€2 to €19) accounts for one of the finest bar menus in town.

COVEN   BAR
Map p302 (📞030-8961 8932; www.thecovenberlin.com; Kleine Präsidentenstrasse 3; ⊙8pm-2am Sun & Tue-Thu, to 3am Fri & Sat; 🚇; 🚇M1, M4, M5, ⓢHackescher Markt) Steel frames, industrial lamps, hard edges – this particular 'witch's lair' has a decidedly stylish, masculine look and feel. Strong and creative drinks, some made with homemade liqueurs and garden-fresh ingredients, make seasoned imbibers of all stripes and persuasions happy.

AUFSTURZ   PUB
Map p302 (📞030-2804 7407; www.aufsturz.de; Oranienburger Strasse 67; ⊙noon-late; 🚇; 🚇M1, M5, ⓤOranienburger Tor, ⓢOranienburger Strasse) Mingle in the warm glow of this unpretentious pub with global DNA, serving some 100 beers on tap and in the bottle alongside a line-up of belly-filling pub grub. The basement club hosts concerts and other cultural events.

ESCHSCHLORAQUE RÜMSCHRÜMP   BAR
Map p302 (www.eschschloraque.de; Rosenthaler Strasse 39; ⊙from 2pm; 🚇M1, ⓢHackescher Markt) A project by the artists' collective Dead Chicken, this subculture survivor is filled with metal monster sculptures and hosts hand-picked experimental concerts, parties and performance art – from Dada burlesque to Balkan postpunk concerts.

🍸 Hauptbahnhof & Oranienburger Tor

MELODY NELSON   BAR
Map p304 (Novalisstrasse 2; ⊙7pm-2am Mon-Thu, to 4am Fri & Sat; 🚇M1, M5, ⓤOranienburger Tor) Everything about this bar speaks of refinement, but without an iota of stuffiness: the dim lighting, the plush seating, the carpeted floors and the luxe cocktails. It helps that sexy siren Jane Birkin is winking at you from behind the bar. Decide whether to go for a 'classic' or a 'new face', or just order a Black Mojito, the can't-go-wrong signature drink.

HAUS SCHWARZENBERG

The last holdout in the heavily gentrified area around the Hackescher Markt is **Haus Schwarzenberg** (Map p302; www.haus-schwarzenberg.org; Rosenthaler Strasse 39; ⊙courtyard 24hr; ⊠M1, ⓈHackescher Markt). Run by a nonprofit organisation, it's an unpretentious space where art and creativity are allowed to flourish beyond the mainstream and commerce. Festooned with street art and bizarre metal sculptures, the courtyards lead to studios, offices, an underground 'amusement park', the edgy-arty **Eschschloraque Rümschrümp** (p140) bar, an art-house **cinema** (p142) – outdoors in summer – and a trio of exhibits dealing with Jewish persecution during the Third Reich.

Gedenkstätte Stille Helden ('Silent Heroes' Memorial Exhibit; Map p302; ☑030-2759 6865; www.gedenkstaette-stille-helden.de; Rosenthaler Strasse 39; ⊙10am-8pm; ⊠M1, ⓈHackescher Markt) The 'Silent Heroes' Memorial Exhibit is dedicated to ordinary Germans who found the courage to hide and help their persecuted Jewish neighbours. Interactive media tables provide themed background information, while upstairs multimedia information pillars document the fate of individuals, from the point of view of both the helpers and the persecuted.

Museum Blindenwerkstatt Otto Weidt (Museum Otto Weidt Workshop for the Blind; Map p302; ☑030-2859 9407; www.blindes-vertrauen.de; 1st courtyard, Rosenthaler Strasse 39; ⊙10am-8pm; ⊠M1, ⓈHackescher Markt) Otto Weidt was a broom and brush maker who employed mainly blind and deaf Jews during World War II. He risked his own life trying to save those threatened with deportation and death by providing food, organising false papers, bribing Gestapo officials and even hiding people in the back of his workshop. A highlight is a moving video in which survivors recall Weidt's efforts to save their lives.

Anne Frank Zentrum (Map p302; ☑030-288 865 600; www.annefrank.de; Rosenthaler Strasse 39; adult/concession €5/3; ⊙10am-6pm Tue-Sun; ⊠M1, ⓈHackescher Markt, ⓊWeinmeisterstrasse) This exhibit uses artefacts and photographs to tell the extraordinary story of a girl who needs no introduction. Who hasn't read the diary Anne Frank penned while hiding from the Nazis in Amsterdam? Frank perished from typhus at Bergen-Belsen concentration camp just days before her 16th birthday. An entire room is devoted to her diary and its profound impact on postwar generations.

PIER
PUB

Map p304 (☑030-6026 0714; www.the-pier.de; Invalidenstrasse 30; ⊙7pm-1am; ⓊNaturkundemuseum) Subtitled 'Badeanzüge & Bier' (Swimsuits & Beer), this upscale craft-beer bar was inspired by an 1865 Coney Island beach club serving beer. The Berlin incarnation supplies the thirsty with a deftly curated changing roster of about 15 handmade draught beers plus about 30 bottled varieties. Oyster shots, Dorito pies and other bar bites help stave off brain imbalances.

♀ Torstrasse

LARRY
BAR

Map p304 (www.facebook.com/larryclubberlin; Chausseestrasse 131; ⊙10pm-7am Wed-Sat; ⊠M1, ⓊOranienburger Tor) Larry is a small, keep-it-real place with a crowd and drinks menu to match. Cool retro sounds enliven

the two rooms, each decorated with vintage slot machines and a 1977 pinball machine. Beware of the 'instant margarita'!

SHARLIE CHEEN
BAR

Map p302 (☑030-5552 7425; www.sharliecheen bar.berlin; Brunnenstrasse 196; ⊙6pm-late; ⊠M1, ⓊRosenthaler Platz) Charlie Sheen finds his fictitious alter ego in the classily unpretentious Sharlie Cheen bar. Sharlie's apocryphal story is told in cute anecdotes accompanying the dozen signature cocktails, including an intensely ginger-y Moscow Mule and the playful In Thyme with homemade raspberry-thyme syrup.

KAFFEE BURGER
CLUB

Map p302 (www.kaffeeburger.de; Torstrasse 60; ⊙from 9pm Mon-Thu, from 10pm Fri-Sun; ⓊRosa-Luxemburg-Platz) Nothing to do with either coffee or meat patties, this sweaty cult club with lovingly faded Commie-era

SUNDAY CONCERTS

From roughly September to June, clued-in classical music fans gather at 7pm on Sundays amid the faded elegance of the early-20th-century Spiegelsaal (Mirror Hall) of the **Sonntagskonzerte** (Map p302; ☎030-5268 0256; www.sonntagskonzerte.de; Auguststrasse 24; adult/concession €12/8; ☺Sep-Jun; ⓜM1, ⓢOranienburger Strasse, ⓤOranienburger Tor) for piano concerts, opera recitals, string quartets and other musical offerings. It's upstairs from **Clärchens Ballhaus** (p138) in the heart of the Scheunenviertel. It's possible to make reservations online, but there are no assigned seats.

With its cracked and blinded mirrors, elaborate chandeliers and old-timey wallpaper, the hall recalls the grandeur of past eras when it was the domain of the city's elite, while the common folks hit the planks in the ballroom downstairs.

In July and August performances are free and held outdoors against the glorious backdrop of the Bode-Museum on Museumsinsel (8.30pm, weather permitting).

decor is a fun-for-all concert and party pen. The sound policy swings from indie and electro to klezmer punk without missing a beat. Also has readings and poetry slams.

MEIN HAUS AM SEE
BAR

Map p302 (☎030-2759 0873; www.mein-haus -am-see.club; Brunnenstrasse 197/198; ☺24hr; ☻; ⓜM1, ⓤRosenthaler Platz) This 'House by the Lake' is nowhere near anything liquid, unless you count the massive amount of beverages consumed at its multitasking all-hours cafe-bar, gallery, performance space and club. Plop down onto grandma's sofa or grab a seat on the staircase for stadium-style hipster-watching. Separate smoking room.

☆ ENTERTAINMENT

BABYLON
CINEMA

Map p302 (☎030-242 5969; www.babylonberlin. de; Rosa-Luxemburg-Strasse 30; tickets €7-9; ⓤRosa-Luxemburg-Platz) This top-rated indie screens a smartly curated potpourri of cinematic expression, from new German films and international art-house flicks to themed retrospectives and other stuff you'd never catch at the multiplex. For silent movies, the original theatre organ is put through its paces. Also hosts occasional readings and concerts.

CHAMÄLEON VARIETÉ
CABARET

Map p302 (☎030-400 0590; www.chamaeleon berlin.com; Rosenthaler Strasse 40/41; tickets €29-69; ⓜM1, ⓢHackescher Markt) A marriage of art-nouveau charms and high-tech theatre trappings, this intimate 1920s-style ven-

ue in an old ballroom hosts classy variety shows – comedy, juggling acts and singing – often in sassy, sexy and unconventional fashion.

VOLKSBÜHNE AM ROSA-LUXEMBURG-PLATZ
THEATRE

Map p302 (☎030-2406 5777; www.volksbuehne -berlin.de; Rosa-Luxemburg-Platz; tickets €10-40; ⓤRosa-Luxemburg-Platz) Nonconformist, radical and provocative: since Frank Castorf took over the venerable People's Stage in 1992, performances have not been for the squeamish. In 2017 he will be replaced by Chris Dercon, the Belgian art historian and current director of London's Tate Modern.

KINO CENTRAL
CINEMA

Map p302 (☎030-2859 9973; www.kino-central. de; Rosenthaler Strasse 39; tickets €6-8; ⓜM1, ⓢHackescher Markt) This art-house cinema in the back of Haus Schwarzenberg (p141) screens intelligent international films, usually in the original language with German subtitles. In summer, the screenings move into the courtyard.

FRIEDRICHSTADT-PALAST BERLIN
CABARET

Map p304 (☎030-2326 2326; www.palast. berlin; Friedrichstrasse 107; tickets €17-120; ⓜM1, ⓤOranienburger Tor, ⓢFriedrichstrasse, Oranienburger Strasse) Europe's largest revue theatre is coming up to its centenary and is still famous for glitzy-glam Vegas-style variety shows with leggy showgirls, singing, elaborate costuming, a high-tech stage, mind-boggling special effects and abundant artistry. Productions are innovative, highly professional and don't require German-language skills.

B-FLAT

LIVE MUSIC

Map p302 (☎030-283 3123; www.b-flat-berlin.de; Dircksenstrasse 40; tickets €10-14; ☺8pm-late Sun-Thu, 9pm-late Fri & Sat; 🚇100, 200, Ⓤ Alexanderplatz, Ⓢ Hackescher Markt) Cool cats of all ages come out to this intimate jazz and acoustic music venue, where the audience sits within spitting distance of the performers. Mal Waldron, Randy Brecker and even Mikis Theodorakis have graced its stage. Wednesday's free jam session often brings down the house.

🛍 SHOPPING

Along and around Alte Schönhauser Strasse, Neue Schönhauser Strasse, Münzstrasse, Mulackstrasse and inside the Hackesche Höfe are plenty of options for seekers of the latest Berlin fashions, and label hounds addicted to staying ahead of the fashion curve. Contemporary art galleries line Linienstrasse, Auguststrasse and their side streets.

★ BONBONMACHEREI

FOOD

Map p302 (☎030-4405 5243; www.bonbonmacherei.de; Oranienburger Strasse 32, Heckmann Höfe; ☺noon-7pm Wed-Sat Sep-Jun; 🚇M1, Ⓢ Oranienburger Strasse) The aroma of peppermint and liquorice wafts through this old-fashioned basement candy kitchen whose owners use antique equipment and time-tested recipes to churn out such souvenir-worthy treats as their signature leaf-shaped Berliner Maiblätter made with woodruff. Mix and match your own bag for €1.70 per 100g.

DO YOU READ ME?!

BOOKS

Map p302 (☎030-6954 9695; www.doyoureadme.de; Auguststrasse 28; ☺10am-7.30pm Mon-Sat; Ⓢ Oranienburger Strasse, Ⓤ Rosenthaler Platz) Cool hunters could probably spend hours browsing this gallery-style assortment of rare, obscure and small-print magazines from around the world. There's a distinct focus on fashion, design, architecture, art and contemporary trends, and knowledgeable staff to help you navigate, if needed.

SCHWARZER REITER

ADULT

Map p302 (☎030-4503 4438; www.schwarzer-reiter.de; Torstrasse 3; ☺noon-8pm Mon-Sat; 🚇M2, M4, M5, M6, M8, Ⓤ Rosa-Luxemburg-Platz)

If you worship at the altar of hedonism, you'll appreciate the wide range of luxe erotica in this classy shop decked out in sensuous black and purple. Beginner and advanced pleasure needs can be fulfilled, from rubber ducky vibrators, feather teasers and furry blindfolds to unmentionable hard-core stuff.

PAPER & TEA

DRINKS

Map p302 (www.paperandtea.com; Alte Schönhauser Strasse 50; ☺11am-8pm Mon-Sat; Ⓤ Rosa-Luxemburg-Platz) Drink in the calming Zen atmosphere in this apothecary-style concept store where you can peruse, sniff and feel dozens of whole-leaf, hand-processed and single-garden tea varieties presented in little bowls. If it's all too bewildering, ask the expertly schooled 'teaists' for advice or to brew up a cup in the integrated tea bar.

HUNDT HAMMER STEIN

BOOKS

Map p302 (☎030-2345 7669; www.hundthammerstein.de; Alte Schönhauser Strasse 23/24; ☺11am-7pm Mon-Sat; Ⓤ Weinmeisterstrasse) Kurt Hammerstein has a nose for good books beyond the bestseller lists. Feel free to browse through this stylish lit lair with word candy from around the world or ask the affable owner to match a tome to your taste. There's a sizeable English selection, quality books for tots and a sprinkling of travel guides as well.

KAUF DICH GLÜCKLICH

FASHION & ACCESSORIES

Map p302 (☎030-2887 8817; www.kaufdichgluecklich-shop.de; Rosenthaler Strasse 17; ☺11am-8pm Mon-Sat; Ⓤ Weinmeisterstrasse, Rosenthaler Platz) What began as a waffle cafe and vintage shop has turned into a small emporium of indie concept boutiques with this branch being the flagship. It's a prettily arranged and eclectic mix of reasonably priced accessories, music and clothing for him and her from the own-brand KDG-collection and other hand-picked, mostly Scandinavian and Berlin, labels.

TRIPPEN

SHOES

Map p302 (☎030-2839 1337; www.trippen.com; Rosenthaler Strasse 40/41, Hackesche Höfe, Courts IV & VI; ☺11am-8pm Mon-Fri, 10am-8pm Sat; 🚇M1, Ⓢ Hackescher Markt) Forget about 10cm heels! Berlin-based Trippen's shoes are designed with the human anatomy in mind, yet are light years ahead in style compared to the loafers grandma used to buy in the orthopaedic shop. The award-winning brand prides itself on its 'socially responsible' manufacturing and love of unusual shapes. The shops themselves are gorgeous.

EAT BERLIN
FOOD

Map p302 (◻030-5228 3260; www.eatberlin store.de; Rosenthaler Strasse 39, Hackesche Höfe, Court VII; ◷11.30am-7.30pm Mon-Sat; ▣M1, Ⓢ Hackescher Markt) Owner Adam Mikusch's own mustard and salad dressings are just a couple of the artisanal products made in Berlin for sale in this cute little shop. Top picks include Berlin Brandstifter Gin and Berliner Honig (honey). Great for picking up souvenirs for yourself or the folks back home.

AMPELMANN BERLIN
GIFTS & SOUVENIRS

Map p302 (◻030-4472 6438; www.ampelmann. de; Rosenthaler Strasse 40/41, Hackesche Höfe, Court V.; ◷9.30am-9pm Mon-Sat, 1-8pm Sun; ▣M1, Ⓢ Hackescher Markt, Ⓤ Weinmeister-strasse) It took a vociferous grass-roots campaign to save the little Ampelmann, the endearing fellow on East German pedestrian traffic lights. Now the beloved cult figure and global brand graces an entire shop's worth of T-shirts, fridge magnets, pasta, onesies, umbrellas and other knick-knacks.

Check the website for additional branches around town.

PRO QM
BOOKS

Map p302 (◻030-2472 8520; www.pro-qm.de; Almstadtstrasse 48-50; ◷11am-8pm Mon-Sat; Ⓤ Rosa-Luxemburg-Platz) This treasure trove of the printed word (much of it in English) is squarely focused on design, art, architecture, pop and photography, with a sprinkling of political and philosophical tomes and a broad selection of obscure mags from around the world. With floor-to-ceiling shelves and stacks of books throughout, it's a browser's haven.

HAPPY SHOP
FASHION & ACCESSORIES

Map p302 (◻030-2900 9501; www.facebook. com/happyshopglobalalliance; Torstrasse 67; ◷11am-7pm Tue-Fri, noon-7pm Sat; Ⓤ Rosa-Luxemburg-Platz) Fashion outside the mainstream is the mojo of Happy Shop, in an arty wooden pavilion with a striped facade, pink doors and an ingenious floating rack system. Aside from owner-designer Micha Woeste's own Smeilinener label, the global

line-up includes 'Scandinasian' fashions by the Inoue Brothers and Japanese wunderkind Mihara Yasuhiro's Puma Black Label line. Ring the bell to enter.

LALA BERLIN
FASHION & ACCESSORIES

Map p302 (◻030-2009 5563; www.lalaberlin. com; Alte Schönhauser Strasse 3; ◷11am-7pm Mon-Sat; Ⓤ Rosa-Luxemburg-Platz) Ex-MTV editor Leyla Piedayesh makes top-flight women's urban fashion that flatters both the twig-thin and the well upholstered. Originally known for knitwear, her flagship boutique is now also the place to pick up boldly patterned tunics, silk dresses or a sassy Lala Girl T-shirt.

CLAUDIA SKODA WOMEN
FASHION & ACCESSORIES

Map p302 (◻030-4004 1884; www.claudiaskoda. com; Mulackstrasse 8; ◷12.30-6.30pm Mon & Thu-Sat; Ⓤ Rosa-Luxemburg-Platz) Berlin-born Claudia Skoda has been a local design icon since the 1970s, when she used to party with David Bowie and Iggy Pop. Global fashionistas pop by her gorgeous boutique to check out the figure-hugging knitted couture, from bold but classy dresses to colour-happy coats and snug sweaters, all made from top-quality yarns.

IC! BERLIN
FASHION & ACCESSORIES

Map p302 (◻030-2472 7200; www.ic-berlin. de; Max-Beer-Strasse 17; ◷11am-8pm Mon-Sat; Ⓤ Weinmeisterstrasse) What looks like a bachelor pad, with worn sofas, wacky art and turntables, is the flagship store of this internationally famous eyewear maker. The featherweight, patented frames, with their klutz-proof, screwless hinges, are stored in retro airline serving trolleys and have added 'spec appeal' to celebs from Madonna to the king of Morocco. Ask about its free factory tours.

1. ABSINTH DEPOT BERLIN
FOOD & DRINKS

Map p302 (◻030-281 6789; www.erstesabsinth depotberlin.de; Weinmeisterstrasse 4; ◷2pm-midnight Mon-Fri, 1pm-midnight Sat; Ⓤ Weinmeisterstrasse) Van Gogh, Toulouse-Lautrec and Oscar Wilde are among the *fin-de-siècle* artists who drew inspiration from the 'green fairy', as absinthe is also known. This quaint little shop has over 100 varieties of the potent stuff and an expert owner who'll happily help you pick out the perfect bottle for your own mind-altering rendezvous.

Kreuzberg & Neukölln

BERGMANNKIEZ | KOTTBUSSER TOR & THE LANDWEHRKANAL | NEUKÖLLN | SCHLESISCHES TOR & THE SPREE

Neighbourhood Top Five

1 **Club der Visionäre**
(p158) Challenging your
party stamina by dancing
and partying at a day-to-
night location.

2 **Street Food Thursday**
(p155) Eating your way
around the world at the
historic Markthalle Neun.

3 **Jüdisches Museum**
(p147) Stepping back into
the fascinating history of
Jews in Germany at this
Libeskind-designed archi-
tectural masterpiece.

4 **Kotti Bar-Hop** (p160)
Soaking up the punky-funky
alt-feel of eastern

Kreuzberg in search of
your favourite drinking den
around Kottbusser Tor.

5 **Türkischer Markt**
(p162) Immersing yourself
in multicultural bounty on a
crawl through the bustling
market.

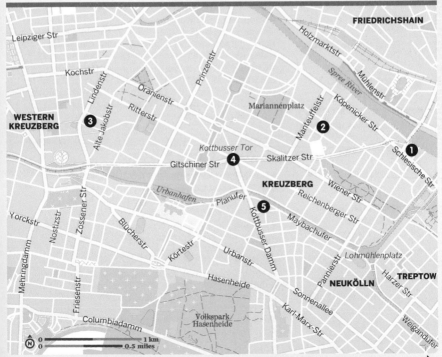

For more detail of this area see Map p312 ➡

Lonely Planet's Top Tip

For the ultimate 'Turkish Delight', head for **Sultan Hamam** (☎030-2175 3375; www.sultanhamamberlin.de;Bülowstrasse 57; 3hr sessions €19; [S]Yorckstrasse, [U]Yorckstrasse) where a traditional Turkish bathhouse meets modern spa culture. Relax in the richly tiled sauna and steam room, then treat yourself to a soapy scrub and *kese* (full body peeling with silken gloves). It's mostly for women, although men are welcome on Sundays and Mondays.

🍴 Best Places to Eat

- Cafe Jacques (p154)
- Burgermeister (p155)
- Max und Moritz (p153)
- Restaurant Richard (p156)
- Chicha (p153)

For reviews, see p152.➡

🍷 Best Places to Drink

- Schwarze Traube (p158)
- Club der Visionäre (p158)
- Thelonius (p157)
- Möbel Olfe (p160)

For reviews, see p156.➡

👁 Best Places to Dance

- Gretchen (p156)
- Loftus Hall (p158)
- Ritter Butzke (p157)
- Tresor (p159)

For reviews, see p156.➡

Explore: Kreuzberg & Neukölln

Kreuzberg and northern Neukölln are epicentres of freewheeling, multicultural and alternative Berlin. There are three quite distinct areas. The western half of Kreuzberg, around Bergmannstrasse, has an upmarket, genteel air and is home to the district's main sights: the Jewish Museum and the German Museum of Technology. Eastern Kreuzberg (around Moritzplatz, Kottbusser Tor, Goerlitzer Platz), meanwhile, is a multicultural mosaic of tousled students, *shisha*-smoking Turks and Arabs, and international artists. Come here to track down fabulous street art, browse vintage stores and hang by the canal, then find out why Kreuzberg is also a night-crawler's paradise.

All that hipness has spilled across the Landwehrkanal to the northern part of Neukölln, sometimes called Kreuzkölln. Once making headlines for its crime and poor schools, the district has had an influx of young, creative neo-Berliners (including many from Italy, Spain and Australia). Trash-trendy bars, performance spaces and galleries pop up almost daily.

Local Life

➡**Bar-hopping** Kreuzberg and northern Neukölln deliver some of the city's most hot-stepping nighttime action, especially around Kottbusser Tor, along Schlesische Strasse and on Weserstrasse.

➡**Shopping** Delightfully devoid of high-street chains, shopping here is all about individual style. Join locals in putting together that inimitable outfit from vintage shops, local designers, pop-up shops and flea markets.

➡**Chilling** The locals don't live to work. Heck, they may not work at all, which is why they have plenty of time to chill in green oases like Tempelhofer Feld, Viktoriapark or Görlitzer Park or watch boats floating by on the Landwehrkanal or Spree River.

Getting There & Away

➡**Bus** M29 links Potsdamer Platz with Oranienstrasse via Checkpoint Charlie; the M41 (also coming from Potsdamer Platz) hits the Bergmannkiez before trudging down to Neukölln via Hermannplatz.

➡**S-Bahn** The Ringbahn (Circle Line) S41/S42 stops at Treptower Park, Sonnenallee, Neukölln and Hermannstrasse.

➡**U-Bahn** Getting off at Kottbusser Tor (U8) puts you in the thick of eastern Kreuzberg, although Görlitzer Bahnhof and Schlesisches Tor (U1) are also handy. For northern Neukölln, Schönleinstrasse, Hermannplatz and Boddinstrasse (all on the U8) as well as Rathaus Neukölln (U7) are key stops. For the Bergmannkiez area, head to Mehringdamm (U6) or Gneisenaustrasse (U7).

TOP SIGHT
JÜDISCHES MUSEUM

In a landmark building by Daniel Libeskind, Berlin's Jewish Museum has, since 2001, offered a chronicle of the trials and triumphs from 2000 years of German history seen through the eyes of the Jewish minority. The exhibit smoothly navigates all major periods, from the Middle Ages via the Enlightenment to the community's current renaissance.

The Building

Libeskind's architectural masterpiece (which he titled *Between the Lines*) is essentially a 3D metaphor for the tortured history of the Jewish people. Its zigzag shape symbolises a broken Star of David; its silvery titanium-zinc walls are sharply angled; and instead of windows there are only small gashes piercing the building's gleaming facade.

The Axes

The museum consists of two buildings. The entrance is via a stately baroque structure that once housed the Prussian supreme court. From here a steep, dark and winding staircase leads down to the Libeskind building where three intersecting walkways called 'axes' represent the experiences of Jews in the 20th century. The **Axis of Emigration** leads to the maze-like Garden of Exile, which consists of 49 tilted concrete columns; Russian willow oak, a symbol of hope, sprouts from each. The **Axis of the Holocaust** ends in the tomb-like 'void' that stands for the loss of Jewish life, culture and humanity in Europe. Only the **Axis of Continuity**, which represents the present and the future, leads to the actual exhibits, but it too is a cumbersome journey up a sloping walkway and several steep flights of stairs.

DON'T MISS

➜ Axis of the Holocaust
➜ *Shalekhet – Fallen Leaves* installation
➜ Moses Mendelssohn exhibit
➜ Garden of Exile

PRACTICALITIES

➜ Jewish Museum
➜ Map p314, C2
➜ ☏030-2599 3300
➜ www.jmberlin.de
➜ Lindenstrasse 9-14
➜ adult/concession €8/3, audioguide €3
➜ ⏰10am-8pm Tue-Sun, to 10pm Mon, last entry 1hr before closing
➜ Ⓤ Hallesches Tor, Kochstrasse

TOP TIPS

➡Budget at least two hours to visit the museum, plus extra time to go through the airport-style entrance security checks.

➡Rent the audioguide (€3) for a more in-depth experience.

➡Free themed tours (in German) take place at 3pm on Saturday and 11am and 2pm on Sunday.

Tickets are also valid for reduced admission on the same day and the next two days to the Berlinische Galerie (p149), a survey of 150 years of Berlin art, located just 500m away.

TAKE A BREAK

For a refuelling stop, pop by the museum's **Café Schmus** (Map p314; ☑030-2579 6751; www.koflerkompanie. com; Jüdisches Museum, Lindenstrasse 9-14; dishes €5.50-8; ☺10am-8pm Tue-Sun, to 10pm Mon; ⓤKochstrasse, Hallesches Tor) for modern takes on traditional Jewish cuisine. At the Berlinische Galerie, **Cafe Dix** (Map p314; ☑030-2392 4109; www.cafe-dix.berlin; Alte Jakobstraße 124-128; mains €6-15; ☺10am-7pm Wed-Mon; ⓤKochstrasse, Moritzplatz) serves salads, German dishes and cakes.

The Exhibit

The permanent exhibit portrays facets and milestones of German-Jewish life and culture through art, daily objects, photographs and letters, media stations and interactive displays. Find out about Jewish cultural contributions, holiday traditions, the difficult road to emancipation, outstanding individuals and the fates of ordinary people and families.

An entire section is dedicated to the philosopher Moses Mendelssohn (1729–86), who paved the way for the Emancipation Edict of 1812 that made Jews full citizens with equal rights and duties. Elsewhere you can learn about holiday traditions old and new (ever heard of 'Chrismukkah'?), what it means to live kosher, or how people such as composer Arnold Schönberg, writer Walter Benjamin or artist Max Liebermann influenced global culture from their Berlin base. The subject of anti-Semitism pops up throughout, culminating in the 'National Socialism' section, where an interactive table traces the paths to exile taken by 276,000 people who fled Nazi Germany.

A new section trains the spotlight on the two largest German Nazi trials: the Auschwitz Trial in Frankfurt (1963–65) and the Majdanek Trial in Düsseldorf (1975–81).

Art Installations

The Jewish Museum is peppered with art installations, of which the late Menashe Kadishman's **Shalekhet – Fallen Leaves** is a poignant standout. More than 10,000 open-mouthed faces cut from rusty iron plates lie arbitrarily scattered on the floor in an ocean of silent screams. The haunting effect is exacerbated by the space itself, a cold and claustrophobic 'void'. Also note Dresden-born artist Via Lewandowsky's **Gallery of the Missing**, which consists of five black glass sculptures set up throughout the exhibition floor near one of these voids. Each contains acoustic descriptions of missing or destroyed objects relating to German-Jewish culture, such as the *Encyclopaedia Judaica,* whose completion came to a sudden halt in 1934.

W Michael Blumenthal Academy

The academy across from the main museum, open since November 2012, houses the museum's archive, library and education department, but for general visitors is mostly of interest for its architecture. Another Libeskind design, the house-in-house concept consists of three inclined cubes with the first forming the entrance and leading to a central hall. From here two more wood-panelled cubes tilted towards one another and intended to evoke Noah's Ark house the auditorium and a library. The inner courtyard called 'Diaspora Garden' is a quiet place of reflection.

◉ SIGHTS

Attractions in these vast districts are rather spread out with the Jewish Museum in the north, the Museum of Technology in the west and Tempelhof airport park in the south. Fortunately, public transport is excellent, making it easy to keep travelling time between sights to a minimum.

◉ Bergmannkiez

JÜDISCHES MUSEUM MUSEUM
See p147.

BERLINISCHE GALERIE GALLERY
Map p314 (Berlin Museum of Modern Art, Photography & Architecture; ☑030-7890 2600; www.berlinischegalerie.de; Alte Jakobstrasse 124-128; adult/concession/under 18 €8/5/free; ☺10am-6pm Wed-Mon; ⓊKochstrasse, Moritzplatz) This gallery in a converted glass warehouse is a superb spot for taking stock of what Berlin's art scene has been up to since 1870. Temporary exhibits occupy the ground floor from where two floating stairways lead upstairs to selections from the permanent collection, which is especially strong when it comes to Dada, New Objectivity, Eastern Europe avant-garde, and art created during the Cold War. Jüdisches Museum (p147)

ticket holders qualify for reduced admission on the same day and the following two days, and vice versa.

KÖNIG GALERIE @ ST AGNES KIRCHE GALLERY
Map p314 (☑030-2610 3080; www.koeniggalerie.com; Alexandrinenstrasse 118-121; ☺11am-6pm Tue-Sun; ⓊPrinzenstrasse) FREE If art is your religion, a pilgrimage to this church-turned-gallery is a must. Tucked into a nondescript part of Kreuzberg, this decommissioned Catholic church was designed in the mid-1960s by architect and city planner Werner Düttmann and is a prime example of Brutalist architecture in Berlin. In 2012, it was leased by the gallerist Johann König and converted into a spectacular space that presents interdisciplinary, concept-oriented and space-based art.

DEUTSCHES TECHNIKMUSEUM MUSEUM
Map p314 (German Museum of Technology; ☑030-902 540; www.sdtb.de; Trebbiner Strasse 9; adult/concession/under 18 €8/4/ after 3pm free, audioguide adult/concession €2/1; ☺9am-5.30pm Tue-Fri, 10am-6pm Sat & Sun; Ⓟⓕ; ⓊGleisdreieck, Möckernbrücke) A roof-mounted 'candy bomber' (the plane used in the 1948 Berlin airlift) is merely the overture to this enormous and hugely engaging shrine to technology. Fantastic for kids, the giant museum counts the

---

LOCAL KNOWLEDGE

ICONIC MURALS OF KREUZBERG

Astronaut Mural (Map p312; Mariannenstrasse, near Skalitzer Strasse; ⓊKottbusser Tor) One of Berlin's best-known works of street art is this monumental stencil-style piece inspired by the US-Soviet space race and created by Victor Ash as part of the 2007 Backjumps urban art festival.

Nature Morte (Map p312; cnr Oranienstrasse & Manteuffelstrasse; ⓈGörlitzer Bahnhof) This five-storey-tall street mural by Belgian artist ROA depicts animal carcasses, including a sheep and a deer, in a distinctive monochrome spray-paint style. The theme of animal conservation is close to ROA's heart and his works often deal with habitat loss due to urbanisation.

Yellow Man Mural (Map p312; Oppelner Strasse 3; ⓈSchlesisches Tor) This wall-sized street mural showing a bizarrely dressed man with bright yellow skin is a signature work by Os Gemeos, aka identical twins Otavio and Gustavo Pandolfo, from São Paulo, Brazil.

Rounded Heads Mural (Map p312; Oppelner Strasse 46-47; ⓊSchlesisches Tor) Rounded Heads is a house-sized mural by internationally renowned Berlin street artist Nomad that shows a faceless person embracing a hooded character.

Pink Man Mural (Map p312; Falckensteinstrasse 48; ⓊSchlesisches Tor) Italian artist Blu created this house-sized mural that depicts a creature composed of hundreds of writhing pink bodies. Note the lone white guy crouched on its finger.

TEMPELHOFER FELD: LEGENDARY AIRPORT TURNS URBAN PLAYGROUND

In Berlin history, Tempelhof Airport is a site of legend. It was here in 1909 that aviation pioneer Orville Wright ran his first flight experiments, managing to keep his home-made flying machine in the air for a full minute. The first Zeppelin landed the same year and in 1926 Lufthansa's first scheduled flight took off for Zurich. The Nazis held massive rallies on the airfield and enlarged the smallish terminal into a massive semi-circular compound that measures 1.23km from one end to the other. Designed by Ernst Sagebiel, it was constructed in only two years and is still one of the world's largest freestanding buildings. Despite its monumentalism, Sagebiel managed to inject some pleasing design features, especially in the grand art deco–style departure hall.

After the war, the US Armed Forces took over the airport and expanded its facilities, installing a power plant, bowling alley and basketball court. In 1948–49, the airport saw its finest hours during the Berlin airlift. After Tegel Airport opened in 1975, passenger volume declined, and flight operations stopped in 2008 after much brouhaha and (initially) against the wishes of many Berliners. That sentiment changed dramatically when the airfield opened as a public **park** (Map p314; ☎030-200 037 441; www.thf-berlin.de; enter via Oderstrasse, Tempelhofer Damm or Columbiadamm; tours adult/concession €13/9; ☉sunrise to sunset, tours in English 1.30pm & 3.30pm Wed & Fri, 3pm Sat, 2pm Sun; Ⓤ Paradestrasse, Boddinstrasse, Leinestrasse) FREE, a wonderfully noncommercial, creative open-sky space where cyclists, bladers and kite-surfers whisk along the tarmac. Fun zones include a beer garden near Columbiadamm, barbecue areas, an artsy mini-golf course, art installations, abandoned aeroplanes and an urban gardening project.

In fact, this vast, untamed urban playground has by now become so intensely beloved by Berliners that plans by the city to build thousands of apartments, offices and a central library along its perimeter were thwarted in a referendum held in May 2014. Critics charge that the steady growth of Berlin's population, coupled with the dearth of affordable housing, will make it untenable to keep this vast open space completely untouched, but for now the so-called ThF-Gesetz (Tempelhofer Feld Law) stands with one exception: the airport building itself is currently the interim home of thousands of refugees fleeing war and persecution in Syria, Irak, Afghanistan and other countries.

English-language **tours** (Map p314; ☎030-200 037 441; www.thf-berlin.de; Tempelhofer Damm 1-7; tours adult/concession €15/10; ☉1.30pm Wed, Fri-Sun; Ⓢ Platz der Luftbrücke) of both airport and airfield are available.

world's first computer, an entire hall of vintage locomotives and extensive exhibits on aerospace and navigation among its top attractions. At the adjacent **Science Center Spectrum** (enter Möckernstrasse 26, same ticket) kids can participate in hands-on experiments.

PARK AM GLEISDREIECK
PARK

Map p314 (www.gruen-berlin.de/gleisdreieck; entrances incl cnr Obentrautstrasse & Möckernstrasse; ☉24hr; Ⓢ Möckernbrücke, Mendelssohn-Bartholdy-Park) FREE Berliners crave green open spaces, and this vast park on a former railway junction is only the latest in a string of urban oases. A railway line still separates the sprawling grounds into the wide-open **Westpark**, with expansive lawns and play zones for kids, and the **Ostpark**, with a nature discovery area, a half-pipe, a little maple and oak forest and even an outdoor dance floor. Historic relics like tracks, signals and ramps are smoothly integrated throughout.

VIKTORIAPARK
PARK

Map p314 (btwn Kreuzbergstrasse, Methfesselstrasse, Dudenstrasse & Katzbachstrasse; ☉24hr; Ⓤ Platz der Luftbrücke) Take a break in this unruly, rambling park draped over the 66m-high Kreuzberg hill, Berlin's highest natural elevation. It's home to a vineyard, lawns for chilling, a waterfall and the Golgatha (p156) beer garden.

LUFTBRÜCKENDENKMAL
MEMORIAL

Map p314 (Berlin Airlift Memorial; Platz der Luftbrücke; Ⓟ; Ⓢ Platz der Luftbrücke) Nicknamed *Hungerharke* (Hunger Rake), the Berlin Airlift Memorial right outside the former Tempelhof Airport honours those who participated in keeping the city fed and free during the 1948 Berlin Blockade. A trio of

WORTH A DETOUR

TREPTOWER PARK & THE SOVIET MEMORIAL
....

Southeast of Kreuzberg, the former East Berlin district of Treptow gets its character from the Spree River and two parks: Treptower Park and Plänterwald. Both are vast sweeps of expansive lawns, shady woods and tranquil riverfront and have been popular for chilling, tanning, picnicking, jogging or just strolling around for well over a century. In summer, **Stern und Kreisschiffahrt** (p271) operates cruises from landing docks just south of the Treptower Park S-Bahn station. A bit further south, you can tuck into German food or swill a beer at **Restaurant & Biergarten Zenner** (☑030-533 7370; www.hauszenner.de; Alt-Treptow 14-17; mains €11.50-23.50; ⊘noon-midnight Wed-Sat, 10am-10pm Sun; Ⓢ Plänterwald, Treptower Park). From the terrace, you'll have a lovely view of the **Insel der Jugend** (☑030-8096 1850; www.inselberlin.de; Alt-Treptow 6; Ⓢ Plänterwald, Treptower Park), a tiny island reached via a 1915 steel bridge that was the first of its kind in Germany. In summer there's a cafe, boat rentals, movie screenings, concerts and parties.

Nearby awaits Treptower Park's main sight: the gargantuan **Sowjetisches Ehrenmal Treptow** (Soviet War Memorial; Treptower Park; ⊘24hr; Ⓡ Treptower Park) **FREE**, which stands above the graves of 5000 Soviet soldiers killed in the 1945 Battle of Berlin. It's a bombastic and sobering testament to the immensity of Russia's wartime losses. Coming from the S-Bahn station, you'll first be greeted by a **statue of Mother Russia** grieving for her dead children. Beyond, two mighty walls fronted by soldiers kneeling in sorrow flank the gateway to the memorial itself; the red marble used here was supposedly scavenged from Hitler's ruined chancellery. Views open up to an enormous sunken lawn lined by **sarcophagi** representing the then 16 Soviet republics, each decorated with war scenes and Stalin quotations. The epic dramaturgy reaches a crescendo at the **mausoleum**, topped by a 13m statue of a Russian soldier clutching a child, his sword resting melodramatically on a shattered swastika. The socialist-realism mosaic within the plinth shows grateful Soviets honouring the fallen.

South of here, near the *Karpfenteich* (carp pond), is the **Archenhold Sternwarte** (Archenhold Observatory; ☑030-536 063 719; www.sdtb.de; Alt-Treptow 1; exhibit free, tours €6/3; ⊘exhibit 2-4.30pm Wed-Sun, tours 8pm Thu, 3pm Sat & Sun; Ⓢ Plänterwald, Treptower Park), Germany's oldest astronomical observatory. It was here in 1915 that Albert Einstein gave his first public speech in Berlin about the theory of relativity. The observatory's pride and joy is its 21m-long refracting telescope, the longest in the world, built in 1896 by astronomer Friedrich Simon Archenhold. Demonstrations of this giant of the optical arts usually take place at 3pm Sunday. Exhibits on the ground floor are a bit ho-hum but still impart fascinating nuggets about the planetary system, astronomy in general and the history of the observatory. Kids love having their picture taken next to a huge meteorite chunk.

spikes represents the three air corridors used by the Western Allies, while a plinth bears the names of the 79 people who died in this colossal effort.

◉ Kottbusser Tor & the Landwehrkanal

FHXB FRIEDRICHSHAIN-KREUZBERG MUSEUM   MUSEUM
Map p312 (☑030-5058 5233; www.kreuzbergmuseum.de; Adalbertstrasse 95a; ⊘10am-7pm Tue-Sun; Ⓤ Kottbusser Tor) **FREE** The ups and downs of one of Berlin's most colourful districts are chronicled in this converted red-brick factory. The permanent exhibit zeros in on Kreuzberg's radical legacy, lets a rainbow of locals show you the 'hood on a virtual iPad tour and goes into depth on six historically significant buildings. The 1928 printing press on the mezzanine level is still cranked into action on occasion.

MUSEUM DER DINGE   MUSEUM
Map p312 (Museum of Things; ☑030-9210 6311; www.museumderdinge.de; Oranienstrasse 25; adult/concession/under 17 €6/4/free; ⊘noon-7pm Thu-Mon; Ⓢ Kottbusser Tor) With its extensive assemblage of everyday items, this museum ostensibly traces German design history from the early 20th century to today but actually feels more like a cross between a cabinet of curiosities and a flea market.

Alongside detergent boxes and cigarette cases are plenty of bizarre items, like a spherical washing machine, inflation money from 1923 and a swastika-adorned mug.

KÜNSTLERHAUS BETHANIEN GALLERY

Map p312 (☎030-616 9030; www.bethanien.de; Kottbusser Strasse 10; ⌚2-7pm Tue-Sun; [S]Kottbusser Tor, Schönleinstrasse) [FREE] Founded in 1975, the Künstlerhaus is an artistic sanctuary and creative cauldron for emerging artists from around the globe. In 2010 it moved into this former light fixture factory where it maintains one of Germany's largest artist-in-residence programs. Exhibits showcase their work, as well as that of former residents and other artists.

⊙ Neukölln

PUPPENTHEATER-MUSEUM BERLIN MUSEUM

Map p312 (Puppet Theatre Museum; ☎030-687 8132; www.puppentheater-museum.de; Karl-Marx-Strasse 135, rear bldg; adult/child €4/3, shows €5; ⌚9am-3pm Mon-Fri, 11am-4pm Sun; [U]Karl-Marx-Strasse) At this little museum, you'll enter a fantasy world inhabited by adorable hand puppets, marionettes, shadow puppets, stick figures and all manner of dolls, dragons and devils from around the world. Many of them hit the stage singing and dancing during shows that enthral both the young and the young at heart.

RIXDORF AREA

Map p312 (Richardplatz; [S]Berlin-Neukölln, [U]Karl-Marx-Strasse, Neukölln) Weavers from Bohemia first settled in quiet Rixdorf, a tiny historic village centred on Richardplatz, in the early 18th century. Some of the original buildings still survive, including a **blacksmith** (Map p312; ☎030-8507 8682; www.feine-klingen.de; Richardplatz 28; ⌚10am-1pm & 2-5pm Mon-Thu), a farmhouse and the 15th-century **Bethlehemskirche** (Map p312; Richardplatz 22; ⌚10am-noon Mon-Fri). A few nice cafes and restaurants make this a lovely spot to relax, especially in the summertime.

KÖRNERPARK GARDENS

(☎030-5682 3939; www.körnerpark.de; Schierker Strasse 8; ⌚park 24hr, gallery noon-8pm Tue-Sun; [S]Neukölln, [U]Neukölln) [FREE] This elegant sunken neo-baroque century-old garden comes with a secret: strolling past the flower beds and cascading fountain, you are actually standing in a reclaimed gravel pit! Ponder this as you sip a cuppa in the cafe, then check out the latest exhibit in the adjacent gallery. In summer join locals for free film nights or alfresco classical, jazz and world-music concerts.

From U-/S-Bahn station Neukölln, follow Karl-Marx-Strasse north for 250m, turn left on Schierker Strasse and continue 125m to the park.

🍴 EATING

Kreuzberg and northern Neukölln are among Berlin's most exciting and diverse foodie districts, with some of the best eating done in low-key neighbourhood restos, ethnic eateries and canal-side cafes. But the area also fields a growing share of high-end restaurants, including two decorated with Michelin stars. Markthalle Neun (p162), ground zero for Berlin's street food craze, is still going strong, and vegan cafes seem to be popping up at a startling rate.

🍴 Bergmannkiez

CURRY 36 GERMAN €

Map p314 (☎030-2580 088 336; www.curry36.de; Mehringdamm 36; snacks €2-6; ⌚9am-5am; [U]Mehringdamm) Day after day, night after night, a motley crowd – cops, cabbies, queens, office jockeys, savvy tourists etc – wait their turn at this top-ranked *Currywurst* snack shop that's been frying 'em up since 1981. Other sausage varieties – bratwurst, wiener and bockwurst – are also available, along with traditional potato and noodle salads.

TOMASA INTERNATIONAL €€

Map p314 (☎030-8100 9885; www.tomasa.de; Kreuzbergstrasse 62; tapas €3.20-5.50, mains €8-17; ⌚9am-1am Mon-Fri, to 2am Fri & Sat; 🍸 👪; [U]Mehringdamm) It's not only breakfast that is a joy at this enchanting late-19th-century villa with a Mediterranean-style garden at the foot of the Viktoriapark. The menu also features inspired salads and vegetarian and vegan mains, *Flammekuche* (Alsatian pizza) and grilled meats. Kids can make new friends in the play room or the adjacent petting zoo.

TULUS LOTREK FRENCH €€€
Map p312 (📞030-4195 6687; www.tuluslotrek.de; Fichtestrasse 24; mains €23-34; ⊘7pm-midnight; Ⓤ Südstern) Artist Henri Toulouse-Lautrec was a bon vivant who embraced good food and wine, which is exactly what the owners of this charismatic newcomer want their guests to do. Blanketing the rustic wooden plank tables is boldly flavoured and sometimes adventurous modern French cooking that doesn't follow any trends. It's an off-beat energy also reflected in the whimsical wallpaper.

✗ Kottbusser Tor & the Landwehrkanal

MAROUSH LEBANESE €
Map 312 (%030-6953 6171; www.maroush-berlin. de; Adalbertstrasse 93; sandwiches €3, platters €5-9; h11am-2am) This warm and woodsy hole-in-the-wall is tailor-made for restoring balance to the brain on a bar hop, with soulful felafel or shawarma paired with a glass of date juice or fresh mint tea. Some of the best Lebanese food in town.

MASANIELLO ITALIAN €
Map p312 (📞030-692 6657; www.masaniello.de; Hasenheide 20; pizza €6-10; ⊘noon-midnight; Ⓤ Hermannplatz) Tables are almost too small for the wagon-wheel-sized certified Neapolitan pizzas tickled by wood fire at this old-timey pizzeria, whose spacious flowery terrace transports you on a balmy summer night. Fresh fish on Friday and Saturday.

CHICHA PERUVIAN €
Map p312 (📞030-6273 1010; www.chicha-berlin. de; Friedelstrasse 34; mains €4-10.50; ⊘6pm-midnight; Ⓤ Schönleinstrasse) What began as a regular appearance at Berlin's street food fairs has evolved into a cheerful permanent nosh spot serving such Peruvian classics as ceviche (marinated raw fish), *tiradito* (Nikkei-style tuna carpaccio) and *anticuchos de corazon* (beef heart skewers).

MAX UND MORITZ GERMAN €€
Map p312 (📞030-6951 5911; www.maxundmoritz berlin.de; Oranienstrasse 162; mains €9.50-17; ⊘5pm-midnight; 📶; Ⓤ Moritzplatz) The patina of yesteryear hangs over this ode to old school brewpub named for the cheeky Wilhelm Busch cartoon characters. Since 1902 it has packed hungry diners and drinkers into its rustic tile-and-stucco ornamented

rooms for sudsy home brews and granny-style Berlin fare. A menu favourite is the *Königsberger Klopse* (veal meatballs in caper sauce).

LOUIS PRETTY DELI €€
Map p312 (📞030-7732 1122; www.facebook.com/ louisprettyberlin; Ritterstrasse 2; mains €8.50-12.50; ⊘11.30am-10pm; 📶; Ⓤ Moritzplatz, Kottbusser Damm) With its orange walls and swimming-pool-blue laminate tables, this hip New York–style Jewish deli dishes up some of the city's best pastrami on rye and other delectable nosh. The meat is magnificent after undergoing an epic four-week prepping process that involves curing, smoking, cooking and marinating.

COCOLO RAMENBAR JAPANESE €€
Map p312 (📞030-9833 9073; www.kuchi.de/res taurant/cocolo-x-berg; Paul-Lincke-Ufer 39-40; soups €8-10.50; ⊘noon-11pm Mon-Sat, 6-11pm Sun; 📶; Ⓤ Kottbusser Tor) For some of Berlin's top Japanese noodles, follow locals to this lantern-lit canal-side charmer. Its hearty soups based on richly flavoured pork broth are filled with homemade noodles and fresh vegetables. In fine weather, the terrace tables with river views beckon.

3 SCHWESTERN GERMAN €€
Map p312 (📞030-600 318 600; www. 3schwestern-berlin.de; Mariannenplatz 2; lunch specials €7.50, dinner mains €15-23; ⊘11am-midnight; Ⓤ Kottbusser Tor) In a beautiful, airy spot with a lovely garden at the Kunst-quartier Bethanien, a hospital turned art centre, the 'Three Sisters' is a dependable pit stop for fresh regional fare inspired by the seasons and sometimes infused by Mediterranean, Asian or Middle Eastern touches. Weekday lunch specials, weekend breakfast, homemade cakes and occasional post-dining concerts.

HENNE GERMAN €€
Map p312 (📞030-614 7730; www.henne-berlin. de; Leuschnerdamm 25; half chicken €8.30; ⊘6pm-midnight Tue-Sat, 5pm-midnight Sun; 🚌 M29, 140, 147, Ⓤ Moritzplatz, Kottbusser Tor) This Old Berlin institution operates on the KISS (keep it simple, stupid!) principle: milk-fed chicken spun on the rotisserie for moist yet crispy perfection. That's all it's been serving for over a century, alongside tangy potato and white cabbage salads. Eat in the garden or in the cosy 1907 dining room. Reservations essential.

KREUZBERG & NEUKÖLLN EATING

A ROYAL GARDEN FOR THE PEOPLE

In 2009, the nonprofit group Nomadic Green inspired a small army of volunteers to help turn wasteland into the fertile gardens **Prinzessinnengärten** (Princess Gardens; Map p312; www.prinz essinnengarten.net; Prinzenstrasse 35-38, Moritzplatz; ⊘garden from 10am, weather permitting, info centre & shop 11am-6pm Mon-Sat; ⓊMoritzplatz). There are workshops on gardening and beekeeping, activities for kids and a cafe (open noon to 6pm) where meals are prepared with the home-grown crop.

DEFNE TURKISH €€

Map p312 (☑030-8179 7111; www.defne-restau rant.de; Planufer 92c; mains €8.50-20; ⊘4pm-1am Apr-Sep, 5pm-1am Oct-Mar; ☑; ⓊKottbusser Tor, Schönleinstrasse) If you thought Turkish cuisine stopped at the doner kebab, canalside Defne will teach you otherwise. The appetiser platter alone elicits intense cravings (fabulous walnut-chilli paste!), but inventive mains such as *ali nacik* (sliced lamb with puréed eggplant and yoghurt) also warrant repeat visits. Good vegetarian choices too. Lovely summer terrace. Fresh fish and seafood on Friday and Saturday.

★HORVÁTH AUSTRIAN €€€

Map p312 (☑030-6128 9992; www.restaurant -horvath.de; Paul-Lincke-Ufer 44a; 5-/7-/9-course menu €89/109/129; ⊘6-11pm Wed-Sun; ⓊKottbusser Tor) At his canal-side restaurant, Sebastian Frank's kitchen talents have earned him two Michelin stars for performing culinary alchemy with Austrian classics, fearlessly combining products, textures and flavours. There is, of course, the classic wine pairing but also a matching non-alcoholic beverage line-up. Despite the fanciful cuisine, the ambience in the elegantly rustic dining room remains relaxed.

✗ Neukölln

CITY CHICKEN MIDDLE EASTERN €

Map p312 (☑030-624 8600; Sonnenallee 59; chicken plate €5.50; ⊘11am-2am; ⓊRathaus Neukölln) There's chicken and then there's City Chicken, an absolute cult destination when it comes to juicy birds sent through the rotisserie for the perfect tan. Well worth ordering with the full complement of sides – especially the wicked garlic sauce and the creamy hummus. Outdoor seating for full-on immersion in Neukölln street life.

BERLIN BURGER INTERNATIONAL AMERICAN €

Map p312 (☑0160 482 6505; www.berlin burgerinternational.com; Pannierstrasse 5; burgers €5-8.50; ⊘noon-midnight Mon-Thu, to 1am Fri, to 10pm Sun; ☑; ⓊHermannplatz) The guys at BBI know that size matters. At least when it comes to burgers: handmade, two-fisted, bulging and sloppy contenders. Get a side of chilli cheese fries or homemade coleslaw and you'll be in fast-food heaven. Paper towels supplied. You'll need 'em.

CABSLAM – CALIFORNIA BREAKFAST SLAM AMERICAN, VEGETARIAN €

Map p312 (☑030-686 9624; www.cabslam.com; Innstrasse 47; mains €6-9; ⊘10am-midnight Fri-Mon, to 4pm Tue-Thu; ☎; ☐104, 171, M41, ⓊRathaus Neukölln) It serves lunch and dinner too, but it's the breakfast that has 'slam' groupies in a headlock. If the prospect of fluffy banana-walnut pancakes, *huevos rancheros* or Israeli *shakshuka* doesn't get you out of bed, what will? The coffee comes from local top microroastery Five Elephant.

★CAFE JACQUES INTERNATIONAL €€

Map p312 (☑030-694 1048; Maybachufer 14; mains €12-20; ⊘6pm-late; ⓊSchönleinstrasse) A favourite with off-duty chefs and loyal foodies, Jacques infallibly charms with flattering candlelight, arty-elegant decor and fantastic wine. It's the perfect date spot but, quite frankly, you only have to be in love with good food to appreciate the French- and North African–inspired blackboard menu. Fish and meat are always tops and the pasta is homemade. Reservations essential.

INDUSTRY STANDARD INTERNATIONAL €€€

Map p312 (☑030-6272 7732; www.industry-standard.de; Sonnenallee 83; small plates €1.50-16; ⊘6-11pm Wed-Sun, 10am-3pm Sum; ☎; ☐M41, ⓊRathaus Neukölln) The folks behind this foodie fave embrace the nose-to-tail concept by serving even such perceived low-brow animal parts as tongue, heart or marrow in a most sophisticated fashion. The rebellious cooking also extends to vegetables, which are harvested fresh from the field by a regional farmer. Natural wines form an agreeable complement.

FILETSTÜCK – PIGALLE
STEAK €€€

Map p312 (☏030-2393 9663; www.filetstueck -berlin.de; Sanderstrasse 17; lunch €17.50, steak €32-55; ⏱noon-11pm Mon-Sat; Ⓤ Schönlein- strasse) Live out your lust for meat in this former brothel under the watchful eye of a neon cupid. Your expertly prepared filet or entrecôte doesn't really need embellish- ment, although it would be a shame to miss out on the aromatic veal bone jus or such terrifically creative sides as potato-endive mash. Carnivores on a budget should opt for the lunch special.

LAVANDERIA VECCHIA
ITALIAN €€€

Map p312 (☏030-6272 2152; www.lavanderia vecchia.de; Flughafenstrasse 46, 2nd courtyard; lunch mains from €5.50, 3 courses from €10, 13-course dinner menu €58; ⏱noon-2.30pm Mon- Sat, dinner 7.30pm Mon-Sat; Ⓤ Boddinstrasse) For a first-class (albeit waist-expanding) culinary journey around Italy, book a table amid the rustic-industrial charm of this historic laundry. Cooked-to-order antipasti courses are followed by pasta or risotto, a fishy or meaty main, and dessert. Dinner starts at 7.30pm and includes half a bottle of wine, plus water, coffee and digestif. Res- ervations essential. The entrance is from the courtyard.

The restaurant has been so successful that the owners have opened a smaller à la carte restaurant called Lava in the front building.

EINS44
FRENCH, GERMAN €€€

Map p312 (☏030-6298 1212; www.eins44. com; Elbestrasse 28/29, 2nd courtyard; mains lunch €8-10, dinner €26, 3-/4-/5-course dinner €43/53/63; ⏱12.30-2.30pm Tue-Fri, 7pm-mid- night Tue-Sat; ☏; ▣M41, 104, 167, Ⓤ Rathaus Neukölln) This outpost in a late-19th-century distillery serves 'elevated Franco-German bistro fare' that ticks all the boxes from old- fashioned to postmodern. Metal lamps, tiles and heavy wooden tables create industrial charm enhanced by large black-and-white photos. Lunches feature just a few classic dishes, while dinners are more elaborate.

✖ Schlesisches Tor & the Spree

★ BURGERMEISTER
BURGERS €

Map p312 (☏030-2388 3840; www.burger -meister.de; Oberbaumstrasse 8; burgers €3.50- 4.80; ⏱11am-3am Sun-Thu, to 4am Fri & Sat; Ⓤ Schlesisches Tor) It's green, ornate, a cen- tury old and...it used to be a toilet. Now it's a burger joint beneath the elevated U-Bahn tracks. Get in line for the plump all-beef patties (try the Meisterburger with fried

KREUZBERG & NEUKÖLLN EATING

LOCAL KNOWLEDGE

STREET FOOD PARTIES

Street Food Thursday (www.markthalleneun.de; Eisenbahnstrasse 42-43; ⏱5-10pm Thu; Ⓤ Görlitzer Bahnhof) Every Thursday evening since 2013, a couple of dozen aspir- ing chefs set up their food stalls in **Markthalle Neun** (p162), a historic market hall in Kreuzberg, to serve up delicious global street food. Pick your favourites and enjoy them with a glass of Heidenpeters, a craft beer brewed right on the premises. Some of the original food purveyors have enjoyed such roaring success that they have opened brick-and-mortar restaurants around the city.

Bite Club (Map p312; www.biteclub.de; Arena Berlin, Eichenstrasse 4; ⏱5pm-midnight every 3rd Fri May-Sep; Ⓢ Treptower Park, Ⓤ Schlesisches Tor) From New Zealand meat pies to Taiwanese burgers, Argentine pulled pork to Korean tacos, there's no limit to the culi- nary creativity at this outdoor street food party right on the Spree River.

To keep things in flux, regular stands and trucks are joined by aspiring newbies as well as craft beer, wine and whisky purveyors. The party continues on the retro Hop- petosse boat with lovely sunset views of river and city.

Burgers & Hip Hop (Map p312; www.facebook.com/burgersandhiphop; Prinzenstrasse 85f; ⏱3pm-6am Sat, dates vary; Ⓤ Moritzplatz) Every few weeks it's grill and grind at this street food burger fest with a residency at the **Prince Charles** (p157) club on Moritzplatz. Fuel up on the city's finest patties, then dance it all off inside the club and in the courtyard.

onions, bacon and barbecue sauce) paired with cheese fries and such homemade dips as peanut or mango curry. There's a second location at Kottbusser Tor.

FREISCHWIMMER INTERNATIONAL €€

Map p312 (☎030-6107 4309; www.freischwimmer-berlin.com; Vor dem Schlesischen Tor 2a; mains €10-16; ⏲noon-late Mon-Fri, 10am-late Sat & Sun; 📶; [S]Treptower Park, [U]Schlesisches Tor) In fine weather, few places are more idyllic than this rustic 1930s boathouse turned canal-side chill zone. The menu runs from meat and fish cooked on a lava rock grill to crisp salads, *Flammekuche* (French pizza) and seasonal specials. It's also a popular Sunday brunch spot (€12.90). Kayak and pedal boat rentals available.

★**RESTAURANT RICHARD** FRENCH €€€

Map p312 (☎030-4920 7242; www.restaurant-richard.de; Köpenicker Strasse 174; 4-course dinner €58, additional courses €10; ⏲7pm-midnight Tue-Sat; [U]Schlesisches Tor) A venue where Nazis partied in the 1930s and leftists debated in the '70s has been reborn as a fine-dining shrine solidly rooted in the French tradition and, since 2015, endowed with a Michelin star. With its coffered ceiling, bubble chandeliers and risqué canvases, the decor is as luscious as the fancy food while the vibe remains charmingly relaxed.

SPINDLER & KLATT INTERNATIONAL €€€

Map p312 (☎030-319 881 860; www.spindlerklatt.com; Köpenicker Strasse 16-17; mains €14.50-29; ⏲restaurant 7-11pm Thu-Sun, club 11pm-late Fri & Sat; [P]📶; [U]Schlesisches Tor) It's not the hot spot it once was, but summer nights on the riverside terrace are magical in this Prussian bread factory turned stylish nosh and party spot serving low-carb, diet-friendly salads and grilled meat and fish. The equally dazzling interior morphs into a dance club after 11pm on Friday and Saturday.

🍷 DRINKING & NIGHTLIFE

Kreuzberg and northern Neukölln have Berlin's greatest density of bars, pubs and clubs, and on weekends you'll have no problem partying nonstop from Friday night to Monday morning. There's a high concentration of bars around Kottbusser Tor and on Oranienstrasse, Skalitzer Strasse, Schlesische Strasse and Weserstrasse, but no matter where you are, the next tipple will likely be within stumbling distance.

🍷 Bergmannkiez

LIMONADIER BAR

Map p314 (☎0170 601 2020; www.limonadier-barkultur.de; Nostitzstrasse 12; ⏲6pm-2am Mon-Thu, 6pm-3am Fri & Sat; [U]Mehringdamm) A big portrait of Harry Johnson, whose 1882 bartenders' manual is still the profession's 'bible', keeps an eye on imbibers at this neighbourhood-adored cocktail cavern. The drinks menu shows tiki, apothecary and classic influences. Worth trying: locally inspired modern drinks like Berlin at Night or Kreuzberg Spritz.

GRETCHEN CLUB

Map p314 (☎030-2592 2702; www.gretchen-club.de; Obentrautstrasse 19-21; ⏲hours vary, always Fri & Sat; [U]Mehringdamm, Hallesches Tor) One of Berlin's finest music venues has set up in the gorgeous brick-vaulted stables of a mid-19th-century Prussian regiment. The low-key crowd defines the word eclectic, as does the music, which hops around contempo trends from electro to dubstep, indie to hip hop, funk to house. Hosts concerts and DJ sets.

GOLGATHA BEER GARDEN

Map p314 (☎030-785 2453; www.golgatha-berlin.de; Dudenstrasse 48-64; ⏲9am-late Apr-Sep; [S]Yorckstrasse, [U]Platz der Luftbrücke) This classic beer garden in idyllic Viktoriapark (p150) draws a changing cast of characters all day long: families in the daytime (there's an adjacent playground), the after-work crowd for the day's final rays on the rooftop terrace, chatty types for beer and brats in the evening and party folk to dance till morning. After 10pm enter the park from Katzbachstrasse.

🍷 Kottbusser Tor & the Landwehrkanal

ANKERKLAUSE PUB

Map p312 (☎030-693 5649; www.ankerklause.de; Kottbusser Damm 104; ⏲from 4pm Mon, from 10am Tue-Sun; [U]Schönleinstrasse) Ahoy there! Drop anchor at this nautical kitsch tavern in an old harbour master's shack and enjoy the arse-kicking jukebox, cold beers and surprisingly good German pub fare. The best seats are on the geranium-festooned terrace where you can wave to the boats puttering along the canal. A cult pit stop until the wee hours.

RITTER BUTZKE CLUB

Map p312 (www.ritterbutzke.de; Ritterstrasse 24; ⊗midnight-late Thu-Sat; ⓤMoritzplatz) Ritter Butzke is a former bathroom fittings factory turned Kreuzberg party circuit fixture. Wrinkle-free hipsters hit the four floors for high-quality electronic music spun by both DJ legends and the latest sound spinners of the deep house and techno scenes. Thanks to the DonnersDuck party session, the Butzke weekend starts on Thursday.

PRINCE CHARLES CLUB

Map p312 (☑030-200 950 933; www. princecharlesberlin.com; Prinzenstrasse 85f; ⊗from 11pm Thu-Sat; ⓤMoritzplatz) Prince Charles is a stylish mix of club and bar ensconced in a former pool and overlooked by a kitschy-cute fish tile mural. Electro, techno and house rule the turntables. The venue also hosts concerts and the Burgers & Hip Hop (p155) street food party. In summer, the action spills into the courtyard.

SO36 CLUB

Map p312 (☑030-6140 1306; www.so36.de; Oranienstrasse 190; ⊗nightly; ⓤKottbusser Tor) This legendary club began as an artist squat in the early 1970s and soon evolved into Berlin's seminal punk venue, known for wild concerts by the Dead Kennedys, Die Ärzte and Einstürzende Neubauten. Today the crowd depends on the night's program: electro party, punk concert, lesbi-gay tea dance, night flea market, '80s, 'Bad Taste' – pretty much anything goes.

BOURBON DOGS BAR

Map p312 (☑0174 862 8388; www.bourbon -dogs.com; Spreewaldplatz 14; ⊗5pm-late Tue-Sat, noon-midnight Sun; ☎; ⓤGörlitzer Bahnhof) Brooklyn meets Kreuzberg in this cosy space that has bet its money on a trifecta of bourbon, gourmet hot dogs and international craft beers. Leather sofas, dark woods and dangling bottles create a feel-good ambience. Crustacean aficionados invade for Lobster Roll Sunday.

🍷 Neukölln

KLUNKERKRANICH BAR

Map p312 (www.klunkerkranich.de; Karl-Marx-Strasse 66; ⊗10am-1.30am Mon-Sat, noon-1.30am Sun, weather permitting; ☎; ⓤRathaus Neukölln) During the warmer months, this club-garden-bar combo is mostly a fab place for day-drinking and chilling to local DJs or bands up on the rooftop parking deck of the Neukölln Arcaden shopping mall. It also does breakfast, light lunches and tapas. Check the website – these folks come up with new ideas all the time (gardening workshops anyone?).

To get up here, take the lifts just inside the 'Bibliothek/Post' entrance on Karl-Marx-Strasse to the 5th floor.

★THELONIUS COCKTAIL BAR

Map p312 (☑030-5561 8232; www.facebook. com/theloniousbarberlin; Weserstrasse 202; ⊗7pm-2am or later; ⓤHermannplatz) Embraced by a mellow soundscape and complexion-friendly lighting, well-mannered patrons pack this narrow burrow named for American jazz giant Thelonius Monk. Owner Laura Maria, who travelled the world before returning to her Neukölln roots, is the consummate host and creator of the drinks menu that ticks all the boxes, from classics to the adventurous.

GRIESSMÜHLE CLUB

(www.griessmuehle.de; Sonnenallee 221; ⓈSonnenallee) Hugging an idyllic canal, Griessmühle is a sprawling indoor-outdoor space with a funky garden strewn with tree houses, Trabis (GDR-era cars) and flower beds. The project by the ZMF artist collective woos attitude-free electro lovers with an events roster that includes not only parties and concerts but also a flea market, movie nights and pop-up dinner parties.

TIER BAR

Map p312 (Weserstrasse 42; ⊗7pm-2am; ☐M41, ⓤRathaus Neukölln) Neukölln barflies with a hankering for finely crafted cocktails flock to this softly lit laid-back lair. With its top-shelf spirits, smartly clad pro bar staff and small-groups-only policy, the vibe feels grown-up for the area. Groups larger than six may be refused entry. Must be 21.

KREUZBERG & NEUKÖLLN DRINKING & NIGHTLIFE

KELLER
CLUB

Map p312 (www.facebook.com/kellerkultur.net; Karl-Marx-Strasse 52, 2nd courtyard; ⊙11.45pm-8am Fri, 8pm-8am Sat; ⓤRathaus Neukölln) Quite literally a bastion of the Berlin 'underground' is this warren-like cellar in a back courtyard. The charmingly improvised dancing den is affiliated with the label 'Keller', which strives to break down the barriers between melodic techno and deep house. The turntable is a platform for young alternative talent of all stripes.

PROMENADEN ECK
BAR

Map p312 (www.promenaden-eck.de; Schillerpromenade 11; ⊙7pm-5am Sun-Thu, to 8am Fri & Sat; ⓤBoddinstrasse) With its daily line-up of Berlin-based electro DJs, table tennis, low prices and 5am closing time (8am on weekends), Promenaden Eck checks all the boxes of a classic 'hipster hang-out'. The finely tuned vintage living-room decor features lots of rustic wood, granny sofas, wallpaper and carpets. High in fun, low in attitude.

VIN AQUA VIN
WINE BAR

Map p312 (☑030-9405 2886; www.vinaquavin.de; Weserstrasse 204; ⊙4pm-midnight or later Mon-Wed, from 3pm Thu & Fri, from 2pm Sat; ☐171, M29, M41, ⓤHermannplatz) Vin Aqua Vin does double duty as a wine shop and wine bar where you can sample hand-picked wines amid candlelight and a homey, anti-snob vibe that takes out the intimidation factor and means even hipsters drop by for a sip.

Instead of expensive trophy wines, owner Jan Kreuzinger pours and sells a shifting set of affordable boutique favourites, many from small German producers with a willingness to experiment. Also try his own sparkling wine.

LOFTUS HALL
CLUB

Map p312 (www.loftushall.de; Maybachufer 48; ⊙usually from 11pm or midnight Fri & Sat; ☐M29, 171, ⓤHermannplatz) This '70s retro haunt in a former slot-machine factory takes its name from a haunted mansion in Ireland – you half expect a ghost to lurk behind the wood-panelled walls and heavy curtains. The sound system and music, however, are very up-to-the-minute, with next-gen electro DJs helming the decks most nights here and in the affiliated Bertrams club in the basement.

Ä
PUB

Map p312 (☑030-3064 8751; www.ae-neukoelln. de; Weserstrasse 40; ⊙5pm-late; ☐M41, ⓤRathaus Neukölln) Always wall-to-wall with globalists, this *Kiez* (neighbourhood) pioneer is a dressed-down watering hole to feed your party animal an appetiser, camp out for the night or turn in for that final drink. Expect to be eclectically entertained by readings, DJs, bands or (get this!) a monthly live soap opera starring cast-off stuffed animals.

SCHWUZ
GAY

Map p312 (☑030-5770 2270; www.schwuz.de; Rollbergstrasse 26; ⊙from 11pm Thu-Sat; ☐104, 167, ⓤRathaus Neukölln) This long-running queer party institution is the go-to spot for high-energy flirting and dancing. Different nightly parties draw different punters, so check what's on before heading out. Regular parties include Electronic Thursdays and the L-Tunes lesbian party. Good for easing into Berlin's LGBTIQ party scene.

⚑ Schlesisches Tor & the Spree

CLUB DER VISIONÄRE
CLUB

Map p312 (☑030-6951 8942; www.clubdervisionaere.com; Am Flutgraben 1; ⊙3pm-late Mon-Fri, noon-late Sat & Sun; ⓈTreptower Park, ⓤSchlesisches Tor) It's cold beer, crispy pizza and fine electro at this summertime day-to-night-and-back-to-day chill and party playground in an old canal-side boatshed. Park yourself beneath the weeping willows, stake out some turf on the upstairs deck or hit the tiny dance floor. To keep the party going year-round, CDV has expanded to the Hoppetosse boat moored nearby in the Spree.

★ SCHWARZE TRAUBE
COCKTAIL BAR

Map p312 (☑030-2313 5569; www. schwarzetraube.de; Wrangelstrasse 24; ⊙7pm-2am Sun-Thu, to 5am Fri & Sat; ⓤGörlitzer Bahnhof) Mixologist Atalay Aktas was Germany's Best Bartender of 2013 and this pint-sized drinking parlour is where he and his staff create their magic potions. Since there's no menu, each drink is calibrated to the taste and mood of each patron using premium spirits, expertise and a dash of psychology.

SEX & THE CITY

The decadence of the Weimar years is alive and kicking in this city long known for its libertine leanings. While full-on sex clubs are most common in the gay scene (eg **Lab. oratory** p173), places such as **Insomnia** (www.insomnia-berlin.de; Alt-Tempelhof 17-19; ⊘Tue-Sun; ⓤAlt-Tempelhof), the **KitKatClub** (Map p312; www.kitkatclub.de; Köpenicker Strasse 76; ⊘from 11pm Fri, Sat & Mon, 8am Sun; ⓤHeinrich-Heine-Strasse) and **Club Culture Houze** (Map p312; ☑030-6170 9669; www.club-culture-houze.de; Görlitzer Strasse 71; ⊘7pm-late Mon, 8pm-late Wed-Sat; ⓤGörlitzer Bahnhof) allow straights, gays, lesbians, the bi-curious and polysexuals to live out their fantasies in a safe if public setting.

Surprisingly, there's nothing seedy about this, but you do need to check your inhibitions – and much of your clothing – at the door. If fetish gear doesn't do it for you, wear something sexy or glamorous; men can usually get away with tight pants and an open (or no) shirt. No normal street clothes, no tighty-whities. As elsewhere, couples and girl groups get in more easily than all-guy crews. And don't forget Mum's 'safe sex only' speech (condoms are usually provided).

BIRGIT&BIER BEER GARDEN, CLUB

Map p312 (☑0152 3392 0930; www.facebook.com/birgitundbier; Schleusenufer 3; ⊘2pm-3am or later; ☒165, 265, N65, ⓢTreptower Park, ⓤSchlesisches Tor) To describe this venue merely as a beer garden would only be telling part of the story. With its twinkle lights, carousel, wacky carnival decor and small indoor electro club, it's more of an adult playground in the spirit of the former Bar 25. DJs are often top dogs from such local labels as Katermukke, Get Physical and Ritter Butzke.

MADAME CLAUDE PUB

Map p312 (☑030-8411 0859; www.madameclaude.de; Lübbener Strasse 19; ⊘7pm-2am or later; ⓤSchlesisches Tor, Görlitzer Bahnhof) Gravity is literally upended at this David Lynchian booze burrow where the furniture dangles from the ceiling and the moulding is on the floor. There are concerts, DJs and events every night, including Experimontag, Wednesday's music quiz night and open-mike Sundays. The name honours a famous French prostitute – *très apropos* given the place's bordello pedigree.

PRIVATCLUB CLUB

Map p312 (☑030-6167 5962; www.privatclub-berlin.de; Skalitzer Strasse 85-86; tickets around €12-15; ⊘daily, hours vary; ⓤSchlesisches Tor, Görlitzer Bahnhof) In a former red-brick postal office, this retro-styled venue draws an easygoing crowd with concerts and parties that don't chase the latest trends. Expect a timeless beat potpourri that may even include ska, cumbia and indietronic.

HOPFENREICH PUB

Map p312 (☑030-8806 1080; www.hopfenreich.de; Sorauer Strasse 31; ⊘4pm-2am Mon-Thu, to 3am Fri-Sun; ⓤSchlesisches Tor) Berlin's first dedicated craft beer bar has a changing roster of 22 global ales, IPAs and other brews on tap, including local heroes Heidenpeters and Hops & Barley, plus dozens of bottled varieties, both known and obscure. It's all served with hipster flourish in a corner pub near the Schlesische Strasse party mile. Tastings, tap takeovers and guest brewers keep things in flux.

WATERGATE CLUB

Map p312 (☑030-6128 0394; www.water-gate.de; Falckensteinstrasse 49a; ⊘11.55pm-5am or later Wed, Fri & Sat; ⓤSchlesisches Tor) For a short night's journey into day, check into this high-octane riverside club with two floors, panoramic windows and a floating terrace overlooking the Oberbaumbrücke and Universal Music. Top DJs keep electro-hungry hipsters hot and sweaty till way past sunrise. Long queues, tight door.

TRESOR CLUB

Map p312 (www.tresorberlin.com; Köpenicker Strasse 70; ⊘midnight-10am or noon Mon, Wed, Fri & Sat; ⓤHeinrich-Heine-Strasse) One of Berlin's original techno labels and dance temples, Tresor has not only the pedigree but all the right ingredients for success: the industrial maze of a derelict power station, awesome sound and a great DJ line-up. Look for the namesake vault in the basement at the end of a 30m-long tunnel. The door is relatively easy.

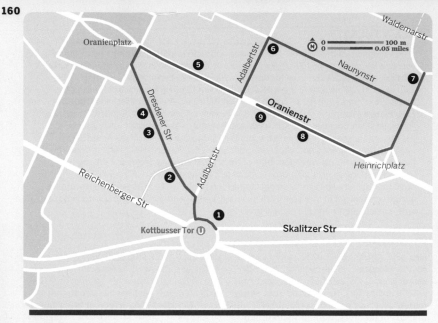

🏃 Local Life
Kotti Bar-Hop

Noisy, chaotic and sleepless, the area around Kottbusser Tor U-Bahn station (Kotti, for short) defiantly retains the alt feel that's defined it since the 1970s. More gritty than pretty, this beehive of snack shops, cafes, pubs and bars delivers some of the city's most hot-stepping night-time action and is tailor-made for bar-hopping.

❶ Elevated Speakeasy

An anonymous steel door next to the doner shop Misir Carsisi points the way to **Monarch Bar** (Map p312; www.kottimonarch.de; Skalitzer Strasse 134; ⊘9pm-2am or later Tue-Sat; Ⓤ Kottbusser Tor), a drinking den and DJ bar that draws a motley crowd of expats, Berliners and visitors. The vibe is friendly, the music eclectic and the drinks fairly priced.

❷ Funky Salon

Tucked behind a pile of Turkish kebab shops, grocers and *shisha* bars, **Möbel Olfe** (Map p312; ☑030-2327 4690; www.moebel-olfe.de; Reichenberger Strasse 177; ⊘6pm-3am or later Tue-Sun; Ⓤ Kottbusser Tor) is a queer-leaning drinking saloon that channels the area's alternative vibe with boho decor, strong Polish beers and a chatty vibe. It's a popular with lesbians on Tuesday and gays on Thursday.

❸ Grape Delights

A charming wine lair with woodsy fixtures and a bar covered in slate, **Otto Rink** (Map p312; www.ottorink.de; Dresdener Strasse 124; ⊘6pm-2am or later Mon-Sat; Ⓤ Kottbusser Tor) is an easygoing place to discover just how wonderful German wines can be. There's an emphasis on white varietals from the Moselle region, but wines from other German areas as well as from France, Spain and South America also feature on the monthly changing menu.

❹ '50s Cocktail Cave

For a swish night out, point the compass to **Würgeengel** (Map p312; ☑030-615 5560; www.wuergeengel.de; Dresdener Strasse 122; ⊘7pm-2am or later; Ⓤ Kottbusser Tor), a stylish art-deco-style bar with operatic chandeliers and black-glass surfaces. It serves great cocktails, as well as pizza and other Italian dishes from the adjacent restaurant.

❺ Luscious Lair

Luzia (Map p312; ☑030-8179 9958; www.facebook.com/luziabar; Oranienstrasse 34; ⊘noon-5am; Ⓤ Kottbusser Tor) is an excellent place to get the party started with a few beers or long drinks. A fixture on Kreuzberg's hipster circuit, the vintage decor gets updated with a mural by street artist chinchin. Tables behind the panoramas windows are great people-watching perches, and there's a smoker's lounge as well.

⑥ 'Gateway to Hell'

Popular with punks and alternative types, the **Trinkteufel** (Map p312; ☑030-614 7128; www.trinkteufel.de; Naunynstrasse 60; ☺1pm-4am Mon-Thu, 24hr Fri-Sun; ⓤKottbusser Tor) – 'Drink Devil' – is the dive bar where Pete Doherty downed a few before getting briefly arrested in 2009 after smashing a car window. Ponder this as you hang out by the bar and check out the trippy decor while swilling a cold brew.

⑦ Easy Medicine

Whatever ails you may well be fixed after dropping by the **Apotheken Bar** (Map p312; ☑030-6951 8108; www.apothekenbar. de; Mariannenplatz 6; ☺7pm-2am Mon, 6pm-2am Tue-Thu, 6pm-4am Fri & Sat; ⓤKottbusser Tor), a vintage-styled outpost in a 19th-century pharmacy. The original fixtures and old objects like a scale, bottles and signs form the atmospheric setting for expert cocktails, some featuring homemade tonic water and other potions.

⑧ Den of Debauchery

A mashup of trash, camp and fun, **Roses** (Map p312; ☑030-615 6570; Oranienstrasse 187; ☺9pm-6am or later; ⓤKottbusser Tor) is a beloved pit stop on the Kreuzberg party scene, especially among lesbigays and friends. Don't let the furry walls and a predominance of the colour pink distract you from the fact that this is a place that takes drinking seriously until the early morning hours.

⑨ Burlesque Boite

A jewel-box-sized burlesque bar, **Prinzipal** (Map p312; ☑030-6162 7326; www.prinzipal-kreuzberg.com; Oranienstrasse 178; ☺8pm-3am or later Mon-Sat; ⓤKottbusser Tor) celebrates the glamour of the Golden Twenties with plenty of eye-candy detail, an apothecary-style bar and servers in custom-designed corsets and glamorous make-up. A bestseller among the 10 signature cocktails is 'Date with Dita', a refreshing blend of bourbon, grapefruit, lemon, dates and homemade bitters.

RAUSCHGOLD · BAR

Map p314 (☑030-9227 4178; www.rauschgold.berlin; Mehringdamm 62; ☺8pm-late; ⓢ; ⓤMehringdamm) German for tinsel, Rauschgold's name is the game at this shimmering gay girl-boy lair with outlandish theme parties, karaoke contest, potent cocktails and sing-a-long hits from the '60s to today. Heteros welcome.

☆ ENTERTAINMENT

LIDO · LIVE MUSIC

Map p312 (☑030-6956 6840; www.lido-berlin. de; Cuvrystrasse 7; ⓤSchlesisches Tor) A 1950s cinema has been recycled into a rock-indie-electro-pop mecca with mosh-pit electricity and a crowd that cares more about the music than about looking good. Global DJs and talented upwardly mobile live noise-makers pull in the punters. Its monthly Balkanbeats party is legendary.

BI NUU · LIVE MUSIC

Map p312 (☑030-6956 6840; www.bi-nuu.de; Im Schlesischen Tor; ⓤSchlesisches Tor) This smallish, frill-free indie and alternative venue, in the crimson-lit catacombs below the U-Bahn station Schlesisches Tor, presents genre-spanning gigs by up-and-coming musicians alongside a weekly rap competition, record releases and dance parties. The curious name, by the way, pays homage to the third album by the Neue Deutsche Welle band Ideal, which was released in 1982.

WILD AT HEART · LIVE MUSIC

Map p312 (☑030-611 9231; www.wildatheart berlin.de; Wiener Strasse 20; ☺from 8pm Thu-Sat; ⓤGörlitzer Bahnhof) Named after a David Lynch road movie, this kitsch-cool dive with blood-red walls, tiki gods and Elvis paraphernalia hammers home punk, ska, surf-rock and rockabilly. It's really, REALLY loud, so if your ears need a break, head to the tiki-themed restaurant-bar next door. Free concerts on Wednesday.

HEBBEL AM UFER · THEATRE

Map p314 (HAU 1; ☑030-259 0040; www.hebbel -am-ufer.de; Stresemannstrasse 29; tickets €8-30; ⓤHallesches Tor) Germany's most avant-garde and trailblazing theatre comes with a mission to explore the changes in the social and political fabric of society, often by blurring the lines between theatre, dance and art. Performances are held in this 1907 art nouveau theatre called Hau 1 (the main performance venue), as well as in two smaller venues nearby, **Hau 2** (Map p314; Hallesches Ufer 32; tickets €8-30; ⓤHallesches Tor, Möckernbrücke) and **Hau 3** (Map p314; Tempelhofer Ufer 10; tickets €8-30; ⓤHallesches Tor, Möckernbrücke).

ENGLISH THEATRE BERLIN   THEATRE

Map p314 (☎030-691 1211; www.etberlin.de; Fidicinstrasse 40; ⓤPlatz der Luftbrücke) Berlin's oldest English-language theatre puts on an engaging roster of in-house productions, plays by international visiting troupes, concerts, comedy, dance and cabaret by local performers. Quality is high, the cast international and the programming intelligent. Tickets usually cost around €15.

NEUKÖLLNER OPER   THEATRE

Map p312 (☎tickets 030-6889 0777; www.neukoellneroper.de; Karl-Marx-Strasse 131-133; ⓤKarl-Marx-Strasse) Neukölln's refurbished prewar ballroom has an anti-elitist crossover repertoire ranging from intelligent musical theatre to original productions and experimental interpretations of classics. Many performances pick up on contemporary themes or topics relevant to Berlin and some are suitable for non-German speakers.

YORCKSCHLÖSSCHEN   LIVE MUSIC

Map p314 (☎030-215 8070; www.yorckschloesschen.de; Yorckstrasse 15; tickets €4-8; ⓣ5pm-3am Mon-Sat, from 10am Sun; ⓤMehringdamm) Cosy and knick-knack-laden, this Kreuzberg institution has plied an all-ages, all-comers crowd of jazz and blues lovers with tunes and booze for over 30 years. Toe-tapping bands invade several times a week, but there's also a pool table, beer garden, local beer on tap, and European soul food served till 1am. Jazz brunch on Sunday.

🛍 SHOPPING

Kreuzberg and northern Neukölln have a predictably eclectic shopping scene. Bergmannstrasse in the western district and Oranienstrasse both offer a fun cocktail of vintage frocks, hot-label street- and clubwear alongside music and accessories. Nearby Kottbusser Damm is almost completely in Turkish hands, with vendors selling everything from billowing bridal gowns to roasted nuts and gooey baklava. On Tuesday and Friday the Türkischer Markt (Turkish Market; Map p312; www.tuerkenmarkt.de; Maybachufer; ⓣ11am-6.30pm Tue & Fri; ⓤSchönleinstrasse) **lures big crowds with its inexpensive fresh produce and other goods.**

★MARKTHALLE NEUN   MARKET

Map p312 (☎030-6107 3473; www.markthalleneun.de; Eisenbahnstrasse 42-43; ⓣ5-10pm Thu, 10am-8pm Tue & Fri, 10am-6pm Sat; ⓤGörlitzer Bahnhof) This delightful 1891 market hall with its iron-beam-supported ceiling was saved by dedicated locals in 2009. On market days, local and regional producers present their wares, while on Street Food Thursday (p155) a couple of dozen amateur or semipro chefs set up their stalls to serve delicious snacks from around the world. There's even an on-site craft brewery.

★VOOSTORE   FASHION & ACCESSORIES

Map p312 (☎030-6957 972 710; www.vooberlin.com; Oranienstrasse 24; ⓣ10am-8pm Mon-Sat; ⓤKottbusser Tor) Kreuzberg's first concept store opened in an old backyard locksmith shop off gritty Oranienstrasse, stocking style-forward designer threads and accessories by such crave-worthy labels as Acne Studios, Soulland, Henrik Vibskov, Carven and dozens more, along with tightly curated books, gadgets, mags and spirits. The in-house cafe is a nice touch.

HARD WAX   MUSIC

Map p312 (☎030-6113 0111; www.hardwax.com; Paul-Lincke-Ufer 44a, 3rd fl, door A, 2nd courtyard; ⓣnoon-8pm Mon-Sat; ⓤKottbusser Tor) This well-hidden outpost has been on the cutting edge of electronic music for about two decades and is a must-stop for fans of techno, house, minimal, dubstep and whatever permutation comes along next.

★ANOTHER COUNTRY   BOOKS

Map p314 (☎030-6940 1160; www.anothercountry.de; Riemannstrasse 7; ⓣ2-8pm Mon, 11am-8pm Tue-Fri, noon-6pm Sat; ☎; ⓤGneisenaustrasse) Run by the eccentric Sophie Raphaeline, this nonprofit boho outfit is really more a library and (countercultural) salon than a bookshop. Pick a tome from around 20,000 used English-language books – classic lit to science fiction – and, if you want, sell it back, minus a €1.50 borrowing fee. Also hosts an English Filmclub (9pm Tuesday) and dinners (8pm Friday).

⭐HALLESCHES HAUS HOMEWARES

Map p314 (www.hallescheshaus.com; Tempelhofer Ufer 1; ⊗9am-7pm Mon-Fri, 11am-4pm Sat; ⓤHallesches Tor) IKEA graduates with a mod penchant will go ga-ga at this pretty pad packed with stylish whimsies for the home. Even day-to-day items get a zany twist in this airy space converted from an old post office. The in-store cafe serves locally roasted coffee, baked goods and light meals at lunchtime, much of it organic and local.

OTHER NATURE ADULT

Map p314 (✆030-2062 0538; www.other-nature.de; Mehringdamm 79; ⊗noon-6pm Mon & Tue, noon-8pm Wed-Sat; ⓤMehringdamm, Platz der Luftbrücke) At this alternative sex shop with a feminist slant you can stock up on vegan condoms, kegel balls, menstrual cups, dildos in all shapes, sizes and materials, and other fun stuff presented in a non-sexist environment. Owner Sara is happy to offer advice on any and all subjects. Also ask about its workshops.

NOWKOELLN FLOWMARKT MARKET

Map p312 (www.nowkoelln.de; Maybachufer; ⊗10am-6pm 2nd & 4th Sun of month Mar-Oct or later; ⓤKottbusser Tor, Schönleinstrasse) This hipster-heavy flea market sets up twicemonthly along the scenic Landwehrkanal and delivers secondhand bargains galore along with handmade threads and jewellery.

GROBER UNFUG BOOKS

Map p314 (✆030-6940 1490; www.groberunfug.de; Zossener Strasse 33; ⊗11am-7pm Mon-Fri, to 6pm Sat; ⓤGneisenaustrasse) Fans of international comics and graphic novels can easily lose a few hours in this very cool repository of books, DVDs, soundtracks and knickknacks. There's a mega-selection of indie and mainstream imports from the US, Japan and elsewhere.

MARHEINEKE MARKTHALLE FOOD

Map p314 (www.meine-markthalle.de; Marheinekeplatz; ⊗8am-8pm Mon-Fri, to 6pm Sat; ⓤGneisenaustrasse) Beautifully renovated, this historic market hall is like a giant deli where vendors ply everything from organic sausage to handmade cheese, artisanal honey and other delicious bounty, both local and international. Take a break from shopping with a glass of Prosecco or a snack. Snack stands feed tummy pangs.

COLOURS VINTAGE

Map p314 (✆030-694 3348; www.kleidermarkt-vintage.de; Bergmannstrasse 102, 1st fl; ⊗11am-7pm Mon-Sat; ⓤMehringdamm) This huge, light-filled loft has great used clothes going back to the 1960s for both men and women, plus a smaller selection of new street- and club-wear threads. Items are clean, in good condition and priced by the kilo (€18); there's a 30% discount during happy hour, 11am to 1pm Tuesday. Entrance is via the courtyard.

SAMEHEADS FASHION & ACCESSORIES

Map p312 (✆030-7012 1060; www.sameheads.com; Richardstrasse 10; ⊗2pm-late Tue-Sat; ⓤKarl-Marx-Strasse) The living room of Neukölln hipsters, Sameheads is all over the place: it's a shop-gallery-bar-party-space as well as soapbox for budding talent of all stripes. Aside from stocking out-there fashion, art and music, it hosts live shows at 8pm on Friday and Saturday and also operates Radio Rixdorf, which streams live during opening hours.

🏃 SPORTS & ACTIVITIES

BADESCHIFF SWIMMING

Map p312 (✆030-533 2030; www.arena-berlin.de; Eichenstrasse 4; adult/concession €5/3; ⊗8am-midnight May-Sep; 🚌265, 🚆Treptower Park, ⓤSchlesische Strasse) Take an old river barge, fill it with water, moor it in the Spree and – voila! – you get an artist-designed urban lifestyle pool that is a popular swim-and-chill spot. With music blaring, a sandy beach, wooden decks, lots of hot bods and a bar to fuel the fun, the vibe is distinctly 'Ibiza on the Spree'. Come early on scorching days as it's often filled to capacity (1500 people max) by noon. Or show up for sunset and night-time parties or concerts.

STADTBAD NEUKÖLLN SWIMMING

Map p312 (✆030-2219 0011; www.berliner-baeder.de/baeder/stadtbad-neukoelln; Ganghoferstrasse 3; adult €5-7, concession €3.50-5; ⊗hours vary; ⓤRathaus Neukölln, Karl-Marx-Strasse) This gorgeous bathing temple from 1914 wows swimmers with mosaics, frescos, marble and brass. There are two pools (20m and 25m) and a Russian-Roman bath with sauna (€15.50). Mondays are reserved for women only.

Friedrichshain

BOXHAGENER PLATZ & NORDKIEZ | WESTERN FRIEDRICHSHAIN | BOXHAGENER PLATZ | REVALER STRASSE & OSTKREUZ

Neighbourhood Top Five

❶ East Side Gallery (p166) Confronting the ghosts of the Cold War at the world's longest outdoor artwork.

❷ RAW Gelände (p167) Partying till sunrise in the rough-around-the-edges bars and clubs of this former train repair station.

❸ Flea market (p174) Foraging for treasure at this Sunday sell-a-thon on Boxhagener Platz, followed by brunch in a nearby cafe.

❹ Karl-Marx-Allee (p167) Marvelling at the bombastic architecture of this grand socialist boulevard in eastern Berlin.

❺ Volkspark Friedrichshain (p169) Relaxing over a beer, a barbecue or an open-air movie in Berlin's oldest public park.

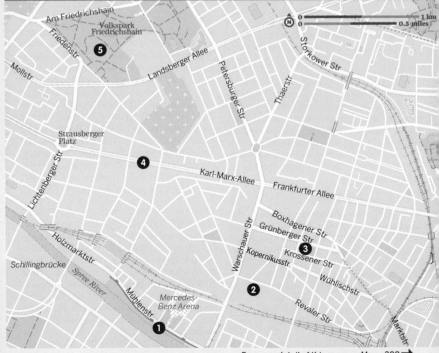

For more detail of this area see Map p308 ➡

Explore: Friedrichshain

Friedrichshain is the only central district where major vestiges of the GDR have survived. The prime sight is the East Side Gallery, the longest surviving stretch of Berlin Wall, closely followed by the Karl-Marx-Allee, a grand boulevard that is the epitome of Stalinist pomposity. To delve deep into the extinct country's sinister part, swing by the HQ of the Stasi, the GDR's omnipresent secret police, or head out to the Stasi Prison in the adjacent district of Hohenschönhausen, where regime critics wound up. More-pleasant daytime diversions include relaxing in sprawling Volkspark Friedrichshain or picking through the indie boutiques around Boxhagener Platz.

But it's at night when Friedrichshain truly comes into its own. From the late afternoon onward waves of international party pilgrims stream out of the Warschauer Strasse S-Bahn or U-Bahn stations and make their way, beer bottle in hand, to the happy-hour bars along Simon-Dach-Strasse. Later the action moves on to the drinking holes, clubs and concert venues on the graffiti-slathered industrial grounds of the RAW Gelände, a derelict former train repair station. Those still standing in the small hours might power on through Sunday in the electro clubs around Ostkreuz or drift into the Berghain/Panorama Bar.

Local Life

→**Marketeering** Forage for vintage finds at flea markets on Boxhagener Platz (p174), at the RAW Flohmarkt (p174) and at Ostbahnhof (p174).

→**Picnic in the park** Berlin's long summer evenings are perfect for chilling in rambling Volkspark Friedrichshain (p169), whether barbecue or sunset with a six-pack.

→**Party town** Become the master of the lost weekend, partying at Berghain/Panorama Bar (p172) or less hyped – though no less fun – clubs like Suicide Circus (p172) or ://about blank (p172).

Getting There & Away

→**S-Bahn** Ostbahnhof is handy for the East Side Gallery; Warschauer Strasse and Ostkreuz for Boxhagener Platz and Revaler Strasse. Ringbahn (circle line) trains S41 and S42 stop at Frankfurter Allee and Ostkreuz.

→**U-Bahn** U1 links Warschauer Strasse with Kreuzberg, Schöneberg and Charlottenburg; the U5 runs east from Alexanderplatz down Karl-Marx-Allee and beyond.

→**Tram** M10 links Warschauer Strasse with Prenzlauer Berg; M13 runs from Warschauer Strasse to Boxhagener Platz.

→**Bus** Take bus 200 for Volkspark Friedrichshain from Mitte (eg Alexanderplatz); bus 240 from Ostbahnhof to Boxhagener Platz.

Lonely Planet's Top Tip

To peel away the layers of Friedrichshain on a self-guided 2.5km walk, rent the audio tour by **Stadt im Ohr** (www.stadt-im-ohr.de, €9) from **Café Sibylle** (p167) and turn it in at **Kaufbar** (☑030-2390 9470; www.kaufbar-berlin.de; Gärtnerstrasse 4; ⊙10am-1am Wed-Mon; 🐾; 🚋M13, Ⓤ Warschauer Strasse, ⓈWarschauer Strasse).

✖ Best Places to Eat

→ Fame Restaurant (p170)
→ Schneeweiss (p169)
→ Schönbrunn (p170)
→ Vöner (p168)

For reviews, see p168. ➡

🍷 Best Places to Drink

→ Hops & Barley (p170)
→ Chapel Bar (p172)
→ Briefmarken Weine (p170)
→ Kater Blau (p172)

For reviews, see p170. ➡

◉ Best Places to Dance

→ Berghain/Panorama Bar (p172)
→ ://about blank (p172)
→ Magdalena (p172)
→ Salon zur Wilden Renate (p172)

For reviews, see p172 ➡

TOP SIGHT
EAST SIDE GALLERY

The year was 1989. After 28 years the Berlin Wall, that grim divider of humanity, met its maker. Most of it was quickly dismantled, but a 1.3km stretch along Mühlenstrasse, between Oberbaumbrücke and Ostbahnhof, became the East Side Gallery, the world's largest open-air mural strip. Today it's a memorial to the fall of the Wall and the peaceful reunification that followed.

In more than 100 paintings, 129 artists from 20 countries translated the era's global euphoria and optimism into a mix of political statements, drug-induced musings and truly artistic visions. Birgit Kinder's *Test the Rest*, showing a Trabi bursting through the Wall, *My God, Help Me To Survive This Deadly Love* by Dimitri Vrubel, which has Erich Honecker and Leonid Brezhnev locking lips, and Thierry Noir's bright cartoon faces called *Homage to the Young Generation* are all shutterbug favourites.

Alas, time, taggers and disrespectful tourists getting a kick out of signing their favourite picture is taking a toll on this protected historic landmark. In 2009 the entire stretch got its first costly makeover; a second one to remove graffiti and fix other damage got under way in 2015.

The East Side Gallery has also come under threat from property developers. Construction has brought about the removal of two sections of the wall, one 45m long and one 6m long, despite large-scale protests in 2013 that even inspired David Hasselhoff and Roger Waters to join the fight.

Check out the list of Top Five murals on p168.

DON'T MISS

➡ Taking a picture in front of your favourite mural

➡ Sunset drinks on the riverside lawn

PRACTICALITIES

➡ Map p308, C7

➡ www.eastsidegallery-berlin.de

➡ Mühlenstrasse btwn Oberbaumbrücke & Ostbahnhof

➡ admission free

➡ ⊘24hr

➡ Ⓤ Warschauer Strasse, Ⓢ Ostbahnhof, Warschauer Strasse

⊙ SIGHTS

EAST SIDE GALLERY   LANDMARK
See p166.

BOXHAGENER PLATZ   SQUARE
Map p308 (Boxhagener Platz; ⊘24hr; **P**; ⊡240, **S**Warschauer Strasse, **U**Samariterstrasse, Warschauer Strasse) **FREE** The heart of Friedrichshain, Boxhagener Platz is a lovely, leafy square with benches and a playground. It's framed by restored 19th-century buildings harbouring boho cafes and shabby-chic boutiques. The area is busiest during the Saturday **farmers' market** (Map p308; ⊘9am-3.30pm Sat; ⊡M10, M13, **U**Samariterstrasse, Frankfurter Tor) 🍴 and on Sundays when a flea market (p174) brings in folks from all over town.

KARL-MARX-ALLEE   AREA
Map p308 (⊘24hr; **U**Strausberger Platz, Weberwiese, Frankfurter Tor) **FREE** It's easy to feel like Gulliver in the Land of Brobdingnag when walking down monumental Karl-Marx-Allee, one of Berlin's most impressive GDR-era relics. Built between 1952 and 1960, the 90m-wide boulevard runs for 2.3km between Alexanderplatz and Frankfurter Tor and is a fabulous showcase of East German architecture. A considerable source of national pride back then, it provided modern flats for comrades and served as a backdrop for military parades.

CAFÉ SIBYLLE   HISTORIC SITE
Map p308 (☎030-2935 2203; www.cafe-sibylle.de; Karl-Marx-Allee 72; exhibit free; ⊘11am-7pm Mon, 10am-7pm Tue-Sun; 🛜; **U**Weberwiese, Strausberger Platz) Open since 1953, this was once one of East Berlin's most popular cafes and still makes for a delightfully retro coffee break. It also features a small exhibit charting the milestones of Karl-Marx-Allee from its inception to today. Note the original mural and the stucco ornamentation.

The exhibit features portraits and biographies of the architects of KMA, alongside posters, toys and other items from socialist times. There's even a piece of Stalin's moustache scavenged from the nearby statue that was torn down in 1961.

COMPUTERSPIELEMUSEUM   MUSEUM
Map p308 (Computer Games Museum; ☎030-6098 8577; www.computerspielemuseum.de; Karl-Marx-Allee 93a; adult/concession €8/5; ⊘10am-8pm; ⊡240, 347, **U**Weberwiese) No matter if you grew up with Nimrod, Pac-Man, World of Warcraft or no games at all, this well-curated museum takes you on a fascinating trip down computer-game memory lane while putting the industry's evolution into historical and cultural context. Colourful and engaging, it features interactive stations amid hundreds of original exhibits, including an ultrarare 1972 Pong arcade machine and its twisted modern cousin, the 'PainStation' (must be over 18 to play...).

RAW GELÄNDE   ARTS CENTRE
Map p308 (www.raw-tempel.de; along Revaler Strasse; **S**Warschauer Strasse, Ostkreuz, **U**Warschauer Strasse) This jumble of derelict buildings is one of the last subcultural compounds in central Berlin. Founded in 1867 as a train repair station ('Reichsbahn-Ausbesserungs-Werk', aka RAW), it remained in operation until 1994. Since 1999 the graffiti-slathered grounds have been a thriving offbeat sociocultural centre for creatives of all stripes. They also harbour clubs, bars, an indoor skate park, a swimming pool club and a bunker-turned-climbing-wall.

URBAN SPREE   ARTS CENTRE
Map p308 (www.urbanspree.com; Revaler Strasse 99; ⊘noon-11pm; 🛜; **U**Warschauer Strasse, **S**Warschauer Strasse) This artistic collective and grass-roots gallery of street, photographic and urban art is a top stop in the RAW compound along Revaler Strasse. Several times a week, concerts from garage to psych rock and electronic music broaden the range of visitors, while the beer garden is a great summertime chill zone.

OBERBAUMBRÜCKE   BRIDGE
Map p308 (Oberbaumstrasse; **S**Warschauer Strasse, **U**Schlesisches Tor, Warschauer Strasse) With its jaunty towers and turrets, the Oberbaumbrücke (1896) gets our nod for being Berlin's prettiest bridge. Linking Kreuzberg and Friedrichshain across the Spree, it smoothly integrates a steel middle section by Spanish bridgemeister Santiago Calatrava. In summer, street musicians and artists turn the bridge into an impromptu party zone.

There's an added bonus: the fabulous views. Looking southeast along the river, you'll spot the Universal Music HQ, MTV Europe and the extravagantly designed nhow hotel. On the Kreuzberg side is the Watergate club, the Badeschiff and, in the distance, a giant aluminium sculpture called **Molecule Man** (Map p312; An den Treptowers 1; ⊡Treptower

TOP FIVE EAST SIDE GALLERY MURALS

You'll likely find your own favourite among the 100 or so murals, but here's our take:

➡ **It Happened in November** (Kani Alavi) A wave of people being squeezed through a breached Wall in a metaphorical rebirth reflects Alavi's recollection of the events of 9 November 1989. Note the different expressions on the faces, ranging from hope, joy and euphoria to disbelief and fear.

➡ **Test the Rest** (Birgit Kinder) Another shutterbug favourite is Kinder's painting of a GDR-era Trabant car (known as a Trabi) bursting through the Wall with the licence plate reading 'November 9, 1989'. Originally called 'Test the Best', the artist renamed her work after the image's 2009 restoration.

➡ **Homage to the Young Generation** (Thierry Noir) This Berlin-based French artist has done work for Wim Wenders and U2, but he's most famous for these cartoonlike heads. Naive, simple and boldly coloured, they symbolise the new-found freedom that followed the Wall's collapse. Noir was one of the few artists who had painted the western side of the Wall before its demise.

➡ **Detour to the Japanese Sector** (Thomas Klingenstein) Born in East Berlin, Klingenstein spent time in a Stasi prison for dissent before being extradited to West Germany in 1980. This mural was inspired by his childhood love for Japan, where he ended up living from 1984 to the mid-'90s.

➡ **My God, Help Me To Survive This Deadly Love** (Dimitry Vrubel) The gallery's best-known painting – showing Soviet and GDR leaders Leonid Brezhnev and Erich Honecker locking lips with eyes closed – is based on an actual photograph taken by French journalist Remy Bossu during Brezhnev's 1979 Berlin visit. This kind of fraternal kiss was an expression of great respect in socialist countries.

Park) by American artist Jonathan Borofsky. Right in the river, it shows three bodies embracing and is a symbol of the joining of the three districts of Kreuzberg, Friedrichshain and Treptow across the former watery border.

🍴 EATING

🍴 Boxhagener Platz & Nordkiez

VÖNER VEGAN €

Map p308 (☎030-9926 5423; www.voener.de; Boxhagener Strasse 56; dishes €3.50-6.50; 🕒noon-11pm; 🌿; [S]Ostkreuz) Vöner inventor Holger used to live in a so-called *Wagenburg*, a countercultural commune made up of old vans, buses and caravans. The alt-spirit lives on in his original vegan doner outlet, which has since sprouted branches in other German cities. The eponymous 'Vöner' is a spit-roasted blend of wheat protein, vegetables and herbs.

LEMON LEAF ASIAN €€

Map p308 (☎030-2900 9428; www.lemonleaf.de; Grünberger Strasse 69; mains €8-14; 🕒noon-midnight; 🌿; 🚋M10, [U]Frankfurter Tor) Cheap, cheerful and stylish, this place is always swarmed by loyal locals, and for good reason: light, inventive and fresh, the South Asian menu has few false notes. Intriguing choice: the sweet-sour Indochine salad with banana blossoms.

LISBOA BAR PORTUGUESE €€

Map p308 (☎030-9362 1978; www.lisboa-bar-berlin.de; Krossener Strasse 20; tapas €3-10; 🕒noon-10pm; 🚋M13, [U]Warschauer Strasse, Samariterstrasse, [S]Warschauer Strasse) This colour-drenched bistro is an inspired Portuguese port of call. Regulars pop by for a leisurely breakfast (served until 4pm) or just for a *galão* coffee pick-me-up paired with a *pastel de nata* pastry. In the evening, hearty tapas, including classic chicken in hot piri-piri sauce, provide a good base for an extended bar-hop.

SPÄTZLE & KNÖDEL GERMAN €€

Map p308 (☎030-2757 1151; www.spaetzleknoedel.de; Wühlischstrasse 20; mains €7-14; 🕒5-11pm Mon-Fri, 3-11pm Sat & Sun; [U]Samariterstrasse) This elbows-on-the-table gastropub provides a southern German comfort-food fix, from roast pork with dark-beer gravy to goulash with red cabbage, and, of course, the epony-

TOP SIGHT
VOLKSPARK FRIEDRICHSHAIN

Berlin's oldest public park has provided relief from urbanity since 1840, but has been hilly only since the late 1940s when wartime debris was piled here to create two 'mountains' – **Mont Klamott** is the taller, at 78m. Diversions include expansive lawns, tennis courts, a halfpipe, the outdoor cinema **Freiluftkino Friedrichshain** (p173) and a couple of good beer gardens, including **Schönbrunn** (p170) by a little pond. Kids in tow? Head for the themed playgrounds and enchanting 1913 **Märchenbrunnen** (Fairy Tale Fountain), where frolicking turtles and frogs are flanked by Cinderella, Snow White and other Brothers Grimm stars.

Fans of communist-era memorials (and who isn't?) will find a trio of treats. Along Friedenstrasse, the sculpture **Denkmal der Spanienkämpfer** pays respect to the German communists who died in the Spanish Civil War (1936–39) fighting for the International Brigades. The **Friedhof der Märzgefallenen** (☉10am-6pm) is a cemetery for the victims of the revolutionary riots of March 1848, and the fallen of the November Revolution 1918. Finally, there's the **Denkmal des Polnischen Soldaten und des deutschen Antifaschisten** (Memorial to Polish Soldiers and German Antifascists).

DON'T MISS

➡ Märchenbrunnen
➡ A picnic on Mont Klamott
➡ Cold beers in Schönbrunn
➡ Alfresco movies at Freiluftkino Friedrichshain

PRACTICALITIES

➡ Map p308, B1
➡ bounded by Am Friedrichshain, Friedenstrasse, Danziger Strasse & Landsberger Allee
➡ ☉24hr
➡ 🚌142, 200, 🚊M5, M6, M8, M10, Ⓤ Schillingstrasse

---

mous *spaetzle* (German mac 'n' cheese) and Knödel (dumplings). Bonus: Bavarian Riegele, Maisel and Weihenstephan beers on tap.

SCHALANDER
GERMAN €€

Map p308 (☏030-8961 7073; www.schalander-berlin.de; Bänschstrasse 91; snacks €4-11, mains €7-22; ☉4pm-late Mon-Fri, 3pm-late Sat, noon-late Sun; 🛜👶; 🚊21, Ⓢ Frankfurter Allee, Ⓤ Samariterstrasse) See the pub action reflected in the very shiny steel vats that churn out the full-bodied Pilsner, *Dunkel* (dark) and *Weizen* (wheat) at this old-school gastropub far off the tourist track. The menu is big on beer-hall-type meaty mains along with *Flammkuche* (Alsatian pizza). For an unusual finish, order the wheat-beer crème brûlée.

SCHNEEWEISS
GERMAN €€

Map p308 (☏030-2904 9704; www.schneeweiss-berlin.de; Simplonstrasse 16; mains €11-18; ☉noon-4pm Mon-Fri May-Oct, 6pm-1am Mon-Fri, 10am-1am Sat & Sun year-round; 👶; 🚊M13, Ⓤ Warschauer Strasse, Ⓢ Warschauer Strasse) The chilly-chic all-white decor with an eye-catching 'ice' chandelier hints at the Alpine menu at this fine dining pioneer in Friedrichshain. Classics like schnitzel or cheese

spaetzle to more innovative creations like braised pork belly with scallops all feature on the menu. Reservations essential for weekend brunch (10am to 4pm).

✖ Western Friedrichshain

CANTINA UNIVERSALE
CAFE €

Map p308 (www.universal-osthafen.de; Stralauer Allee 1; mains €5.50-7.50; ☉8am-8pm Mon-Fri Apr-Sep, to 6pm Mon-Fri Oct-Mar; @🛜🖋; Ⓢ Warschauer Strasse, Ⓤ Warschauer Strasse) The cafeteria at the European headquarters of Universal Music is open to all. Choose from four daily mains or fill up at the salad bar (priced by weight), then savour your food with a view of the Spree River and the fanciful Oberbaumbrücke (Oberbaum bridge).

MICHELBERGER
MEDITERRANEAN €€

Map p308 (☏030-2977 8590; www.michelberger hotel.com; Warschauer Strasse 39-40; mains lunch €8-10, dinner €12-23; ☉7-11am, noon-3pm & 7-11pm; 🛜🖋; Ⓢ Warschauer Strasse, Ⓤ Warschauer Strasse) 🖋 Ensconced in one of Berlin's hippest hotels (p225), Michelberger makes mouthwatering Mediterranean-influenced dishes that often combine unusual organic ingredients in creative ways. Also a nice place for breakfast and a launch pad for a stroll along the East Side Gallery (p166).

FAME RESTAURANT INTERNATIONAL €€

Map p308 (⌨030-5105 2134; www.fame.kater schmaus.de; Holzmarktstrasse 25; mains €12-21; ☉noon-3pm Tue-Fri, 7-11pm Tue-Sat; ☏; ⓤJannowitzbrücke, ⓢJannowitzbrücke) From the homemade bread to the wicked crème brûlée, dining at this carefully designed ramshackle space under the U-Bahn tracks is very much a Berlin experience. Run by the legendary Bar 25/Katerschmaus folks, Fame features meaty, fishy and vegetarian mains meant to be paired with a selection of seasonal side dishes. Reservations essential.

SCHÖNBRUNN AUSTRIAN €€

Map p308 (⌨030-453 056 525; www.schoen brunn.net; Am Schwanenteich, Volkspark Friedrichshain; mains €11.50-20, pizza €6.50-10; ☉10am-11pm; ⊞; ⌗200, 240, ⌗M4, M5, M6, M8) Watch snow-white swans drift around their pond at this fairy-tale setting in the middle of Volkspark Friedrichshain (p169) while tucking into Austrian fare with Mediterranean touches. If you're not in the mood for the formal restaurant, report to the beer garden for a cold one with pizza or sausage. Breakfast is served until 2pm.

🍷 DRINKING & NIGHTLIFE

Along with Kreuzberg, Friedrichshain is Berlin's seminal fun and party zone with hot-stepping venues centred on the RAW Gelände, along Simon-Dach-Strasse and around the Ostkreuz train station. The neighbourhood is also home to the city's best techno-electro clubs, from big bad Berghain to hole-in-the-wall underground joints. On weekends, the action never stops.

🍷 Boxhagener Platz

⭐BRIEFMARKEN WEINE WINE BAR

Map p308 (⌨030-4202 5292; www.briefmark enweine.de; Karl-Marx-Allee 99; ☉7pm-midnight; ⓤWeberwiese) For *dolce vita* right on socialist Karl-Marx-Allee, head to this charmingly nostalgic Italian wine bar ensconced in

a former stamp shop. The original wooden cabinets cradle a hand-picked selection of Italian bottles that complement a snack menu of yummy cheeses, prosciutto and salami, plus a pasta dish of the day.

HOPS & BARLEY PUB

Map p308 (⌨030-2936 7534; www.hopsand barley-berlin.de; Wühlischstrasse 22/23; ☉from 5pm Mon-Fri, from 3pm Sat & Sun; ⌗M13, ⓤWarschauer Strasse, ⓢWarschauer Strasse) Conversation flows as freely as the unfiltered Pilsner, malty *Dunkel* (dark) and fruity *Weizen* (wheat) produced right here at one of Berlin's oldest craft breweries. The pub is inside a former butcher's shop and still has the tiled walls to prove it. Two projectors show soccer games.

AUNT BENNY CAFE

Map p308 (⌨030-6640 5300; www.auntbenny. com; Oderstrasse 7, enter on Jessnerstrasse; ☉9am-1am Tue-Fri, 11am-1am Sat & Sun; ☏; ⓢFrankfurter Allee, ⓤFrankfurter Allee) This Canadian-owned daytime cafe in an unhurried yet central section of Friedrichshain combines urban sophistication with downhomey treats. Catch up on your reading (lots of international magazines) over potent coffee and homemade carrot cake or banana bread. Turns into a bar at night.

KPTN A MÜLLER PUB

Map p308 (⌨030-5473 2257; www.kptn.de; Simon-Dach-Strasse 32; ☉6pm-late; ☏; ⌗M13, ⓢWarschauer Strasse, ⓤWarschauer Strasse) Arrgh, matey, the captain's in town. Pretensions are checked at the door of this self-service joint where drinks are cheap and table football and wi-fi are free. The Matterhorn photo wallpaper in the DJ room out back makes for an easy conversation starter.

SÜSS WAR GESTERN BAR

Map p308 (⌨0176 2441 2940; Wühlischstrasse 43; ☉8pm-2am; ⌗M13, ⓤWarschauer Strasse, Samariterstrasse, ⓢWarschauer Strasse) Chilled electro and well-mixed cocktails fuel the party spirit, and the low light makes everyone look good. Beware of the ubercomfy retro sofas – they make it hard to get up for that next drink, even if it's the eponymous house cocktail made with real root ginger, ginger ale and whisky.

BADEHAUS SZIMPLA MUSIKSALON BAR

Map p308 (⌨030-2593 3042; www.badehaus-berlin.com; Revaler Strasse 99, RAW Gelände, en-

STASI SIGHTS IN EAST BERLIN

In East Germany, the walls had ears. Modelled after the Soviet KGB, the GDR's Ministerium für Staatssicherheit (Ministry of State Security, 'Stasi' for short) was founded in 1950. It was secret police, central intelligence agency and bureau of criminal investigation all rolled into one. Called the 'shield and sword' of the SED (the sole East German party), it put millions of GDR citizens under surveillance in order to suppress internal opposition. The Stasi grew steadily in power and size and, by the end, had 91,000 official full-time employees and 189,000 IMs (*inoffizielle Mitarbeiter,* unofficial informants). The latter were regular folks recruited to spy on their coworkers, friends, family and neighbours. There were also 3000 IMs based in West Germany.

When the Wall fell, the Stasi fell with it. Thousands of citizens stormed the organisation's headquarters in January 1990, thus preventing the shredding of documents that reveal the full extent of institutionalised surveillance and repression through wiretapping, videotape observation, opening private mail and other methods. The often cunningly low-tech surveillance devices (hidden in watering cans, rocks, even neckties) are among the more intriguing exhibits in the **Stasimuseum** (☏030-553 6854; www.stasimuseum.de; Haus 1, Ruschestrasse 103; adult/concession €6/4.50; ☺10am-6pm Mon-Fri, 11am-6pm Sat & Sun; ⓊMagdalenenstrasse), which occupies several floors of the former fortresslike ministry. At its peak, more than 8000 people worked in this compound alone; the scale model in the entrance foyer will help you grasp its vast dimensions.

Another museum highlight is the 'lion's den' itself, the stuffy offices, private quarters and conference rooms of Erich Mielke, head of the Stasi for an incredible 32 years, from 1957 until the bitter end. Other rooms introduce the ideology, rituals and institutions of East German society. There's also background on the SED party and on the role of the youth organisation *Junge Pioneere* (Young Pioneers). Information panels are partly in English.

Few words are needed to understand the purpose of the van in the foyer. Outfitted with five teensy, lightless cells, it was used to transport suspects to the **Stasi prison** (Gedenkstätte Berlin-Hohenschönhausen; ☏030-9860 8230; www.stiftung-hsh.de; Genslerstrasse 66; tours adult/concession €6/3, exhibit free; ☺tours in English 10.30am, 12.30pm & 2.30pm Mar-Oct, 2.30pm daily & 11.30am Sat & Sun Nov-Feb, exhibit 9am-6pm, German tours more frequent; ℙ; ⓂM5) a few kilometres from the ministry. It too is a memorial site today – officially called Gedenkstätte Berlin-Hohenschönhausen – and is, if anything, even more creepy than the Stasi Museum.

Tours, sometimes led by former prisoners, reveal the full extent of the terror and cruelty perpetrated upon thousands of suspected political opponents, many utterly innocent. If you've seen the Academy Award–winning film *The Lives of Others,* you may recognise many of the original settings. An **exhibit** uses photographs, objects and a free audioguide to document daily life behind bars and also allows for a look at the offices of the former prison administration. Old maps of East Berlin show a blank spot where the prison was: officially, it did not exist. .

ter near Simon-Dach-Strasse; ☺Tue-Sun; ⓂM10, ⓊWarschauer Strasse, ⓈWarschauer Strasse) The little sister of the famous Szimpla Kert ruin bar in Budapest is making a splash in an old Berlin bathhouse. Head past the golden tub for eclectic bathhouse-themed decor, cheap drinks and a relaxed vibe. With parties and concerts spanning a musical arc from punk to electro swing, this place covers all the bases.

HIMMELREICH   GAY & LESBIAN

Map p308 (☏030-2936 9292; www.himmelreich-berlin.de; Simon-Dach-Strasse 36; ☺6pm-2am or later Mon-Sat, 4pm-1am or later Sun; ⓂM13, ⓈWarschauer Strasse, ⓊWarschauer Strasse) Confirming all those stereotypes about gay people having good taste, this candlelit and pretence-free drinking cove makes most of the competition look like a straight guy's bedsit. Try the Prosit Beer, which is especially brewed for Himmelreich.

🍷 Revaler Strasse & Ostkreuz

★://ABOUT BLANK CLUB

Map p308 (www.aboutparty.net; Markgrafendamm 24c; ⏱hours vary, always Fri & Sat; [S]Ostkreuz) At this gritty multifloor party pen with lots of nooks and crannies, a steady line-up of top DJs feed a diverse bunch of revellers dance-worthy electronic gruel. Intense club nights usually segue into the morning and beyond. Run by a collective, the venue also hosts cultural, political and gender events. In summer the action spills out into the garden (sometimes in winter, too, around a bonfire).

SISYPHOS CLUB

(☎030-9836 6839; www.sisyphos-berlin.net; Hauptstrasse 15; ⏱hours vary, usually midnight Fri-10am Mon Jun-Aug, weather permitting; 🚌21, [S]Ostkreuz) On summer weekends, an old dog-food factory about 2km southeast of S-Bahn station Ostkreuz turns into a hedonistic party village that proves that Berlin can still 'do underground'. Climb to the viewing platform to take in the space, which includes a pond and a fire truck. Techno dominates the turntables on the main floor with its great sound system, while a second floor is more house oriented.

SALON ZUR WILDEN RENATE CLUB

(☎030-2504 1426; www.renate.cc; Alt-Stralau 70; ⏱hours vary, always from midnight Fri & Sat; [S]Ostkreuz) Yes, things can indeed get pretty wild at Renate. Stellar local spinners feed self-ironic free-thinkers with sweat-inducing electro in the rambling rooms of an abandoned residential building. Sofas, a fireplace room and several bars provide suitable chill zones, as does the garden in summer.

SUICIDE CIRCUS CLUB

Map p308 (www.suicide-berlin.com; Revaler Strasse 99; ⏱11am-10am Wed, Thu & Sun, midnight-noon Fri & Sat; [S]Warschauer Strasse, [U]Warschauer Strasse) Tousled hipsters hungry for an eclectic electro shower invade this gritty midsize dancing den, where the top-notch sound system occasionally brings DJ royalty to the decks. In summer, watch the stars fade from the outdoor floor.

HAUBENTAUCHER BAR

Map p308 (www.haubentaucher.berlin; Revaler Strasse 99, Gate 1; admission varies, usually under €5; ⏱from noon Mon-Fri, from 10.30am Sat & Sun May-Sep, weather permitting; 📶; 🚌M10, [U]Warschauer Strasse, [S]Warschauer Strasse) Behind the brick walls of the graffiti-festooned RAW Gelände (p167) hides this ingenious urban beach club with industrial charm and Med-flair. At its heart is a heated outdoor swimming pool wrapped in a wooden sun deck; shade is provided by a vine-festooned garden lounge. An adjacent hall with bar and club carries the party into the night.

CHAPEL BAR COCKTAIL BAR

Map p308 (☎0157 3200 0032; www.chapelberlin.com; Sonntagstrasse 30; ⏱6pm-1am Sun-Wed, to 2am Thu, to 3.30am Fri & Sat; [S]Ostkreuz) A star in the Friedrichshain cocktail firmament, the Chapel Bar has a delightfully cluttered look and a convivial vibe thanks to a crowd more interested in good drinks than looking good. The folks behind the bar wield the shaker with confidence, be it to create classics or their own 'liquid dreams' like the whisky-based Köppernickel.

MAGDALENA CLUB

(☎030-293 641 240; www.magdalena-club.de; Alt-Stralau 1-2; ⏱Wed & Fri-Sun; [S]Ostkreuz, Treptower Park) This venerable club has found refuge in an historic harbour generating plant, which also had a stint as a newspaper office. After a total makeover, the venue now has a state-of-the-art Pioneer DJ Pro Audio System powering the usual stellar electronic line-up on the dance floors and in the pool bar in the cellar. The Sunday after-party kicks off at 10am.

🍷 Western Friedrichshain

★BERGHAIN/PANORAMA BAR CLUB

Map p308 (www.berghain.de; Am Wriezener Bahnhof; ⏱midnight Fri-Mon am; [S]Ostbahnhof) Only world-class spinmasters heat up this hedonistic bass-junkie hellhole inside a labyrinthine ex–power plant. Hard-edged minimal techno dominates the ex–turbine hall (Berghain) while house dominates at Panorama Bar, one floor up. Strict door, no cameras. Check the website for midweek concerts and record-release parties at the main venue and the adjacent Kantine am Berghain (p173).

★KATER BLAU CLUB

Map p308 (www.katerblau.de; Holzmarktstrasse 25; ⏱parties Fri-Sun; [U]Jannowitzbrücke, [S]Jannowitzbrücke) With the opening of Kater Blau, the Bar 25 crew returned to its original riverbank location. Once again a top roster of DJs, including stalwart residents Sven Dohse and Dirty Doering, showers freewheeling hipsters with fine electro in a rambling indoor-outdoor playground spread over two floors, plus a wooden boat moored in the Spree for chilling.

LAB.ORATORY GAY

Map p308 (www.lab-oratory.de; Am Wriezener Bahnhof; ⏰Thu-Mon; [S]Ostbahnhof) Part of the Berghain complex, this well-equipped 'lab' has plenty of toys and rooms for advanced male sexual experimentation in what looks like the engine room of an aircraft carrier. Party names like Yellow Facts, Naked Sex Party and Fausthouse leave little to the imagination. Hedonism pure. Come before midnight and skip the aftershave.

YAAM CLUB CLUB

Map p308 (☎030-615 1354; www.yaam.de; An der Schillingsbrücke 3; ⏰10am-late; [S]Ostbahn hof) A slice of the Caribbean on the Spree River, this reggae and dancehall institution attracts an all-ages, multicultural crowd to its live concerts, parties and beach bar with outdoor sports, art, food and fun in the sand.

There's even a kids' corner with face painting, theatre and other activities.

MONSTER RONSON'S ICHIBAN KARAOKE KARAOKE

Map p308 (☎030-8975 1327; www.karaokemonster.de; Warschauer Strasse 34; ⏰7pm-4am; [S]Warschauer Strasse, [U]Warschauer Strasse) Knock back a couple of brewskis if you need to loosen your nerves before belting out your best Beyoncé or Lady Gaga at this mad, great karaoke joint. *Pop Idol* wannabes too shy to hit the stage can book a booth for music and mischief in private. Some nights are GLBT-geared, like Monday's MultiSEXxual BOXhopping. Must be 21 to enter.

☆ ENTERTAINMENT

ASTRA KULTURHAUS LIVE MUSIC

Map p308 (☎030-2005 6767, tickets 030-6110 1313; www.astra-berlin.de; Revaler Strasse 99; ⏰hours vary, always Thu-Sat; 🚋M13, [S]Warschauer Strasse, [U]Warschauer Strasse) With space for 1500, easygoing Astra is one of the bigger indie venues in town, yet it often fills up easily, and not just when international headliners hit the stage. The party roster lures punters with electro swing, indie rock, techno and other sounds across the spectrum. Bonus: the gold-and-red colour scheme and sweet '50s East Berlin decor vestiges.

FREILUFTKINO FRIEDRICHSHAIN CINEMA

Map p308 (☎030-2936 1629; www.freiluftkino-berlin.de; Volkspark Friedrichshain; tickets €7; ⏰mid-May–mid-Sep; 🚌142, 🚋M5, M6, M8) Cradled by Volkspark Friedrichshain (p169), this open-air cinema has seating for 1500 on comfortable benches with backrests, plus a lawn with space for 300 more film fans. A kiosk sells drinks and snacks, and you're free to bring a picnic. Unless flagged otherwise, movies are shown dubbed into German.

KANTINE AM BERGHAIN LIVE MUSIC

Map p308 (☎030-2936 0210; www.berghain.de; Am Wriezener Bahnhof; admission varies; ⏰hours vary; [S]Ostbahnhof) Big bad Berghain's (p172) little sister has taken over the former staff *cantina* of the giant ex-power station. The space holds up to 200 people and mostly puts on concerts starting around 9pm. In summer, the attached beer garden with outdoor fireplace is an ideal chill zone. Easy door.

RADIALSYSTEM V PERFORMING ARTS

Map p308 (☎030-2887 8850; www.radialsystem.de; Holzmarktstrasse 33; 📶; [S]Ostbahnhof) 'Space for arts and ideas' is the motto of this progressive performance space in an old riverside pump station, which blurs the boundaries between the arts to nurture new forms of creative expression. Contemporary dance meets medieval music, poetry meets pop tunes, painting meets digital. The nice cafe-bar with riverside terrace opens from 10am on weekends and event days.

KINO INTERNATIONAL CINEMA

Map p308 (☎030-2475 6011; www.yorck.de; Karl-Marx-Allee 33; tickets €6.50-9.50; ⏰daily; [U]Schillingstrasse) The East German film elite once held its movie premieres in this 1960s cinema, whose potpourri of chandeliers and glitter curtains is a show in itself. Today it presents smartly curated international indie hit flicks, usually in the original language with German subtitles. Mondays are reserved for gay-themed movies and the first Saturday of the month for the gay megabash **Klub International** (Map p308; ☎030-2475 6011; www.klub-international.com; Kino International; ⏰from 11.45pm first Sat of month).

MARKETS GALORE

If you're into marketeering, Sundays are a great time to swing by Friedrichshain.

Flohmarkt am Boxhagener Platz (Map p308; Boxhagener Platz; ⏰10am-6pm Sun; 🚋M13, [S]Warschauer Strasse, [U]Warschauer Strasse, Samariterstrasse) Wrapped around leafy Boxhagener Platz, this fun flea market is just a java whiff away from Sunday brunch cafes. It's easy to sniff out the pro vendors from the regular folks here to unload their spring-cleaning detritus. Usually a good selection of vinyl and books.

RAW Flohmarkt (Map p308; www.raw-flohmarkt-berlin.de; Revaler Strasse 99, RAW Gelände; ⏰9am-7pm Sun; 🚋M10, M13, [S]Warschauer Strasse, [U]Warschauer Strasse) Bargains abound at this smallish flea market right on the grounds of **RAW Gelände** (p167), a former train repair station turned party village. It's wonderfully free of professional sellers, meaning you'll find everything from the proverbial kitchen sink to 1970s go-go boots. Bargains are plentiful, and food, a beer garden and cafes are nearby.

Antikmarkt am Ostbahnhof (Map p308; Erich-Steinfurth-Strasse; ⏰9am-5pm Sun; [S]Ostbahnhof) If you're after antiques and collectibles, head to this sprawling market outside the Ostbahnhof station's north exit. The 'Grosser Antikmarkt' (large antiques market) is more professional and brims with old coins, Iron Curtain–era relics, gramophone records, books, stamps, jewellery etc. It segues neatly into the 'Kleiner Antikmarkt' (small antiques market), which has more bric-a-brac and lower prices.

🛍 SHOPPING

Friedrichshain has come along in the shopping department, with increasingly chic indie clothing boutiques and speciality stores sprinkled around Boxhagener Platz (especially Wühlischstrasse) and along Sonntagstrasse and its side streets near Ostkreuz station.

HERR & FRAU NITSCHKE — CLOTHING

Map p308 (☎030-6040 5830; www.herrundfraunitschke.de; Wühlischstrasse 32; ⏰11.30am-7.30pm Mon-Fri, 11am-7pm Sat; 🚋M13, [U]Warschauer Strasse, [S]Warschauer Strasse) 🍃 Organic and fair trade are more than just buzzwords at this cute little shop with a hand-picked assortment of clothing for eco-conscious men and women. Look for trendy jeans by Kuyichi, Koi and Kings of Indigo, backpacks by Ethnotek and T-shirts by Dedicated.

SOMETIMES COLOURED — VINTAGE

Map p308 (☎030-2935 2075; www.facebook.com/sometimescoloured; Grünberger Strasse 90; ⏰noon-8pm Mon-Fri, to 7pm Sat; [U]Samariterstrasse) Never mind the minimal decor – there are some excellent vintage and secondhand treasures to be ferreted out from the racks, both for women and men (more for women). The selection turns over frequently but focuses on barely worn garments, including many contemporary labels (Adidas, Chucks, Stella McCartney), and even couture by Dior and Armani.

STRAWBETTY — CLOTHING

Map p308 (☎030-8999 3663; www.strawbetty.com; Gärtnerstrasse 32; ⏰noon-7pm Mon-Fri, to 6pm Sat; 🚋M13, [U]Warschauer Strasse, [S]Warschauer Strasse) No matter if you're a dedicated rockabilly girl or just want to look good at the next theme party, this boutique will kit you out with petticoats, sailor dresses, capri pants, boleros and other feminine vintage threads. It also stocks the right bag, hat and jewellery to perfect the fashion time warp.

PRACHTMÄDCHEN — FASHION & ACCESSORIES

Map p308 (☎030-9700 2780; www.prachtmaedchen.de; Wühlischstrasse 28; ⏰11am-8pm Mon-Fri, to 4pm Sat; 🚋M13, [S]Warschauer Strasse, [U]Warschauer Strasse) This store was a pioneer on Wühlischstrasse, aka Friedrichshain's 'fashion mile'. Low-key and friendly, it's great for kitting yourself out head to toe in grown-up streetwear by such labels as Blutsgeschwister, skunkfunk and Tokyo Jane. Also, chic undies by Pussy Deluxe and Vive Maria.

Prenzlauer Berg

MAUERPARK & THE NORTH KIEZ | KOLLWITZPLATZ & THE SOUTH KIEZ

Neighbourhood Top Five

❶ Gedenkstätte Berliner Mauer (p177) Coming to grips with the absurdity of a divided city at this memorial exhibit that follows the course of a 1.4km-long stretch of the Berlin Wall.

❷ Mauerpark (p179) Spending a sunny Sunday digging for flea-market treasures and cheering on karaoke crooners in this popular park reclaimed from a section of the Berlin Wall death strip.

❸ Kulturbrauerei (p179) Catching a concert, movie or street-food market at this venerable red-brick brewery turned cultural centre.

❹ Kollwitzplatz (p179) Taking a leisurely ramble around this leafy square and its side streets lined with beautiful townhouses, convivial cafes and indie boutiques.

❺ Prater Biergarten (p185) Guzzling a big mug of cold beer under the chestnut trees of Berlin's oldest beer garden.

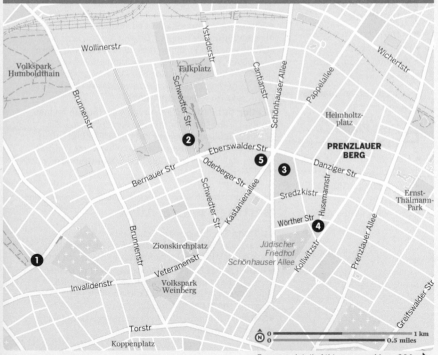

For more detail of this area see Map p306 ➡

Lonely Planet's Top Tip

Stop by the local **tourist office** (☐030-4435 2170; www.tic-berlin.de; Schönhauser Allee 36, Kulturbrauerei; ☺11am-7pm; ⓤEberswalder Strasse) in the Kulturbrauerei, which has maps, flyers and booklets to help you plug into the Prenzlauer Berg neighbourhood. It also sells tickets to events around town.

✗ Best Places to Eat

➡ Nalu Diner (p182)

➡ Kanaan (p179)

➡ Pizzeria L'Antica Dogana (p180)

➡ Umami (p183)

For reviews, see p179.➡

☐ Best Places to Drink

➡ Prater Biergarten (p185)

➡ Bryk Bar (p186)

➡ Weinerei Forum (p185)

➡ Deck 5 (p187)

For reviews, see p185.➡

☐ Best Places to Shop

➡ Flohmarkt im Mauerpark (p187)

➡ Saint Georges (p187)

➡ Ta(u)sche (p187)

➡ Upcycling Deluxe (p187)

For reviews, see p187.➡

Explore: Prenzlauer Berg

Once a neglected backwater, Prenzlauer Berg went from rags to riches after reunification to emerge as one of Berlin's most desirable and well-heeled neighbourhoods. The one must-see sight is the Gedenkstätte Berliner Mauer, the city's best place to understand the layout and impact of the Berlin Wall. The 1.4km-long indoor-outdoor exhibit actually starts in the adjoining district of Wedding but ends in Prenzlauer Berg near the Mauerpark. Generally speaking, though, Prenzlauer Berg's ample charms reveal themselves in subtler, often unexpected ways and are best experienced on a leisurely daytime meander. The prettiest area, and a good place to start, is around Kollwitzplatz, which is packed with congenial cafes and boutiques. Be sure to look up at pastel-coloured townhouse facades that not long ago bore the scars of war – polished Rykestrasse is a prime example.

Local Life

➡**Outdoor quaffing** Days get long, temperatures climb and spirits soar. Time to celebrate summer beneath the chestnut trees of the Prater (p185) beer garden, on the Deck 5 (p187) rooftop terrace or at a sunny pavement cafe on Knaackstrasse. Alternatively, score a beverage at a *Späti* (convenience market) and watch the sunset in the Mauerpark.

➡**Shopping** Kastanienallee and smaller side streets are nirvana for indie shoppers. Browse for practical bags at Ta(u)sche (p187), Berlin designers at **Flagshipstore** (Map p306; ☐030-4373 5327; www.flagshipstore-berlin.de; Oderberger Strasse 53; ☺noon-8pm Mon-Fri, 11am-8pm Sat; ⓜM1, 12, ⓤEberswalder Strasse) or retro threads at the Flohmarkt im Mauerpark (p187).

➡**Eating out** Favourites for foodies on the run include Habba Habba (p182) for Middle Eastern wraps, Zia Maria (p182) for pizza, and Konnopke's Imbiss (p183) for *Currywurst*. On Saturdays, join locals for gourmet snacks and a glass of bubbly at the bountiful farmers market (p188) on Kollwitzplatz.

Getting There & Away

➡**U-Bahn** The U2 stops at Schönhauser Allee, Eberswalder Strasse and Senefelderplatz en route to Alexanderplatz, Gendarmenmarkt and western Berlin.

➡**Tram** The M1 links Museumsinsel and Prenzlauer Berg via the Scheunenviertel, Kastanienallee and Schönhauser Allee. The M13 goes straight into Friedrichshain party central.

➡**S-Bahn** Ringbahn (Circle Line) trains S41 and S42 stop at Schönhauser Allee.

TOP SIGHT
GEDENKSTÄTTE BERLINER MAUER

For an insightful primer on the Berlin Wall, visit this 1.4km-long outdoor memorial, which explains the physical layout of the barrier and the death strip, how the border fortifications were enlarged and perfected over time and what impact they had on the daily lives of people on both sides of the Wall.

The memorial exhibit extends along Bernauer Strasse, one of the streets that played a pivotal role in Cold War history. The Berlin Wall ran along its entire length, with one side of the street located in West Berlin and the other in East Berlin. The exhibit is divided into four sections with overarching themes. Integrated within are an original section of Wall, vestiges of the border installations and escape tunnels, a chapel and a monument. Multimedia stations, 'archaeological windows' and markers provide context and details about events that took place along here.

Gartenstrasse to Ackerstrasse

This is the most important segment of the memorial. It focuses on explaining how the Berlin Wall restricted citizens' freedom of movement and secured the East German government's power. An emotional highlight is the **Window of Remembrance**, where photographic portraits give identity to would-be escapees who lost their lives at the Berlin Wall, one of them only six years young. The parklike area surrounding the installation was once part of the adjacent cemetery.

Near Ackerstrasse the **National Monument to German Division** consists of a 70m section of original Berlin Wall bounded by two rusted steel flanks and embedded in an

DON'T MISS

- Exhibit at the Documentation Centre and the view from its tower
- Remembrance service at the Chapel of Reconciliation
- Ghost Station exhibit
- National Monument to German Division

PRACTICALITIES

- Berlin Wall Memorial
- ☎030-467 986 666
- www.berliner-mauer-gedenkstaette.de
- Bernauer Strasse btwn Schwedter Strasse & Gartenstrasse
- admission free
- ⏰visitor & documentation centre 10am-6pm Tue-Sun, open-air exhibit 8am-10pm daily
- [S]Nordbahnhof, Bernauer Strasse, wEberswalder Strasse

TOP TIPS

➡If you have limited time, spend it in the first section between Gartenstrasse and Ackerstrasse.

➡Enjoy sweeping views of the memorial from the viewing tower of the Documentation Centre near Ackerstrasse.

➡The visitors centre has free maps and screens a short introductory film.

The Berlin Wall also divided the city's transport system. Three lines (today's U6, U8 and the north–south S-Bahn rails) that originated in West Berlin had to travel along tracks that happened to run beneath the eastern sector before returning to stations back on the western side. Trains slowed down but did not stop at these so-called 'ghost stations' on East Berlin turf, which were closed and patrolled by heavily armed GDR border guards. An exhibit inside the Nordbahnhof S-Bahn station describes underground escape attempts and the measures taken by the East German government to prevent them.

artistic representation of the border complex. Walk down Ackerstrasse to enter the monument from the back. Through gaps in a wall, you can espy a reconstructed death strip complete with a guard tower, a security patrol path and the lamps that bathed it in fierce light at night.

Ackerstrasse to Brunnenstrasse

In this section, the linear exhibit focuses on the division's human toll and especially on the daring and desperate escapes that took place along Bernauer Strasse. Just past Ackerstrasse, the modern **Chapel of Reconciliation** stands in the spot of an 1894 brick church detonated in 1985 to make room for a widening of the border strip. A 15-minute remembrance service for Wall victims is held at noon Tuesday to Friday. Other information stations deal with the physical construction of the Wall and the continuous expansion of the border complex.

Brunnenstrasse to Schwedter Strasse

In the final section, info stations and exhibits must skirt private property and new apartment buildings and are mostly restricted to a narrow strip along the former border patrol path. Information stations address such topics as West Germany's take on the Berlin Wall, what daily life was like for an East German border guard and the eventual fall of the Wall in 1989. A highlight is the dramatic story of the world-famous **Tunnel 29**, which ran for 135m below Bernauer Strasse and helped 29 people escape from East Berlin in September 1962.

Documentation Centre

Across the street from the National Monument to German Division, a former church building now houses a two-floor Documentation Centre. The exhibit – called '1961/1989. The Berlin Wall' – opened on 9 November 2014, the 25th anniversary of the fall of the Wall. It puts the barrier's construction and demise into a political context and uses artefacts, documents and videos to show how it affected daily life on both sides. Upstairs, GDR propaganda posters are juxtaposed with photographs depicting the reality, such as food shortages and Stasi persecution. The exhibit concludes with a look at the massive transformation Berlin has undergone in glueing the two halves back together after reunification.

⊙ SIGHTS

Apart from the city's most important exhibit on the Berlin Wall, the Gedenkstätte Berliner Mauer (Berlin Wall Memorial), Prenzlauer Berg doesn't have any blockbuster sights, and most of what it does have is concentrated in the pretty southern section around Kollwitzplatz.

GEDENKSTÄTTE
BERLINER MAUER   MEMORIAL
See p177.

MAUERPARK   PARK
Map p306 (www.mauerpark.info; btwn Bernauer Strasse, Schwedter Strasse & Gleimstrasse; 🚋M1, M10, 12, Ⓤ Eberswalder Strasse) With its wimpy trees and anaemic lawn, Mauerpark is hardly your typical leafy oasis, especially given that it was forged from a section of Cold War–era death strip (a short stretch of Berlin Wall survives). It's this mystique combined with an unassuming vibe and a hugely popular Sunday flea market and karaoke show that has endeared the place to locals and visitors alike.

KULTURBRAUEREI   HISTORIC BUILDING
Map p306 (☎030-4431 5152; www.kulturbrauerei.de; btwn Schönhauser Allee, Knaackstrasse, Eberswalder Strasse & Sredzskistrasse; 🚋M1, Ⓤ Eberswalder Strasse) The fanciful red-and-yellow brick buildings of this 19th-century brewery have been recycled into a cultural powerhouse with a small village's worth of venues, from concert and theatre halls to nightclubs, shops, a multiplex cinema and a free GDR history museum. From spring to fall, foodies invade for the Sunday street-food market (p183).

MUSEUM IN DER
KULTURBRAUEREI   MUSEUM
Map p306 (☎030-467 777 911; www.hdg.de; Knaackstrasse 97; ⊘10am-6pm Tue, Wed & Fri-Sun, to 8pm Thu; 🚋M1, 12, Ⓤ Eberswalder Strasse) FREE This exhibit uses original documents and objects (including a camper-style Trabi car) to teach the rest of us about daily life in East Germany. Four themed sections juxtapose the lofty aspirations of the socialist state with the sobering realities of material shortages, surveillance and oppression. Case studies show the different paths individuals took to deal with their living conditions.

KOLLWITZPLATZ   SQUARE
Map p306 (🚌; Ⓤ Senefelderplatz) Triangular Kollwitzplatz is the epicentre of Prenzlauer Berg gentrification. To pick up on the local vibe, linger with macchiato mamas and media daddies in a street cafe or join them at the farmers market (p188). The park in the square's centre is tot heaven with three playgrounds plus a bronze sculpture of the artist Käthe Kollwitz for clambering on.

JÜDISCHER FRIEDHOF
SCHÖNHAUSER ALLEE   CEMETERY
Map p306 (☎030-441 9824; www.jg-berlin.org; Schönhauser Allee 23-25; ⊘8am-4pm Mon-Thu, 7.30am-2.30pm Fri; Ⓤ Senefelderplatz) Berlin's second Jewish cemetery opened in 1827 and hosts many well-known dearly departed, such as the artist Max Liebermann and the composer Giacomo Meyerbeer. It's a pretty place with dappled light filtering through big old trees and a sense of melancholy emanating from overgrown graves and toppled tombstones. The nicest and oldest have been moved to the Lapidarium by the main entrance. Liebermann's tomb is next to his family's crypt roughly in the centre along the back wall. Men must cover their heads; pick up a free skullcap by the entrance.

ZEISS
GROSSPLANETARIUM   PLANETARIUM
Map p306 (☎030-421 8450; www.sdtb.de; Prenzlauer Allee 80; ⊘currently closed; Ⓢ Prenzlauer Allee) The people of East Berlin were not allowed to see what was across the Wall, but at least they could gaze at the entire universe at this planetarium, which opened in 1987 as one of the largest star theatres in Europe. It is currently being upgraded into a state-of-the-art facility and may reopen in 2016.

✗ EATING

✗ Mauerpark & the North Kiez

★KANAAN   MIDDLE EASTERN €
Map p306 (☎0176 2258 6673; www.facebook.com/kanaanrestaurantberlin; Kopenhagener Strasse 17; dishes €4-7; ⊘noon-4pm Mon-Fri, to 10pm Sat & Sun; 🚋M1, Ⓤ Schönhauser Allee, Ⓢ Schönhauser Allee) In this feel-good venture, an Israeli biz whiz and a Palestinian

LOCAL KNOWLEDGE

SPOTLIGHT ON WEDDING

Amorphous, multiethnic and rough around the edges – Wedding is a draw for urban explorers of neighbourhoods still exhibiting pre-gentrification authenticity. Sights are fairly scarce but if you're keen on the offbeat, down-to-earth locals and improvised DIY bars and creative venues, you'll still find them in this working-class northern district. Here are our five top picks to give you a taste of this emerging 'hood:

Sight

Siedlung Schillerpark (approach via Barfussstrasse; ⓤRehberge, Seestrasse) The Siedlung Schillerpark is the oldest of Berlin's five sprawling, modernist, 1920s housing estates that were inscribed on Unesco's list of World Cultural Heritage Sites in 2008. Designed by Bruno Taut, it was inspired by red-brick Dutch-style architecture and sits east of the Schiller Park.

Eating

Moos Restaurant (☎030-4606 1205; www.facebook.com/moosrestaurant; Gerichtstrasse 35; dishes €3-8; ⓘnoon-6pm Mon-Wed, to midnight Thu & Fri, 10am-midnight Sat, 10am-7pm Sun; ☎; ⓢWedding, ⓤLeopoldplatz, Wedding) Part of the Silent Green Kulturquartier (☎030-4606 7324; www.silent-green.net) in a decommissioned crematorium, this contemporary cafe provides daytime feedings of coffee, cake and light meals, including vegan and vegetarian fare, in a cosy environment with panoramic windows and a large wooden counter.

Drinking

Vagabund Brauerei (☎030-5266 7668; www.vagabundbrauerei.com; Antwerpener Strasse 3; ⓘ5pm-late Mon-Fri, 1pm-late Sat & Sun; ☎; ⓤSeestrasse) American friends Tom, Matt and David became Berlin craft beer pioneers when they started their small batch brewery in 2011. In their earthy-chic tap room, they pour hoppy American as well as double and triple Indian pale ales alongside a mean wheat beer, a smokey beer and the exotic 'Szechuan Saison' with crushed coriander seeds and peppercorns.

Entertainment

Piano Salon Christofori (☎0176 3900 7753; www.konzertfluegel.com; Uferhallen 8; admission by donation; ⓘconcerts 8.30pm; ⓤPankstrasse) Fancy taking in a piano concert at a piano repair shop in a former bus and tram repair station in industrial Wedding? The brainchild of Christoph Schreiber, this unusual nonprofit venue hosts concerts, mostly by young but highly talented soloists, several times weekly on a donation basis. Make online reservations as early as possible.

Shopping

Marc Cain Factory Outlet (☎030-455 0090; www.marc-cain.com; Oudenarder Strasse 16; ⓘ10am-8pm Mon-Fri, to 6pm Sat; ⓠ50, M13, ⓤNauener Platz) This German fashion label makes stylish clothing, shoes and accessories for grown-up women, sold at least at a 40% discount in its nicely designed factory outlet in the Osram-Höfe, a former light bulb factory.

chef have teamed up to bring a progressive blend of Middle Eastern fare to Berlin. Top menu picks are hummus, *shakshuka* and *sabich*. For now, weekday lunch is served from a rakishly ramshackle hut, while on weekends a bigger menu is dished up across the street at Kohlenquelle, a funky bar in a former coal cellar.

PIZZERIA L'ANTICA DOGANA   ITALIAN €

(☎030-4737 6372; www.wbb-pankow.de/pizzeria; Berliner Strasse 80-82; pizza €4.50-8.50; ⓘ5-10pm; ❋; ⓠM1, ⓤVinetastrasse) In the frills-free surroundings of the former custom house of the defunct Willner Brewery, Lino di Napoli and Sebastiano Micieli crank out authentic thin-crust pies, best consumed with a posse of friends and

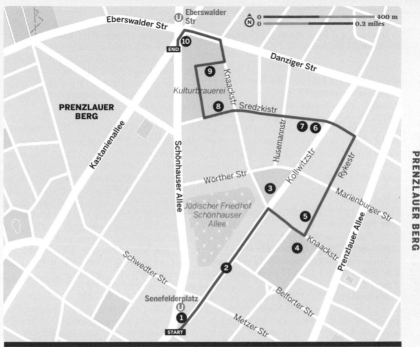

🏃 Neighbourhood Walk
Poking Around Prenzlauer Berg

START SENEFELDER PLATZ
END KONNOPKE'S IMBISS
LENGTH 1.2KM; 1½ HOURS

Start out at **1 Senefelder Platz**, a patch of green named for Alois Senefelder, an Austro-German actor who invented lithography. Note the marble statue with his name chiselled into the pedestal in mirror-writing, just as it would be using his printing technique. Head northeast on **2 Kollwitzstrasse**, where the huge LPG organic supermarket and the ultradeluxe Palais KolleBelle apartment complex are solid indicators of the neighbourhood's upmarket demographics.

You'll soon arrive at **3 Kollwitzplatz** (p179), a square named for the artist Käthe Kollwitz, who lived here with her husband for over 40 years while tending to the destitute. Follow Knaackstrasse to Rykestrasse, past a row of popular cafes, and note the circular **4 Wasserturm**, Berlin's oldest water tower (1877), which is now honeycombed with pie-sliced flats. In Nazi Germany, its

machine room went through a sinister stint as an improvised prison and torture centre. Follow Rykestrasse to the **5 Synagoge Rykestrasse**, which survived WWII and once again hosts Shabbat services.

Continue on Rykestrasse to Sredzkistrasse, perhaps stopping for a cuppa and delicious homemade cakes at **6 Anna Blume** or a browse at **7 Bücher Tauschbaum**, a free book exchange made from tree trunks.

Further up on the right looms the sprawling **8 Kulturbrauerei** (p179), a brewery-turned-cultural-complex. Admire the gorgeous architecture whose fanciful turrets and towers conjure visions of a fairytale fortress. In its northern wing, the free **9 Museum in der Kulturbrauerei** (p179) invites you to get an eyeful of daily life in East Germany.

Exit the Kulturbrauerei on to Knaackstrasse and turn left on Danziger Strasse to wrap up your walk with a *Currywurst* (slivered sausage with 'secret' tomato sauce and a sprinkling of curry powder) from cultkitchen **10 Konnopke's Imbiss** (p183).

several carafes of cheap, tasty red wine. Some of the furniture is made from bric-a-brac scavenged from the brewery grounds. Beer garden in summer.

VAN HOA
VIETNAMESE €

Map p306 (☑030-4057 4197; www.vanhoa-berlin. de; Stargarder Strasse 79; mains €4.90; ☺noon-midnight; ⓤSchönhauser Allee, ⓢSchönhauser Allee) Empty tables are a rare sight at this uncluttered cafe with its small blackboard menu of simply satisfying bowls of beef or chicken piled high with fresh veg and herbs. In winter, the *pho* soups go a long way towards staving off the chills.

NALU DINER
AMERICAN €

Map p306 (☑030-8975 8633; www.nalu-diner. com; Dunckerstrasse 80a; mains €4-11; ☺10am-9pm Wed-Fri, 9am-9pm Sat & Sun; ☒M10, ⓤEberswalder Strasse, ⓢPrenzlauer Allee) With its wall of baseball cards, iced tap water and free coffee refills, Nalu is as authentic an American roadside diner as you'll find this side of the Atlantic. The breakfast (served any time) with maple-syrup-drenched pancakes, hash browns and bacon makes homesick Yankees tear up, and the burgers, sandwiches and shakes are also worthwhile cholesterol spikers.

ZIA MARIA
ITALIAN €

Map p306 (www.pizzaziamaria.de; Pappelallee 32a; pizza slices €1.50-3.50; ☺noon-11.30pm; ☒12, ⓢSchönhauser Allee, ⓤSchönhauser Allee) This pizza kitchen-cum-gallery gets a big thumbs up for its freshly made crispy-crust pies with classic and eclectic toppings, including wafer-thin prosciutto, nutmeg-laced artichokes and pungent Italian sausage. Two slices are enough to fill up most bellies. Pour your own wine from the barrel.

KAUF DICH GLÜCKLICH
CAFE €

Map p306 (☑030-4862 3292; www.kaufdich gluecklich-shop.de/berlin; Oderberger Strasse 44; meals €3-6; ☺10am-1am; ☎; ☒M10, M1, 12, ⓤEberswalder Strasse) This retro-styled cafe on one of Prenzlauer Berg's prettiest streets is famous for its fresh waffles and home-made ice cream. Order at the counter, grab a table and start salivating.

HÜFTENGOLD
CAFE €

Map p306 (☑030-4171 4500; Oderberger Strasse 27; mains €4-8; ☺10am-11pm; ☒M1, M10, 12, ⓤEberswalder Strasse) This shoebox-sized cafe really comes into its own on sunny days when the vintage benches and tables on the flowery pavement terrace become the perfect people-watching perch. While kicking back with breakfast, coffee or a light meal, look up to admire the beautiful facades of the restored 19th-century town-houses that were saved from demolition in the late '70s.

SALT 'N BONE
BRITISH €€

Map p306 (☑030-9144 8885; www.saltnbone.de; Schliemannstrasse 31; mains €13-22; ☺5pm-2am Tue-Sun; ☎; ☒12, ⓢPrenzlauer Allee, Schön-hauser Allee, ⓤSchönhauser Allee) Run by an Irish couple, this rustic gastropub draws upon the zeitgeist with unpolished furniture, naked light bulbs and vintage photos. The soulful menu puts local meat to good use in such dishes as rum and cola-glazed ribs, homemade bangers with mash, and 'meat on a stick' (pork belly). Homesick Brits invade for the Sunday roast.

ZUM SCHUSTERJUNGEN
GERMAN €€

Map p306 (☑030-442 7654; www.zumschus terjungen.com; Danziger Strasse 9; mains €9-17; ☺11am-midnight; ⓤEberswalder Strasse) At this old-school gastropub, rustic Berlin charm is doled out with as much abandon as the delish home cooking. Big platters of goulash, roast pork and *sauerbraten* feed both tummy and soul, as do the regionally brewed Berliner Schusterjunge Pilsner and Märkischer Landmann black beer.

✖ Kollwitzplatz & the South Kiez

CHUTNIFY
INDIAN €

Map p306 (☑030-4401 0795; www.chutnify.com; Sredzkistrasse 43; mains €6.50-8.50; ☺noon-11pm Tue-Sun; ☎; ☒M2, M10, ⓤEberswalder Strasse) Aparna Aurora's little restaurant is spicing up Berlin's rather bland Indian food scene. Here the focus is on authentic South Indian street food with a special nod to do-sas (a type of crêpe) filled with everything from potato masala to tandoori chicken.

HABBA HABBA
MIDDLE EASTERN €

Map p306 (☑030-3674 5726; www.habba-habba. de; Kastanienallee 15; dishes €4.50-9; ☺10am-10pm; ☎; ☒M1, 12, ⓤEberswalder Strasse) This tiny *Imbiss* (snack bar) makes the best

---

LOCAL KNOWLEDGE

STREET FOOD SUNDAYS
••••••••••••••••••••••••••••••

Street Food auf Achse (Map p306; ☑030-4431 0737; www.streetfoodaufachse.de; Kulturbrauerei, btwn Schönhauser Allee, Knaackstrasse, Eberswalder Strasse & Sredzkistrasse; ⊙noon-6pm Sun spring-autumn) On Sunday, the **Kulturbrauerei** (p179) gets mobbed by hungry folk keen on a first-class culinary journey at economy prices. Dozens of mobile kitchens set up in the courtyard of this 19th-century red-brick brewery turned cultural complex, and there's a beer garden as well as occasional live music and other entertainment.

---

wraps in town for our money, especially the one stuffed with tangy pomegranate-marinated chicken and nutty buckwheat dressed in a minty yoghurt sauce. Other faves include the halloumi salad and the coriander kofta. All dishes are available in vegetarian and vegan versions.

FRÄULEIN KIMCHI   KOREAN €
Map p306 (☑030-8975 5102; www.fraeulein kimchi.com; Kollwitzstrasse 46; mains €6.50-9; ⊙5-10pm Tue-Thu & Sun, noon-10pm Fri & Sat; ⓤSenefelder Platz) 'Fräulein Kimchi' is really Lauren Lee, a Korean-American whirlwind with a degree in opera whose 'Seoul-Food' proved to be such a big hit at local street-food markets that she decided to open a bricks-and-mortar branch. Try the signature ramen burger made with slow-cooked beef, kimchi and condiments served on a homemade 'ramen bun'.

KONNOPKE'S IMBISS   GERMAN €
Map p306 (☑030-442 7765; www.konnopke-imbiss.de; Schönhauser Allee 44a; sausages €1.30-2; ⊙9am-8pm Mon-Fri, 11.30am-8pm Sat; ⓐM1, M10, ⓤEberswalder Strasse) Brave the inevitable queue at this famous sausage kitchen, ensconced in the same spot below the elevated U-Bahn tracks since 1930, but now equipped with a heated pavilion and an English menu. The 'secret' sauce topping its classic *Currywurst* comes in a four-tier heat scale from mild to wild.

W-DER IMBISS   FUSION €
Map p306 (☑030-4435 2206; www.w-derimbiss. de; Kastanienallee 49; dishes €5-12; ⊙noon-10pm

Sun-Thu, to 11pm Fri & Sat; ☒; ⓐM1, ⓤRosenthaler Platz) The self-described home of 'indo-mexi-cal-ital' fusion, W has for years been delighting fans with its signature naan pizza freshly baked in the tandoor oven and decorated with anything from avocado to smoked salmon. The fish tacos, thali curry spread and tandoori salmon also have their fans.

UMAMI   VIETNAMESE €€
Map p306 (☑030-2886 0626; www.umami-restaurant.de; Knaackstrasse 16-18; mains €7.50-15; ⊙noon-11.30pm; ☎☒; ⓐM2, ⓤSenefelderplatz) A mellow 1950s lounge-vibe and an inspired menu of Indochine home cooking divided into 'regular' and 'vegetarian' choices are the main draws of this restaurant with large pavement terrace. Leave room for the green-tea apple pie or a Vietnamese cupcake called 'popcake'. The six-course family meal is a steal at €20 (€9 per additional person).

LUCKY LEEK   VEGAN €€
Map p306 (☑030-6640 8710; www.lucky-leek. de; Kollwitzstrasse 54; mains €14-20, 3-/5-course dinners €33/55; ⊙6-10pm Wed-Sun; ☒; ⓤSenefelderplatz) Josita Hartanto has a knack for coaxing maximum flavour out of the vegetable kingdom and for boldly combining ingredients in unexpected ways. Hers is one of the best vegan restaurants in town and is especially lovely in the summer, when seating expands to a leafy pavement terrace. No à la carte on Fridays and Saturdays.

STANDARD – SERIOUS PIZZA   ITALIAN €€
Map p306 (☑030-4862 5614; www.standard-berlin.de; Templiner Strasse 7; pizza €8.50-12.50; ⊙6pm-midnight Tue-Fri, 1pm-midnight Sat & Sun; ☎; ⓤSenefelderplatz) The name is definitely not the game, for the Neapolitan-style pizzas here are anything but standard. Topped with such quality ingredients as San Marzano tomatoes, from the heel of Vesuvius, they are tickled to perfection in a ferociously hot cupola furnace.

MUSE   INTERNATIONAL €€
Map p306 (☑030-4005 6289; www.museberlin. de; Immanuelkirchstrasse 31; burgers €8.50-14.50, small plates €4.50-5; ⊙noon-3.30pm Tue-Fri, 6-10.30pm Mon-Sat, 11am-5pm Sun; ☎; ⓐM2) What began as a supper club in the home of owners Caroline and Tobias has grown into a rustic-chic neighbourhood

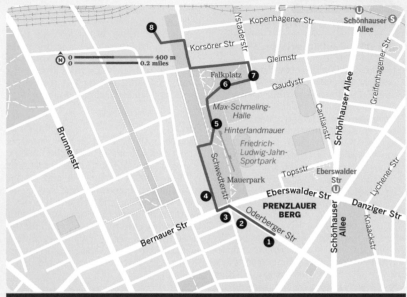

🏃 Local Life
Sundays Around the Mauerpark

Locals, neo-Berliners and tourists – everyone flocks to the Mauerpark on Sundays. It's an energetic urban tapestry where a flea market, karaoke and bands provide entertainment, and people gather for barbecues, basketball and boules. A graffiti-covered section of the Berlin Wall recalls the time when the park was part of the death strip separating East and West Berlin.

① Bright Beginnings

Start your day on Oderberger Strasse, with breakfast at Hüftengold (p182) or waffles at Kauf Dich Glücklich (p182), and admire the beautiful facades of the restored 19th-century townhouses that were saved from demolition in the late '70s when the street still dead-ended at the Berlin Wall. On sunny days, grab an outside table and watch a multicultural passel of people on parade.

② Coffee Deluxe

The pioneers of third-wave coffee in Berlin, Yumi and Kiduk make a mean cuppa java from freshly roasted top-flight beans in their tiny industrial-flavoured cafe, **Bonanza Coffee Heroes** (Map p306; www.bonanzacoffee.de; Oderberger Strasse 35; ⏰8.30am-6.30pm Mon-Fri, 10am-6.30pm Sat & Sun; 📞; 🚊M1, M10, 12, 🚇Eberswalder Strasse). Lines can be long, giving you plenty of time to inhale the tempting aroma and to admire the hip laboratory-like set up with its shiny machines, mills and filters.

③ Confronting Cold War History

During the Cold War, East met West at Bernauer Strasse, now paralleled by a 1.4km-long linear multimedia memorial (p177) that vividly illustrates the realities of life with the Berlin Wall. It ends at Schwedter Strasse and follows the former border-patrol path. This is the best place in town to learn about the Berlin Wall, and even walking just a short stretch is an eye-opening experience.

④ Urban Archaeology

After this dose of history, hit the Flohmarkt im Mauerpark (p187) for some quality hunting and gathering of retro threads, cool stuff by local designers, GDR-era household items and vintage vinyl. Afterwards, fortify yourself at a street food stall or drag your loot to a market beer garden and chillout in the sun.

5 Bearpit Karaoke

On most summer Sundays, Berlin's best free entertainment kicks off around 3pm when Joe Hatchiban sets up his custom-made mobile **karaoke** (Map p306; www.bearpitkaraoke.de; Amphitheatre Mauerpark; ⏰around 3-8pm Sun spring-autumn; 🚋M1, M10, 12, [U]Eberswalder Strasse) unit in the Mauerpark's amphitheatre. As many as 2000 people cram on to the stone bleachers to cheer and clap for eager crooners ranging from giggling 11-year-olds to Broadway-calibre belters.

6 Falkplatz

Studded with ancient chestnut, oak, birch, ash and poplar trees, this leafy park was a parade ground for Prussian soldiers back in the 19th century and used to grow vegetables right after WWII. Today, it's a great place to relax on the grass and watch kids frolicking around the sea-lion fountain or searching for other animal sculptures tucked among the shrubs.

7 Burgermania

New York meets Berlin at expat favourite **Bird** (Map p306; ☎030-5105 3283; www.thebirdinberlin.com; Am Falkplatz 5; burgers €9.50-14, steaks from €22.50; ⏰6pm-midnight Mon-Thu, 4pm-midnight Fri, noon-midnight Sat & Sun; 📶; 🚋M1, [U]Schönhauser Allee, [S]Schönhauser Allee), whose dry-aged steaks, burgers and hand-cut fries might just justify the hype. Sink your teeth into a dripping half-pounder made from freshly ground premium German beef trapped between a toasted English muffin.

8 Northern Mauerpark

To escape the Mauerpark frenzy and see where the locals relax, head north of the Gleimstrasse tunnel. This is where you'll find an enchanting birch grove; the **Jugendfarm Moritzhof** (Map p306; ☎030-4402 4220; www.jugendfarm-moritzhof.de; Schwedter Strasse 90; ⏰noon-6pm Mon-Fri, 1-6pm Sat; 🚋M1, [U]Schönhauser Allee, [S]Schönhauser Allee), a farm playground complete with barnyard animals; and daredevils scaling the **Schwedter Nordwand** (Map p306; ☎0179 172 7577; www.alpinclub-berlin.de; Schwedter Strasse, near Kopenhagener Strasse; ⏰24hr; 🚋M1, [U]Schönhauser Allee, [S]Schönhauser Allee) climbing wall operated by the German Alpine Club.

bistro. The all-day gourmet burger menu gets an added dimension in the evening with an international small-plate potpourri. On some Saturdays, either they or guest chefs host multicourse meals in the supper-club tradition.

DER HAHN IST TOT! FRENCH €€

Map p306 (☎030-6570 6756; www.der-hahn-ist-tot.de; Zionskirchstrasse 40; 4-course dinners €21; ⏰6.30-11pm Tue-Sun; 🥕; 🚋M1, [U]Senefelderplatz, Bernauer Strasse) A French children's ditty inspired the curious name, which translates as 'The rooster is dead!'. At this homey restaurant the deceased chicken is turned into *coq au vin*, the classic French country stew, which always features on one of the three weekly changing four-course dinners (one of them meat-free) that shine a spotlight on the best of French and German rural cooking.

ODERQUELLE GERMAN €€

Map p306 (☎030-4400 8080; www.oderquelle.de; Oderberger Strasse 27; mains €12-20; ⏰6-11pm Mon-Sat, noon-11pm Sun; 🚋M1, 12, [U]Eberswalder Strasse) It's always fun to pop by this woodsy resto and see what's inspired the chef today. Most likely it will be a well-crafted hearty German meal, perhaps with a slight Mediterranean nuance. On the standard menu, the crispy *Flammkuche* (Alsatian pizza) is a reliable standby. Best seat: on the pavement so you can keep an eye on the parade of passers-by.

DRINKING & NIGHTLIFE

★PRATER BIERGARTEN BEER GARDEN

Map p306 (☎030-448 5688; www.pratergarten.de; Kastanienallee 7-9; snacks €2.50-6; ⏰noon-late Apr-Sep, weather permitting; [U]Eberswalder Strasse) Berlin's oldest beer garden has seen beer-soaked nights since 1837 and is still a charismatic spot for guzzling a custom-brewed Prater Pilsner beneath the ancient chestnut trees (self-service). Kids can romp around the small play area.

In foul weather, and in winter, the adjacent beer hall is a fine place to sample classic Berlin dishes (mains €10 to €20).

★WEINEREI FORUM WINE BAR

Map p306 (☎030-440 6983; www.weinerei.com; Fehrbelliner Strasse 57; ⏰10am-midnight;

☎; ⊟M1, Ⓤ Rosenthaler Platz) After 8pm, this living-room-style cafe turns into a wine bar that works on the honour principle: you 'rent' a wine glass for €2, then help yourself to as much vino as you like and in the end decide what you want to pay. Please be fair to keep this fantastic concept going.

ZUM STARKEN AUGUST PUB

Map p306 (☑030-2520 9020; www.zumstarken august.de; Schönhauser Allee 56; ⊘11am-1am Sun & Mon, to 2am Tue, to 3am Wed, to 4am Thu, to 5am Fri & Sat; ⊟M1, M10, Ⓤ Eberswalder Strasse) Part circus, part burlesque bar, this vibrant venue dressed in Victorian-era exuberance is a fun and friendly addition to the Prenzlauer Berg pub culture. Join the unpretentious, international crowd over cocktails and craft beers while being entertained with drag-hosted bingo, burlesque divas, wicked cabaret or the hilarious 'porno karaoke'.

BRYK BAR COCKTAIL BAR

Map p306 (☑030-3810 0165; www.bryk-bar.com; Rykestrasse 18; ⊘noon-2am Sun-Thu, to 3am Fri & Sat; ⊟M2, M10, ⓈPrenzlauer Allee) Both vintage and industrial elements contribute to the unhurried, dapper ambience at this darkly lit cocktail lab. Bar chef Frank Grosser whips unusual ingredients into such experimental liquid teasers as Kamasutra with a Hangover, which blends rum with lemon, honey and white chocolate–horseradish foam.

The free dill popcorn is positively addictive. In fine weather, the terrace beckons.

EMILS BIERGARTEN BEER GARDEN

(www.wbb-pankow.de/biergarten; Berliner Strasse 80-82; ⊘3-10pm Apr-Oct, weather permitting; ⊟M1, Ⓤ Vinetastrasse) This simple, urban beer garden on the grounds of a former brewery has a pedigree going back to the early 20th century and, after a 20-year hiatus, was finally revived in 2013. The good beer selection, relaxed local crowd, pizza and bratwurst, all at down-to-earth prices, fill tables to capacity on balmy summer nights.

HERMAN PUB

Map p306 (☑030-4431 2854; www.bravebel gians.be; Schönhauser Allee 173; ⊘6pm-3am; Ⓤ Senefelderplatz) Named for owner Bart Neirynck's German teacher, Herman offers up a bewildering range of Belgian beers, 100 in all, from abbey ale and wheat beer to

Lambic and India pale ale. If you're feeling flush, order a *bière brut*, a potent top-shelf brew cave-aged in the Champagne region of France.

CASTLE PUB PUB

(☑0151 6767 6757; www.castlepub.de; Hochstrasse 2; ⊘6pm-late; ☎; Ⓤ Gesundbrunnen, ⓈGesundbrunnen) What started out as a regular Irish pub has morphed into an oasis of craft beer with over 30 varieties on tap plus 100 more in bottles. There's even a resident microbrewery, Two Fellas Brewery. Fun events like a pub quiz, karaoke and comedy shows give this Castle a grungy hipster vibe.

CAFE CHAGALL BAR

Map p306 (☑030-441 5881; www.cafe-chagall. com; Kollwitzstrasse 2; ⊘10am-3am Mon-Sat, to 2am Sun; Ⓤ Senefelderplatz) Proof that the boho spirit is not dead in Prenzlauer Berg, Chagall is flooded with a congenial mix of locals, expats and visitors. They come for cold drinks served by staff who make everyone feel welcome. Separate smoking room in back, big pavement terrace in summer and Russian food in the affiliated restaurant next door.

GREIFBAR GAY

Map p306 (☑030-8975 1498; www.greifbar.com; Wichertstrasse 10; ⊘10pm-6am; ⓈSchönhauser Allee, Ⓤ Schönhauser Allee) Men-Drinks-Cruising: Greifbar's motto says it all. This traditional Prenzlauer Berg gay bar draws a mixed crowd of jeans, sneakers, leather and skin, sniffing each other out below the big-screen video in the bar, before retiring to the private play zone in the back.

BASSY CLUB

Map p306 (☑030-3744 8020; www.bassy-club. de; Schönhauser Allee 176a; ⊘9pm-late, concerts 11pm; Ⓤ Senefelderplatz) Most punters here have a post-Woodstock birth date, but happily ride the retro wave at this trashy-charming concert and party den dedicated 'strictly' to pre-1969 sounds on vinyl – surf music, rockabilly, swing and country among them. Concerts, burlesque cabaret and the infamous **Chantals House of Shame** (Map p306; www.facebook.com/ChantalsHouseof Shame; Bassy Club; ⊘11pm-8am Thu) gay party on Thursdays beef up the schedule. Dress creatively.

DECK 5   BAR
Map p306 (www.freiluftrebellen.de; Schönhauser
Allee 80; ⏰noon-midnight, weather permitting
usually Apr-Sep; 🚊M1, Ⓢ Schönhauser Allee,
Ⓤ Schönhauser Allee) Soak up the rays, grand
city views and colourful cocktails at this
beach bar in the sky while sinking your
toes into tons of sand lugged to the top
parking deck of the Schönhauser Arkaden
mall. After mall hours (10am to 9pm, Monday to Saturday) access is via the never-
ending flight of stairs from Greifenhagener
Strasse.

BECKETTS KOPF   COCKTAIL BAR
Map p306 (📞030-9900 5188; www.becketts-
kopf.de; Pappelallee 64; ⏰8pm-late; 🚊12,
Ⓢ Schönhauser Allee, Ⓤ Schönhauser Allee)
Past Samuel Beckett's portrait, the art of
cocktail-making is taken very seriously. Settle into a heavy armchair in the warmly lit
lounge and take your sweet time perusing
the extensive – and poetic – drinks menu.
All the classics are accounted for, of course,
but it's the seasonal special concoctions
that truly stimulate the senses.

Reservations recommended as there is
no standing allowed.

AUGUST FENGLER   BAR
Map p306 (www.augustfengler.de; Lychener
Strasse 11; ⏰7pm-4am; 🚊M1, Ⓤ Eberswalder
Strasse) With its flirty vibe, tiny dance floor
and foosball in the cellar, this local institution scores a trifecta on key ingredients for a
good night out. Wallet-friendly drinks prices and a pretension-free crowd don't hurt
either. Music-wise anything goes, from new
wave, rock and Latin to soul, indie and ska.

☆ ENTERTAINMENT

KOOKABURRA   COMEDY
Map p306 (📞030-4862 3186; www.comedy
club.de; Schönhauser Allee 184; tickets €12-16;
⏰7.30pm Tue-Thu, 7pm Fri & Sat, 6pm Sun; Ⓤ Rosa-Luxemburg-Platz) This living-room-style
comedy club delivers an assembly line of
belly laughs in cosy digs at a former bank
building. Check the schedule for English-
speaking funny folk spinning everyday
material into comedy gold. Also recommended: Karsten Kaie's 'How to Become
a Berliner in One Hour?'. Food and drink
served.

🛍 SHOPPING

★ UPCYCLING
DELUXE   FASHION & ACCESSORIES
Map p306 (📞030-338 4892; www.upcycling-
deluxe.com; Kastanienallee 22; ⏰noon-8pm
Mon-Fri, 11am-8pm Sat; 🚊M1, Ⓤ Eberswalder
Strasse) 🧦 Door mats made from flip-flops,
hats from coffee bags, paper from elephant
poo – there's no telling what's in store at
this bilevel shop packed with affordable
and useful products created from what is,
essentially, garbage by some 50 upcycling
designers and eco-conscious co-ops around
the world.

★ TA(U)SCHE   FASHION & ACCESSORIES
Map p306 (📞030-4030 1770; www.tausche.de;
Raumerstrasse 8; ⏰10am-8pm Mon-Fri, to 6pm
Sat; Ⓤ Eberswalder Strasse) Heike Braun and
Antje Strubels now sell their ingenious
messenger-style bags around the world,
but this is the shop where it all began. Bags
come in 11 sizes with exchangeable flaps
that zip off and on in seconds. There's a
huge range of designs to match your mood
or outfit, plus various inserts, depending on
whether you need to lug a laptop, a camera
or nappies (diapers).

FLOHMARKT IM MAUERPARK   MARKET
Map p306 (www.flohmarktimmauerpark.de; Bernauer Strasse 63-64; ⏰9am-6pm Sun; 🚊M1, M10,
12, Ⓤ Eberswalder Strasse) Join the throngs of
thrifty trinket hunters, bleary-eyed clubbers and excited tourists sifting for treasure
at this always busy flea market with cult
status, running right where the Berlin Wall
once ran. Source new faves among retro
threads, local-designer T-shirts, vintage vinyl and offbeat stuff. Street-food stands and
beer gardens, including **Mauersegler** (Map
p306; 📞030-9788 0904; www.mauersegler-
berlin.de; ⏰2pm-2am May-Oct; 🕯; 🚊M10,
Ⓤ Eberswalder Strasse), provide sustenance.

RATZEKATZ   TOYS
Map p306 (📞030-681 9564; www.ratzekatz.de;
Raumerstrasse 7; ⏰10am-7pm Mon-Sat; 🚊12,
Ⓤ Eberswalder Strasse) Packed with quality playthings, this adorable shop made
headlines a few years ago when Angelina
Jolie and son Maddox picked out a Jurassic
Park's worth of dinosaurs. Even without the
celeb glow, it's a fine place to source everything from Siku cars and trucks to Ravens-
burger jigsaws, Lego and piles of plush toys.

LUXUS INTERNATIONAL   GIFTS & SOUVENIRS
Map p306 (📞030-8643 5500; www.luxus-inter national.de; Kastanienallee 84; ⊙11am-8pm Mon-Sat; 🚇M1, Ⓤ Eberswalder Strasse) There's no shortage of creative spirits in Berlin, but not many of them can afford their own shop. In comes Luxus International, a unique concept store that rents these creatives a shelf or two to display their original designs: T-shirts, tote bags, ashtrays, lamps, candles, mugs etc. You never know what you'll find, but you can bet it won't be run of the mill.

KOLLWITZPLATZMARKT   MARKET
Map p306 (Kollwitzstrasse; ⊙noon-7pm Thu, 9am-4pm Sat; Ⓤ Senefelderplatz) On the edge of lovely and leafy Kollwitzplatz square, Berlin's poshest farmers market has everything you need to put together a gourmet picnic or meal. Velvety gorgonzola, juniper-berry smoked ham, crusty sourdough bread and homemade pesto are among the exquisite morsels scooped up by well-heeled locals. The Saturday edition also features handicrafts. Cap a spree with a glass of sparkling wine.

SAINT GEORGES   BOOKS
Map p306 (📞030-8179 8333; www.saintgeorges bookshop.com; Wörther Strasse 27; ⊙11am-8pm Mon-Fri, to 7pm Sat; 🐾; Ⓤ Senefelderplatz) Laid-back and low-key, Saint Georges bookshop is a sterling spot to track down new and used English-language fiction and non-fiction. The selection includes plenty of rare and out-of-print books as well as literature by foreign authors translated into English.

TRÖDELMARKT ARKONAPLATZ   MARKET
Map p306 (www.troedelmarkt-arkonaplatz. de; Arkonaplatz; ⊙10am-4pm Sun; 🚇M1, M10, Ⓤ Bernauer Strasse) Surrounded by cafes perfect for carbo-loading, this smallish flea market on a leafy square lets you ride the retro frenzy with plenty of groovy furniture, accessories, clothing, vinyl and books, including some East German vintage items. It's easily combined with a visit to the nearby Flohmarkt im Mauerpark (p187).

THATCHERS   FASHION & ACCESSORIES
Map p306 (www.thatchers.de; Kastanienallee 21; ⊙11am-7pm Mon-Sat; 🚇M1, Ⓤ Eberswalder Strasse) Founded in 1989, this pioneering Berlin fashion label specialises in well-tailored clothing that's feminine and versatile and divided into basics, classics and couture, with prices to match. Its hand-stitched smart dresses, skirts and shirts look almost plain on the rack, but actually go well from office to dinner to nightclub – but not quickly out of fashion.

City West & Charlottenburg

KURFÜRSTENDAMM & AROUND | SAVIGNYPLATZ & KANTSTRASSE

Neighbourhood Top Five

1 **Schloss Charlottenburg** (p191) Marvelling at the Prussian royal lifestyle, then relaxing with a picnic by the carp pond in the palace park.

2 **Story of Berlin** (p195) Finishing up an engaging survey of city history with a tour of a creepy Cold War–era atomic bunker.

3 **Kaiser-Wilhelm-Gedächtniskirche** (p196) Meditating upon the futility of war at this majestically ruined 19th-century church.

4 **Berlin Zoo** (p195) Communing with creatures from apes to zebras at the world's most species-rich animal park.

5 **Bikini Berlin** (p201) Shopping for idiosyncratic Berlin fashions and accessories at this architecturally stunning concept mall.

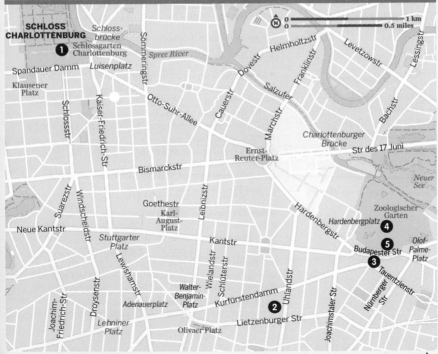

For more detail of this area see Map p316 ➡

Lonely Planet's Top Tip

Leaving from Zoologischer Garten, bus 100 and 200 pass many blockbuster sights (including Potsdamer Platz and the Reichstag) on their route through the central city to Alexanderplatz.

✕ Best Places to Eat

➡ Restaurant am Steinplatz (p198)

➡ Restaurant Faubourg (p197)

➡ Good Friends (p198)

➡ Butcher (p198)

For reviews, see p197.➡

⊖ Best Places to Drink

➡ Bar am Steinplatz (p198)

➡ Diener Tattersall (p199)

➡ Monkey Bar (p199)

For reviews, see p198.➡

◉ Best Museums

➡ Museum Berggruen (p193)

➡ C/O Berlin (p196)

➡ Museum für Fotografie (p196)

➡ Käthe-Kollwitz-Museum (p195)

For reviews, see p193.➡

Explore: City West & Charlottenburg

West Berlin's commercial hub during the city's division, Charlottenburg still counts its famous shopping boulevard, the Kurfürstendamm, among its biggest drawcards. Fashionable boutiques mix it up with high-street chains and department stores along this strip and its leafy side streets. It continues east as Tauentzienstrasse, which culminates at the humongous KaDeWe department store.

En route, witness the new construction and revitalisation of the City West area around the landmark Kaiser-Wilhelm-Gedächtniskirche, a church ruin turned antiwar memorial. Nearby, elephants trumpet and lions roar in the famous Berlin Zoo, a sure-fire hit with kids.

After satisfying your shopping urges, head out to must-see Schloss Charlottenburg for a glimpse of how the Prussian royalty spent its money in centuries past. Tour the fancifully decorated living quarters, then relax with a stroll in lushly landscaped gardens. In fine weather, consider bringing a picnic. A trip to the palace is easily combined with a spin around the trio of excellent art museums nearby.

Throughout Charlottenburg, you'll never be far from a smart cafe in which to indulge in a coffee-and-cake break. Though the area was a giddy nightlife district during the Golden Twenties, today's after-dark action is mostly confined to restaurants and bars, along with a couple of jazz and mainstream dance clubs.

Local Life

➡**Shopping** Shop till you drop at high-street chains and high-fashion boutiques along Ku'damm (p195) and its side streets or at the Bikini Berlin (p201) concept mall.

➡**The Asian mile** Find your favourite among the authentic Chinese eateries in Berlin's Little Asia (p197) along Kantstrasse.

➡**Views** Enjoy sunset drinks at the Monkey Bar (p199).

Getting There & Away

➡**Bus** Zoologischer Garten is the western terminus for buses 100 and 200. M19, M29 and X10 travel along Kurfürstendamm. Lines 309 and M45 go to Schloss Charlottenburg, X9 and 109 to Tegel airport.

➡**S-Bahn** S5 and S7 link to Hauptbahnhof and Alexanderplatz via Zoologischer Garten. The circle line S41/S42 passes through the district's western edge.

➡**U-Bahn** Uhlandstrasse, Kurfürstendamm and Wittenbergplatz stations (U1) put you right into shopping central.

TOP SIGHT
SCHLOSS CHARLOTTENBURG

Schloss Charlottenburg is an exquisite baroque palace and the best place in Berlin to soak up the one-time grandeur of the royal Hohenzollern clan. A visit is especially pleasant in summer when you can fold a stroll around the palace garden into a day of peeking at royal treasures and lavishly furnished period rooms reflecting centuries of royal tastes and lifestyles.

The palace started out rather modestly, as a petite summer retreat built for Sophie-Charlotte, wife of Elector Friedrich III, and was expanded in the mode of Versailles after the elector's promotion to king in 1701. Subsequent royals dabbled with the compound, most notably Frederick the Great who added the spectacular Neuer Flügel. Reconstruction of the Schloss after its WWII drubbing was completed in 1966.

The grand Schloss complex consists of the main building and three smaller structures scattered about the sprawling **Schlossgarten Charlottenburg** (Palace Park; www.spsg. de; Spandauer Damm 20-24; M45, 109, 309, USophie-Charlotte-Platz, Richard-Wagner-Platz) FREE, which is part formal French baroque garden, part unruly English landscape and all idyllic playground. Hidden among the shady paths, flower beds, lawns, mature trees and carp pond are the sombre Mausoleum, the playful Belvedere and the elegant Neuer Pavillion.

Altes Schloss

Also known as the Nering-Eosander Building after its two architects, the **Altes Schloss** (Old Palace; 030-320 911; closed for renovation) is the central, and oldest, section of the palace, and is fronted by Andreas Schlüter's grand

DON'T MISS

➡ Frederick the Great's apartments in the Neuer Flügel

➡ A stroll around the Schlossgarten

➡ Paintings by Watteau and other French masters

➡ Picasso & Co in the Museum Berggruen

PRACTICALITIES

➡ 030-320 910

➡ www.spsg.de

➡ Spandauer Damm 10-22

➡ day passes to all 4 buildings adult/concession €12/9

➡ hours vary by building

➡ P

➡ M45, 109, 309, URichard-Wagner-Platz, Sophie-Charlotte-Platz

TOP TIPS

➡The Ticket charlottenburg+ (adult/concession €12/9) is a day pass valid for one-day admission to every open building within Charlottenburg Palace Gardens.

➡Arrive early, especially on weekends and in summer when queues can be long.

➡A palace visit is easily combined with a spin around the trio of adjacent art museums.

The Schloss is at its most photogenic from outside the gate in front and the carp pond in the Schlossgarten. If you want to take photographs inside the palaces, you need to buy a photo permit (€3).

BAROQUE CONCERTS

Feel like a member of the Prussian court during the **Berliner Residenz Konzerte** (☑030-2581 0350; www.residenzkonzerte.berlin; various locations at Schloss Charlottenburg, Spandauer Damm 22-24; concert only €29-79, with dinner €66-116; ☺dinner 6pm, concert 8pm), a series of concerts held by candlelight with musicians dressed in powdered wigs and historical costumes playing works by baroque and early classical composers.

equestrian statue of the Great Elector (1699). Inside, the baroque living quarters of Friedrich I and Sophie-Charlotte are an extravaganza in stucco, brocade and overall opulence. Highlights include the **Oak Gallery**, a wood-panelled festival hall draped in family portraits; the charming **Oval Hall** overlooking the park; Friedrich I's bedchamber, with the first-ever bathroom in a baroque palace; and the **Eosander Chapel**, with its trompe l'œil arches. The king's passion for precious china is reflected in the dazzling **Porcelain Chamber**, which is smothered in nearly 3000 pieces of Chinese and Japanese blue ware.

Please note that the Altes Schloss will be closed for much-needed renovation until at least 2017.

Neuer Flügel

The palace's most beautiful rooms are the flamboyant private chambers of Frederick the Great in the **Neuer Flügel** (New Wing; ☑030-320 910; adult/concession incl tour or audioguide €10/7; ☺10am-6pm Tue-Sun Apr-Oct, to 5pm Nov-Mar; ℗) extension, designed in 1746 by royal buddy and star architect of the period Georg Wenzeslaus von Knobelsdorff. The confectionlike **White Hall** banquet room and the **Golden Gallery**, a rococo fantasy of mirrors and gilding, are both standouts. Other rooms display one of the largest collections of 18th-century French paintings outside France, including masterworks by Watteau and Pesne. Also note the apartment of Luise (1776–1810; a popular queen and wife of King Friedrich Wilhelm III), with its stunning bedroom designed by Karl Friedrich Schinkel.

Neuer Pavillion

Returning from a trip to Italy, Friedrich Wilhelm III (r 1797–1848) commissioned Karl Friedrich Schinkel to design the **Neuer Pavillon** (New Pavilion; ☑030-320 910; adult/concession incl audioguide €4/3; ☺10am-6pm Tue-Sun Apr-Oct, to 5pm Nov-Mar) as a summer retreat modelled on neoclassical Italian villas. Today, the minipalace shows off Schinkel's many talents as architect, painter and designer while also presenting sculpture by Christian Daniel Rauch and master paintings by such Schinkel contemporaries as Caspar David Friedrich and Eduard Gaertner.

Belvedere

The late-rococo **Belvedere** (☑030-320 910; adult/concession €4/3; ☺10am-6pm Tue-Sun Apr-Oct) palace, with its distinctive cupola, got its start in 1788 as a private sanctuary for Friedrich Wilhelm II. These days it houses porcelain masterpieces by the royal manufacturer KPM, which was established in 1763 by Frederick the Great. Among the exhibit highlights are the dainty tea cups painted with cheeky cherubs.

Mausoleum

The 1810 temple-shaped **Mausoleum** (⏰030-320 910; adult/concession €2/1; ⏰10am-6pm Tue-Sun Apr-Oct) was conceived as the final resting place of Queen Luise, and was twice expanded to make room for other royals, including Kaiser Wilhelm I and his wife Augusta. Their marble sarcophagi are exquisitely sculpted works of art. More royals are in the crypt (closed to the public).

Sammlung Scharf-Gerstenberg

The stellar **Scharf-Gerstenberg Collection** (⏰030-266 424 242; www.smb.museum/ssg; Schlossstrasse 70; adult/concession incl Museum Berggruen €10/5; ⏰10am-6pm Tue-Fri, 11am-6pm Sat & Sun; ⬛M45, 109, 309, ⓊSophie-Charlotte-Platz, Richard-Wagner-Platz) showcases 250 years of surrealist art, with large bodies of work by such protagonists as René Magritte, Max Ernst and Salvador Dalí. Standouts among their 18th-century forerunners include Goya's spooky etchings and the creepy dungeon scenes by Italian engraver Giovanni Battista Piranesi. Post-WWII surrealist interpretations are represented by Jean Dubuffet.

The collection was founded in the early 20th century by insurance mogul Otto Gerstenberg, a man with a Midas touch and a passion for the arts. Although much of it was destroyed in WWII or disappeared to Russia as war booty, his grandsons used the remainder as a starting point for their own collection, mostly of surrealist art.

A Sammlung Scharf-Gerstenberg ticket will also get you into the Museum Berggruen and vice versa.

Museum Berggruen

Fans of classical modern art will be in their element at the delightful **Museum Berggruen** (⏰030-266 424 242; www.smb.museum/mb; Schlossstrasse 1; adult/concession incl Sammlung Scharf-Gerstenberg €10/5; ⏰10am-6pm Tue-Fri, 11am-6pm Sat & Sun; Ⓟ; ⬛M45, 109, 309, ⓊRichard-Wagner-Platz, Sophie-Charlotte-Platz). Picasso is especially well represented with paintings, drawings and sculptures from all major creative phases. Standouts include the *Seated Harlequin* from his early blue and rose periods and bold cubist canvases like his portrait of Georges Braque. Elsewhere it's off to Paul Klee's emotional world, Matisse's paper cut-outs, Giacometti's famous sculptures and a sprinkling of African art that inspired both Klee and Picasso. Behind the building is a landscaped culture garden.

Tickets also include admission to the Sammlung Scharf-Gerstenberg across the street.

Bröhan Museum

The **Bröhan Museum** (⏰030-3269 0600; www.broehan-museum.de; Schlossstrasse 1a; adult/concession/under 18 €8/5/free; ⏰10am-6pm Tue-Sun; ⬛M45, 109, 309, ⓊSophie-Charlotte-Platz, Richard-Wagner-Platz) trains the spotlight on applied arts from the late 19th century until the outbreak of WWII. Pride of place goes to the **art nouveau collection**, with period rooms, furniture, porcelain and glass art from England, France, Germany, Scandinavia and Austria. A secondary focus is on **art deco** and **functionalism**, styles of the 1920s and 30s. A picture gallery with works by Berlin Secession artists complements the exhibits.

SCHLOSS BY BOAT

From mid-April to early October, a lovely way to travel to or from Schloss Charlottenburg is by the Spree River cruise operated by Stern und Kreisschiffahrt (p271). Boats make the trip twice daily from landing docks in Treptow (1¾ hours) and **Jannowitzbrücke** (Map p300; Ⓤ Jannowitzbrücke; 1¼ hour) and go through Berlin's scenic historic centre to the **palace boat landing** (Bonhoefferufer) just outside the east corner of the park. The return trip also drops off at Friedrichstrasse. Tickets cost €15.50 one way or €23 round trip.

Schloss Charlottenburg is about 3.5km northwest of Zoologischer Garten. For the most scenic approach take the U2 to Sophie-Charlotte-Platz, then walk 1km north on Schlossstrasse, a leafy avenue flanked by dignified town houses built for senior court officials.

TAKE A BREAK

There's a pretty cafe with tree-shaded outdoor seating in the **Kleine Orangerie** (⊘10am-6pm Tue-Sun ; mains €7-17) building near the entrance to the palace gardens.

Belvedere palace (p192)

Abguss-Sammlung Antiker Plastik Berlin

If you are a fan of classical sculpture or simply enjoy studying naked guys who are missing noses or other bodily protrusions, make the **Abguss-Sammlung Antiker Plastik Berlin** (Antique Plaster-Cast Collection; ☏030-342 4054; www.abguss-sammlung-berlin.de; Schlossstrasse 69b; ⊘2-5pm Thu-Sun; Ⓟ; ▣M45, 109, 309, Ⓤ Richard-Wagner-Platz, Sophie-Charlotte-Platz) FREE a stopover. It has works spanning 3500 years, created by cultures as diverse as the Minoan, Roman or Byzantine, allowing you to trace the evolution of this ancient art form. The shop sells plaster-cast copies.

⊙ SIGHTS

Concentrate your sightseeing in the City West around Zoologischer Garten and along the famous Kurfürstendamm boulevard, Berlin's major shopping strip. From here it's about 3.5km northwest to western Berlin's top sight: Schloss Charlottenburg, the grand 18th-century Prussian park-and-palace ensemble.

SCHLOSS CHARLOTTENBURG PALACE
See p191.

KURFÜRSTENDAMM AREA
Map p316 (Kurfürstendamm; Ⓤ Kurfürstendamm, Uhlandstrasse) The 3.5km Kurfürstendamm is a ribbon of commerce that began as a bridle path to the royal hunting lodge in the Grunewald forest. In the early 1870s, Otto von Bismarck, the Iron Chancellor, decided that the capital of the newly founded German Reich needed its own representative boulevard, which he envisioned as even bigger and better than the Champs-Élysées. Today it is Berlin's busiest shopping strip, especially towards its eastern end.

STORY OF BERLIN MUSEUM
Map p316 (☏030-8872 0100; www.story-of-berlin.de; Kurfürstendamm 207-208, enter via Ku'damm Karree mall; adult/concession €12/9; ⊙10am-8pm, last admission 6pm; ▢X9, X10, 109, 110, M19, M29, TXL, Ⓤ Uhlandstrasse) This engaging museum breaks 800 years of Berlin history down into bite-size chunks that are easy to swallow but substantial enough to be satisfying. Each of the 23 rooms uses sound, light, technology and original objects to zero in on a specific theme or epoch in the city's history, from its founding in 1237 to the fall of the Berlin Wall. The creepily fascinating climax is a tour (in English) of a still-functional atomic bunker beneath the building.

KÄTHE-KOLLWITZ-MUSEUM MUSEUM
Map p316 (☏030-882 5210; www.kaethe-kollwitz.de; Fasanenstrasse 24; adult/concession/under 18 €6/3/free, audioguide €3; ⊙11am-6pm; Ⓤ Uhlandstrasse) This museum in a charming villa is devoted to German artist Käthe Kollwitz (1867–1945), whose social and political awareness lent a tortured power to her lithographs, graphics, woodcuts, sculptures and drawings. In the newly revamped

⊙ TOP SIGHT
BERLIN ZOO & AQUARIUM

Berlin's zoo holds a triple record as Germany's oldest, most species-rich and most popular animal park. It gained international fame when the polar bear cub Knut, born at the zoo in 2006, was successfully nursed by a zookeeper after his mother had abandoned him. He died in 2011.

In 1844 King Friedrich Wilhelm IV donated land plus animals from the royal family's private reserve, establishing the zoo. Today's menagerie includes orangutans, koalas, rhinos, giraffes and penguins, many housed in open enclosures designed to resemble their habitat. Under a new director, more than a dozen habitats are currently being modernised. **Feeding sessions** are a major visitor magnet – pick up a schedule at the ticket counter. The adjacent **Zoo-Aquarium** (Map p316; www.aquarium-berlin.de; Budapester Strasse 32; adult/child €14.50/7.50, with zoo €20/10; ⊙9am-6pm; ▥) presents three floors of exotic fish, amphibians and reptiles in darkened halls and glowing tanks. Its tropical **Crocodile Hall** could be the stuff of nightmares, but jellyfish, iridescent poison frogs and a real-life 'Nemo' should bring smiles to most youngsters. The zoo's architecture deserves a special mention, especially the exotic **Elephant Gate**.

DON'T MISS
➜ Great apes
➜ Crocodile Hall
➜ Jellyfish tanks

PRACTICALITIES
➜ Map p316, G4
➜ ☏030-254 010
➜ www.zoo-berlin.de
➜ Hardenbergplatz 8
➜ adult/child €14.50/7.50, with aquarium €20/10
➜ ⊙9am-6.30pm Apr-Sep, to 6pm Mar & Oct, to 4.30pm Nov-Feb
➜ ▢100, 200, Ⓢ Zoologischer Garten, Ⓤ Zoologischer Garten, Kurfürstendamm

TOP SIGHT
KAISER-WILHELM-GEDÄCHTNISKIRCHE

One of Berlin's most photographed landmarks is actually a ruin, albeit an impressive one. Allied bombing on 23 November 1943 left only the husk of the west tower of the magnificent neo-Romanesque church, built in honour of Kaiser Wilhelm I, standing. Now an antiwar memorial, the original was designed by Franz Schwechten and completed in 1895. Historic photographs in the **Gedenkhalle** (Hall of Remembrance), at the bottom of the tower, help you visualise its former grandeur. The hall also contains remnants of the elaborate mosaics that once swathed the entire interior, depicting heroic moments from Kaiser Wilhelm I's life, among other scenes. Note the marble reliefs, liturgical objects and two symbols of reconciliation: an icon cross donated by the Russian Orthodox church and a copy of the Cross of Nails from Coventry Cathedral, which was destroyed by Luftwaffe bombers in 1940.

In 1961 a bell tower and **octagonal church** designed by Egon Eiermann were completed next to the ruined tower; the latter is especially striking thanks to its glowing midnight-blue glass walls. The golden statue of Christ 'floating' above the altar is made of tombac, a type of brass with a high copper content, and weighs 300kg. Admission is free.

DON'T MISS

→ Memorial hall mosaics

→ Blue glass walls

PRACTICALITIES

→ Map p316, G5

→ ☎030-218 5023

→ www.gedaechtnis kirche.com

→ Breitscheidplatz

→ ⊙church 9am-7pm, memorial hall 10am-6pm Mon-Fri, 10am-5.30pm Sat, noon-5.30pm Sun

→ ☒100, 200, ⓊZoologischer Garten, Kurfürstendamm, ⓈZoologischer Garten

---

four-floor exhibit, you first get to meet this extraordinary woman who lived in Berlin for 52 years, then study her artistic visions, including the powerful antihunger lithography *Brot!* (Bread!, 1924) and the woodcut series *Krieg* (War, 1922–23).

MUSEUM FÜR FOTOGRAFIE　　　MUSEUM
Map p316 (☎030-266 424 242; www.smb. museum/mf; Jebensstrasse 2; adult/concession €10/5; ⊙10am-6pm Tue, Wed & Fri, 10am-8pm Thu, 11am-6pm Sat & Sun; ⓈZoologischer Garten, ⓊZoologischer Garten) In a converted Prussian officers' casino, this museum showcases the artistic legacy of Helmut Newton (1920–2004), the Berlin-born enfant terrible of fashion and lifestyle photography, with the two lower floors dedicated to his life and work. On the top floor, the gloriously restored barrel-vaulted **Kaisersaal** (Emperor's Hall) forms a grand backdrop for changing high-calibre photography exhibits drawn from the archive of the Kunstbibliothek (Art Library).

C/O BERLIN　　　GALLERY
Map p316 (☎030-284 441 662; www.co-berlin. org; Amerika Haus, Hardenbergstrasse 22-24; adult/concession/under 18 €10/5/free; ⊙11am-8pm; ⓈZoologischer Garten, ⓊZoologischer Garten) The C/O Berlin is Berlin's most respected private, nonprofit exhibition centre for international photography. Founded in 2000 it moved into its current digs in the historic Amerika Haus near Zoo Station in 2014. Its roster of highbrow exhibits has featured many members of the shutterbug elite, including Annie Leibovitz, Stephen Shore, Nan Goldin and Anton Corbijn.

EUROPA-CENTER　　　LANDMARK
Map p316 (www.europa-center-berlin.de; Breitscheidplatz; ⊙24hr; ℗; ⓈZoologischer Garten, ⓊKurfürstendamm, Zoologischer Garten) The 103m-high Europa-Center shopping mall was Berlin's first 'skyscraper' at its 1965 opening, the giant Mercedes star spinning on its rooftop a symbol of capitalist West Germany's miraculous economic recovery. Today, the gracefully ageing structure has 70 shops and exudes charming retro flair enlivened by such quirky sights as the **Lotus Fountain** and the psychedelic **Flow of TimeClock** by Bernard Gitton.

EATING

The dining quality in Charlottenburg is dependably high and the number of trail-blazing kitchens is growing steadily. Savignyplatz exudes the relaxed and bustling vibe of an Italian piazza on balmy summer nights, while Kantstrasse is lined with many excellent Asian and Spanish eateries.

✗ Kurfürstendamm & Around

CAFÉ-RESTAURANT WINTERGARTEN IM LITERATURHAUS   INTERNATIONAL €€
Map p316 (☑030-882 5414; www.literaturhaus -berlin.de/wintergarten-cafe-restaurant.html; Fasanenstrasse 23; mains €8-16; ⊙9am-midnight; ☑; ⓤUhlandstrasse) The hustle and bustle of Ku'damm is only a block away from this genteel art nouveau villa with attached literary salon and bookshop. Tuck into seasonal bistro cuisine amid elegant Old Berlin flair in the gracefully stucco-ornamented rooms or, if weather permits, in the idyllic garden. Breakfast is served until 2pm.

NENI   INTERNATIONAL €€
Map p316 (☑030-120 221 200; www.neniberlin. de; Budapester Strasse 40; dishes €5-26; ⊙noon-11pm Mon-Fri, 12.30-11pm Sat & Sun; ☑100, 200, Ⓢ Zoologischer Garten, ⓤZoologischer Garten) This bustling greenhouse-style dining hall at the 25hours Hotel Bikini Berlin (p226) presents a spirited menu of meant-to-share dishes inspired by the cuisines of Morocco, Israel, Iran and Spain. Top billing goes to the homemade falafel, the Jerusalem platter, the Reuben sandwich and the chia lemon-curd crumble. The 10th-floor views of the zoo and the rooftops are a bonus.

WOLFF & EBER   SYRIAN, GERMAN €€
(☑030-6881 1018; www.wolffundereber.de; Kulmbacher Strasse 15; mains €10.50-18.50; ⊙6-11pm Sun & Tue-Thu, to midnight Fri & Sat; ⓤSpichernstrasse) This happy fusion of Arab cooking and local ingredients is the brainchild of kitchen chef – and Aleppo refugee – Hadi Nseeny. In a rustic-chic setting he fearlessly pairs venison ragout with figs and cumin for his signature dish. Game – clearly a menu focus – also finds its destiny in the appetiser platter with various pâtés and sausages.

BERLIN'S LITTLE ASIA

It's not quite Chinatown, but if you're in the mood for Asian food, simply head to Kantstrasse between Savignyplatz and Wilmersdorfer Strasse to find the city's densest concentration of authentic Chinese, Vietnamese and Thai restaurants, including the perennially popular **Good Friends** (p198). At lunchtime most offer value-priced specials, perfect for filling up on the cheap.

SCHLEUSENKRUG   GERMAN €€
Map p316 (☑030-313 9909; www.schleusen krug.de; Müller-Breslau-Strasse; mains €4-15; ⊙10am-midnight May-Sep, to 7pm Oct-Apr; Ⓢ Zoologischer Garten, ⓤZoologischer Garten) Sitting pretty on the edge of the Tiergarten, next to a canal lock, Schleusenkrug truly comes into its own during beer garden season. People from all walks of life hunker over big mugs and comfort food – from grilled sausages to *Flammkuche* (Alsatian pizza) and weekly specials. Breakfast is served until 2pm.

★RESTAURANT FAUBOURG   FRENCH €€€
Map p316 (☑030-800 999 7700; www.sofitel -berlin-kurfurstendamm.com; Augsburger Strasse 41; mains €20-42; ⊙noon-11pm; ⓤKurfürstendamm) At this château-worthy French restaurant, head chef Felix Mielke applies punctilious artisanship to top-notch regional ingredients, creating intensely flavoured and beautifully plated dishes. For maximum palate exposure, put together a meal from the appetiser menu, although the mains – prepared either in classic or contemporary fashion – also command attention, as does the wine list. Gorgeous Bauhaus-inspired decor.

GROSZ   EUROPEAN €€€
Map p316 (☑030-652 142 199; www.grosz-berlin. de; Kurfürstendamm 193/194; lunch specials Mon-Fri €13.50, dinner mains €18-74; ⊙9am-11pm Sun-Thu, to 11.30pm Fri & Sat; ⓤUhlandstrasse) This high-ceilinged symphony of marble, brass, mirrors and glossy wood does a masterful job of recreating the elegant aura of a Golden Twenties cafe. Drop by for coffee and a slice of Princess Victoria tart (a mash-up of white chocolate and pistachios), or feast on fine crustaceans, meats and fish prepared in time-honoured continental fashion.

🍴 Savignyplatz & Kantstrasse

ALI BABA ITALIAN €

Map p316 (☎030-881 1350; www.alibaba-berlin.de; Bleibtreustrasse 45; dishes €3-11.50; ⏰11am-2am Sun-Thu, to 3am Fri & Sat; 🌶; [S]Savignyplatz) In business for more years than there are robbers in the eponymous fairy tale, Ali Baba is a bustling port-of-call beloved by shoppers, students, cabbies and party people. They come for its delicious thin-crust pizza and generous portions of pasta served with a side of crusty homemade bread for sopping up the juices.

KOSHARY LUX MIDDLE EASTERN €

Map p316 (☎030-8140 6190; www.facebook.com/klxkosharylux; Grolmanstrasse 27; mains €4.50-7; ⏰noon-3pm & 6-9pm Mon-Thu, noon-10pm Fri & Sat; [S]Savignyplatz, [U]Uhlandstrasse) This darling snack shack deals in North African and Middle Eastern street-food staples like *murtabak* sandwiches from Yemen, orange-olive salad from Morocco and, of course, the namesake Egyptian *koshary*, a mix of lentils, macaroni and rice served with caramelised onions, chickpeas, tomato sauce and a pistachio-spice blend.

BUTCHER BURGERS €€

Map p316 (☎030-323 015 600; www.the-butcher.com; Kantstrasse 144; burgers €9-11.50; ⏰7am-late; 📶; [S]Savignyplatz) No matter if you fancy the Daddy, the Cow Boy or the Ugly – this place knows how to build one hell of a burger. Prime ingredients like Aberdeen Angus beef, house-baked buns and a secret (what else?) sauce make these patty-and-bun combos shine. With its bar and DJ line-up, the Butcher also injects a dose of hip into the 'hood.

★GOOD FRIENDS CHINESE €€

Map p316 (☎030-313 2659; www.goodfriends-berlin.de; Kantstrasse 30; 2-course lunches €7, dinner mains €7-20; ⏰noon-1am; [S]Savignyplatz) Good Friends is widely considered Berlin's best Cantonese restaurant. The ducks dangling in the window are merely an overture to a menu long enough to confuse Confucius, including plenty of authentic home-style dishes. If sea cucumber with fish belly proves too challenging, you can always fall back on sweet-and-sour pork or fried rice with shrimp.

DICKE WIRTIN GERMAN €€

Map p316 (☎030-312 4952; www.dicke-wirtin.de; Carmerstrasse 9; mains €6-16.50; ⏰11am-late; [S]Savignyplatz) Old Berlin charm oozes from every nook and cranny of this been-here-forever pub, which pours nine draught beers (including the superb Kloster Andechs) and nearly three dozen homemade schnapps varieties. Hearty local and German fare like smoked veal dumplings, boiled eel, beef liver and pork roast keeps brains balanced. Bargain lunches, too.

RESTAURANT AM STEINPLATZ GERMAN €€€

Map p316 (☎030-5544 447 053; www.hotelsteinplatz.com; Steinplatz 4; mains €18-38, 4-/5-course dinners €56/65; ⏰noon-2.30pm & 6.30-10.30pm; [P]; 🚌M45, [U]Ernst-Reuter-Platz, Zoologischer Garten, [S]Zoologischer Garten) The 1920s get a 21st-century makeover at this stylish outpost with an open kitchen where Marcus Zimmer feeds regional products into classic German and Berlin recipes. Even rustic beer-hall dishes such as *Eisbein* (boiled pork knuckle) are imaginatively reinterpreted and beautifully plated. A perennial favourite is the Königsberger Klopse (veal dumplings with capers, beetroot and mashed potatoes).

🍷 DRINKING & NIGHTLIFE

Today's Charlottenburg may no longer be the glamorous party pit of the Golden Twenties, but that's not to say that a good time can't still be had. You'll find it in fancy cocktail bars (many of them in hotels) and lovably nostalgic Old Berlin pubs. If you don't want to go home around midnight, a few mainstream dance clubs towards the eastern end of Kurfürstendamm keep the action going.

★BAR AM STEINPLATZ BAR

Map p316 (☎030-554 4440; www.hotelamsteinplatz.com; Steinplatz 4; ⏰4pm-late; [U]Ernst-Reuter-Platz) Christian Gentemann's liquid playground may reside at art-deco Hotel am Steinplatz (p226), but it hardly whispers 'stuffy hotel bar'. The classic and creative drinks (how about a Red Beet Old Fashioned?) often showcase regionally produced spirits and ingredients, and even the draught beer hails from the Berlin-based

ⓘ HAVE A BLAST ON THE BUS

It's a poorly kept secret that one of Berlin's best bargains is a self-guided city tour aboard **bus 100 or 200**, whose routes check off nearly every major sight in the city centre for the price of a public transport ticket (tariff AB, €2.70). You can even get on and off within the two hours of its validity period as long as you continue in the same direction. If you plan to explore all day, a *Tageskarte* (day pass, €7) is your best bet.

Bus 100 travels from Zoologischer Garten (Zoo Station) to Alexanderplatz, passing the Gedächtniskirche, the Siegessäule in the Tiergarten, the Reichstag, the Brandenburger Tor (Brandenburg Gate) and Unter den Linden. **Bus 200** also starts at Bahnhof Zoo, and follows a more southerly route via the Kulturforum museums and Potsdamer Platz before hooking up with Unter den Linden. Without traffic, trips take about 30 minutes. There's no commentary, of course, but it's still a great overview and useful for orientation and understanding the layout of the central city.

Buses run every few minutes but they do get crowded, so be wary of pickpockets. To snag a seat on the upper deck, it's best to board at either terminus, ie Bahnhof Zoo or Alexanderplatz.

Rollberg brewery. Inventive bar bites complement the drinks.

★DIENER TATTERSALL PUB

Map p316 (☎030-881 5329; www.diener-berlin.de; Grolmanstrasse 47; ⏲6pm-2am; [S]Savignyplatz) In business for over a century, this Old Berlin haunt was taken over by German heavyweight champion Franz Diener in the 1950s and has since been one of West Berlin's preeminent artist pubs. From Billy Wilder to Harry Belafonte, they all came for beer and *Bulette* (meat patty), and left behind signed black-and-white photographs that grace Diener's walls to this day.

★MONKEY BAR BAR

Map p316 (☎030-120 221 210; www.25hours-hotel.com; Budapester Strasse 40; ⏲noon-1am Sun-Thu, to 2am Fri & Sat; 📶; 🚌100, 200, [S]Zoologischer Garten, [U]Zoologischer Garten) On the 10th floor of the 25hours Hotel Bikini Berlin (p226), this 'urban jungle' hot spot delivers fabulous views of the city and the Berlin Zoo. On balmy days, the sweeping terrace is a handy perch for sunset drinks selected from a menu that gives prominent nods to tiki concoctions (including the original Trader Vic's Mai Tai) and gin-based cocktail sorcery.

BAR ZENTRAL COCKTAIL BAR

Map p316 (www.barzentral.de; Lotte-Lenya-Bogen 551; ⏲from 5pm; [S]Zoologischer Garten, [U]Zoologischer Garten, Kurfürstendamm) Even though palm trees decorate the walls, there's not a cocktail umbrella in sight at this elegant drinking den tucked into a brick-vaulted S-Bahn arch. Helmed by two Berlin bar gurus, it delivers the gamut of cocktail mainstays alongside adventurous new concoctions.

CONNECTION CLUB GAY

(☎030-218 1432; www.connectionclub.de; Fuggerstrasse 33; ⏲11pm-6am Fri & Sat; [U]Wittenbergplatz) This legendary men-only party den, with two dance floors, a huge cruising area and a three-floor cinema, was a techno pioneer way back in the '80s; despite a recent makeover it still hasn't lost its grip on the scene. Its predecessor, run by drag queen Romy Haag, was a favourite David Bowie hang-out.

☆ ENTERTAINMENT

STAATSOPER IM SCHILLER THEATER OPERA

Map p316 (☎030-2035 4455; www.staatsoper-berlin.de; Bismarckstrasse 110; tickets €18-230; [U]Ernst-Reuter-Platz) Point your highbrow compass towards the Daniel Barenboim-led Staatsoper, Berlin's top opera company. While its historic digs on Unter den Linden are getting a facelift, the high-calibre productions are staged at the Schiller Theater in Charlottenburg. All operas are sung in their original language.

DEUTSCHE OPER BERLIN OPERA

Map p316 (☎030-3438 4343; www.deutscheoperberlin.de; Bismarckstrasse 35; tickets €18-198; [U]Deutsche Opera) The German Opera was founded by local citizens in 1912 as a

WORTH A DETOUR

OLYMPIASTADION & AROUND

The main attraction in far western Berlin is the **Olympiastadion** (Olympic Stadium; ☎030-2500 2322; www.olympiastadion-berlin.de; Olympischer Platz 3; adult/concession self-guided tour €7/5.50, highlights tour €11/9.50; 🕘9am-7pm Apr-Jul, Sep & Oct, 9am-8pm Aug, 10am-4pm Nov-Mar; [S]Olympiastadion, [U]Olympiastadion). Even though it was put through a total modernisation for the 2006 FIFA World Cup, it's hard to ignore the fact that this massive coliseum-like stadium was built by the Nazis for the 1936 Olympic Games. The bombastic bulk of the structure remains but has been softened by the addition of a spidery oval roof, snazzy VIP boxes and top-notch sound, lighting and projection systems. It seats up to 74,650 people for games played by the local premier league Hertha BSC football (soccer) team, concerts, the Pope or Bruce Springsteen.

On nonevent days you can explore the stadium on your own, although renting a multilingual audioguide is recommended (€4). Several times daily, guided tours (some in English, phone ahead) take you into the locker rooms, warm-up areas and VIP areas that are otherwise off limits. Access the stadium via the visitors' centre at the Osttor (eastern gate).

To truly appreciate the grandeur of the stadium, head west past the Maifeld parade grounds to the outdoor viewing platform of the 77m-high **Glockenturm** (Olympic Bell Tower; ☎030-305 8123; www.glockenturm.de; Am Glockenturm; adult/child €4.50/3; 🕘9am-6pm Apr-Oct; [P]; [S]Pichelsberg), which was also built for the 1936 Olympics. En route you'll pass a replica of the Olympic bell (the damaged original is displayed south of the stadium). In the foyer, an exhibit chronicles the ground's history, including the 1936 games, with panels in German and English. A documentary features rare original footage.

About 1.3km south of the stadium is the **Georg Kolbe Museum** (☎030-304 2144; www.georg-kolbe-museum.de; Sensburger Allee 25; adult/concession/under 18 €7/5/free; 🕘10am-6pm Tue-Sun; [P]; 🚌Heerstrasse), dedicated to one of Germany's most influential early-20th-century sculptors (1877–1947). A member of the Berlin Secession, Kolbe distanced himself from traditional sculpture and became a chief exponent of the idealised nude, which later found favour with the Nazis. The newly renovated museum in his former studio and home mounts several exhibits per year with a focus on sculpture by Kolbe and his contemporaries, often juxtaposed with the works by contemporary artists. Built in the late 1920s, it consists of two rectangular brick buildings flanking a sculpture garden. Its **Cafe K** is one of Berlin's most charming museum cafes.

About 2km southeast of the stadium, overlooking the trade fairgrounds, looms another Berlin landmark, the 147m-high **Funkturm** (Radio Tower; ☎030-3038 1905; www.funkturm-messeberlin.de; Messedamm 22; adult/concession platform €5/3, restaurant €3/2; 🕘platform 10am-8pm Mon, to 11pm Tue-Sun, weather permitting; [P]; [U]Kaiserdamm, [S]Messe Nord/ICC). The filigree structure bears an uncanny resemblance to Paris' Eiffel Tower and looks especially attractive when lit up at night. It started transmitting signals in 1926; nine years later the world's first regular TV program was broadcast from here. From the viewing platform at 126m or the restaurant at 55m you can enjoy sweeping views of the Grunewald forest and the western city, as well as the **AVUS**, Germany's first car-racing track, which opened in 1921; AVUS stands for Automobil-, Verkehrs- und Übungsstrasse (auto, traffic and practice track). The Nazis made it part of the autobahn system, which it still is today.

counterpoint to the royal opera (today's Staatsoper) on Unter den Linden. The original building was destroyed in WWII and replaced in 1961 by an introverted modernist venue with seating for nearly 1900 opera aficionados. It presents mostly a classic 19th-century opera repertory with a focus on Verdi, Puccini, Wager and Strauss, all sung in their original language.

BAR JEDER VERNUNFT CABARET

Map p316 (☎030-883 1582; www.bar-jeder-vernunft.de; Schaperstrasse 24; tickets €24.50; [U]Spichernstrasse) Life's still a cabaret at this intimate 1912 mirrored art nouveau tent, which puts on sophisticated song-and-dance shows, comedy and *chansons* nightly. Seating is in upholstered booths or at little cafe tables, both with waiter service.

Many shows are suitable for patrons without German-language skills.

A-TRANE JAZZ

Map p316 (☎030-313 2550; www.a-trane.de; Bleibtreustrasse 1; admission varies; 🕒8pm-1am Sun-Thu, to late Fri & Sat; [S]Savignyplatz) Herbie Hancock and Diana Krall have graced the stage of this intimate jazz club, but mostly it's emerging talent bringing their A-game to the A-Trane. Entry is free on Monday, when local boy Andreas Schmidt and his band get everyone toe-tapping, and after midnight on Saturday for the late-night jam session.

SCHAUBÜHNE THEATRE

Map p316 (☎030-890 023; www.schaubuehne.de; Kurfürstendamm 153; tickets €7-48; [U]Adenauerplatz) In a converted 1920s expressionist cinema by Erich Mendelsohn, this is western Berlin's main stage for experimental, contemporary theatre, usually with a critical and analytical look at current social and political issues. The cast of dedicated actors is led by director Thomas Ostermeier. Some performances feature English subtitles.

SHOPPING

Kurfürstendamm and Tauentzienstrasse are chock-a-block with multiple outlets of international chains flogging fashion and accessories. Further west on Ku'damm are the more high-end boutiques such as Hermès, Cartier and Bulgari. Kantstrasse is the go-to zone for home designs. Connecting side streets, such as Bleibtreustrasse and Schlüterstrasse, house upscale indie and designer boutiques, bookshops and galleries, while Bikini Berlin features cutting-edge concept and flagship stores.

★MANUFACTUM HOMEWARES

Map p316 (☎030-2403 3844; www.manufactum.de; Hardenbergstrasse 4-5; 🕒10am-8pm Mon-Fri, to 6pm Sat; [U]Ernst-Reuter-Platz) 🍃 Long before sustainable became a buzzword, this shop (the brainchild of a German Green party member) stocked traditionally made quality products from around the world, many of which have stood the test of time. Cool finds include hand-forged iron pans by Turk, fountain pens by Pelikan and Japanese knives by Kenyo.

GOLDHAHN UND SAMPSON FOOD

Map p316 (www.goldhahnundsampson.de; Wilmersdorfer Strasse 102/103; 🕒8am-9pm Mon-Sat; [U]Wilmersdorfer Strasse, [S]Charlottenburg) Arctic sea salt, wild sumac and green chai are among the global pantry stockers tastefully displayed at this stylish food emporium. Items are hand-sourced from small artisanal suppliers and usually organic. There's a huge cookbook selection (many in English) and fun classes at the on-site cooking school (in German).

BIKINI BERLIN MALL

Map p316 (www.bikiniberlin.de; Budapester Strasse 38-50; 🕒shops 10am-8pm Mon-Sat, building 9am-9pm Mon-Sat, 1-6pm Sun; 📶; 🚌100, 200, [U]Zoologischer Garten, [S]Zoologischer Garten) Germany's first concept mall opened in 2014 in a spectacularly rehabilitated 1950s architectural icon nicknamed 'Bikini' because of its design: 200m-long upper and lower sections separated by an open floor, now chastely covered by a glass facade. Inside are three floors of urban indie boutiques and short-lease pop-up 'boxes' that offer a platform for up-and-coming designers.

STILWERK HOMEWARES

Map p316 (☎030-315 150; www.stilwerk.de/berlin; Kantstrasse 17; 🕒10am-7pm Mon-Sat; [S]Savignyplatz) This four-storey temple of good taste will have devotees of the finer things itching to redecorate. Everything you could possibly want for home and hearth is here – from key rings to grand pianos and vintage lamps – representing over 500 brands in 52 stores. It's all housed in an open atrium clad in natural stone, maple and glass.

KÄTHE WOHLFAHRT ARTS & CRAFTS

Map p316 (☎09861-4090; wohlfahrt.com; Kurfürstendamm 225-226; 🕒10am-7pm Mon-Sat, 1-6pm Sun; [U]Kurfürstendamm) With its mind-boggling assortment of traditional German Yuletide decorations and ornaments, this shop lets you celebrate Christmas year-round. It's accessed via a ramp that spirals around an 8m-high Christmas tree.

BERLINER TRÖDELMARKT MARKET

Map p316 (☎030-2655 0096; www.berliner-troedelmarkt.de; Strasse des 17 Juni; 🕒10am-5pm Sat & Sun; [S]Tiergarten) Vendors vie for your euros with yesteryear's fur coats, silverware, jewellery, lamps, dolls, hats and other stuff one might find in granny's attic. West of Tiergarten S-Bahn station, this is Berlin's oldest flea market (since 1973). The adjacent arts and crafts market sells mostly new items.

Day Trips from Berlin

Potsdam & Schloss Sanssouci p203
It's practically impossible to not be enchanted by this rambling park and palace ensemble starring Schloss Sanssouci.

Sachsenhausen Concentration Camp p209
The horrors of the Third Reich become all too real at what's left of one of Germany's oldest Nazi-built concentration camps.

Spandau p210
Anchored by a delightful Altstadt (old town), this northwestern Berlin district flaunts its historic pedigree.

Grunewald & Dahlem p211
Tree-lined streets with mansions and manicured lawns lace Berlin's poshest area, which also boasts plenty of culture cred.

Wannsee p213
Hemmed in by the Havel River, Berlin's southwestern-most district counts palaces, forests and historical sights among its assets.

Köpenick p215
Home to Berlin's largest lake, a sprawling forest, a handsome baroque castle and a medieval centre.

TOP SIGHT
POTSDAM & SCHLOSS SANSSOUCI

Potsdam, on the Havel River just 25km southwest of central Berlin, is the capital and crown jewel of the federal state of Brandenburg. Easily reached by S-Bahn, the former Prussian royal seat is the most popular day trip from Berlin, luring visitors with its splendid gardens and palaces, which garnered Unesco World Heritage status in 1990.

Headlining the roll call of royal pads is Schloss Sanssouci, the private retreat of King Friedrich II (Frederick the Great), who was also the mastermind behind many of Potsdam's other fabulous parks and palaces. Most miraculously survived WWII with nary a shrapnel wound. When the shooting stopped, the Allies chose Schloss Cecilienhof for the Potsdam Conference of August 1945 to lay the groundwork for Germany's postwar fate.

Schloss & Park Sanssouci

This glorious park and palace ensemble is what happens when a king has good taste, plenty of cash and access to the finest architects and artists of the day. Sanssouci was dreamed up by Frederick the Great (1712–86) and is anchored by the eponymous palace, which was his favourite summer retreat, a place where he could be *'sans souci'* (without cares).

Schloss Sanssouci

The biggest stunner, and what everyone comes to see, is Schloss Sanssouci, Frederick the Great's famous summer palace. Designed by Georg Wenzeslaus von Knobelsdorff in 1747, the rococo gem sits daintily above vine-draped terraces with the king's grave nearby.

Standouts on the tours (guided or self-guided) include the **Konzertsaal** (Concert Hall), whimsically decorated with vines, grapes and even a cobweb where sculpted spiders frolic.

DON'T MISS
➡ Tour of Schloss Sanssouci
➡ Chinesisches Haus
➡ View of Sanssouci palace from below the vineyard terrace

PRACTICALITIES
➡ ☎0331-969 4200
➡ www.spsg.de
➡ Maulbeerallee
➡ adult/concession incl tour or audioguide €12/8
➡ ⊙10am-6pm Tue-Sun Apr-Oct, to 5pm Nov-Mar
➡ 🚌614, 650, 695

INFORMATION

There are two visitors' centres in Park Sanssouci: the **Besucherzentrum an der Historischen Mühle** (☑0331-969 4200; An der Orangerie 1; ⊘8.30am-5.30pm Tue-Sun Apr-Oct, to 4.30pm Nov-Mar) and the **Besucherzentrum im Neuen Palais** (☑0331-969 4200; Am Neuen Palais; ⊘9am-6pm Wed-Mon Apr-Oct, to 5pm Nov-Mar).

Regional trains leaving from Berlin Hauptbahnhof and Zoologischer Garten take only 25 minutes to reach Potsdam Hauptbahnhof; some continue on to Potsdam Charlottenhof and Potsdam Sanssouci. The S7 from central Berlin makes the trip in 40 minutes. You need a ticket covering zones ABC (€3.30) for either service. Buses for Sanssouci (lines 605 and 695) leave from outside Potsdam Hauptbahnhof.

PARK SANSSOUCI

The oldest and most resplendent of Potsdam's many green patches **Park Sanssouci** (⊘8am-dusk; ☑614, 650, 695) **FREE** is open from dawn til dusk year-round and is dotted with numerous palaces and outbuildings.

The king himself gave flute recitals here. Also note the intimate **Bibliothek** (library), lidded by a gilded sunburst ceiling, where the king would seek solace amid 2000 leather-bound tomes ranging from Greek poetry to the latest releases by his friend Voltaire. Another highlight is the **Marmorsaal** (Marble Room), an elegant white Carrara marble symphony modelled after the Pantheon in Rome.

As you exit the palace, note the **Ruinenberg**, a pile of fake classical ruins looming in the distance.

Bildergalerie

The **Picture Gallery** (Gallery of Old Masters; Im Park Sanssouci 4; adult/concession €6/5; ⊘10am-6pm Tue-Sun May-Oct) shelters Frederick the Great's prized collection of Old Masters, including such pearls as Caravaggio's *Doubting Thomas*, Anthony van Dyck's *Pentecost* and several works by Peter Paul Rubens. Behind the rather plain facade hides a sumptuous symphony of gilded ornamentation, yellow and white marble and a patterned stone floor that is perhaps just as impressive as the mostly large-scale paintings that cover practically every inch of wall space.

Neue Kammern

The **Neue Kammern** (New Chambers; ☑0331-969 4200; www.spsg.de; Park Sanssouci; adult/concession incl tour or audioguide €6/5; ⊘10am-6pm Tue-Sun Apr-Oct; ☑614, 650, 695), built by Knobelsdorff in 1748, were originally an orangery and later converted into a guest palace. The interior drips with rococo opulence, most notably the square **Jasper Hall**, which is drenched in precious stones and lidded by a Venus fresco, and the **Ovidsaal**, a grand ballroom with gilded wall reliefs depicting scenes from *Metamorphosis*.

Chinesisches Haus

The 18th-century fad for the Far East is strongly reflected in the adorable **Chinesisches Haus** (Chinese House; Am Grünen Gitter; adult/concession €3/2; ⊘10am-6pm Tue-Sun May-Oct; ☑605, 606, ☑91). The cloverleaf-shaped pavilion is among the park's most photographed buildings thanks to its enchanting exterior of exotically dressed, gilded figures shown sipping tea, dancing and playing musical instruments amid palm-shaped pillars. Inside is a precious collection of Chinese and Meissen porcelain.

Orangerieschloss

Modelled after an Italian Renaissance villa, the 300m-long, 1864-built **Orangerieschloss** (Orangery Palace; An der Orangerie 3-5; adult/concession €4/3; ⊘10am-6pm Tue-Sun May-Oct, Sat & Sun Apr; ☑695) was

Potsdam

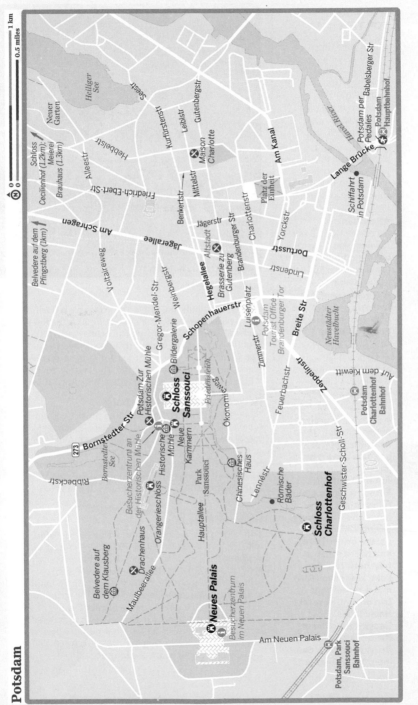

0.5 miles
1 km

Cecilienhof (1.2km); Meierei Brauhaus (1.3km); Schloss

Belvedere auf dem Pfingstberg (1km)

Heiliger See

Neuer Garten

Seestr

Kurfürstenstr

Gutenbergstr

Leiblstr

Hebbelstr

Alleestr

Maison Charlotte

Mittelstr

Friedrich-Ebert-Str

Benkertstr

Am Kanal

Am Schragen

Jägerallee

Voltaireweg

Gregor-Mendel-Str

Weinbergstr

Jägerstr

Altstadt

Brasserie zu Gutenberg

Hegelallee

Brandenburger Str

Charlottenstr

Platz der Einheit

Yorckstr

Dortustr

Lindenstr

Schopenhauerstr

Luisenplatz

Zimmerstr

Potsdam Tourist Office - Brandenburger Tor

Breite Str

Neustädter Havelbucht

Lange Brücke

Schiffahrt in Potsdam

Potsdam per Pedales; Potsdam Hauptbahnhof

Ribbeckstr

Bornstedter See

Bornstedter Str

Besucherzentrum an der Historischen Mühle

Potsdam Zur Historischen Mühle

Bildergalerie

Schloss Sanssouci

Historische Mühle

Neue Kammern

Friedenskirche

Feuerbachstr

Zeppelinstr

Auf dem Kiewitt

Potsdam Charlottenhof Bahnhof

Belvedere auf dem Klausberg

Drachenhaus

Orangerieschloss

Maulbeerallee

Hauptallee

Park Sanssouci

Ökonomieweg

Chinesisches Haus

Lennéstr

Römische Bäder

Schloss Charlottenhof

Geschwister-Scholl-Str

Neues Palais

Besucherzentrum im Neuen Palais

Am Neuen Palais

Potsdam, Park Sanssouci Bahnhof

273

TOP TIPS

➡Book your timed ticket to Schloss Sanssouci online to avoid wait times and/or disappointment.

➡Avoid visiting on Monday when most palaces are closed.

➡Ticket sanssouci+, a one-day pass to palaces in Potsdam, costs €19 (concession €14) and is sold online and at each building.

➡Picnicking is permitted throughout the park, but cycling is limited to Ökonomieweg and Maulbeerallee.

➡There's a €3 day fee for taking pictures (*Fotoerlaubnis*) inside the palaces.

➡Palaces are fairly well spaced – it's almost 2km between the Neues Palais and Schloss Sanssouci.

A relaxing way to enjoy Potsdam is from the deck of a cruise boat. The most popular trip run by Schiffahrt in Potsdam (www.schiffahrt-in-potsdam. de) is the 90-minute Schlösserundfahrt palace cruise (€14), and there's also a two-hour tour to Lake Wannsee (€16) and a three-hour trip around several Havel lakes (€16). Boats depart from the docks near Lange Brücke. English commentary available.

Wall decoration at Neues Palais

the favourite building project of Friedrich Wilhelm IV – a passionate Italophile. Its highlight is the **Raffaelsaal** (Raphael Hall), which brims with 19th-century copies of the famous painter's masterpieces. The greenhouses are still used for storing potted plants in winter. Note that the observation tower will be closed for renovation until at least April 2018.

Belvedere auf dem Klausberg

Frederick the Great's final building project was this templelike **belvedere** (An der Orangerie 1; ⊘open for special events only; ▣695), modelled on Nero's palace in Rome. The panorama of park, lakes and Potsdam is predictably fabulous from up here. The upstairs hall has an impressive frescoed dome, oak parquet and fanciful stucco marble but, alas, it can be seen during special events only.

Historische Mühle

This reconstructed 18th-century Dutch-style **windmill** (Historic Windmill; ☏0331-550 6851; www.spsg.de; Maulbeerallee 5; adult/concession €3/2; ⊘10am-6pm daily Apr-Oct, to 4pm Sat & Sun Nov & Jan-Mar; ▣650, 695) contains exhibits about the history of the mill and mill technology, and offers a close-up of the grinding mechanism and a top-floor viewing platform.

According to legend, Frederick the Great ordered its owner to demolish the original mill because of the noise. However, when the miller refused and threatened to go to court, the king acquiesced.

Neues Palais

The final palace commissioned by Frederick the Great, the **Neues Palais** (New Palace; ☎0331-969 4200; www.spsg.de; Am Neuen Palais; adult/concession incl tour or audioguide €8/6; ⏲10am-6pm Wed-Mon Apr-Oct, to 5pm Nov-Mar; 🚌605, 606, 695, [S]Potsdam Charlottenhof) has made-to-impress dimensions, a central dome and a lavish exterior capped with a parade of sandstone figures. The interior attests to the high level of artistry and craftwork of the 18th century. It's an opulent symphony of ceiling frescos, gilded stucco ornamentation, ornately carved wainscoting and fanciful wall coverings alongside paintings (by Antoine Pesne, for example) and richly crafted furniture.

The palace was built in just six years, largely to demonstrate the undiminished power of the Prussian state following the bloody Seven Years War (1756–63). The king himself rarely camped out here, preferring the intimacy of Schloss Sanssouci and using it for representational purposes only. Only the last German Kaiser, Wilhelm II, used it as a residence, until 1918.

After extensive restoration, most of the building highlights are once again accessible, including the shimmering festival hall called **Grottensaal** (Grotto Hall) and the magnificent **Marmorsaal** (Marble Hall). Also looking splendid is the redone **Unteres Fürstenquartie**r (Lower Royal Suite), which consists of a concert room, an oval-shaped chamber, an antechamber and, most impressively, a dining room with walls sheathed in red silk damask with gold-braided trim.

The pair of lavish buildings behind the Schloss is called the **Communs**. It originally housed the palace servants and kitchens and is now part of Potsdam University.

Schloss Charlottenhof

Originally a baroque country manor, this small **palace** (Charlottenhof Palace; ☎0331-969 4200; www.spsg.de; Geschwister-Scholl-Strasse 34a; tours adult/concession €6/5; ⏲tours 10am-6pm Tue-Sun May-Oct; 🚌605, 606, 610, X5, 🚋91, 94, 98) was

EATING & DRINKING

Brasserie zu Gutenberg (☎0331-7403 6878; www.brasserie-zu-gutenberg.de; Jägerstrasse 10, cnr Gutenbergstrasse; mains €9-28; ⏲noon-midnight; 🚌604, 609, 638, 🚋92, 96) This charming little brasserie with dark-wood tables and chocolate-brown banquettes is great for a quick bite of quiche and coffee or for a hearty meal, perhaps featuring the signature *coq au vin* and a glass of fine Bordeaux.

Meierei Brauhaus (☎0331-704 3211; www.meierei-potsdam.de; Im Neuen Garten 10; mains €5-13; ⏲noon-10pm Tue-Fri, 11am-10pm Sat & Sun Apr-Oct, noon-10pm Tue-Sat, noon-8pm Sun Nov-Mar; 🚌603 to Höhenstrasse) The Berlin Wall once ran right past this brewpub, where the beer garden invites you to count the boats sailing on the Jungfernsee in summer. The hearty dishes are a perfect match for the delicious craft beers, including the classic Helles (pale lager) and seasonal suds brewed on the premises. In summer, try its Weizen (wheat beer) and the top-fermented Berliner Weisse.

Maison Charlotte (☎0331-280 5450; www.maison-charlotte.de; Mittelstrasse 20; Flammkuchen €8.50-13.50, 3-/4-course menus €43/53; ⏲noon-11pm; 🚌604, 609, 638, 🚋92, 96) There's a rustic lyricism to the French country cuisine in this darling Dutch Quarter bistro, no matter whether your appetite runs towards a simple *Flammkuchen* (Alsatian pizza), Breton fish soup or a multicourse menu. Budget *bon vivants* come for the daily lunch special (€7.50), which includes a glass of wine and is best enjoyed on the patio in summer.

TAKE A BREAK

Right in the park, **Drachenhaus** (📞0331-505 3808; www.drachen haus.de; Maulbeerallee 4; mains €12-20; ⊘11am-8pm or later Apr-Oct, to 6pm Tue-Sun Nov, Dec & Mar, & Sat & Sun Jan & Feb; 🚌695) is pagoda-style minipalace serving coffee, cakes and seasonal cuisine.For international favourites, head to **Potsdam Zur Historischen Mühle** (📞0331-281 493; www. moevenpick-restaurants. com; Zur Historischen Mühle 2; mains €11.50-25; ⊘8am-10pm; P 🔥; 🚌614, 650, 695) with beer garden and children's playground.

Potsdam per Pedales (📞0331-748 0057; www. potsdam-per-pedales.de; Potsdam Hauptbahnhof, platform 6/7; adult/ concession per day from €11/9; ⊘7am-8pm Mon-Fri, 9.30am-8pm Sat & Sun Apr-Oct; Ⓢ Potsdam Hauptbahnhof), right on the station platform, rents quality bicycles and offers guided and self-guided bike tours. If you want to see more of Potsdam than Park Sanssouci, a bike is ideal.

Belvedere auf dem Pfingstberg

enlarged by Karl Friedrich Schinkel for Friedrich Wilhelm IV in the late 1820s. The building is modelled on classical Roman villas and features a Doric portico and a bronze fountain. Peter Joseph Lenné designed the surrounding park, creating a harmonious blend of architecture and nature. Schinkel also designed the Biedermeier-style furniture.

Römische Bäder

Karl Friedrich Schinkel, aided by his student Ludwig Persius, dreamed up the so-called **Römische Bäder** (Roman Baths; 📞0331-969 4200; www.spsg.de; Park Charlottenhof; adult/concession €5/4; ⊘10am-6pm Tue-Sun May-Oct; 🚌605, 606, 610, X5, 🚋91, 94, 98) in Park Charlottenhof. Despite the name, it's actually a romantic cluster of 15th-century Italian country-estate buildings, complete with vine-draped pergola.

Views

For splendid views over Potsdam and surrounds, ascend the spiralling wrought-iron staircases of the twin-towered **Belvedere auf dem Pfingstberg** (📞0331-2005 7930; www.pfingstberg.de; Pfingstberg; adult/concession €4.50/3.50, audioguides €1; ⊘10am-6pm daily Apr-Oct, 10am-4pm Sat & Sun Mar & Nov; 🚌92, 96), commissioned by Friedrich Wilhelm IV and modelled on an Italian Renaissance–style villa. There's a small exhibit chronicling the history of the building and the 1801 Pomonatempel just below it. The latter was Karl Friedrich Schinkel's very first architectural commission at age 19.

Sachsenhausen Concentration Camp

Explore

Sachsenhausen was built by prisoners and opened in 1936 as a prototype for other concentration camps. By 1945 about 200,000 people had passed through its sinister gates, initially mostly political opponents, but later also gypsies, gays, Jews and, after 1939, POWs from eastern Europe, especially the Soviet Union. Tens of thousands died here from hunger, exhaustion, illness, exposure, medical experiments and executions. Thousands more succumbed during the death march of April 1945, when the Nazis evacuated the camp in advance of the Red Army. Note the memorial plaque to these victims as you walk towards the camp (at the corner of Strasse der Einheit and Strasse der Nationen). After the war, the Soviets held some 60,000 German POWs in what was then called Speziallager No 7 (Special Camp No 7); about 12,000 died of malnutrition and disease before it was dissolved in 1950. Soviet and GDR military used the grounds for another decade until the camp became a memorial site in 1961.

Top Tip

Although the memorial site is open daily, it's best not to visit on a Monday when the indoor exhibits are closed.

Getting There & Away

Train The S1 makes the trip thrice hourly from central Berlin (eg Friedrichstrasse station) to Oranienburg (ABC ticket €3.30, 45 minutes). Hourly regional RE5 and RB12 trains leaving from Hauptbahnhof are faster (ABC ticket €3.30, 25 minutes). The camp is about 2km from the Oranienburg train station. Turn right onto Stralsunder Strasse, right on Bernauer Strasse, left on Strasse der Einheit and right on Strasse der Nationen. Alternatively, bus 804 makes hourly trips.

Need to Know

➡ **Area Code** ☑03301

➡ **Location** About 35km north of central Berlin.

◉ SIGHTS

Unless you're on a guided tour of the camp, officially called **Gedenkstätte und Museum Sachsenhausen** (Memorial & Museum Sachsenhausen; ☑03301-200 200; www.stiftung-bg.de; Strasse der Nationen 22, Oranienburg; ☺8.30am-6pm mid-Mar–mid-Oct, to 4.30pm mid-Oct–mid-Mar, museums closed Mon mid-Oct–mid-Mar; Ⓟ; ⓈOranienburg) FREE, pick up a leaflet (€0.50) or, better yet, an audioguide (€3, including leaflet) at the visitor centre to get a better grasp of this huge site. The approach to the camp takes you past photographs taken during the death march and the camp's liberation in April 1945. Just beyond the perimeter, the **Neues Museum** (New Museum) has exhibits on Sachsenhausen's precursor, the nearby Oranienburg concentration camp, and on the history of the memorial site during the GDR-era (1950 to 1990).

Proceed to **Tower A**, the entrance gate, cynically labelled, as at Auschwitz, *Arbeit Macht Frei* (Work Sets You Free). Beyond here is the roll-call area, with barracks and other buildings fanning out beyond. Off to the right, two restored barracks illustrate the abysmal living conditions prisoners endured. **Barrack 38** has an exhibit on Jewish inmates, while **Barrack 39** graphically portrays daily life at the camp. The **prison**, where famous inmates included Hitler's would-be assassin Georg Elser and the minister Martin Niemöller, is next door. Exhibits in the **infirmary barracks** on the other side of the roll-call area illustrate the camp's poor medical care and the horrific medical experiments performed on prisoners. Moving towards the centre, the **Prisoners' Kitchen** chronicles key moments in the camp's history. Exhibits include instruments of torture, the original gallows that stood in the roll-call area, and, in the cellar, heart-wrenching artwork scratched into the wall by prisoners.

The most sickening displays, though, are about the extermination area called **Station Z**, which was separated from the rest of the grounds and consisted of an execution trench, a crematorium and a gas chamber. The most notorious mass executions took place in autumn 1941 when over 10,000 Soviet POWs were executed here in the course of four weeks. In the far right corner, a new building and two original barracks house the **Soviet Special Camp exhibit**, which documents Sachsenhausen's stint as Speziallager No 7, a German POW camp run by the Soviets from 1945 until 1950.

✗ EATING & DRINKING

No food is available at the memorial site, although a vending machine in the Neues Museum dispenses hot drinks. There are cafes, bakeries and small markets outside Oranienburg train station.

Spandau

Explore

Spandau is a congenial mix of green expanses, rivers, industry and almost rural residential areas wrapped around a medieval core famous for its 16th-century bastion, the Zitadelle Spandau (Spandau Citadel). Older than Berlin by a few years, it sits at the confluence of Havel and Spree and thrived as an independent city for nearly eight centuries and only became part of Berlin in 1920. To this day, its people still talk about 'going to Berlin' when heading to any other city district. Nearly all sights handily cluster in and around the Altstadt. The suburb of Gatow, with the Museum of Military History, is about 10km south of here.

The Best...

➡ **Sight** Zitadelle Spandau (p210)
➡ **Place to Eat** Satt und Selig (p211)
➡ **Place to Drink** Brauhaus in Spandau (p211)

Top Tip

In summer, big international acts like Billy Idol, Lana del Rey and Limp Bizkit gig to appreciative audiences alfresco during the Citadel Music Festival (www.citadelmusicfestival.de). Year-round concerts take place in the Gothic Hall.

Getting There & Away

➡ **U-Bahn** The recommended route is via the U7, which travels to Spandau in 30 to 40 minutes and stops at the Zitadelle, the Altstadt and the Rathaus.
➡ **S-Bahn** The S5 makes the trip to central Spandau in about 30 to 40 minutes.

Need to Know

➡ **Area Code** ☑030
➡ **Location** About 13km northwest of central Berlin.
➡ **Tourist Office** (☑030-333 9388; www.partner-fuer-spandau.de; Breite Strasse 32; ◷10am-6pm Tue-Sat; Ⓢ Spandau, Ⓤ Altstadt Spandau)

◉ SIGHTS

ZITADELLE SPANDAU CASTLE
(Spandau Citadel; ☑030-354 9440; www.zitadelle-spandau.de; Am Juliusturm 64; adult/concession €4.50/2.50, audioguide €2; ◷10am-5pm, last entry 4.30pm; Ⓤ Zitadelle) The 16th-century Spandau Citadel, on a little island in the Havel River, is one of the world's best-preserved Renaissance fortresses. With its moat, drawbridge and arrowhead-shaped bastions, it is also a veritable textbook in military architecture. These days, the impressive complex multitasks as museum, cultural venue and wintering ground for thousands of bats. Climb the 30m-high **Julius Tower** for sweeping views. Top international artists perform at the Citadel Music Festival in summer.

NIKOLAIKIRCHE CHURCH
(Church of St Nicholas; ☑030-333 5639; www.nikolai-spandau.de; Reformationsplatz 6; tower €1; ◷noon-4pm Mon-Fri, 11am-4pm Sat, 11.30am-4pm Sun, tower tours 12.30pm Sat, noon 1st & 3rd Sun Apr-Oct; Ⓤ Altstadt Spandau) The Gothic Church of St Nicholas is famous for hosting Brandenburg's first public Lutheran-style worship service back in 1539, under Elector Joachim II whose bronze statue stands outside the church. Inside, important treasures include a baptismal font (1398), a baroque pulpit (1714) and a late-Renaissance altar (1582). Tours up the 77m-high tower are available.

GOTISCHES HAUS HISTORIC BUILDING
(☑030-333 9388; Breite Strasse 32; ◷noon-6pm Mon-Sat; Ⓤ Altstadt Spandau) FREE Whoever built this Gothic House in the 15th century must not have been hurting for money, for it's made of stone not wood, as was customary in those times. The well-preserved Altstadt gem sports ornate net-ribbed vaulting on the ground floor, which houses the local tourist office.

MILITARY AVIATION HISTORY ON THE RUNWAY

Operated by the Bundeswehr, the **Militärhistorisches Museum – Flugplatz Berlin-Gatow** (Museum of Military History – Airfield Berlin-Gatow; ☑030-3687 2601; www. mhm-gatow.de; Am Flugplatz Gatow 33; ☺10am-6pm Tue-Sun; ℗; ☐135) is a fascinating destination for fans of aviation, technology, history and the military. It spreads its wings over a military airfield used both by the Nazis and the Royal Air Force. Exhibits in the control tower and two hangars focus on various aspects of aerial warfare with plenty of old planes, air defense guns and engines on display. Over 100 fighter jets, bombers, helicopters and weapons systems litter the runway, including such gems as WWI biplanes, a Russian MiG-21, a Messerschmidt ME-163 Komet and a GDR-era Antonov An-14. The museum is about 10km south of central Spandau. Take bus 135 from S- or U-Bahn Rathaus Spandau to 'Kurpromenade', then walk for 1km.

Upstairs, 13 rooms document living styles and conditions in Spandau through the centuries. Check out the Biedermeier-era living room and late-19th-century kitchen upstairs.

KOLK AREA

(Ⓤ Altstadt Spandau) Separated from the Altstadt by the busy Strasse am Juliusturm, the Kolk quarter was the site of Spandau's first settlement and exudes medieval village flair with its romantic narrow lanes, crooked, half-timbered houses and 78m-long section of town wall. Its key sight is the church of **St Marien am Behnitz** (☑030-353 9630; www.behnitz.de; Behnitz 9; ☺2-5pm; Ⓤ Altstadt Spandau) **FREE**, which is now privately owned and used as a concert venue.

EATING & DRINKING

SATT UND SELIG INTERNATIONAL €€

(☑030-3675 3877; www.sattundselig.de; Carl-Schurz-Strasse 47; mains €10-18; ☺9am-11pm; Ⓤ Altstadt Spandau) In a baroque half-timbered house in the historic centre, this local favourite gets things right from morning to night. The breakfast selection is legendary, the cakes homemade and the main dishes creative, fresh and ample. In summer, terrace tables spill out onto the pedestrian zone.

BRAUHAUS IN SPANDAU BEER GARDEN

(☑030-353 9070; www.brauhaus-spandau.de; Neuendorfer Strasse 1; ☺10am-midnight; Ⓤ Altstadt Spandau) In summer there are few nicer places to while away an evening in central Spandau than in the tree-canopied beer garden of this brewery in a historic red-brick building. On tap are the Spandau-er Havelbräu as well as monthly changing seasonal brews alongside hearty German pub grub (€5 to €15).

It's right in the Kolk quarter, the oldest area in town.

Grunewald & Dahlem

Explore

Berlin's most upper-crust neighbourhoods, Dahlem and Grunewald are packed with cultural and natural appeal. Set between their leafy streets and lavish villa colonies (especially around Grunewald S-Bahn station) are gardens, parks, palaces and a sprinkling of museums, most of them with an art focus. After WWII, the area was part of the American sector, a legacy reflected in such institutions as the AlliertenMuseum (Allied Museum) and the hulking US Consulate. A respite for Berliners and residents alike is the **Grunewald forest**, a vast fresh-air refuge crisscrossed by paths and dotted with lakes extending all the way west to the Havel River. Wild boar, deer and other animals make their home here.

The Best...

➡ **Sight** Brücke-Museum (p212)
➡ **Place to Eat & Drink** Luise (p212)

Top Tip

The fragrant Botanischer Garten is the glorious backdrop for alfresco summer concerts – jazz to flamenco to classical – held every Friday from 6pm to 8pm in July and August. Tickets (€15) include garden access.

Getting There & Away

➡ **U-Bahn** The U3 meanders through this area, with key stops being Dahlem-Dorf for the museums and Krumme Lanke for easy access to the southern Grunewald forest.

➡ **S-Bahn** The S1 skirts southern Dahlem, while the S7 runs straight through the Grunewald forest.

Need to Know

➡ **Area Code** ☑ 030
➡ **Location** About 11km southwest of central Berlin.

◉ SIGHTS

BRÜCKE-MUSEUM   GALLERY

(☑ 030-831 2029; www.bruecke-museum.de; Bussardsteig 9; adult/concession €6/4; ⊙ 11am-5pm Wed-Mon; Ⓟ; Ⓢ Oskar-Helene-Heim, then bus 115 to Pücklerstrasse) In 1905 Karl Schmidt-Rottluff, Erich Heckel and Ernst Ludwig Kirchner founded Germany's first modern-artist group, called Die Brücke (The Bridge). Rejecting traditional techniques taught in the academies, they experimented with bright, emotional colours and warped perspectives that paved the way for German expressionism and modern art in general. Schmidt-Rottluff's personal collection forms the core of this lovely presentation of expressionist art.

KUNSTHAUS DAHLEM   MUSEUM

(☑ 030-832 227 258; www.kunsthaus-dahlem.de; Käuzchensteig 8; adult/concession €6/4; ⊙ 11am-5pm Wed-Mon; Ⓟ; Ⓤ Oskar-Helene-Heim, then bus 115 or X10) This new private art museum in the monumental studio of Nazi-era sculptor Arno Breker presents works created in eastern and western Germany in the years between WWII and the construction of the Berlin Wall in 1961. Its inaugural exhibit, which runs until June 2017, presents stunning works by Gerhard Marcks, Bernhard Heiliger, Jeanne Mammen and Hans Uhlmann in lofty rooms with floor-to-ceiling windows.

A visit here is easily combined with the nearby Brücke-Museum (combination tickets €8/5).

ALLIIERTENMUSEUM BERLIN   MUSEUM

(Allied Museum; ☑ 030-818 1990; www.alliierten-museum.de; Clayallee 135; ⊙ 10am-6pm Tue-Sun; Ⓟ; Ⓤ Oskar-Helene-Heim) **FREE** The original Checkpoint Charlie guard cabin, a Berlin Airlift plane and a reconstructed spy tunnel are among the dramatic exhibits at the Allied Museum, which documents historical milestones and the challenges faced by the Western Allies during the Cold War. There's also a survey of events leading to the collapse of communism and the fall of the Berlin Wall. An original piece of the Wall sits in the yard.

'BERLIN BRAIN'   ARCHITECTURE

(☑ 030-8385 8888; www.fu-berlin.de/sites/philbib; Habelschwerdter Allee 45; ⊙ 9am-10pm Mon-Fri, 10am-8pm Sat & Sun; Ⓤ Thielplatz) British architect Norman Foster was the brain behind the 'Berlin Brain', a 2005 masterpiece of modern architecture that houses the Freie Universität Berlin's Philology Library. It was its cranial shape that inspired the unusual nickname. Inside are four floors sheltered within a naturally ventilated,

---

TRACKS OF DEATH

Between 1941 and 1942, more than 50,000 Jewish Berliners were deported from Gleis 17 (platform 17) next to the S-Bahn station Grunewald. Some 186 trains left for Theresienstadt, Riga, Lodz and Auschwitz, carrying their Jewish cargo like cattle to the slaughter. In their honour, memorial plaques recording the departure dates, number of people and destinations of the trains have been fastened to the edge of the platform.

It's quiet at the **Gleis 17 Memorial** (Platform 17 Memorial; www.memorialmuseums.org; Am Bahnhof Grunewald; ⊙ 24hr; Ⓢ Grunewald) , with only the trees rustling in the breeze, but the silence speaks loudly.

bubble-like enclosure draped in aluminium and glazed panels. An inner membrane of translucent glass fibre filters the daylight, while scattered transparent openings allow momentary glimpses of the sky.

 EATING & DRINKING

LUISE INTERNATIONAL €€
(☎030-841 8880; www.luise-dahlem.de; Königin-Luise-Strasse 40-42; pizza €6.50-15, mains €10-19; ⊙10am-1am; 🔊🚼; Ⓤ Dahlem-Dorf) This cafe-restaurant-beer-garden combo is a Dahlem institution with a long menu likely to please everyone from salad heads to schnitzel fiends to pizza punters. Scrumptious breakfasts are served until 2pm and there are seven beers on tap to enjoy beneath the chestnut trees. Children can romp around in a playground.

RISTORANTE GALILEO ITALIAN €€
(☎030-831 2377; www.ristorantegalileo.de; Otto-von-Simson-Strasse 26; mains €6.50-16.50; ⊙10am-10pm Mon-Fri; 🔊; Ⓤ Dahlem-Dorf) On the edge of the Free University campus, Galileo has plied students, faculty and clued-in locals with cheap, authentic Italian fare for about a quarter century. If homemade pasta and pizza don't do it for you, go for the daily specials, which might feature grilled tuna or rosemary-scented lamb filet.

Wannsee

Explore
Leafy Wannsee, Berlin's southwestern-most suburb, is named for the enormous Wannsee lake, which is really just a bulge in the Havel River. In fine weather, it's a fantastic place to leave the city bustle behind. You can cruise around the lake, walk in the forest, visit an enchanting island, tour a Prussian palace or work on your tan in the Strandbad Wannsee, a lakeside lido with a 1km-long sandy beach, or at one of the other spots for taking a quick dip. On the western edge of the lake (and easily reached by bus) are a couple of major sights linked to the Nazis and the painter Max Liebermann. Wannsee is linked to Spandau via the F10 ferry.

The Best...
➡ **Sight** Pfaueninsel (p213)
➡ **Place to Eat** Restaurant Seehaase (p214)
➡ **Place to Drink** Loretta am Wannsee (p214)

Top Tip
For cruising on the cheap, catch the 20-minute ride on public transport ferry F10 from Wannsee to the Spandau suburb of Alt-Kladow (tariff AB, €2.70).

Getting There & Away
➡ **S-Bahn** Take S1 or S7 from central Berlin to Wannsee, then walk or bus depending on where you're headed.

Need to Know
➡ **Area Code** ☑ 030
➡ **Location** Twenty-five kilometres southwest of central Berlin.

SIGHTS

★ PFAUENINSEL PARK
(☎030-8058 6830; www.spsg.de; Nikolskoer Weg; adult/concession ferry €4/3, palace €6/5, Meierei €2/1.50; ⊙ferry 9am-8pm May-Aug, shorter hours Sep-Apr, palace 10am-5.30pm Tue-Sun Apr-Oct, Meierei 10am-5.30pm Sat & Sun Apr-Oct; Ⓢ Wannsee, then bus 218) Back to nature was the dictum in the 18th century, so Friedrich Wilhelm II had this little island turned into an idyllic playground, perfect for retreating from state affairs and for frolicking with his mistress in a snowy-white fairy-tale palace. To heighten the romance factor, he brought in a flock of peacocks that gave the island its name and that are still strutting their stuff to this day. A stand-out among the smattering of other buildings is the **Meierei**, a dairy farm in the shape of a Gothic monastery at the island's northern end.

The island is a nature preserve, so no smoking, cycling or swimming. Picnicking, though, remains legal. There are no cafes or restaurants. The island is about 4km northwest of the Wannsee S-Bahn station, from where it's served several times hourly by bus 218.

IN & ON THE WANNSEE

Stern und Kreisschiffahrt – Wannsee Cruise (☎030-536 3600; www.sternundkreis.de; 2hr cruise €11.50; ⏲hourly 10.30am-5.30pm Apr–mid-Oct; [S]Wannsee) From April to mid-October, Stern und Kreisschiffahrt operates two-hour cruises around seven lakes from landing docks near Wannsee S-Bahn station.

Strandbad Wannsee (☎030-2219 0011; www.berlinerbaeder.de/baeder/strandbad-wannsee; Wannseebadweg 25; adult/concession €5.50/3.50; ⏲10am-6pm, longer hours May-Sep; [S]Nikolassee) This lakeside public beach has delighted water rats for over a century. Although 1km long, the broad sandy strip can get very busy on hot days, especially on weekends. Besides swimming, you can rent boats, play volleyball, basketball or table tennis or grab a snack or drink. Note that the northern end of the beach is reserved for nude bathing.

The Strandbad is about 1.3km northwest of the S-Bahn station Nikolassee. Walk north on Borussenstrasse, then turn left onto Wannseebadweg.

HAUS DER WANNSEE-KONFERENZ — MEMORIAL

(☎030-805 0010; www.ghwk.de; Am Grossen Wannsee 56-58; ⏲10am-6pm; [S]Wannsee, then bus 114) [FREE] In January 1942 a group of 15 high-ranking Nazi officials met in a stately villa near Lake Wannsee to hammer out the details of the 'Final Solution': the systematic deportation and murder of European Jews in Eastern Europe. The 13-room exhibit in the very rooms where discussions took place illustrates the sinister meeting but also examines the racial policies and persecution leading up to it and the question of how aware ordinary Germans were of the genocidal actions.

LIEBERMANN-VILLA AM WANNSEE — MUSEUM

(☎030-8058 5900; www.liebermann-villa.de; Colomierstrasse 3; adult/concession €7/4 Apr-Sep, €6/4 Oct-Mar, audioguide €3; ⏲10am-6pm Mon, Wed, Fri & Sat, 10am-7pm Thu & Sun Apr-Sep, 11am-5pm Wed-Mon Oct-Mar; [S]Wannsee, then bus 114) This lovely villa was the summer home of Berlin Secession founder Max Liebermann from 1909 until his death in 1935. Liebermann loved the lyricism of nature and often painted the gardens as seen through the window of his barrel-vaulted upstairs studio. A selection of these works is on permanent display.

SCHLOSS GLIENICKE — PALACE

(☎030-8058 6750; www.spsg.de; Königstrasse 36; palace tours adult/concession €6/5; ⏲10am-6pm Tue-Sun Apr-Oct, to 5pm Sat & Sun Nov-Mar; [P]; [S]Wannsee, then bus 316) Glienicke Palace is the result of a rich royal kid travelling to Italy and falling in love with the country. Prince Carl of Prussia (1801–83) was only 21 when he returned to Berlin giddy with dreams of building his own Italian villa, so he hired starchitect du jour Karl Friedrich Schinkel to turn an existing garden estate into an elegant, antique-looking compound. It's richly decorated with marble fireplaces, sparkling crystal chandeliers, gold-framed paintings and fine furniture.

🍴 EATING & DRINKING

LORETTA AM WANNSEE — GERMAN €€

(☎030-8010 5333; www.loretta-berlin.de; Kronprinzessinnenweg 260; mains beer garden €2.60-9, restaurant €12-17; ⏲11am-11pm; [P]; [S]Wannsee) Robust Bavarian cooking is on the menu at this traditional restaurant with an enchanting beer garden overlooking Wannsee lake. Have a grilled sausage in the beer garden, a light meal or go the whole hog with *Grillhaxe* (pork leg) braised in black beer. König Pilsner, Augustiner and Erdinger are on tap. It's about 300m south of Wannsee S-Bahn station.

RESTAURANT SEEHAASE — INTERNATIONAL €€

(☎030-8049 6474; www.restaurant-seehaase.de; Am Grossen Wannsee 58-60; mains €8.50-16; ⏲11am-9pm Sun-Thu, 10am-10pm Fri & Sat; [P]; [S]Wannsee, then bus 114) Most of the Wannsee waterfront lots are in private hands, so the Seehaase with its lake views is justifiably popular. The menu is mostly classic German, but also features pasta, *Flammkuche* and an interesting array of Turkish appetisers.

Köpenick

Explore

The southeastern suburb of Köpenick was founded around 1240, making it only three years younger than Berlin itself. A 20-minute S-Bahn ride away from central Berlin, it's famous for its handsome baroque castle, a picturesque Altstadt (old town) and a trio of superlative natural assets: Berlin's largest lake (Müggelsee), biggest forest (Köpenicker Stadtforst) and highest natural elevation (Müggelberge, 115m). A leisurely ramble, relaxed boat ride or cooling dip in the water quickly restores balance to a brain overstimulated by life in the city – or too much sightseeing.

Many of the cobblestone streets in the Altstadt still follow their medieval layout. The main street, called Alt-Köpenick, is lined with baroque beauties and the historic Rathaus (town hall).

Urban trendspotters, meanwhile, might want to keep an eye on developments in **Oberschöneweide**, a one-time industrial area northwest of central Köpenick that's being discovered by artists and creatives.

The Best...

➡**Sight** Schloss Köpenick (p215)
➡**Place to Eat & Drink** Ratskeller Köpenick (p216)

Top Tip

For a more in-depth understanding of Köpenick's history, take a self-guided tour with the help of a multimedia audioguide (€5) dispensed by the tourist office.

Getting There & Away

➡**S-Bahn** For the Altstadt, take the S3 to S-Bahn station Köpenick, then walk 1.5km south along Bahnhofstrasse or take tram 62 to the Schloss Köpenick. For the Müggelsee get off at S-Bahn station Friedrichshagen and take tram 60 or walk 1.5km south on Bölschestrasse.

Need to Know

➡**Area Code** ✆030

➡**Location** About 16km southeast of central Berlin.
➡**Tourist Office** (✆030-655 7550; www. tkt-berlin.de; Alt-Köpenick 31-33, enter via Grünstrasse; ☺9am-6.30pm Mon-Fri, 10am-4pm Sat; ☑62, Ⓢ Köpenick)

⊙ SIGHTS

SCHLOSS KÖPENICK PALACE

(✆030-266 424 242; www.smb.museum; Schlossinsel 1; adult/concession/under 18 €6/3/free; ☺11am-6pm Tue-Sun Apr-Sep, to 5pm Thu-Sun Oct-Mar; ☑62, Ⓢ Köpenick) Berlin's only surviving baroque palace, on a little island just south of the Altstadt, houses a branch of the **Kunstgewerbemuseum** (Museum of Decorative Arts). It's a rich and eclectic collection of furniture, tapestries, porcelain, silverware, glass and other frilly objects from the Renaissance, baroque and rococo periods. Note elaborate ceiling paintings and stucco ornamentation. Highlights include four lavishly panelled rooms and the recreated **Wappensaal** (Coat of Arms Hall).

GROSSER MÜGGELSEE LAKE

(☑60, Ⓢ Friedrichshagen) At 4km long and 2.5km wide, the Müggelsee is Berlin's largest lake. Hemmed in by forest on two sides, it's hugely popular for swimming and boating on hot summer days and easily reached by public transport in less than an hour from central Berlin.

The **Müggelpark** on its north shore has restaurants and beer gardens as well as the landing docks of **Reederei Kutzker** (✆03362-6251; www.reederei-kutzker. de; Müggelpark, Müggelseedamm; 1hr tours €7; ☺tours late Mar–early Oct; ☑60, Ⓢ Friedrichshagen), which runs one-hour lake tours several times daily from late March to early October.

For a walk in the woods, head to the other side of the Spree via the nearby Spree-tunnel. The closest public lake beach, with boat rental, **Strandbad Friedrichshagen** (✆030-645 5756; www.seebad-friedrichshagen. de; Müggelseedamm 216; adult/concession €5/2.80; ☺10am-7pm May-Aug; ☑60, Ⓢ Friedrichshagen), is about 300m west of the Müggelpark.

DAY TRIPS FROM BERLIN KÖPENICK

WORTH A DETOUR

DEUTSCH-RUSSISCHES MUSEUM BERLIN-KARLSHORST

On 8 May 1945, the madness of six years of WWII in Europe ended with the unconditional surrender of the Wehrmacht in the headquarters of the Soviet army in what is today a memorial exhibit that documents this fateful day and the events leading up to it from both the Russian and German perspective. The **Deutsch-Russisches Museum Berlin-Karlshorst** (German-Russian Museum Berlin-Karlshorst; ☎030-5015 0810; www.museum-karlshorst.de; Zwieseler Strasse 4; 🕐10am-6pm Tue-Sun; [S]Karlshorst) is a 10- to 15-minute walk from the S-Bahn station; take the Treskowallee exit, then turn right onto Rheinsteinstrasse.

🍴 EATING & DRINKING

RATSKELLER KÖPENICK GERMAN €€

(☎030-655 5178; www.ratskellerkoepenick.de; Alt-Köpenick 21; mains €8-23; 🕐11am-11pm Mon-Sat, to 10pm Sun; 🚋62, 68, [S]Köpenick) The olde-worlde ambience at this cellar-warren in the local town hall is fun, and the menu full of classic rib-stickers (try the smoked pork knuckle) alongside healthier, seasonal and meatless selections. Many ingredients are locally sourced. Reservations advised for the Friday and Saturday live-jazz nights.

KROKODIL MEDITERRANEAN €€

(☎030-6588 0094; www.der-coepenicker.de; Gartenstrasse 46-48; mains €9-18; 🕐4-11pm Mon-Thu, 4pm-midnight Fri, 3pm-midnight Sat, 11am-11pm Sun; [P]; 🚋62, 68, [S]Köpenick) The seasonal fare at this urban getaway is delish, but even more memorable is the idyllic setting on the Dahme River some 700m south of the Altstadt. Join locals in capping a day of lounging on Krokodil's beach with a leisurely sunset dinner or book ahead for the legendary Sunday brunch. The attached **guesthouse** (☎030-6588 0094; www.hotel-pension-berlin.eu; tw €79) has twin rooms.

From S-Bahn station Köpenick take tram 62 or 68 to Schlossplatz, then walk east on Müggelheimer Strasse for 300m and turn south on Kietz for another 400m.

Sleeping

Berlin offers the gamut of places to unpack your suitcase. Just about every international chain now has a flagship in the German capital, but more interesting options that better reflect the city's verve and spirit abound. You can sleep in a former bank, boat or factory, in the home of a silent-movie diva or in a 'flying bed'.

Hotels

With around 137,000 beds in 815 properties, Berlin has more beds than New York and more are scheduled to come online in the coming years. You'll find the entire range of hotels in Berlin, from no-frills cookie-cutter chains to all-out boutique hotels with top-notch amenities and fall-over-backwards service.

The best beds often sell out early, so make reservations, especially around major holidays, cultural events and trade shows. Most properties can be booked online, usually with a best-price guarantee. You might also get better rates (or a better room) by contacting the property directly.

Most smaller and midsized hotels are now entirely nonsmoking; a few of the larger ones (especially the international chains) still set aside rooms or entire floors for smokers.

BUDGET, DESIGNER & ART HOTELS

Berlin being an art- and design-minded city, it's not surprising that there's a large number of smaller indie hotels catering to the needs of savvy urban nomads with at least a mid-range budget. Properties often integrate distinguished architecture with a customised design concept that projects a sense of place and tends to appeal to creative spirits and travellers searching for an authentic and localised experience. There's usually great emphasis on the latest tech trends and on such lifestyle essentials as iPod docks and brand-name espresso machines and sound systems. The antithesis of cookie-cutter chains, these types of abodes are sprinkled around the city but are especially prevalent in the Mitte dis-

trict. Many have succeeded in cultivating the local community with hip rooftop lounges, cocktail bars, progressive restaurants, chic spas and one-off parties and events.

CHAIN HOTELS

In recent years, practically all international hotel chains have opened one or multiple properties in Berlin. Since most conform to certain standards of decor, service and facilities, they're great for people who enjoy predictability and privacy (or simply want to use up those frequent flyer points). Most have several categories of comfort, from cramped singles to high-roller suites, with rates reflecting size and amenities. Generally, prices fluctuate dramatically, with last-minute, weekend or low-occupancy bargains a possibility. Besides the international chains, there are also some Berlin-based contenders, including Amano (www.amanogroup.de) and Meininger (www.meininger-hotels.com) and German chains like Motel One (www.motelone.com) and Leonardo (www.leonardo-hotels.com).

Hostels

Berlin's hostel scene is as vibrant as ever and consists of both classic backpacker hostels with large dorms and a communal spirit to modern 'flashpacker' crashpads catering to wallet-watching city-breakers. Also increasingly popular are hostel-hotel hybrids that have a standard similar to budget hotels. Many also have private quarters with bathrooms and even apartments with kitchens. You'll find them in all districts, but especially in Mitte and Kreuzberg, putting you within stumbling distance of bars and clubs.

Dorm beds can be had for as little as €9, but spending a little more gets you a dorm with fewer beds, private quarters with attached bathroom, or a self-catering apartment. Dorms tend to be mixed, though some hostels also offer women-only units. Indie hostels have no curfew and staff tend to be savvy, multilingual and keen to help with tips and advice.

B&Bs

Nostalgic types seeking Old Berlin flavour should check into a charismatic B&B, called *Hotel-Pension* or simply *Pension*. But better do it quickly because these types of abodes are a dying breed in the digital age! *Pensions* typically occupy one or several floors of a historic residential building and offer local colour and personal attention galore. Amenities, room size and decor vary, often within a single establishment. The cheapest rooms may have shared facilities or perhaps a sink and a shower cubicle in the room but no private toilet. Travellers in need of buckets of privacy, high comfort levels or the latest tech amenities may not feel as comfortable, although wi-fi, cable TV and other mod cons are becoming increasingly available. You'll still find a few of these time warps in the western district of Charlottenburg, around Kurfürstendamm.

Short-Term Rentals

Renting a furnished flat is a hugely popular – and economical – lodging option. The benefit of space, privacy and independence makes flats especially attractive to families and small groups. Alas, since May 2016 a new law has cracked down on peer-to-peer rentals such as those offered through Airbnb or Wimdu, so that the supply of legal short-term rental apartments has dwindled significantly.

Rates

Fierce competition has kept prices low compared to other capital cities in Europe. Prices spike during major trade shows, festivals and public holidays, when early reservations are essential. Business-traveller-geared hotels often have good deals at weekends. In winter, prices often plummet outside holidays, with five-star rooms costing as little as €120.

Amenities

Midrange options generally offer the best value for money. Expect clean, comfortable and decent-sized rooms with at least a modicum of style, a private bathroom, TV and wi-fi. Top-end hotels provide the full spectrum of international-standard amenities and perhaps a scenic location, designer decor or historical ambience. Budget places are generally hostels or other simple establishments where bathrooms may be shared.

Overall, rooms tend to be on the small side. You'll usually find that BBC and CNN are the only English-language channels on TV (nearly all foreign shows and films are dubbed into German) and that air-con is a rare commodity. Wi-fi is commonplace and usually free, although some hotels (especially international chains) may still charge as much as €20 per day for access. In smaller hotels, access may be restricted to the lobby. Few hotels have their own parking lot or garage and even if they do, space will be limited and the cost as high as €25 per day. Public garages are widely available, but also cost a pretty penny.

Useful Websites

➡ **Lonely Planet** (lonelyplanet.com/germany/hotels) Lonely Planet's online booking service with insider low-down on the best places to stay.

➡ **Visit Berlin** (www.visitberlin.de) Official Berlin tourist office books rooms at partner hotels with a best-price guarantee.

➡ **Boutique Hotels Berlin** (www.boutiquehotels-berlin.com) Booking service for about 20 handpicked boutique hotels.

➡ **Berlin30** (www.berlin30.com) Online low-cost booking agency for hotels, hostels, apartments and B&Bs.

Lonely Planet's Top Choices

Casa Camper (p223) Infectious irreverence paired with all the zeitgeist essentials global nomads crave.

Michelberger Hotel (p225) Fun base with eccentric design, party pedigree and unpretentious attitude beautifully captures the Berlin vibe.

Das Stue (p222) Charismatic refuge from the urban bustle with understated grandeur and the Tiergarten park as a front yard.

EastSeven Berlin Hostel (p225) Small, personable and spotless crash pad perfect for making new friends.

Hotel am Steinplatz (p226) Golden 1920s glamour still radiates from the listed walls of this recently revivified art-deco jewel.

Brilliant Apartments (p224) Stylish mash-up of modern and historic in spacious units on trendy street.

Best By Budget

€

Grand Hostel Berlin (p223) Connect to the magic of yesteryear at this historic lair imbued with both character and modern amenities.

Wombats City Hostel Berlin (p222) Fun seekers should thrive at this well-run hostel with hip in-house bar.

EastSeven Berlin Hostel (p225) Friendly and low-key hostel with communal vibe ideal for solo travellers.

€€

Circus Hotel (p223) Perennial pleaser thanks to being a perfect synthesis of style, comfort, location and value.

Hotel Amano (p223) Top value-for-money pick beloved by global nomads on a budget.

Adina Apartment Hotel Berlin Checkpoint Charlie (p221) Ideal base for budget-conscious space-craving self-caterers.

€€€

Mandala Hotel (p222) All-suite city slicker with uncluttered urban feel and top eats.

Louisa's Place (p226) Personal attention is key at this refined outpost with XL-sized suites.

Hotel de Rome (p221) Posh player in former bank building with rooftop bar and bank vault spa.

Best Cool Factor

Michelberger Hotel (p225) With its funky industrial DIY aesthetics, this crash pad hits on all zeitgeist cylinders.

Soho House Berlin (p223) Members-only club with A-lister clientele meets posh boutique hotel in Bauhaus building.

25hours Hotel Bikini Berlin (p226) Inner-city playground with easy access to top shopping and rooms overlooking the Berlin Zoo.

nhow (p225) Karim Rashid–designed shagadelic riverside hotel with recording studio.

Best for Romance

Honigmond Garden Hotel (p222) Urban oasis with antique-filled rooms backed by dreamy 'Garden of Eden'.

Ackselhaus & Blue Home (p225) This cocoon of quiet and sophistication lets you match mood to room.

Das Stue (p222) Stylish boutique pad with luxe spa and park access for long walks.

SLEEPING

Where to Stay

Neighbourhood	For	Against
Historic Mitte	Close to major sights like Reichstag and Brandenburger Tor; great transport links; mostly high-end hotels; Michelin-starred and other top restaurants; close to theatre, opera and classical concert venues	Touristy, expensive, pretty dead at night
Museumsinsel & Alexanderplatz	Supercentral sightseeing quarter; easy transport access; close to blockbuster sights and mainstream shopping; large and new hotels	Noisy, busy and dusty thanks to lots of major construction; hardly any nightlife
Potsdamer Platz & Tiergarten	Urban flair in Berlin's newest quarter; cutting-edge architecture; high-end international hotels; top museums, Philharmonie and multiplex cinemas; next to huge Tiergarten city park	Limited eating options; pricey; practically no street life at night
Scheunenviertel	Hipster quarter; trendy, historic, central; brims with boutique and designer hotels; superb indie and trendy chain shopping; international eats and strong cafe scene; top galleries and plenty of great street art	Pricey, busy, noisy, no parking, bit touristy
Kreuzberg & Neukölln	Vibrant arty, underground and multicultural party quarter; best for bar-hopping and clubbing; cheap; lots of hostels; high-vibe; great foodie scene; excellent street art	Gritty, noisy and busy; U-Bahn ride(s) away from major sights
Friedrichshain	Student and young family quarter; bubbling nightlife; superb Cold War–era sights	Limited sleeping options; not so central for sightseeing; transport difficult in some areas
Prenzlauer Berg	Well-heeled, clean, charming residential area; lively cafe and restaurant scene; indie boutiques and Mauerpark flea market	Limited late-night action, few essential sights
City West & Charlottenburg	The former 'West Berlin'; great shopping at KaDeWe and on Kurfürstendamm; stylish lounges, 'Old Berlin' bars and top restaurants; best range of good-value lodging; historic B&Bs	Sedate; far from key sights and happening nightlife

🛏 Historic Mitte

ADINA APARTMENT
HOTEL BERLIN
CHECKPOINT CHARLIE   APARTMENT €€
Map p296 (☑030-200 7670; www.tfehotels.
com/de/brands/adina-apartment-hotels; Krausenstrasse 35-36; d from €100, 1-bedroom apt from
€145; P❋@🛜🏊♿; ⓊStadtmitte, Spittelmarkt) Adina's contemporary one- and two-bedroom apartments with full kitchens are tailor-made for cost-conscious families, anyone in need of elbow room, and self-caterers (a supermarket is a minute away). Rooms without kitchens are also available. There are toys for children and a pool and sauna for combating post-flight fatigue. See the website for other Adina properties in town. Optional breakfast is €19.

COSMO HOTEL BERLIN   HOTEL €€
Map p296 (☑030-5858 2222; www.cosmo
-hotel.de; Spittelmarkt 13; d €100-210; P❋@🛜; ⓊSpittelmarkt) Despite its ho-hum location on a busy street, this hotel scores high for comfort, design and a 'with it' vibe. The lobby, with its extravagant lamps and armchairs, sets the tone for modern rooms decked out in shades of cinnamon, charcoal and chocolate. All have floor-to-ceiling windows with blackout blinds. Free wi-fi in public areas only. The breakfast buffet is €18.

HOTEL DE ROME   LUXURY HOTEL €€€
Map p296 (☑030-460 6090; www.hotel
derome.com; Behrenstrasse 37; d from €295; P♿❋@🛜🏊♿; 🅿100, 200, ⓊHausvogteiplatz) A delightful alchemy of history and contemporary flair, this luxe contender in a 19th-century bank has richly furnished rooms with extra-high ceilings, marble baths and heated floors. Wind down in the former vault that is now the pool and spa area or over cocktails in the bar or, in summer, on the rooftop terrace. Optional breakfast is €37.

🛏 Museumsinsel & Alexanderplatz

MOTEL ONE BERLIN-
HACKESCHER MARKT   HOTEL €
Map p300 (☑030-2005 4080; www.motel-one.
de; Dircksenstrasse 36; d from €73; P♿❋🛜; ⓢAlexanderplatz, ⓊAlexanderplatz) If you val-

ue location over luxury, this budget designer chain comes with excellent crash-pad credentials. Smallish rooms feature sleek touches (granite counters, rain showers, air-con, flat-screen TVs) that are normally the reserve of posher players. Arne Jacobsen's turquoise egg chairs add hipness to the lobby. Check the website for the other eight Berlin locations. Optional breakfast is €9.50.

HOSTEL ONE80°   HOSTEL €
Map p300 (☑030-2804 4620; www.one80
hostels.com; Otto-Braun-Strasse 65; dm €20-47; ♿@🛜; ⓢAlexanderplatz, ⓊAlexanderplatz) With its designer sofas, ambient music and industrial-chic public areas, One80° is a next-gen lifestyle hostel. There's space for over 700 people in dorms (some with private bathroom) sleeping four to eight in comfy bunk beds with individual reading lamps and two electrical outlets each. Optional breakfast is €6.40. Minimum age 18.

HOTEL ALEXANDER PLAZA   HOTEL €€
Map p300 (☑030-240 010; www.hotel-alexander-
plaza.de; Rosenstrasse 1; d €115-135; P♿🛜; ⓢHackescher Markt) This 94-room city hotel in a sensitively restored 19-century merchant home retains such period details as a mosaic floor and a stucco-adorned floating stairway. Rooms are dressed in soothing tan, black and carmine and get plenty of natural light filtering in through panoramic windows. Kick back in the sauna. Breakfast is €15.

RADISSON BLU HOTEL   HOTEL €€€
Map p300 (☑030-238 280; www.radisson
blu.com/hotel-berlin; Karl-Liebknecht-Strasse 3; d from €150; P♿❋@🛜♿; 🅿100, 200, ⓢHackescher Markt) 🟢 At this swish and super-central contender, you quite literally

'sleep with the fishes', thanks to the lobby's 25m-high tropical aquarium. Streamlined design radiates urban poshness in the 427 rooms and throughout the two restaurants and various social nooks. Thoughtful perks include a 24/7 spa with pool and sauna. Optional breakfast is €25.

🛏 Potsdamer Platz & Tiergarten

SCANDIC BERLIN
POTSDAMER PLATZ   HOTEL €€
Map p294 (📞030-700 7790; www.scandichotels.com; Gabriele-Tergit-Promenade 19; d €90-170; P❄@🤶; ⓤMendelssohn-Bartholdy-Park) 🍃 This Scandinavian import gets kudos for its central location and spacious blond-wood rooms with big bathrooms, as well as for going the extra mile when it comes to being green. Distinctive features include the 8th-floor gym-with-a-view, honey from the rooftop beehive and free bikes. Optional (partly organic) breakfast is €12.

MÖVENPICK HOTEL BERLIN   HOTEL €€
Map p294 (📞030-230 060; www.moevenpick.com; Schöneberger Strasse 3; d €110-320; P⊖❄@🤶; ⓢAnhalter Bahnhof) 🍃 This snazzy Green Globe–certified hotel smoothly marries contemporary boldness with the industrial flair of the listed Siemenshöfe factory. Rooms vamp it up with bright colours and sensuous olive-wood furniture, while the courtyard restaurant is lidded by a retractable glass roof for alfresco dining. Optional breakfast is €22.

⭐DAS STUE   BOUTIQUE HOTEL €€€
Map p294 (📞030-311 7220; www.das-stue.com; Drakestrasse 1; d from €220; ❄@🤶🏊; 🚌100, 106, 200) This charismatic refuge in a 1930s Danish diplomatic outpost flaunts understated grandeur and has the Tiergarten park (p122) as a front yard. A crocodile sculpture flanked by sweeping staircases fluidly leads the way to a hip bar (p127), a Michelin-starred restaurant and sleekly furnished and spacious rooms (some with terrace or balcony). The elegant spa has a pool, a sauna and top-notch massages. Optional breakfast is €25.

⭐MANDALA HOTEL   HOTEL €€€
Map p294 (📞030-590 050 000; www.themandala.de; Potsdamer Strasse 3; ste from €170;

P❄@🤶; 🚌200, ⓢPotsdamer Platz, ⓤPotsdamer Platz) How 'suite' it is to be staying at this sophisticated yet unfussy cocoon. Uncluttered, zeitgeist-compatible units come in 10 sizes (40 to 200 sq metres) and are equipped with a kitchenette, walk-in closets and spacious desks in case you're here to ink that deal. Day spa and 24/7 fitness centre for relaxation, plus on-site two-Michelin-star **restaurant** (Map p294; 📞030-590 051 234; www.facil.de; 5th fl; 1-/2-/3-course lunches €21/36/48, 4-8 course dinners €109-185; 🕐noon-3pm & 7-11pm Mon-Fri; P🤶). Breakfast is €30.

🛏 Scheunenviertel

WOMBAT'S BERLIN   HOSTEL €
Map p302 (📞030-8471 0820; www.wombats-hostels.com/berlin; Alte Schönhauser Strasse 2; dm €20-26, d €68-78; ⊖@🤶; ⓤRosa-Luxemburg-Platz) Sociable and central, Wombat's gets hostelling right. From backpack-sized in-room lockers to individual reading lamps and a guest kitchen with dishwasher, the attention to detail here is impressive. Spacious and clean en-suite dorms are as much part of the deal as free linen and a welcome drink, best enjoyed with fellow party pilgrims at sunset on the rooftop.

CIRCUS HOSTEL   HOSTEL €
Map p302 (📞030-2000 3939; www.circus-berlin.de; Weinbergsweg 1a; dm €19-31, d without/with bathroom €58/75; ⊖@🤶; ⓤRosenthaler Platz) Clean, cheerfully painted singles, doubles and dorms (sleeping three to 10) plus abundant shared facilities, helpful staff and a great location are among the factors that have kept Circus at the top of the hostel heap for around two decades. There's a cute on-site cafe and a basement bar with its own craft brewery. Ask about its guided and DIY tours.

⭐HONIGMOND
GARDEN HOTEL   BOUTIQUE HOTEL €€
Map p304 (📞030-2844 5577; www.honigmond-berlin.de; Invalidenstrasse 122; r €121-186; P⊖@🤶; ⓤNaturkundemuseum, ⓢNordbahnhof) Never mind the busy thoroughfare: this 20-room guesthouse built in 1845 is an utterly sweet retreat. Reach your comfortable, classically styled rooms via an enchanting garden with koi pond, chirping birds, and rich foliage and flowers. Days start with a

sumptuous breakfast (€10) in the winter garden. Avoid rooms facing the road.

⭐**CIRCUS HOTEL** HOTEL €€

Map p302 (☑030-2000 3939; www.circus-berlin.de; Rosenthaler Strasse 1; d €85-120, apt €120-190; ⊖ @ 🛜; Ⓤ Rosenthaler Platz) At this super-central budget boutique hotel, none of the compact, mod rooms are alike, but all feature upbeat colours, thoughtful design touches, a small desk, a tea and coffee station and organic bath products. Unexpected perks include a roof terrace, bike rentals and a fabulous breakfast buffet (€9) served until 1pm. Need more space? Go for an apartment.

BOUTIQUE HOTEL I31 BOUTIQUE HOTEL €€

Map p304 (☑030-338 4000; www.hotel-i31. de; Invalidenstrasse 31; r €90-167; Ⓟ⊖🌸🛜; Ⓤ Naturkundemuseum) This contemporary contender has modern, if smallish, rooms in soothing colours and various relaxation zones, including a sauna, a sunny terrace and a small garden with sun lounges. Nice touch: the minibar with free soft drinks. For a little more space and luxury (designer bath products, for example) book a 'comfort room plus' on one of the upper floors. Continental breakfast/buffet: €5.80/17.50.

ARTE LUISE KUNSTHOTEL BOUTIQUE HOTEL €€

Map p304 (☑030-284 480; www.luise-berlin. com; Luisenstrasse 19; d €89-299, with shared bathroom €53-119; ⊖🌸@🛜; Ⓢ Friedrichstrasse, Ⓤ Friedrichstrasse) At this 'gallery with rooms' each of the 50 units was designed by a different artist, who receive royalties whenever it's rented. All sport high ceilings, oak floors and wonderfully imaginative, poetic or bizarre decor – we're especially fond of number 107 with its giant bed. For cash-strapped art fans there are smaller rooms with shared baths. Avoid those facing the train tracks. Breakfast €12.

HOTEL AMANO HOTEL €€

Map p302 (☑030-809 4150; www.amanogroup. de; Auguststrasse 43; d €70-165, apt €90-185; Ⓟ⊖🌸🛜; Ⓤ Rosenthaler Platz) This sleek, budget, designer hotel has efficiently styled, mod con–laden rooms, where white furniture teams up with oak floors and grey hues to create crisp cosiness. For space-cravers there are apartments in three sizes and with kitchens. Optional breakfast buffet for €15.

⭐**CASA CAMPER** DESIGN HOTEL €€€

Map p302 (☑030-2000 3410; www.casacamper. com; Weinmeisterstrasse 1; r/ste incl breakfast €193-319; Ⓟ⊖🌸🛜; Ⓤ Weinmeisterstrasse) Catalan shoemaker Camper has translated its concept of chic yet sensible footwear into this style-pit for trend-conscious global nomads. Minimalist-mod rooms come with day-lit bathrooms with natural amenities, and beds that invite hitting the snooze button. Minibars are eschewed for a top-floor lounge with stellar views and free 24/7 hot and cold snacks and drinks.

SOHO HOUSE BERLIN DESIGN HOTEL €€€

Map p302 (☑030-405 0440; www.soho houseberlin.com; Torstrasse 1; d from €200; Ⓟ⊖🌸🛜🏊; Ⓤ Rosa-Luxemburg-Platz) The Berlin edition of the eponymous members' club and celeb-fave doubles as a hotel open to all. The vintage-eclectic rooms vary dramatically in size, decor and amenities, but may include vinyl record players, huge flatscreen TVs and free-standing tubs. Staying here also buys access to members-only areas such as the club floor with bar and restaurant, the rooftop pool/bar/restaurant and a small movie theatre.

It's all in a Bauhaus building that's seen stints as a department store, Hitler Youth HQ and East German party elite offices.

🛏 Kreuzberg & Neukölln

⭐**GRAND HOSTEL BERLIN** HOSTEL €

Map p314 (☑030-2009 5450; www.grandhostel -berlin.de; Tempelhofer Ufer 14; dm €10-32, tw with/without bathroom from €49/38; ⊖@🛜; Ⓤ Möckernbrücke) Cocktails in the library bar? Check. Rooms with stucco-ornamented ceilings? Got 'em. Canal views? Yep. Ensconced in a fully renovated 1870s building, the 'five-star' Grand Hostel is one of Berlin's most supremely comfortable, convivial and atmospheric hostels. Private rooms are spacious and nicely furnished and dorms come with freestanding quality beds and large lockers. Breakfast is €6.50.

HÜTTENPALAST HOSTEL €

Map p312 (☑030-3730 5806; www.huetten palast.de; Hobrechtstrasse 66; d campervans & cabins incl breakfast €69, hotel €80; ⊙ check-in 8am-6pm or by arrangement; ⊖🛜; Ⓤ Hermannplatz) This indoor camping ground in an old vacuum-cleaner factory is an unusual place to hang your hat, even by Berlin standards. Sure, it has hotel-style rooms with private bath, but who wants those when you can sleep in a romantic wooden hut with rooftop terrace or in a snug vintage caravan? The little garden with plants and flowers in recycled barrels and tubs invites socialising.

HOTEL SAROTTI-HÖFE
HOTEL €€

Map p314 (⌚030-6003 1680; www.hotel-sarottihoefe.de; Mehringdamm 57; d €100-180; P ⊖ @ ⓢ; Ⓤ Mehringdamm) You'll have sweet dreams in this 19th-century ex-chocolate factory whose courtyard-cloistered rooms are quiet despite being in the middle of the bustling Bergmannkiez quarter. Rooms come in five categories and exude yesteryear flair with high ceilings, red carpets and dark-wood furniture. The nicest (deluxe category) come with private terrace. Breakfast buffet €12.

HOTEL JOHANN
HOTEL €€

Map p314 (⌚030-225 0740; www.hotel-johann-berlin.de; Johanniterstrasse 8; d €86-120; P @ ⓢ; Ⓤ Prinzenstrasse) This 33-room hotel consistently tops the popularity charts, thanks to its eager-to-please service and good-sized rooms with uncluttered modern design and occasional historic flourishes such as scalloped ceilings and exposed brick walls. The small garden is perfect for summery breakfasts, while happening Bergmannstrasse and the Jüdisches Museum (p147) are within strolling distance. Breakfast €8.50.

🛏 Friedrichshain

⭐PLUS BERLIN
HOSTEL €

Map p308 (⌚030-311 698 820; www.plushostels.com/plusberlin; Warschauer Platz 6; dm/d from €12/54; P ✴ @ ⓢ ⊠; Ⓢ Warschauer Strasse, Ⓤ Warschauer Strasse) A hostel with an indoor pool, steam room and yoga classes? Yep. Within stumbling distance of Berlin's best nightlife, Plus is a flashpacker favourite. There's a bar for easing into the night and a tranquil courtyard to soothe that hangover. Spacious dorms have four or six bunks, desks and lockers, while private rooms have TV and air-con. All have ensuites. Optional breakfast is €7.

EASTERN COMFORT HOSTELBOAT
HOSTEL €

Map p308 (⌚030-6676 3806; www.eastern-comfort.com; Mühlenstrasse 73-77; dm €16, d €55-78; ⊙reception 8am-midnight; @ ⓢ; Ⓢ Warschauer Strasse, Ⓤ Warschauer Strasse) Let the Spree River murmur you to sleep while you're snugly ensconced in this two-boat, floating hostel right by the East Side Gallery (p166). Cabins are carpeted and trimmed in wood, but sweetly snug (except

---

TOP THREE FURNISHED APARTMENTS

Miniloft Berlin (Map p304; ⌚030-847 1090; www.miniloft.com; Hessische Strasse 5; apt €95-245; P ⊖ ⓢ; Ⓤ Naturkundemuseum) Eight stunning lofts in an architect-converted building, some with south-facing panorama windows, others with cosy alcoves, all outfitted with modern designer furniture and kitchenettes.

Classic and Compact units are in the old wing (no lift), while the larger Introverted and Extroverted lofts are in the new building.

Brilliant Apartments (Map p306; ⌚030-8061 4796; www.brilliant-apartments.de; Oderberger Strasse 38; apt from €93; ⓢ; Ⓤ Eberswalder Strasse) These 11 stylish and modern units have full kitchens and neat historic touches such as exposed red-brick walls and parquet floors. Four have balconies, one a little garden. They're located on Oderberger Strasse, one of the hippest drags in Prenzlauer Berg, which puts you close to good eats, bars, boutiques and the Mauerpark (p179). Apartments facing out back are quieter.

Gorki Apartments (Map p302; ⌚030-4849 6480; www.gorkiapartments.de; Weinbergsweg 25; apt €145-285; ⊖ ✴ ⓢ; ⓜ M1, 12, Ⓤ Rosenthaler Platz) Idiosyncratic modern furniture and decor meet retro touches like sparkling parquet floors and stucco ornamentation in these 34 spacious, super-central luxury apartments with kitchens. Style mavens will appreciate tea by Berlin-based Paper & Tea, cookies from Friedl and classic soap by Dr Bronner. Breakfast €13.

for '1st-class'); most have their own shower and toilet. The party zones of Kreuzberg and Friedrichshain are handily within staggering distance. Optional breakfast is €6.

⭐ **MICHELBERGER HOTEL** HOTEL €€
Map p308 (☑030-2977 8590; www.michel bergerhotel.com; Warschauer Strasse 39; d €90-160; ☎; ⓤWarschauer Strasse, ⓢWarschauer Strasse) The ultimate in creative crash pads, Michelberger perfectly encapsulates Berlin's offbeat DIY spirit without being self-consciously cool. Rooms don't hide their factory pedigree, but are comfortable and come in sizes suitable for lovebirds, families or rock bands. Staff are friendly and clued-up, and the restaurant (p169) is popular with both guests and locals. Breakfast is €16.

⭐ **NHOW BERLIN** DESIGN HOTEL €€
Map p308 (☑030-290 2990; www.nhow-hotels.com/berlin; Stralauer Allee 3; d €135-215; ℗❄☎; ⓢWarschauer Strasse, ⓤWarschauer Strasse) This riverside behemoth bills itself as a music and lifestyle hotel and underscores the point by having two on-site recording studios. The look is definitely dynamic, what with a sideways tower jutting out over the Spree and Karim Rashid's digipop-pink design, which would make Barbie proud. Kudos for the party-people-friendly Sunday 5pm check-out. Massive breakfast buffet is €24 (served till 3pm).

ALMODÓVAR HOTEL HOTEL €€
Map p308 (☑030-692 097 080; www.almodovar hotel.de; Boxhagener Strasse 83; d €99-136; ℗❄☎; 🚇240, 🚌M13, ⓢOstkreuz) 🌿 A certified organic hotel, Almodóvar is perfect for those wanting to keep their healthy ways while travelling. A yoga mat is a standard amenity in the 60 rooms dressed in crisp white, red and black, while the locavore restaurant turns out vegan, raw, lactose- and gluten-free dishes, and the spa offers Ayurvedic treatments. Breakfast is €16.50.

🛏 Prenzlauer Berg

⭐ **EASTSEVEN BERLIN HOSTEL** HOSTEL €
Map p306 (☑030-9362 2240; www.eastseven.de; Schwedter Strasse 7; dm €14-23, d €52; ❄@☎; ⓤSenefelderplatz) An excellent choice for solo travellers, this small indie hostel has personable staff that go out of their way to make all feel welcome. Make new friends

while chilling in the lounge or garden (hammocks!), firing up the BBQ or hanging out in the 24-hour kitchen. Brightly painted dorms feature comfy pine beds and lockers. Linen is free, breakfast €3.

MEININGER HOTEL BERLIN ALEXANDERPLATZ HOTEL €
Map p306 (☑030-9832 1074; www.meininger-hotels.com; Schönhauser Allee 19; dm/d from €18/54; ❄@☎; ⓤSenefelderplatz) This well-run hostel-hotel combo draws school groups, flashpackers and business types, which makes for an interesting guest mix. A lift whisks you to mod and spacious en-suite rooms and dorms with quality furnishings, flat-screen TVs and handy blackout blinds to combat jet lag (or hangovers). It's close to bars, markets and transport. Breakfast is €6.90.

Note that it's actually 1.5km north of Alexanderplatz but still quite central. Check the website for the three other Meininger locations in town.

HOTEL KASTANIENHOF HOTEL €€
Map p306 (☑030-443 050; www.kastanienhof. biz; Kastanienallee 65; d €105-160; ℗@☎📶; 🚇M1 to Zionskirchstrasse, ⓤRosenthaler Platz, Senefelderplatz) Right on Kastanienallee with its cafes, restaurants and boutiques, this family run traditional charmer has caring staff and 35 good-sized rooms that pair historical touches with flat-screen TVs, modern bathrooms and free wi-fi. New ones under the roof have air-con, a balcony and great views, and there are family rooms as well. Breakfast is €9.

HOTEL ODERBERGER HOTEL €€
Map p306 (☑030-780 089 760; www.hotel-oderberger.de; Oderberger Strasse 56/57; d incl breakfast €158; ❄❄☎📺; 🚇M1, ⓤEberswalder Strasse) These stately public baths established in a neo-Renaissance building in 1902 have been recycled into a modern hotel that nicely integrates original tiles, lamps, doors, wall hooks and other design details. A head-turner is the actual swimming pool in a cathedral-like hall, which can be turned into an event space. At night, a cosy fireplace bar invites winding down.

⭐ **ACKSELHAUS & BLUE HOME** BOUTIQUE HOTEL €€€
Map p306 (☑030-4433 7633; www.acksel-haus.de; Belforter Strasse 21; ste incl breakfast €120-180, apt €150-340; ❄@☎; 🚇M10,

Ⓤ Senefelderplatz) At this charismatic retreat in a 19th-century building you'll sleep in large, classily decorated themed rooms (eg Africa, Rome, Maritime), each with thoughtfully picked special features: a free-standing tub, perhaps, a four-poster bed or Chinese antiques. Many face the enchanting courtyard garden. The breakfast buffet is served – beneath crystal chandeliers – until 11am (until 12.30pm at weekends).

🛏 City West & Charlottenburg

★ 25HOURS HOTEL
BIKINI BERLIN
DESIGN HOTEL €€

Map p316 (📞030-120 2210; www.25hours-hotels.com; Budapester Strasse 40; r €130-330; Ⓟ❄✳@🛜; 🚌100, 200, ⓈZoologischer Garten, ⓊZoologischer Garten) The 'urban jungle' theme of this lifestyle outpost in the iconic 1950s Bikini Haus plays on its location between the zoo and main shopping district. Rooms are stylish, if a tad compact, with the nicer ones facing the animal park. Quirk factors include an on-site bakery, hammocks in the public areas and a sauna with zoo view.

★ HOTEL AM
STEINPLATZ
BOUTIQUE HOTEL €€

Map p316 (📞030-554 4440; www.hotelstein platz.com; Steinplatz 4; r €135-165; Ⓟ✳❄🛜; 🚌M45, 245, ⓊErnst-Reuter-Platz) Vladimir Nabokov and Romy Schneider were among the guests of the original Hotel am Steinplatz, which got a second lease on life in 2013, a century after it first opened. Rooms in this elegant art-deco jewel reinterpret the 1920s in contemporary style with fantastic lamps, smartphone docks and black-and-white bathrooms. Classy bar (p198) and restaurant (p198), to boot. Optional breakfast: €35.

HOTEL-PENSION FUNK
B&B €€

Map p316 (📞030-882 7193; www.hotel-pension funk.de; Fasanenstrasse 69; d incl breakfast €82-129; Ⓟ❄🛜; ⓊUhlandstrasse, Kurfürstendamm) This charismatic *Pension* in the home of silent-movie siren Asta Nielsen is a time-warp back to the Golden Twenties. Stuffed with art nouveau furniture and decor, it's perfect if you value old-fashioned charm over modcons. The 14 rooms vary quite significantly, so if size matters bring up the

subject when booking. Cheaper ones have partial or shared facilities.

HOTEL SIR FK SAVIGNY
BOUTIQUE HOTEL €€

Map p316 (📞030-323 015 600; www.hotel-sir savigny.de; Kantstrasse 144; r €90-160; ❄✳🛜; ⓈSavignyplatz) Not only pictures but also hotels tell a story, and this is the story of Sir FK Savigny, a fictional character who welcomes savvy travellers to his cosmopolitan crash pad with a hip bar and burger joint on the ground floor. Smartly dressed rooms are equipped with such lifestyle essentials as smartphone docks, espresso-pod machines and complimentary minibar. Breakfast is €18.

HOTEL OTTO
HOTEL €€

Map p316 (📞030-5471 0080; www.hotelotto. com; Knesebeckstrasse 10; d €80-140; Ⓟ🛜; ⓊErnst-Reuter-Platz) Otto would feel like 'just' a business hotel were it not for cool perks like fair-trade beauty products and complimentary coffee and cake in the afternoon. Rooms are contemporary-functional and get dimension from colour accents and tactile fabrics. 'Standard' rooms are teensy. Top marks to the slow-food breakfast (€18) served till noon and best enjoyed on the leafy rooftop terrace.

ELLINGTON HOTEL
DESIGN HOTEL €€

Map p316 (📞030-683 150; www.ellington-hotel. com; Nürnberger Strasse 50-55; d €128-268; Ⓟ✳❄@🛜; ⓊAugsburger Strasse) Duke and Ella gave concerts in the jazz cellar and Bowie partied in the Dschungel nightclub, then the lights went out in the '90s. Now the handsome 1920s building has been resuscitated as a high-concept hotel that wraps all that's great about Berlin – history, innovation, *laissez-faire* – into one attractive package. Rooms are stylishly minimalist. Optional breakfast is €20.

★ LOUISA'S PLACE
BOUTIQUE HOTEL €€€

Map p316 (📞030-631 030; www.louisas-place. de; Kurfürstendamm 160; ste from €120-220; Ⓟ🛜♿; 🚌M19, M29, ⓊAdenauerplatz) The all-suite Louisa's, in a charismatic 1904 building, is the kind of place that dazzles with class not glitz. The family-friendly suites brim with individual character, elegant furnishings and full kitchens. Though small, the pool provides a refreshing dip after a session in the sauna or on the treadmill. A high-end restaurant shares the premises. Optional breakfast is €26.

Understand Berlin

Berlin Today

Berlin is truly a 24/7 city, where a spirit of innovation, tolerance and levity roars with unapologetic abandon. Perpetually in flux, Berlin refuses to be pigeonholed, preferring to knit together a new identity from the yarn of its complex history. You can fairly feel the collision between past and future, what is possible and what is realistic, and the hopes and aspirations of people who've joined together from around the globe in one big experiment.

Best on Film

Symphony of a City (1927) Fascinating silent documentary captures a day in the life of Berlin in the 1920s.
Downfall (2004) Chilling account of Hitler's last 12 days holed up in his Berlin bunker.
Good Bye, Lenin! (2003) Cult comedy about a young East Berliner who replicates the GDR for his ailing mother after the fall of the Wall.
The Lives of Others (2006) This Academy Award–winner reveals the stranglehold the East German secret police had on innocent people.

Best in Print

Goodbye to Berlin (Christopher Isherwood; 1939) Brilliant semi-autobiographical account of early 1930s Berlin through the eyes of a gay Anglo-American journalist.
Berlin Alexanderplatz (Alfred Döblin; 1929) This stylised meander through the seamy 1920s is still an essential Berlin text.
Alone in Berlin (Hans Fallada; 1947) A working-class Berlin couple become unlikely Nazi resistors following their son's battlefield death.
Stasiland (Anna Funder; 2004) The Stasi's vast spying apparatus seen from the perspectives of both victims and perpetrators.

Strengthening Economy

It's been a long road to recovery but Berlin is finally seeing slivers of sunlight on the horizon. Since 2005 its economic growth has consistently outpaced that of Germany as a whole, and the city is also leading the nation in job creation. Although still 3.3% above the national average, unemployment dropped to 9.7% in May 2016, the lowest since reunification in 1990.

Berlin's transformation from an industrial to a knowledge-based society is the cause. The growth of the digital economy especially has stimulated the job market. The city today attracts some of the world's brightest minds and invests heavily in such high-tech fields as biotechnology, communication and environmental technologies and transport. In fact, Berlin is ranked among the EU's top three innovative regions.

Tourism continues to be a key force economically, with the number of overnight visitors breaking new records every year; in 2015 the city registered over 12 million visitors, accounting for 30 million overnight stays – more than ever before. And that's not even counting the roughly 100 million day trippers per year. The creative and cultural fields are booming too, and their financial impact, though less tangible, cannot be discounted.

Still, the news is not all good. Berlin has the highest number of welfare recipients of any of the 17 German federal states. And although spending has been reined in, balancing the books remains tough with a debt legacy hovering around €60 billion.

Europe's Start-up Capital

Over the past decade, Berlin has become a breeding ground for Europe's start-up economy, attracting young global talent with its multicultural make-up, relative affordability and open-mindedness. Dubbed 'Silicon Valley on the Spree', the city has given birth to such companies as Zalando, SoundCloud and ResearchGate, plus the Google-funded Factory, which seeks to stimulate dialogue between start-ups and established tech ventures.

As the digital industry gains critical mass, it's becoming a driving force behind Berlin's economy, generating over €8 billion in revenue and employing over 60,000 people. There is no end in sight, especially once 'Berlin TXL: The Urban Tech Republic', a huge new start-up campus on the grounds of Tegel Airport, takes flight. Of course, that won't happen until the new Berlin Brandenburg Airport becomes operational. But that's another story...

Population Growth & Housing Shortages

Berlin's population is growing rapidly, fuelled by a slight increase in the birth rate but mostly by migration from other European countries and asylum seekers. Current estimates predict a population of about four million by 2030, about 10% more than today.

Even with the current population, housing is a major issue. Affordable housing is in especially short supply as investors, most of them from abroad, prefer to build top-flight units or convert existing housing into luxury condominiums. Although not yet at London or New York levels, Berlin's famously low rents are definitely becoming a thing of the past.

Multicultural Society

Berlin's multiculturalism is one of its greatest assets, even if social and economic integration remain challenges. Since 2015, upwards of 100,000 refugees have arrived, mostly from war-torn Syria, Iraq and Afghanistan. The immediate task is finding short-term accommodation, schooling, German-language courses and employment for the new arrivals.

As of early 2016, about 620,000 non-German nationals from around 190 countries lived in Berlin, accounting for about 17% of the total population. Turks constitute the largest community, a legacy of the worker migration of the 1960s and '70s to West Berlin. In East Berlin, contract labour came in smaller numbers from Vietnam, Cuba and Poland. Since reunification, the city has absorbed about 100,000 people from the former Soviet republics. In recent years the global fiscal crisis and high youth unemployment have resulted in a wave of new arrivals from southern Europe, especially Romania and Bulgaria.

Among certain groups, the arrival of migrants and their perceived drain on the economy and society has given rise to new nationalist and anti-immigrant movements like Pegida ('Patriotic Europeans Against the Islamisation of the West') and parties such as AfD (Alternative fuer Deutschland, Alternative for Germany). At least for now these movements have gained only moderate support in Berlin, compared to some other parts of Germany.

if Berlin were 100 people

94 would be German
3 would be Turkish
2 would be Polish
1 would be Italian

belief systems

(% of population)

60 Non-religious
19 Protestant
9 Roman Catholic
Muslim
Other

population per sq km

BERLIN   GERMANY

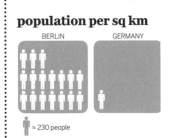

≈ 230 people

History

Berlin has long been in the cross hairs of history: it staged a revolution, was headquartered by fascists, bombed to bits, ripped in half and finally reunited – all just in the 20th century! An accidental capital whose medieval birth was a mere blip on the map of history, Berlin puttered along in relative obscurity until becoming the royal capital of Prussia some 400 years later. It was only in fairly recent times that it significantly impacted on world history.

Medieval Berlin

The recent discovery of an oak beam suggests that Berlin may have roots going back to 1183 but, for now, history records that the city was officially founded in 1237 by itinerant merchants as twin trading posts called Berlin and Cölln. The modest settlements flanked the Spree River in an area just southwest of today's Alexanderplatz. They grew in leaps and bounds and, in 1307, merged into a single town for power and protection. As the centre of the March (duchy) of Brandenburg, it continued to assert its political and economic independence and even became a player in the Hanseatic League in 1360.

Such confidence did not sit well with Sigismund, king of the Germans, who, in 1411, put one of his cronies, Friedrich von Hohenzollern, in charge of Brandenburg, thereby ushering in five centuries of uninterrupted rule by the House of Hohenzollern.

Berlin's medieval birthplace, around the Nikolaikirche, was devastated during WWII bombing raids. Today's 'Nikolaiviertel' is actually a replica of the quarter, dreamed up by the East German government in celebration of the city's 750th anniversary in 1987.

Reformation & the Thirty Years' War

The Reformation, kick-started in 1517 by Martin Luther in nearby Wittenberg, was slow to arrive in Berlin. Eventually, though, the wave of reform reached Brandenburg, leaving Elector Joachim II (r 1535–71) no choice but to subscribe to Protestantism. On 1 November 1539 the court celebrated the first Lutheran-style service in the Nikolaikirche in Spandau. The event is still celebrated as an official holiday (Reformationstag) in Brandenburg, the German federal state that surrounds Berlin, although not in the city state of Berlin itself.

TIMELINE	1244	1307	1360
	Berlin is referenced in a document for the first time in recorded history, although the city's birthday is pegged to the first mention of its sister settlement, Cölln, seven years earlier.	Berlin and Cölln join forces by merging into a single town to assert their independence from local rulers.	The twin town of Berlin-Cölln joins the Hanseatic League, but never plays a major role in the alliance and quits its membership in 1518.

Berlin prospered for the ensuing decades until drawn into the Thirty Years' War (1618–48), a conflict between Catholics and Protestants that left Europe's soil drenched with the blood of millions. Elector Georg Wilhelm (r 1620–40) tried to maintain a policy of neutrality, only to see his territory repeatedly pillaged and plundered by both sides. By the time the war ended, Berlin lay largely in shambles – broke, ruined and decimated by starvation, murder and disease.

Road to a Kingdom

Stability finally returned during the long reign of Georg Wilhelm's son, Friedrich Wilhelm (r 1640–88). Also known as the Great Elector, he took several steps that helped chart Brandenburg's rise to the status of a European powerhouse. His first order of business was to increase Berlin's safety by turning it into a garrison town encircled by fortifications with 13 bastions. He also levied a new sales tax, using the money to build three new neighbourhoods (Friedrichswerder, Dorotheenstadt and Friedrichstadt) and a canal linking the Spree and Oder Rivers (thereby cementing Berlin's position as a trading hub), as well as the Lustgarten and Unter den Linden.

But the Great Elector's most lasting legacy was replenishing Berlin's population by encouraging the settlement of refugees. In 1671, 50 Jewish families arrived from Vienna, followed by thousands of Protestant Huguenots – many of them highly skilled – who had been expelled from France by Louis XIV in 1685. The Französischer Dom (French Cathedral) on Gendarmenmarkt serves as a tangible reminder of Huguenot influence.

The Great Elector's son, Friedrich III, presided over a lively and intellectual court, founding the Academy of Arts in 1696 and the Academy of Sciences in 1700. One year later, he advanced his career by promoting himself to King Friedrich I (elector 1688–1701, king 1701–13) of Prussia, making Berlin a royal residence and the capital of the new state of Brandenburg-Prussia.

The Age of Prussia

All cultural and intellectual life screeched to a halt under Friedrich's son, Friedrich Wilhelm I (r 1713–40), who laid the groundwork for Prussian military might. History quite appropriately knows him as the *Soldatenkönig* (soldier king).

Ironically these soldiers didn't see action until his son and successor Friedrich II (aka Frederick the Great; r 1740–86) came to power. Friedrich fought tooth and nail for two decades to wrest Silesia (in today's Poland) from Austria and Saxony. When not busy on the battlefield, 'Old Fritz', as he was also called, sought greatness through building. His

An 8m-long section is all that survives of Berlin's original city wall, built around 1250 from crude boulders and bricks and standing up to 2m tall. See it on Littenstrasse, near Alexanderplatz.

HISTORY ROAD TO A KINGDOM

1411	1415	1539	1618
German King Sigismund puts Friedrich von Hohenzollern in charge as administrator of Brandenburg, marking the beginning of 500 years of Hohenzollern rule.	Friedrich von Hohenzollern's grip on power solidifies when Sigismund promotes him to elector and margrave of Brandenburg at the Council of Constance.	Elector Joachim II celebrates the first Lutheran service and a year later passes a church ordinance making the new religion binding throughout Brandenburg.	Religious conflict and territorial power struggles escalate into the bloody Thirty Years' War, devastating Berlin financially and halving its population to a mere 6000 people.

Top Five Prussian Sites

Brandenburger Tor (Historic Mitte)

Schloss and Park Sanssouci (Potsdam)

Schloss Charlottenburg (Charlottenburg)

Reichstag (Historic Mitte)

Siegessäule (Tiergarten)

Forum Fridericianum, a grand architectural master plan for Unter den Linden, although never completed, gave Berlin the Staatsoper Unter den Linden (State Opera House); Sankt-Hedwigs-Kathedrale, a former palace now housing the Humboldt Universität (Humboldt University); and other major attractions.

Fredrich also embraced the ideas of the Enlightenment, abolishing torture, guaranteeing religious freedom and introducing legal reforms. With some of the leading thinkers in town (Moses Mendelssohn, Voltaire and Gotthold Ephraim Lessing among them), Berlin blossomed into a great cultural capital that came to be known as 'Athens on the Spree'.

Napoleon & Reforms

Old Fritz' death sent Prussia into a downward spiral, culminating in a serious trouncing of its army by Napoleon at Jena-Auerstedt in 1806. The French marched triumphantly into Berlin on 27 October and left two years later, their coffers bursting with loot. Among the pint-sized conqueror's favourite souvenirs was the *Quadriga* sculpture from atop the Brandenburg Gate.

The post-Napoleonic period saw Berlin caught up in the reform movement sweeping through Europe. Public servants, academics and merchants now questioned the right of the nobility to rule. Friedrich Wilhelm III (r 1797–1840) instituted a few token reforms (easing guild regulations, abolishing bonded labour and granting Jews civic equality), but meaningful constitutional reform was not forthcoming. Power continued to be centred in the Prussian state.

The ensuing period of political stability was paired with an intellectual flourishing in Berlin's cafes and salons. The newly founded Universität zu Berlin (Humboldt Universität) was helmed by the philosopher Johann Gottlieb Fichte and, as it grew in status, attracted other leading thinkers of the day, including Hegel and Ranke. This was also the age of Karl Friedrich Schinkel, whose many projects – from the Neue Wache (New Guardhouse) to the Altes Museum (Old Museum) – still beautify Berlin.

Industrial Revolution

The Industrial Revolution snuck up on Berliners in the second quarter of the 19th century, with companies like Siemens and Borsig vastly stimulating the city's growth. In 1838 trains began chuffing between Berlin and Potsdam, giving birth to the Prussian railway system and spurring the foundation of more than 1000 factories, including electrical giants AEG and Siemens. In 1840 August Borsig built the world's fastest locomotive, besting even the British in a race.

One of the definitive histories of Prussia, Christopher Clark's *Iron Kingdom: The Rise and Downfall of Prussia* covers the period from 1600 to 1947 and shows the central role this powerhouse played in shaping modern Europe.

1631	1640	1671	1685
An outbreak of the plague kills around 2000 Berliners, about a fifth of the population.	Friedrich Wilhelm, who will go down in history as the Great Elector, comes to power and restores a semblance of normality by building fortifications and infrastructure.	Berlin's first Jewish community forms with just a few families arriving from Vienna at the invitation of the Great Elector. It grows to more than 1000 people by 1700.	Friedrich Wilhelm issues the Edict of Potsdam, allowing French Huguenot religious refugees to settle in Berlin, giving a 10-year tax break and granting them the right to hold services.

Tens of thousands of people now streamed into Berlin to work in the factories, swelling the population to more than 400,000 by 1847 and bringing the city's infrastructure close to collapse.

Bismarck & the Birth of an Empire

When Friedrich Wilhelm IV suffered a stroke in 1857, his brother Wilhelm became first regent and then, in 1861, King Wilhelm I (r 1861–88). Unlike his brother, Wilhelm had his finger on the pulse of the times and was not averse to progress. One of his key moves was to appoint Otto von Bismarck as Prussian prime minister in 1862.

Bismarck's glorious ambition was the creation of a unified Germany with Prussia at the helm. An old-guard militarist, he used intricate diplomacy and a series of wars with neighbouring Denmark and Austria to achieve his aims. By 1871 Berlin stood as the proud capital of the German Reich (empire), a bicameral, constitutional monarchy. On 18 January the Prussian king was crowned Kaiser at Versailles, with Bismarck as his 'Iron Chancellor'.

The early years of the German empire – a period called *Gründerzeit* (the foundation years) – were marked by major economic growth, fuelled in part by a steady flow of French reparation payments. Hundreds of thousands of people poured into Berlin in search of work in the factories. Housing shortages were solved by building labyrinthine tenements (*Mietskasernen,* literally 'rental barracks'), where entire families subsisted in tiny and poorly ventilated flats without indoor plumbing.

New political parties gave a voice to the proletariat; foremost was the Socialist Workers' Party (SAP), the forerunner of the Sozialdemokratische Partei Deutschlands (SPD; Social Democratic Party of Germany). Founded in 1875, the SAP captured 40% of the Berlin vote just two years later. Bismarck tried to make the party illegal but eventually, under pressure from the growing and increasingly antagonistic socialist movement, he enacted Germany's first modern social reforms, though this went against his true nature. When Wilhelm II (r 1888–1918) came to power, he wanted to extend social reform while Bismarck wanted stricter antisocialist laws. Finally, in March 1890, the Kaiser's scalpel excised his renegade chancellor from the political scene. After that, the legacy of Bismarck's diplomacy unravelled and a wealthy, unified and industrially powerful Germany paddled into the new century.

WWI & Revolution

The assassination of Archduke Franz Ferdinand, the heir to the Austrian throne, on 28 June 1914, triggered a series of diplomatic decisions

The green octagonal public *pissoirs* occasionally seen around Berlin are a legacy of the late 19th century when the municipal sanitation system could not keep up with the exploding population. About two dozen survive, including one on Chamissoplatz in Kreuzberg and another on Senefelderplatz in Prenzlauer Berg. Their nickname is *cafe achteck* (cafe octagon).

HISTORY BISMARCK & THE BIRTH OF AN EMPIRE

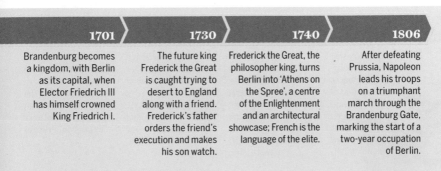

1701	1730	1740	1806
Brandenburg becomes a kingdom, with Berlin as its capital, when Elector Friedrich III has himself crowned King Friedrich I.	The future king Frederick the Great is caught trying to desert to England along with a friend. Frederick's father orders the friend's execution and makes his son watch.	Frederick the Great, the philosopher king, turns Berlin into 'Athens on the Spree', a centre of the Enlightenment and an architectural showcase; French is the language of the elite.	After defeating Prussia, Napoleon leads his troops on a triumphant march through the Brandenburg Gate, marking the start of a two-year occupation of Berlin.

that led to WWI, the bloodiest European conflict since the Thirty Years' War. In Berlin and elsewhere, initial euphoria and faith in a quick victory soon gave way to despair as casualties piled up in the battlefield trenches and stomachs grumbled on the home front. When peace came with defeat in 1918, it also ended domestic stability, ushering in a period of turmoil and violence.

On 9 November 1918, Kaiser Wilhelm II abdicated, bringing an inglorious end to the monarchy and 500 years of Hohenzollern rule. Power was transferred to the SPD, the largest party in the Reichstag, and its leader, Friedrich Ebert. Shortly after the Kaiser's exit, prominent SPD member Philipp Scheidemann stepped to a window of the Reichstag to announce the birth of the German Republic. Two hours later, Karl Liebknecht of the Spartakusbund (Spartacist League) proclaimed a socialist republic from a balcony of the royal palace on Unter den Linden. The struggle for power was on.

Founded by Liebknecht and Rosa Luxemburg, the Spartacist League sought to establish a left-wing, Marxist-style government; by year's end it had merged with other radical groups into the German Communist Party. The SPD's goal, meanwhile, was to establish a parliamentary democracy.

Supporters of the SPD and the Spartacist League took their rivalry to the streets, culminating in the Spartacist Revolt of early January 1919. On the orders of Ebert, government forces quickly quashed the uprising. Liebknecht and Luxemburg were arrested and murdered en route to prison by Freikorps soldiers (right-leaning war volunteers); their bodies were dumped in the Landwehrkanal.

Discover stat after stat on Berlin at the website of the Office of Statistics in Berlin (www.statistik-berlin-brandenburg.de).

The Weimar Republic

In July 1919 the federalist constitution of the fledgling republic – Germany's first serious experiment with democracy – was adopted in the town of Weimar, where the constituent assembly had sought refuge from the chaos of Berlin. It gave women the vote and established basic human rights, but it also gave the chancellor the right to rule by decree – a concession that would later prove critical in Hitler's rise to power.

The so-called Weimar Republic (1920–33) was governed by a coalition of left and centre parties, headed by Friedrich Ebert and later Paul von Hindenburg – both of the SPD, which remained Germany's largest party until 1932. The republic, however, pleased neither communists nor monarchists. Trouble erupted as early as March 1920 when right-wing militants led by Wolfgang Kapp forcibly occupied the government quarter in Berlin. The government fled to Dresden, and in Berlin a general strike soon brought the 'Kapp Putsch' to a collapse.

1810	1830	1837	1838
After the Napoleonic occupation ends, Berlin embarks on a period of reconstruction and reform that includes the creation of its first university by Wilhelm von Humboldt.	The Altes Museum opens as the first of five institutions on Museumsinsel (Museum Island). The last (the Pergamonmuseum) opens exactly 100 years later.	The industrial age kicks into high gear with the founding of August Borsig's machine factory, which in 1840 builds Germany's first locomotive.	Berlin's first train embarks on its maiden voyage from Berlin to Potsdam, making the city the centre of an expanding rail network throughout Prussia.

The Golden Twenties

The giant metropolis of Berlin as we know it today was forged in 1920 from the region's many independent towns and villages (Charlottenburg, Schöneberg, Spandau etc), making Berlin one of the world's largest cities, with around 3.8 million inhabitants.

Otherwise, the 1920s began as anything but golden, marked by the humiliation of a lost war, social and political instability, hyperinflation, hunger and disease. Around 235,000 Berliners were unemployed, and strikes, demonstrations and riots became nearly everyday occurrences. Economic stability gradually returned after a new currency, the *Rentenmark,* was introduced in 1923 and with the Dawes Plan in 1924, which limited the crippling reparation payments imposed on Germany after WWI.

Berliners responded like there was no tomorrow and made their city as much a den of decadence as it was a cauldron of creativity (not unlike today...). Cabaret, Dada and jazz flourished. Pleasure pits popped up everywhere, turning the city into a 'sextropolis' of Dionysian dimensions. Bursting with energy, it became a laboratory for anything new and modern, drawing giants of architecture (Bruno Taut, Martin Wagner, Hans Scharoun and Walter Gropius), fine arts (George Grosz, Max Beckmann and Lovis Corinth) and literature (Bertolt Brecht, Kurt Tucholsky, WH Auden and Christopher Isherwood).

The fun came to an instant end when the US stock market crashed in 1929, plunging the world into economic depression. Within weeks, half a million Berliners were jobless, and riots and demonstrations again ruled the streets. The volatile, increasingly polarised political climate led to clashes between communists and members of a party that had been patiently waiting in the wings – the Nationalsozialistische Deutsche Arbeiterpartei (National Socialist German Workers' Party, NSDAP, or Nazi Party), led by a failed Austrian artist and WWI corporal named Adolf Hitler. Soon jackboots, brown shirts, oppression and fear would dominate daily life in Germany.

Hitler's Rise to Power

The Weimar government's inability to improve conditions during the Depression spurred the popularity of Hitler's NSDAP, which gained 18% of the national vote in the 1930 elections. In the 1932 presidential election, Hitler challenged Hindenburg and won 37% of the second-round vote. A year later, on 30 January 1933, faced with failed economic reforms and persuasive right-wing advisers, Hindenburg appointed Hitler chancellor. That evening, NSDAP celebrated its rise to power with a torchlit procession through the Brandenburg Gate. Not everyone cheered. Observing the scene from his Pariser Platz home, artist Max

Historical Reads

....

Berlin Rising: Biography of a City (Anthony Read, David Fisher)

....

Berlin: Portrait of a City Through the Centuries (Rory MacLean)

....

Berlin Diary: Journal of a Foreign Correspondent 1934–41 (William Shirer)

....

The Candy Bombers (Andrei Cherny)

....

The Berlin Wall (Frederick Taylor)

HISTORY THE GOLDEN TWENTIES

1848	1862	1871	1877
Berlin is swept up in the popular revolutions for democratic reform and a united Germany, but after a few months the Prussian army restores the old order.	Chief city planner James Hobrecht solves the housing shortage by constructing claustrophobic working-class ghettos of tenement blocks.	Employing an effective strategy of war and diplomacy, Prussian chancellor Otto von Bismarck forges a unified Germany with Prussia at its helm and Berlin as its capital.	Berlin's population reaches the one million mark, and this almost doubles by 1900.

Liebermann famously commented: 'I couldn't possibly eat as much as I would like to puke'.

As chancellor, Hitler moved quickly to consolidate absolute power and turn the nation's democracy into a one-party dictatorship. The Reichstag fire in March 1933 gave him the opportunity to request temporary emergency powers to arrest communists and liberal opponents and push through his proposed Enabling Law, allowing him to decree laws and change the constitution without consulting parliament. When Hindenburg died a year later, Hitler fused the offices of president and chancellor to become Führer of the Third Reich.

The Siegessäule (Victory Column) in Tiergarten park has had starring roles in Wim Wenders' movie *Wings of Desire* and U2's 'Stay' music video. It also inspired Paul van Dyk's 1998 trance hit 'For an Angel' and the name of Berlin's leading gay magazine.

Nazi Berlin

The rise of the Nazis had instant, far-reaching consequences for the entire population. Within three months of Hitler's power grab, all non-Nazi parties, organisations and labour unions ceased to exist. Political opponents, intellectuals and artists were rounded up and detained without trial; many went underground or into exile. There was a burgeoning culture of terror and denunciation, and the terrorisation of Jews escalated.

Hitler's brown-shirted Nazi state police, the Sturmabteilung (SA), pursued opponents, arresting, torturing and murdering people in improvised concentration camps, such as the one in the Wasserturm in Prenzlauer Berg. North of Berlin, construction began on Sachsenhausen concentration camp. During the so-called Köpenicker Blutwoche (Bloody Week) in June 1933, around 90 people were murdered. On 10 May, right-wing students burned 'un-German' books on Bebelplatz, prompting countless intellectuals and artists to rush into exile.

Jewish Persecution

Jews were a Nazi target from the start. In April 1933 Joseph Goebbels, *Gauleiter* (district leader) of Berlin and head of the well-oiled Ministry of Propaganda, announced a boycott of Jewish businesses. Soon after, Jews were expelled from public service and banned from many professions, trades and industries. The Nuremberg Laws of 1935 deprived 'non-Aryans' of German citizenship and many other rights.

The international community, meanwhile, turned a blind eye to the situation in Germany, perhaps because many leaders were keen to see some order restored to the country after decades of political upheaval. Hitler's success at stabilising the shaky economy – largely by pumping public money into employment programs – was widely admired. The 1936 Olympic summer games in Berlin were a PR triumph, as Hitler launched a charm offensive. Terror and persecution resumed soon after the closing ceremony.

1891	1902	1918	1919
Berlin engineer Otto Lilienthal, known as the 'Glider King', makes the world's first successful glider flight, travelling over 25m. Five years later he dies in an air accident.	After two decades of debate and eight years of construction, the first segment of the Berlin U-Bahn network is inaugurated, between Warschauer Strasse and Ernst-Reuter-Platz.	WWI ends on 11 November with Germany's capitulation, following the resignation of Kaiser Wilhelm II and his escape to Holland. The Prussian monarchy is dead.	The Spartacist Revolt, led by Liebknecht, Luxemburg and Pieck, is violently suppressed and ends with the murder of Liebknecht and Luxemburg by right-wing Freikorps troops.

OLYMPICS UNDER THE SWASTIKA

When the International Olympics Committee awarded the 1936 games to Germany in 1931, the gesture was supposed to welcome the country back into the world community after its defeat in WWI and the tumultuous 1920s. No one could have known that only two years later, the fledgling democracy would be helmed by a dictator with an agenda to take over the world.

As Hitler opened the games on 1 August in Berlin's Olympic Stadium, prisoners were putting the finishing touches on the first large-scale Nazi concentration camp at Sachsenhausen, just north of town. As famous composer Richard Strauss conducted the Olympic hymn during the opening ceremony, fighter squadrons were headed to Spain in support of Franco's dictatorship. Only while the Olympic flame was flickering were political and racial persecution suspended and anti-Semitic signs taken down.

The Olympics were truly a perfect opportunity for the Nazi propaganda machine, which excelled at staging grand public spectacles and rallies, as was so powerfully captured by Leni Riefenstahl in her epic movie *Olympia*. Participants and spectators were impressed by the choreographed pageantry and warm German hospitality. The fact that these were the first Olympics to be broadcast internationally on radio did not fail to impress either.

The games were also a big success from an athletic point of view, with around 4000 participants from 49 countries competing in 129 events and setting numerous records. The biggest star was African-American track-and-fieldster Jesse Owens, who was awarded four gold medals for the 100m sprint, 200m sprint, 4 x 100m relay and long jump, winning the hearts of the German public. German Jews, meanwhile, were excluded from participating, with the one token exception being half-Jewish fencer Helene Mayer. She took home a silver medal.

For Jews, the horror escalated on 9 November 1938, with the Reichspogromnacht (often called Kristallnacht, or Night of Broken Glass). Using the assassination of a German consular official by a Polish Jew in Paris as a pretext, Nazi thugs desecrated, burned and demolished synagogues and Jewish cemeteries, property and businesses across the country. Jews had begun to emigrate after 1933, but this event set off a stampede.

The fate of those Jews who stayed behind deteriorated after the outbreak of WWII in 1939. At Hitler's request, a conference in January 1942 in Berlin's Wannsee came up with the *Endlösung* (Final Solution): the systematic, bureaucratic and meticulously documented annihilation of European Jews. Sinti and Roma, political opponents, priests, homosexuals and habitual criminals were targeted as well. Of the roughly seven million people who were sent to concentration camps, only 500,000 survived.

1920	1920s	1921	1923
On 1 October Berlin becomes Germany's largest city after seven independent towns, 59 villages and 27 estates are amalgamated into a single administrative unit. The population reaches 3.8 million.	Berlin evolves into a cultural metropolis, exerting a pull on leading artists, scientists and philosophers of the day, including Einstein, Brecht and Otto Dix.	The world's first highway – called AVUS – opens in the Grunewald after eight years of construction.	The Golden Twenties show their dark side when inflation reaches its peak and a loaf of bread costs 3.5 million marks – an entire wheelbarrow's worth.

WWII & the Battle of Berlin

Top Five WWII Sites

Topographie des Terrors (Historic Mitte)

Sachsenhausen concentration camp (Oranienburg)

Holocaust Memorial (Historic Mitte)

Gedenkstätte Deutscher Widerstand (Potsdamer Platz)

Haus der Wannsee-Konferenz (Wannsee)

WWII began on 1 September 1939 with the Nazi attack on Poland. Although France and Britain declared war on Germany two days later, this could not prevent the quick defeat of Poland, Belgium, the Netherlands and France. Other countries, including Denmark and Norway, were also soon brought into the Nazi fold.

In June 1941 Germany broke its nonaggression pact with Stalin by attacking the USSR. Though successful at first, Operation Barbarossa quickly ran into problems, culminating in defeat at Stalingrad (today Volgograd) the following winter, forcing the Germans to retreat.

With the Normandy invasion of June 1944, Allied troops arrived in formidable force on the European mainland, supported by unrelenting air raids on Berlin and most other German cities. The final Battle of Berlin began in mid-April 1945. More than 1.5 million Soviet soldiers barrelled towards the capital from the east, reaching Berlin on 21 April and encircling it on 25 April. Two days later they were in the city centre, fighting running street battles with the remaining troops, many of them boys and elderly men. On 30 April the fighting reached the government quarter where Hitler was ensconced in his bunker behind the chancellery, with his long-time mistress Eva Braun, whom he'd married just a day earlier. Finally accepting the inevitability of defeat, Hitler shot himself that afternoon; his wife swallowed a cyanide pill. As their bodies were burned in the chancellery courtyard, Red Army soldiers raised the Soviet flag above the Reichstag.

RESISTANCE

Resistance to Hitler was quashed early by the powerful Nazi machinery of terror, but it never vanished entirely, as is thoroughly documented in the excellent Topographie des Terrors exhibit (p85). One of the best known acts of defiance was the 20 July 1944 assassination attempt on the Führer, led by senior army officer Claus Graf Schenk von Stauffenberg. On that fateful day, Stauffenberg brought a briefcase packed with explosives to a meeting of the high command at the Wolfschanze (Wolf's Lair), Hitler's eastern-front military headquarters. He placed the briefcase under the conference table near Hitler's seat, then excused himself and heard the bomb detonate from a distance. What he didn't know was that Hitler had escaped with minor injuries thanks to the solid oak table that shielded him from the blast.

Stauffenberg and his co-conspirators were quickly identified and shot by firing squad at the army headquarters in the Bendlerblock in Berlin. The rooms where they hatched their plot now house the Gedenkstätte Deutscher Widerstand, an exhibit about German resistance against the Nazis.

1929	1933	1935	1936
The Great Depression hits Berlin, leaving half a million people unemployed. Thirteen members of the National Socialist German Workers' Party (the Nazi Party) are elected to parliament.	Hitler is appointed chancellor; the Reichstag burns; construction starts on Sachsenhausen concentration camp; the National Socialist German Workers' Party rules Germany.	Germany's first public TV broadcast is made from Berlin on 22 March; it's followed by three weekly broadcasts of 90 minutes each. Most people can only watch it in TV parlours.	The 11th modern Olympic Games, held in Berlin in August, are a PR triumph for Hitler and a showcase of Nazi power. Anti-Jewish propaganda is suspended during the period.

Defeat & Aftermath

The Battle of Berlin ended on 2 May with the unconditional surrender of Helmuth Weidling, the commander of the Berlin Defence Area, to General Vasily Chuikov of the Soviet army. Peace was signed at the US military headquarters in Reims (France) and at the Soviet military headquarters in Berlin-Karlshorst, now a German-Soviet history museum (Deutsch-Russisches Museum Berlin-Karlshorst). On 8 May 1945, WWII in Europe officially came to an end.

The fighting had taken an enormous toll on Berlin and its people. Entire neighbourhoods lay in smouldering rubble and at least 125,000 Berliners had lost their lives. With around one million women and children evacuated, only 2.8 million people were left in the city in May 1945 (compared to 4.3 million in 1939), two-thirds of them women. It fell to them to start clearing up the 25 million tons of rubble, earning them the name *Trümmerfrauen* (rubble women). In fact, many of Berlin's modest hills are actually *Trümmerberge* (rubble mountains), built from wartime debris and reborn as parks and recreational areas. The best known are the Teufelsberg in the Grunewald and Mont Klamott in the Volkspark Friedrichshain.

Some small triumphs came quickly: U-Bahn service resumed on 14 May 1945, newspaper printing presses began rolling again on 15 May, and the Berliner Philharmoniker gave its first postwar concert on 26 May.

One of many fabulous films by Germany's best-known female director, Margarethe von Trotta, *Rosenstrasse* (2003) is a moving portrayal of a 1943 protest by a group of non-Jewish women trying to save their Jewish husbands from deportation. There's a memorial on the site today.

Occupation

At the Yalta Conference in February 1945, Winston Churchill, Franklin D Roosevelt and Joseph Stalin agreed to carve up Germany and Berlin into four zones of occupation controlled by Britain, the USA, the USSR and France. By July 1945, Stalin, Clement Attlee (who replaced Churchill after a surprise election win) and Roosevelt's successor, Harry S Truman, were at the table in Schloss Cecilienhof in Potsdam to hammer out the details.

Berlin was sliced up into 20 administrative areas. The British sector encompassed Charlottenburg, Tiergarten and Spandau; the French got Wedding and Reinickendorf; and the US was in charge of Zehlendorf, Steglitz, Wilmersdorf, Tempelhof, Kreuzberg and Neukölln. All these districts later formed West Berlin. The Soviets held on to eight districts in the east, including Mitte, Prenzlauer Berg, Friedrichshain, Treptow and Köpenick, which would later become East Berlin. The Soviets also occupied the land surrounding Berlin, leaving West Berlin completely encircled by territories under Soviet control.

Did you know that 9 November is Germany's 'destiny date'? It was the end of the monarchy in 1918, the day of the 1923 Hitler putsch in Munich, the Night of Broken Glass (Kristallnacht) in 1938 and the day the Wall fell in 1989.

1938	1942	1944	1945
On 9 November Nazis set fire to nine of Berlin's 12 synagogues, vandalise Jewish businesses and terrorise Jewish citizens during a night of pogroms called Kristallnacht.	At the so-called Wannsee Conference, leading members of the SS decide on the systematic murder of European Jews, cynically called the 'Final Solution'.	On 20 July senior army officers led by Claus Graf Schenk von Stauffenberg stage an assassination attempt on Hitler. Their failure costs their own and countless other lives.	Soviet troops advance on Berlin in the final days of the war, devastating the city. Hitler commits suicide on 30 April, fighting stops on 2 May and the armistice is signed on 8 May.

The Big Chill

Friction between the Western Allies and the Soviets quickly emerged. For the Western Allies, a main priority was to help Germany get back on its feet by kick-starting the devastated economy. The Soviets, though, insisted on massive reparations and began brutalising and exploiting their own zone of occupation. Tens of thousands of able-bodied men and POWs ended up in labour camps deep in the Soviet Union. In the Allied zones, meanwhile, democracy was beginning to take root, and Germany elected state parliaments in 1946–47.

The showdown came in June 1948 when the Allies introduced the Deutschmark in their zones. The USSR regarded this as a breach of the Potsdam Agreement, under which the powers had agreed to treat Germany as one economic zone. The Soviets issued their own currency, the Ostmark, and promptly announced a full-scale economic blockade of West Berlin. The Allies responded with the remarkable Berlin airlift.

Two German States

In 1949 the division of Germany – and Berlin – was formalised. The western zones evolved into the Bundesrepublik Deutschland (BRD, Federal Republic of Germany or FRG) with Konrad Adenauer as its first chancellor and Bonn, on the Rhine River, as its capital. An American economic aid package dubbed the Marshall Plan created the basis for West Germany's *Wirtschaftswunder* (economic miracle), which saw the economy grow at an average of 8% per year between 1951 and 1961. The recovery was largely engineered by economics minister Ludwig Erhard, who dealt with an acute labour shortage by inviting about 2.3 million foreign workers, mainly from Turkey, Yugoslavia and Italy, to Germany, thereby laying the foundation for today's multicultural society.

The Soviet zone, meanwhile, grew into the Deutsche Demokratische Republik (DDR, German Democratic Republic or GDR), making East Berlin its capital and Wilhelm Pieck its first president. From the outset, though, the Sozialistische Einheitspartei Deutschlands (SED, Socialist Unity Party of Germany), led by Walter Ulbricht, dominated economic, judicial and security policy. In order to counter any opposition, the Ministry for State Security, or Stasi, was established in 1950, with its headquarters based in Lichtenberg (now the Stasimuseum). Regime opponents were incarcerated at the super-secret Gedenkstätte Hohenschönhausen (Stasi Prison) nearby.

Economically, East Germany stagnated, in large part because of the Soviets' continued policy of asset stripping and reparation payments. Stalin's death in 1953 raised hopes for reform but only spurred the GDR government to raise production goals even higher. Smouldering discon-

1948	1949	1950	1950s
After the Western Allies introduce the Deutschmark currency, the Soviets blockade West Berlin; in response the US and Britain launch the Berlin airlift, ferrying necessities to the city.	Two countries are born – the Bundesrepublik Deutschland (West Germany) and the Deutsche Demokratische Republik (East Germany)	GDR leaders raze the remains of the Prussian city palace for ideological reasons, despite worldwide protest.	Hundreds of thousands of East Germans move to West Berlin and West Germany, depleting the GDR's brain and brawn power.

tent erupted in violence on 17 June 1953 when 10% of GDR workers took to the streets. Soviet troops quashed the uprising, with scores of deaths and the arrest of about 1200 people.

The Wall: What Goes Up...

Through the 1950s the economic gulf between the two Germanys widened, prompting hundreds of thousands of East Berliners to seek a future in the West. Eventually, the exodus of mostly young and well-educated East Germans strained the troubled GDR economy so much that – with Soviet consent – its government built a wall to keep them in. Construction of the Berlin Wall, the Cold War's most potent symbol, began on the night of 13 August 1961.

This stealthy act left Berliners stunned. Formal protests from the Western Allies, as well as massive demonstrations in West Berlin, were ignored. Tense times followed. In October 1961, US and Soviet tanks faced off at Checkpoint Charlie, pushing to the brink of war.

The appointment of Erich Honecker (1912–94) as leader of East Germany in 1971 opened the way for rapprochement with the West and enhanced international acceptance of the GDR. In September that year the Western Allies and the Soviet Union signed a new Four Power Accord in the Kammergericht (courthouse) in Schöneberg. It guaranteed

Australian journalist Anna Funder documents the Stasi, East Germany's vast domestic spy apparatus, by letting both victims and perpetrators tell their stories in her 2004 book *Stasiland*.

HISTORY THE WALL: WHAT GOES UP...

THE BERLIN AIRLIFT

The Berlin airlift was a triumph of determination and a glorious chapter in Berlin's post-WWII history. On 24 June 1948, the Soviets cut off all rail and road traffic into the city to force the Western Allies to give up their sectors and bring the entire city under Soviet control.

Faced with such provocation, many in the Allied camp urged responses that would have become the opening barrages of WWIII. In the end wiser heads prevailed, and a mere day after the blockade began the US Air Force launched 'Operation Vittles'. The British followed suit on 28 June with 'Operation Plane Fare'.

For the next 11 months Allied planes flew in food, coal, machinery and other supplies to the now-closed Tempelhof airport in West Berlin. By the time the Soviets backed down, the Allies had made 278,000 flights, logged a distance equivalent to 250 round trips to the moon and delivered 2.5 million tons of cargo. The Luftbrückendenkmal (Berlin Airlift Memorial) outside the airport honours the effort and those who died carrying it out.

It was a monumental achievement that profoundly changed the relationship between Germany and the Western Allies, who were no longer regarded merely as occupying forces but as *Schutzmächte* (protective powers).

1951	1953	1961	1963
Berlin enters the celluloid spotlight with the inaugural Berlin International Film Festival (Berlinale).	The uprising of construction workers on the Stalinallee (Karl-Marx-Allee) spreads across the GDR before being crushed by Soviet tanks, leaving several hundred dead and more injured.	Tragedy strikes 11 days after the first stone of the Berlin Wall is laid. On 24 August, 24-year-old Günter Litfin is gunned down by border guards while attempting to swim across Humboldt Harbour.	US president John F Kennedy professes solidarity with the people of Berlin when giving his famous 'Ich bin ein Berliner' speech at the town hall in West Berlin's Schöneberg on 26 June.

access to West Berlin from West Germany and eased travel restrictions between East and West Berlin. The accord paved the way for the Basic Treaty, signed a year later, in which the two countries recognised each other's sovereignty and borders and committed to setting up 'permanent missions' in Bonn and East Berlin, respectively.

Life in the Divided City

For 45 years, Berlin was a political exclave in the cross hairs of the Cold War. After the Berlin Wall was built in 1961, the city's halves developed as completely separate entities.

West Berlin

Daring Young Men: the Heroism and Triumph of the Berlin Airlift (2011), by Richard Reeves, examines this 'first battle of the Cold War' by telling the stories of the American and British pilots who risked their lives to save their former enemies.

West Berlin could not have survived economically without heavy subsidies from the West German government in the form of corporate tax incentives and a so-called *Berlinzulage,* a monthly tax-free bonus of 8% on pretax income for every working Berliner. West Berliners had access to the same aspects of capitalism as all other West Germans, including a wide range of quality consumer goods, the latest technology and imported foods. Then, as now, the main shopping spine was Kurfürstendamm and its extension, Tauentzienstrasse, the crown jewel of which, the KaDeWe department store, left no shopping desire unfulfilled.

Since West Berlin was completely surrounded by East Berlin and East Germany, its residents liked to joke that no matter in which direction you travelled, you were always 'going east'. Still, West Berliners suffered no restrictions on travel and were free to leave and return as they pleased, as well as to choose their holiday destinations. Berlin was linked to West Germany by air, train and four transit roads, which were normal autobahns or highways also used by East Germans. Transit travellers were not allowed to leave the main road. Border checks were common and often involved harassment and time-consuming searches.

East Berlin

From the outset, East Germany's economic, judicial and security policy was dominated by a single party, the SED. Among its prime objectives was the moulding of its citizens into loyal members of a new socialist society. Children as young as six years old were folded into a tight network of state-run mass organisations, and in the workplace the unions were in charge of ideological control and conformity. Officially, membership of any of these groups was voluntary, but refusing to join usually led to limits on access to higher education and career choices. It could also incite the suspicion of the much-feared Stasi.

1964	1967	1971	1976
A master plan to turn Alexanderplatz, East Berlin's central square, into a socialist architectural showcase begins. The square's crowning glory, the TV Tower, opens in 1969.	The death of Benno Ohnesorg, an unarmed student who is shot by a police officer while demonstrating against the Shah of Persia's visit to West Berlin, draws attention to the student movement.	The four Allies sign the Four Power Accord, which confirms Berlin's independent status. A year later, East and West Germany recognise each other's sovereignty in the Basic Treaty.	The Palace of the Republic, which houses the GDR parliament and an entertainment centre, opens on 23 April, on the site where the royal Hohenzollern palace had been demolished in 1950.

The standard of living in East Berlin was higher than in the rest of East Germany, with the Centrum Warenhaus on Alexanderplatz (today's Galeria Kaufhof) a flagship store. While basic foods (bread, milk, butter, some produce) were cheap and plentiful, fancier foods and high-quality goods were in short supply and could often only be obtained with connections and patience. Queues outside shops were a common sight and many items were only available as so-called *Bückware*, meaning that they were hidden from plain view and required the sales clerk to bend *(bücken)* to retrieve them from beneath the counter. Bartering for goods was also common practice. Western products could only be purchased in government-run retail shops, called *Intershops*, and only by the privileged few who had access to hard currency – the East German mark was not accepted.

After the Wall went up in 1961, East Berliners, along with other East Germans, were only allowed to travel within the GDR and to other Eastern Bloc countries. Most holiday trips were state-subsidised and union-organised, and who was allowed to go where, when and for how long depended on such factors as an individual's productivity and level of social and political engagement. Those who could afford it could book a package holiday abroad through the Reisebüro der DDR (GDR Travel Agency).

Women enjoyed greater equality in East Germany. An extensive government-run childcare system made it easier to combine motherhood and employment, and nearly 90% of all women were gainfully employed, many in such 'nontraditional' fields as engineering and construction. However, this gender equality did not necessarily translate into the private sphere, where women remained largely responsible for child-raising and domestic chores. Rising through the ranks at work or in organisations was also rare for women. In fact, the only female member of the Ministerrat (Council of Ministers) was Erich Honecker's wife, Margot Honecker.

The Wall: ...Must Come Down

Hearts and minds in Eastern Europe had long been restless for change, but German reunification came as a surprise to the world and ushered in a new and exciting era. The so-called Wende (turning point, ie the fall of communism) came about as a gradual development that ended in a big bang – the collapse of the Berlin Wall on 9 November 1989.

The Germany of today, with 16 unified federal states, was hammered out through a volatile political debate and negotiations to end post-WWII occupation zones. The first significant step towards unification occurred on 1 July 1990 when monetary, economic and social union became realities, leading to the abolition of border controls and to the

To alleviate acute housing shortages, three new satellite cities – Marzahn, Hohenschönhausen and Hellersdorf – consisting of massive prefab housing blocks for 300,000 people were built in the 1970s and '80s on East Berlin's outskirts. Equipped with mod cons like central heating and indoor plumbing, these modern apartments were much coveted.

The first Love Parade, a techno cavalcade that would draw millions of people to Berlin each summer between 1989 and 2006, actually kicked off modestly with just one truck and 150 ravers partying on West Berlin's Kurfürstendamm.

1987	1989	1989	1990
East and West Berlin celebrate the city's 750th birthday separately. On 12 June Ronald Reagan stands before the Brandenburg Gate to say 'Mr Gorbachev, tear down this Wall!'.	On 9 October East Germany celebrates the 40th anniversary of its founding as demonstrations in favour of reforms reverberate through East Berlin.	On 4 November half a million Berliners in Alexanderplatz demand freedom of speech, press and assembly. The Berlin Wall opens on 9 November without a single bullet being fired.	'The Wall – Live in Berlin' concert, starring Pink Floyd's Roger Waters, celebrates the Wall's demise on the former Potsdamer Platz death strip.

Deutschmark becoming the common currency. On 31 August of the same year, the Unification Treaty, in which both East and West pledged to create a unified Germany, was signed in the Kronprinzenpalais on Unter den Linden. Around the same time, representatives of East and West Germany and the four victorious WWII allied powers (the USSR, France, the UK and the US), who had held the right to determine Germany's future since 1945, met in Moscow. Their negotiations resulted in the signing of the Two-Plus-Four Treaty, which ended postwar oc-

JEWISH BERLIN: MENDELSSOHN TO LIBESKIND

Since reunification, Berlin has had the fastest-growing Jewish community in the world. Their backgrounds are diverse: most are Russian Jewish immigrants but there are also Jews of German heritage, Israelis wishing to escape their war-torn homeland and American expats lured by Berlin's low-cost living and limitless creativity. Today there are about 13,000 active members of the Jewish community, including 1000 belonging to the Orthodox congregation Adass Yisroel. And since not all Jews choose to be affiliated with a synagogue, the actual population is estimated to be at least twice as high.

The community supports 10 synagogues, two *mikve* ritual baths, several schools, numerous cultural institutions and a handful of kosher restaurants and shops. The golden-domed Neue Synagoge (New Synagogue) on Oranienburger Strasse is the most visible beacon of Jewish revival, even though today it's not primarily a house of worship but a community and exhibition space. In Kreuzberg, the Jüdisches Museum, a spectacular structure by Daniel Libeskind, tracks the ups and downs of Jewish life in Germany for almost 2000 years. Another key Jewish site is the Friedhof Grosse Hamburger Strasse, Berlin's oldest Jewish cemetery and final resting home of Enlightenment philosopher Moses Mendelssohn, who arrived in Berlin in 1743. His progressive thinking and lobbying paved the way for the Emancipation Edict of 1812, which made Jews full citizens of Prussia, with equal rights and duties.

By the end of the 19th century, many of Berlin's Jews, then numbering about 5% of the population, had become thoroughly German in speech and identity. When a wave of Hasidic Jews escaping the pogroms of Eastern Europe arrived around the same time, they found their way to today's Scheunenviertel, which at that time was an immigrant slum with cheap housing.

By 1933 Berlin's Jewish population had grown to around 160,000 and constituted one-third of all Jews living in Germany. The well-known horrors of the Nazi years sent most into exile and left 55,000 dead. Only about 1000 to 2000 Jews are believed to have survived the war years in Berlin, often with the help of their non-Jewish neighbours; their acts of courage are commemorated at the Gedenkstätte Stille Helden. Many memorials throughout the city commemorate the Nazi's victims. The most prominent is, of course, the Holocaust Memorial, near the Brandenburg Gate.

1990	1991	1994	1999
The official reunification of the two Germanys goes into effect on 3 October. The date becomes a national holiday.	Members of the Bundestag (German parliament) vote to reinstate Berlin as Germany's capital and to move the federal government here. Berliners elect the first joint city government.	The last British, French, Russian and American troops withdraw from Berlin, ending nearly half a century of occupation and protection.	On 19 April the German parliament holds its first session in the historic Reichstag building, after complete restoration by Lord Norman Foster.

cupation zones and fully transferred sovereignty to a united Germany. Formal unification became effective on 3 October 1990, now Germany's national holiday. In December 1990 Germany held its first unified post-WWII elections.

In 1991 a small majority (338 to 320) of members in the Bundestag (German parliament) voted in favour of moving the government to Berlin and of making Berlin the German capital once again. On 8 September 1994 the last Allied troops stationed in Berlin left the city after a festive ceremony.

The Postunification Years

With reunification, Berlin once again became the seat of government in 1999. Mega-sized construction projects such as Potsdamer Platz and the government quarter eradicated the physical scars of division but did little to improve the city's balance sheet or unemployment statistics. It didn't help that Berlin lost the hefty federal subsidies it had received during the years of division. More than 250,000 manufacturing jobs were lost between 1991 and 2006, most of them through closures of unprofitable factories in East Berlin. Add to that mismanagement, corruption, a banking scandal and excessive government spending and it's no surprise that the city ran up a whopping debt of €60 million.

Elected in 2001, the new governing mayor Klaus Wowereit responded by making across-the-board spending cuts, but with a tax base eroded by high unemployment and ever-growing welfare payments, they did little initially to get Berlin out of the poorhouse. Eventually, though, the economic restructure away from a manufacturing base and towards the service sector began to bear fruit. Job creation in the capital has outpaced that of Germany in general for almost 10 years. No German city has a greater number of business start-ups. Its export quota has risen steadily, as has its population. The health, transport and green-technology industries are growing in leaps and bounds.

On the cultural front, Berlin exploded into a hive of cultural cool with unbridled nightlife, a vibrant art scene and booming fashion and design industries. In 2006 it became part of Unesco's Creative Cities Network. Some 170,000 people are employed in the cultural sector, which generates an annual turnover of around €13 billion. An especially important subsector is music, with nearly 10% of all related companies, including Universal and MTV, moving their European headquarters to Berlin over the past 20 years.

Great Quote

'Berlin is the testicle of the West. When I want the West to scream, I squeeze on Berlin.' – Nikita Khrushchev, Soviet Communist Party Secretary, 1963

HISTORY THE POSTUNIFICATION YEARS

In December 2015, 620,000 people living in Berlin (17% of the city's population) were foreigners. There are people from 185 nations, including 15,710 Americans, 13,456 Brits, 2541 Australians and 2112 Canadians. Berlin's Turkish community represents the single largest foreign population with 98,659 people.

2001	2006	2011	2015
Openly gay politician Klaus Wowereit is elected governing mayor of Berlin.	Berlin's first central train station, the Hauptbahnhof, opens on 26 May. Two weeks later Germany kicks off the 2006 FIFA World Cup.	Berlin's population passes the 3.5 million mark, growing 1.2%, the most within a single year since reunification in 1990. Most of the growth comes from people moving to Berlin.	Chancellor Angela Merkel's offer of temporary asylum to refugees brings 79,034 new arrivals to Berlin, mostly from Syria, Iraq and Afghanistan.

Architecture

From the Schloss Charlottenburg to the Reichstag, the TV Tower to Berliner Philharmonie, the Jewish Museum to the Sony Center – Berlin boasts some mighty fine architecture. It's an eclectic mix, to be sure, shaped by the city's unique history, especially the destruction of WWII and the contrasting urban-planning visions during the years of division. Since reunification, though, Berlin has become a virtual laboratory for the world's elite architects, David Chipperfield, Norman Foster and Daniel Libeskind among them.

Modest Beginnings

Above: The Reichstag dome (p78)

Very few buildings from the Middle Ages until the 1700s have survived time, war and modernist town planning. Only two Gothic churches – the red-brick Nikolaikirche (1230) and Marienkirche (1294) – bear silent witness to the days when today's metropolis was just a small trading town. The former anchors the Nikolaiviertel, a mock-medieval quarter built on the site of the city's original settlement as East Germany's contribution to Berlin's 750th anniversary celebrations in 1987. It's a hodgepodge of genuine historic buildings like the Knoblauchhaus and replicas of historic buildings such as the inn Zum Nussbaum.

A smidgeon of residential medieval architecture also survives in the outer district of Spandau, both in the Gotisches Haus and the half-timbered houses of the Kolk quarter.

Traces of the Renaissance, which reached Berlin in the early 16th century, are rarer still; notable survivors include the Jagdschloss Grunewald and the Zitadelle Spandau.

Going for Baroque

As the city grew, so did the representational needs of its rulers, especially in the 17th and 18th centuries. In Berlin, this role fell to Great Elector Friedrich Wilhelm, who systematically expanded the city by adding three residential quarters, a fortified town wall and a tree-lined boulevard known as Unter den Linden.

This was the age of baroque, a style merging architecture, sculpture, ornamentation and painting into a single *Gesamtkunstwerk* (complete work of art). In Berlin and northern Germany it retained a formal and precise bent, never quite reaching the exuberance favoured in regions further south.

The Great Elector may have laid the groundwork, but it was only under his son, Elector Friedrich III, that Berlin acquired the stature of an exalted residence, especially after he crowned himself *King* Friedrich I in 1701. Two major baroque buildings survive from his reign, both blueprinted by Johann Arnold Nering: Schloss Charlottenburg, which Johann Friedrich Eosander later expanded into a Versailles-inspired three-wing palace; and the Zeughaus (armoury; today's Deutsches Historisches Museum) on Unter den Linden. The museum's modern annexe, named the IM Pei Bau (IM Pei Building) after its architect, was added in the 1990s. Fronted by a transparent, spiral staircase shaped like a snail shell, it's a harmonious interplay of glass, natural stone and light and an excellent example of Pei's muted postmodernist approach.

Meanwhile, back in the early 18th century, two formidable churches were taking shape on Gendarmenmarkt in the heart of the immigrant Huguenot community, who at the time accounted for about 25% of the population. These were the Deutscher Dom (German Church) by Martin Grünberg, and the Französischer Dom (French Church) by Louis Cayart.

No king had a greater impact on Berlin's physical layout than Frederick the Great (Friedrich II). Together with his childhood friend architect Georg Wenzeslaus von Knobelsdorff, he masterminded the Forum Fridericianum, a cultural quarter centred on today's Bebelplatz. It was built in a style called 'Frederician rococo', which blends baroque and neoclassical elements. Since the king's war exploits had emptied his coffers, he could only afford to partially realise his vision by building

Built as a summer palace for King Friedrich I's wife Sophie-Charlotte, Schloss Charlottenburg was originally called Schloss Lietzenburg but was renamed after the popular queen's sudden death in 1705.

BERLIN AND ITS WALLS

1250 The first defensive wall is built of boulders and stands 2m high.

14th century The wall is fortified with bricks and raised to a height of 5m.

1648–1734 The medieval wall is replaced by elaborate fortifications.

1734–1866 A customs wall with 18 city gates replaces the bastion.

1961–1989 The Berlin Wall divides the city.

the neoclassical Staatsoper (State Opera House); the Sankt-Hedwigs-Kathedrale (St Hedwig Cathedral), inspired by Rome's Pantheon; the playful Alte Bibliothek (Old Royal Library); and the Humboldt Universität (Humboldt University), originally a palace for the king's brother Heinrich. Knobelsdorff also designed the Neuer Flügel (New Wing) expansion of Schloss Charlottenburg. His crowning achievement, though, was Schloss Sanssouci (Sanssouci Palace) in Potsdam.

After Knobelsdorff's death in 1753, two architects continued in his tradition: Philipp Daniel Boumann – who designed Schloss Bellevue (Bellevue Palace) for Frederick's youngest brother, August Ferdinand – and Carl von Gontard, who added the domed towers to the Deutscher Dom and Französischer Dom on Gendarmenmarkt.

Top Four Prussian Palaces

Schloss Sanssouci (Potsdam)

Schloss Charlottenburg (Charlottenburg)

Neues Palais (Potsdam)

Schlösschen auf der Pfaueninsel (Wannsee)

The Schinkel Touch

The architectural style that most shaped Berlin was neoclassicism, thanks in large part to one man: Karl Friedrich Schinkel (p250), arguably Prussia's most prominent architect. Turning away from baroque flourishes, neoclassicism drew upon columns, pediments, domes and other design elements that had been popular throughout antiquity.

Schinkel assisted with the design of Queen Luise's mausoleum in Schloss Charlottenburg's park in 1810, but didn't truly make his mark until his first major solo commission, the Neue Wache (New Guardhouse) on Unter den Linden, was completed in 1818. Originally an army guardhouse, it is now an antiwar memorial accented with a haunting sculpture by Käthe Kollwitz.

The nearby Altes Museum (Old Museum) on Museumsinsel (Museum Island), with its colonnaded front, is considered Schinkel's most mature work. Other neoclassical masterpieces include the Schauspielhaus (now the Konzerthaus Berlin) on Gendarmenmarkt and the Neue Pavillon (New Pavilion) in Schlossgarten Charlottenburg. Schinkel's most significant departure from neoclassicism, the turreted Friedrichswerdersche Kirche, was inspired by a Gothic Revival in early-19th-century England.

After Schinkel's death in 1841, several of his disciples kept his legacy alive, notably Friedrich August Stüler, who built the original Neues Museum (New Museum) and the Alte Nationalgalerie (Old National Gallery), both on Museumsinsel, as well as the Matthäuskirche (Church of St Matthew) in today's Kulturforum.

Housing for the Masses

In his 1930 book *Das Steinerne Berlin* (Stony Berlin), Werner Hegemann fittingly refers to Berlin as 'the largest tenement city in the world'. The onset of industrialisation in the middle of the 19th century lured to the capital hundreds of thousands, who dreamed of improving their lot in the factories. Something had to be done to beef up the city's infrastructure and provide cheap housing for the masses, and quick. A plan drawn up in 1862 under chief city planner James Hobrecht called for a city expansion along two circular ring roads bisected by diagonal roads radiating in all directions from the centre – much like the spokes of a wheel. The land in between was divided into large lots and sold to speculators and developers. Building codes were limited to a maximum building height of 22m (equivalent to five stories) and a minimum courtyard size of 5.34m by 5.34m, just large enough for fire-fighting equipment to operate in.

Such lax regulations led to the uncontrolled spread of sprawling working-class tenements called *Mietskasernen* (literally 'rental barracks') in newly created peripheral districts such as Prenzlauer Berg, Kreuzberg, Wedding and Friedrichshain. Each was designed to squeeze the maximum number of people into the smallest possible space. Entire families

Berliner Dom (p108)

crammed into tiny, lightless flats reached via internal staircases that also provided access to shared toilets. Many flats doubled as workshops or sewing studios. Only those in the street-facing front offered light, space and balconies – and they were reserved for the bourgeoisie.

The Empire Years

The architecture in vogue after the creation of the German Empire in 1871 reflected the representational needs of the united Germany and tended towards the pompous. No new style, as such, emerged as architects essentially recycled earlier ones (eg Romanesque, Renaissance, baroque, sometimes weaving them all together) in an approach called *Historismus* (historicism) or *Wilhelmismus*, after Kaiser Wilhelm I. As a result, many buildings in Berlin look much older than they actually are. Prominent examples include the Reichstag by Paul Wallot and the Berliner Dom (Berlin Cathedral) by Julius Raschdorff, both in neo-Renaissance style. Franz Schwechten's Anhalter Bahnhof and the Kaiser-Wilhelm-Gedächtniskirche (Memorial Church), both in ruins, reflect the neo-Romanesque, while the Bode-Museum by Ernst von Ihne is a neobaroque confection.

While squalid working-class neighbourhoods hemmed in neighbourhoods in the north, east and south of the city centre, western Berlin (Charlottenburg, Wilmersdorf) was developed for the middle and upper classes under none other than the 'Iron Chancellor' Otto von Bismarck himself. He had the Kurfürstendamm widened, lining it and its side streets with attractive townhouses. Those with serious money and status moved even further west, away from the claustrophobic centre. The villa colonies in leafy Grunewald and Dahlem are another Bismarck legacy and still among the ritziest residential areas today.

Berlin's architectural growth was notably influenced by advancements in transportation. The first train chugged from Berlin to Potsdam in 1838, the first S-Bahn rumbled along in 1882 and the U-Bahn kicked into service in 1902.

The Birth of Modernism

While most late-19th-century architects were looking to the past, a few progressive minds managed to make their mark, mostly in industrial and commercial design. Sometimes called the 'father of modern architecture', Peter Behrens (1868–1940) taught later modernist luminaries such as Le Corbusier, Walter Gropius and Ludwig Mies van der Rohe. One of his earliest works, the 1909 AEG Turbinenhalle at Huttenstrasse 12-14 in Moabit, is considered an icon of early industrial architecture.

After WWI the 1920s spirit of innovation lured some of the finest avant-garde architects to Berlin, including Bruno and Max Taut, Le Corbusier, Mies van der Rohe, Erich Mendelsohn, Hans Poelzig and Hans Scharoun. In 1924 they formed an architectural collective called Der Ring (The Ring) whose members were united by the desire to break with traditional aesthetics (especially the derivative historicism) and to promote a modern, affordable and socially responsible approach to building.

Their theories were put into practice as Berlin entered another housing shortage. Led by chief city planner Martin Wagner, Ring members devised a new form of social housing called *Siedlungen* (housing estates). In contrast to the claustrophobic tenements, it opened up living space and incorporated gardens, schools, shops and other communal areas that facilitated social interaction. Together with Bruno Taut, Wagner himself designed the Hufeisensiedlung (Horseshoe Colony) in Neukölln, which, in 2008, became one of six Berlin housing estates recognised as a Unesco World Heritage site (p254).

In nonresidential architecture, expressionism flourished with Erich Mendelsohn as its leading exponent. This organic, sculptural approach is nicely exemplified by the Universum Kino (Universum Cinema; 1926), which is today's Schaubühne at Lehniner Platz; it greatly influenced the Streamline Moderne movie palaces of the 1930s. Emil Fahrenkamp's 1931 Shell-Haus at Reichspietschufer 60 follows similar design principles. Reminiscent of a giant upright staircase, it was one of Berlin's earliest steel-frame structures, concealed beneath a skin of travertine. Its extravagant silhouette is best appreciated from the southern bank of the Landwehrkanal.

Walking around Berlin, it's hard to visualise what the city looked like before WWII. In comes Nick Gay's book *Berlin Then and Now*, which handily juxtaposes historical and recent images of major landmarks, streets and squares.

PRUSSIA'S BUILDING MASTER: KARL FRIEDRICH SCHINKEL

Few architects have shaped the Berlin cityscape as much as Karl Friedrich Schinkel (1781–1841). After studying under David Gilly at the Prussian Building Academy in Berlin, he decamped to Italy for a couple of years to examine classical architecture in situ. He returned to a Prussia hamstrung by Napoleonic occupation and was forced to scrape by as a Romantic painter and furniture and set designer for a few years.

Things improved dramatically as soon as the French left Berlin in 1808, allowing Schinkel to quickly climb the career ladder within the Prussian civil service and eventually to become chief building director for the entire kingdom. He travelled tirelessly throughout the land, designing buildings, supervising construction and even developing principles for the protection of historic monuments.

Drawing inspiration from classical Greek architecture, Schinkel very much defined Prussian architecture between 1810 and 1840. His designs strive for the perfect balance between functionality and beauty, achieved through clear lines, symmetry and an impeccable sense for aesthetics. Berlin, which came to be known as 'Athens on the Spree', is littered with his buildings (p248).

Schinkel fell into a coma in 1840 and died one year later in Berlin. He's buried on the Dorotheenstädtischer Friedhof in Mitte.

Nazi Monumentalism

Modernist architecture had its legs cut out from under it as soon as Hitler came to power in 1933. The new regime immediately shut down the Bauhaus School, one of the most influential forces in 20th-century building and design. Many of its visionary teachers, including Gropius, Mies van der Rohe, Wagner and Mendelsohn, went into exile in the USA.

Back in Berlin, Hitler, who was a big fan of architectural monumentalism, put Albert Speer in charge of turning Berlin into the Welthauptstadt Germania, the future capital of the Reich. Today, only a few buildings offer a hint of what Berlin might have looked like had history taken a different turn. These include the coliseumlike Olympiastadion, Tempelhof airport and the former air force ministry that now houses Germany's Federal Finance Ministry.

A Tale of Two Cities

Even before the Wall was built in 1961, the clash of ideologies and economic systems between East and West also found expression in the architectural arena.

East Berlin

East Germans looked to Moscow, where Stalin favoured a style that was essentially a socialist reinterpretation of good old-fashioned neo-classicism. The most prominent East German architect was Hermann Henselmann, the brains behind the Karl-Marx-Allee (called Stalin-allee until 1961) in Friedrichshain. Built between 1952 and 1965, it was East Berlin's showcase 'socialist boulevard' and, with its Moscow-style 'wedding-cake buildings', the epitome of Stalin-era pomposity. It culminates at Alexanderplatz, the historic central square that got a distinctly socialist makeover in the 1960s.

While Alexanderplatz and the Karl-Marx-Allee were prestige projects, they did not solve the need for affordable modern housing, which reached a crescendo in the early 1970s. The government responded by building three massive satellite cities on the periphery – Marzahn, Hohenschönhausen and Hellersdorf – which leapt off the drawing board in the 1970s and '80s. Like a virtual Legoland for giants, these huge housing developments largely consist of row upon row of rectangular high-rise *Plattenbauten,* buildings made from large, precast concrete slabs. Marzahn alone could accommodate 165,000 people in 62,000 flats. Since they offered such mod cons as private baths and lifts, this type of housing was very popular among East Germans, despite the monotony of the design.

West Berlin

In West Berlin, urban planners sought to eradicate any references to Nazi-style monumentalism and to rebuild the city in a modernist fashion. Their prestige project became the Hansaviertel, a loosely structured leafy neighbourhood of midrise apartment buildings and single-family homes, northwest of Tiergarten. Built from 1954 to 1957, it drew the world's top architects, including Gropius, Alvar Aalto and Le Corbusier and was intended to be a model for other residential quarters.

The 1960s saw the birth of a large-scale public building project, the Kulturforum, a museum and concert-hall complex conceptualised by Hans Scharoun. His Berliner Philharmonie, the first building to be completed in 1963, is considered a masterpiece of sculptural modernism. Among the museums, Mies van der Rohe's templelike Neue Nationalgalerie (New National Gallery) is a standout. A massive

The only remaining prewar buildings on Alexanderplatz are the Berolina-haus (1930) and the Alexander-haus (1932), both by Peter Behrens.

Akademie der Künste – Pariser Platz (p86)

glass-and-steel cube, it perches on a raised granite podium and is lidded by a coffered, steel-ribbed roof that seems to defy gravity.

The West also struggled with a housing shortage and built its own versions of mass-scale housing projects, including Gropiusstadt in southern Neukölln and the Märkisches Viertel in Reinickendorf, in northwest Berlin.

Interbau 1987

While mass housing mushroomed on the peripheries, the inner city suffered from decay and neglect on both sides of the Wall. In West Berlin, an international architectural exposition called Interbau (IBA) 1987 was to set new initiatives in urban renewal by blending two architectural principles: 'Careful Urban Renewal' would focus on rehabilitating existing buildings; and 'Critical Reconstruction' would require any new buildings to fit in with the existing urban fabric.

Planning director Josef Paul Kleihues invited the royalty of international architecture to take up the challenges of Interbau, among them Rob Krier, Peter Eisenman, James Stirling, Aldo Rossi, Arata Isozaki and OM Ungers. Eastern Kreuzberg and the area south of the Tiergarten received the most attention. Good places to study the legacy of Interbau 1987 are on a stroll along the Fraenkelufer in Kreuzberg and along the streets surrounding the Jüdisches Museum such as Lindenstrasse, Ritterstrasse and Alte Jakobstrasse.

In the 1920s Adolf Hitler's half-brother Alois was a waiter at Weinhaus Huth, the only building on Potsdamer Platz to survive WWII intact. During the Cold War, it stood forlorn in the middle of the death strip for decades.

The New Berlin

Reunification presented Berlin with both the challenge and the opportunity to redefine itself architecturally. With the Wall and death strip gone, the two city halves had to be physically rejoined across huge gashes of empty space. Critical Reconstruction continued to be the guiding vision under city planning director Hans Stimmann. Architects had to follow a long catalogue of parameters with regard to building heights, facade materials and other criteria with the goal of rebuilding Berlin within its historic forms rather than creating a modern, vertical city.

Potsdamer Platz

The biggest and grandest of the post-1990 Berlin developments, Potsdamer Platz is a modern reinterpretation of the historic square that was Berlin's bustling heart until WWII. From terrain once bifurcated by the Berlin Wall has sprung an urban quarter laid out along a dense, irregular street grid in keeping with a 'European city'. Led by Renzo Piano, it's a collaboration of an international roster of renowned architects, including Helmut Jahn, Richard Rogers and Rafael Moneo. Structures are of medium height, except for three gateway high-rises overlooking the intersection of Potsdamer Strasse and Ebertstrasse.

Pariser Platz

Pariser Platz was reconstructed from the ground up. It's a formal, introspective square framed by banks, embassies and the Hotel Adlon Kempinski that, in keeping with Critical Reconstruction, had to have natural stone facades. The one exception is the glass-fronted Akademie der Künste (Academy of Arts). Its architect, Günter Behnisch, had to fight tooth and nail for this facade, arguing that the square's only public building should feel open, inviting and transparent. The Adlon, meanwhile, is practically a spitting image of the 1907 original.

Diplomatenviertel

Some of Berlin's most exciting new architecture is clustered in the revitalised Diplomatenviertel (Diplomatic Quarter) on the southern edge of Tiergarten, where many countries rebuilt their embassies on their historic pre-WWII sites.

Regierungsviertel

The 1991 decision to move the federal government back to Berlin resulted in a flurry of building activity in the empty space between the Reichstag and the Spree River. Designed by Axel Schultes and Charlotte Frank, and arranged in linear east–west fashion, are the Federal Chancellery, the Paul-Löbe-Haus and the Marie-Elisabeth-Lüders-Haus. Together they form the Band des Bundes (Band of Federal Buildings) in a symbolic linking of the formerly divided city halves across the Spree.

Overlooking all these shiny new structures is the Reichstag, home of the Bundestag (German parliament), the glass cupola of which is the most visible element of the building's total makeover masterminded by Norman Foster.

The glass-and-steel 'spaceship' on the northern riverbank is Berlin's first-ever central train station, the sparkling Hauptbahnhof designed by the Hamburg firm of Gerkan, Marg und Partner and completed in 2006.

More Architectural Trophies

In Kreuzberg, Daniel Libeskind's deconstructivist Jüdisches Museum (1999) is among the most daring and provocative structures in the new Berlin. With its irregular, zigzagging floor plan and shiny zinc skin pierced by gashlike windows, it is not merely a museum but a powerful

If you want to learn more about Berlin's contemporary architecture, arrange for a tour (also in English) with Ticket B (www.ticket-b.de), an architect-run guide company.

ARCHITECTURE THE NEW BERLIN

Top Five Buildings since 1990

Jüdisches Museum (Daniel Libeskind; Kreuzberg)

Reichstag Dome (Norman Foster; Historic Mitte)

Sony Center (Helmut Jahn; Potsdamer Platz)

Neues Museum (David Chipperfield; Museumsinsel)

Hauptbahnhof (Gerkan, Marg und Partner; Historic Mitte)

UNCOMMON ENVIRONS FOR THE COMMON FOLK

Architecturally speaking, Museumsinsel, Schloss Sanssouci and the Hufeisen-siedlung in Neukölln could not be more different. Yet all have one thing in common: they are Unesco World Heritage Sites. Along with five other working-class housing estates throughout Berlin, the Hufeisensiedlung was inducted on to this illustrious list in July 2008.

Created between 1910 and 1933 by such leading architects of the day as Bruno Taut and Martin Wagner, these icons of modernism are the earliest examples of innovative, streamlined and functional – yet human-scale – mass housing and stand in stark contrast to the slumlike, crowded tenements of the late 19th century. The flats, though modest, were functionally laid out and had kitchens, private baths and balconies that let in light and fresh air. For further details, see whc.unesco.org.

Hufeisensiedlung, Neukölln (Lowise-Reuter-Ring; Ⓤ Parchimer Allee) Taut and Wagner dreamed up a three-storey-high horseshoe-shaped colony (1933–35) with 1000 bal-conied flats wrapping around a central park. From the station follow Fritz-Reuter-Allee north.

Gartenstadt Falkenberg, Köpenick (Akazienhof, Am Falkenberg & Gartenstadtweg; Ⓢ Grünau) Built by Taut between 1910 and 1913, the oldest of the six Unesco-honoured estates is a cheerful jumble of colourfully painted cottages. Approach from Am Falk-enberg.

Siemensstadt, Spandau (Geisslerpfad, Goebelstrasse, Heckerdamm, Jungfernheideweg, Mäckeritzstrasse; Ⓤ Siemensdamm) This huge development (1929–31) combines Walter Gropius' minimalism, Hugo Häring's organic approach and Hans Scharoun's ship-inspired designs. Best approach is via Jungfernheideweg.

Schillerpark Siedlung, Wedding (Barfussstrasse, Bristolstrasse, Corker Strasse, Dub-liner Strasse, Oxforder Strasse, Windsorer Strasse, Wedding; Ⓤ Rehberge) Inspired by Dutch architecture, this large colony was masterminded by Taut (1924–30) and sports a dynamic red-and-white-brick facade. Best approach is via Barfussstrasse.

Weisse Stadt, Reinickendorf (Aroser Allee, Baseler Strasse, Bieler Strasse, Emmentaler Strasse, Genfer Strasse, Gotthardstrasse, Romanshorner Weg, Schillerring, Sankt-Galler-Strasse; Ⓤ Residenzstrasse) Martin Wagner's 'White City' (1929–31) in-cludes shops, a kindergarten, a cafe, a central laundry and other communal facilities. Best approach is via Aroser Allee.

Wohnstadt Carl Legien, Prenzlauer Berg (streets around Erich-Weinert-Strasse; Ⓢ Prenzlauer Allee) For this development (1928–30) in Prenzlauer Berg, Taut arranged rows of four-to-five-storey-high houses and garden areas in a semi-open space. Approach via Erich-Weinert-Strasse.

---

metaphor for the troubled history of the Jewish people. Libeskind also designed the museum's extension, which opened in a nearby converted flower market in June 2013.

Near Gendarmenmarkt, along Friedrichstrasse, the Friedrichstadt-passagen (1996) is a trio of luxurious shopping complexes, including the glamorous Galeries Lafayette, that hide their jewel-like interiors behind postmodern facades.

Across town in the City West, several new structures have added some spice to the rather drab postwar architecture around Kurfürstendamm. The Ludwig-Erhard-Haus (1997), home of the Berlin stock market, is a great example of the organic architecture of the UK's Nicholas Grim-shaw. Nearby, Kleihues' Kantdreieck (1995) establishes a visual accent on Kantstrasse by virtue of its rooftop metal 'sail'. Noteworthy build-ings along Ku'damm itself are Helmut Jahn's Neues Kranzler Eck (2000) and the Neues Ku-Damm-Eck (2001), a corner building with a gradated and rounded facade, designed by Gerkan, Marg und Partner and festooned with sculptures by Markus Lüpertz.

Another highlight is David Chipperfield's reconstruction of the Neues Museum (2009) on Museumsinsel. Like a giant jigsaw puzzle, it beautifully blends fragments from the original structure, which was destroyed in WWII, with modern elements. The result is so harmonious and impressive, it immediately racked up the accolades, including a prestigious award from the Royal Institute of British Architects (RIBA) in 2010.

Recent Developments & the Future

You'd think that, more than 25 years after reunification, the ballet of cranes would finally have disappeared, but there are still plenty of large-scale projects on the drawing board or under construction.

In 2013 construction kicked off on the replica of the former Prussian city palace (Berliner Stadtschloss) on Schlossplatz opposite Museumsinsel. To be known as Humboldt-Forum, it will resemble its historic predecessor only from the outside, with the modern interior housing museums and cultural institutions.

The first spies have started moving into the new Berlin HQ of the Bundesnachrichtendienst (BND; Germany's federal intelligence agency) on Chausseestrasse, just north of the Scheunenviertel. Designed by Kleihues + Kleihues, the giant compound sits on a lot once occupied by the GDR-era Stadium of the World Youth and will provide work space for 4000 people.

The City West has also garnered several high-profile additions including the towering Waldorf Astoria Hotel and its yet-to-be-completed neighbour, the Upper West residential and commercial tower. Construction has also commenced on Zoom, a new office-and-retail building opposite the Astoria/Upper West twin towers.

Nearby, a couple of 1950s buildings have been reinvented for the 21st century. The iconic Bikini Berlin became Germany's first 'concept mall' after a total refurb in 2014. The curious name was inspired by its design: two 200m-long upper and lower sections are separated by an open floor supported by a curtain of columns. Today the middle section is chastely covered by a glass facade. Nearby, the sensitively restored 1950s Amerika Haus now houses the prestigious photography gallery C/O Berlin.

The biggest upcoming building project is the Europa-City north of the Hauptbahnhof, an entire neighbourhood to be built on 40 hectares, complete with S-Bahn station, a bridge across the canal and leafy squares.

The Berliner Architekturpreis 2016, which is awarded every three years, went to the St Agnes Kirche, a brutalist church in Kreuzberg that was minimally converted into the spectacular art gallery König by Arno Brandlhuber.

With its cool, calm facade, the DZ Bank on Pariser Platz seems untypical for its exuberant architect, Frank Gehry. The surprise, though, lurks beyond the foyer leading to a light-flooded atrium anchored by an enormous sci-fi-esque stainless-steel sculpture used as a conference room.

The opening of Berlin's Brandenburg Airport in Schönefeld has been delayed repeatedly. A referendum in May 2014, however, prevented the city from partly developing Tempelhof Airport, which closed in 2008. Much to the delight of Berliners, it will remain a public park.

Painting & Visual Arts

The arts are fundamental to everything Berlin holds dear, and the sheer scope of creative activity in the city is astounding. The city itself provides an iconic setting for a spectrum of visual arts, its unmistakable presence influencing artists and residents just as it does those canny visitors who take the time to dive in.

Early Beginnings

Fine art only began to flourish in Berlin in the late 17th century, when self-crowned King Friedrich I founded the Akademie der Künste (Academy of Arts) in 1696, egged on by court sculptor Andreas Schlüter. Schlüter repaid the favour with outstanding sculptures, including the *Great Elector on Horseback,* now in front of Schloss Charlottenburg, and the haunting masks of dying warriors in the courtyard of today's Deutsches Historisches Museum (German Historical Museum). Artistic accents in painting were set by Frenchman Antoine Pesne, who became Friedrich I's court painter in 1710. His main legacy is his elaborate portraits of the royal family members.

The arts also reached a heyday under Friedrich I's grandson, Friedrich II (Frederick the Great), who became king in 1740. Friedrich drew heavily on the artistic expertise of his friend Georg Wenzeslaus von Knobelsdorff, a student of Pesne, and amassed a sizeable collection of works by such French artists as Jean Antoine Watteau.

The 19th Century

A student of Christian Daniel Rauch, the sculptor Reinhold Begas developed a neobaroque, theatrical style that met with a fair amount of controversy in his lifetime. Major works include the Neptune fountain near the TV Tower, and the Schiller memorial on Gendarmenmarkt.

Neoclassicism emerged as a dominant sculptural style in the 19th century. Johann Gottfried Schadow's *Quadriga* – the horse-drawn chariot atop the Brandenburg Gate – epitomises the period. Schadow's student Christian Daniel Rauch had a special knack for representing idealised, classical beauty in a realistic fashion. His most famous work is the 1851 monument of Frederick the Great on horseback on Unter den Linden.

In painting, heart-on-your-sleeve romanticism that drew heavily on emotion and a dreamy idealism dominated the 19th century. A reason for this development was the awakening of a nationalist spirit in Germany, spurred by the Napoleonic Wars. Top dog of the era was Caspar David Friedrich, best known for his moody, allegorical landscapes. Although more famous as an architect, Karl Friedrich Schinkel also created some fanciful canvases. Eduard Gärtner's paintings documenting Berlin's evolving cityscape found special appeal among the middle classes.

A parallel development was the so-called Berliner Biedermeier, a more conservative and painstakingly detailed style that appealed to the emerging Prussian middle class. The name itself is derived from the German word for conventional *(bieder)* and the common surname of Meier; visit the Knoblauchhaus in the Nikolaiviertel for fine examples. The Alte Nationalgalerie on Museumsinsel and the Neuer Pavillon of Schloss Charlottenburg are both showcases of 19th-century paintings.

Into the 20th Century

Berliner Secession

The Berliner Secession was formed in 1898 by a group of progressively minded artists who rejected the traditional teachings of the arts academies that stifled any new forms of expression. The schism was triggered in 1891, when the established Verein Berliner Künstler (Berlin Artist Association) refused to show paintings by Edvard Munch at its annual salon, and reached its apex in 1898 when the salon jury rejected a landscape painting by Walter Leistikow. Consequently, 65 artists banded together under the leadership of Leistikow and Max Liebermann and seceded from the Verein. Other famous Berliner Secession members included Lovis Corinth, Max Slevogt, Ernst Ludwig Kirchner, Max Beckmann and Käthe Kollwitz.

Expressionism

In 1905 Kirchner, along with Erich Heckel and Karl Schmidt-Rottluff, founded the artists' group Die Brücke (The Bridge) in Dresden: it turned the art world on its head with groundbreaking visions that paved the way for German expressionism. Abstract forms, a flattened perspective and bright, emotional colours characterised this new aesthetic. Die Brücke moved to Berlin in 1911 and disbanded in 1913. The small Brücke-Museum in the Grunewald has a fantastic collection of these influential artists.

Ironically, it was the expressionists who splintered off from the Berliner Secession in 1910 after their work was rejected by the Secession jury. With Max Pechstein at the helm, they formed the Neue Secession. The original Berliner Secession group continued on but saw its influence wane, especially after the Nazi power grab in 1933.

The Bauhaus & Art under the Nazis

The year 1919 saw the founding of the Bauhaus movement and school in Weimar. It was based on practical anti-elitist principles bringing form and function together, and had a profound effect on all modern design – visit the Bauhaus Archiv for ample examples. Although the school moved to Dessau in 1925 and only came to Berlin in 1932, many of its most influential figures worked in Berlin. The Nazis forced it to close down in 1933.

After the Nazi takeover many artists left the country and others ended up in prison or concentration camps, their works confiscated or destroyed. The art promoted instead was often terrible, favouring straightforward 'Aryan' forms and epic styles. Propaganda artist Mjölnir defined the typical look of the time with block Gothic scripts and idealised figures.

Art-world honchos descend upon Berlin in late April for the annual Gallery Weekend, when you can hop-scotch around 40 galleries, and again for the Berlin Biennale, a curated forum for contemporary art held over two months in spring or summer every other year.

The coppersmith Emanuel Jury, who cast the *Quadriga* sculpture atop the Brandenburg Gate, used his cousin as a model for the Goddess Victoria, pilot of the chariot.

PAINTING & VISUAL ARTS INTO THE 20TH CENTURY

ZILLE SEASON

Born in Dresden in 1858, Heinrich Zille moved to Berlin with his family when he was a child. A lithographer by trade, he became the first prominent artist to evoke the social development of the city as the tendrils of modernity reached Berlin. His instantly recognisable style depicted everyday life and real people, often featuring the bleak *Hinterhöfe* (back courtyards) around which so much of their lives revolved. Even during his lifetime Zille was acknowledged as one of the definitive documenters of his time, and since his death in 1929 his prolific photographic work has also come to be seen as a valuable historical record. When he died, thousands of Berliners turned out to pay their respects to the man whose pictures chronicled their daily lives with sharp humour and unsentimental honesty. There's a Zille Museum in the Nikolaiviertel dedicated to his life and work.

Berlin Dada

Dada was an avant-garde art movement formed in Zurich in 1916 in reaction to the brutality of WWI. It spread to Berlin in 1918 with the help of Richard Huelsenbeck, who held the first Dada event in a gallery in February that year and later produced the *First German Dada Manifesto*. Founding members included George Grosz, photomontage inventor John Heartfield and Hannah Höch; Marcel Duchamp, Kurt Schwitters and Hans Arp were among the many others who dabbled in Dada.

Dada artists had an irrational, satirical and often absurdist approach, imbued with a political undercurrent and a tendency to shock and provoke. The First International Dada Fair in 1920, for instance, took place beneath a suspended German officer dummy with a pig's head.

One artist greatly influenced by Dadaism was Otto Dix, who, in the 1920s, produced a series of dark and sombre paintings depicting war scenes – disfigured, dying and decomposing bodies – in graphic detail. Dix and Grosz went on to become key figures of the late 1920s Neue Sachlichkeit (New Objectivity), an offshoot of expressionism distinguished by an unsentimental, practical and objective look at reality.

To keep a tab on the contemporary art scene, check out the latest shows at the city's many high-calibre galleries, such as Galerie Eigen+Art or Contemporary Fine Arts, and visit the collections at Hamburger Bahnhof and the Sammlung Boros.

Post WWII

After WWII, Berlin's art scene was as fragmented as the city itself. In the east, artists were forced to toe the social realism line, at least until the late 1960s when artists of the so-called Berliner Schule, including Manfred Böttcher and Harald Metzkes, sought to embrace a more interpretative and emotional form of expression inspired by the colours and aesthetic of Beckmann, Matisse, Picasso and other classical modernists. In the '70s, when conflicts of the individual in society became a prominent theme, underground galleries flourished in Prenzlauer Berg and art became a collective endeavour.

In postwar West Berlin, artists eagerly embraced abstract art. Pioneers included Zone 5, which revolved around Hans Thiemann, and surrealists Heinz Trökes and Mac Zimmermann. In the 1960s politics was a primary concern and a new style called 'critical realism' emerged, propagated by artists like Ulrich Baehr, Hans-Jürgen Diehl and Wolfgang Petrick. The 1973 movement, Schule der Neuen Prächtigkeit (School of New Magnificence), had a similar approach. In the late 1970s and early 1980s, expressionism found its way back on to the canvases of Salomé, Helmut Middendorf and Rainer Fetting, a group known as the Junge Wilde (Young Wild Ones). One of the best-known German neoexpressionist painters is Georg Baselitz, who lives in Berlin and became internationally famous in the 1970s with his 'upside-down' works.

The Present

Art aficionados will find their compass on perpetual spin in Berlin, which has developed one of the most exciting and dynamic arts scenes in Europe. With an active community of some 10,000 artists, there have been notable successes, most famously perhaps Danish-Icelandic artist Olafur Eliasson. Other major leaguers like Thomas Demand, Jonathan Meese, Via Lewandowsky, Isa Genzken, Tino Seghal, Esra Ersen, John Bock and the artist duo Ingar Dragset and Michael Elmgreen all live and work in Berlin, or at least have a second residence here.

Berlin has also emerged as a European street art capital with some major international artists like Blu, JR and Os Gemeos leaving their mark on the city. Local top talent includes Alias and El Bocho. Street art is especially prevalent in eastern Kreuzberg (especially around the U-Bahn station Schlesisches Tor) as well as in Mitte (Haus Schwarzenberg) and at the Urban Spree gallery in Friedrichshain.

Literature & Film

Since its beginnings, Berlin's literary scene has reflected a peculiar blend of provincialism and worldliness, but the city's pioneering role in movie history is undeniable: in 1895 Max Skladanowsky screened early films on a bioscope, in 1912 one of the world's first film studios was established in Potsdam and since 1951 Berlin has hosted a leading international film festival.

Literature

First Words

Berlin's literary history began during the 18th-century Enlightenment, an epoch dominated by humanistic ideals. A major author from this time was Gotthold Ephraim Lessing, noted for his critical works, fables and tragedies, who wrote the play *Minna von Barnhelm* (1763) in Berlin. During the Romantic period, an outgrowth of the Enlightenment, it was the poets who stood out, including Achim von Arnim, Clemens Brentano, and Heinrich von Kleist, who committed suicide at Wannsee lake in 1811.

In the mid-19th century, realist literature captured the imagination of the newly emerging middle class. Theodor Fontane raised the Berlin society novel to an art form by showing both the aristocracy and the middle class mired in their societal confinements. His 1894 novel, *Effi Briest,* is among his best-known works. Naturalism, a spin-off of realism, painstakingly recreated the milieus of entire social classes. Gerhard Hauptmann's portrayal of social injustice and the harsh life of the working class won him the Nobel Prize for Literature in 1912.

Modernism & Modernity

In the 1920s, Berlin became a literary hotbed, drawing writers like Alfred Döblin, whose definitive *Berlin Alexanderplatz* is a stylised meander through the seamy 1920s, and Anglo-American import Christopher Isherwood, whose brilliant semiautobiographical *Berlin Stories* formed the basis of the musical and film *Cabaret.* Other notables include the political satirists Kurt Tucholsky and Erich Kästner. Many artists left Germany after the Nazis came to power, and those who stayed often kept their mouths shut and worked underground, if at all.

In West Berlin, the postwar literary revival was led by *The Tin Drum* (1958), by Nobel Prize–winner Günter Grass, which traces recent German history through the eyes of a child who refuses to grow. In the mid-1970s, a segment of the East Berlin literary scene began to detach itself slowly from the socialist party grip. Christa Wolf is one of the best and most controversial East German writers, while Heiner Müller had the distinction of being unpalatable in both Germanys. His dense, difficult works include *The Man Who Kept Down Wages* and the *Germania* trilogy of plays.

New Berlin Novel

In the 1990s, a slew of novels dealt with German reunification; many are set in Berlin, including Thomas Brussig's tongue-in-cheek *Heroes*

Berlin Cult Novels

Berlin Alexanderplatz, Alfred Döblin (1929)

Goodbye to Berlin, Christopher Isherwood (1939)

Alone in Berlin, Hans Fallada (1947)

Wall Jumper, Peter Schneider (1983)

Berlin Blues, Sven Regener (2001)

For an in-depth study of literature that emerged in Berlin after the fall of the Wall, pick up a copy of *Writing the New Berlin* (2008) by Katharina Gerstenberger.

Like Us (1998), Peter Schneider's *Edward's Homecoming* (1999) and Jana Hensel's *After the Wall: Confessions from an East German Childhood and the Life that Came Next* (2002). The late Nobel Prize–winner Günter Grass contributed *A Wide Field* (1995) to the debate. Also worth reading is Cees Nooteboom's *All Souls Day* (2002).

The lighter side of contemporary Berlin is represented by Sven Regener, frontman of the Berlin band Element of Crime, whose hugely successful *Berlin Blues* (2001) is a boozy trawl through Kreuzberg nights at the time of the fall of the Wall. The runaway success story, however, was Russian-born author Wladimir Kaminer's *Russendisko* (Russian Disco, 2000), a collection of amusing, stranger-than-fiction vignettes about life in Berlin. Both *Berlin Blues* and *Russendisko* were made into feature films.

Foreign authors too continue to be inspired by Berlin. Ian McEwan's *The Innocent* (1990) and Joseph Kanon's *Leaving Berlin: A Novel* (2015) are both spy stories set in the 1950s. Kanon also wrote *The Good German* (2002), which was made into a motion picture. The *Berlin Noir* trilogy (1989–91), by British author Philip Kerr, features a private detective solving crimes in Nazi Germany. Berlin history unfolds in a dreamlike sequence in *Book of Clouds* (2009) by Chloe Aridjis.

> Film-fan tourism generates Berlin over €330 million in yearly revenue. To visit famous film locations, sign up for the multimedia 'Filmstadt Berlin' tour by videoBustour (www.videosight seeing.de). Sta Tours (www. sta-tours.de) has tours to the homes of German film legends.

Film

Before 1945

The legendary UFA (Universum Film AG), one of the world's first film studios, began shooting in Potsdam, near Berlin, in 1912 and continues to churn out both German and international blockbusters in its modern incarnation as the Filmstudios Babelsberg. The 1920s and early '30s were a boom time for Berlin cinema, with UFA emerging as Germany's flagship dream factory and Marlene Dietrich's bone structure and distinctive voice seducing the world. As early as 1919, Ernst Lubitsch produced historical films and comedies such as *Madame Dubarry,* starring Pola Negri and Emil Jannings; the latter went on to win the Best Actor Award at the very first Academy Awards ceremony in 1927. The same year saw the release of Walter Ruttmann's classic *Berlin: Symphony of a City,* a fascinating silent documentary that captures a day in the life of Berlin in the '20s.

Other 1920s movies were heavily expressionistic, using stark contrast, sharp angles, heavy shadows and other distorting elements. Well-known flicks employing these techniques include *Nosferatu,* a 1922 Dracula adaptation by FW Murnau, and the groundbreaking *Metropolis* (1927) by Fritz Lang. One of the earliest seminal talkies was Josef von Sternberg's *Der Blaue Engel* (1930) starring Dietrich. After 1933, though, film-makers

> Cool places to plug into German movie history are the Museum für Film und Fernsehen at Potsdamer Platz, the Filmmuseum Potsdam and the Filmpark Babelsberg.

FAMOUS FILM LOCATIONS

Wings of Desire (1987) The top of the Siegessäule (Victory Column) in Tiergarten is a place where angels congregate and listen to people's thoughts.

Good Bye, Lenin! (2003) The flat where Alexander Kerner (Daniel Brühl) recreates life in East Berlin for his ailing mother is in a modern high-rise at Berolinastrasse 21.

Bourne Supremacy (2004) The epic car chase where Bourne (Matt Damon) forces Russian assassin Kirill (Karl Urban) to crash his car into a concrete divider in a tunnel was filmed in the Tiergartentunnel a year and a half before its official opening in 2006.

The Lives of Others (2006) The apartment where two of the main characters, the playwright Georg Dreymann (Sebastian Koch) and his actor wife Christa-Maria Sieland (Martina Gedeck), make their home is at Wedekindstrasse 21 in Friedrichshain.

The Hunger Games: Mockingjay Part 2 (2015) Scenes from the third instalment in this successful series were filmed at Tempelhof Airport.

MARLENE DIETRICH
··

Marlene Dietrich (1901–92) was born Marie Magdalena von Losch into a middle-class Berlin family. After acting school, she first captivated audiences as a hard-living, libertine flapper in 1920s silent movies, but quickly carved a niche as the dangerously seductive femme fatale. The 1930 talkie *Der Blaue Engel* (The Blue Angel) turned her into a Hollywood star and launched a five-year collaboration with director Josef von Sternberg. Dietrich built on her image of erotic opulence – dominant and severe but always with a touch of self-irony.

Dietrich stayed in Hollywood after the Nazi rise to power, though Hitler, not immune to her charms, reportedly promised perks and the red-carpet treatment if she moved back to Germany. She responded with an empty offer to return if she could bring along Sternberg – a Jew and no Nazi favourite. She took US citizenship in 1937 and entertained Allied soldiers on the front.

found their artistic freedom, not to mention funding, increasingly curtailed, and by 1939 practically the entire industry had fled to Hollywood.

Films made during the Nazi period were mostly of the propaganda variety, with brilliant if controversial Berlin-born director Leni Riefenstahl (1902–2003) greatly pushing the genre's creative envelope. Her most famous film, *Triumph of the Will,* documents the 1934 Nuremberg Nazi party rally. *Olympia,* which chronicles the 1936 Berlin Olympic Games, was another seminal work.

After 1945
Like most of the arts, film-making has generally been well funded in Berlin since 1945, especially in the West. During the 1970s in particular, large subsidies lured directors back to the city, including such New German Film luminaries as Rainer Werner Fassbinder, Volker Schlöndorf, Wim Wenders and Werner Herzog. It was Wenders who made the highly acclaimed *Wings of Desire* (1987), an angelic love story swooping around the old, bare no-man's-land of Potsdamer Platz.

Some of the best films about the Nazi era include Wolfgang Staudte's *Die Mörder sind unter uns* (Murderers among Us, 1946); Fassbinder's *Die Ehe der Maria Braun* (The Marriage of Maria Braun, 1979); Margarethe von Trotta's *Rosenstrasse* (2003), and Oliver Hierschbiegel's extraordinary *Der Untergang* (Downfall, 2004), depicting Hitler's final days.

The first round of postreunification flicks were light-hearted comedy dramas. A standout is the cult classic *Good Bye, Lenin!* (2003), Wolfgang Becker's witty and heartwarming tale of a son trying to recreate the GDR life to save his sick mother. It was Florian von Donnersmarck who first trained the filmic spotlight on the darker side of East Germany, with *The Lives of Others* (2006), an Academy Award–winner that reveals the stranglehold the East German secret police (Stasi) had on ordinary people.

Today
These days, 'Germany's Hollywood' is no longer in Munich or Hamburg but in Berlin, with an average of 300 German and international productions being filmed on location and at the Filmstudios Babelsberg each year. Well-trained crews, modern studio and postproduction facilities, government subsidies and authentic 'old world' locations regularly attract such Hollywood royalty as Quentin Tarantino (*Inglourious Basterds,* 2009) and George Clooney (*The Monuments Men,* 2014). Other recent big productions include *The Grand Budapest Hotel* (2014), *The Hunger Games: Mockingjay Part 2* (2015), Tom Hanks' *A Hologram for the King* (2015) and the entire fifth season of the TV series *Homeland* (2015).

Aside from the headline-grabbing Berlinale, dozens of other film festivals are held throughout the year, including the Jewish Film Festival, Feminist Film Week and Too Drunk to Watch Punk. See www.berliner-filmfestivals.de for the schedule.

LITERATURE & FILM FILM

Music

Just like the city itself, Berlin's music scene is a shape-shifter, fed by the city's appetite for diversity and change. With at least 2000 active bands and dozens of indie labels, Berlin is Germany's undisputed music capital. About 60% of the country's music revenue is generated here, and it's where Universal Music and MTV have their European headquarters.

Beginnings

The Beauty of Transgression: a Berlin Memoir (2011) by US-born artist Danielle de Picciotto (partner of Einstürzende Neubauten bassist Andreas Hacke) beautifully captures the atmosphere and history of Berlin's creative underground from the 1980s to recent times.

For centuries, Berlin was largely eclipsed by Vienna, Leipzig and other European cities when it came to music. One notable exception is Carl Maria von Weber's *Der Freischütz* (The Marksman), which premiered in 1821 at today's Konzerthaus on Gendarmenmarkt and is considered the first important German Romantic opera. Weber's music also influenced Berlin-born Felix Mendelssohn-Bartholdy's *A Midsummer Night's Dream* from 1843. The same year, fellow composer Giacomo Meyerbeer became Prussian General Music Director.

The Berliner Philharmoniker was established in 1882 and quickly gained international stature under Hans von Bülow and, after 1923, Wilhelm Furtwängler. In East Germany, a key figure was Hanns Eisler, composer of the country's national anthem.

The 1920s

Cabaret may have been born in 1880s Paris, but it became a wild and libidinous grown-up in 1920s Berlin. Jazz was the dominant sound, especially after American performer Josephine Baker's headline-grabbing performances at the Theater des Westens dressed in nothing but a banana skirt. More home-grown cabaret music came in the form of the Berlin *Schlager* – light-hearted songs with titles like 'Mein Papagei frisst keine harten Eier' ('My parakeet doesn't eat hard-boiled eggs'), which teetered on the silly and surreal. The most successful *Schlager* singing group was the *a cappella* Comedian Harmonists, who were famous for their perfect vocal harmonies, which sounded like musical instruments.

Another runaway hit was *The Threepenny Opera,* written by Bertolt Brecht with music by Kurt Weill. Friedrich Hollaender was also a key composer in the cabaret scene, noted for his wit, improvisational talent and clever lyrics. Among his most famous songs is 'Falling in Love Again', sung by Marlene Dietrich in *Der Blaue Engel.* Like so many other talents (including Weill and Brecht), Hollaender left Germany when the Nazis brought down the curtain, and continued his career in Hollywood.

The pulsating 1920s drew numerous classical musicians to Berlin, including Arnold Schönberg and Paul Hindemith, who taught at the Akademie der Künste and the Berliner Hochschule, respectively.

Pop, Punk & Rock before 1990

Since the end of WWII, Berlin has spearheaded many of Germany's popular-music innovations. In West Berlin, Tangerine Dream helped to propagate the psychedelic sound of the late 1960s, while the Ton Steine Scherben, led by Rio Reiser, became a seminal German-language rock band in the '70s and early '80s. Around the same time, Kreuzberg's subculture launched the punk movement at SO36 and other famous clubs. Regular visitors included the late David Bowie and Iggy Pop, who were Berlin flat buddies on Hauptstrasse in Schöneberg in the 1970s. Trying to kick a drug addiction and greatly inspired by Berlin's brooding mood, Bowie partly wrote and recorded his Berlin Trilogy (*Low, Heroes, Lodger*) at the famous Hansa Studios, which he dubbed the 'Hall by the Wall'. Check out Thomas Jerome Seabrook's *Bowie in Berlin: A New Career in a New Town* (2008) for a cool insight into those heady days.

In East Germany, access to Western rock and other popular music was restricted and few Western stars were invited to perform live. The artistic freedom of East German talent was greatly compromised as all lyrics had to be approved and performances were routinely monitored. Nevertheless, a slew of home-grown *Ostrock* (eastern rock) emerged. Some major ones like The Puhdys, Karat, Silly and City managed to get around the censors by disguising criticism with seemingly innocuous metaphors, or by deliberately inserting provocative lyrics that they fully expected to be deleted by the censorship board. All built up huge followings on both sides of the Wall.

Many nonconformists were placed under an occupational ban and prohibited from performing. Singer-songwriter Wolf Biermann became a cause célèbre when, in 1976, he was not allowed to return to the GDR from a concert series in the West despite being an avid – albeit regime-critical – socialist. When other artists rallied to his support, they too were expatriated, including Biermann's stepdaughter Nina Hagen, an East Berlin pop singer who later became a West Berlin punk pioneer. The small but vital East Berlin punk scene produced Sandow and Feeling B, members of whom went on to form the industrial metal band Rammstein in 1994, still Germany's top musical export.

Once in West Berlin, Hagen helped chart the course for *Neue Deutsche Welle* (German New Wave). This early '80s sound produced such West Berlin bands as D.A.F, Trio, Neonbabies, Ideal and UKW, as well as Rockhaus in East Berlin. The '80s also saw the birth of Die Ärzte, who released their last album, the live recording *Die Nacht der Dämonen*, in 2013. Einstürzende Neubauten pioneered a proto-industrial sound that transformed oil drums, electric drills and chainsaws into musical instruments. Its founder Blixa Bargeld joined The Bad Seeds, helmed by Nick Cave who spent some heroin-addled time in Berlin in the early 1980s.

Pop, Rock & Hip Hop after 1990

Since reunification, hundreds of indie, punk, alternative and goth bands have gigged to appreciative

BERLIN TRACKS

1973
Berlin (Lou Reed) Dark song about the tragedy of two star-crossed junkies.

1977
Heroes (David Bowie) Two lovers in the shadow of the 'Wall of Shame'.

1980
Wir stehen auf Berlin (Ideal) Love declaration by the seminal *Neue Deutsche Welle* band.

1991
Zoo Station (U2) Bono embarks on a surreal journey inspired by a Berlin train station.

1995
Born to Die in Berlin (The Ramones) Drug-addled musings revealing Berlin's dark side.

2000
Dickes B (Seeed) Reggae ode to the 'Big B' (ie Berlin).

2007
Kreuzberg (Bloc Party) Looking for true love...

2008
Schwarz zu Blau (Peter Fox) Perfect portrait of Kottbusser Tor grit and grunge.

2013
Where are We Now? (David Bowie) Melancholic reminiscence of Bowie's time in 1970s Berlin.

Berlin audiences. The still active Die Ärzte, Element of Crime and Einstürzende Neubauten were joined by other successful exports, such as alternative punk rockers Beatsteaks, and the pop-rock band Wir sind Helden, helmed by the charismatic Judith Holofernes, who released her first solo album in 2014.

Other fine Berlin music originates from a jazz/breaks angle (electrojazz and breakbeats, favouring lush grooves, obscure samples and chilled rhythms). Remix masters Jazzanova are top dogs of the downtempo scene. Their Sonar Kollektiv label also champions similar artists, including Micatone. Reggae-dancehall has been huge in Berlin ever since Seeed was founded in 1998; frontperson Peter Fox' solo album *Stadtaffe* (2008) was one of the best-selling albums in Germany and also won the 2010 Album of the Year Echo Award (the 'German Grammy'). Also commercially successful is Culcha Candela, who have essentially pop-ified the Seeed sound and released their fifth studio album, *Flätrate*, in 2011.

Home-grown rap and hiphop have a huge following, thanks to Sido, Fler, Bushido and Kool Savas, who cofounded Masters of Rap (MOR) in 1996. Also hugely successful are Berlin-based Casper and Marteria. K.I.Z., meanwhile, are more of a gangsta rap parody. Other famous Berlin-based artists include eccentric Canadian transplant King Khan, who fuelled the garage rock revival; the country and western band Boss Hoss; the electro-folky singer-songwriter Clara Hill; the indie rock band Gods of Blitz; and the uncategorisable 17 Hippies.

Techno Town

Call it techno, electro, house, minimal – electronic music is the sound of Berlin and its near-mythical club culture has defined the capital's cool factor and put it on the map of global hedonists. The sound may have been born in Detroit but it came of age in Berlin.

The seed was sown in dark and dank cellar club UFO on Köpenicker Strasse in 1988. The 'godfathers' of the Berlin sound, Dr Motte, Westbam and Kid Paul, played their first gigs here, mostly sweat-driven acid house all-night raves. It was Motte who came up with the idea to take the party to the street with a truck, loud beats and a bunch of friends dancing behind it – and the Love Parade was born (it peaked in 1999 with 1.5 million people swarming Berlin's streets).

The Berlin Wall's demise, and the vacuum of artistic freedom it created, catapulted techno out of the underground. The associated euphoria, sudden access to derelict and abandoned spaces in eastern Berlin and lack of control by the authorities were all defining factors in making Berlin a techno mecca. In 1991 the techno-sonic gang followed UFO founder Dimitri Hegemann to the label Tresor, which launched camouflage-sporting DJ Tanith along with trance pioneer Paul van Dyk. Today Tresor is still a seminal brand representing Jeff Mills, Blake Baxter and Cristian Vogel, among many others.

Key label BPitch Control, founded by Ellen Allien in 1999, launched the careers of Modeselektor, Apparat, Sascha Funke and Paul Kalkbrenner. Another heavyweight is the collective Get Physical, which includes Booka Shade, Nôze and the dynamic duo M.A.N.D.Y., who fuse house and electro with minimal and funk to create a highly danceable sound. The charmingly named Shitkatapult, founded in 1997 by Marco Haas (aka T.Raumschmiere), does everything from cutting-edge electronica to tech-rock and mellow ambient. Another mainstay is the house duo Tiefschwarz.

Other leading Berlin DJs include Berghain residents Ben Klock, Marcel Dettmann, Tama Sumo and Steffi, who are all represented by the Ostgut label. New Berlin-based labels to keep an eye on are Nous and the Italian-Spanish Slow Life.

The 2014 documentary *B-Movie: Lust & Sound in West Berlin 1979–1989*, by Mark Reeder, is a tour de force through the subcultural 1980 music scene, featuring Joy Division, Nick Cave, Die Ärzte, Einstürzende Neubauten and others.

Survival Guide

Transport

ARRIVING IN BERLIN

Most visitors arrive in Berlin by air. The opening of Berlin's new central airport, about 24km southeast of the city centre, next to Schönefeld airport, has been delayed indefinitely. Check www.berlin-airport.de for the latest. In the meantime, flights continue to land at the city's Tegel and Schönefeld airports.

Lufthansa and practically all other major European airlines and low-cost carriers (including easyJet, Ryanair and Germanwings) operate direct flights to Berlin from throughout Europe. There are a few direct flights from US gateway cities such as Miami and New York, but normally travel from outside Europe involves changing planes in another European city such as Frankfurt or Amsterdam.

Depending on your departure point, travel to Berlin by train or bus is a viable alternative. Coming from London, for instance, you could be in Berlin in as little as nine hours by taking a combination of the Eurostar and German high-speed trains.

Flights, cars and tours can be booked online at lonely planet.com/bookings.

Air

Tegel Airport

Tegel Airport (TXL; ✆030-6091 1150; www.berlin-airport.de; ☒Tegel Flughafen) In the northwestern suburb of Tegel, about 8km northwest of Zoologischer Garten and 13km northwest of Alexanderplatz. It is served directly only by bus and taxi. Buy bus tickets from official transport staff, from vending machines at the bus stop or directly from the bus driver (change given).

BUS
➡ The TXL express bus connects Tegel to Alexanderplatz (€2.70, Tariff AB; 40 minutes) via Hauptbahnhof (central train station) and Unter den Linden every 10 minutes.

➡ For the City West around Zoologischer Garten take bus X9 (€2.70, Tariff AB; 20 minutes), which also runs at 10-minute intervals.

➡ Bus 109 heads to U-/S-Bahn station Zoologischer Garten every 10 minutes; it's slower and useful only if you're headed somewhere along Kurfürstendamm (€2.70, Tariff AB; 20 to 30 minutes).

U-BAHN
➡ The U-Bahn station closest to the airport is Jakob-Kaiser-Platz, which is served by bus 109 and X9. From here, the U7 takes you directly to Schöneberg and Kreuzberg. Trips cost €2.70 (Tariff AB).

S-BAHN
➡ The closest S-Bahn station is Jungfernheide, which is a stop on the S41/S42 (the Ringbahn, or circle line). It is linked to the

---

CLIMATE CHANGE & TRAVEL

Every form of transport that relies on carbon-based fuel generates CO_2, the main cause of human-induced climate change. Modern travel is dependent on aeroplanes, which might use less fuel per kilometre per person than most cars but travel much greater distances. The altitude at which aircraft emit gases (including CO_2) and particles also contributes to their climate change impact. Many websites offer 'carbon calculators' that allow people to estimate the carbon emissions generated by their journey and, for those who wish to do so, to offset the impact of the greenhouse gases emitted with contributions to portfolios of climate-friendly initiatives throughout the world. Lonely Planet offsets the carbon footprint of all staff and author travel.

PUBLIC TRANSPORT TICKETS

➡ One ticket is valid for all forms of public transport.

➡ The network comprises fare zones A, B and C with tickets available for zones AB, BC or ABC.

➡ AB tickets, valid for two hours, cover most city trips (interruptions and transfers allowed, round-trips not). Exceptions: Potsdam and Schönefeld Airport (ABC tariff).

➡ Children aged six to 14 qualify for reduced (ermässigt) rates; kids under six travel free.

➡ Buy tickets from bus drivers, vending machines at U- or S-Bahn stations and aboard trams, station offices, and news kiosks sporting the yellow BVG logo. Some vending machines accept debit cards. Bus drivers and tram vending machines only take cash.

➡ Single tickets, except those bought from bus drivers and in trams, must be validated at station platform entrances.

➡ On-the-spot fine for travelling without a valid ticket: €40.

➡ A range of travel passes (p269) offer good value.

airport by bus X9. Another Ringbahn station, Beusselstrasse, links up with the TXL bus route. Trips cost €2.70 (Tariff AB).

TAXI
Taxi rides cost about €20 to Zoologischer Garten and €27 to Alexanderplatz and take 30 to 45 minutes. There's a €0.50 surcharge for trips originating at Tegel Airport.

Schönefeld Airport
Schönefeld Airport (SXF; ☑030-6091 1150; www.berlin -airport.de; ℝAirport-Express, RE7 & RB14) About 22km southeast of Alexanderplatz this small airport is directly served by S-Bahn and regional trains. Travel to the city centre requires a transport ticket covering zones ABC (€3.30), available from vending machines in the station tunnel and on platforms (cash and debit cards; change given). Tickets must be validated before boarding (machines are on the station platforms).

S-BAHN & REGIONAL TRAINS
➡ The airport train station is 400m from the terminals. Free shuttle buses run every 10 minutes; walking takes five to 10 minutes.

➡ Airport-Express trains make

the trip to central Berlin twice hourly. Note: these are regular Deutsche Bahn regional trains denoted as RE7 and RB14 in timetables. The journey takes 20 minutes to Alexanderplatz and 30 minutes to Zoologischer Garten.

➡ The S-Bahn S9 runs every 20 minutes and is slower, but useful if you're headed to Friedrichshain (eg Ostkreuz, 30 minutes) or Prenzlauer Berg (eg Schönhauser Allee, 45 minutes).

➡ For the Messe (trade fairgrounds), take the S45 to Südkreuz and change to the S41 to Messe Nord/ICC. Trains run every 20 minutes and the journey takes 55 minutes.

➡ All journeys cost €3.30.

U-BAHN
Schönefeld is not served by the U-Bahn. The nearest station, Rudow, is about a 10-minute ride on bus X7 or bus 171 from the airport. From Rudow, the U7 takes you straight into town. This connection is useful if you're headed for Neukölln or Kreuzberg. You will need an ABC transport ticket (€3.30).

TAXI
A cab ride to central Berlin averages €42 and takes 40 minutes to an hour.

Berlin Brandenburg Airport
Berlin's new central airport is taking shape about 24km southeast of the city center, next to Schönefeld airport. Once operational, it will be served by train and taxi. Check www.berlin-airport.de for the latest.

Bus
Thanks to the 2013 lifting of an anachronistic ban on long-distance domestic bus travel (passed in 1931 to protect the state-owned railway system), travelling to Berlin by coach has become easy, affordable and popular. Buses are comfortable, clean and air-conditioned; some offer free on-board wi-fi and sell snacks and soft drinks. **Mein Fernbus/Flixbus** (www.meinfernbus.de), **Berlin Linien Bus** (www.berlin linienbus.de) and **Eurolines** (www.eurolines.de) are the biggest operators. A handy site for finding out which company goes where, when and for how much is www. busliniensuche.de.

Zentraler Omnibusbahnhof
➡ Most long-haul buses arrive at the **Zentraler Omnibusbahnhof** (ZOB;

(☎030-3010 0175; www.iob-berlin.de; Masurenallee 4-6; [S]Messe/ICC Nord, [U]Kaiserdamm) near the trade fairgrounds on the western city edge. Some stop at Alexanderplatz or other points in town.

➡ The closest U-Bahn station to ZOB is Kaiserdamm, about 400m north and served by the U2 line, which travels to Zoologischer Garten in about eight minutes and to Alexanderplatz in 28 minutes. Tickets cost €2.70 (Tariff AB).

➡ The nearest S-Bahn station is Messe Süd/ICC, about 200m east of ZOB. It is served by the Ringbahn (circle line) S41/42 and handy for such districts as Prenzlauer Berg, Friedrichshain and Neukölln. You need an AB ticket (€2.70).

➡ Budget about €14 for a taxi ride to the western city centre and €22 to the eastern city centre.

Train

Berlin's **Hauptbahnhof** (Main Train Station; www.berliner-hbf.de; Europaplatz, Washingtonplatz; [S]Hauptbahnhof, [U]Hauptbahnhof) is in the heart of the city, just north of the Government Quarter and within walking distance of major sights and hotels. From here, the U-Bahn, the S-Bahn, trams and buses provide links to all parts of town. Taxi ranks are located outside the north exit (Europaplatz) and the south exit (Washingtonplatz).

➡ Buy tickets in the Reisezentrum (travel centre) located between tracks 14 and 15 on the first upper level (OG1), online at www.bahn.de or, for shorter distances, at station vending machines.

➡ The left-luggage office (€5 per piece, per 24 hours) is behind the Reisebank currency exchange on level OG1, opposite the Reisezentrum.

GETTING AROUND BERLIN

Berlin's extensive and efficient public transport system is operated by BVG (www.bvg.de) and consists of the U-Bahn (underground, or subway), the S-Bahn (light rail), buses and trams. For trip planning and general information, call the 24-hour hotline (☎030-194 49) or check the website.

The U-Bahn is usually the most efficient way of getting around town. The S-Bahn comes in handy for covering longer distances, while buses, trams and bicycles are useful for shorter journeys.

U-Bahn

➡ Lines (referred to as U1, U2 etc) operate from 4am until about 12.30am and throughout the night on Friday, Saturday and public holidays (all lines except the U4 and U55). From Sunday to Thursday, night buses take over in the interim.

➡ Individual listings in this guide indicate the closest station.

S-Bahn & Regional Trains

➡ S-Bahn trains (S1, S2 etc) don't run as frequently as the U-Bahn, but they make fewer stops and are thus useful for covering longer distances. Trains operate from 4am to 12.30am and all night on Friday, Saturday and public holidays.

➡ Individual listings indicate the closest station.

➡ Destinations further afield are served by RB and RE trains. You'll need an ABC or **Deutsche Bahn** (☎01806 99 66 33; www.bahn.de) ticket to use these trains.

Bus

➡ Buses are slow but useful for sightseeing on the cheap (especially routes 100 and 200). They run frequently between 4.30am and 12.30am. Night buses (N19, N23 etc) take over after 12.30am.

➡ MetroBuses, designated M19, M41 etc, operate 24/7.

➡ Tickets bought from bus drivers don't need to be validated.

Tram

➡ Trams *(Strassenbahn)* operate almost exclusively in the eastern districts.

➡ Those designated M1, M2 etc run 24/7.

➡ A useful line is the M1, which links Prenzlauer Berg with Museum Island via Hackescher Markt.

➡ Individual listings mention the nearest tram stop.

Taxi

➡ You can order a **taxi** (☎030-443 311, 030-202 020; www.taxi-in-berlin.de) by phone, flag one down or pick one up at a rank. At night, cars often line up outside theatres, clubs and other venues.

➡ Flag fall is €3.90, then it's €2 per kilometre up to 7km and €1.50 for each additional kilometre. There's a surcharge of €1.50 if paying by credit or debit card, but none for night trips. Bulky luggage that does not fit into the boot is charged at €1 per piece.

➡ Tip about 10%.

➡ Some sample fares include: Alexander Platz to Zoologischer Garten €18; East Side Gallery to Brandenburger Tor €16; Jüdisches Museum to Hackescher Markt €11; Kollwitzplatz to Gendarmenmarkt €13.

TRAVEL FARES & PASSES

➡ If you're taking more than two trips in a day, a day pass (*Tageskarte*) will save you money. It's valid for unlimited rides on all forms of public transport until 3am the following day. The group day pass (*Kleingruppen-Tageskarte*) is valid for up to five people travelling together.

➡ For short trips, buy the *Kurzstreckenticket*, which is good for three stops on the U-Bahn or S-Bahn, or six stops on any bus or tram; no changes allowed.

➡ For longer stays, consider the seven-day pass (*Wochenkarte*), which is transferable and lets you take along another adult and up to three children aged six to 14 for free after 8pm Monday to Friday and all day on Saturday, Sunday and holidays.

TICKET TYPE	AB (€)	BC (€)	ABC (€)
Einzelfahrschein (single)	2.70	3	3.30
Ermässigt (reduced single)	1.70	2.10	2.40
Tageskarte (day pass)	7	7.30	7.60
Kleingruppen-Tageskarte (group day pass)	17.30	17.60	17.80
Wochenkarte (7-day pass)	30	31.10	37.20

Bicycle

➡ Bicycles are handy both for in-depth explorations of local neighbourhoods and for getting across town. More than 650km of dedicated bike paths make getting around less intimidating even for riders who are not experienced or confident.

➡ Having said that, always be aware of dangers caused by aggressive or inattentive drivers. Watch out for car doors opening and for cars turning right in front of you at intersections. Getting caught in tram tracks is another problem.

➡ Bicycles may be taken aboard designated U-Bahn and S-Bahn carriages (look for the bicycle logo) as well as on night buses (Sunday to Thursday only) and trams. You need a separate bicycle ticket called a *Fahrradkarte* (€1.90). Taking a bike on regional trains (RE, RB) costs €3.30 per trip or €6 per day.

➡ The websites www.bbbike.de and www.vmz-info.de are handy for route planning.

Hire

Many hostels and hotels have guest bicycles, often for free or a nominal fee, and rental stations are at practically every corner. These include not only the expected locations (bike shops, gas stations) but also convenience stores, cafes and even clothing boutiques.

Prices start at €6 per day, although the definition of 'day' can mean anything from eight hours to 24 hours. A cash or credit-card deposit and/or photo ID is usually required.

The following outfits are recommended. Call or check the website for branches and be sure to book ahead, especially in summer.

Fahrradstation (☏0180 510 8000; www.fahrradstation. com; bike rentals from per day/week €15/49) Large fleet of quality bikes, English-speaking staff and seven branches across Mitte, Kreuzberg, Charlottenburg, Prenzlauer Berg and Potsdam. Bike rentals start at €15 per day or €49 per week. The Friedrichstrasse branch rents e-bikes. Offers online bookings.

Prenzlberger Orange Bikes (Map p306;☏030-4435 6852; www.orange-bikes.de; Kollwitzstrasse 37; per 24hr €7; ☉noon-6pm Apr-Nov; Ⓤ Senefelderplatz) The cheapest bike rentals in town with proceeds going to social projects for kids and youth.

Lila Bike (Map p306;☏0176 9957 9089; www.berlin-city tours-by-bike.de; Schönhauser Allee 41; 1st 24hr €8, additional 24hr €5; ☉10am-8pm Mon-Sat, 1-8pm Sun Apr-Oct, to 6pm Nov-Mar; ⓶M1, 12, Ⓤ Eberswalder Strasse) Small outfit in Prenzlauer Berg with quality bikes and great prices.

Car & Motorcycle

Driving in Berlin is more hassle than it's worth, especially since parking is expensive and difficult to find. If you're bringing in your own car, be aware that central Berlin (defined as the area bounded by the S-Bahn circle line) is a restricted low-emission zone, meaning that all cars entering (yes, even foreign ones) must display a special green sticker called an *Umweltplakette*, available only for eligible, low-emission cars (which includes pretty much all modern cars). Drivers caught without one will be fined €80. Buy one online in advance (eg at www.green-zones.eu). Once in Germany, stickers are available from designated repair centres, car dealers and vehicle-licensing offices. The introduction of an even more restrictive 'blue' sticker (called a *Stickoxid-Plakette*, nitric oxide sticker) is expected for early 2017.

Hire

➔ All the big internationals maintain branches at the airports, major train stations and throughout town. Book in advance for the best rates.

➔ Taking your rental vehicle into an Eastern European country, such as the Czech Republic or Poland, is often a no-no; check in advance if you're planning a side trip from Berlin.

TOURS

Walking Tours

Several English-language walking tour companies run introductory spins that take in both blockbuster and offbeat sights, plus themed tours(eg Third Reich, Cold War, Sachsenhausen). Tours don't require reservations - just show up at one of the meeting points. Check the websites for the latest timings and locations.

Alternative Berlin Tours (☑0162 819 8264; www.alternativeberlin.com; tours €10-20) Not your run-of-the-mill tour company, this outfit

runs tip-based subculture tours that get beneath the skin of the city, plus an excellent street-art tour and workshop, an alternative pub crawl, a craft beer tour, the surreal 'Twilight Tour', an eco-tour, and a food and drink tour.

Original Berlin Walks (☑030-301 9194; www.berlinwalks.de; adult/concession from €14/12) Berlin's longest-running English-language walking tour company has a large roster of general and themed tours (eg Hitler's Germany, Jewish Life, Berlin Wall), as well as trips out to Sachsenhausen concentration camp, Potsdam and Wittenberg. The website has details on timings and meeting points.

Brewer's Berlin Tours (☑0177 388 1537; www.brewersberlintours.com; adult/concession €15/12) Local experts run an epic six-hour Best of Berlin tour (€15) and a shorter donation-based Berlin Free Tour, as well as a Craft Beer & Breweries tour with tastings (€35), a Spies & Escapes tour (€12) and an excursion to Potsdam (May to October). Details and booking online.

Insider Tour Berlin (☑030-692 3149; www.insidertour.com; adult/concession €14/12) Insightful general and themed tours of Berlin (eg Cold

War, Third Reich, Jewish Berlin), plus a pub crawl, six-hour trips to Sachsenhausen concentration camp and Potsdam (€17), and day trips to Dresden (€49). No prebooking required. Check the website for timings and meeting points.

New Berlin Tours (www.newberlintours.com; adult/concession from €12/10; ☺free tour 10am, 11am, 2pm & 4pm) Entertaining and informative city spins by the pioneers of the donation-based 'free tour' and the pub crawl (€12). Also offers tours to Sachsenhausen concentration camp, themed tours (Red Berlin, Third Reich, Alternative Berlin) and a trip to Potsdam. Check the website for timings, prices and meeting points.

Bicycle Tours

Fat Tire Tours Berlin (Map p300; ☑030-2404 7991; www.fattiretours.com/berlin; Panoramastrasse 1a; adult/concession/under 12 incl bicycle from €28/26/14; Ⓢ Alexanderplatz, Ⓤ Alexanderplatz) This top-rated outfit runs English-language tours by bike, e-bike and Segway. Options include a classic city spin; tours with a focus on Nazi Germany, the Cold War or 'Modern Berlin'; a trip to Potsdam; and an evening food tour. Tours leave from the TV Tower main entrance. Reservations advised.

Berlin on Bike (Map p306; ☑030-4373 9999; www.berlinonbike.de; Knaackstrasse 97, Kulturbrauerei, Court 4; tours incl bike adult/concession €21/18; ☺8am-8pm mid-Mar–mid-Nov, 10am-4pm Mon-Sat mid-Nov–mid-Mar; ⒨M1, Ⓤ Eberswalder Strasse) This well-established company has a busy schedule of insightful and fun bike tours led by locals. There are daily English-language city tours

CALL A BIKE

Call a Bike (☑069-4272 7722; www.callabike.de; annual membership €3, plus per 30min/24hr €1/15) is an automated cycle-hire scheme offered by Deutsche Bahn (German Rail). In order to use it, you need a credit card to preregister, for free, online or at one of the dozens of docking stations scattered around the central districts. The website has a map but, alas, it is in German only at this point. Machines at the docking stations, though, have English instructions.

Short-term visitors should select the *Basis-Tarif* (basic tariff), which costs €3 for annual membership plus €1 for each 30 minutes or €15 per 24 hours. Fees are charged to your credit card.

(Berlin's Best) and Berlin Wall tours as well as an Alternative Berlin tour three times weekly. Other tours (eg street art, night tours) run in German or in English on request.
New in 2016: the fun Bike 'n' Bite tour for foodies. Reservations recommended for all tours. Also rents bicycles for €10 per 24 hours.

Boat Tours

Stern und Kreisschiffahrt (☎030-536 3600; www.sternundkreis.de; 🕒Mar-Dec) A lovely way to experience Berlin on a warm day is from the deck of a boat cruising along the city's rivers, canals and lakes. Tours range from one-hour spins around the historic centre (from €14) to longer trips to Schloss Charlottenburg and beyond (from €15.50). Commentary is provided in eight languages by GPS-linked audioguide.

Bus Tours

You'll see them everywhere around town: colourful buses (in summer, often open-top double-deckers) that tick off all the key sights on two-hour loops with basic taped commentary in multiple languages. You're free to get off and back on at any of the stops during the day. Buses depart roughly every 15 to 30 minutes between 10am and 5pm or 6pm daily; tickets cost from €10 to €20 (half-price for teens, free for children). Traditional tours (where you stay on the bus), combination boat/bus tours or excursions to Potsdam are also available. Look for flyers in hotel lobbies or in tourist offices.

Speciality Tours

Berlin Music Tours (☎030-3087 5633; www.musictours-berlin.com; Bowie walk €14; 🕒Bowie walk noon-3pm Sun) Berlin's music history – Bowie to U2 and Rammstein, cult clubs to the Love Parade – comes to life during expertly guided tours run by this well-respected outfit. There is a regularly scheduled walk in Bowie's footsteps, but other options such as a multimedia bus tour, a walking tour, and U2 and Depeche Mode tours run only by request. Some even get you inside the storied Hansa Studios. English tours on request (price depends on group size).

Berliner Unterwelten (☎030-4991 0517; www.berliner-unterwelten.de; Brunnenstrasse 105; adult/concession €11/9; 🕒Dark Worlds tours in English 1pm Mon & 11am Thu-Mon year-round, 11am Wed Mar-Nov, 3pm Wed-Mon & 1pm Wed-Sun Apr-Oct; [S]Gesundbrunnen, [U]Gesundbrunnen) After you've checked off the Brandenburg Gate and the TV Tower, why not explore Berlin's dark and dank underbelly? Join Berliner Unterwelten on its 'Dark Worlds' tour of a WWII underground bunker (available in English) and pick your way through a warren of claustrophobic rooms, past heavy steel doors, hospital beds, helmets, guns, boots and lots of other wartime artefacts.

Berlinagenten (☎030-4372 0701; www.berlinagenten.com; tours from €200) Get a handle on all facets of Berlin's urban lifestyle with an insider private guide who opens doors to hot and/or secret bars, boutiques, restaurants, clubs, private homes and sights. Dozens of culinary, cultural and lifestyle tours on offer, including the best-selling 'Gastro Rallye' for the ultimate foodie. Prices depend on group size.

Trabi Safari (Map p296; ☎030-3020 1030; www.trabi-safari.de; Zimmerstrasse 97; per person from €39; 🕒daily; [U]Kochstrasse) Catch the *Good Bye, Lenin!* vibe on tours of Berlin with you driving or riding as a passenger in a convoy of GDR-made Trabant cars (Trabi) or classic American Mustangs with live commentary (in English by prior arrangement) piped into your vehicle. Options include tours of eastern Berlin or western Berlin, or with Berlin Wall–related stops. Drivers need to bring their licence and a valid credit card. Children under 15 ride for free.

videoSightseeing (Map p296; www.videosightseeing.de; bus tour €15-25, walking tour €25, 4-person minimum; 🚌100, 200, [U]Friedrichstrasse) For more insightful sightseeing, join one of these multimedia bus and walking tours that use historical footage, photographs, documents, animations, movie clips and other visuals to bring history into the present. There are four themed public bus tours (Historical Berlin, Movie City Berlin, Famous Crime Scenes and Culinary Berlin), so far with live narration in German only. The new walking tours with iPad are also in English.

Directory A–Z

Customs Regulations

➡ Goods brought in and out of countries within the EU incur no additional taxes provided duty has been paid somewhere within the EU and the goods are only for personal use.

➡ Duty-free shopping is only available if you're leaving the EU.

Discount Cards

Berlin Welcome Card
(travel in AB zones 48/72 hours €19.50/27.50, travel in ABC zones 48/72 hours €21.50/29.50, AB zones 72 hours plus admission to Museumsinsel €42 or €44 for ABC zones. Valid for unlimited public transport for one adult and up to three children under 14; up to 50% discount to 200 sights, attractions and tours; available for up to six days. Sold online, at the tourist offices, from U-Bahn and S-Bahn station ticket vending machines, on buses and at BVG sales points. Details www.berlin-welcomecard.de.

CityTourCard (travel in AB zone 48 hours/72 hours/five days €17.50/25.50/33.50, ABC zone €19.50/26.50/38.50) Operates on a similar scheme as the Berlin Welcome Card; it's a bit cheaper, but offers fewer discounts. Available for up to six days from tourist offices, bus drivers and U-Bahn and S-Bahn vending machines.

Museumspass Berlin (adult/concession €24/12) Buys admission to the permanent exhibits of about 50 museums for three consecutive days, including big draws like the Pergamon-museum. Sold at tourist offices and participating museums.

Electricity

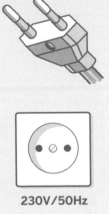

230V/50Hz

IMPORT RESTRICTIONS

ITEM	DUTY-FREE	TAX & DUTY PAID WITHIN EU
beer & wine	16L beer, 4L wine	110L beer, 90L wine (with no more than 60L sparkling wine)
tobacco	200 cigarettes or 100 cigarillos or 50 cigars or 250g tobacco or a combination thereof	800 cigarettes or 400 cigarillos or 200 cigars or 1kg tobacco
spirits & liqueurs	1L spirits or 2L fortified wine	10L spirits or 20L fortified wine
other goods	up to a value of €300 if arriving by land or €430 if arriving by sea or air (€175 for those under 15yr)	n/a

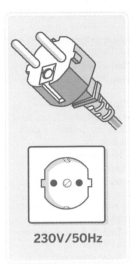

230V/50Hz

Emergency

➜ **Ambulance** (☑112)
➜ **Fire Department** (☑112)
➜ **Police** (☑110)

Internet Access

➜ Since June 2016 'Project Wi-Fi Berlin' has provided free public wi-fi – the 100 access points at launch time are expected to grow to 650 by 2017. Locations include public squares, landmarks like the Brandenburger Tor, libraries and town halls. Check www.audible.de/free wifiberlin for the full list.

➜ Most hotels and hostels now provide free wi-fi access (W-LAN in Germany; pronounced vay-lan) or an internet corner for their guests (those that do are identified with a wi-fi icon 🛜 in our listings).

➜ Many cafes, bars, and even bakeries and boutiques, have free wi-fi hot spots, although you usually need to ask for a password. In our listings, such places are identified with a wi-fi icon.

➜ Note that in some proper-ties (free) wi-fi may be limited to some rooms and/or public areas, so if you need in-room access, be sure to specify at the time of booking.

➜ A few hotels (usually top-end and business hotels) charge as much as €25 per day for wi-fi access.

➜ Internet cafes tend to have the lifespan of a fruit fly, so we have not listed any. If you need one, ask at your hotel.

Legal Matters

➜ By law you must possess some form of photographic identification, such as your passport, national identity card or driving licence.

➜ The permissible blood-alcohol limit is 0.05% for drivers and 0.16% for cyclists. Anyone caught exceeding this amount is subject to stiff fines, a confiscated licence or even jail time. Drinking in public is not illegal, but be discreet about it.

➜ Cannabis *consumption* is not illegal, but its possession, acquisition, sale and cultivation is considered a criminal offence. There is usually no persecution for possession of 'small quantities' (defined as up to 10g in Berlin). Dealers face much stiffer penalties, as do people caught with any other recreational drugs. Searches upon entering clubs are common.

➜ If arrested, you have the right to make a phone call and are presumed innocent until proven guilty, although you may be held in custody until trial. If you don't know a lawyer, contact your embassy.

Medical Services

➜ High-level health care is available from a *Rettungsstelle* (emergency department) at a *Krankenhaus* (hospital) or from an *Arztpraxis* (doctor's office). Most doctors speak at least some English, especially in the hospitals.

➜ The most central hospital with a 24-hour emergency room is the renowned **Charité Mitte** (☑030-450 50; www. charite.de; emergency room Luisenstrasse 65,; ⊙24hr; 🚌147, ⓤOranienburger Tor).

➜ For minor illnesses (headache, bruises, diarrhoea), pharmacists can provide advice, sell over-the-counter medications and make doctors' referrals if further help is needed.

➜ Condoms are widely available in drugstores, pharmacies and supermarkets. Birth control pills require a doctor's prescription.

Pharmacies

➜ German chemists (drugstores, *Drogerien*) do not sell any kind of medication, not even aspirin. Even over-the-counter *(rezeptfrei)* medications for minor health concerns, such as a cold or upset stomach, are only available at a pharmacy *(Apotheke)*.

➜ For more serious conditions, you will need to produce a prescription *(Rezept)* from a licensed physician. If you take regular medication, be sure to bring a full supply for your entire trip, as the same brand may not be available in Germany.

➜ The names and addresses of pharmacies open after hours (these rotate) are posted in every pharmacy window, or call ☑011 41 for a recorded message of after-hour pharmacies.

Money
ATMs & Debit Cards

➜ The easiest and quickest way to obtain cash is by using your debit (bank) card at an ATM *(Geldautomat)* linked to international networks such as Cirrus, Plus, Star and Maestro.

PRACTICALITIES

→ **Clothing** For women's clothing sizes, a German size 36 equals a size 6 in the US and a size 10 in the UK, then increases in increments of two, making size 38 a US 8 and UK 12, and so on.

→ **Laundry** There are dry cleaners (*Reinigung*) and self-service laundrettes (*Waschsalon*) scattered all over Berlin. Most hostels have washing machines for guest use, while hotels offer a cleaning service as well, although this is quite pricey.

→ **DVD** Germany is in region code 2.

→ **Newspapers** Widely read local dailies include *Tagess-piegel, Berliner Zeitung, Berliner Morgenpost* and *taz*.

→ **Magazines** *Zitty* and *Tip* are the main listings magazines for Berlin. *Siegessäule* is a freebie for the LGBTIQ community.

ATMs are ubiquitous and accessible 24/7.

→ Be wary of ATMs not affiliated with major banks as they may charge exorbitant transaction fees. ATMs do not recognise pins with more than four digits.

→ Since many ATM cards double as debit cards, they can often be used for payment in shops, hotels, restaurants and other businesses, especially MasterCard and Visa cards.

→ Most places use the 'chip and pin' system: instead of signing, you enter your PIN. If your card isn't chip-and-pin enabled, you may be able to sign the receipt, but not always – ask first.

Cash

Cash is king in Germany, so always carry some with you and plan to pay in cash in most places. It's a good idea to set aside a small amount of euros as an emergency stash.

Changing Money

Currency exchange offices (*Wechselstuben*) can be found at airports and major train stations. They usually have better hours and charge lower fees than commercial banks.

Some convenient offices include:

→ **Reisebank** (www.reisebank. de) Zoologischer Garten, Hauptbahnhof, Ostbahnhof and Bahnhof Friedrichstrasse.

→ **Euro-Change** (www.euro -change.de) Zoologischer Garten and Alexanderplatz stations; Friedrichstrasse 80.

Reisebank keeps slightly longer hours (at least until 8pm); on Sundays, the airports are your only option.

Credit Cards

→ Credit cards are becoming more widely accepted (especially in hotels and upmarket shops and restaurants), but it's best not to assume that you'll be able to use one – enquire first.

→ Visa and MasterCard are more commonly accepted than American Express and Diner's Club.

→ Some places require a minimum purchase with credit card use.

→ Cash advances on credit cards via ATMs usually incur steep fees – check with your card issuer.

→ Report lost or stolen cards to the central number 🗐116 116 or to the following:

American Express 🗐069-9797 1000
MasterCard 🗐0800-819 1040
Visa 🗐0800-814 9100

Tipping

→ **Hotels** Room cleaners €1 to €2 per day, porters the same per bag.

→ **Restaurants** For good service 5% to 10%.

→ **Bars/Pubs** 5% to 10% for table service, rounded to the nearest euro, no tip for self-service.

→ **Taxis** 10%, always rounding to a full euro.

→ **Toilet attendants** €0.50.

It's considered rude to leave the tip on the table. Instead, tell the server the total amount you want to pay. If you don't want change back, say '*Stimmt so*' (that's fine).

Opening Hours

The following are typical opening hours, although these may vary seasonally and by location (city centre or the suburbs).

Banks 9.30am–6pm Monday to Friday, some to 1pm Saturday

Bars 7pm–1am or later

Boutiques 11am–7pm Monday to Friday, to 4pm Saturday

Cafes 8am–8pm

Clubs 11pm–5am or later

Post Offices 9am–6pm Monday to Friday, to 1pm Saturday

Restaurants 11am–11pm

Shops 10am–8pm Monday to Saturday

Supermarkets 8am–8pm or later; some 24 hours

Post

→ You can buy stamps at post

offices and at convenience stores offering postal services. The rate for standard-sized letters up to 20g is €0.70 to destinations within Germany and €0.90 elsewhere in the world. For other rates, see www.deutschepost.de.

➡ Mail takes a day or two within Germany, two or three within Europe, and three or four to the USA and Australia.

➡ Central post office branches with late hours can be found in **Charlottenburg** (Map p316; Tauentzienstrasse 9, Europa Presse Center; ⏰7.30am-10.30pm; 🚌100, 200, Ⓢ Zoologischer Garten, Ⓤ Zoologischer Garten) and near **Alexanderplatz** (Map p300; Grunerstrasse 20; ⏰8am-9pm Mon-Sat; Ⓢ Alexanderplatz, Ⓤ Alexanderplatz).

Public Holidays

Shops, banks and public and private offices are closed on the following *gesetzliche Feiertage* (public holidays):

Neujahrstag (New Year's Day) 1 January

Ostern (Easter) March/April; Good Friday, Easter Sunday and Easter Monday

Christi Himmelfahrt (Ascension Day) Forty days after Easter, always on a Thursday

Maifeiertag (Labour Day) 1 May

Pfingsten (Whitsun/Pentecost Sunday and Monday) May/June

Tag der Deutschen Einheit (Day of German Unity) 3 October

Reformationstag (Reformation Day; Brandenburg state only) 31 October

Weihnachtstag (Christmas Day) 25 December

Zweiter Weihnachtstag (Boxing Day) 26 December

Taxes & Refunds

Value-added tax (VAT, *Mehrwertsteuer*) is a 19% sales tax levied on most goods. The rate for food, books and services is usually 7%. VAT is always included in the price. If your permanent residence is outside the EU, you may be able to partially claim back the VAT you paid on purchased goods.

Telephone

Mobile Phones

➡ Mobile phones (*Handys*) work on GSM900/1800. If your home country uses a different standard, you'll need a multiband GSM phone in Germany. Check your contract for roaming charges.

➡ If you have an unlocked phone that works in Germany, you should be able to cut down on roaming charges by buying a prepaid, rechargeable local SIM card. These are sold at supermarkets, pharmacies, convenience stores and electronics shops and can be topped up as needed.

➡ Calls made from landlines to German mobile phone numbers are charged at higher rates than those to other landlines. Incoming calls on mobile numbers are free.

Phone Codes

German phone numbers consist of an area code, starting with 0, and the local number. The area code for Berlin is ☎030. When dialling a Berlin number from a Berlin-based landline, you don't need to dial the area code. When you're using a landline outside Berlin, or a mobile phone, you must dial it.

German mobile numbers begin with a four-digit prefix such ☎0151, ☎0157 or ☎0173.

Calling Berlin from abroad Dial your country's international access code, then ☎49 (Germany's country code), then the area code (dropping the initial 0, so just ☎30) and the local number.

Calling internationally from Berlin Dial ☎00 (the international access code), then the country code, the area code (without the zero if there is one) and the local number.

Phonecards

➡ In the smartphone age, public payphones are going the way of the dinosaurs. Existing ones only work with Deutsche Telecom (DT) phonecards, available in denominations of €5, €10 and €20 from DT shops, post offices, newsagents and tourist offices.

SMOKING REGULATIONS

➡ Except in designated areas, smoking (including e-cigarettes) is not allowed in public buildings or at airports and train stations.

➡ Smoking is not allowed in restaurants and clubs unless there is a completely separate and enclosed room set aside for smokers.

➡ Owners of single-room bars and pubs smaller than 75 sq metres, who don't serve anything to eat and keep out customers under 18 years of age, may choose to be a '*Raucherbar*', ie allow smoking. The venue must be clearly designated as such.

➡ *Shisha* bars may operate as long as no alcohol is available and no one under 18 is allowed in.

➡ The minimum age for purchasing tobacco products or e-cigarettes is 18.

→ For long-distance and international calls, prepaid calling cards issued by other providers tend to offer better rates, but check for per-call connection fees.

Time

Clocks in Germany are set to central European time (GMT/UTC plus one hour). Daylight-savings time kicks in on the last Sunday in March and ends on the last Sunday in October. The 24-hour clock is the norm (eg 6.30pm is 18.30). As daylight-savings time differs across regions, the following times are indicative only:

CITY	NOON IN BERLIN
Auckland	11pm
Cape Town	1pm
London	11am
New York	6am
San Francisco	3am
Sydney	9pm
Tokyo	8pm

Toilets

→ German toilets are sit-down affairs; men are expected to sit when peeing.

→ Free-standing, 24-hour self-cleaning public toilet pods have become quite commonplace. The cost is €0.50 and you have 15 minutes to finish your business. Most are wheelchair-accessible.

→ Toilets in malls, clubs, beer gardens etc often have an attendant who expects a tip of around €0.50.

Tourist Information

Visit Berlin (www.visitberlin. de) has branches at the airports, the main train station, the Brandenburg Gate, the

TV Tower and on Kurfürstendamm, plus a **call centre** (☑030-2500 2333; ◷9am-7pm Mon-Fri, 10am-6pm Sat, 10am-2pm Sun) for information and bookings.

Travellers with Disabilities

→ Access ramps and/or lifts are available in many public buildings, including train stations, museums, concert halls and cinemas. Newer hotels have lifts and rooms with extra-wide doors and spacious bathrooms. For a databank assessing the accessibility of cafes, restaurants, hotels, theatres and other public spaces (in German), check with Mobidat (www.mobidat.de).

→ Most buses, trains and trams are wheelchair-accessible and many U-Bahn and S-Bahn stations are equipped with ramps or lifts. For trip-planning assistance, contact the BVG (☑030-194 49; www.bvg.de). Many stations also have grooved platforms to assist blind and vision-impaired passengers. Seeing-eye dogs are allowed everywhere. Hearing-impaired passengers can check upcoming station names on displays installed in all forms of public transport.

→ **Rollstuhlpannendienst** (☑0177 833 5773; www.roll stuhlpannendienst.de; ◷24hr) provides 24-hour wheelchair repairs and rentals.

→ Download Lonely Planet's free *Accessible Travel* guide from http://lptravel.to/Acces sibleTravel.

Visas

→ Unless you're an EU national or from a nation without visa requirements, you need a Schengen Visa to enter Germany. Visa applications must be filed with the embassy or consulate of the Schengen country that is your primary destination. It is valid

for stays of up to 90 days. Legal permanent residency in any Schengen country makes a visa unnecessary, regardless of your nationality.

→ EU nationals need only their national identity card or passport to enter Germany. If you intend to stay for an extended period, you must register with the authorities (Bürgeramt, or Citizens' Office) within two weeks of arrival.

→ Citizens of Australia, Canada, Israel, Japan, New Zealand, Switzerland and the US are among those who need only a valid passport (no visa) if entering as tourists for a stay of up to three months within a six-month period.

→ Passports must be valid for at least another four months beyond the planned departure date.

→ For full details and current regulations, see www.auswaertiges-amt.de or check with a German consulate in your country.

Women Travellers

→ Berlin is remarkably safe for women to explore, even solo. Simply use the same common sense you would at home.

→ Going alone to cafes and restaurants is perfectly acceptable, even at night.

→ It's quite normal to split dinner bills, even on dates.

→ In bars and nightclubs, solo women are likely to attract some attention, but if you don't want company, most men will respect a firm 'no, thank you'. Don't leave your drink unattended!

→ If assaulted, call the police (☑110). For help in dealing with the emotional and physical trauma associated with an attack, contact the **Women's Crisis Hotline** (☑030-615 4243; ◷10am-noon Mon & Thu, 3-5pm Tue, 7-9pm Wed & Fri, 5-7pm Sat & Sun).

Language

German belongs to the West Germanic language family and has around 100 million speakers. It is commonly divided into Low German (*Plattdeutsch*) and High German (*Hochdeutsch*). Low German is an umbrella term used for the dialects spoken in Northern Germany. High German is the standard form; it's also used in this chapter.

German is easy for English speakers to pronounce because almost all of its sounds are also found in English. If you read our coloured pronunciation guides as if they were English, you should be understood just fine. Note that kh sounds like the 'ch' in 'Bach' or in the Scottish 'loch' (pronounced at the back of the throat), r is also pronounced at the back of the throat, zh is pronounced as the 's' in 'measure', and ü as the 'ee' in 'see' but with rounded lips. The stressed syllables are indicated with italics in our pronunciation guides. The markers (pol) and (inf) indicate polite and informal forms.

BASICS

Hello.	*Guten Tag.*	goo·ten tahk
Goodbye.	*Auf Wiedersehen.*	owf vee·der·zay·en
Yes./No.	*Ja./Nein.*	yah/nain
Please.	*Bitte.*	bi·te
Thank you.	*Danke.*	dang·ke
You're welcome.	*Bitte.*	bi·te
Excuse me.	*Entschuldigung.*	ent·shul·di·gung
Sorry.	*Entschuldigung.*	ent·shul·di·gung

WANT MORE?

For in-depth language information and handy phrases, check out Lonely Planet's *German Phrasebook*. You'll find it at **shop. lonelyplanet.com**, or you can buy Lonely Planet's iPhone phrasebooks at the Apple App Store.

How are you?
Wie geht es Ihnen/dir? (pol/inf) — vee gayt es ee·nen/deer

Fine. And you?
Danke, gut. Und Ihnen/dir? (pol/inf) — dang·ke goot unt ee·nen/deer

What's your name?
Wie ist Ihr Name? (pol) — vee ist eer *nah*·me
Wie heißt du? (inf) — vee haist doo

My name is ...
Mein Name ist ... (pol) — main *nah*·me ist ...
Ich heiße ... (inf) — ikh *hai*·se ...

Do you speak English?
Sprechen Sie Englisch? (pol) — *shpre*·khen zee *eng*·lish
Sprichst du Englisch? (inf) — *shprikhst* doo *eng*·lish

I don't understand.
Ich verstehe nicht. — ikh fer·*shtay*·e nikht

ACCOMMODATION

guesthouse	*Pension*	pahng·*zyawn*
hotel	*Hotel*	ho·*tel*
inn	*Gasthof*	gast·hawf
youth hostel	*Jugend-herberge*	*yoo*·gent·her·ber·ge

Do you have a ... room?	*Haben Sie ein ...?*	hah·ben zee ain ...
double	*Doppelzimmer*	do·pel·tsi·mer
single	*Einzelzimmer*	ain·tsel·tsi·mer

How much is it per ...?	*Wie viel kostet es pro ...?*	vee feel *kos*·tet es praw ...
night	*Nacht*	nakht
person	*Person*	per·*zawn*

Is breakfast included?
Ist das Frühstück inklusive? — ist das frü·*shtük* in·kloo·*zee*·ve

DIRECTIONS

Where's ...?
Wo ist ...? — vaw ist ...

What's the address?
Wie ist die Adresse? — vee ist dee a·dre·se

How far is it?
Wie weit ist es? — vee vait ist es

Can you show me (on the map)?
Können Sie es mir — ker·nen zee es meer
(auf der Karte) zeigen? — (owf dair kar·te) tsai·gen

How can I get there?
Wie kann ich da — vee kan ikh dah
hinkommen? — hin·ko·men

Turn ...	*Biegen Sie ... ab.*	bee·gen zee ... ab
at the corner	*an der Ecke*	an dair e·ke
at the traffic lights	*bei der Ampel*	bai dair am·pel
left	*links*	lingks
right	*rechts*	rekhts

EATING & DRINKING

I'd like to reserve a table for ...
Ich möchte einen Tisch für ... reservieren. — ikh merkh·te ai·nen tish für ... re·zer·vee·ren

| **(eight) o'clock** | *(acht) Uhr* | (akht) oor |
| **(two) people** | *(zwei) Personen* | (tsvai) per·zaw·nen |

I'd like the menu, please.
Ich hätte gern die Speisekarte, bitte. — ikh he·te gern dee shpai·ze·kar·te bi·te

What would you recommend?
Was empfehlen Sie? — vas emp·fay·len zee

What's in that dish?
Was ist in diesem Gericht? — vas ist in dee·zem ge·rikht

I'm a vegetarian.
Ich bin Vegetarier/ Vegetarierin. (m/f) — ikh bin ve·ge·tah·ri·er/ ve·ge·tah·ri·e·rin

That was delicious.
Das hat hervorragend geschmeckt. — das hat her·fawr·rah·gent ge·shmekt

Cheers!
Prost! — prawst

Please bring the bill.
Bitte bringen Sie die Rechnung. — bi·te bring·en zee dee rekh·nung

Key Words

| **bar (pub)** | *Kneipe* | knai·pe |
| **bottle** | *Flasche* | fla·she |

To get by in German, mix and match these simple patterns with words of your choice:

When's (the next flight)?
Wann ist (der nächste Flug)? — van ist (dair naykhs·te flook)

Where's (the station)?
Wo ist (der Bahnhof)? — vaw ist (dair bahn·hawf)

Where can I (buy a ticket)?
Wo kann ich (eine Fahrkarte kaufen)? — vaw kan ikh (ai·ne fahr·kar·te kow·fen)

Do you have (a map)?
Haben Sie (eine Karte)? — hah·ben zee (ai·ne kar·te)

Is there (a toilet)?
Gibt es (eine Toilette)? — gipt es (ai·ne to·a·le·te)

I'd like (a coffee).
Ich möchte (einen Kaffee). — ikh merkh·te (ai·nen ka·fay)

I'd like (to hire a car).
Ich möchte (ein Auto mieten). — ikh merkh·te (ain ow·to mee·ten)

Can I (enter)?
Darf ich (hereinkommen)? — darf ikh (her·ein·ko·men)

Could you please (help me)?
Könnten Sie (mir helfen)? — kern·ten zee (meer hel·fen)

Do I have to (book a seat)?
Muss ich (einen Platz reservieren lassen)? — mus ikh (ai·nen plats re·zer·vee·ren la·sen)

bowl	*Schüssel*	shü·sel
breakfast	*Frühstück*	frü·shtük
cold	*kalt*	kalt
cup	*Tasse*	ta·se
daily special	*Gericht des Tages*	ge·rikht des tah·ges
delicatessen	*Feinkost- geschäft*	fain·kost· ge·sheft
desserts	*Nachspeisen*	nahkh·shpai·zen
dinner	*Abendessen*	ah·bent·e·sen
drink list	*Getränke- karte*	ge·treng·ke· kar·te
fork	*Gabel*	gah·bel
glass	*Glas*	glahs
grocery store	*Lebensmittel- laden*	lay·bens·mi·tel· lah·den
hot (warm)	*warm*	warm
knife	*Messer*	me·ser

lunch	Mittagessen	mi·tahk·e·sen
market	Markt	markt
plate	Teller	te·ler
restaurant	Restaurant	res·to·rahng
set menu	Menü	may·nü
spicy	würzig	vür·tsikh
spoon	Löffel	ler·fel
with/without	mit/ohne	mit/aw·ne

Meat & Fish

beef	Rindfleisch	rint·flaish
carp	Karpfen	karp·fen
fish	Fisch	fish
herring	Hering	hay·ring
lamb	Lammfleisch	lam·flaish
meat	Fleisch	flaish
pork	Schweinefleisch	shvai·ne·flaish
poultry	Geflügelfleisch	ge·flü·gel·flaish
salmon	Lachs	laks
sausage	Wurst	vurst
seafood	Meeresfrüchte	mair·res·frükh·te
shellfish	Schaltiere	shahl·tee·re
trout	Forelle	fo·re·le
veal	Kalbfleisch	kalp·flaish

Fruit & Vegetables

apple	Apfel	ap·fel
banana	Banane	ba·nah·ne
bean	Bohne	baw·ne
cabbage	Kraut	krowt
capsicum	Paprika	pap·ri·kah
carrot	Mohrrübe	mawr·rü·be
cucumber	Gurke	gur·ke
fruit	Frucht/Obst	frukht/awpst
grapes	Weintrauben	vain·trow·ben
lemon	Zitrone	tsi·traw·ne
lentil	Linse	lin·ze
lettuce	Kopfsalat	kopf·za·laht
mushroom	Pilz	pilts
nuts	Nüsse	nü·se
onion	Zwiebel	tsvee·bel
orange	Orange	o·rahng·zhe
pea	Erbse	erp·se
plum	Pflaume	pflow·me
potato	Kartoffel	kar·to·fel
spinach	Spinat	shpi·naht

strawberry	Erdbeere	ert·bair·re
tomato	Tomate	to·mah·te
vegetable	Gemüse	ge·mü·ze
watermelon	Wasser-melone	va·ser·me·law·ne

Other

bread	Brot	brawt
butter	Butter	bu·ter
cheese	Käse	kay·ze
egg/eggs	Ei/Eier	ai/ai·er
honey	Honig	haw·nikh
jam	Marmelade	mar·me·lah·de
pasta	Nudeln	noo·deln
pepper	Pfeffer	pfe·fer
rice	Reis	rais
salt	Salz	zalts
soup	Suppe	zu·pe
sugar	Zucker	tsu·ker

Drinks

beer	Bier	beer
coffee	Kaffee	ka·fay
juice	Saft	zaft
milk	Milch	milkh
orange juice	Orangensaft	o·rang·zhen·zaft
red wine	Rotwein	rawt·vain
sparkling wine	Sekt	zekt
tea	Tee	tay
water	Wasser	va·ser
white wine	Weißwein	vais·vain

EMERGENCIES

| Help! | Hilfe! | hil·fe |

SIGNS

Ausgang	Exit
Damen	Women
Eingang	Entrance
Geschlossen	Closed
Herren	Men
Toiletten (WC)	Toilets
Offen	Open
Verboten	Prohibited

Go away!	Gehen Sie weg!	gay·en zee vek
Call the police!		
Rufen Sie die Polizei!		roo·fen zee dee po·li·tsai
Call a doctor!		
Rufen Sie einen Arzt!		roo·fen zee ai·nen artst
Where are the toilets?		
Wo ist die Toilette?		vo ist dee to·a·le·te
I'm lost.		
Ich habe mich verirrt.		ikh hah·be mikh fer·irt
I'm sick.		
Ich bin krank.		ikh bin krangk
It hurts here.		
Es tut hier weh.		es toot heer vay
I'm allergic to ...		
Ich bin allergisch		ikh bin a·lair·gish
gegen ...		gay·gen ...

SHOPPING & SERVICES

I'd like to buy ...		
Ich möchte ... kaufen.		ikh merkh·te ... kow·fen
I'm just looking.		
Ich schaue mich nur um.		ikh show·e mikh noor um
Can I look at it?		
Können Sie es mir		ker·nen zee es meer
zeigen?		tsai·gen
How much is this?		
Wie viel kostet das?		vee feel kos·tet das
That's too expensive.		
Das ist zu teuer.		das ist tsoo toy·er
Can you lower the price?		
Können Sie mit dem		ker·nen zee mit dem
Preis heruntergehen?		prais he·run·ter·gay·en
There's a mistake in the bill.		
Da ist ein Fehler		dah ist ain fay·ler
in der Rechnung.		in dair rekh·nung

ATM	Geldautomat	gelt·ow·to·maht
post office	Postamt	post·amt
tourist office	Fremdenverkehrsbüro	frem·den·fer·kairs·bü·raw

TIME & DATES

What time is it?		
Wie spät ist es?		vee shpayt ist es
It's (10) o'clock.		
Es ist (zehn) Uhr.		es ist (tsayn) oor

QUESTION WORDS

What?	Was?	vas
When?	Wann?	van
Where?	Wo?	vaw
Who?	Wer?	vair
Why?	Warum?	va·rum

At what time?		
Um wie viel Uhr?		um vee feel oor
At ...		
Um ...		um ...

morning	Morgen	mor·gen
afternoon	Nachmittag	nahkh·mi·tahk
evening	Abend	ah·bent
yesterday	gestern	ges·tern
today	heute	hoy·te
tomorrow	morgen	mor·gen
Monday	Montag	mawn·tahk
Tuesday	Dienstag	deens·tahk
Wednesday	Mittwoch	mit·vokh
Thursday	Donnerstag	do·ners·tahk
Friday	Freitag	frai·tahk
Saturday	Samstag	zams·tahk
Sunday	Sonntag	zon·tahk
January	Januar	yan·u·ahr
February	Februar	fay·bru·ahr
March	März	merts
April	April	a·pril
May	Mai	mai
June	Juni	yoo·ni
July	Juli	yoo·li
August	August	ow·gust
September	September	zep·tem·ber
October	Oktober	ok·taw·ber
November	November	no·vem·ber
December	Dezember	de·tsem·ber

TRANSPORT

Public Transport

boat	Boot	bawt
bus	Bus	bus
metro	U-Bahn	oo·bahn
plane	Flugzeug	flook·tsoyk
train	Zug	tsook

At what time's the ... bus?	Wann fährt der ... Bus?	van fairt dair... bus
first	erste	ers·te
last	letzte	lets·te
next	nächste	naykhs·te

NUMBERS

1	eins	ains
2	zwei	tsvai
3	drei	drai
4	vier	feer
5	fünf	fünf
6	sechs	zeks
7	sieben	zee·ben
8	acht	akht
9	neun	noyn
10	zehn	tsayn
20	zwanzig	tsvan·tsikh
30	dreißig	drai·tsikh
40	vierzig	feer·tsikh
50	fünfzig	fünf·tsikh
60	sechzig	zekh·tsikh
70	siebzig	zeep·tsikh
80	achtzig	akht·tsikh
90	neunzig	noyn·tsikh
100	hundert	hun·dert
1000	tausend	tow·sent

A ... to (Cologne).	*Eine ... nach (Köln).*	ai·ne ... nahkh (kerln)
1st-/2nd-class ticket	*Fahrkarte erster/zweiter Klasse*	fahr·kar·te ers·ter/tsvai·ter kla·se
one-way ticket	*einfache Fahrkarte*	ain·fa·khe fahr·kar·te
return ticket	*Rückfahrkarte*	rük·fahr·kar·te

At what time does it arrive?
Wann kommt es an? — van komt es an

Is it a direct route?
Ist es eine direkte Verbindung? — ist es ai·ne di·rek·te fer·bin·dung

Does it stop at ...?
Hält es in ...? — helt es in ...

What station is this?
Welcher Bahnhof ist das? — vel·kher bahn·hawf ist das

What's the next stop?
Welches ist der nächste Halt? — vel·khes ist dair naykh·ste halt

I want to get off here.
Ich möchte hier aussteigen. — ikh merkh·te heer ows·shtai·gen

Please tell me when we get to ....
Könnten Sie mir bitte sagen, wann wir in ... ankommen? — kern·ten zee meer bi·te zah·gen van veer in ... an·ko·men

Please take me to (this address).
Bitte bringen Sie mich zu (dieser Adresse). — bi·te bring·en zee mikh tsoo (dee·zer a·dre·se)

platform	*Bahnsteig*	bahn·shtaik
ticket office	*Fahrkarten-verkauf*	fahr·kar·ten·fer·kowf
timetable	*Fahrplan*	fahr·plan

Driving & Cycling

I'd like to hire a ...	*Ich möchte ein ... mieten.*	ikh merkh·te ain ... mee·ten
4WD	*Allrad-fahrzeug*	al·raht·fahr·tsoyk
bicycle	*Fahrrad*	fahr·raht
car	*Auto*	ow·to
motorbike	*Motorrad*	maw·tor·raht

How much is it per ...?	*Wie viel kostet es pro ...?*	vee feel kos·tet es praw ...
day	*Tag*	tahk
week	*Woche*	vo·khe

bicycle pump	*Fahrradpumpe*	fahr·raht·pum·pe
child seat	*Kindersitz*	kin·der·zits
helmet	*Helm*	helm
petrol	*Benzin*	ben·tseen

Does this road go to ...?
Führt diese Straße nach ...? — fürt dee·ze shtrah·se nahkh ...

(How long) Can I park here?
(Wie lange) Kann ich hier parken? — (vee lang·e) kan ikh heer par·ken

Where's a petrol station?
Wo ist eine Tankstelle? — vaw ist ai·ne tangk·shte·le

I need a mechanic.
Ich brauche einen Mechaniker. — ikh brow·khe ai·nen me·khah·ni·ker

My car/motorbike has broken down (at ...).
Ich habe (in ...) eine Panne mit meinem Auto/Motorrad. — ikh hah·be (in ...) ai·ne pa·ne mit mai·nem ow·to/maw·tor·raht

I've run out of petrol.
Ich habe kein Benzin mehr. — ikh hah·be kain ben·tseen mair

I have a flat tyre.
Ich habe eine Reifenpanne. — ikh hah·be ai·ne rai·fen·pa·ne

Are there cycling paths?
Gibt es Fahrradwege? — geept es fahr·raht·vay·ge

Is there bicycle parking?
Gibt es Fahrrad-Parkplätze? — geept es fahr·raht·park·ple·tse

GLOSSARY

You may encounter the following terms and abbreviations while in Berlin.

Bahnhof (Bf) – train station
Berg – mountain
Bibliothek – library
BRD – Bundesrepublik Deutschland (abbreviated in English as FRG – Federal Republic of Germany); see also *DDR*
Brücke – bridge
Brunnen – fountain or well
Bundestag – German parliament

CDU – Christliche Demokratische Union (Christian Democratic Union), centre-right party

DDR – Deutsche Demokratische Republik (abbreviated in English as GDR – German Democratic Republic); the name for the former East Germany; see also *BRD*
Denkmal – memorial, monument
Dom – cathedral

ermässigt – reduced (eg admission fee)

Fahrrad – bicycle
Flohmarkt – flea market
Flughafen – airport
FRG – Federal Republic of Germany; see also *BRD*

Gasse – lane or alley
Gästehaus, Gasthaus – guesthouse
GDR – German Democratic Republic (the former East Germany); see also *DDR*
Gedenkstätte – memorial site
Gestapo – Geheime Staatspolizei (Nazi secret police)

Gründerzeit – literally 'foundation time'; early years of German empire, roughly 1871–90

Hafen – harbour, port
Hauptbahnhof (Hbf) – main train station
Hof (Höfe) – courtyard(s)

Imbiss – snack bar, takeaway stand
Insel – island

Kaiser – emperor; derived from 'Caesar'
Kapelle – chapel
Karte – ticket
Kiez(e) – neighbourhood(s)
Kino – cinema
König – king
Konzentrationslager (KZ) – concentration camp
Kristallnacht – literally 'Night of Broken Glass'; Nazi pogrom against Jewish businesses and institutions on 9 November 1938
Kunst – art
Kunsthotels – hotels either designed by artists or liberally furnished with art

Mietskaserne(n) – tenement(s) built around successive courtyards

Ostalgie – fusion of the words Ost and Nostalgie, meaning nostalgia for East Germany

Palais – small palace
Palast – palace
Passage – shopping arcade
Platz – square

Rathaus – town hall
Reich – empire
Reisezentrum – travel centre in train or bus stations

Saal (Säle) – hall(s), large room(s)
Sammlung – collection
S-Bahn – metro/regional rail service with fewer stops than the U-Bahn
Schiff – ship
Schloss – palace
See – lake
SPD – Sozialdemokratische Partei Deutschlands (Social Democratic Party of Germany)
SS – Schutzstaffel; organisation within the Nazi Party that supplied Hitler's bodyguards, as well as concentration camp guards and the Waffen-SS troops in WWII
Stasi – GDR secret police (from Ministerium für Staatssicherheit, or Ministry of State Security)
Strasse (Str) – street

Tageskarte – daily menu; day ticket on public transport
Tor – gate
Trabant – GDR-era car boasting a two-stroke engine
Turm – tower
Trümmerberge – rubble mountains

U-Bahn – rapid transit railway, mostly underground; best choice for metro trips
Ufer – bank

Viertel – quarter, neighbourhood

Wald – forest
Weg – way, path
Weihnachtsmarkt – Christmas market
Wende – 'change' or 'turning point' of 1989, ie the collapse of the GDR and the resulting German reunification

Behind the Scenes

SEND US YOUR FEEDBACK

We love to hear from travellers – your comments keep us on our toes and help make our books better. Our well-travelled team reads every word on what you loved or loathed about this book. Although we cannot reply individually to your submissions, we always guarantee that your feedback goes straight to the appropriate authors, in time for the next edition. Each person who sends us information is thanked in the next edition – the most useful submissions are rewarded with a selection of digital PDF chapters.

Visit **lonelyplanet.com/contact** to submit your updates and suggestions or to ask for help. Our award-winning website also features inspirational travel stories, news and discussions.

Note: We may edit, reproduce and incorporate your comments in Lonely Planet products such as guidebooks, websites and digital products, so let us know if you don't want your comments reproduced or your name acknowledged. For a copy of our privacy policy visit lonelyplanet.com/privacy.

OUR READERS

Many thanks to the travellers who used the last edition and wrote to us with helpful hints, useful advice and interesting anecdotes: Rod Hastie, Darren McAteer, George & Linda Moss, Harvey Schwartz, Maggie Trewhitt, Eilis Webser, Sabine Will

WRITER THANKS
Andrea Schulte-Peevers

Big heartfelt thanks to all the wonderful people who supplied me with tips, insights, information, ideas and encouragement, including (in no particular order): Henrik Tidefjaerd, Barbara Woolsey, Frank Engster, Claudia Scheffler, Ubin Eoh, Patricia Kurowski, Shachar and Dorit Elkanati, Renate Freiling, Bernd Olsson, Christian Tänzler, Nicole Röbel, Julia Rautenberg, Claudi Sult and many more too numerous to mention here.

ACKNOWLEDGEMENTS

Berlin S+U-Bahn Map © 2016 Kartographie Berliner Verkehrsbetrieben (BVG).

Cover photograph: Berlin skyline, Matthias Makarinus/Getty

THIS BOOK

This 10th edition of Lonely Planet's *Berlin* guidebook was researched and written by Andrea Schulte-Peevers. The previous two editions were also written by Andrea. This guidebook was produced by the following:

Destination Editor Gemma Graham
Product Editors Kate Kiely, Catherine Naghten
Senior Cartographer Valentina Kremenchutskaya
Book Designer Mazzy Prinsep
Assisting Editors Imogen Bannister, Michelle Bennett, Carly Hall, Gabrielle Innes, Ross Taylor
Assisting Book Designers Jessica Rose, Wibowo Rusli
Cover Researcher Naomi Parker
Thanks to Kate Chapman, Sasha Drew, Mark Griffiths, Alison Lyall, Luna Soo, Tony Wheeler, Amanda Williamson

See also separate subindexes for:

✗ EATING P288

● DRINKING & NIGHTLIFE P289

☆ ENTERTAINMENT P290

🔒 SHOPPING P290

🛏 SLEEPING P290

🏃 SPORTS & ACTIVITIES 290

Index

✗ EATING

INDEX DRINKING & NIGHTLIFE

Berlin Maps

Sights
- Beach
- Bird Sanctuary
- Buddhist
- Castle/Palace
- Christian
- Confucian
- Hindu
- Islamic
- Jain
- Jewish
- Monument
- Museum/Gallery/Historic Building
- Ruin
- Shinto
- Sikh
- Taoist
- Winery/Vineyard
- Zoo/Wildlife Sanctuary
- Other Sight

Activities, Courses & Tours
- Bodysurfing
- Diving
- Canoeing/Kayaking
- Course/Tour
- Sento Hot Baths/Onsen
- Skiing
- Snorkelling
- Surfing
- Swimming/Pool
- Walking
- Windsurfing
- Other Activity

Sleeping
- Sleeping
- Camping

Eating
- Eating

Drinking & Nightlife
- Drinking & Nightlife
- Cafe

Entertainment
- Entertainment

Shopping
- Shopping

Information
- Bank
- Embassy/Consulate
- Hospital/Medical
- Internet
- Police
- Post Office
- Telephone
- Toilet
- Tourist Information
- Other Information

Geographic
- Beach
- Gate
- Hut/Shelter
- Lighthouse
- Lookout
- Mountain/Volcano
- Oasis
- Park
- Pass
- Picnic Area
- Waterfall

Population
- Capital (National)
- Capital (State/Province)
- City/Large Town
- Town/Village

Transport
- Airport
- Border crossing
- Bus
- Cable car/Funicular
- Cycling
- Ferry
- Metro station
- Monorail
- Parking
- Petrol station
- S-Bahn/Subway station
- Taxi
- T-bane/Tunnelbana station
- Train station/Railway
- Tram
- Tube station
- U-Bahn/Underground station
- Other Transport

Note: Not all symbols displayed above appear on the maps in this book

Routes
- Tollway
- Freeway
- Primary
- Secondary
- Tertiary
- Lane
- Unsealed road
- Road under construction
- Plaza/Mall
- Steps
- Tunnel
- Pedestrian overpass
- Walking Tour
- Walking Tour detour
- Path/Walking Trail

Boundaries
- International
- State/Province
- Disputed
- Regional/Suburb
- Marine Park
- Cliff
- Wall

Hydrography
- River, Creek
- Intermittent River
- Canal
- Water
- Dry/Salt/Intermittent Lake
- Reef

Areas
- Airport/Runway
- Beach/Desert
- Cemetery (Christian)
- Cemetery (Other)
- Glacier
- Mudflat
- Park/Forest
- Sight (Building)
- Sportsground
- Swamp/Mangrove

MAP INDEX

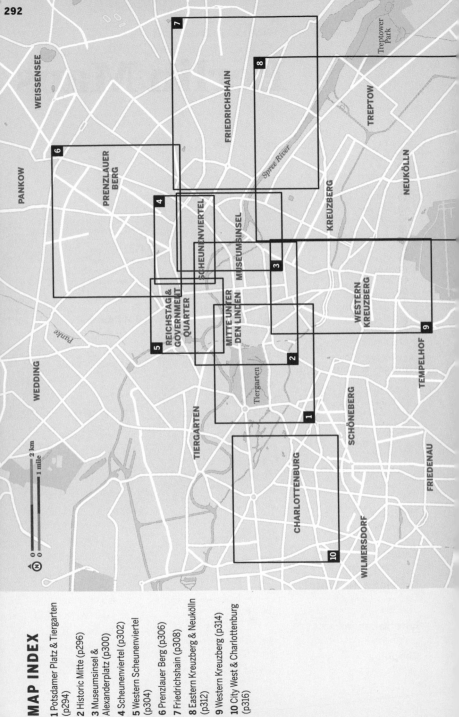

POTSDAMER PLATZ & TIERGARTEN

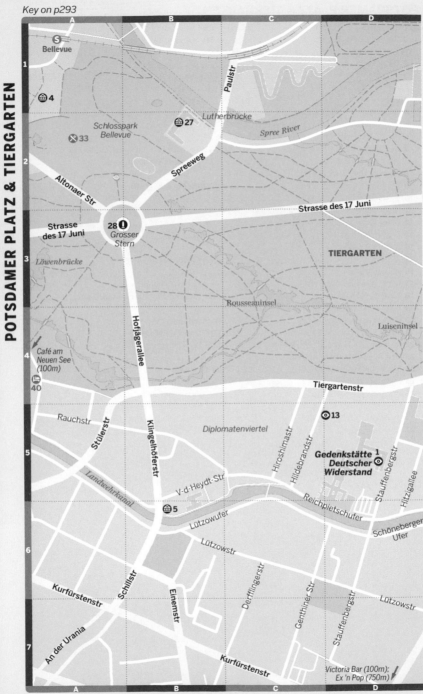

Bellevue

4

Schlosspark
Bellevue

33

27

Paulstr

Lutherbrücke

Spree River

Spreeweg

Altonaer Str

Strasse des 17 Juni

28
Grosser
Stern

Strasse
des 17 Juni

TIERGARTEN

Löwenbrücke

Rousseauinsel

Luiseninsel

Hofjägerallee

Café am
Neuen See
(100m)

40

Tiergartenstr

Rauchstr

Stülerstr

Klingelhöferstr

Diplomatenviertel

13

Hiroshimastr

Hildebrandstr

Gedenkstätte
Deutscher
Widerstand

1

Stauffenbergstr

Hitzigallee

Landwehrkanal

V-d-Heydt-Str

5

Lützowufer

Reichpietschufer

Schöneberger
Ufer

Kurfürstenstr

Schillstr

Einemstr

Lützowstr

Derfflingerstr

Genthiner Str

Stauffenbergstr

Lützowstr

An der Urania

Kurfürstenstr

Victoria Bar (100m);
Ex 'n Pop (750m)

N 0 ——— 200 m
0 ——— 0.1 miles

See map p304

See map p296

See map p314

Bundeskanzleramt

Haus der Kulturen der Welt

Bundestag Ⓤ

Paul-Löbe-Haus

Paul-Löbe-Allee

Platz der Republik

Reichstag

Reichstagufer

John-Foster-Dulles-Allee

Scheidemannstr

Dorotheenstr

Yitzhak-Rabin-Str

Brandenburger Tor Ⓤ

Pariser Platz

Ⓢ Brandenburger Tor

Brandenburger Tor

Ebertstr

Behrenstr

Wilhelmstr

Holocaust Memorial

Cora-Berliner-Str

Hannah-Arendt-Str

Tiergartentunnel

In den Ministergärten

Bellevueallee

Lennéstr

Beisheim Center

Vossstr

Am Park

Bellevuestr

Ben-Gurion-Str

23 🏛

37 ⭐
29 📷

🏛 43

Leipziger Platz

📷 38

Leipziger Str

8 📷

🏛 17

Gemäldegalerie

Potsdamer Platz

19 📷

🏛 22

📷 9

📷 6
📷 3

Potsdamer Str

🏛 2

18 🏛

Matthäikirchplatz

📷 41

📷 5
25

Ⓢ

12

Potsdamer Platz

🏛 30

Potsdamer Platz

Daimler City

10 ❶

🏛 11

Erna-Berger-Str

❶ 7

21 ❶

Sigismundstr

Alte Potsdamer Str

31 🍴

Stresemannstr

24 🏛

26 ❶

Marlene-Dietrich-Platz

39 🔒

Niederkirchner Str

🏛 20

34 ✖

15 ❶

📷 16

14 ❶

Potsdamer Brücke

Linkstr

Gabriele-Tergit-Promenade

Köthener Str

Dessauer Str

Askanischer Platz

Anhalter Str

Stresemannstr

Potsdamer Str

Reichpietschufer

Schöneberger Ufer

44

Mendessohn-Bartholdy-Platz

Anhalter Bahnhof Ⓢ

42

36

35 🏛

32 ✖

Lützowstr

Flottwellstr

Schöneberger Str

See map p314

Key on p298

HISTORIC MITTE

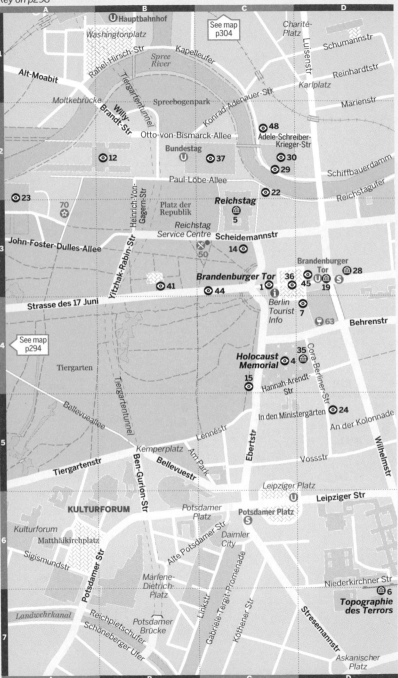

Ⓤ **Hauptbahnhof**

Washingtonplatz

See map
p304

Charité-
Platz

Rahel-Hirsch-Str

Kapelleufer

Luisenstr

Schumannstr

Alt-Moabit

Spree
River

Reinhardtstr

Tiergartentunnel

Moltkebrücke

Spreebogenpark

Karlplatz

Konrad-Adenauer-Str

Marienstr

**Willy-
Brandt-Str**

Otto-von-Bismarck-Allee

⊙ 48

Adele-Schreiber-
Krieger-Str

⊙ 12

Bundestag
Ⓤ

⊙ 37

⊙ 30

⊙ 29

Schiffbauerdamm

Paul-Löbe-Allee

Reichstagufer

⊙ 22

◉ 23

70
☆

Heinrich-von-
Gagern-Str

Platz der
Republik

Reichstag

🏛
5

Yitzhak-Rabin-Str

Reichstag
Service Centre

Scheidemannstr

14 ⊙

John-Foster-Dulles-Allee

⊗
50

Brandenburger
Tor 🏛 28
Ⓤ🏛 Ⓢ

⊙ 41

Brandenburger Tor

36
⊙

45

19

1 ⊙
ℹ

**Berlin
Tourist
Info**

⊙ 44

Strasse des 17 Juni

7 ⊙

🚻 63

Behrenstr

See map
p294

Tiergarten

Bellevueallee

Tiergartentunnel

**Holocaust
Memorial** ⊙ 4

35
⊙

Cora-Berliner-Str

15
⊙

Hannah-Arendt-
Str

In den Ministergärten

⊙ 24

An der Kolonnade

Lennéstr

Ebertstr

Vossstr

Wilhelmstr

Kemperplatz

Am Park

Ben-Gurion-Str

Bellevuestr

Tiergartenstr

Leipziger Platz
Ⓤ

Leipziger Str

KULTURFORUM

Potsdamer
Platz

Potsdamer Platz
Ⓢ

Kulturforum

Matthäikirchplatz

Alte Potsdamer Str

Daimler
City

Sigismundstr

Potsdamer Str

Marlene-
Dietrich-
Platz

Gabriele-Tergit-Promenade

Linkstr

Köthener Str

Niederkirchner Str

🏛 6

**Topographie
des Terrors**

Landwehrkanal

Reichpietschufer

Schöneberger Ufer

Potsdamer
Brücke

Stresemannstr

Askanischer
Platz

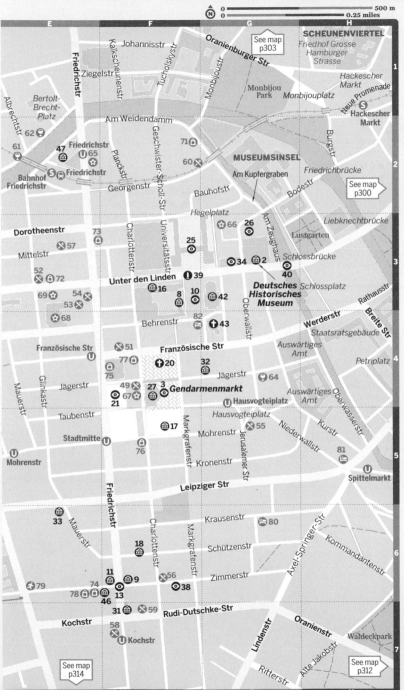

HISTORIC MITTE *Map on p296*

HISTORIC MITTE

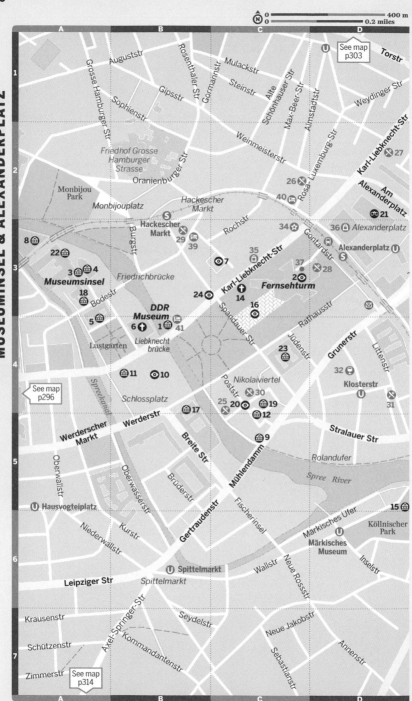

MUSEUMINSEL & ALEXANDERPLATZ

SCHEUNENVIERTEL

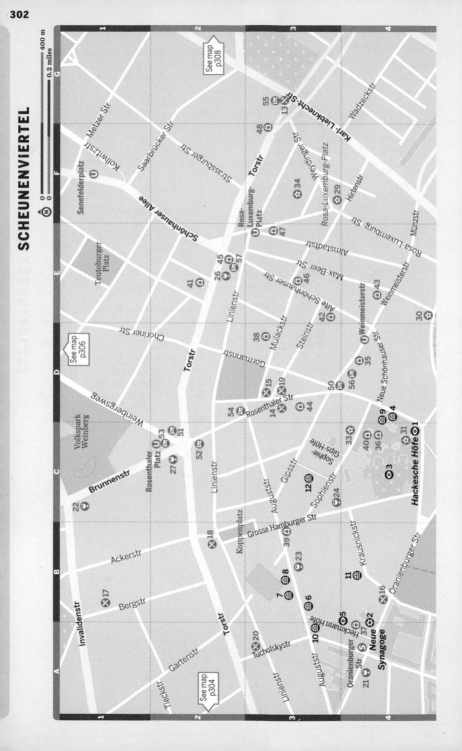

See map p308

See map p306

See map p304

Hackesche Höfe

Neue
Synagoge

Volkspark
Weinberg

Teutoburger
Platz

Senefelderplatz

Rosenthaler
Platz

Sophie-
Gips-Höfe

Heckmann Höfe

Scale:
0 — 400 m
0 — 0.2 miles

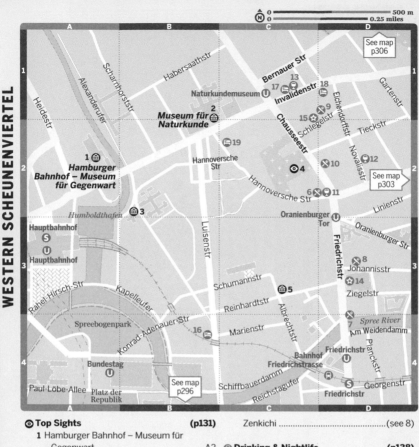

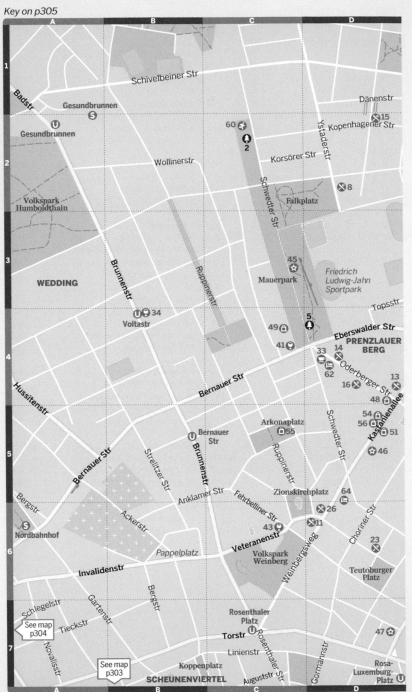

PRENZLAUER BERG

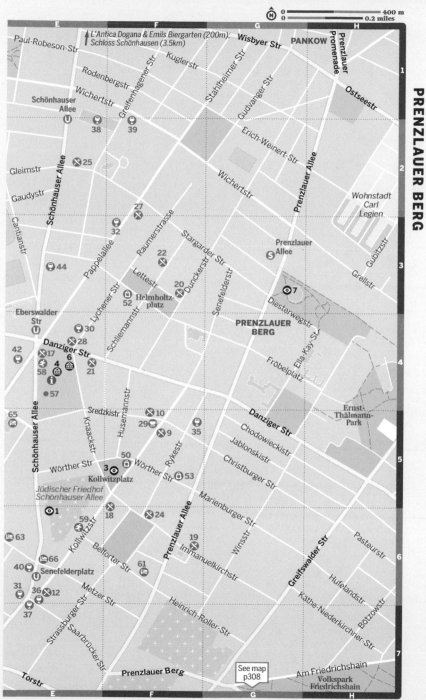

L'Antica Dogana & Emils Biergarten (200m);
Schloss Schönhausen (3.5km)

Paul-Robeson-Str

Wisbyer Str   PANKOW

Prenzlauer Promenade

Ostseestr

Rodenbergstr

Kuglerstr

Greifenhagener Str

Wichertstr

Schönhauser Allee

Stahlheimer Str

Gudvanger Str

Erich-Weinert-Str

Prenzlauer Allee

Wohnstadt Carl Legien

Gleimstr

25

Wichertstr

Gaudystr

Schönhauser Allee

Cantianstr

27

Raumerstrasse

32

Pappelallee

22

Stargarder Str

Dunckerstr

Prenzlauer Allee

Gubitzstr

Grellstr

44

Lettestr

Lychener Str

20

52 Helmholtz-platz

Schliemannstr

Senefelderstr

7

Diesterwegstr

Eberswalder Str

30

PRENZLAUER BERG

Danziger Str

28

42

17

6

Ella-Kay-Str

58 4

21

Fröbelplatz

i
57

Husemannstr

Ernst-Thälmann-Park

65

Sredzkistr

10

Danziger Str

Schönhauser Allee

Knaackstr

29

9

35

Chodowieckistr

Jablonskistr

50

Rykestr

Christburger Str

Wörther Str

3

Wörther Str

53

Kollwitzplatz

Marienburger Str

Jüdischer Friedhof Schönhauser Allee

1

18

24

Winsstr

63

59

Kollwitzstr

Prenzlauer Allee

19

Greifswalder Str

Pasteurstr

66

Immanuelkirchstr

40 Senefelderplatz

Belforter Str

61

Hufelandstr

31 36 12

Metzer Str

Käthe-Niederkirchner-Str

Bötzowstr

37

Strassburger Str

Saarbrücker Str

Heinrich-Roller-Str

Torstr

Prenzlauer Berg

See map p308

Am Friedrichshain

Volkspark Friedrichshain

FRIEDRICHSHAIN

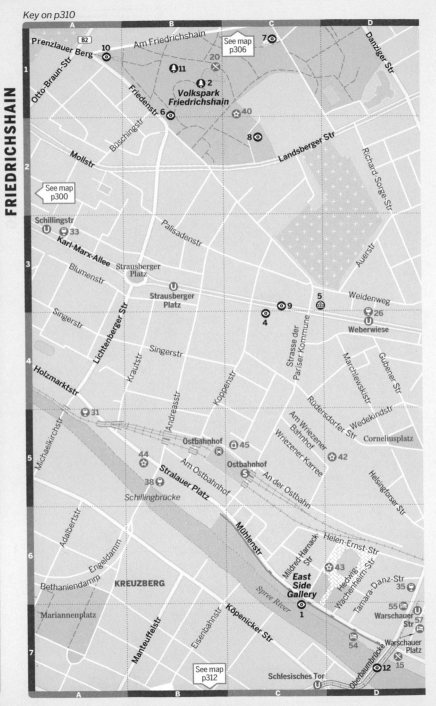

Key on p310

Prenzlauer Berg
B2
Am Friedrichshain

See map
p306

Otto-Braun-Str

10

11

20

2

Friedenstr 6

**Volkspark
Friedrichshain**

40

Büschingstr

8

Landsberger Str

Mollstr

Danziger Str

Richard-Sorge-Str

See map
p300

Schillingstr

33

Karl-Marx-Allee

Palisadenstr

Auerstr

Blumenstr

Strausberger
Platz

Weidenweg

Singerstr

Strausberger
Platz

5

26

Lichtenberger Str

9

4

Weberwiese

Singerstr

Krautstr

Strasse der Pariser Kommune

Marchlewskistr

Gubener Str

Holzmarktstr

31

Andreasstr

Koppenstr

Rüdersdorfer Str

Wedekindstr

Am Wriezener Bahnhof

Corneliusplatz

Michaelkirchstr

44

Ostbahnhof

45

Wriezener Karree

42

Helsingforser Str

38

Stralauer Platz

Am Ostbahnhof

Ostbahnhof

An der Ostbahn

Schillingbrücke

Adalbertstr

Engeldamm

Mühlenstr

Helen-Ernst-Str

Mildred-Harnack-Str

Bethaniendamm

KREUZBERG

43

Hedwig-Wachenheim-Str

35

Marianenplatz

Spree River

**East
Side
Gallery**

Tamara-Danz-Str

55

Warschauer
Str

57

Manteuffelstr

Eisenbahnstr

Köpenicker Str

1

54

Warschauer
Platz

Oberbaumbrücke

12

15

See map
p312

Schlesisches Tor

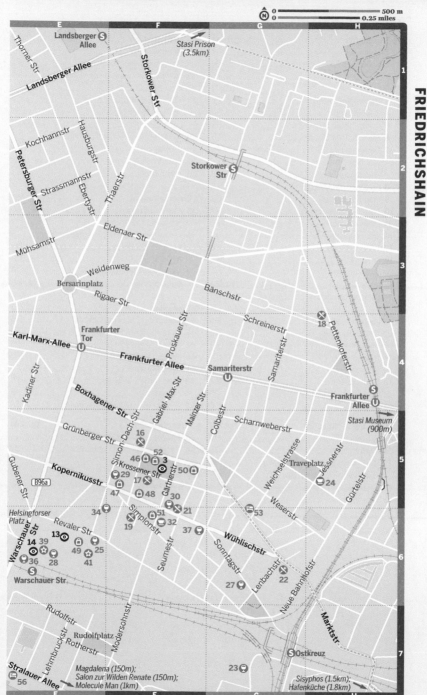

0 500 m
0 0.25 miles

Landsberger Allee

Thorner Str

Landsberger Allee

Storkower Str

Stasi Prison
(3.5km)

Kochhannstr

Hausburgstr

Petersburger Str

Strassmannstr

Ebertstr

Thaerstr

Storkower Str

Eldenaer Str

Mühsamstr

Weidenweg

Bersarinplatz

Rigaer Str

Bänschstr

Schreinerstr

Samariterstr

Pettenkoferstr

18

Karl-Marx-Allee

Frankfurter Tor

Frankfurter Allee

Proskauer Str

Samariterstr

Frankfurter Allee

Stasi Museum
(900m)

Kadiner Str

Boxhagener Str

Gabriel-Max-Str

Mainzer Str

Colbestr

Scharnweberstr

Weichselstrasse

Jessnerstr

Güntzelstr

Grünberger Str

Simon-Dach-Str

16

Kopernikusstr

52

46 3

Krossener Str

50

29

17

Gärtnerstr

30

Weserstr

Traveplatz

24

Gubener Str

B96a

47

48

21

53

Helsingforser Platz

34

Simplonstr

51

32

37

Wühlischstr

Revaler Str

19

Warschauer Str

13

14 39

49 25

Seumestr

Sonntagstr

Lenbachstr

22

36 28

41

27

Warschauer Str

Rudolfstr

Modersohnstr

Neue Bahnhofstr

Markstr

Ostkreuz

Rudolfplatz

Rotherstr

Lehmbruckstr

Stralauer Allee

56

Magdalena (150m);
Salon zur Wilden Renate (150m);
Molecule Man (1km)

23

Sisyphos (1.5km);
Hafenküche (1.8km)

FRIEDRICHSHAIN *Map on p309*

FRIEDRICHSHAIN

EASTERN KREUZBERG & NEUKÖLLN

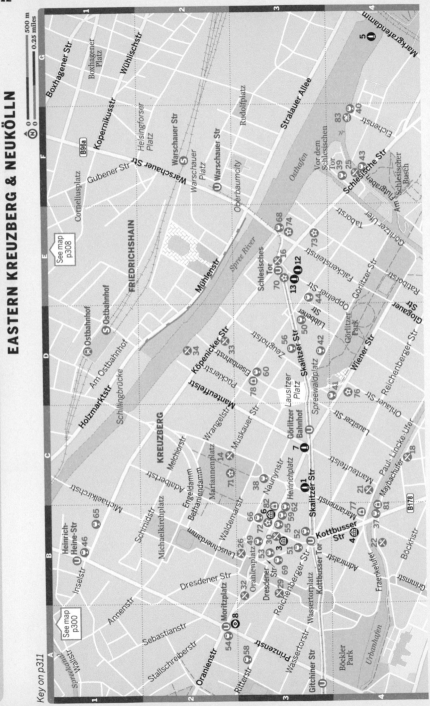

Key on p311

See map p308

See map p300

500 m
0.25 miles

FRIEDRICHSHAIN

KREUZBERG

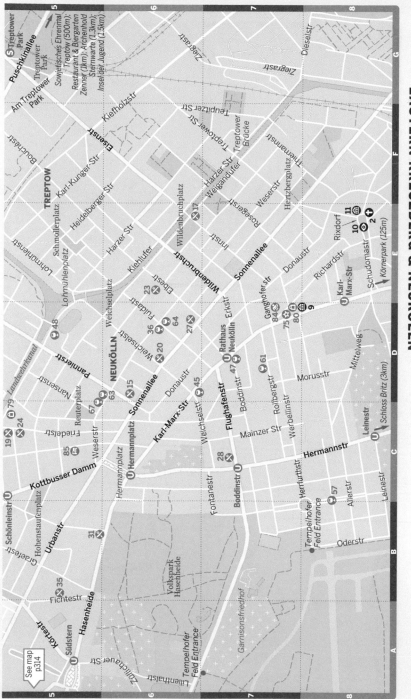

EASTERN KREUZBERG & NEUKÖLLN

TREPTOW

NEUKÖLLN

Treptower Park

Puschkinallee

Am Treptow Park

Sowjetisches Ehrenmal
Treptow (500m);
Restaurant & Biergarten
Zenner (1km); Archenhold
Sternwarte (1.3km);
Insel der Jugend (1.5km)

Bouchéstr

Eisenstr

Karl-Kunger-Str

Heidelberger Str

Kiefholzstr

Harzer Str

Teupitzer Str

Treptower Str

Treptower
Brücke

Thiemannstr

Ziegrastr

Dieselstr

Hertzbergplatz

Weserstr

Harzer Str

Weigandufer

Rosegerstr

Wildenbruchplatz

17

Sonnenallee

Donaustr

Rixdorf

11

10

2

Schudomastr

Körnerpark (125m)

Richardstr

Karl-
Marx-Str

Ganghofer str

84

75

80

9

Erkstr

Innstr

Wildenbruchstr

Elbestr

Fuldastr

Kiehlufer

Weichselplatz

Weichselstr

Lohmühlenstr

Lohmühlenplatz

Schmollerplatz

23

36

64

27

48

20

Rathaus
Neukölln

47

61

Morusstr

Mittelweg

Schloss Britz (3km)

Pannierstr

Landwehrkanal

Nansenstr

Reuterplatz

67

63

15

Donaustr

Flughafenstr

45

Boddinstr

Rollbergstr

Werbellinstr

Leinestr

Leinestr

79

24

19

85

Friedelstr

Weserstr

Hermannplatz

Hermannstr

Weichselstr

28

Fontanestr

Boddinstr

Mainzer Str

Hermannstr

Herrfurthstr

57

Allerstr

Oderstr

Kottbusser Damm

Schönleinstr

Hohenstaufenplatz

Graefestr

Urbanstr

31

Hasenheide

Fichtestr

35

Kärtestr

Südstern

Zülpichstr

Lilienthalstr

Zülpichstr

Volkspark
Hasenheide

Tempelhofer
Feld Entrance

Garnisonsfriedhof

Tempelhofer
Feld Entrance

See map
p314

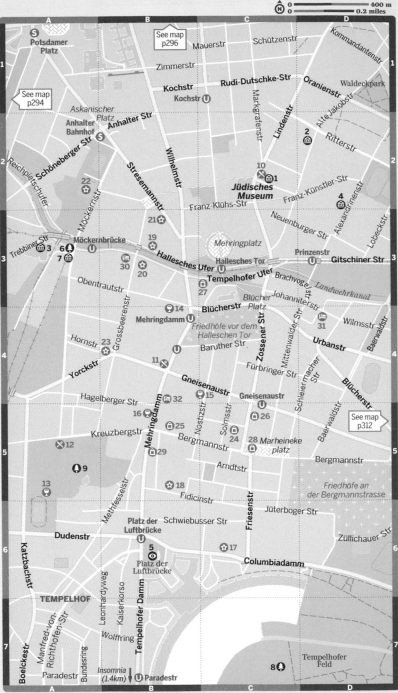

0 400 m
0 0.2 miles

Potsdamer Platz

See map p296

See map p294

Mauerstr
Schützenstr
Kommandantenstr
Zimmerstr
Kochstr
Rudi-Dutschke-Str
Oranienstr
Waldeckpark
Kochstr
Markgrafenstr
Lindenstr
Alte-Jakobstr
Rritterstr
Askanischer Platz
Anhalter Str
Anhalter Bahnhof
Schöneberger Str
Reichpietschufer
Stresemannstr
Wilhelmstr
Franz-Klühs-Str
Jüdisches Museum
10
1
Franz-Künstler-Str
4
Alexandrinenstr
Neuenburger Str
Lobeckstr
22
Möckernstr
21
19
Möckernbrücke
Hallesches Ufer
Mehringplatz
Prinzenstr
Gitschiner Str
Trebbiner Str
3
6
7
30
20
Halleches Tor
Tempelhofer Ufer
27
Landwehrkanal
Brachvoge
Johanniterstr
Obentrautstr
14
Blücherstr
Blücher Platz
Mehringdamm
Friedhöfe vor dem Hallelschen Tor
Zossener Str
Mittenwalder Str
31
Wilmsstr
Baerwaldstr
Hornstr
23
Grossbeerenstr
Baruther Str
Urbanstr
Yorckstr
11
Fürbringer Str
Schleiermacher Str
Blücherstr
Gneisenaustr
15
Gneisenaustr
See map p312
Hagelberger Str
32
16
Mehringdamm
25
Nostizstr
Solmsstr
26
Baerwaldstr
Kreuzbergstr
24
28
Marheineke platz
12
29
Bergmannstr
Bergmannstr
9
13
18
Arndtstr
Friedhöfe an der Bergmannstrasse
Fidicinstr
Friesenstr
Jüterboger Str
Platz der Luftbrücke
Schwiebusser Str
Dudenstr
5
17
Columbiadamm
Züllichauer Str
Platz der Luftbrücke
Katzbachstr
TEMPELHOF
Manfred-von-Richthofen-Str
Leonhardyweg
Kaiserkorso
Tempelhofer Damm
Wolfflring
Tempelhofer Feld
Boelckestr
Paradestr
Bundesring
Insomnia (1.4km)
Paradestr
8

WESTERN KREUZBERG

CITY WEST & CHARLOTTENBURG

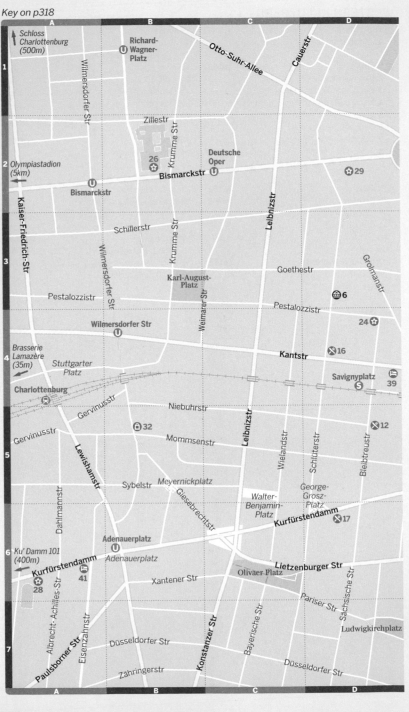

Schloss
Charlottenburg
(500m)

Richard-
Wagner-
Platz

Otto-Suhr-Allee

Cauerstr

A **B** **C** **D**

1

Wilmersdorfer Str

Zillestr

Krumme Str

26

Deutsche
Oper

Bismarckstr

29

2
Olympiastadion
(5km)

Bismarckstr

Leibnizstr

Kaiser-Friedrich-Str

Schillerstr

Krumme Str

Wilmersdorfer Str

3

Karl-August-
Platz

Goethestr

Grolmanstr

Pestalozzistr

Weimarer Str

Pestalozzistr

6

24

Wilmersdorfer Str

Kantstr

16

Brasserie
Lamazère
(35m)

Stuttgarter
Platz

Savignyplatz

39

4

Charlottenburg

Gervinusstr

Niebuhrstr

Leibnizstr

Wielandstr

Schlüterstr

Bleibtreustr

12

Gervinusstr

32

Mommsenstr

5

Lewishamstr

Sybelstr

Meyernickplatz

Giesebrechtstr

Walter-
Benjamin-
Platz

George-
Grosz-
Platz

Kurfürstendamm

17

Dahlmannstr

Adenauerplatz

Adenauerplatz

Lietzenburger Str

6
Ku' Damm 101
(400m)

Kurfürstendamm

Olivaer Platz

Sächsische Str

Albrecht-Achilles-Str

41

28

Xantener Str

Pariser Str

Ludwigkirchplatz

Paulsborner Str

Eisenzahnstr

Düsseldorfer Str

Konstanzer Str

Bayerische Str

Düsseldorfer Str

7

Zähringerstr

A **B** **C** **D**

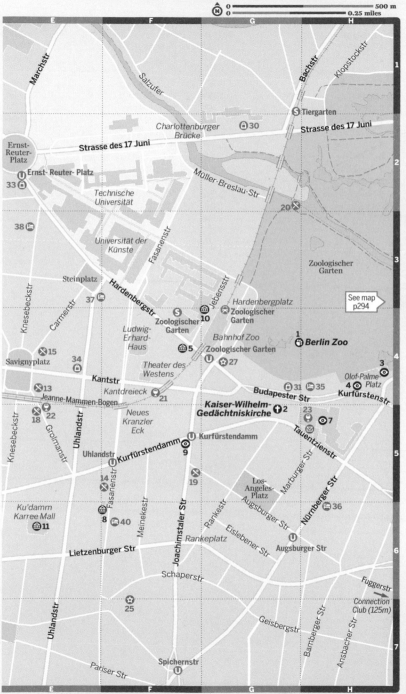

CITY WEST & CHARLOTTENBURG *Map on p316*

CITY WEST & CHARLOTTENBURG

CITY WEST & CHARLOTTENBURG

Our Story

A beat-up old car, a few dollars in the pocket and a sense of adventure. In 1972 that's all Tony and Maureen Wheeler needed for the trip of a lifetime – across Europe and Asia overland to Australia. It took several months, and at the end – broke but inspired – they sat at their kitchen table writing and stapling together their first travel guide, *Across Asia on the Cheap*. Within a week they'd sold 1500 copies. Lonely Planet was born.

Today, Lonely Planet has offices in Franklin, London, Melbourne, Oakland, Dublin, Beijing and Delhi, with more than 600 staff and writers. We share Tony's belief that 'a great guidebook should do three things: inform, educate and amuse'.

Our Writer

Andrea Schulte-Peevers

Born and raised in Germany and educated in London and at UCLA, Andrea has travelled the distance to the moon and back in her visits to some 75 countries. She has earned her living as a professional travel writer for over two decades and authored or contributed to nearly 100 Lonely Planet titles, as well as to newspapers, magazines and websites around the world. She also works as a travel consultant, translator and editor. Andrea's destination expertise is especially strong when it comes to Germany, Dubai and the United Arab Emirates, Crete and the Caribbean Islands. She makes her home in Berlin.

Andrea grew up in Bochum, a charmingly industrial town deep in western Germany put on the map by Germany's top rock bard Herbert Grönemeyer. Despite a passion for her home town, she packed her bags right after school, decamping first to London, then to Los Angeles, where she haunted the hallowed halls of UCLA in pursuit of a degree in English literature. Equipped with such highly sought-after credentials, she fearlessly embarked on a career in journalism, soon getting tapped by Lonely Planet for her Germany expertise. It's been a great ride so far.

Published by Lonely Planet Global Limited
CRN 554153
10th edition – Feb 2017
ISBN 978 1 78657 225 7
© Lonely Planet 2017   Photographs © as indicated 2017
10 9 8 7 6 5 4 3 2 1
Printed in China